PHILIP'S

STREET ATLAS
East Yorkshire
Northern Lincolnshire

First published in 2002 by
Philip's, a division of
Octopus Publishing Group Ltd
2–4 Heron Quays, London E14 4JP

First colour edition 2002
First impression 2002

ISBN 0-540-08146-9

Printed and bound in Spain
by Cayfosa-Quebecor

Contents

III **Key to map symbols**

IV **Key to map pages**

VI **Route planning**

X **Administrative and Postcode boundaries**

1 **Street maps** at 1¼ inches to 1 mile

122 **Street maps** at 2½ inches to 1 mile

154 **Street maps of centres of Beverley, Kingston-upon-Hull and York** at 5 inches to 1 mile

157 **Town maps** of Doncaster and Scarborough

158 **Index** of towns and villages

160 **Index** of streets, hospitals, industrial estates, railway stations, schools, shopping centres, universities and places of interest

Digital Data

The exceptionally high-quality mapping found in this atlas is available as digital data in TIFF format, which is easily convertible to other bit mapped (raster) image formats.

The index is also available in digital form as a standard database table. It contains all the details found in the printed index together with the National Grid reference for the map square in which each entry is named and feature codes for places of interest in eight categories such as education and health.

For further information and to discuss your requirements, please contact Philip's on 020 7531 8440 or george.philip@philips-maps.co.uk

Key to map symbols

22a	**Motorway** with junction number
	Primary route – dual/single carriageway
	A road – dual/single carriageway
	B road – dual/single carriageway
	Minor road – dual/single carriageway
	Other minor road – dual/single carriageway
— — —	**Road under construction**
	Pedestrianised area
DY7 •••••••••	**Postcode boundaries**
—·—	**County and unitary authority boundaries**
——	**Railway**
- - - - - -	**Railway under construction**
——	**Tramway, miniature railway**
	Rural track, private road or narrow road in urban area
	Gate or obstruction to traffic (restrictions may not apply at all times or to all vehicles)
- - - - - -	**Path, bridleway, byway open to all traffic, road used as a public path**
	The representation in this atlas of a road, track or is no evidence of the existence of a of a right of way
187 / 210 / 84	**Adjoining page indicators** (The colour of the arrow indicates the scale of the adjoining page - see scales below)
211 / 203	**The map areas within the pink and blue bands are shown at a larger scale on the page, indicated by the red and blue blocks and arrows**

Walsall	**Railway station**
	Private railway station
	Bus, coach station
◆	**Ambulance station**
◆	**Coastguard station**
◆	**Fire station**
◆	**Police station**
✚	**Accident and Emergency entrance to hospital**
H	**Hospital**
+	**Place of worship**
i	**Information Centre** (open all year)
P	**Parking**
P&R	**Park and Ride**
PO	**Post Office**
	Camping site
	Caravan site
	Golf course
	Picnic site
Prim Sch	**Important buildings, schools, colleges, universities and hospitals**
River Medway	**Water name**
	River, stream
	Lock, weir
	Water
	Tidal water
	Woods
	Houses
Church	**Non-Roman antiquity**
ROMAN FORT	**Roman antiquity**

Acad	**Academy**	Mkt	**Market**
Allot Gdns	**Allotments**	Meml	**Memorial**
Cemy	**Cemetery**	Mon	**Monument**
C Ctr	**Civic Centre**	Mus	**Museum**
CH	**Club House**	Obsy	**Observatory**
Coll	**College**	Pal	**Royal Palace**
Crem	**Crematorium**	PH	**Public House**
Ent	**Enterprise**	Recn Gd	**Recreation Ground**
Ex H	**Exhibition Hall**	Resr	**Reservoir**
Ind Est	**Industrial Estate**	Ret Pk	**Retail Park**
IRB Sta	**Inshore Rescue Boat Station**	Sch	**School**
		Sh Ctr	**Shopping Centre**
Inst	**Institute**	TH	**Town Hall/House**
Ct	**Law Court**	Trad Est	**Trading Estate**
L Ctr	**Leisure Centre**	Univ	**University**
LC	**Level Crossing**	Wks	**Works**
Liby	**Library**	YH	**Youth Hostel**

■ The small numbers around the edges of the maps identify the 1 kilometre National Grid lines ■ The dark grey border on the inside edge of some pages indicates that the mapping does not continue onto the adjacent page

The scale of the maps on pages numbered in blue is 3.92 cm to 1 km • 2½ inches to 1 mile • 1: 25344

0 — ¼ — ½ — ¾ — 1 mile
0 — 250 m — 500 m — 750 m — 1 kilometre

The scale of the maps on pages numbered in green is 1.96 cm to 1 km • 1¼ inches to 1 mile • 1: 50688

0 — ¼ — ½ — ¾ — 1 mile
0 — 250m — 500m — 750m — 1kilometre

The scale of the maps on pages numbered in red is 7.84 cm to 1 km • 5 inches to 1 mile • 1: 12672

0 — 220 yards — 440 yards — 660 yards — ½ mile
0 — 125m — 250m — 375m — ½ kilometre

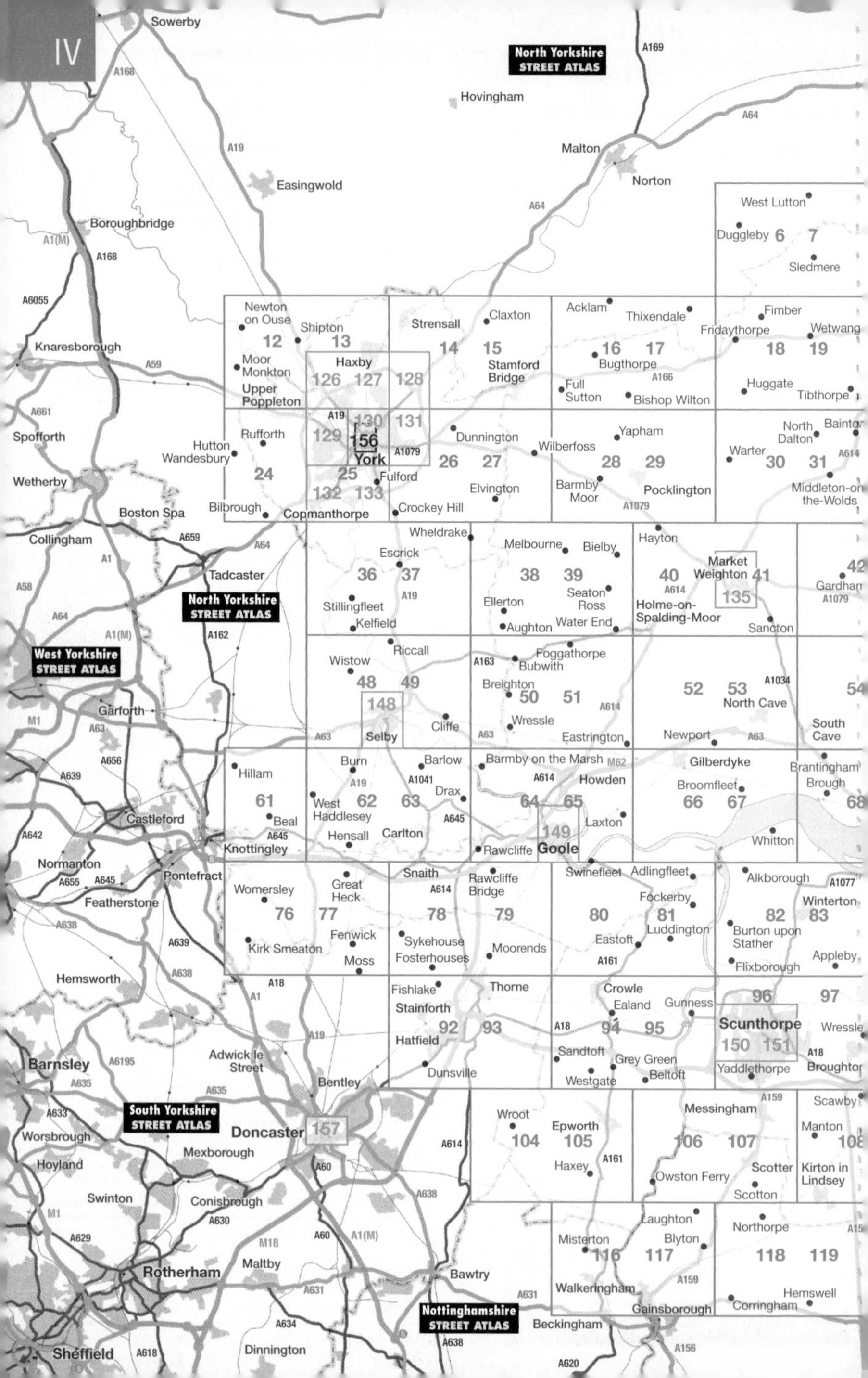
North Yorkshire STREET ATLAS
Sowerby
A169
A168
Hovingham
A64
A19
Malton
Norton
Easingwold
A64
West Lutton
Boroughbridge
A1(M)
Duggleby 6 7
A168
Sledmere
A6055
Newton on Ouse
Shipton
12 13
Strensall
Claxton
14 15
Acklam
Thixendale
16 17
Fimber
Fridaythorpe
Wetwang
18 19
Knaresborough
A59
Moor Monkton
Haxby
126 127 128
Stamford Bridge
Bugthorpe
A166
Full Sutton
Bishop Wilton
Huggate
Tibthorpe
Upper Poppleton
A661
A19
130
131
Rufforth
129
156
Dunnington
Wilberfoss
Yapham
North Dalton
Bainton
Spofforth
Hutton Wandesbury
York
A1079
26 27
28 29
Warter
30 31
A614
24
25
Fulford
Barmby Moor
Pocklington
Middleton-on-the-Wolds
Wetherby
132 133
Elvington
A1079
Boston Spa
Bilbrough
Copmanthorpe
Crockey Hill
Wheldrake
Collingham
A659
A64
Escrick
Melbourne
Bielby
Hayton
Market Weighton
42
A1
Tadcaster
36 37
38 39
40
41
Gardham
A58
Stillingfleet
A19
Ellerton
Seaton Ross
A614
135
A1079
North Yorkshire STREET ATLAS
A64
Kelfield
Aughton
Water End
Holme-on-Spalding-Moor
Sancton
A1(M)
A162
Riccall
Foggathorpe
West Yorkshire STREET ATLAS
Wistow
A163
Bubwith
48 49
Breighton
50 51
52 53
A1034
North Cave
54
148
A614
Garforth
M1
A63
Cliffe
Wressle
South Cave
A63
Selby
A63
Eastrington
Newport
A63
A656
Burn
Barlow
Barmby on the Marsh
M62
Gilberdyke
Brantingham
Hillam
A639
A19
A1041
A614
Howden
Broomfleet
Brough
61
62 63
Drax
64 65
66 67
68
West Haddlesey
A645
Beal
Laxton
149
Castleford
A645
Hensall
Carlton
A642
Knottingley
Rawcliffe
Goole
Whitton
Normanton
Snaith
Rawcliffe Bridge
Swinefleet
Adlingfleet
Alkborough
A1077
A655
A645
Pontefract
Womersley
Great Heck
A614
Fockerby
Winterton
Featherstone
76 77
78 79
80
81
82 83
A638
Burton upon Stather
Luddington
Fenwick
Sykehouse
Eastoft
A639
Kirk Smeaton
Moorends
Moss
Fosterhouses
A161
Flixborough
Appleby
Hemsworth
A638
A18
Fishlake
Thorne
Crowle
96 97
A1
Stainforth
Ealand
Gunness
Scunthorpe
92 93
A18
94 95
Wressle
A19
Hatfield
150 151
Sandtoft
A18
Adwick le Street
Grey Green
Broughton
Barnsley
A6195
Dunsville
Yaddlethorpe
Belton
Westgate
A635
A635
Bentley
A159
Scawby
A633
South Yorkshire STREET ATLAS
Messingham
Wroot
Manton
Worsbrough
Doncaster
157
Epworth
104 105
106 107
108
Mexborough
A614
Hoyland
Haxey
A161
Scotter
Kirton in Lindsey
A60
Owston Ferry
Scotton
Swinton
Conisbrough
A638
M1
A630
Laughton
Northorpe
A629
M18
A60
A1(M)
Misterton
Blyton
116 117
118 119
Rotherham
Maltby
Bawtry
A159
A631
Walkeringham
A631
Hemswell
Corringham
Gainsborough
Nottinghamshire STREET ATLAS
A634
Beckingham
A638
Sheffield
A618
Dinnington
A156
A620

Key to map pages

Map pages at 5 inches to 1 mile (156)

Map pages at 2½ inches to 1 mile (141)

Map pages at 1¼ inches to 1 mile (113)

Scale: 0, 5, 10, 15, 20 km; 0, 5, 10 miles

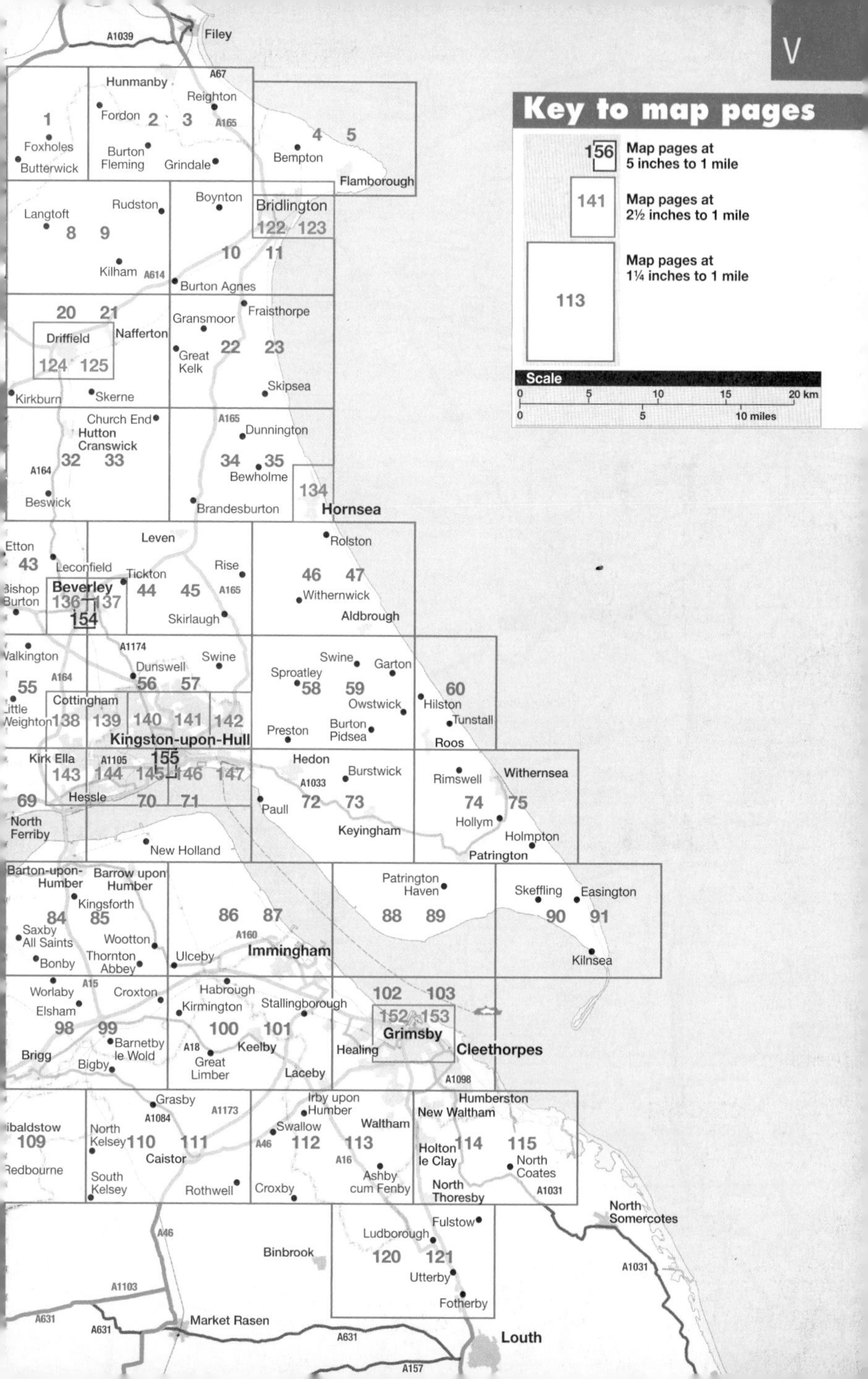

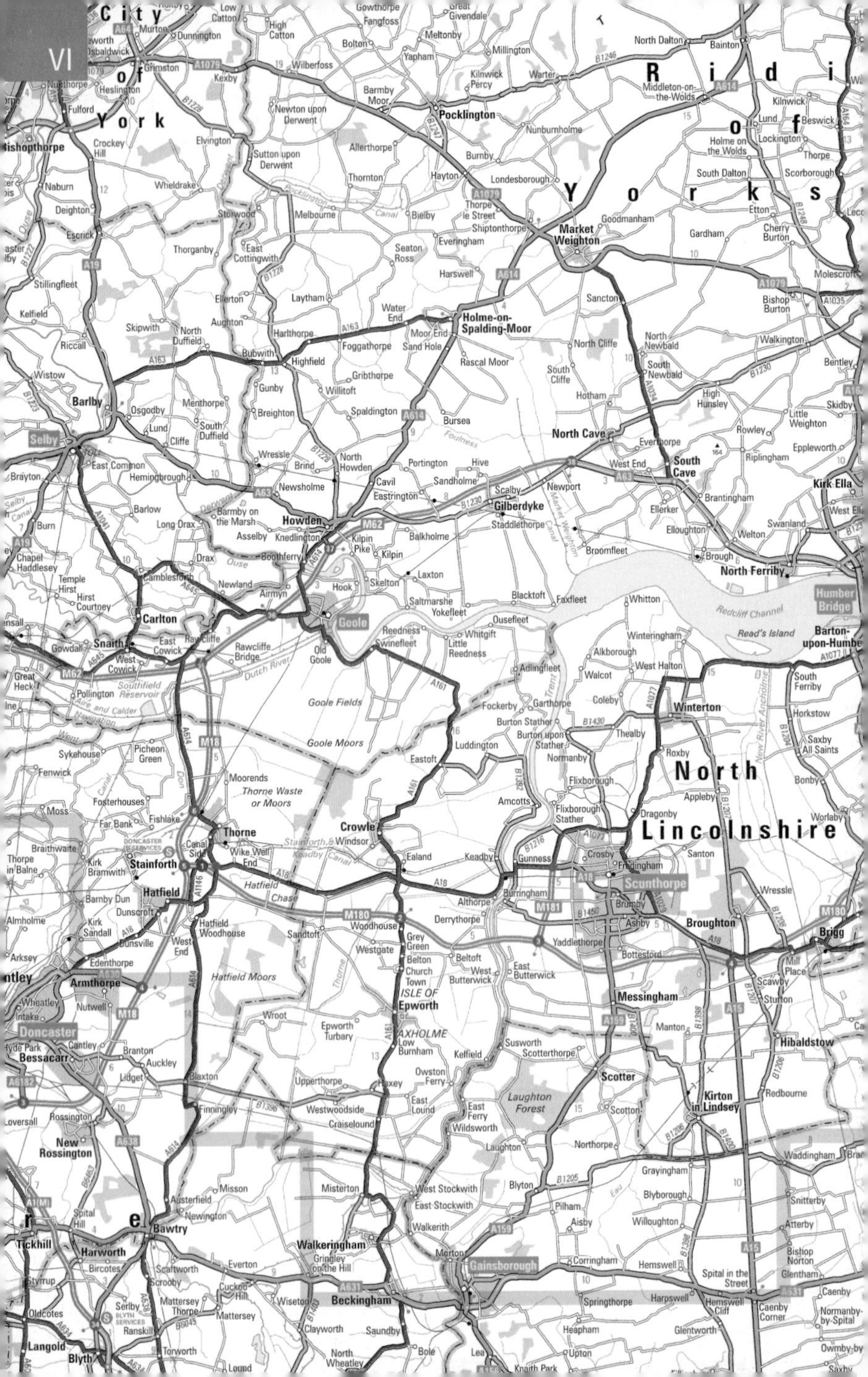
City of York
Riding of Yorkshire
North Lincolnshire
Murton
Dunnington
Low Catton
High Catton
Gowthorpe
Fangfoss
Great Givendale
Bolton
Meltonby
Yapham
Millington
North Dalton
Bainton
Osbaldwick
Grimston
Heslington
Kexby
Wilberfoss
Barmby Moor
Pocklington
Kilnwick Percy
Warter
Middleton-on-the-Wolds
Kilnwick
Beswick
Lund
Lockington
Holme on the Wolds
Thorpe
South Dalton
Scorborough
Fulford
Newton upon Derwent
Nunburnholme
Bishopthorpe
Crockey Hill
Elvington
Sutton upon Derwent
Allerthorpe
Burnby
Hayton
Londesborough
Naburn
Wheldrake
Thornton
Pocklington Canal
Deighton
Storwood
Melbourne
Bielby
Thorpe le Street
Shiptonthorpe
Market Weighton
Goodmanham
Etton
Cherry Burton
Gardham
Escrick
Thorganby
East Cottingwith
Seaton Ross
Everingham
Harswell
Stillingfleet
Kelfield
Ellerton
Laytham
Water End
Holme-on-Spalding-Moor
Sancton
Bishop Burton
Molescroft
Skipwith
North Duffield
Aughton
Harlthorpe
Foggathorpe
Moor End
Sand Hole
Rascal Moor
North Cliffe
North Newbald
South Newbald
Walkington
Bentley
Riccall
Bubwith
Highfield
Gribthorpe
Willitoft
South Cliffe
Wistow
Barlby
Gunby
Osgodby
Menthorpe
Lund
South Duffield
Breighton
Spaldington
Bursea
Hotham
High Hunsley
Little Weighton
Skidby
Selby
Cliffe
Wressle
Brind
North Howden
Portington
Hive
North Cave
Everthorpe
Rowley
Eppleworth
Riplingham
Brayton
East Common
Hemingbrough
Newsholme
Cavil
Eastrington
Sandholme
Scalby
Gilberdyke
Newport
West End
South Cave
Kirk Ella
Barlow
Barmby on the Marsh
Howden
Staddlethorpe
Ellerker
Brantingham
West Ella
Burn
Long Drax
Asselby
Knedlington
Kilpin Pike
Kilpin
Balkholme
Market Weighton Canal
Broomfleet
Elloughton
Welton
Swanland
Chapel Haddlesey
Drax
Boothferry
Brough
North Ferriby
Temple Hirst
Hirst Courtney
Camblesforth
Newland
Airmyn
Hook
Skelton
Laxton
Blacktoft
Faxfleet
Whitton
Humber Bridge
Redcliff Channel
Read's Island
Carlton
Goole
Saltmarshe
Yokefleet
Ousefleet
Barton-upon-Humber
Snaith
Gowdall
East Cowick
Rawcliffe
Rawcliffe Bridge
Old Goole
Reedness
Swinefleet
Whitgift
Little Reedness
Winteringham
Alkborough
West Halton
Great Heck
West Cowick
Dutch River
Adlingfleet
Walcot
South Ferriby
Pollington
Southfield Reservoir
Aire and Calder Navigation
Goole Fields
Fockerby
Garthorpe
Coleby
Winterton
Horkstow
Burton Stather
Burton upon Stather
Thealby
Goole Moors
Luddington
Saxby All Saints
Sykehouse
Picheon Green
Eastoft
Roxby
Normanby
Fenwick
Moorends
Thorne Waste or Moors
Flixborough
Bonby
Fosterhouses
Amcotts
Appleby
Moss
Fishlake
Flixborough Stather
Dragonby
Worlaby
Far Bank
Thorne
Crowle
Windsor
Braithwaite
Doncaster Services
Canal Side
Stainforth & Keadby Canal
Ealand
Keadby
Gunness
Crosby
Frodingham
Santon
Thorpe in Balne
Kirk Bramwith
Stainforth
Wike Well End
Scunthorpe
Hatfield
Hatfield Chase
Burringham
Wressle
Barnby Dun
Dunscroft
Althorpe
Brumby
Almholme
Kirk Sandall
Hatfield Woodhouse
Woodhouse
Derrythorpe
Ashby
Broughton
Brigg
Dunsville
West End
Sandtoft
Grey Green
Yaddlethorpe
Arksey
Edenthorpe
Westgate
Belton
Bottesford
Church Town
Beltoft
West Butterwick
East Butterwick
Mill Place
Scawby
Armthorpe
Hatfield Moors
Isle of Axholme
Epworth
Messingham
Sturton
Wheatley
Nutwell
Intake
Doncaster
Wroot
Epworth Turbary
Low Burnham
Manton
Hibaldstow
Hyde Park
Cantley
Bessacarr
Branton
Auckley
Kelfield
Susworth
Scotterthorpe
Owston Ferry
Lidget
Blaxton
Upperthorpe
Haxey
Scotter
Redbourne
Kirton in Lindsey
Laughton Forest
Loversall
Rossington
Finningley
Westwoodside
East Lound
East Ferry
Wildsworth
Scotton
Craiselound
New Rossington
Laughton
Northorpe
Waddingham
Misson
Misterton
West Stockwith
East Stockwith
Blyton
Grayingham
Blyborough
Snitterby
Austerfield
Newington
Pilham
Aisby
Willoughton
Atterby
Spital Hill
Bawtry
Walkerith
Tickhill
Harworth
Walkeringham
Gringley on the Hill
Morton
Gainsborough
Corringham
Hemswell
Bishop Norton
Glentham
Bircotes
Scaftworth
Everton
Scrooby
Cuckoo Hill
Spital in the Street
Styrrup
Wiseton
Beckingham
Springthorpe
Harpswell
Hemswell Cliff
Caenby
Caenby Corner
Normanby-by-Spital
Oldcotes
Serlby
Mattersey Thorpe
Mattersey
Blyth Services
Ranskill
Clayworth
Saundby
Heapham
Glentworth
Langold
Blyth
Torworth
North Wheatley
Bole
Lea
Upton
Knaith Park
Lound
Owmby-by-Spital
Saxby
Derwent
Ouse
Foulness
Trent
Eau
Don
Thorne
New River Ancholme
A64
A1079
A19
A614
A163
A1034
A63
M62
A645
A1041
A161
M18
A18
M180
A1146
M181
A1077
A1029
A159
A15
A630
A6182
A638
A1(M)
A631
A634
B1228
B1246
B1247
B1248
B1222
B1223
B1230
B1430
B1392
B1216
B1450
B1204
B1207
B1206
B1398
B1400
B1205
B1396
B6463
B6045
B1403

Route planning

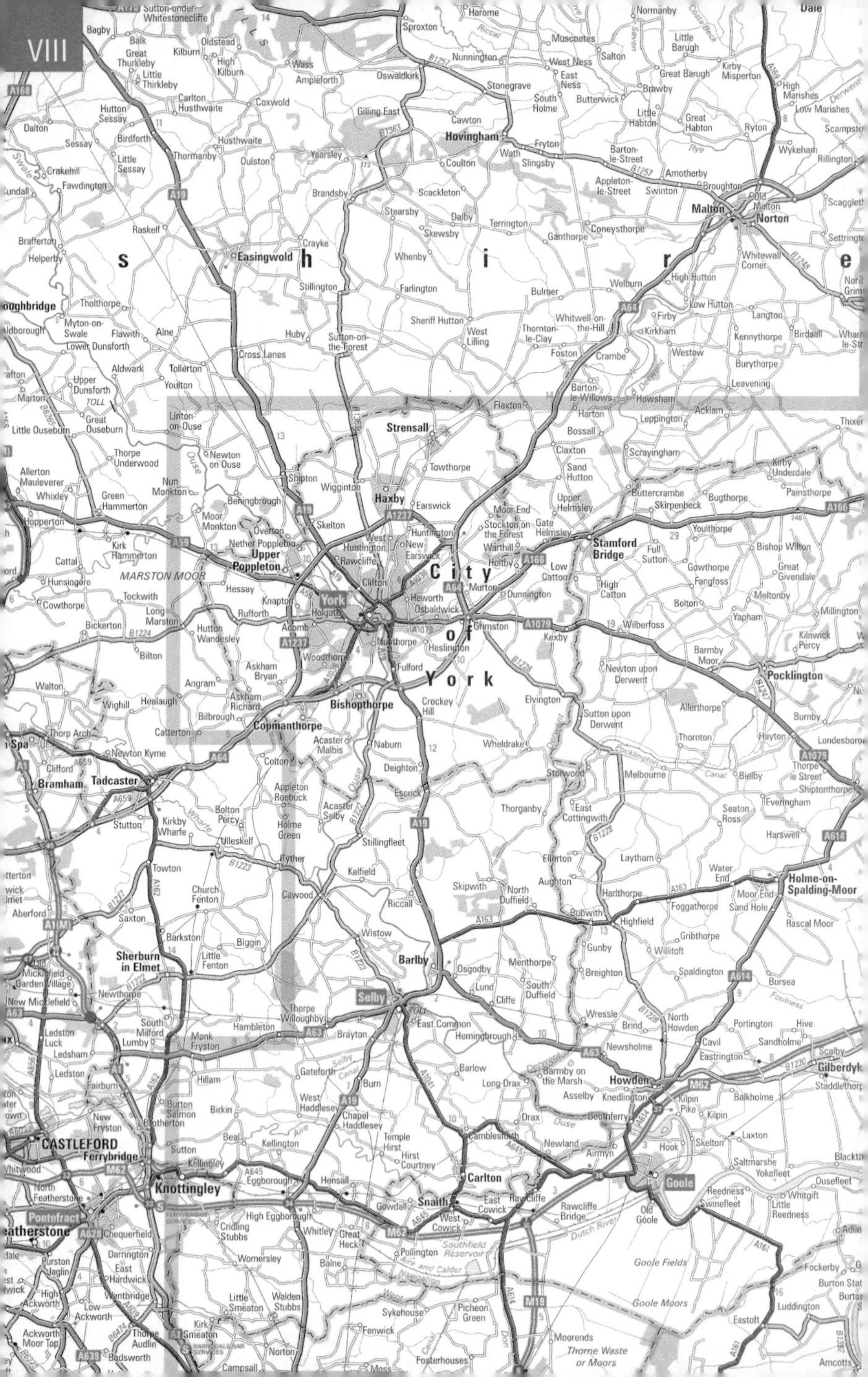
Sutton-under-Whitestonecliffe
Bagby
Balk
Great Thirkleby
Little Thirkleby
Kilburn
Oldstead
High Kilburn
Carlton Husthwaite
Coxwold
Hutton Sessay
Dalton
Sessay
Birdforth
Little Sessay
Husthwaite
Thormanby
Oulston
Crakehill
Fawdington
Raskelf
Brafferton
Helperby
Easingwold
Tholthorpe
Myton-on-Swale
Flawith
Alne
Lower Dunsforth
Aldwark
Tollerton
Youlton
Upper Dunsforth
Great Ouseburn
Little Ouseburn
Linton-on-Ouse
Newton on Ouse
Thorpe Underwood
Allerton Mauleverer
Whixley
Green Hammerton
Nun Monkton
Beningbrough
Moor Monkton
Hopperton
Kirk Hammerton
Cattal
Hunsingore
MARSTON MOOR
Cowthorpe
Tockwith
Long Marston
Bickerton
Bilton
Walton
Wighill
Healaugh
Thorp Arch
Clifford
Bramham
Tadcaster
Newton Kyme
Stutton
Kirkby Wharfe
Towton
Saxton
Barkston
Church Fenton
Biggin
Little Fenton
Sherburn in Elmet
Aberford
Micklefield
New Micklefield
South Milford
Lumby
Ledston Luck
Ledsham
Ledston
Fairburn
Monk Fryston
Hambleton
Hillam
Burton Salmon
Brotherton
New Fryston
CASTLEFORD
Ferrybridge
Knottingley
Kellingley
Sutton
Pontefract
Featherstone
Chequerfield
Darrington
East Hardwick
Wentbridge
High Ackworth
Low Ackworth
Purston Jaglin
Ackworth Moor Top
Thorpe Audlin
Badsworth
Kirk Smeaton
Little Smeaton
Walden Stubbs
Womersley
Cridling Stubbs
High Eggborough
Eggborough
Whitley
Beal
Kellington
Birkin
Hensall
Gowdall
Snaith
Great Heck
Pollington
Balne
Sykehouse
Fenwick
Campsall
Norton
Moss
Fosterhouses
Picheon Green
Moorends
Thorne Waste or Moors
Sproxton
Harome
Wass
Ampleforth
Oswaldkirk
Gilling East
Yearsley
Brandsby
Stearsby
Crayke
Stillington
Huby
Sutton-on-the-Forest
Cross Lanes
Whenby
Farlington
Sheriff Hutton
West Lilling
Strensall
Towthorpe
Haxby
Wigginton
Shipton
Skelton
Earswick
Huntington
New Earswick
Overton
Nether Poppleton
Upper Poppleton
Rawcliffe
Clifton
Hessay
Knapton
Rufforth
York
Holgate
Acomb
Heworth
Osbaldwick
Murton
Hutton Wandesley
Askham Bryan
Askham Richard
Angram
Bilbrough
Catterton
Woodthorpe
Dringhouses
Heslington
Fulford
Bishopthorpe
Copmanthorpe
Acaster Malbis
Naburn
Deighton
Escrick
Colton
Appleton Roebuck
Bolton Percy
Acaster Selby
Holme Green
Ulleskelf
Ryther
Stillingfleet
Kelfield
Cawood
Riccall
Wistow
Barlby
Selby
Thorpe Willoughby
Brayton
Gateforth
Burn
West Haddlesey
Chapel Haddlesey
Temple Hirst
Hirst Courtney
Camblesforth
Carlton
Drax
Long Drax
Barlow
East Cowick
West Cowick
Rawcliffe
Rawcliffe Bridge
Airmyn
Newland
Boothferry
Goole
Old Goole
Hook
Skelton
Saltmarshe
Laxton
Kilpin
Kilpin Pike
Balkholme
Knedlington
Howden
Asselby
Barmby on the Marsh
Hemingbrough
East Common
Osgodby
Lund
Cliffe
South Duffield
Menthorpe
Wressle
Brind
Newsholme
North Howden
Cavil
Eastrington
Portington
Sandholme
Hive
Scalby
Gilberdyke
Staddlethorpe
Blacktoft
Yokefleet
Ouseflee
Whitgift
Reedness
Swinefleet
Little Reedness
Goole Fields
Goole Moors
Adlingfleet
Fockerby
Burton Stather
Luddington
Eastoft
Amcotts
Hovingham
Nunnington
Stonegrave
Cawton
Coulton
Scackleton
Dalby
Skewsby
Terrington
Wath
Slingsby
Fryton
Ganthorpe
Coneysthorpe
Bulmer
Whitwell-on-the-Hill
Thornton-le-Clay
Foston
Crambe
Flaxton
Barton-le-Willows
Harton
Bossall
Claxton
Sand Hutton
Upper Helmsley
Gate Helmsley
Stockton on the Forest
Warthill
Holtby
Dunnington
Grimston
Kexby
Low Catton
High Catton
Stamford Bridge
Full Sutton
Elvington
Sutton upon Derwent
Wheldrake
Storwood
Thorganby
East Cottingwith
Ellerton
Aughton
Skipwith
North Duffield
Bubwith
Highfield
Gunby
Breighton
Willitoft
Spaldington
Laytham
Harlthorpe
Foggathorpe
Gribthorpe
Melbourne
Newton upon Derwent
Wilberfoss
Allerthorpe
Thornton
Barmby Moor
Pocklington
Bielby
Everingham
Seaton Ross
Harswell
Holme-on-Spalding-Moor
Water End
Moor End
Sand Hole
Rascal Moor
Bursea
Hayton
Burnby
Londesborough
Thorpe le Street
Shiptonthorpe
Yapham
Meltonby
Bolton
Fangfoss
Gowthorpe
Bishop Wilton
Great Givendale
Kilnwick Percy
Millington
Youlthorpe
Skirpenbeck
Buttercrambe
Bugthorpe
Painsthorpe
Kirby Underdale
Scrayingham
Leppington
Acklam
Howsham
Leavening
Burythorpe
Westow
Kirkham
Firby
Welburn
Langton
Kennythorpe
Birdsall
High Hutton
Low Hutton
Whitewall Corner
Malton
Norton
Old Malton
Broughton
Amotherby
Swinton
Appleton-le-Street
Barton-le-Street
Great Habton
Little Habton
Ryton
Butterwick
South Holme
Muscoates
West Ness
East Ness
Salton
Normanby
Little Barugh
Great Barugh
Brawby
Kirby Misperton
High Marishes
Low Marishes
Wykeham
Rillington
Scampston
Scagglethorpe
Settrington
City of York
Ouse
Derwent
Wharfe
Aire
Rye
Riccal
Pocklington Canal
Dutch River
Southfield Reservoir
Aire and Calder Navigation
Selby Canal
Foulness
A19
A64
A59
A1237
A1036
A1079
A166
A163
A614
A63
A1
A1(M)
A162
A645
A1041
A659
A656
A628
A638
M62
M18
A161
A169
B1257
B1363
B1224
B1223
B1222
B1228
B1230
B1248
B1247
B6474

Brompton
Lebberston
Gristhorpe
Filey Brigg
Filey
Flixton
Folkton
Muston
Willerby
Staxton
Filey Bay
Primrose Valley
Yedingham
THE CARRS
Ganton
Hunmanby
Hunmanby Moor
Reighton Sands
Reighton Gap
East Heslerton
Sherburn
West Knapton
East Knapton
West Heslerton
Potter Brompton
Fordon
Reighton
Speeton
Thorpe Bassett
Wintringham
Place Newton
Foxholes
Wold Newton
Burton Fleming
Buckton
Bempton
FLAMBOROUGH HEAD
Butterwick
Grindale
Flamborough
Helperthorpe
Weaverthorpe
Octon
Thwing
Sewerby
East Lutton
West Lutton
Octon Cross Roads
Boynton
Rudston
Bridlington
Kirby Grindalythe
Duggleby
Langtoft
Bessingby
Carnaby
West Hill
Hilderthorpe
Sledmere
Cottam
Haisthorpe
Thornholme
Kilham
BRIDLINGTON BAY
THE WOLDS
Burton Agnes
Ruston Parva
Harpham
Fraisthorpe
Fimber
Lowthorpe
Garton-on-the-Wolds
Gransmoor
Nafferton
Fridaythorpe
Wetwang
Barmston
Great Kelk
Lissett
Elmswell
Little Driffield
Driffield
Gembling
Ulrome
Kelleythorpe
Foston on the Wolds
Wansford
Driffield Canal
Skipsea
Huggate
Tibthorpe
Skerne
Kirkburn
Southburn
Brigham
Church End
Beeford
Skipsea Brough
Hutton
North Frodingham
Hutton Cranswick
Dunnington
Rotsea
North Dalton
Bainton
Hempholme
Bewholme
Atwick
Middleton-on-the-Wolds
Watton
North Cliff
Kilnwick
Watton Beck
Burshill
Hornsea
Lund
Beswick
Lockington
Holme on the Wolds
Thorpe
Baswick Steer
Brandesburton
Seaton
Hornsea Bridge
Hornsea Mere
Sigglesthorne
Rolston
South Dalton
Scorborough
Aike
Hull
Leven Canal
Leven
Catwick
Goxhill
Mappleton
Arram
East Riding of Yorkshire
Little Hatfield
Great Cowden
Goodmanham
Etton
Leconfield
Eske
Routh
Rise
Market Weighton
Gardham
Cherry Burton
Long Riston
Great Hatfield
Tickton
Arnold
Withernwick
Molescroft
Beverley
Weel
Meaux
Skirlaugh
New Ellerby
Sancton
Bishop Burton
Marton
West Newton
Aldbrough
East Newton
Woodmansey
North Newbald
North Cliffe
Walkington
Wawne
Old Ellerby
Flinton
Thearne
South Newbald
Bentley
Garton
South Cliffe
Dunswell
Swine
Coniston
Grimston
Hotham
High Hunsley
Skidby
Bransholme
Thirtleby
Sproatley
Humbleton
Fitling
Hilston
Kingston-upon-Hull
Sutton on Hull
Ganstead
Little Weighton
Cottingham
Rowley
Inglemire
North Cave
Everthorpe
Sutton Ings
Bilton
Lelley
Owstwick
Elstronwick
Riplingham
Eppleworth
Newland
Stoneferry
Burton Pidsea
Roos
West End
Willerby
Sculcoates
Summergangs
Preston
South Cave
Newport
Kirk Ella
East Ella
Marfleet
West End
Brantingham
West Ella
Salt End
Hedon
Ellerker
Anlaby
Haven Side
Rimswell
Swanland
Burstwick
Halsham
Elloughton
Welton
Market Weighton Canal
Northfield
Hessle
KINGSTON UPON HULL
Paull
Camerton
Broomfleet
Brough
Thorngumbald
Ryehill
Keyingham
North Ferriby
HUMBER
Ottringham
Faxfleet
Whitton
Humber Bridge
Goxhill Haven
Redcliff Channel
Barton Waterside
New Holland
Little Humber
Patrington
Read's Island
Barton-upon-Humber
Winteringham
Barrow Haven
Thorney Crofts
Alkborough
Cherry Cob Sands
West Halton
Goxhill
Walcot
Barrow upon Humber
South Ferriby
South End
East Halton
Coleby
Winterton
Horkstow
Kingsforth
Sunk Island
Thealby
River Trent
New River Ancholme
Saxby All Saints
Thornton Curtis
North Killingholme
Roxby
Burnham
Normanby
Wootton
North
Flixborough
Bonby
Ulceby Skitter
South Killingholme
Ulceby
Immingham
Appleby

Administrative and Postcode boundaries

County and unitary authority boundaries

Postcode boundaries

Area covered by this atlas

Scale

0 5 10 15 20 25 30 35 40 km

0 5 10 15 20 25 miles

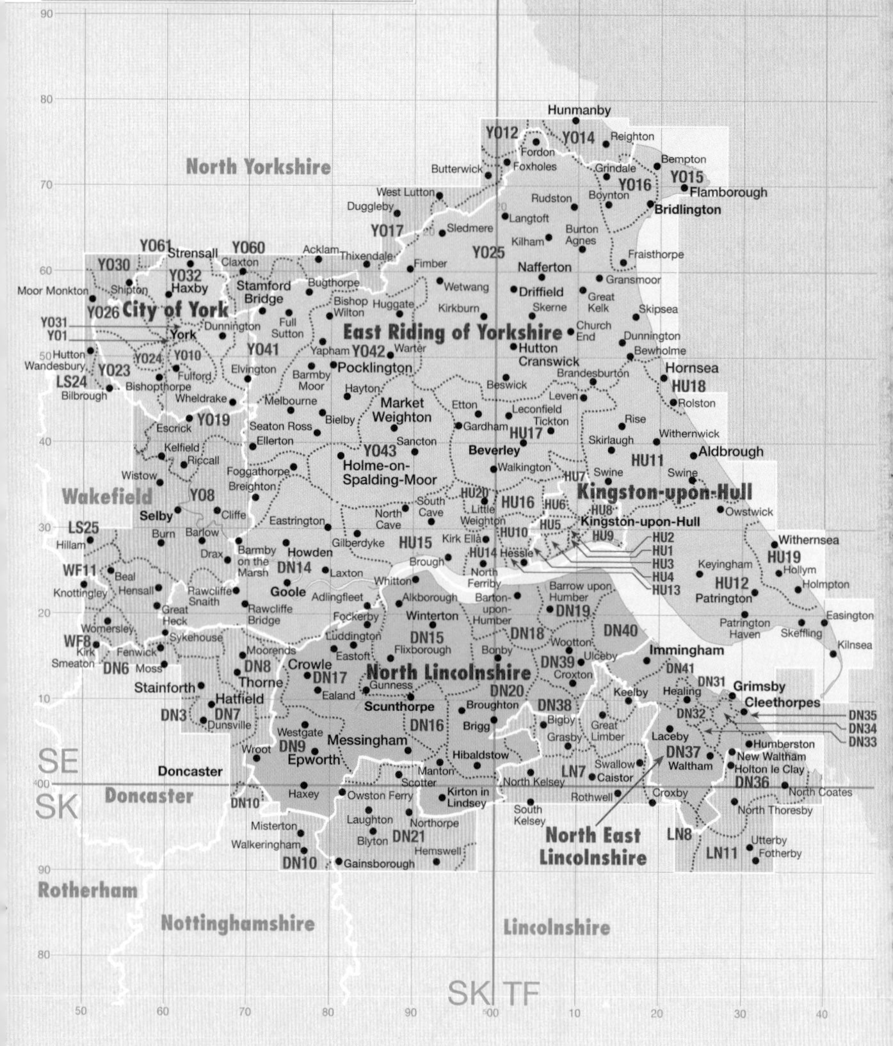
NZ
SE TA
SE
SK
SK TF
North Yorkshire
City of York
East Riding of Yorkshire
Kingston-upon-Hull
North Lincolnshire
North East Lincolnshire
Lincolnshire
Nottinghamshire
Doncaster
Rotherham
Wakefield
Hunmanby
Reighton
Bempton
Flamborough
Bridlington
Fordon
Foxholes
Butterwick
Grindale
Boynton
Rudston
West Lutton
Duggleby
Sledmere
Langtoft
Kilham
Burton Agnes
Fraisthorpe
Nafferton
Gransmoor
Driffield
Great Kelk
Skipsea
Fimber
Thixendale
Acklam
Wetwang
Kirkburn
Skerne
Church End
Dunnington
Bewholme
Hutton Cranswick
Hornsea
Brandesburton
Rolston
Leven
Leconfield
Tickton
Rise
Beverley
Walkington
Skirlaugh
Withernwick
Aldbrough
Swine
Owstwick
Withernsea
Hollym
Holmpton
Keyingham
Patrington
Patrington Haven
Skeffling
Easington
Kilnsea
Strensall
Claxton
Shipton
Haxby
Moor Monkton
Stamford Bridge
Bugthorpe
Bishop Wilton
Huggate
York
Dunnington
Full Sutton
Yapham
Warter
Pocklington
Hutton Wandesbury
Fulford
Elvington
Barmby Moor
Bilbrough
Bishopthorpe
Wheldrake
Hayton
Melbourne
Bielby
Market Weighton
Etton
Gardham
Escrick
Seaton Ross
Ellerton
Sancton
Kelfield
Riccall
Holme-on-Spalding-Moor
Wistow
Foggathorpe
Breighton
South Cave
North Cave
Little Weighton
Selby
Cliffe
Eastrington
Burn
Barlow
Hillam
Drax
Barmby on the Marsh
Howden
Gilberdyke
Kirk Ella
Hessle
Brough
North Ferriby
Beal
Knottingley
Hensall
Rawcliffe Snaith
Goole
Laxton
Adlingfleet
Whitton
Alkborough
Barton-upon-Humber
Barrow upon Humber
Great Heck
Rawcliffe Bridge
Fockerby
Winterton
Womersley
Sykehouse
Luddington
Flixborough
Bonby
Wootton
Immingham
Ulceby
Kirk Smeaton
Fenwick
Moss
Moorends
Eastoft
Crowle
Thorne
Gunness
Croxton
Keelby
Healing
Grimsby
Cleethorpes
Stainforth
Hatfield
Ealand
Scunthorpe
Broughton
Brigg
Bigby
Great Limber
Grasby
Laceby
Humberston
Dunsville
Westgate
Messingham
Waltham
New Waltham
Holton le Clay
Wroot
Epworth
Hibaldstow
Swallow
Caistor
Doncaster
Manton
Scotter
North Kelsey
Haxey
Owston Ferry
Kirton in Lindsey
Rothwell
Croxby
North Coates
South Kelsey
North Thoresby
Misterton
Laughton
Northorpe
Walkeringham
Blyton
Hemswell
Gainsborough
Utterby
Fotherby
Y012
Y014
Y015
Y016
Y017
Y025
Y061
Y060
Y030
Y032
Y026
Y031
Y01
Y010
Y024
Y023
Y041
Y042
Y019
Y043
Y08
LS24
LS25
WF11
WF8
DN6
DN3
DN7
DN8
DN14
DN17
DN15
DN9
DN16
DN20
DN18
DN19
DN39
DN38
DN40
DN41
DN31
DN32
DN33
DN34
DN35
DN36
DN37
DN10
DN21
LN7
LN8
LN11
HU1
HU2
HU3
HU4
HU5
HU6
HU7
HU8
HU9
HU10
HU11
HU12
HU13
HU14
HU15
HU16
HU17
HU18
HU19
HU20
90
80
70
60
50
40
30
20
10
00
50
60
70
80
90
00
10
20
30
40

2

Scale: 1¼ inches to 1 mile

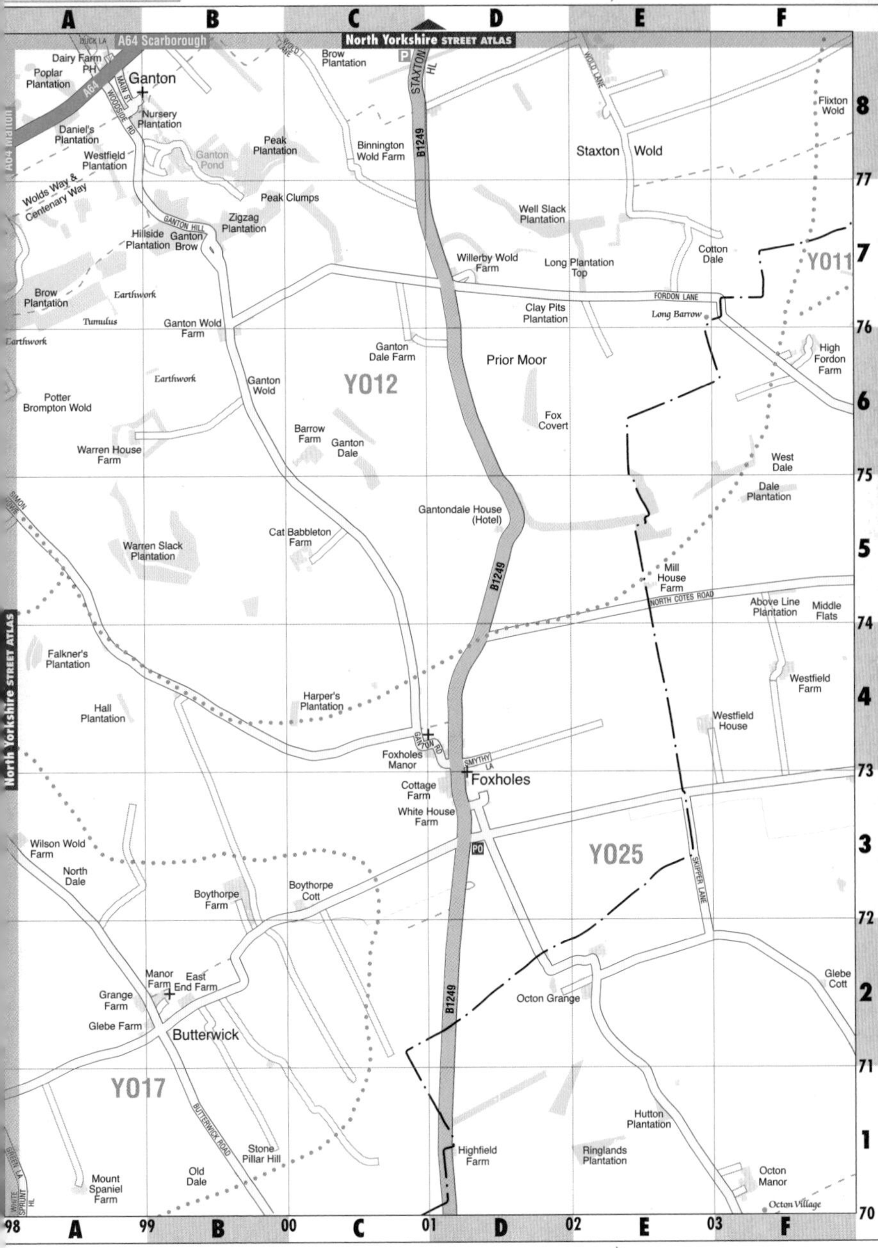

¼ ½ mile
250m 500m 750m 1 km
A
B
C
D
E
F
North Yorkshire STREET ATLAS
A64 Scarborough
DUCK LA
Dairy Farm PH
Poplar Plantation
Ganton
MAIN ST
WOODSIDE RD
A64
A64 Malton
Nursery Plantation
Daniel's Plantation
Westfield Plantation
Ganton Pond
Peak Plantation
Wolds Way & Centenary Way
Peak Clumps
GANTON HILL
Zigzag Plantation
Hillside Plantation
Ganton Brow
Brow Plantation
Earthwork
Tumulus
Earthwork
Ganton Wold Farm
Earthwork
Potter Brompton Wold
Warren House Farm
Ganton Wold
WOLD LANE
Brow Plantation
STAXTON HL
B1249
Binnington Wold Farm
Barrow Farm
Ganton Dale
Y012
Ganton Dale Farm
Willerby Wold Farm
WOLD LANE
Staxton Wold
Well Slack Plantation
Long Plantation Top
Cotton Dale
FORDON LANE
Clay Pits Plantation
Long Barrow
Prior Moor
Fox Covert
Flixton Wold
Y011
High Fordon Farm
West Dale
Dale Plantation
Gantondale House (Hotel)
SIMON HOWE
Warren Slack Plantation
Cat Babbleton Farm
Mill House Farm
NORTH COTES ROAD
Above Line Plantation
Middle Flats
Falkner's Plantation
Harper's Plantation
Hall Plantation
Westfield Farm
Westfield House
GANTON RD
Foxholes Manor
SMYTHY LA
Foxholes
Cottage Farm
White House Farm
PO
Y025
Wilson Wold Farm
North Dale
Boythorpe Farm
Boythorpe Cott
SKIPPER LANE
Manor Farm
East End Farm
Grange Farm
Glebe Farm
Butterwick
Octon Grange
Glebe Cott
Y017
BUTTERWICK ROAD
Hutton Plantation
Stone Pillar Hill
Highfield Farm
Ringlands Plantation
Old Dale
Mount Spaniel Farm
Octon Manor
Octon Village
GREEN LA
WHITE SPRUNT HL
8
77
7
76
6
75
5
74
4
73
3
72
2
71
1
70
98
99
00
01
02
03

8

2

1

F8
1 OWSTON RD
2 MITFORD RD
3 MITFORD CL
4 OUTGAITS CL
5 WENTWORTH WY
6 SIMPSON AV
7 HIGH CFT
8 CASTLE HL
9 BOWLING GN LA
10 CHURCH HL
11 HUNGATE CT
12 VICARAGE CL
13 FONTAYNE RD
14 BARDNEY RD
15 ROWEDALE CL
16 AMBREY CL
17 PARK RISE
18 OLIVER'S CL
19 ROSEMOOR CL
20 HARBOROUGH CL

Scale: 1¼ inches to 1 mile
0 ¼ ½ mile
0 250m 500m 750m 1 km

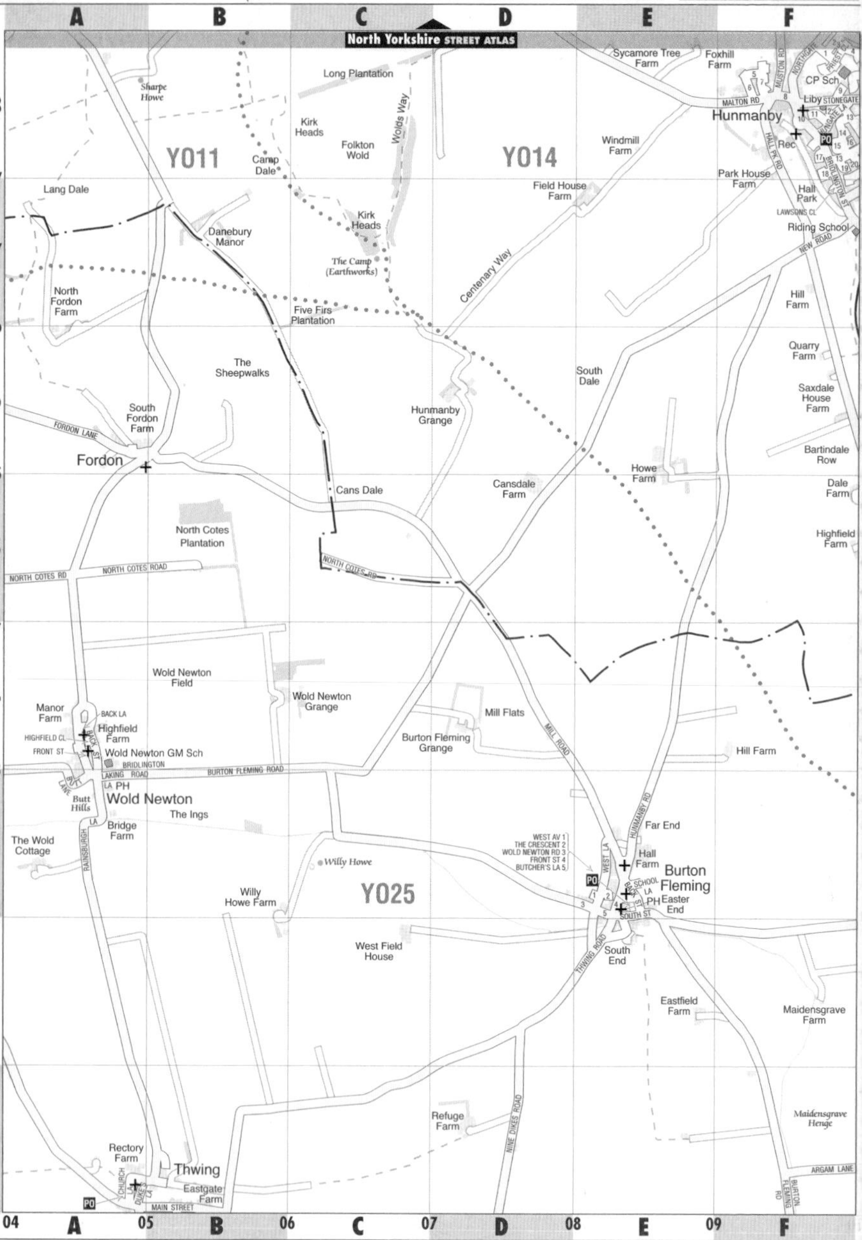

1

9

Scale: 1¼ inches to 1 mile
0 ¼ ½ mile
0 250m 500m 750m 1 km

A8
1 WRANGHAM DR
2 LENNOX CL
3 BURLYN RD
4 CHERRY RD
5 HAWKE GARTH
6 MANOR GD
7 CECIL RD
8 HOWES RD
9 WATSON CL
10 HAMERTON RD
11 HAMERTON CL
12 GRIMSTON RD
13 STRICKLAND RD
14 PERCY RD
15 HAVERCROFT RD
16 COWLINGS CL

4

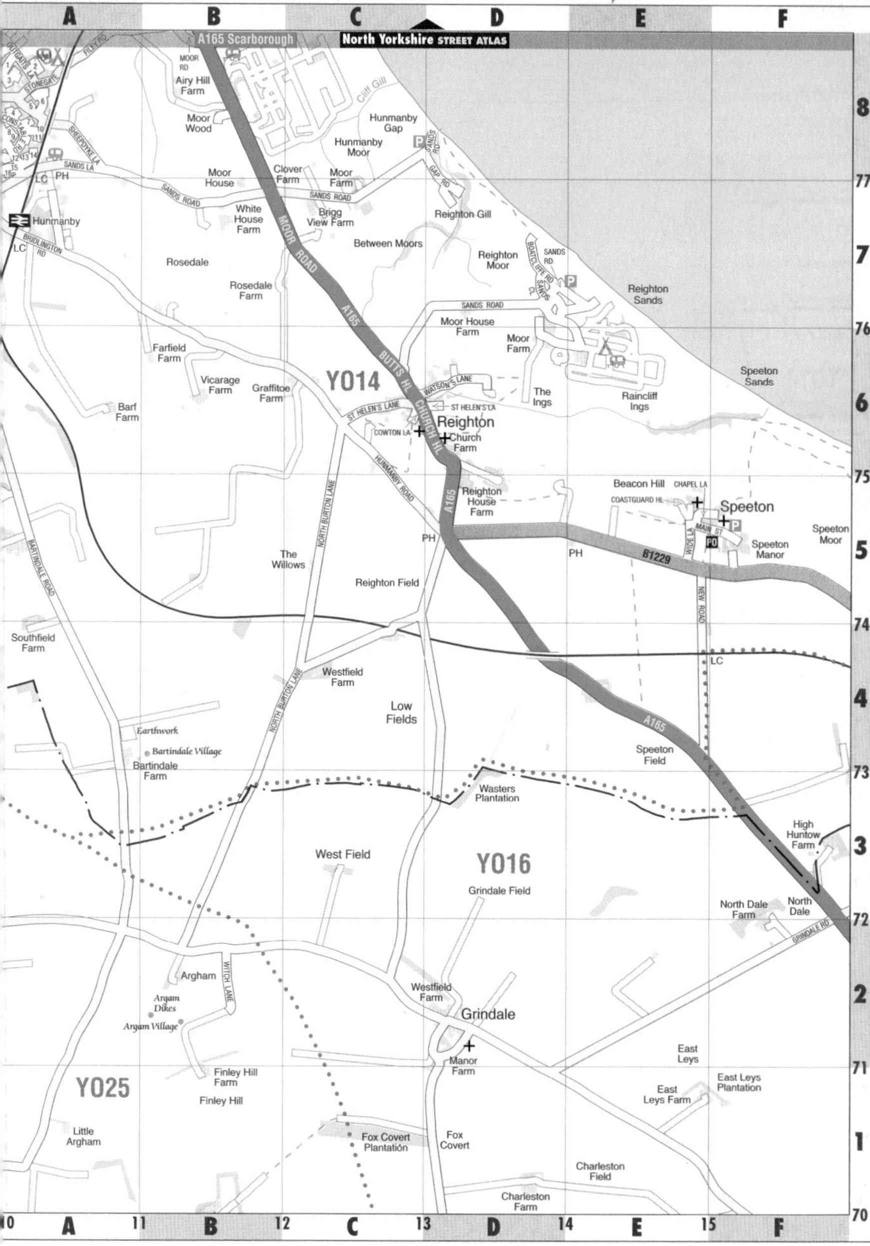

10
4

Scale: 1¼ inches to 1 mile

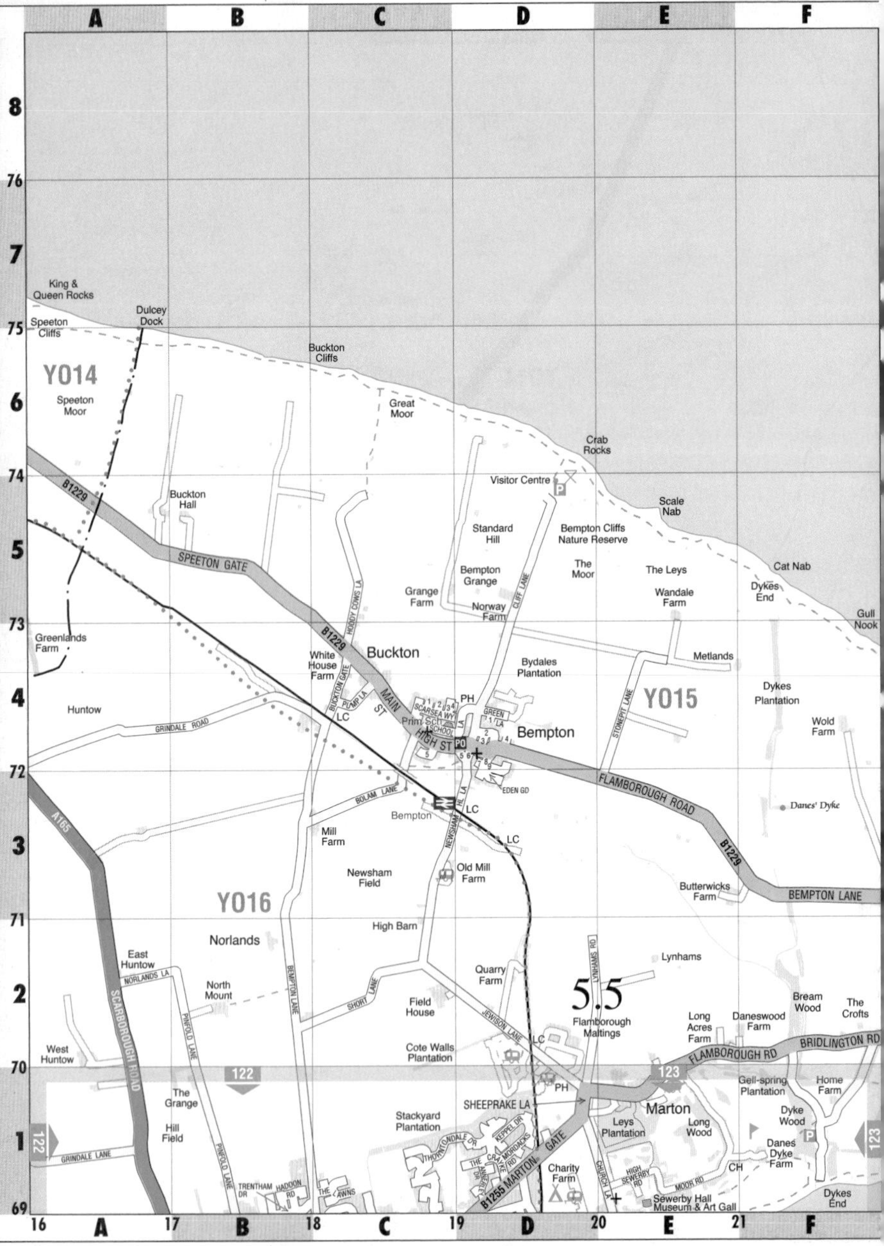
A
B
C
D
E
F
King &
Queen Rocks
Dulcey
Dock
Speeton
Cliffs
Buckton
Cliffs
YO14
Speeton
Moor
Great
Moor
Crab
Rocks
Visitor Centre
Scale
Nab
Buckton
Hall
B1229
Standard
Hill
Bempton Cliffs
Nature Reserve
SPEETON GATE
The
Moor
The Leys
Cat Nab
Bempton
Grange
Grange
Farm
Wandale
Farm
Dykes
End
Norway
Farm
CLIFF LANE
HODDY COWS LA
Gull
Nook
Greenlands
Farm
B1229
Buckton
Metlands
White
House
Farm
Bydales
Plantation
Dykes
Plantation
YO15
Huntow
BUCKTON GATE
MAIN ST
PUMP LA
PH
SCARSEA WY
SCHOOL LA
GREEN LA
Bempton
Wold
Farm
GRINDALE ROAD
LC
Prim Sch
HIGH ST
PO
STONEPIT LANE
FLAMBOROUGH ROAD
EDEN GD
A165
BOLAM LANE
LC
Danes' Dyke
Bempton
NEWSHAM HL LA
LC
Mill
Farm
B1229
Newsham
Field
Old Mill
Farm
Butterwicks
Farm
BEMPTON LANE
YO16
High Barn
Norlands
LYNHAMS RD
Lynhams
East
Huntow
NORLANDS LA
Quarry
Farm
North
Mount
SHORT LANE
Field
House
5.5
Bream
Wood
The
Crofts
SCARBOROUGH ROAD
PINFOLD LANE
BEMPTON LANE
JEWISON LANE
Flamborough
Maltings
Long
Acres
Farm
Daneswood
Farm
West
Huntow
Cote Walls
Plantation
LC
FLAMBOROUGH RD
BRIDLINGTON RD
122
123
Gell-spring
Plantation
Home
Farm
PH
The
Grange
Stackyard
Plantation
SHEEPRAKE LA
Marton
Hill
Field
Leys
Plantation
Long
Wood
Dyke
Wood
122
THORNTONDALE DR
KEPPEL DR
Danes
Dyke
Farm
123
GRINDALE LANE
PINFOLD LANE
THE CRAYKE
MORDACKS RD
B1255 MARTON GATE
Charity
Farm
CHURCH LA
HIGH SEWERBY RD
MOOR RD
CH
TRENTHAM DR
HADDON RD
THE LAWNS
Sewerby Hall
Museum & Art Gall
Dykes
End
8
76
7
75
6
74
5
73
4
72
3
71
2
70
1
69
16
17
18
19
20
21

C4
1 WALMSLEY CL
2 GRANGE CL
3 COLLINGWOOD RD
4 THE MEADOWS
5 RINGLEY MS

D4
1 THE PADDOCK
2 SPRING LA
3 ST MICHAEL'S WK
4 BYEDALES
5 GILLUS LA
6 CHURCH LA
7 ACREDYKES
8 VICARAGE LA
9 CLARK CR

For full street detail of the highlighted area see pages 122 and 123.

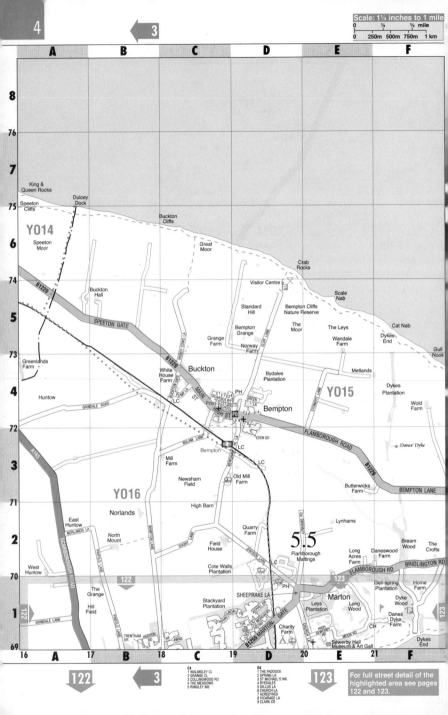

A2
1 WOODCOCK RD
2 BEECH GR
3 BEECH AV
4 GARENDS RD
5 NORTH END
6 CHAPEL ST
7 HIGH ST
8 GREENSIDE
9 MERESIDE
10 SCHOOL LA
11 OGLE RD
12 POST OFFICE ST
13 DOG AND DUCK SQ
14 ALLISON LA
15 STYLEFIELD RD
16 CASTLE CR
17 STOTTLEBINK
18 CONSTABLE CL
19 CHURCH ST
20 WATER LA
21 WEST ST
22 HARTENDALE CL
23 BUTLERS LA
24 CHURCH LA
25 CHURCH CL
26 SOUTH SEA AV

Scale: 1¼ inches to 1 mile

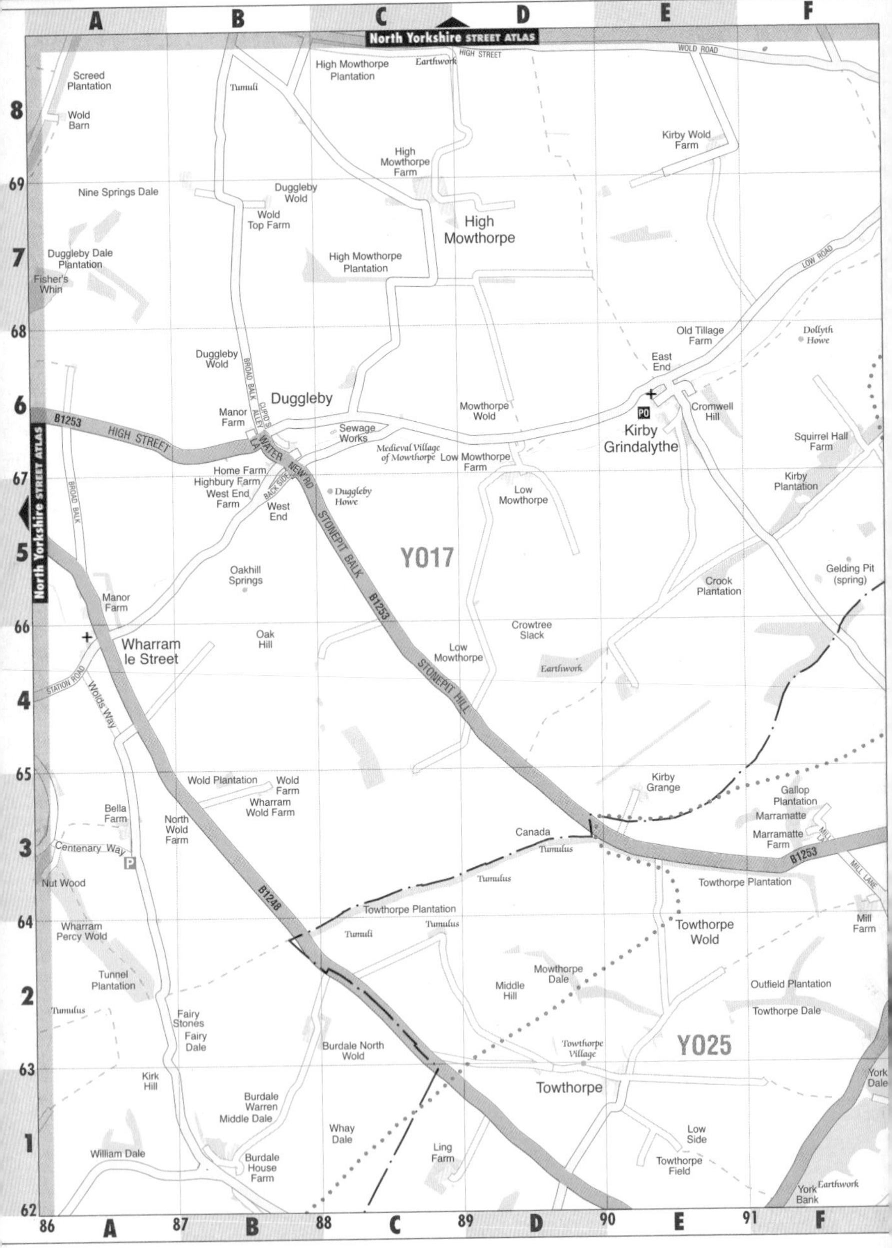
North Yorkshire STREET ATLAS
A
B
C
D
E
F
Screed Plantation
Wold Barn
High Mowthorpe Plantation
Earthwork
HIGH STREET
WOLD ROAD
Tumuli
High Mowthorpe Farm
Kirby Wold Farm
Nine Springs Dale
Duggleby Wold
Wold Top Farm
High Mowthorpe
Duggleby Dale Plantation
High Mowthorpe Plantation
Fisher's Whin
LOW ROAD
Old Tillage Farm
Dollyth Howe
Duggleby Wold
East End
BROAD BALK
CUPIDS ALLEY
Duggleby
Mowthorpe Wold
Cromwell Hill
Manor Farm
Sewage Works
Kirby Grindalythe
B1253
HIGH STREET
WATER LA
NEW RD
Medieval Village of Mowthorpe
Low Mowthorpe Farm
Squirrel Hall Farm
Home Farm
Highbury Farm
West End Farm
BACK SIDE
West End
Duggleby Howe
Low Mowthorpe
Kirby Plantation
BROAD BALK
STONEPIT BALK
YO17
Oakhill Springs
Crook Plantation
Gelding Pit (spring)
Manor Farm
B1253
Wharram le Street
Oak Hill
Crowtree Slack
Low Mowthorpe
STONEPIT HILL
Earthwork
STATION ROAD
Wolds Way
Wold Plantation
Wold Farm
Wharram Wold Farm
Kirby Grange
Gallop Plantation
Bella Farm
North Wold Farm
Marramatte
Canada
Marramatte Farm
MILL LA
Centenary Way
Tumulus
B1253
Nut Wood
Tumulus
Towthorpe Plantation
MILL LANE
B1248
Towthorpe Plantation
Towthorpe Wold
Mill Farm
Wharram Percy Wold
Tumuli
Tumulus
Tunnel Plantation
Mowthorpe Dale
Middle Hill
Outfield Plantation
Tumulus
Towthorpe Dale
Fairy Stones
Fairy Dale
Burdale North Wold
Towthorpe Village
YO25
Kirk Hill
Towthorpe
York Dale
Burdale Warren Middle Dale
Whay Dale
Low Side
Ling Farm
William Dale
Burdale House Farm
Towthorpe Field
York Bank
Earthwork
86
87
88
89
90
91
62
63
64
65
66
67
68
69
1
2
3
4
5
6
7
8

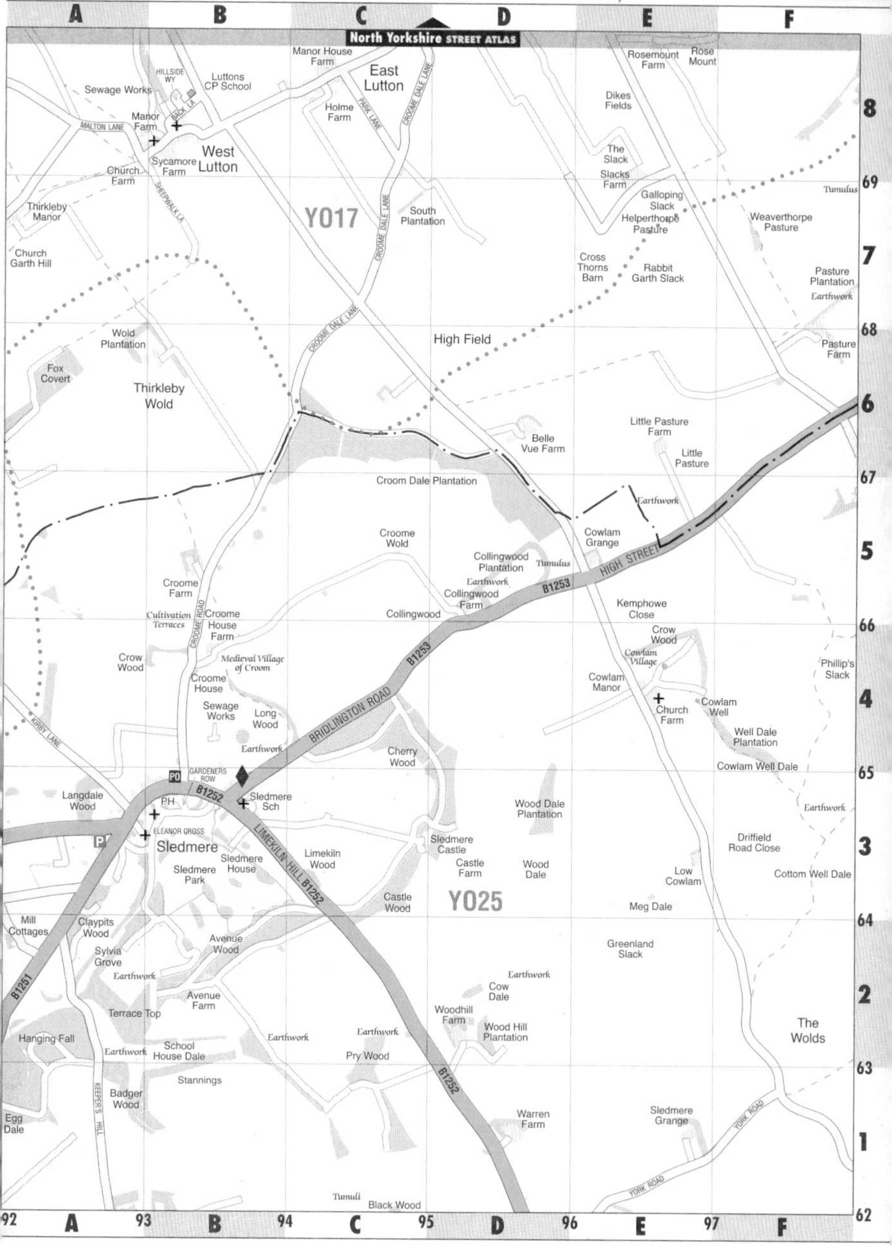
A
B
C
D
E
F
North Yorkshire STREET ATLAS
Manor House Farm
East Lutton
Rosemount Farm
Rose Mount
Luttons CP School
Sewage Works
HILLSIDE WY
BACK LA
MALTON LANE
Manor Farm
Holme Farm
PARK LANE
CROOME DALE LANE
Dikes Fields
West Lutton
Sycamore Farm
Church Farm
The Slack
Slacks Farm
SHEEPWALK LA
Thirkleby Manor
YO17
South Plantation
Galloping Slack
Helperthorpe Pasture
Weaverthorpe Pasture
Tumulus
Church Garth Hill
Cross Thorns Barn
Rabbit Garth Slack
Pasture Plantation
Earthwork
Wold Plantation
High Field
Pasture Farm
Fox Covert
Thirkleby Wold
Little Pasture Farm
Belle Vue Farm
Little Pasture
Croom Dale Plantation
Earthwork
Croome Wold
Cowlam Grange
Collingwood Plantation
Tumulus
HIGH STREET
B1253
Earthwork
Croome Farm
Collingwood Farm
Kemphowe Close
Cultivation Terraces
CROOME ROAD
Croome House Farm
Collingwood
Crow Wood
Cowlam Village
Medieval Village of Croom
B1253
Crow Wood
Croome House
Cowlam Manor
Phillip's Slack
BRIDLINGTON ROAD
Sewage Works
Long Wood
Church Farm
Cowlam Well
KIRBY LANE
Earthwork
Cherry Wood
Well Dale Plantation
Cowlam Well Dale
PO
GARDENERS ROW
Langdale Wood
B1252
PH
Sledmere Sch
Wood Dale Plantation
Earthwork
ELEANOR CROSS
P
Sledmere
Sledmere Castle
Driffield Road Close
Sledmere House
Limekiln Wood
LIMEKILN HILL B1252
Sledmere Park
Castle Farm
Wood Dale
Low Cowlam
Cottom Well Dale
Castle Wood
YO25
Meg Dale
Mill Cottages
Claypits Wood
Avenue Wood
Greenland Slack
Sylvia Grove
Earthwork
Earthwork
B1251
Avenue Farm
Cow Dale
Terrace Top
Woodhill Farm
Wood Hill Plantation
The Wolds
Hanging Fall
Earthwork
Earthwork
School House Dale
Earthwork
Pry Wood
Stannings
B1252
Badger Wood
KEEPER'S HILL
Egg Dale
Warren Farm
Sledmere Grange
YORK ROAD
YORK ROAD
Tumuli
Black Wood
8
69
7
68
6
67
5
66
4
65
3
64
2
63
1
62
92
93
94
95
96
97

7 1

Scale: 1¼ inches to 1 mile
0 ¼ ½ mile
0 250m 500m 750m 1 km

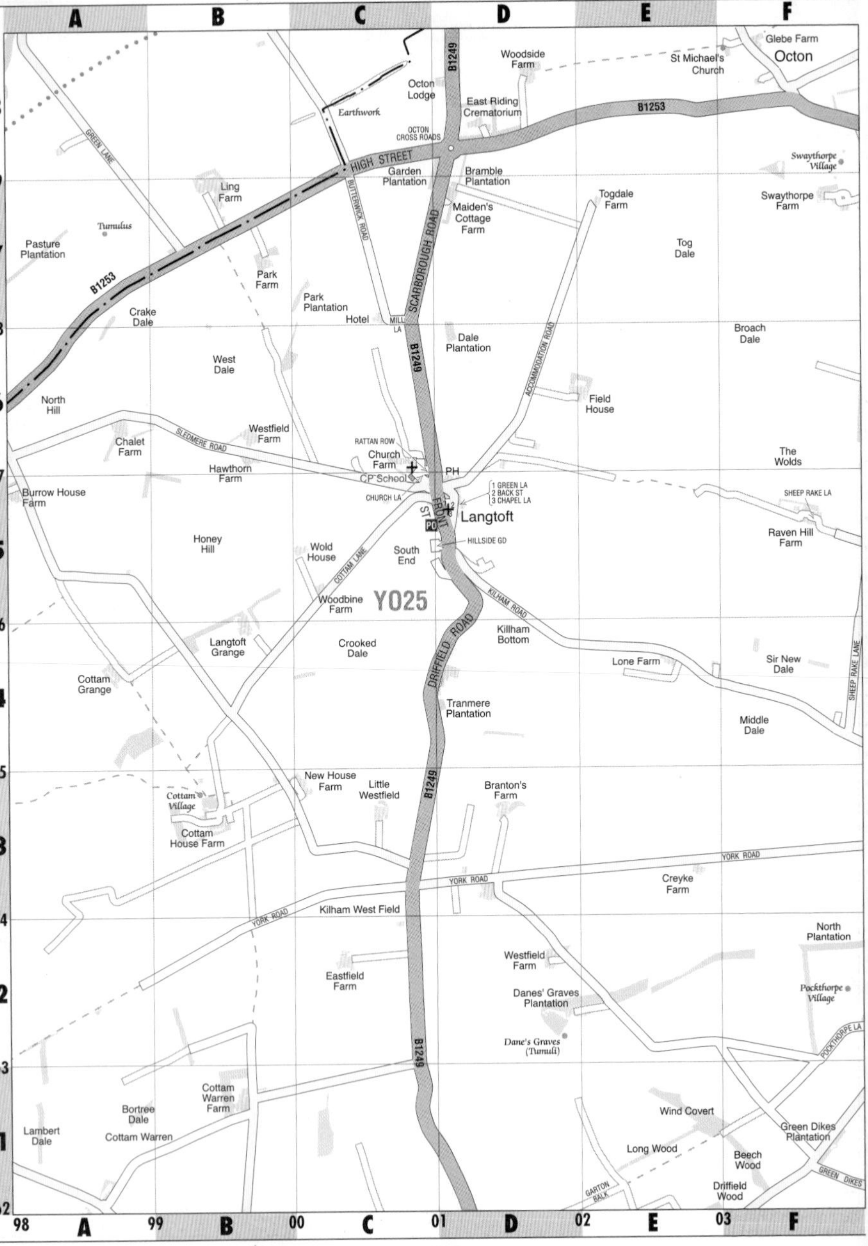

7 20

Scale: 1¼ inches to 1 mile
0 ¼ ½ mile
0 250m 500m 750m 1 km

2
10

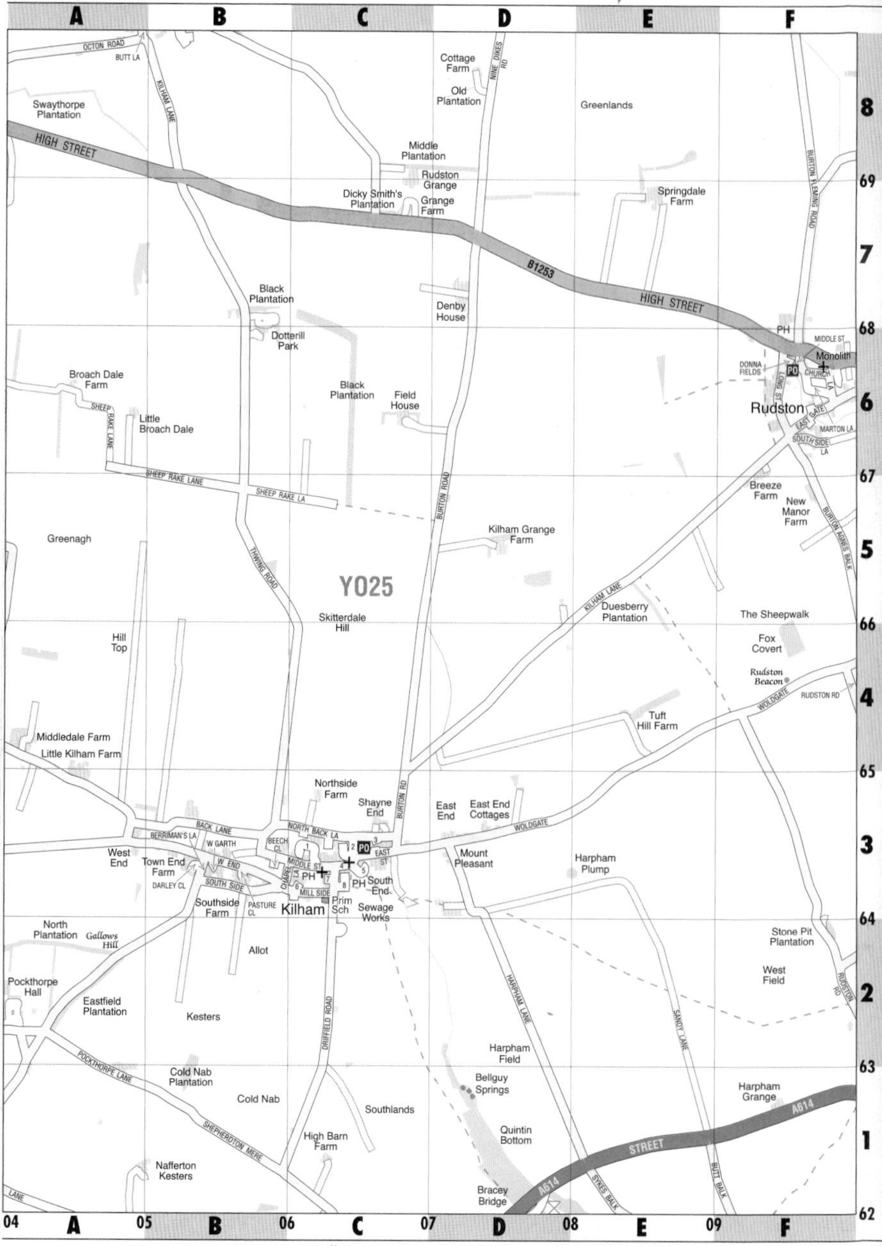

C3
1 CHANTRY MS
2 CHURCH LA
3 ROPERY CL
4 CHURCH ST
5 BAKEHOUSE LA
6 MILL SIDE CL
7 SOUTH CL
8 SOUTH GR

21
10

9
3

Scale: 1¼ inches to 1 mile
0 ¼ ½ mile
0 250m 500m 750m 1 km

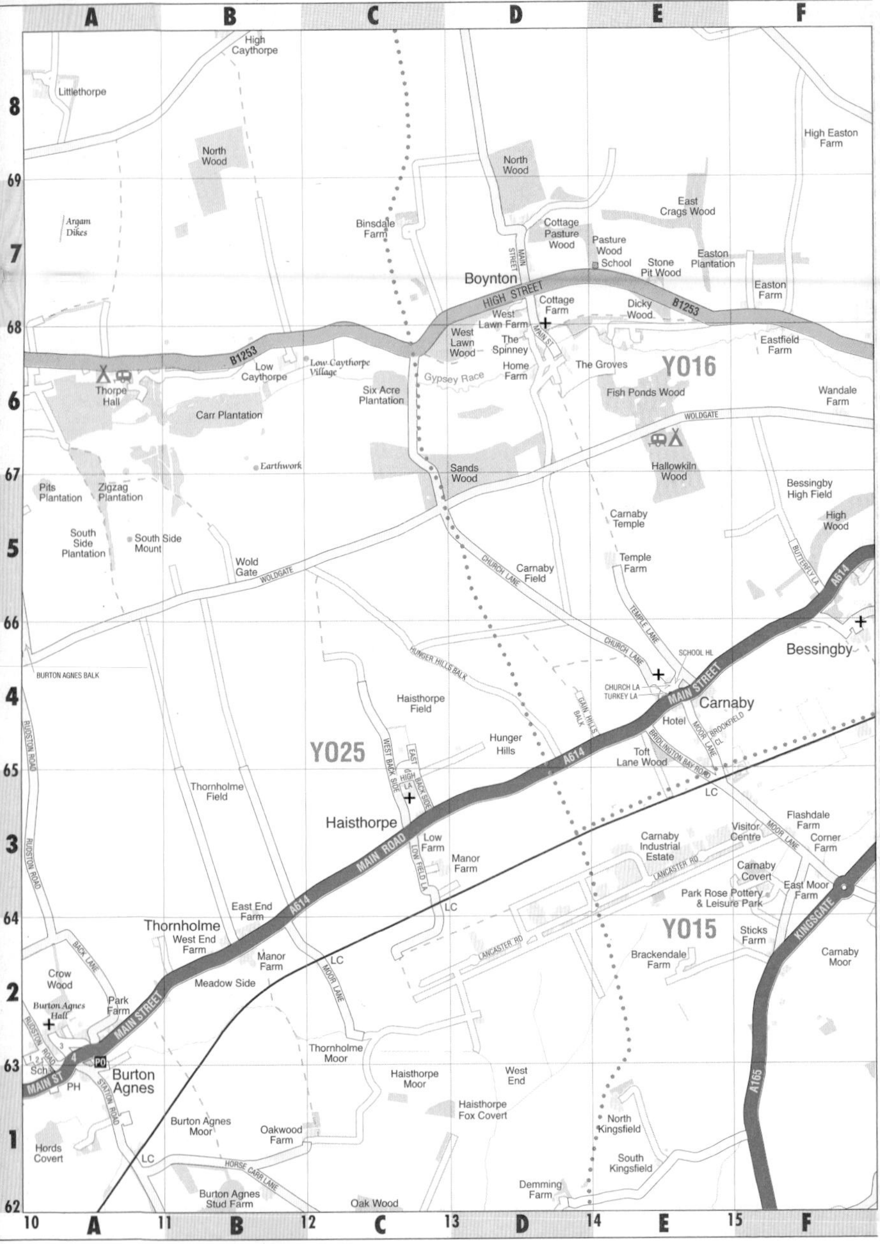

A2
1 ST MARTIN'S DR
2 ST MARTIN'S CL
3 SHADY LA
4 HOSPITAL HL

9
22

Scale: 1¼ inches to 1 mile

4

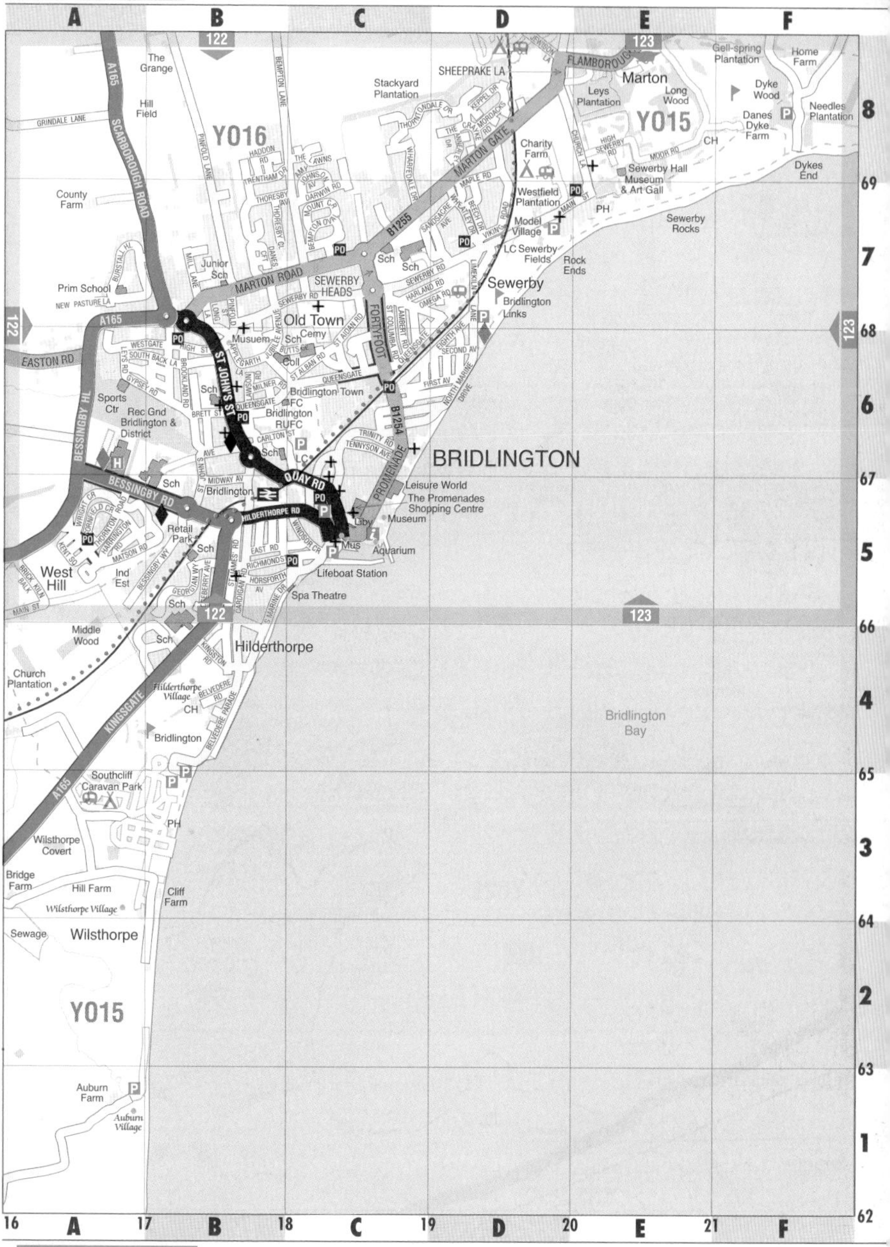

For full street detail of the highlighted area see pages 122 and 123.

23

Scale: 1¼ inches to 1 mile

0 ¼ ½ mile

0 250m 500m 750m 1 km

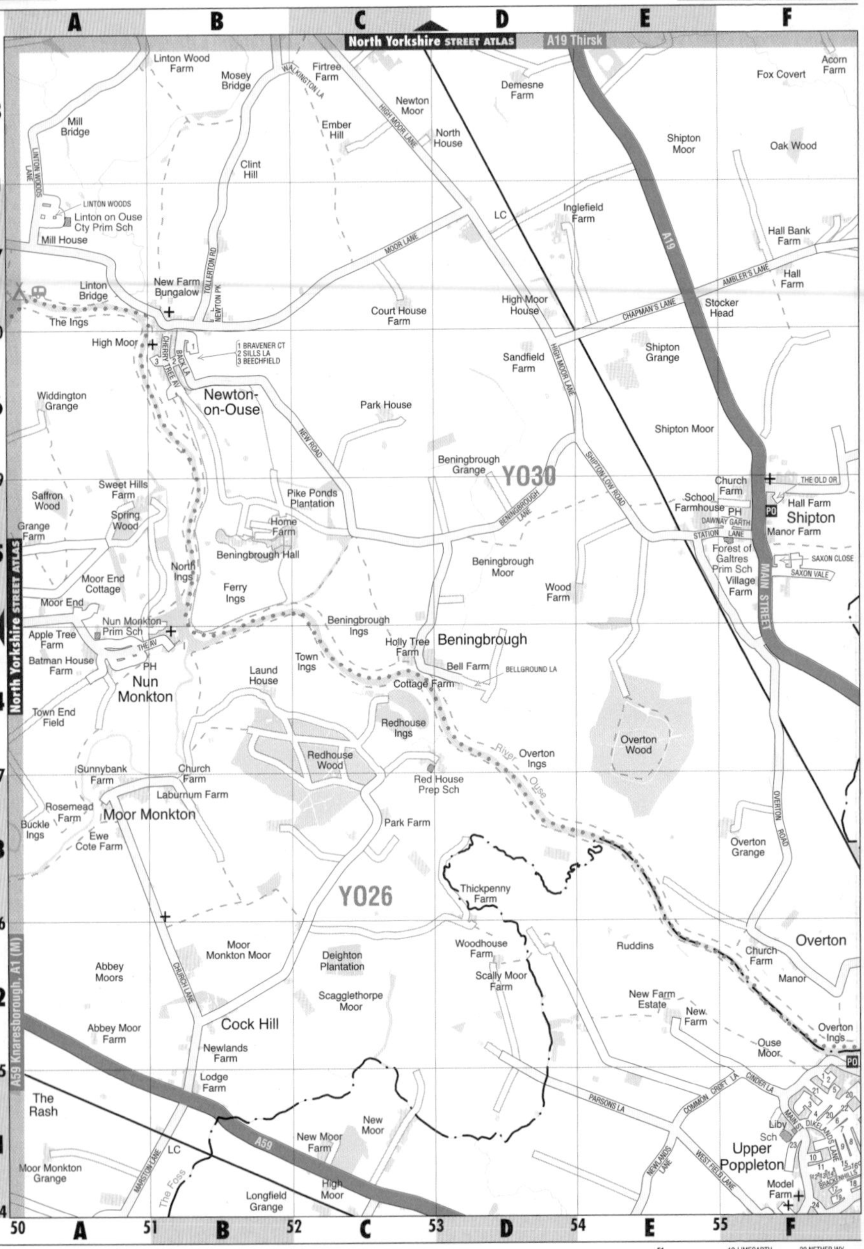

A
B
C
D
E
F
North Yorkshire STREET ATLAS
A19 Thirsk
Linton Wood Farm
Mosey Bridge
WALKINGTON LA
Firtree Farm
Newton Moor
Ember Hill
HIGH MOOR LANE
North House
Demesne Farm
Fox Covert
Acorn Farm
Mill Bridge
Shipton Moor
Oak Wood
LINTON WOODS LANE
Clint Hill
LINTON WOODS
Linton on Ouse Cty Prim Sch
Mill House
LC
Inglefield Farm
A19
Hall Bank Farm
TOLLERTON RD
MOOR LANE
AMBLER'S LANE
Linton Bridge
New Farm Bungalow
NEWTON PK
Hall Farm
Court House Farm
High Moor House
CHAPMAN'S LANE
Stocker Head
The Ings
High Moor
CHERRY TREE AV
BACK LA
1 BRAVENER CT
2 SILLS LA
3 BEECHFIELD
Sandfield Farm
HIGH MOOR LANE
Shipton Grange
Widdington Grange
Newton-on-Ouse
Park House
Shipton Moor
NEW ROAD
Beningbrough Grange
YO30
SHIPTON LOW ROAD
Church Farm
THE OLD OR
Saffron Wood
Sweet Hills Farm
Pike Ponds Plantation
School Farmhouse
PH
Hall Farm
Shipton
PO
Spring Wood
BENINGBROUGH LANE
DAWNAY GARTH
Grange Farm
Home Farm
STATION LANE
Manor Farm
Beningbrough Hall
Forest of Galtres Prim Sch
SAXON CLOSE
North Ings
Beningbrough Moor
SAXON VALE
Moor End Cottage
Ferry Ings
Wood Farm
Village Farm
MAIN STREET
Moor End
Nun Monkton Prim Sch
Beningbrough Ings
Apple Tree Farm
THE AV
Holly Tree Farm
Beningbrough
Batman House Farm
PH
Town Ings
Laund House
Bell Farm
BELLGROUND LA
Nun Monkton
Cottage Farm
Town End Field
Redhouse Ings
Overton Wood
Redhouse Wood
River Ouse
Overton Ings
Sunnybank Farm
Church Farm
Red House Prep Sch
Laburnum Farm
Rosemead Farm
Moor Monkton
OVERTON ROAD
Buckle Ings
Park Farm
Ewe Cote Farm
Overton Grange
Thickpenny Farm
YO26
Moor Monkton Moor
Woodhouse Farm
Ruddins
Overton
Abbey Moors
Deighton Plantation
Church Farm
CHURCH LANE
Scally Moor Farm
Manor
Scagglethorpe Moor
New Farm Estate
Abbey Moor Farm
Cock Hill
New Farm
Overton Ings
Ouse Moor
Newlands Farm
PO
Lodge Farm
The Rash
COMMON CROFT LA
CINDER LA
PARSONS LA
New Moor
Liby
MAIN ST
DIKELANDS LANE
A59
Sch
New Moor Farm
LC
Upper Poppleton
NEWLANDS LANE
WEST FIELD LANE
Moor Monkton Grange
MARSTON LANE
The Foss
High Moor
Longfield Grange
Model Farm
BRACKENHILLS
A59 Knaresborough, A1 (M)
54
55
56
57
58
59
60
61
50
51
52
53

F1
1 RIVERSIDE WALK
2 RIVERSIDE GD
3 BANKSIDE CL
4 SPRINGFIELD RD
5 LITTLEFIELD CL
6 MONTAGUE WALK
7 EBOR WAY
8 PEAR TREE AV
9 ELM TREE AV
10 LIMEGARTH
11 CHANTRY GAP
12 GROVE GD
13 CHANTRY GR
14 CHANTRY AV
15 APPLE GARTH
16 CHERRY GROVE
17 SYCAMORE VIEW
18 FAIRWAY DR
19 DIKELANDS CL
20 NETHER WY
21 RIVERSVALE DR
22 ALLERTON DR
23 SCHOOL LA
24 STATION RD

24

E5
1 VILLAGE GARTH
2 LONGCROFT
3 RIPLEY GR
4 SOUTHLANDS
5 THE AVENUE
6 REDWOOD DR
7 MULBERRY DR
8 ASH LANE
9 ELM END
10 COPPICE CL
11 LITTLE LANE
12 HAWTHORN AV
13 BIRCH LANE
14 FLETCHER CT
15 ST MARY'S CL
16 SANDY LANE
17 CHURCH LANE
18 BROAD OAK LA
19 WESTFIELD PL
20 WESTFIELD RD
21 WESTFIELD CL
22 ST NICHOLAS WAY
23 PLANTATION WAY
24 MIDDLE BANKS
25 HORNSEY GARTH
26 GLEBE WAY
27 FOREST CL
28 CHURCHFIELD DR
29 SANDYLAND
30 HEADLAND CL
31 WANDHILL
32 KENNEDY DR
33 ABELTON GR
34 ORCHARD PADDOCK

D5
1 CASTLE CL
2 WINDSOR DR
3 TOWN END GDNS
4 STEEPLE CL
5 HAREWOOD CL
6 DELAMERE CL
7 ETON DR
8 SAXFORD WAY
9 CANTERBURY CL
10 HAMBLETON VIEW
11 BACK LANE
12 WESTFIELD GR
13 BURRILL DR
14 TWIN PIKE WAY
15 STABLER CL
16 HELMSLEY GR
17 CORNER CL
18 LANCAR CL
19 WATERINGS
20 BUTTERS CL
21 CORBAN WY
22 BUTT HILL

F5
1 FARNDALE CL
2 SANDHOLME
3 NEWDALE
4 KELDALE
5 NORTHCROFT
6 RUSHWOOD CL
7 LANSDOWN WY
8 SCRIVEN GR
9 WOODCOCK CL
10 FALCON CL
11 MALLARD WY
12 HALL RISE
13 FOLKS CL
14 OLD COPPICE
15 NEW FORGE CT
16 CHATSWORTH DR
17 RIVERSDALE
18 NETHERWINDINGS
19 THORNHILLS
20 GARTHS END
21 THE LANDINGS
22 LANDING LA

For full street detail of the highlighted area see pages 126 and 127.

129

128

130

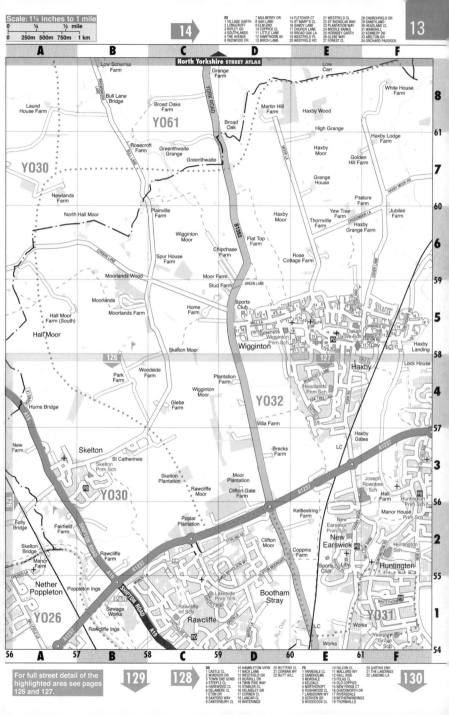

B8
1 LAKESIDE GR
2 THOMPSON DR
3 JAYWICK CL
4 BLACKLEE CL
5 NORTHFIELDS
6 NETHERWOODS

C8
1 CHAPMAN CL
2 BRUNSWICK CL
3 PULLEYN CL
4 STUART CL
5 COULSON CL
6 CUNDALL CL

13

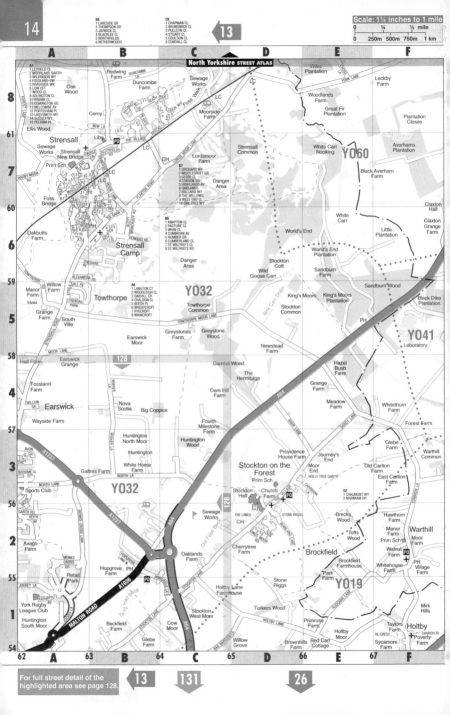

Scale: 1¼ inches to 1 mile
0 ¼ ½ mile
0 250m 500m 750m 1 km

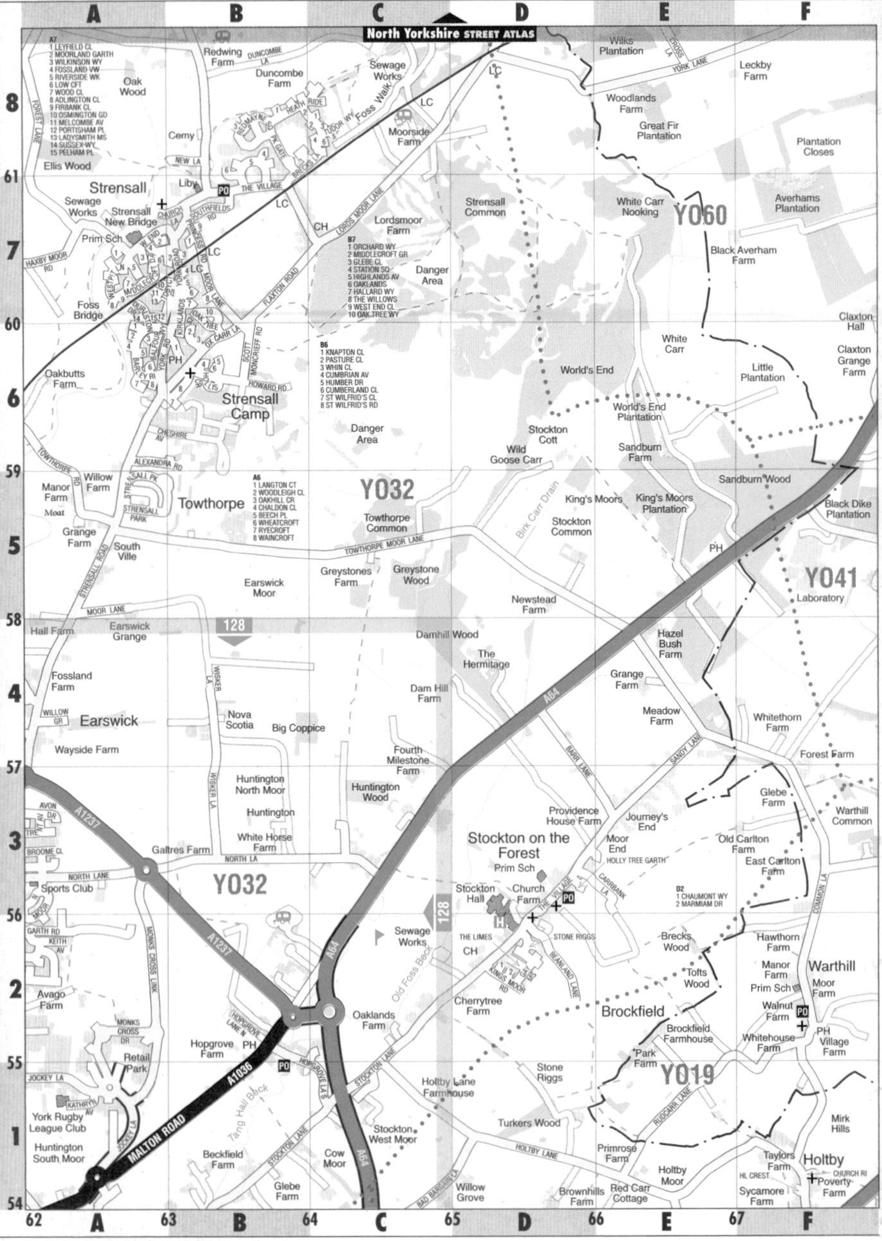

Scale: 1¼ inches to 1 mile
0 ¼ ½ mile
0 250m 500m 750m 1 km

16

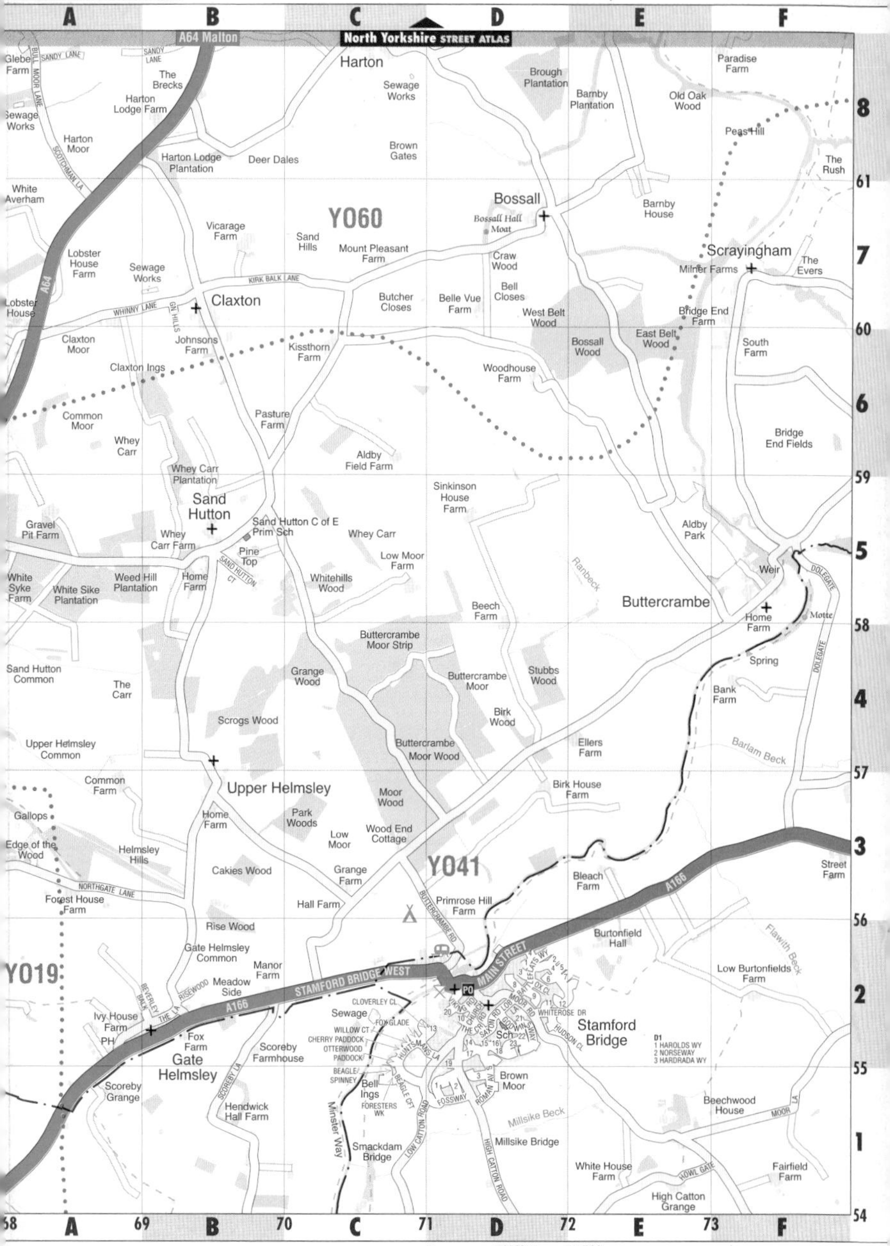

North Yorkshire STREET ATLAS
A64 Malton
A B C D E F
8 61 7 60 6 59 5 58 4 57 3 56 2 55 1 54
68 69 70 71 72 73
YO60
YO41
YO19
Harton
Sewage Works
Brough Plantation
Barnby Plantation
Old Oak Wood
Paradise Farm
Peas Hill
The Rush
Glebe Farm
SANDY LANE
BULL MOOR LANE
The Brecks
Harton Lodge Farm
Sewage Works
Harton Moor
SCOTCHMAN LA
Harton Lodge Plantation
Deer Dales
Brown Gates
White Averham
Bossall
Bossall Hall Moat
Barnby House
Vicarage Farm
Sand Hills
Mount Pleasant Farm
Craw Wood
Scrayingham
Milner Farms
The Evers
Lobster House Farm
Sewage Works
KIRK BALK LANE
Bell Closes
A64
Lobster House
WHINNY LANE
GN HILLS
Claxton
Butcher Closes
Belle Vue Farm
West Belt Wood
Bridge End Farm
Claxton Moor
Johnsons Farm
Kissthorn Farm
East Belt Wood
Bossall Wood
South Farm
Claxton Ings
Woodhouse Farm
Common Moor
Pasture Farm
Whey Carr
Bridge End Fields
Aldby Field Farm
Whey Carr Plantation
Sinkinson House Farm
Sand Hutton
Gravel Pit Farm
Sand Hutton C of E Prim Sch
Whey Carr
Aldby Park
Whey Carr Farm
Pine Top
Low Moor Farm
Ranbeck
White Syke Farm
White Sike Plantation
Weed Hill Plantation
Home Farm
SAND HUTTON CT
Whitehills Wood
Weir
DOLEGATE
Beech Farm
Buttercrambe
Home Farm
Motte
Buttercrambe Moor Strip
Sand Hutton Common
Spring
The Carr
Grange Wood
Buttercrambe Moor
Stubbs Wood
Bank Farm
Scrogs Wood
Birk Wood
Upper Helmsley Common
Buttercrambe Moor Wood
Ellers Farm
Barlam Beck
Common Farm
Upper Helmsley
Birk House Farm
Moor Wood
Gallops
Home Farm
Park Woods
Low Moor
Wood End Cottage
Edge of the Wood
Helmsley Hills
Cakies Wood
Grange Farm
Bleach Farm
Street Farm
A166
NORTHGATE LANE
Forest House Farm
Hall Farm
BUTTERCRAMBE RD
Primrose Hill Farm
Rise Wood
Burtonfield Hall
Flawith Beck
Gate Helmsley Common
Manor Farm
MAIN STREET
Low Burtonfields Farm
Meadow Side
STAMFORD BRIDGE WEST
BEVERLEY BALK
RISEWOOD
THE LA
PO
CLOVERLEY CL
Sewage
FOX GLADE
WILLOW CT
CHERRY PADDOCK
OTTERWOOD PADDOCK
Ivy House Farm
PH
Fox Farm
Gate Helmsley
Scoreby Farmhouse
HUNTSMANS LA
BEAGLE SPINNEY
Bell Ings
BEAGLE CFT
FORESTERS WK
WHITEROSE DR
HUDSON CL
Sch
Stamford Bridge
D1
1 HAROLDS WY
2 NORSEWAY
3 HARDRADA WY
Brown Moor
FOSSWAY
ROMAN AV
Scoreby Grange
SCOREBY LA
Hendwick Hall Farm
Minster Way
Millsike Beck
Beechwood House
MOOR LA
LOW CATTON ROAD
HIGH CATTON ROAD
Smackdam Bridge
Millsike Bridge
White House Farm
HOWL GATE
Fairfield Farm
High Catton Grange

27

D2
1 BRIDLINGTON RD
2 DERWENT CL
3 DANESWELL CL
4 BURTON FIELDS RD
5 GARROWBY VW
6 KINGSWAY
7 DARLEY CL
8 WHARTON RD
9 ST JOHN'S RD
10 CHURCH LA
11 EGREMONT CL
12 BURTON FIELDS CL
13 HEATHER BANK
14 TOSTIG CL
15 FAIRFAX
16 SCHOOL CL
17 ROMAN AV N
18 GODWINSWAY
19 BUTTS CL
20 VIKING CL
21 MIDGLEY CL
22 BROWN MOOR
23 FURLONG RD

16

15

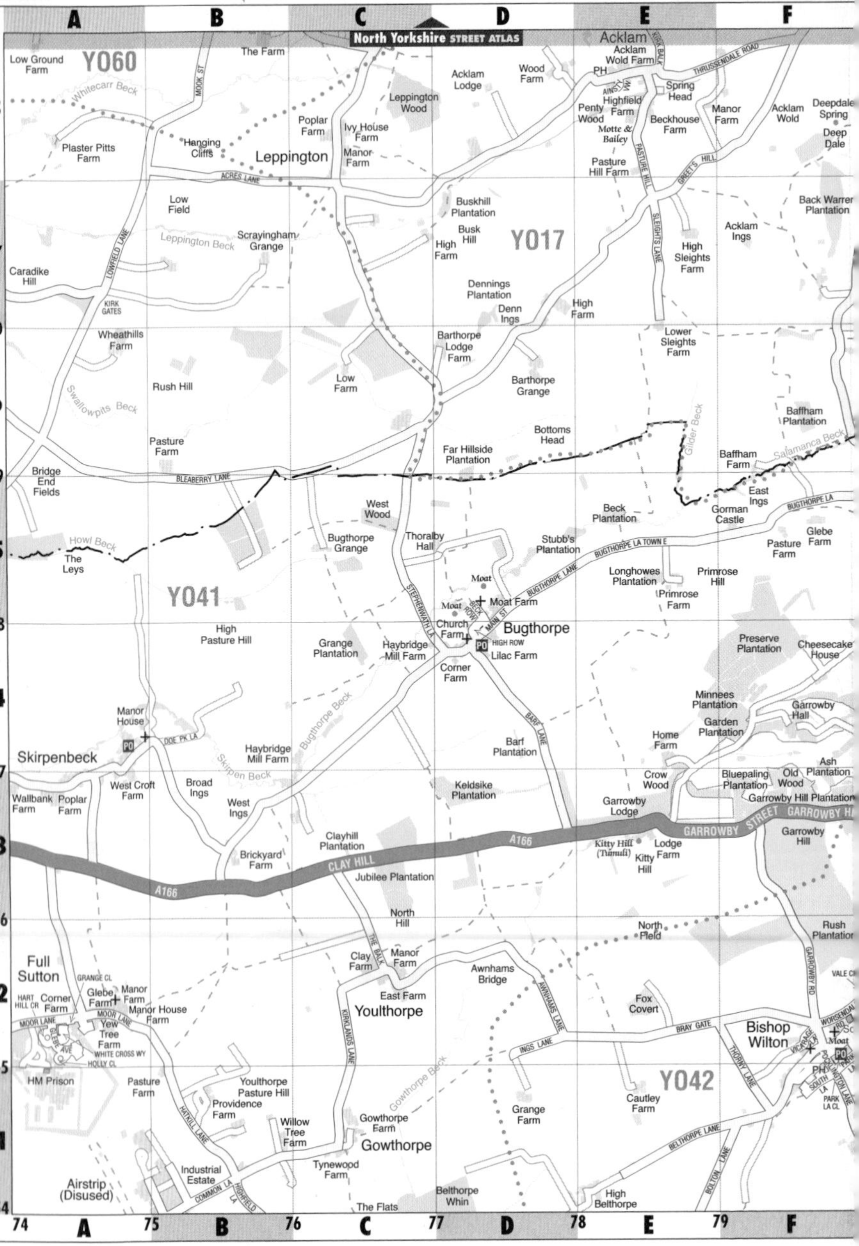
Scale: 1¼ inches to 1 mile
0 ¼ ½ mile
0 250m 500m 750m 1 km
North Yorkshire STREET ATLAS
A B C D E F
8 61 7 60 6 59 5 58 4 57 3 56 2 55 1 54
74 75 76 77 78 79
YO60
YO17
YO41
YO42
Low Ground Farm
Whitecarr Beck
Plaster Pitts Farm
MOOK ST
Hanging Cliffs
The Farm
Poplar Farm
Leppington
Ivy House Farm
Manor Farm
Leppington Wood
Acklam Lodge
Wood Farm
Acklam
Acklam Wold Farm
KIRK BALK
THRUSSENDALE ROAD
PH
AINSTY VW
Highfield Farm
Penty Wood
Motte & Bailey
Spring Head
Beckhouse Farm
Manor Farm
Acklam Wold
Deepdale Spring
Deep Dale
Pasture Hill Farm
PASTURE HILL
GREET'S HILL
ACRES LANE
Low Field
Buskhill Plantation
Busk Hill
High Farm
Back Warren Plantation
Acklam Ings
SLEIGHTS LANE
High Sleights Farm
Leppington Beck
Scrayingham Grange
Caradike Hill
LOWFIELD LANE
KIRK GATES
Dennings Plantation
Denn Ings
High Farm
Wheathills Farm
Barthorpe Lodge Farm
Lower Sleights Farm
Rush Hill
Low Farm
Barthorpe Grange
Swallowpits Beck
Baffham Plantation
Gilder Beck
Pasture Farm
Bottoms Head
Far Hillside Plantation
Baffham Farm
Salamanca Beck
Bridge End Fields
BLEABERRY LANE
East Ings
Gorman Castle
West Wood
Beck Plantation
BUGTHORPE LA
Glebe Farm
Howl Beck
The Leys
Bugthorpe Grange
Thoralby Hall
Stubb's Plantation
BUGTHORPE LA TOWN E
Pasture Farm
Longhowes Plantation
Primrose Hill
Moat
BUGTHORPE LANE
Moat Farm
Primrose Farm
STEPHENWATH LA
BECK ROW
MAIN ST
Church Farm
Bugthorpe
PO
HIGH ROW
Lilac Farm
High Pasture Hill
Grange Plantation
Haybridge Mill Farm
Corner Farm
Preserve Plantation
Cheesecake House
Minnees Plantation
Garrowby Hall
Manor House
Garden Plantation
Skirpenbeck
DOE PK LA
Bugthorpe Beck
Barf Plantation
BARF LANE
Home Farm
Haybridge Mill Farm
Skirpen Beck
Crow Wood
Ash Plantation
Bluepaling Plantation
Old Wood
Garrowby Hill Plantation
Wallbank Farm
Poplar Farm
West Croft Farm
Broad Ings
West Ings
Keldsike Plantation
Garrowby Lodge
GARROWBY STREET
GARROWBY HILL
Clayhill Plantation
A166
Kitty Hill (Tumuli)
Lodge Farm
Kitty Hill
Garrowby Hill
Brickyard Farm
CLAY HILL
Jubilee Plantation
North Hill
North Field
Rush Plantation
THE BALK
Clay Farm
Manor Farm
Awnhams Bridge
Full Sutton
GRANGE CL
Glebe Farm
Manor Farm
HART HILL CR
Corner Farm
Manor House Farm
East Farm
Youlthorpe
AWNHAMS LANE
Fox Covert
GARROWBY RD
VALE CR
MOOR LANE
MOOR LANE
Yew Tree Farm
GLEBE AVE
WHITE CROSS WY
HOLLY CL
KIRKLANDS LANE
INGS LANE
BRAY GATE
Bishop Wilton
THORNY LANE
VICARAGE
WORSENDALE RD
Moat
PO
PH
POCKLINGTON LANE
SOUTH LA
PARK LA CL
HM Prison
Pasture Farm
Youlthorpe Pasture Hill
Providence Farm
Gowthorpe Beck
YO42
Cautley Farm
HATKILL LANE
Willow Tree Farm
Gowthorpe Farm
Gowthorpe
Grange Farm
BELTHORPE LANE
BOLTON LANE
Industrial Estate
Tynewood Farm
Airstrip (Disused)
COMMON LA
HIGHFIELD LA
Belthorpe Whin
The Flats
High Belthorpe

Scale: 1¼ inches to 1 mile
0 ¼ ½ mile
0 250m 500m 750m 1 km

18

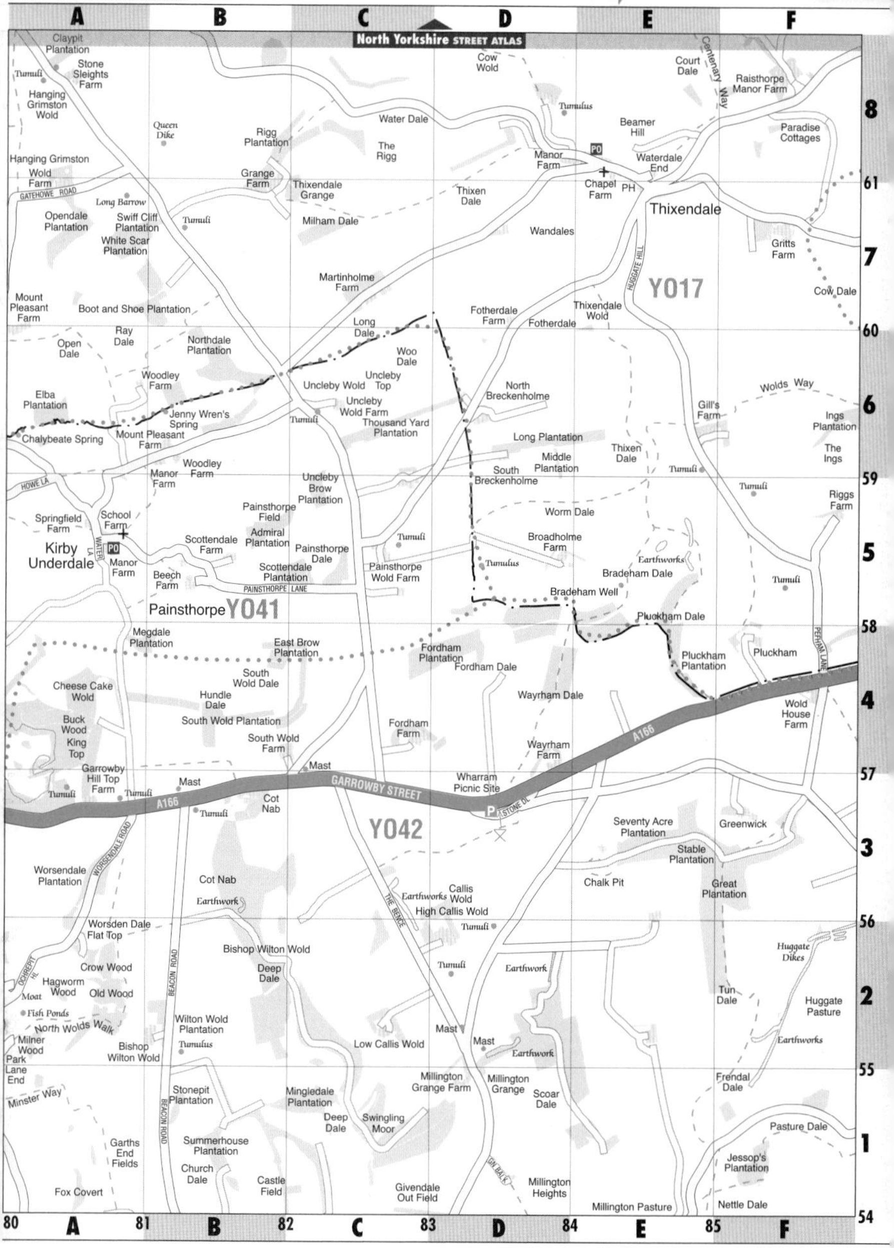
A
B
C
D
E
F
North Yorkshire STREET ATLAS
Claypit Plantation
Tumuli
Stone Sleights Farm
Hanging Grimston Wold
Queen Dike
Rigg Plantation
Water Dale
The Rigg
Cow Wold
Tumulus
Centenary Way
Court Dale
Raisthorpe Manor Farm
Beamer Hill
Paradise Cottages
Hanging Grimston Wold Farm
GATEHOWE ROAD
Grange Farm
Thixendale Grange
Manor Farm
PO
Waterdale End
Chapel Farm
PH
Thixendale
Thixen Dale
Long Barrow
Opendale Plantation
Swift Cliff Plantation
White Scar Plantation
Milham Dale
Wandales
HUGGATE HILL
Gritts Farm
Martinholme Farm
YO17
Mount Pleasant Farm
Boot and Shoe Plantation
Fotherdale Farm
Fotherdale
Thixendale Wold
Cow Dale
Ray Dale
Open Dale
Northdale Plantation
Long Dale
Woo Dale
Woodley Farm
Uncleby Wold
Uncleby Top
North Breckenholme
Wolds Way
Elba Plantation
Jenny Wren's Spring
Uncleby Wold Farm
Thousand Yard Plantation
Gill's Farm
Ings Plantation
Chalybeate Spring
Mount Pleasant Farm
Long Plantation
Thixen Dale
The Ings
Woodley Farm
Manor Farm
HOWE LA
Uncleby Brow Plantation
South Breckenholme
Middle Plantation
Riggs Farm
Springfield Farm
School Farm
Painsthorpe Field
Worm Dale
Kirby Underdale
WATER LA
Manor Farm
Scottendale Farm
Admiral Plantation
Painsthorpe Dale
Broadholme Farm
Earthworks
Beech Farm
Scottendale Plantation
Painsthorpe Wold Farm
Tumulus
Bradeham Dale
PAINSTHORPE LANE
Bradeham Well
Painsthorpe
YO41
Pluckham Dale
Megdale Plantation
East Brow Plantation
Fordham Plantation
Fordham Dale
Pluckham Plantation
Pluckham
PERHAM LANE
South Wold Dale
Cheese Cake Wold
Hundle Dale
Wayrham Dale
Wold House Farm
Buck Wood
King Top
South Wold Plantation
South Wold Farm
Fordham Farm
A166
Wayrham Farm
Garrowby Hill Top Farm
Mast
Wharram Picnic Site
GARROWBY STREET
Cot Nab
STONE DL
YO42
Seventy Acre Plantation
Greenwick
WORSENDALE ROAD
Worsendale Plantation
Stable Plantation
Cot Nab
Chalk Pit
Great Plantation
Earthwork
Callis Wold
THE BENCE
High Callis Wold
Worsden Dale
Flat Top
Bishop Wilton Wold
Huggate Dikes
OCHREPIT HL
Crow Wood
Deep Dale
Hagworm Wood
Old Wood
Moat
BEACON ROAD
Tun Dale
Huggate Pasture
Fish Ponds
North Wolds Walk
Wilton Wold Plantation
Milner Wood
Bishop Wilton Wold
Low Callis Wold
Park Lane End
Millington Grange Farm
Millington Grange
Scoar Dale
Frendal Dale
Minster Way
Stonepit Plantation
Mingledale Plantation
Deep Dale
Swingling Moor
Pasture Dale
Garths End Fields
Summerhouse Plantation
Jessop's Plantation
Church Dale
Castle Field
GN BALK
Fox Covert
Givendale Out Field
Millington Heights
Millington Pasture
Nettle Dale
8
61
7
60
6
59
5
58
4
57
3
56
2
55
1
54
80
81
82
83
84
85

29

18

17
6

Scale: 1¼ inches to 1 mile
0 ¼ ½ mile
0 250m 500m 750m 1 km

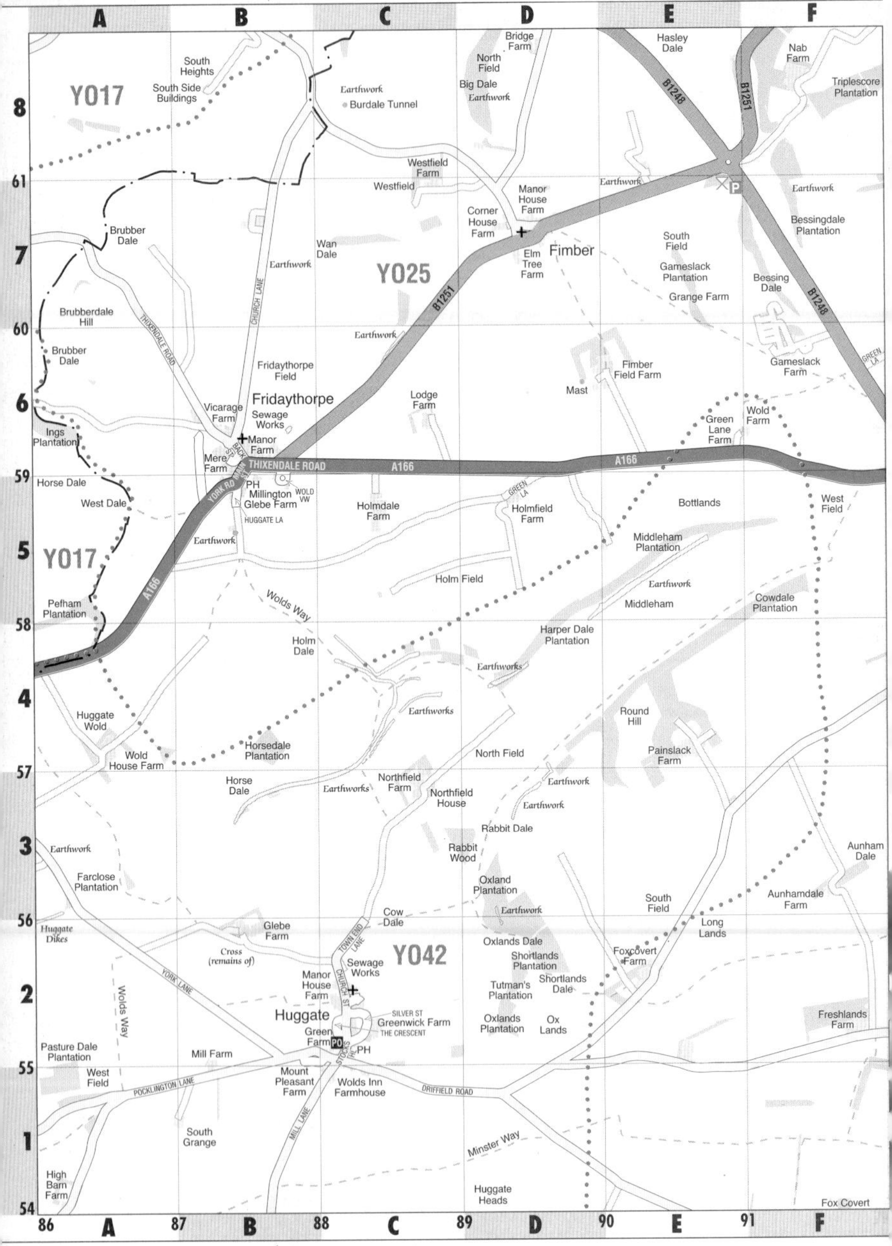
A
B
C
D
E
F
8
61
7
60
6
59
5
58
4
57
3
56
2
55
1
54
86
87
88
89
90
91
YO17
South Heights
South Side Buildings
Earthwork
Burdale Tunnel
Bridge Farm
North Field
Big Dale
Hasley Dale
B1248
B1251
Nab Farm
Triplescore Plantation
Westfield Farm
Westfield
Manor House Farm
Corner House Farm
Elm Tree Farm
Fimber
Earthwork
P
Bessingdale Plantation
Brubber Dale
Wan Dale
YO25
South Field
Gameslack Plantation
Bessing Dale
Grange Farm
Brubberdale Hill
THIXENDALE ROAD
CHURCH LANE
Gameslack Farm
GREEN LA
Fimber Field Farm
Mast
Fridaythorpe Field
Lodge Farm
Vicarage Farm
Fridaythorpe
Sewage Works
Manor Farm
Wold Farm
Green Lane Farm
Ings Plantation
Mere Farm
BACK ST
MAIN ST
A166
Horse Dale
PH
Millington Glebe Farm
WOLD VW
HUGGATE LA
YORK RD
West Dale
Holmdale Farm
Holmfield Farm
Bottlands
West Field
Middleham Plantation
Earthwork
YO17
Holm Field
Middleham
Cowdale Plantation
Pefham Plantation
Wolds Way
Harper Dale Plantation
Holm Dale
Earthworks
Round Hill
Huggate Wold
Horsedale Plantation
North Field
Painslack Farm
Wold House Farm
Horse Dale
Northfield Farm
Northfield House
Rabbit Dale
Rabbit Wood
Aunham Dale
Farclose Plantation
Oxland Plantation
South Field
Aunhamdale Farm
Cow Dale
Long Lands
Huggate Dikes
Glebe Farm
TOWN END LANE
Oxlands Dale
Foxcovert Farm
Cross (remains of)
YO42
Shortlands Plantation
Manor House Farm
Sewage Works
Tutman's Plantation
Shortlands Dale
YORK LANE
CHURCH ST
Wolds Way
Huggate
SILVER ST
Greenwick Farm
THE CRESCENT
Oxlands Plantation
Ox Lands
Freshlands Farm
Green Farm
PO
PH
STOCKS HL
Pasture Dale Plantation
Mill Farm
West Field
Mount Pleasant Farm
Wolds Inn Farmhouse
POCKLINGTON LANE
DRIFFIELD ROAD
MILL LANE
South Grange
Minster Way
High Barn Farm
Huggate Heads
Fox Covert

17
30

Scale: 1¼ inches to 1 mile
0 ¼ ½ mile
0 250m 500m 750m 1 km

7
20

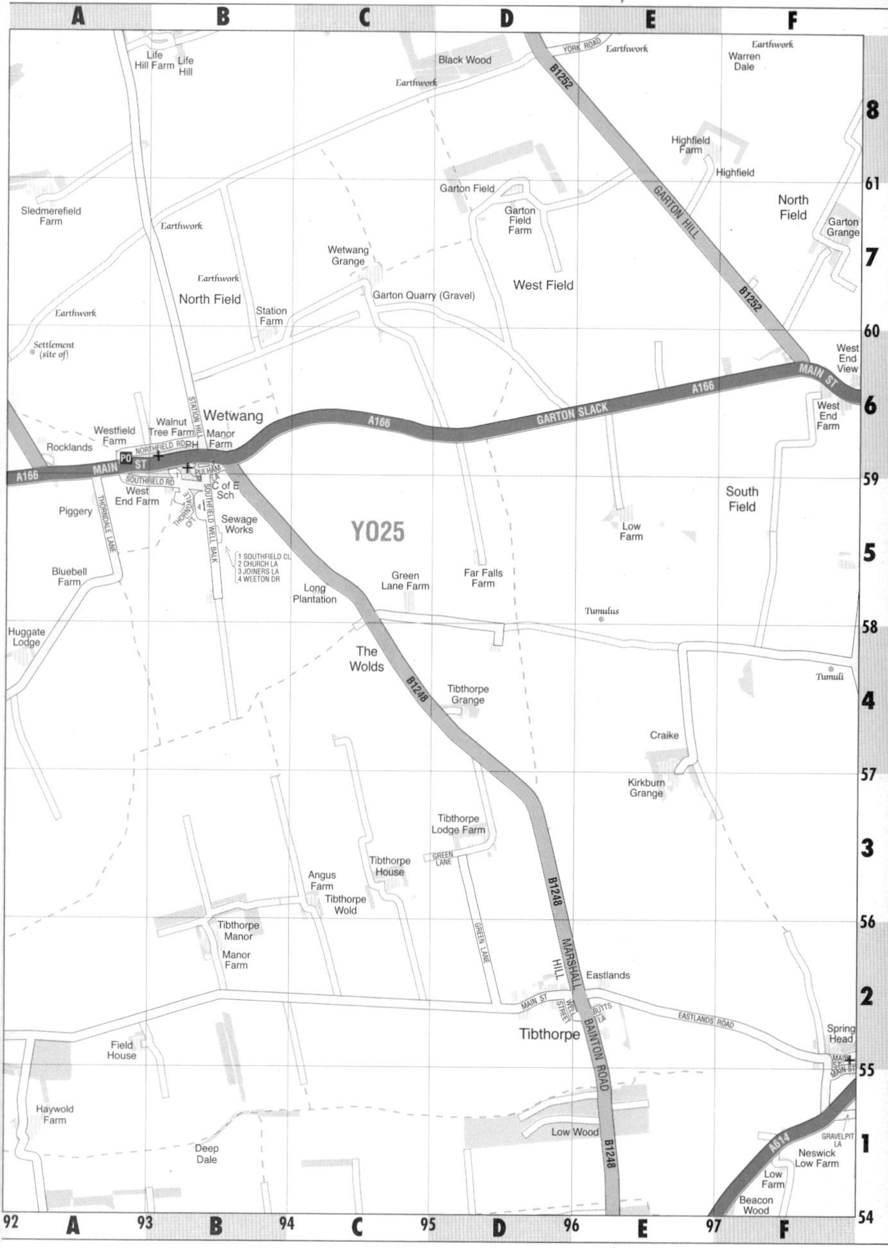

31
20

19
8

Scale: 1¼ inches to 1 mile
0 ¼ ½ mile
0 250m 500m 750m 1 km

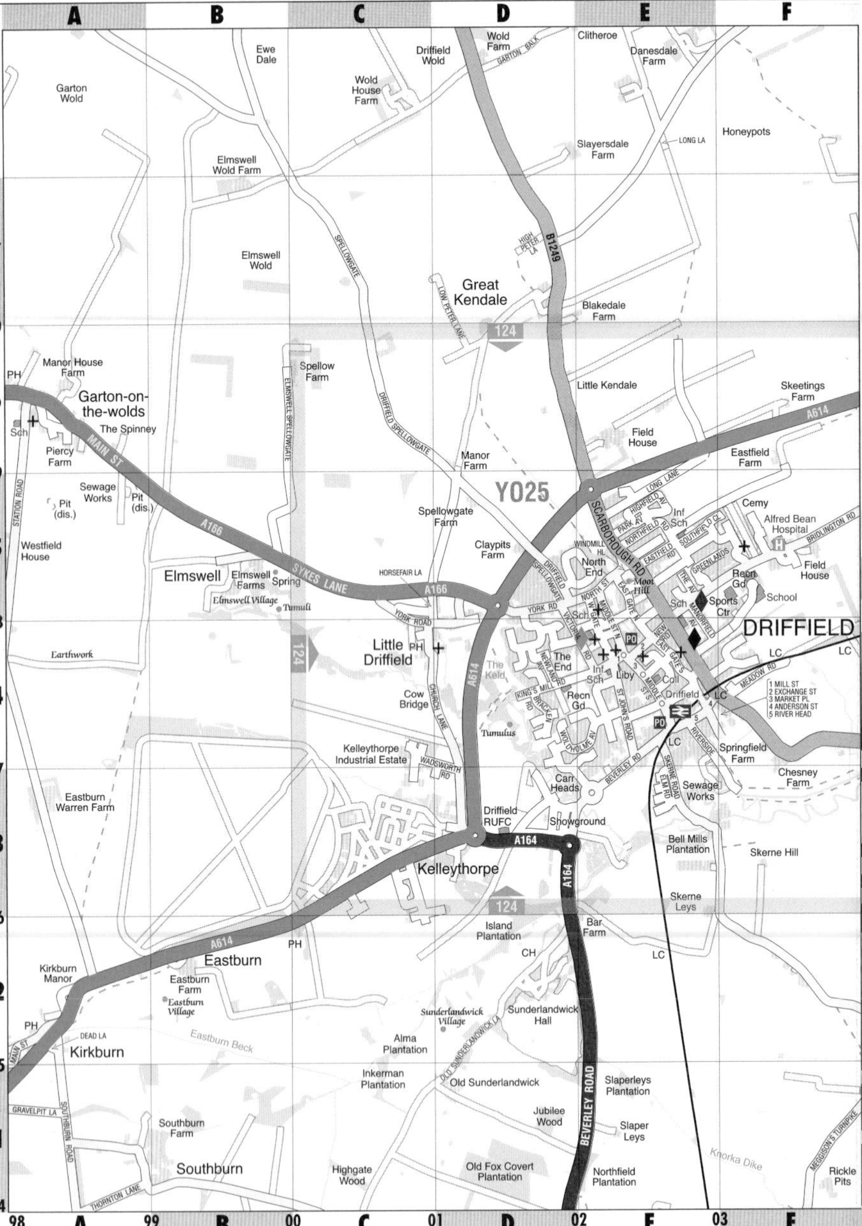
Garton Wold
Ewe Dale
Driffield Wold
Wold Farm
Clitheroe
Danesdale Farm
Wold House Farm
Elmswell Wold Farm
Slayersdale Farm
Honeypots
LONG LA
B1249
Elmswell Wold
SPELLOWGATE
Great Kendale
Blakedale Farm
124
Manor House Farm
Spellow Farm
Little Kendale
Skeetings Farm
A614
Garton-on-the-wolds
The Spinney
MAIN ST
Field House
Eastfield Farm
Piercy Farm
Manor Farm
YO25
Sewage Works
Pit (dis.)
A166
Spellowgate Farm
Cemy
Alfred Bean Hospital
Westfield House
Claypits Farm
SCARBOROUGH RD
Elmswell
Elmswell Farms
Spring
SYKES LANE
HORSEFAIR LA
North End
Moot Hill
Recn Gd
Sports Ctr
School
Elmswell Village
Tumuli
YORK ROAD
DRIFFIELD
Earthwork
Little Driffield
The Keld
The End
Liby
Coll
Driffield
Cow Bridge
CHURCH LANE
Tumulus
Recn Gd
1 MILL ST
2 EXCHANGE ST
3 MARKET PL
4 ANDERSON ST
5 RIVER HEAD
Kelleythorpe Industrial Estate
WADSWORTH RD
Springfield Farm
Chesney Farm
Eastburn Warren Farm
Carr Heads
Sewage Works
Driffield RUFC
Showground
A164
Bell Mills Plantation
Skerne Hill
Kelleythorpe
Skerne Leys
Island Plantation
Bar Farm
Eastburn
Kirkburn Manor
Eastburn Farm
Eastburn Village
Sunderlandwick Village
Sunderlandwick Hall
DEAD LA
Kirkburn
Eastburn Beck
Alma Plantation
Inkerman Plantation
Old Sunderlandwick
Slaperleys Plantation
BEVERLEY ROAD
GRAVELPIT LA
SOUTHBURN ROAD
Southburn Farm
Jubilee Wood
Slaper Leys
Knorka Dike
MEGGISON'S TURNPIKE
Southburn
Highgate Wood
Old Fox Covert Plantation
Northfield Plantation
Rickle Pits
THORNTON LANE

19
32

For full street detail of the highlighted area see pages 124 and 125.

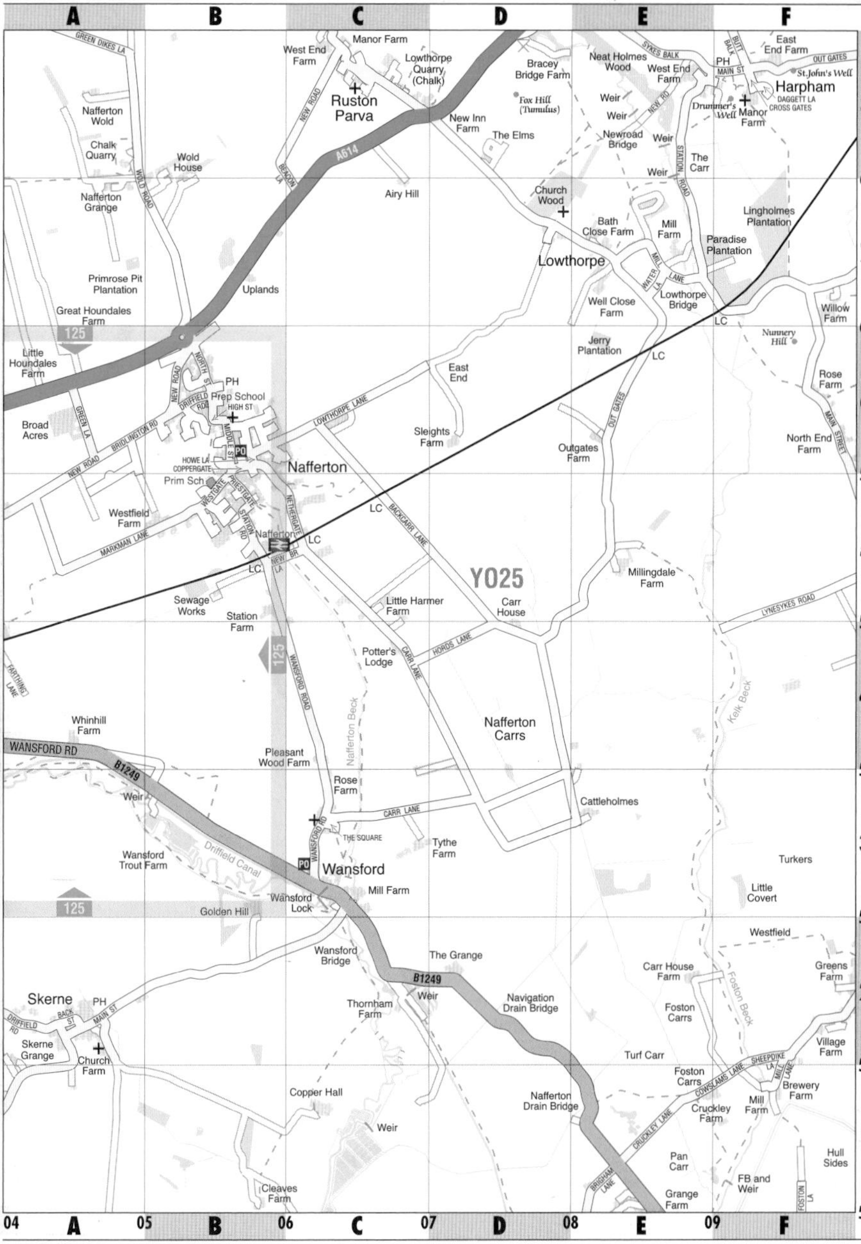

For full street detail of the highlighted area see page 125.

21
10

Scale: 1¼ inches to 1 mile
0 ¼ ½ mile
0 250m 500m 750m 1 km

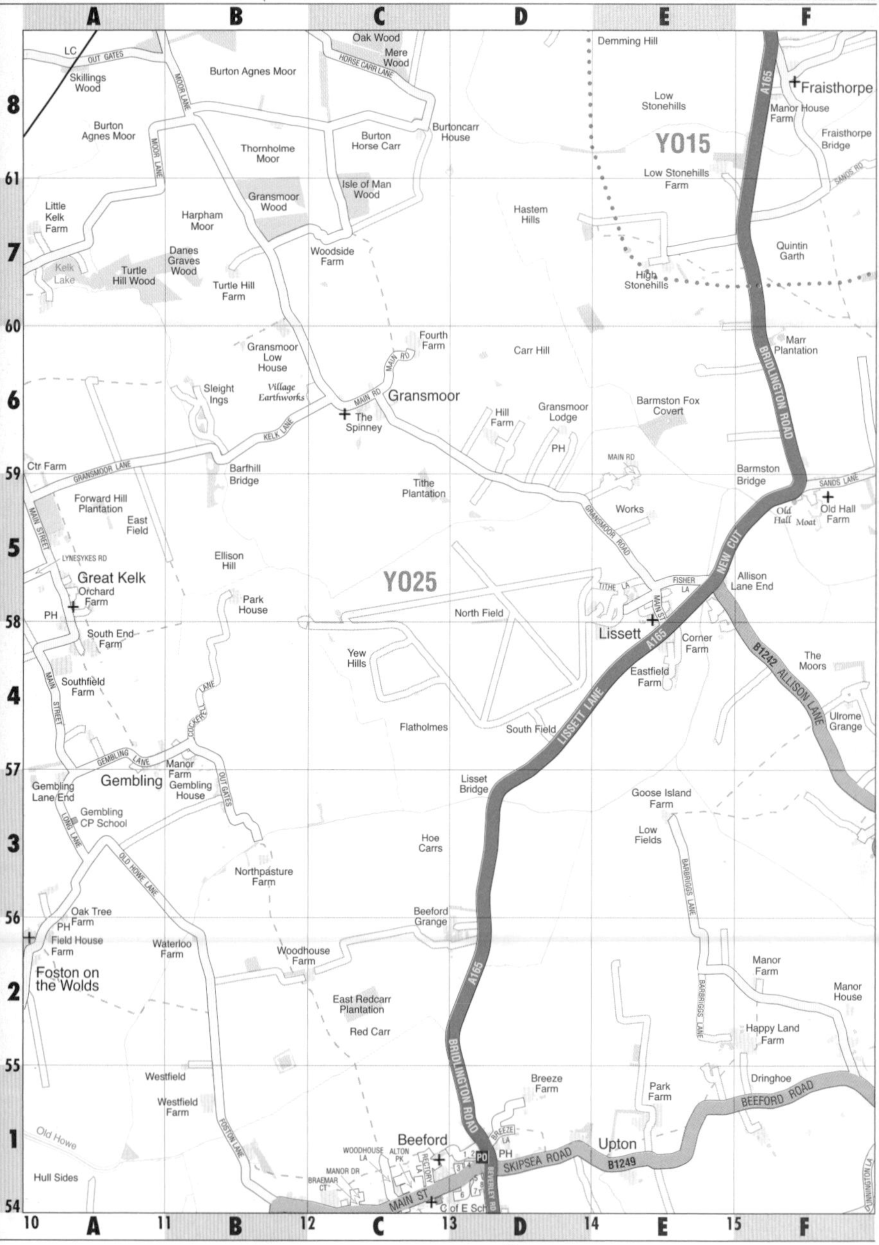
A B C D E F
8 61 7 60 6 59 5 58 4 57 3 56 2 55 1 54
10 11 12 13 14 15
LC
OUT GATES
Skillings Wood
Burton Agnes Moor
MOOR LANE
Oak Wood
Mere Wood
HORSE CARR LANE
Demming Hill
A165
Fraisthorpe
Manor House Farm
Low Stonehills
YO15
Fraisthorpe Bridge
Burton Agnes Moor
Thornholme Moor
Burton Horse Carr
Burtoncarr House
Low Stonehills Farm
SANDS RD
Little Kelk Farm
Harpham Moor
Gransmoor Wood
Isle of Man Wood
Hastem Hills
Kelk Lake
Turtle Hill Wood
Danes Graves Wood
Turtle Hill Farm
Woodside Farm
High Stonehills
Quintin Garth
Gransmoor Low House
Fourth Farm
MAIN RD
Carr Hill
Marr Plantation
BRIDLINGTON ROAD
Sleight Ings
Village Earthworks
Gransmoor
The Spinney
KELK LANE
Hill Farm
Gransmoor Lodge
PH
Barmston Fox Covert
Ctr Farm
GRANSMOOR LANE
Barfhill Bridge
Tithe Plantation
MAIN RD
Barmston Bridge
SANDS LANE
Old Hall Farm
Old Hall
Moat
Forward Hill Plantation
East Field
MAIN STREET
Works
GRANSMOOR ROAD
NEW CUT
LYNESYKES RD
Ellison Hill
Great Kelk
Orchard Farm
YO25
Allison Lane End
FISHER LA
TITHE LA
MAIN ST
Park House
PH
North Field
Lissett
South End Farm
A165
Corner Farm
B1242 ALLISON LANE
The Moors
Yew Hills
Eastfield Farm
Southfield Farm
COCKERILL LANE
Ulrome Grange
Flatholmes
South Field
LISSETT LANE
GEMBLING LANE
Manor Farm
Gembling
Gembling Lane End
Gembling House
OUT GATES
Lisset Bridge
Goose Island Farm
Gembling CP School
LONG LANE
Low Fields
Hoe Carrs
OLD HOWE LANE
Northpasture Farm
BARBRIGGS LANE
Oak Tree Farm
PH
Beeford Grange
Field House Farm
Waterloo Farm
Woodhouse Farm
Foston on the Wolds
Manor Farm
Manor House
East Redcarr Plantation
Red Carr
Happy Land Farm
Westfield
Breeze Farm
Dringhoe
Westfield Farm
Park Farm
BEEFORD ROAD
FOSTON LANE
Old Howe
BREEZE LA
Upton
Beeford
WOODHOUSE LA
ALTON PK
RECTORY LA
PO
PH
SKIPSEA ROAD
B1249
MANOR DR
BRAEMAR CT
BEVERLEY RD
Hull Sides
MAIN ST
C of E Sch
DUNNINGTON LA

21
34

D1
1 CHURCH LA
2 ST LEONARD'S CL
3 WHARRAM FIELD
4 NEWSAM CL
5 MEADOW CL
6 ASHLEIGH DR
7 BARONWOOD CR
8 WELBURN CT

11

Scale: 1¼ inches to 1 mile
0 ¼ ½ mile
0 250m 500m 750m 1 km

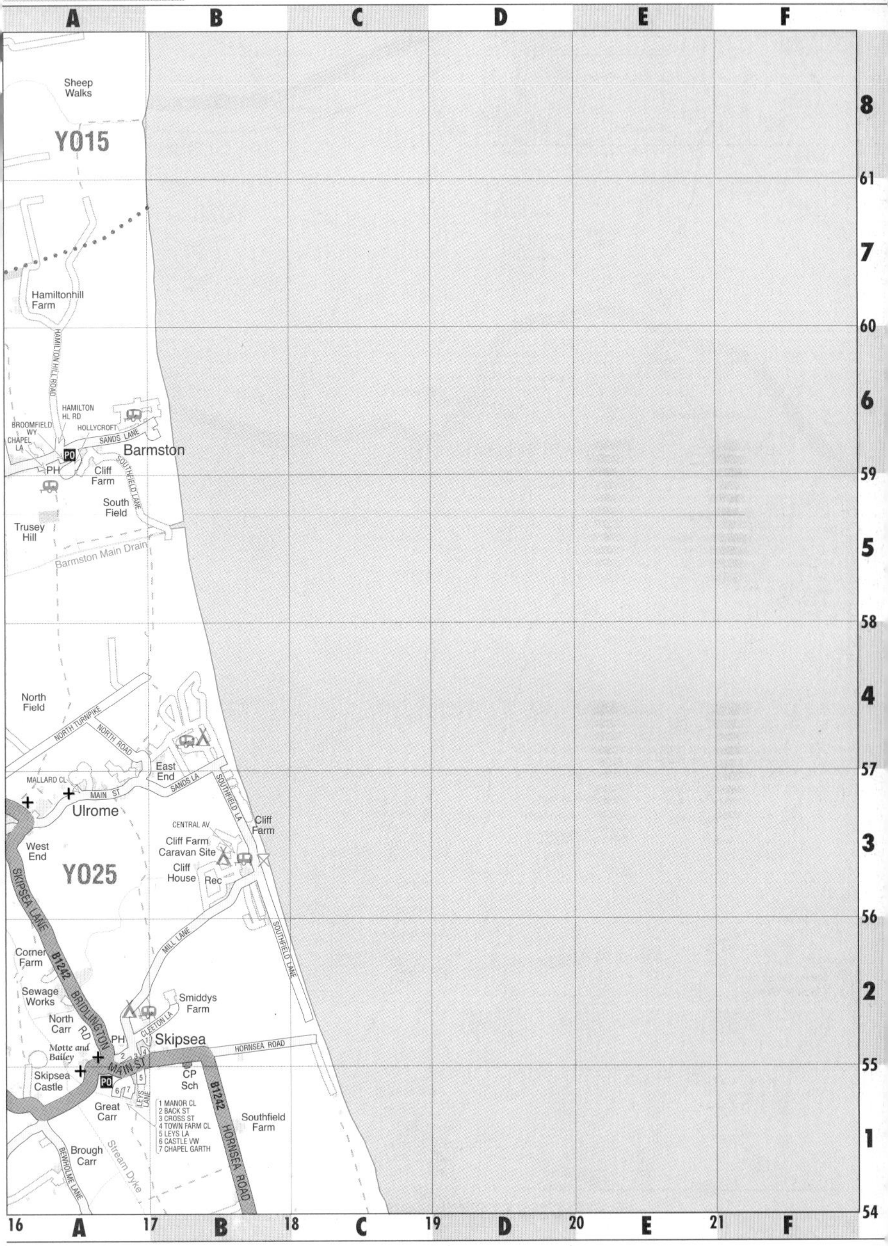

35

12

Scale: 1¼ inches to 1 mile
0 ¼ ½ mile
0 250m 500m 750m 1 km

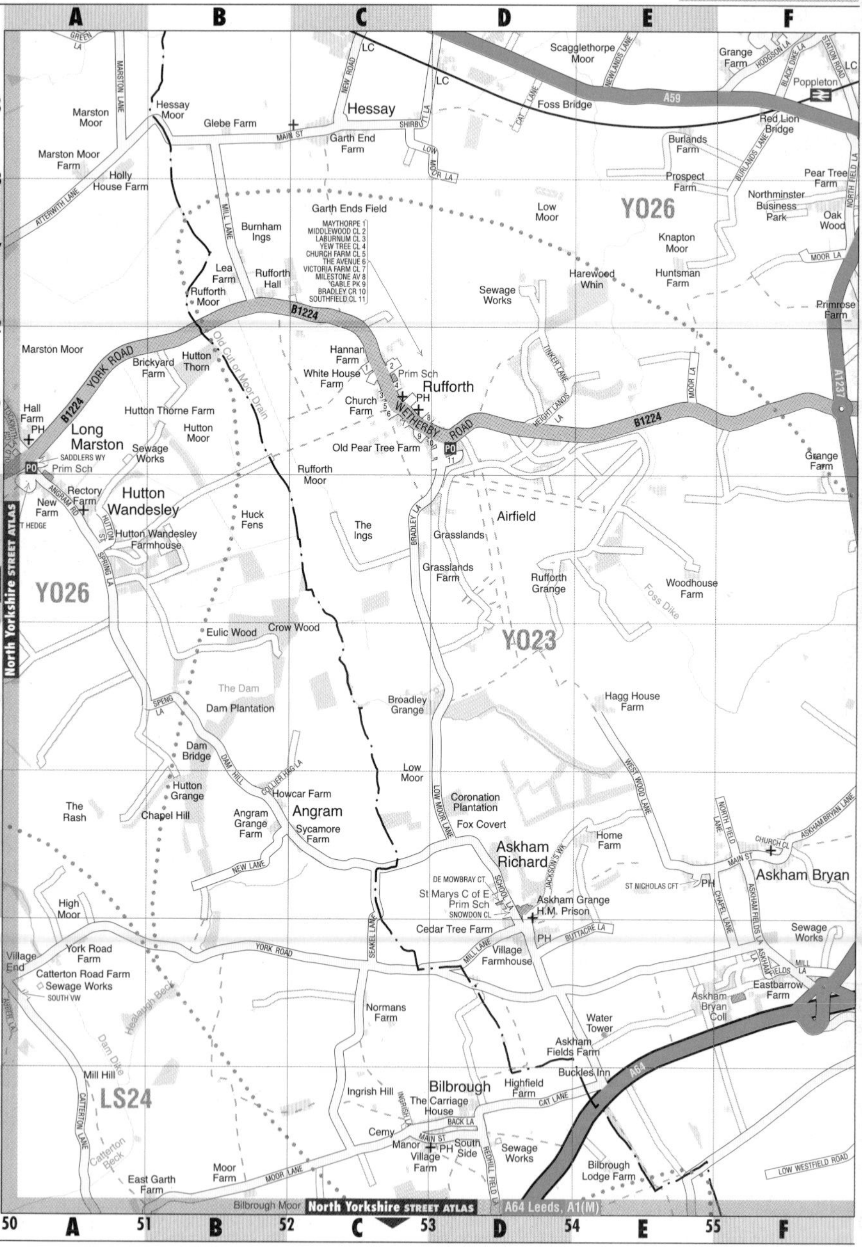
A
B
C
D
E
F
8
53
7
52
6
51
5
50
4
49
3
48
2
47
1
46
50
51
52
53
54
55
Green La
Marston Lane
Hessay Moor
Marston Moor
Marston Moor Farm
Holly House Farm
Atterwith Lane
Glebe Farm
Main St
Hessay
New Road
LC
Garth End Farm
Shirbutt La
Low Moor La
Scagglethorpe Moor
Newlands Lane
Cat Lane
Foss Bridge
A59
Grange Farm
Hodgson La
Black Dike La
Station Road
Poppleton
Red Lion Bridge
Burlands Farm
Burlands Lane
Prospect Farm
Pear Tree Farm
North Field La
Northminster Business Park
Oak Wood
Low Moor
YO26
Knapton Moor
Moor La
Huntsman Farm
Harewood Whin
Primrose Farm
Garth Ends Field
Burnham Ings
Mill Lane
Lea Farm
Rufforth Hall
Rufforth Moor
MAYTHORPE 1
MIDDLEWOOD CL 2
LABURNUM CL 3
YEW TREE CL 4
CHURCH FARM CL 5
THE AVENUE 6
VICTORIA FARM CL 7
MILESTONE AV 8
GABLE PK 9
BRADLEY CR 10
SOUTHFIELD CL 11
Sewage Works
B1224
York Road
Marston Moor
Brickyard Farm
Hutton Thorn
Old Cut or Moor Drain
Hannah Farm
White House Farm
Prim Sch
Rufforth
PH
Church Farm
Wetherby Road
Tinker Lane
Height Lands La
Moor La
A1237
Hall Farm
PH
Long Marston
Hutton Thorne Farm
Hutton Moor
Sewage Works
Saddlers Wy
PO
Prim Sch
Old Pear Tree Farm
Rufforth Moor
Grange Farm
Rectory Farm
New Farm
Angram Rd
Hutton Wandesley
T Hedge
Hutton St
Huck Fens
The Ings
Bradley La
Grasslands
Airfield
Hutton Wandesley Farmhouse
Spring La
Grasslands Farm
Rufforth Grange
Woodhouse Farm
Foss Dike
YO26
Eulic Wood
Crow Wood
YO23
The Dam
Dam Plantation
Speng La
Broadley Grange
Hagg House Farm
Dam Bridge
Dam Hill
Collier Hag La
Low Moor
West Wood Lane
Hutton Grange
The Rash
Chapel Hill
Howcar Farm
Angram Grange Farm
Angram
Low Moor Lane
Coronation Plantation
Fox Covert
Sycamore Farm
Askham Richard
Jackson's Wk
Home Farm
North Field Lane
Askham Bryan Lane
Church Cl
Main St
Askham Bryan
New Lane
De Mowbray Ct
School La
St Nicholas Cft
PH
Chapel Lane
Askham Fields La
St Marys C of E Prim Sch
Askham Grange H.M. Prison
Snowdon Cl
High Moor
Seakel Lane
Cedar Tree Farm
PH
Buttacre La
Sewage Works
York Road Farm
York Road
Mill Lane
Village Farmhouse
Mill La
Village End
Catterton Road Farm
Sewage Works
South Vw
Eastbarrow Farm
Askham Bryan Coll
Normans Farm
Healaugh Beck
Water Tower
Dam Dike
Askham Fields Farm
Mill Hill
Buckles Inn
A64
LS24
Ingrish Hill
Bilbrough
Highfield Farm
The Carriage House
Cat Lane
Catterton Lane
Back La
Cemy
Main St
Manor
PH
South Side
Village Farm
Redhill Field La
Sewage Works
Catterton Beck
Moor Farm
Moor Lane
Bilbrough Lodge Farm
Low Westfield Road
East Garth Farm
Bilbrough Moor
North Yorkshire Street Atlas
A64 Leeds, A1(M)

Scale: 1¼ inches to 1 mile
¼ ½ mile
250m 500m 750m 1 km

126 127 131

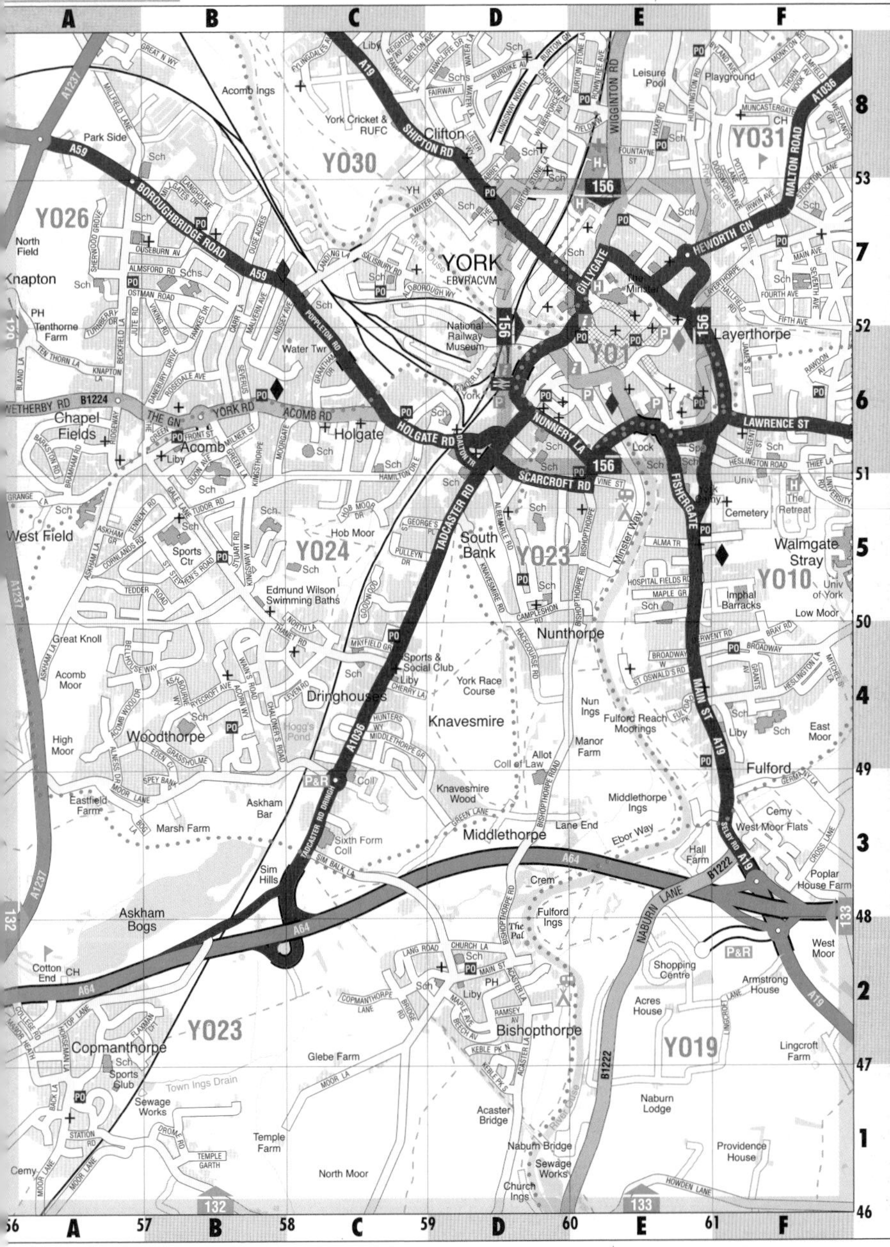

36 26

For full street detail of the highlighted area see pages 129, 130, 132 and 133.

For full street detail of the highlighted area see page 156.

F7
1 GORSE HL
2 HOLLY TREE CFT
3 ASPEN CL
4 ORCHARD CTS
5 PETERCROFT CL
6 KENDAL CL
7 UNDERCROFT
8 THORNCROFT
9 SAWYERS WK
10 CONEYCROFT
11 KEEPERS WY
12 WESTWOOD MS
13 SCAUDERCROFT
14 GREENCROFT CT
15 LIME TREE MS
16 OX CALDER CL
17 GREENCROFT LA
18 GREENSIDE
19 ASHDALE RD
20 THE GREEN
21 HUNTERS WOOD WY
22 DEERSTONE WY
23 GREENSIDE WLK
24 GREENSIDE CL

Scale: 1¼ inches to 1 mile
0 ¼ ½ mile
0 250m 500m 750m 1 km

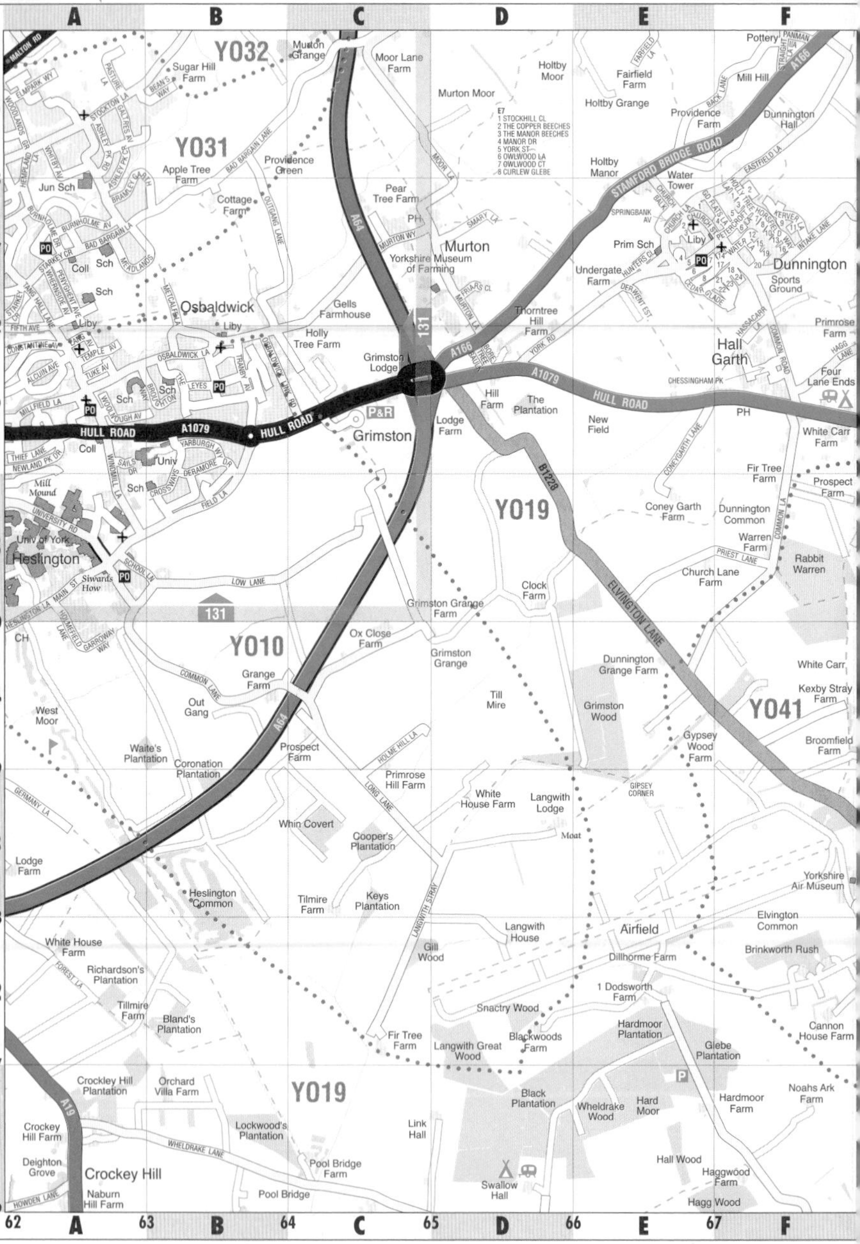

For full street detail of the highlighted area see page 131.

Scale: 1¼ inches to 1 mile
0 ¼ ½ mile
0 250m 500m 750m 1 km

15
28

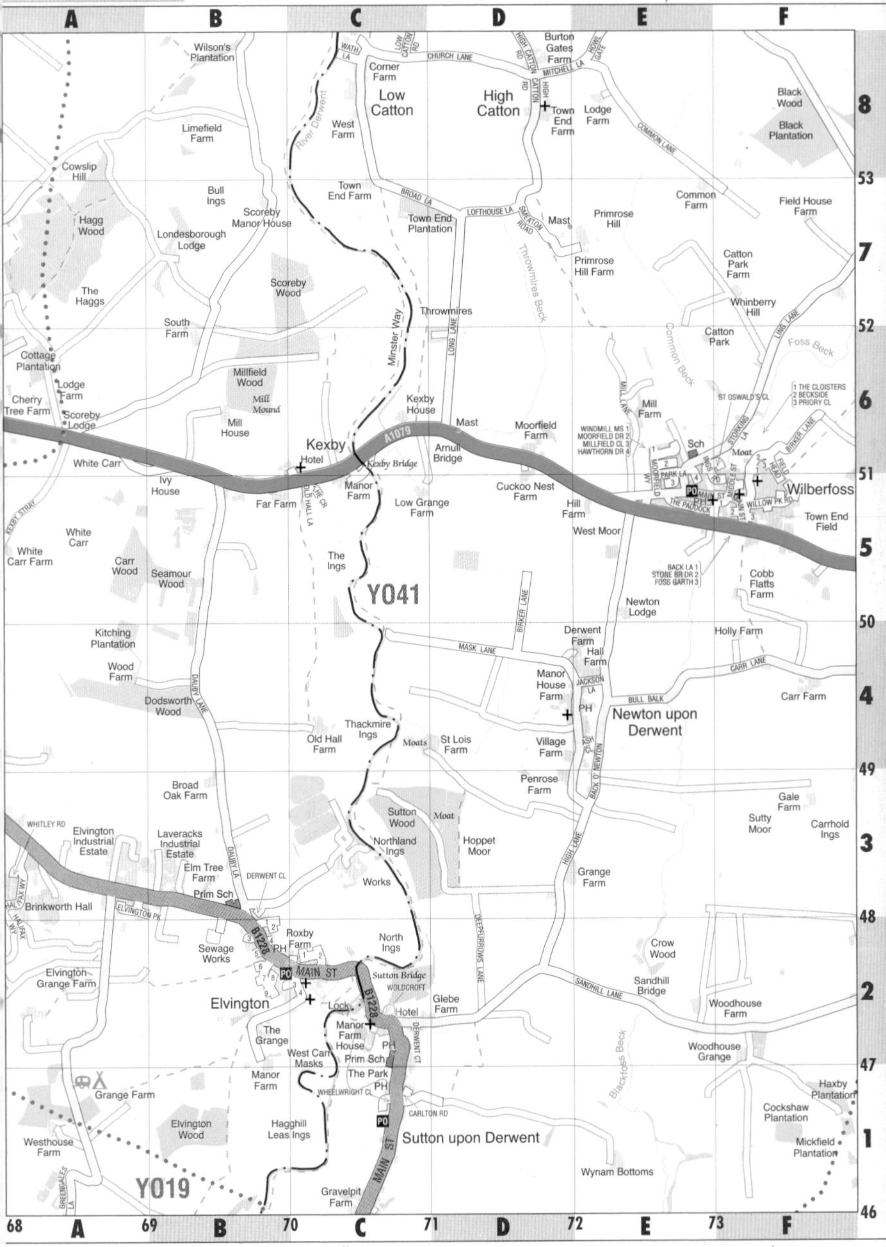

B2
1 WHITE HOUSE GR
2 BEECH CL
3 LORRAINE AV
4 HILLGARTH CT
5 DOVECOTE GARTH
6 BECK CL
7 BECKSIDE
8 BELVOIR AV
9 ALVIN WK

C2
1 RIVERSIDE CL
2 RIVERSIDE GD
3 CHURCH GN
4 CHURCH LA

38
28

27
16

Scale: 1¼ inches to 1 mile
0 ¼ ½ mile
0 250m 500m 750m 1 km

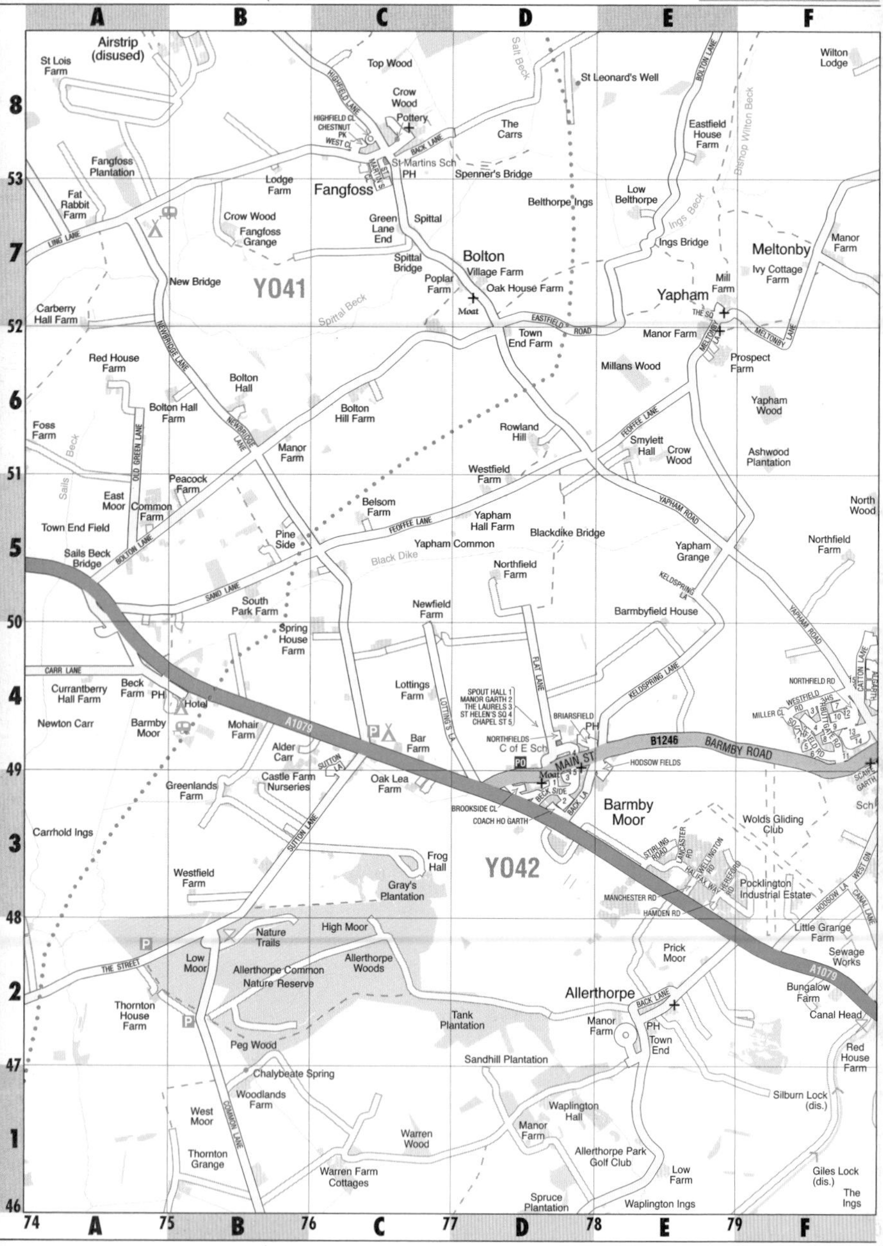
Airstrip (disused)
St Lois Farm
Top Wood
St Leonard's Well
Wilton Lodge
Crow Wood
Pottery
The Carrs
Eastfield House Farm
Fangfoss Plantation
Fat Rabbit Farm
Lodge Farm
Fangfoss
St Martins Sch
PH
Spenner's Bridge
Low Belthorpe
Belthorpe Ings
Crow Wood
Fangfoss Grange
Green Lane End
Spittal
Ings Bridge
Ings Beck
Bolton
Village Farm
Meltonby
Ivy Cottage Farm
Manor Farm
New Bridge
Y041
Spittal Bridge
Poplar Farm
Oak House Farm
Mill Farm
Yapham
Carberry Hall Farm
Spittal Beck
Moat
Town End Farm
Manor Farm
Prospect Farm
Red House Farm
Bolton Hall
Millans Wood
Bolton Hall Farm
Bolton Hill Farm
Yapham Wood
Foss Farm
Rowland Hill
Smylett Hall
Crow Wood
Ashwood Plantation
Manor Farm
Westfield Farm
Peacock Farm
East Moor
Common Farm
Belsom Farm
North Wood
Town End Field
Yapham Hall Farm
Blackdike Bridge
Northfield Farm
Pine Side
Yapham Common
Yapham Grange
Sails Beck Bridge
Black Dike
Northfield Farm
South Park Farm
Newfield Farm
Barmbyfield House
Spring House Farm
Lottings Farm
Currantberry Hall Farm
Beck Farm
PH
Hotel
Newton Carr
Barmby Moor
Mohair Farm
Bar Farm
C of E Sch
PO
Alder Carr
Castle Farm Nurseries
Oak Lea Farm
Greenlands Farm
Barmby Moor
Carrhold Ings
Wolds Gliding Club
Frog Hall
Y042
Westfield Farm
Gray's Plantation
Pocklington Industrial Estate
High Moor
Nature Trails
Little Grange Farm
Sewage Works
Prick Moor
Low Moor
Allerthorpe Woods
Allerthorpe Common Nature Reserve
Allerthorpe
Bungalow Farm
Thornton House Farm
Tank Plantation
Manor Farm
Canal Head
Peg Wood
Town End
Sandhill Plantation
Red House Farm
Chalybeate Spring
Woodlands Farm
Silburn Lock (dis.)
West Moor
Waplington Hall
Manor Farm
Warren Wood
Thornton Grange
Allerthorpe Park Golf Club
Warren Farm Cottages
Low Farm
Giles Lock (dis.)
Spruce Plantation
Waplington Ings
The Ings
LING LANE
NEWBRIDGE LANE
OLD GREEN LANE
BOLTON LANE
SAND LANE
FEOFFEE LANE
EASTFIELD ROAD
YAPHAM ROAD
MELTONBY LANE
KELDSPRING LANE
CARR LANE
A1079
SUTTON LANE
LOTTINGS LA
FLAT LANE
B1246
BARMBY ROAD
MAIN ST
BACK LA
BECK SIDE
COMMON LANE
THE STREET
BACK LANE
HIGHFIELD LANE
HIGHFIELD CL
CHESTNUT PK
WEST CL
BOLTON LANE
SPOUT HALL 1
MANOR GARTH 2
THE LAURELS 3
ST HELEN'S SQ 4
CHAPEL ST 5
BRIARSFIELD
NORTHFIELDS
HODSOW FIELDS
BROOKSIDE CL
COACH HO GARTH
STIRLING ROAD
LANCASTER RD
WELLINGTON RD
HALIFAX WAY
HEREFORD RD
MANCHESTER RD
HAMDEN RD
NORTHFIELD RD
MILLER CL
CATTON LANE
HODSOW LA
CANAL LANE
WEST GN
Sch
A B C D E F
8 53 7 52 6 51 5 50 4 49 3 48 2 47 1 46
74 75 76 77 78 79

F4
1 DALMAIS CL
2 BURNS CL
3 WESTFIELD CL
4 ORCHARD GD
5 WELLINGTON CL
6 MEADOWFIELD CL
7 NORTHFIELD RI
8 HALIFAX CL
9 ORCHARD WY
9 ORCHARD WY
10 ORCHARD CL
11 ST JOHN'S CL
12 NORTHFIELD CL
13 SHERBUTTGATE DR
14 SHERBUTTGATE RD
15 ANDREW'S CT

27
39

Scale: 1¼ inches to 1 mile
0 ¼ ½ mile
0 250m 500m 750m 1 km

17
30

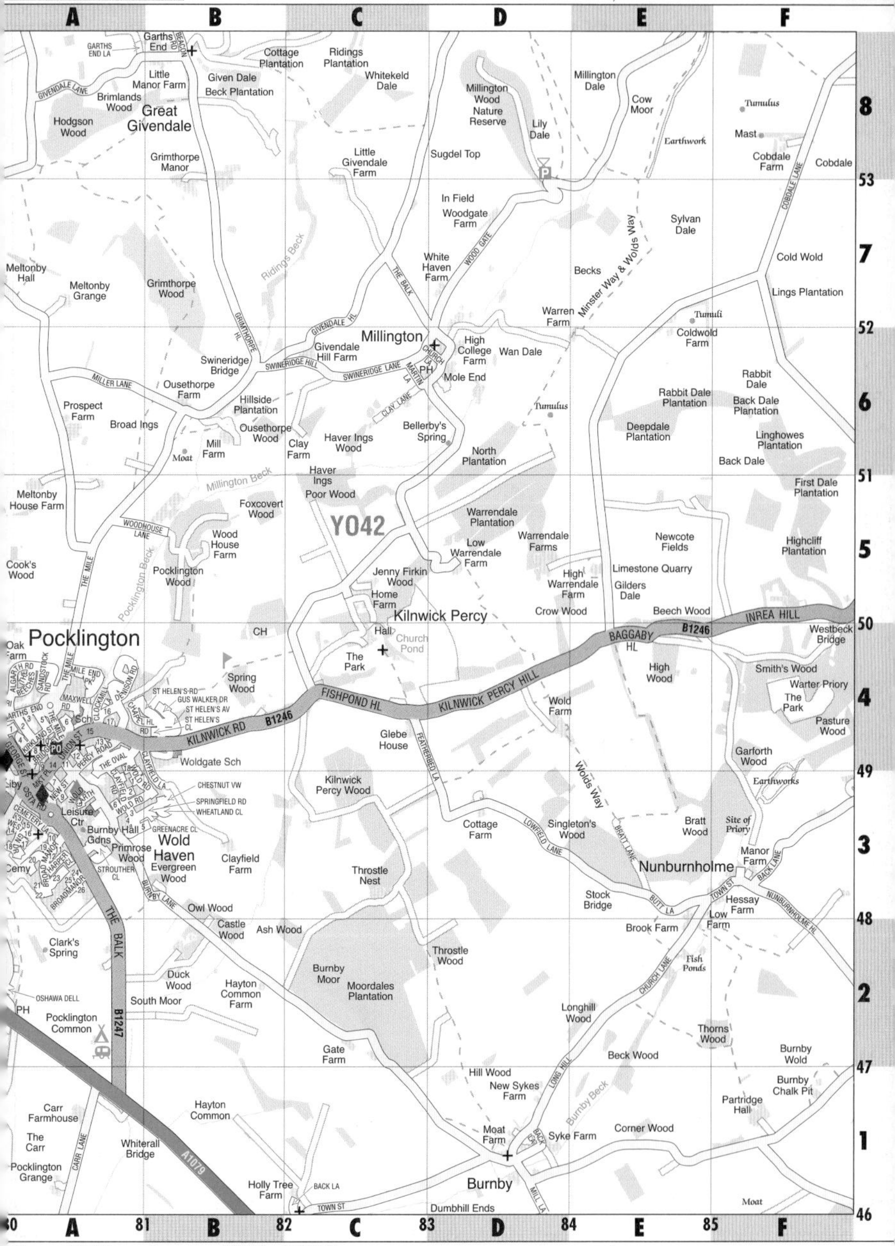

A4
1 EDWARD ST
2 VICTORIA RD
3 MURRAY CL
4 BRINDLEGATE
5 SCHOOL LA
6 BEECH CT
7 PEM LANE
8 KIRKGATE
9 MARKET ST
10 HALLGATE
11 THE AV
12 CHERRY ORCH MS
13 VOLAGE CT
14 ST PETER'S SQ
15 LONDON ST
16 TARGET LA
17 PAYTON CL
18 CLAYFIELD CL

A3
1 WOLDGATE VW
2 KILNWICK GARTH
3 PINEWOOD RD
4 PINEWOOD CT
5 PINEWOOD CL
6 VALENTINE CL
7 DEAN'S LA
8 REGENT ST PAVEMEN
9 WILLOW CT
10 THE LILACS
11 MCSHANE CT
12 MACDONALD CT
13 SYMONS WY
14 BECK VW
15 GARRICK CL
16 COMRIE DR
17 WAITE CL
18 TURNBULL DR
19 FETHERSTON CL
20 BROWNING RD
21 SAUNDERS CRES
22 THURLOW AV
23 DORRINGTON CL
24 KINGS CL
25 MCGRATH CL
26 HART DR

40
30

29
18

Scale: 1¼ inches to 1 mile
0 ¼ ½ mile
0 250m 500m 750m 1 km

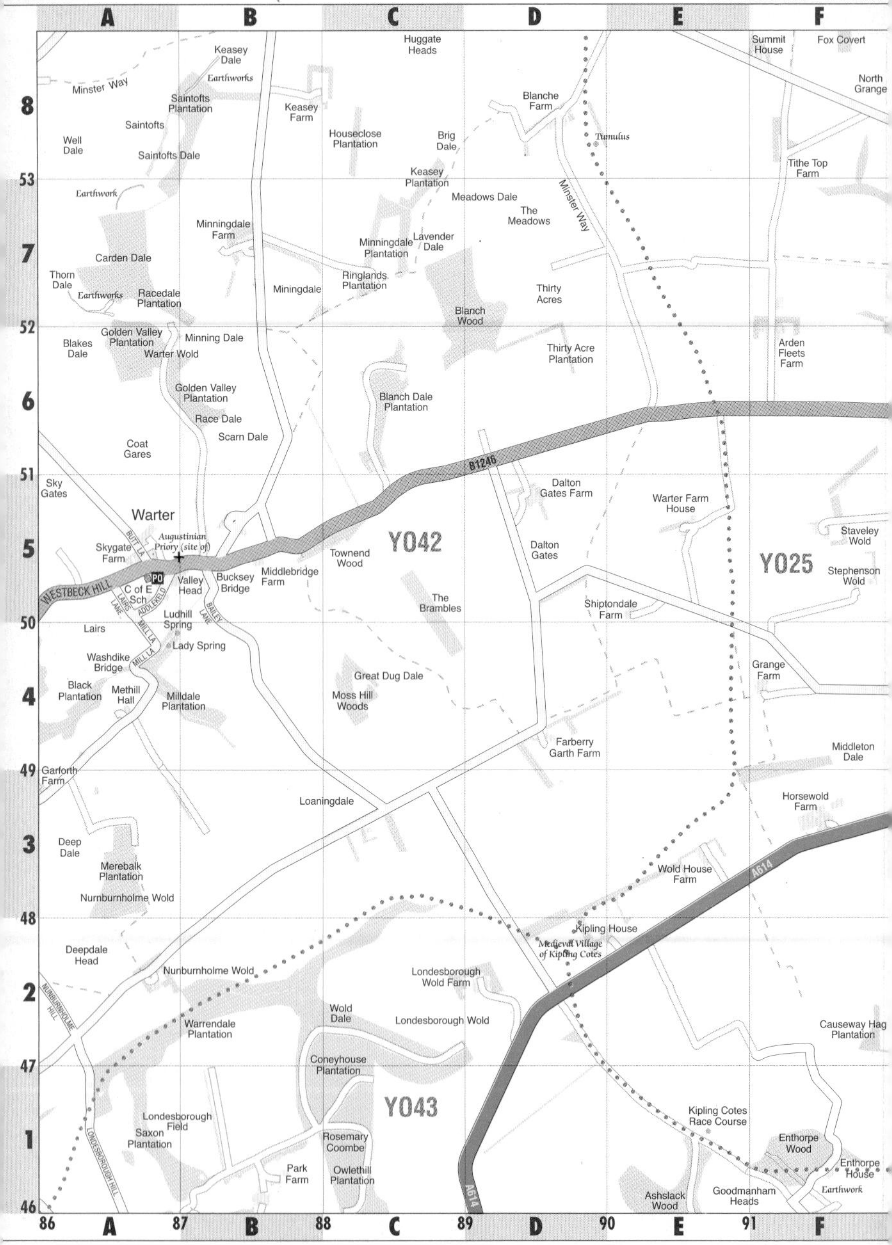

29
41

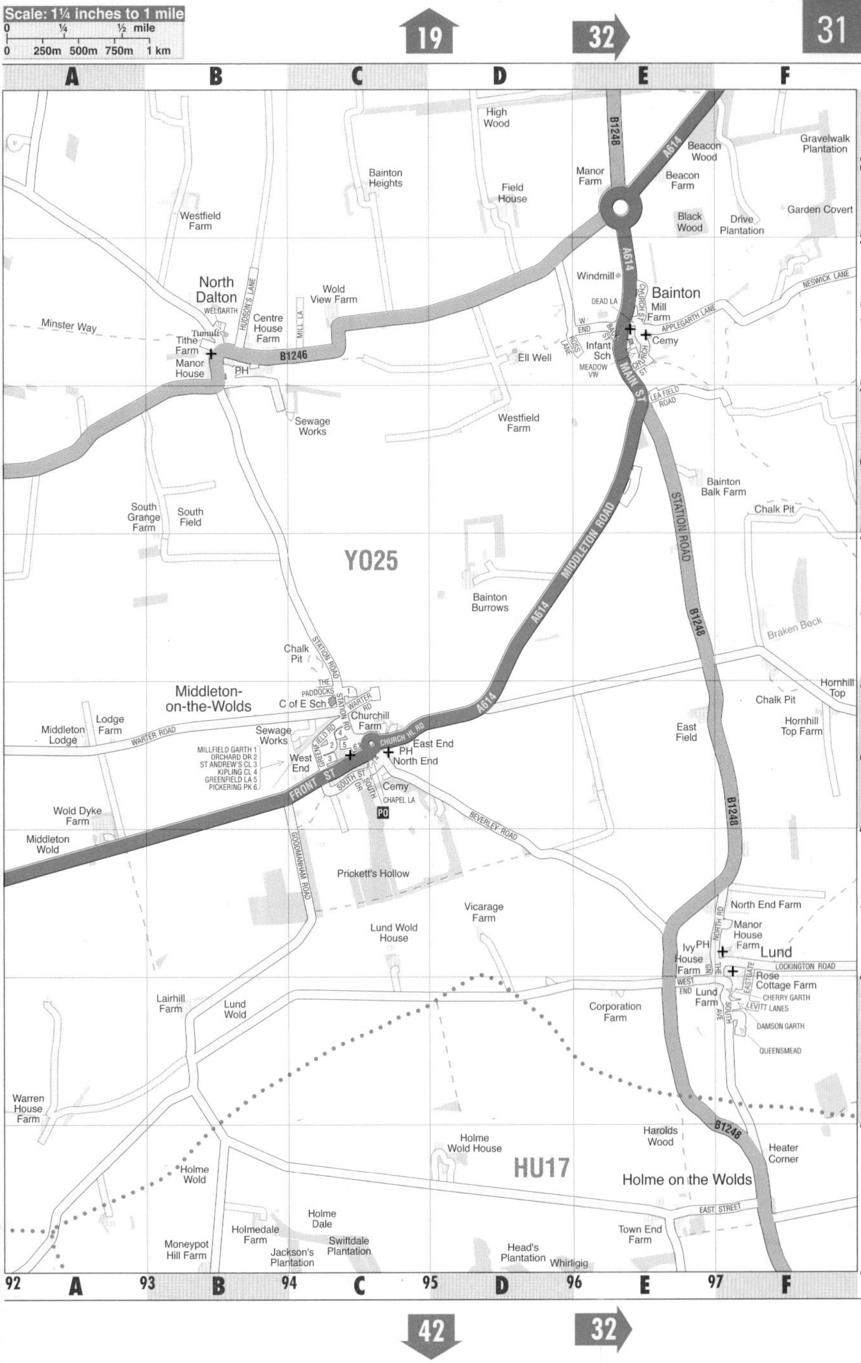
Scale: 1¼ inches to 1 mile
0 ¼ ½ mile
0 250m 500m 750m 1 km
19
32
A B C D E F
High Wood
B1248
A614
Beacon Wood
Gravelwalk Plantation
Bainton Heights
Manor Farm
Beacon Farm
Field House
Garden Covert
Westfield Farm
Black Wood
Drive Plantation
Windmill
Bainton
NESWICK LANE
North Dalton
HUDSON'S LANE
Wold View Farm
DEAD LA
CHURCH ST
Mill Farm
Minster Way
WELGARTH
Centre House Farm
MILL LA
W END
BACK ST
APPLEGARTH LANE
Tumuli
Tithe Farm
B1246
Cemy
Manor House
PH
Ell Well
ROSS LANE
Infant Sch
CHURCH ST
MEADOW VW
MAIN ST
LEA FIELD ROAD
Sewage Works
Westfield Farm
Bainton Balk Farm
STATION ROAD
Chalk Pit
South Grange Farm
South Field
MIDDLETON ROAD
YO25
Bainton Burrows
B1248
Braken Beck
Chalk Pit
STATION ROAD
Hornhill Top
Middleton-on-the-Wolds
THE PADDOCKS
C of E Sch
WARTER RD
Chalk Pit
Lodge Farm
Churchill Farm
Middleton Lodge
WARTER ROAD
Sewage Works
CHURCH HL RD
East End
East Field
Hornhill Top Farm
MILLFIELD GARTH 1
ORCHARD DR 2
ST ANDREW'S CL 3
KIPLING CL 4
GREENFIELD LA 5
PICKERING PK 6
West End
PH
North End
FRONT ST
SOUTH ST
SOUTH DR
Cemy
CHAPEL LA
PO
BEVERLEY ROAD
Wold Dyke Farm
Middleton Wold
GOODMANHAM ROAD
Prickett's Hollow
North End Farm
Vicarage Farm
NORTH RD
Manor House Farm
Lund Wold House
Ivy House Farm
PH
Lund
LOCKINGTON ROAD
Rose Cottage Farm
WEST END
Lund Farm
EASTGATE
CHERRY GARTH
Lairhill Farm
Lund Wold
Corporation Farm
SOUTH AVE
LEVITT LANES
DAMSON GARTH
QUEENSMEAD
Warren House Farm
Harolds Wood
B1248
Holme Wold House
Heater Corner
Holme Wold
HU17
Holme on the Wolds
EAST STREET
Holme Dale
Holmedale Farm
Swiftdale Plantation
Town End Farm
Moneypot Hill Farm
Jackson's Plantation
Head's Plantation
Whirligig
8 53 7 52 6 51 5 50 4 49 3 48 2 47 1 46
92 93 94 95 96 97
42
32

31
20

Scale: 1¼ inches to 1 mile
0 ¼ ½ mile
0 250m 500m 750m 1 km

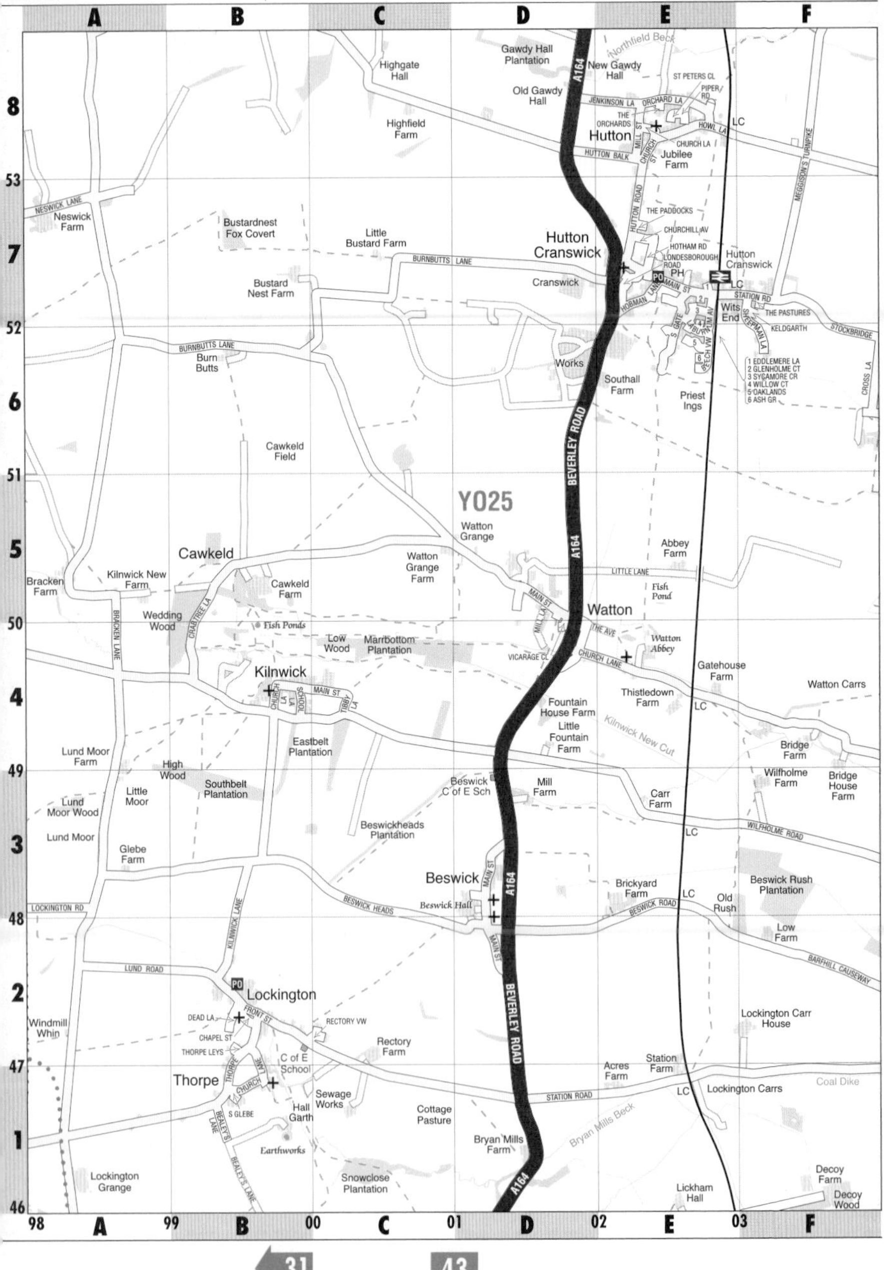

31
43

Scale: 1¼ inches to 1 mile
0 ¼ ½ mile
0 250m 500m 750m 1 km

21
34

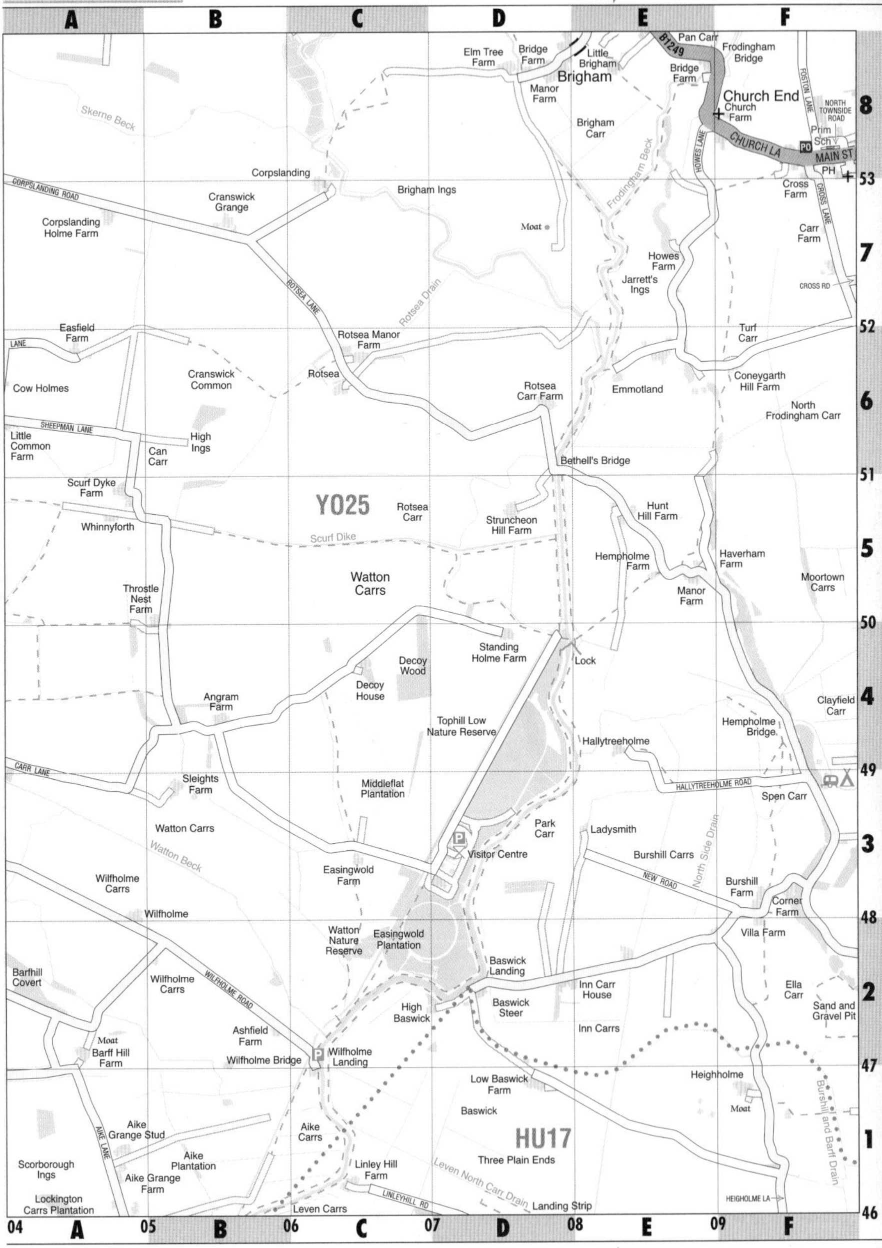

44
34

33
22

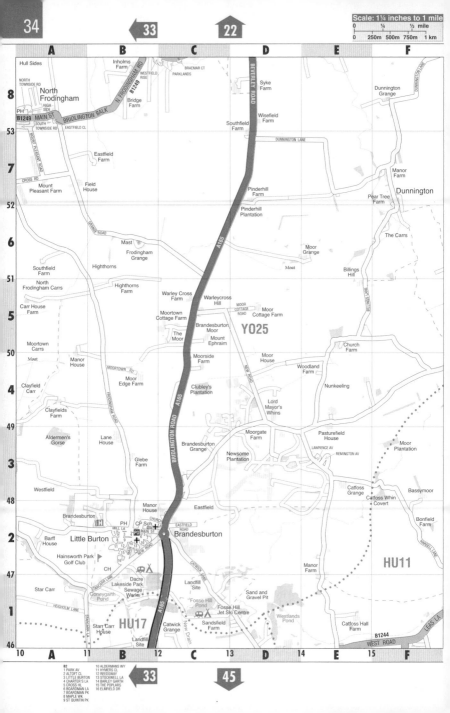

Scale: 1¼ inches to 1 mile
0 ¼ ½ mile
0 250m 500m 750m 1 km

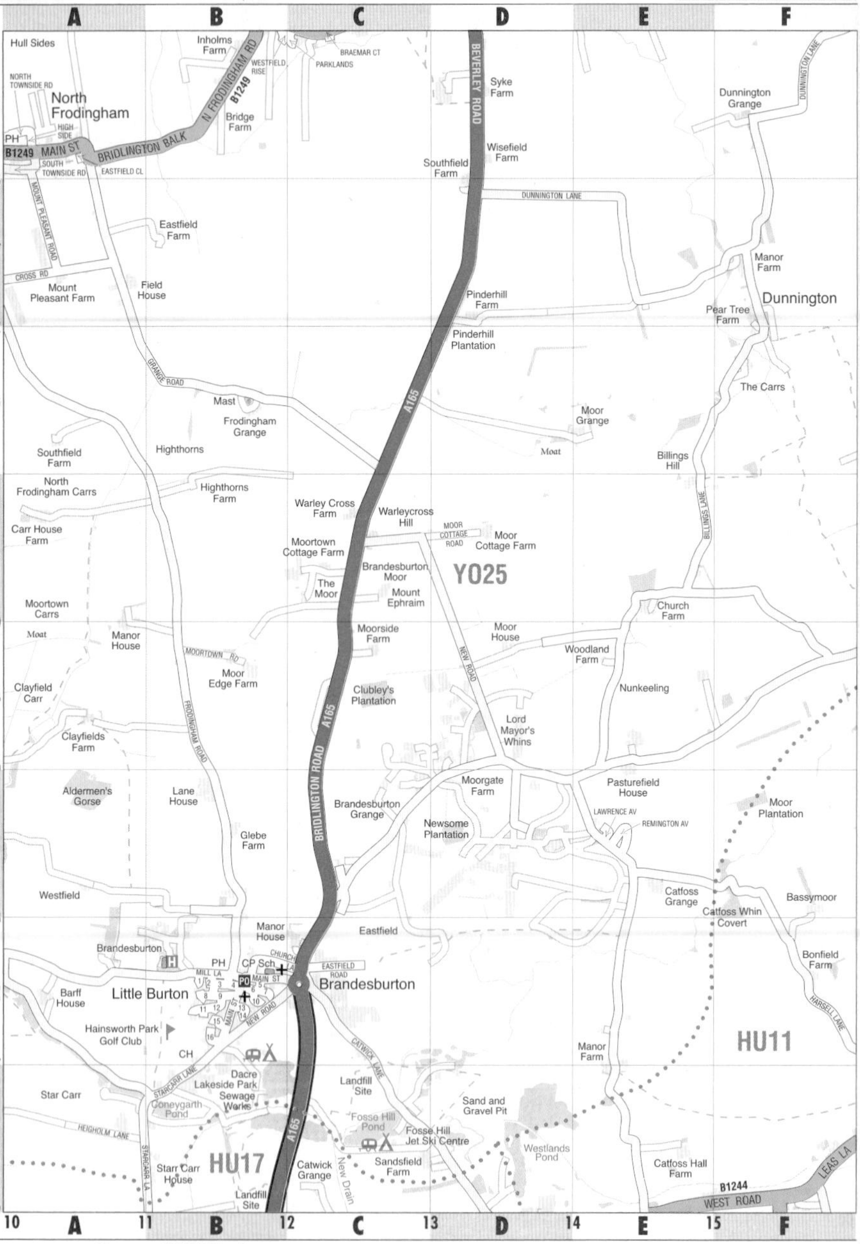

B2
1 PARK AV
2 ALTOFT CL
3 LITTLE BURTON
4 CHARTER'S LA
5 CROSS HL
6 BOARDMAN LA
7 BOARDMAN PK
8 MAPLE WK
9 ST QUINTIN PK
10 ALDERMANS WY
11 HYMERS CL
12 REEDSWAY
13 STOCKWELL LA
14 BARLEY GARTH
15 THE POPLARS
16 ELMFIELD DR

33
45

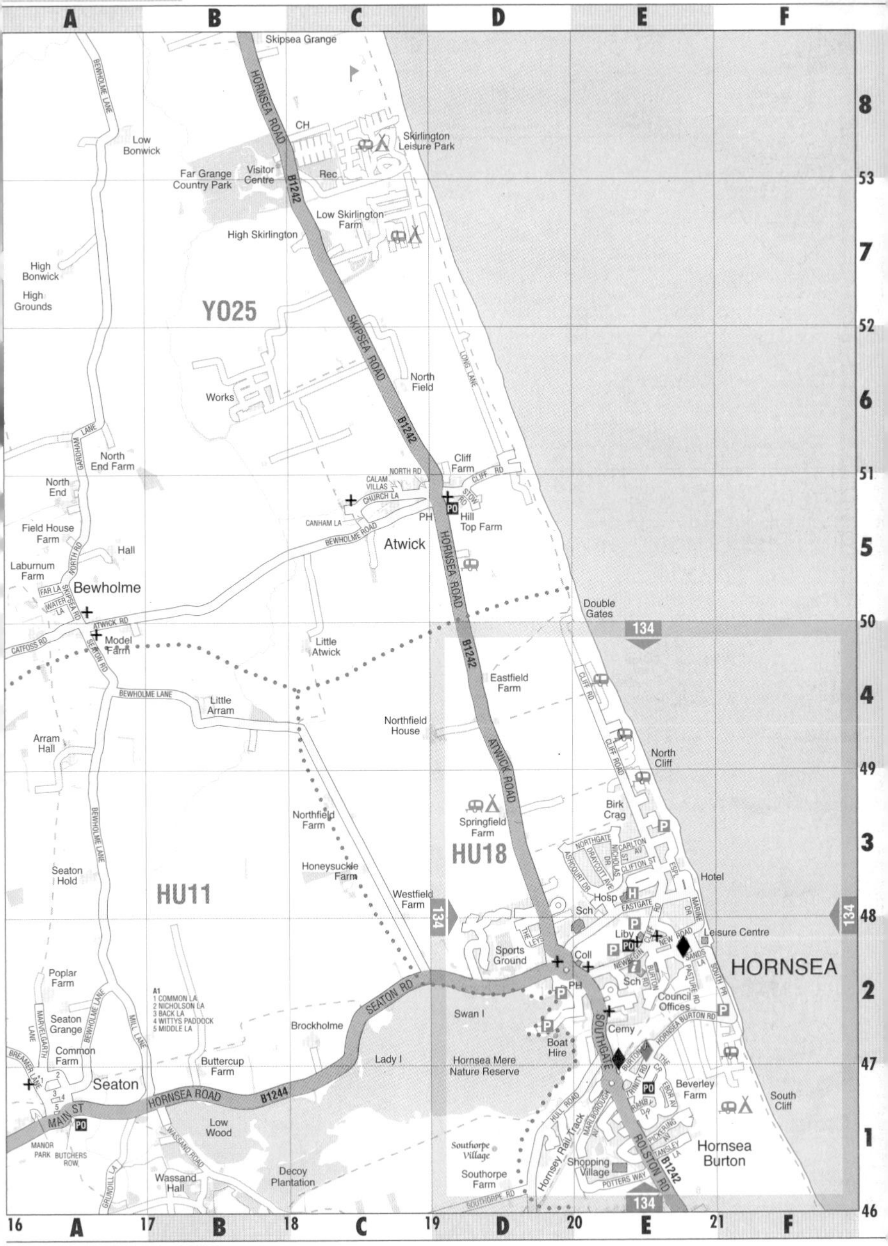
A
B
C
D
E
F
Skipsea Grange
HORNSEA ROAD
BEWHOLME LANE
CH
Skirlington Leisure Park
Low Bonwick
Far Grange Country Park
Visitor Centre
Rec
B1242
Low Skirlington Farm
High Skirlington
High Bonwick
High Grounds
YO25
SKIPSEA ROAD
LONG LANE
North Field
Works
GARDHAM LANE
North End Farm
Cliff Farm
NORTH RD
CALAM VILLAS
CHURCH LA
CLIFF RD
STOW RD
North End
PO
Hill Top Farm
PH
CANHAM LA
BEWHOLME ROAD
Atwick
Field House Farm
Hall
Laburnum Farm
NORTH RD
Bewholme
FAR LA
WATER LA
SKIPSEA RD
Double Gates
ATWICK RD
CATFOSS RD
Model Farm
SEATON RD
Little Atwick
134
Eastfield Farm
CLIFF RD
BEWHOLME LANE
Little Arram
Northfield House
Arram Hall
North Cliff
ATWICK ROAD
Birk Crag
Northfield Farm
Springfield Farm
HU18
NORTHGATE
ASHCOURT DR
DRAYCOTT AVE
NICHOLAS ST
CARLTON AV
CLIFTON ST
ESPL
Honeysuckle Farm
Seaton Hold
HU11
Westfield Farm
Hosp
Hotel
EASTGATE
Sch
MARINE DR
Leisure Centre
THE LEYS
Liby
NEW ROAD
Sports Ground
Coll
SANDS LA
HORNSEA
Poplar Farm
A1
1 COMMON LA
2 NICHOLSON LA
3 BACK LA
4 WITTYS PADDOCK
5 MIDDLE LA
SEATON RD
PH
NEWBEGIN
BURTON RD
Sch
PASTURE RD
SOUTH PR
Council Offices
Seaton Grange
MARVELGARTH LANE
MILL LANE
Brockholme
Swan I
HORNSEA BURTON RD
Cemy
Common Farm
BREAMER LANE
Buttercup Farm
Lady I
Hornsea Mere Nature Reserve
Boat Hire
SOUTHGATE
Seaton
HORNSEA ROAD
B1244
TRINITY RD
EBOR AV
Beverley Farm
South Cliff
MAIN ST
PO
Low Wood
WASSAND ROAD
HULL ROAD
MARLBOROUGH AV
RANBY DR
PICKERING AV
TANSLEY LA
MANOR PARK
BUTCHERS ROW
Wassand Hall
Decoy Plantation
Southorpe Village
Southorpe Farm
Hornsey Rail Track
Shopping Village
POTTERS WAY
ROLSTON RD
Hornsea Burton
GRUNDILL LA
SOUTHORPE RD
8
53
7
52
6
51
5
50
4
49
3
48
2
47
1
46
16
17
18
19
20
21

For full street detail of the highlighted area see page 134.
46

132
133

Scale: 1¼ inches to 1 mile
0 ¼ ½ mile
0 250m 500m 750m 1 km

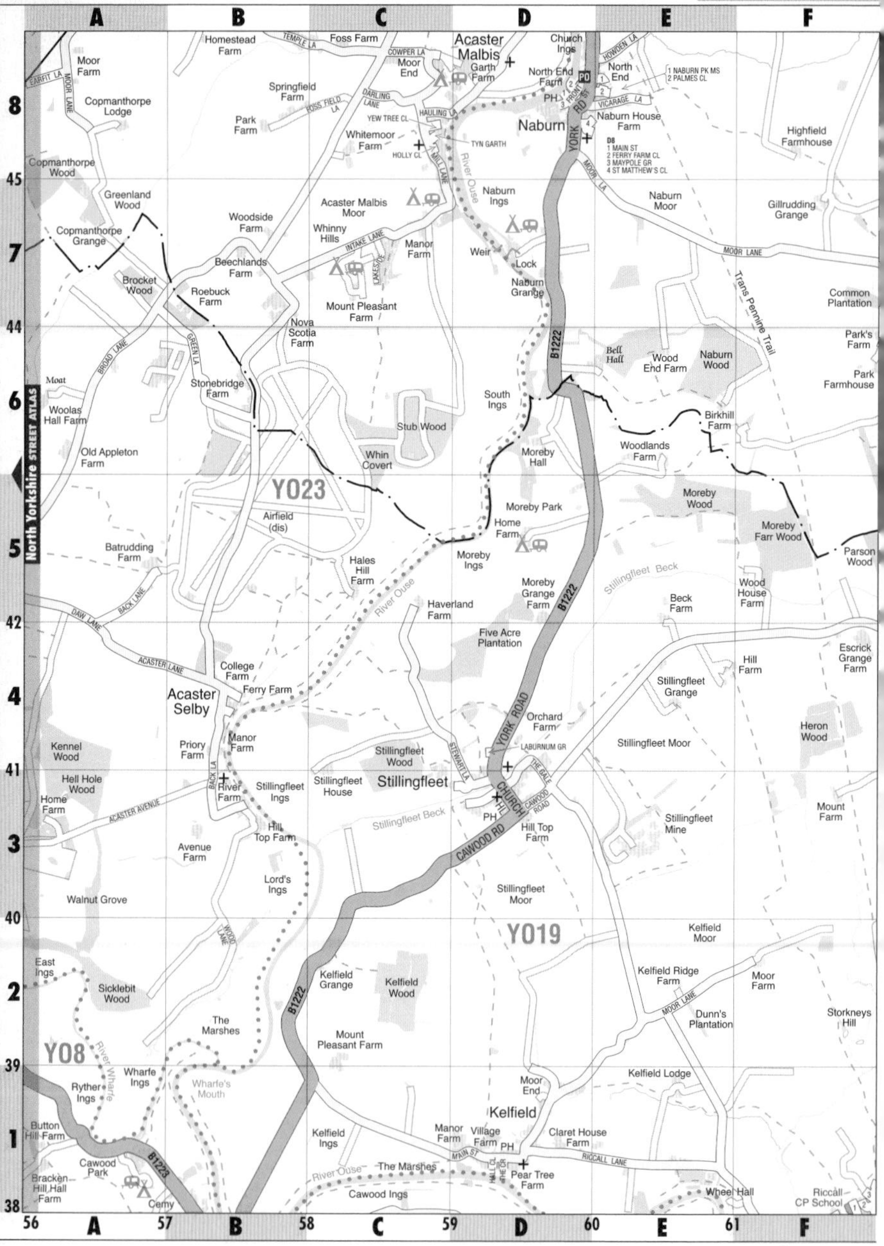

48

F1
1 Coppergate
2 Elms Cl
3 Northfield La

Scale: 1¼ inches to 1 mile
0 ¼ ½ mile
0 250m 500m 750m 1 km

26
38

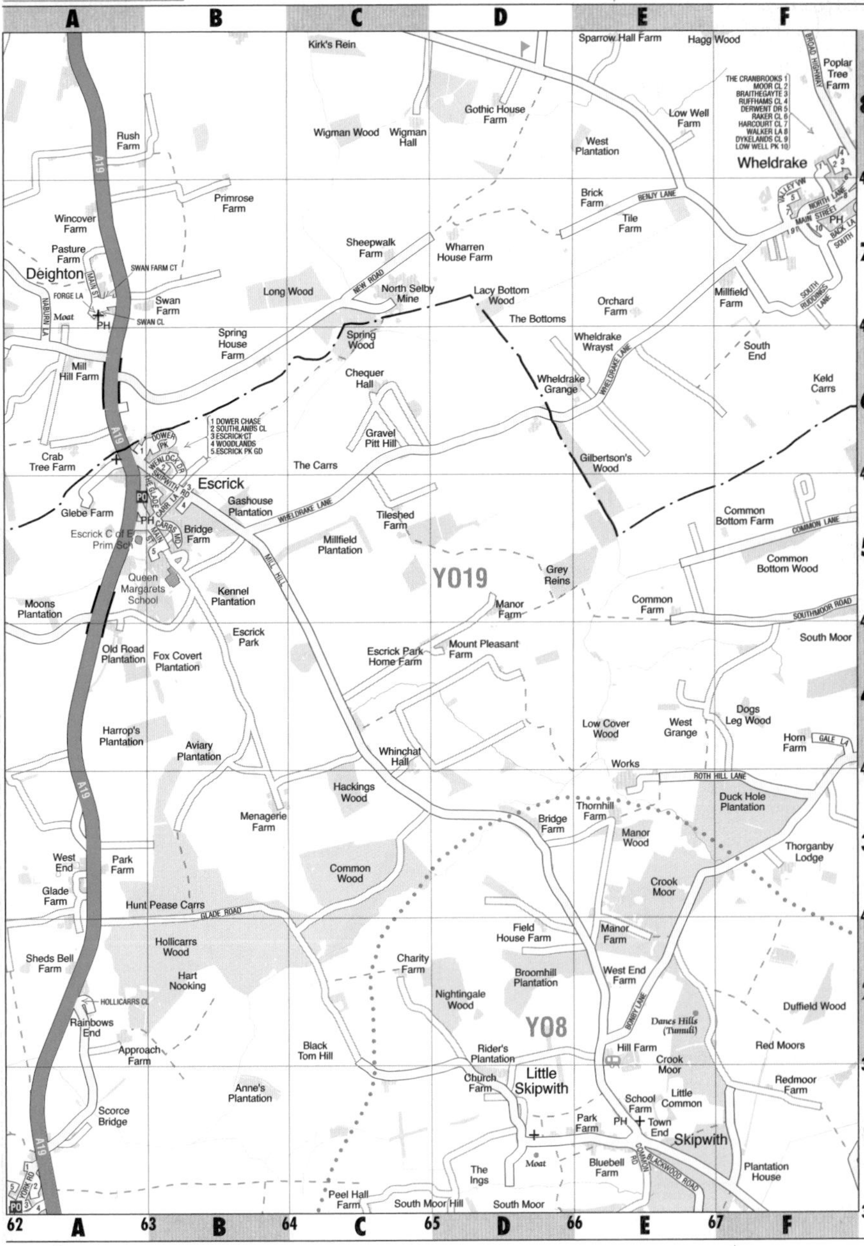
A B C D E F
8 45 7 44 6 43 5 42 4 41 3 40 2 39 1 38
62 63 64 65 66 67
Kirk's Rein
Sparrow Hall Farm
Hagg Wood
Poplar Tree Farm
BROAD HIGHWAY
THE CRANBROOKS 1
MOOR CL 2
BRAITHEGAYTE 3
RUFFHAMS CL 4
DERWENT DR 5
RAKER CL 6
HARCOURT CL 7
WALKER LA 8
DYKELANDS CL 9
LOW WELL PK 10
Gothic House Farm
Low Well Farm
Rush Farm
Wigman Wood
Wigman Hall
West Plantation
Wheldrake
A19
Primrose Farm
Brick Farm
BENJY LANE
Tile Farm
VALLEY VW
NORTH LANE
MAIN STREET
PH
BACK LA
SOUTH
Wincover Farm
Pasture Farm
Sheepwalk Farm
Wharren House Farm
Deighton
SWAN FARM CT
MAIN ST
NEW ROAD
FORGE LA
Long Wood
North Selby Mine
Lacy Bottom Wood
Orchard Farm
Millfield Farm
SOUTH RUDDINGS LANE
NABURN LA
Moat
Swan Farm
SWAN CL
The Bottoms
Spring House Farm
Spring Wood
Wheldrake Wrayst
South End
Mill Hill Farm
Chequer Hall
WHELDRAKE LANE
Wheldrake Grange
Keld Carrs
1 DOWER CHASE
2 SOUTHLANDS CL
3 ESCRICK CT
4 WOODLANDS
5 ESCRICK PK GD
DOWER PK
Gravel Pitt Hill
Gilbertson's Wood
Crab Tree Farm
WENLOCK DR
SKIPWITH RD
The Carrs
Escrick
THE GLADE
CARR LA
PO
Gashouse Plantation
Glebe Farm
Tileshed Farm
Common Bottom Farm
COMMON LANE
PH
CARRS MD
Bridge Farm
Escrick C of E Prim Sch
MAIN
Millfield Plantation
Common Bottom Wood
MILL HILL
YO19
Grey Reins
Queen Margarets School
Kennel Plantation
Moons Plantation
Manor Farm
Common Farm
SOUTHMOOR ROAD
South Moor
Escrick Park
Old Road Plantation
Fox Covert Plantation
Escrick Park Home Farm
Mount Pleasant Farm
Dogs Leg Wood
Low Cover Wood
West Grange
Harrop's Plantation
Horn Farm
GALE LA
Aviary Plantation
Whinchat Hall
Works
ROTH HILL LANE
Hackings Wood
Duck Hole Plantation
Thornhill Farm
Menagerie Farm
Bridge Farm
Manor Wood
Thorganby Lodge
West End
Park Farm
Common Wood
Crook Moor
Glade Farm
Hunt Pease Carrs
GLADE ROAD
Field House Farm
Manor Farm
Sheds Bell Farm
Hollicarrs Wood
Charity Farm
Broomhill Plantation
West End Farm
Hart Nooking
Nightingale Wood
Duffield Wood
HOLLICARRS CL
BONBY LANE
Danes Hills (Tumuli)
Rainbows End
YO8
Red Moors
Approach Farm
Black Tom Hill
Rider's Plantation
Hill Farm
Crook Moor
Church Farm
Little Skipwith
Redmoor Farm
Anne's Plantation
Little Common
School Farm
Scorce Bridge
Park Farm
PH
Town End
Skipwith
COMMON RD
BLACKWOOD ROAD
Moat
Plantation House
Bluebell Farm
The Ings
YORK RD
PO
Peel Hall Farm
South Moor Hill
South Moor

A1
1 MILL LA
2 HOLMES DR
3 CHAPEL LA
4 CHAPEL WK
5 PINFOLD CL

49
38

37
27

Scale: 1¼ inches to 1 mile
0 ¼ ½ mile
0 250m 500m 750m 1 km

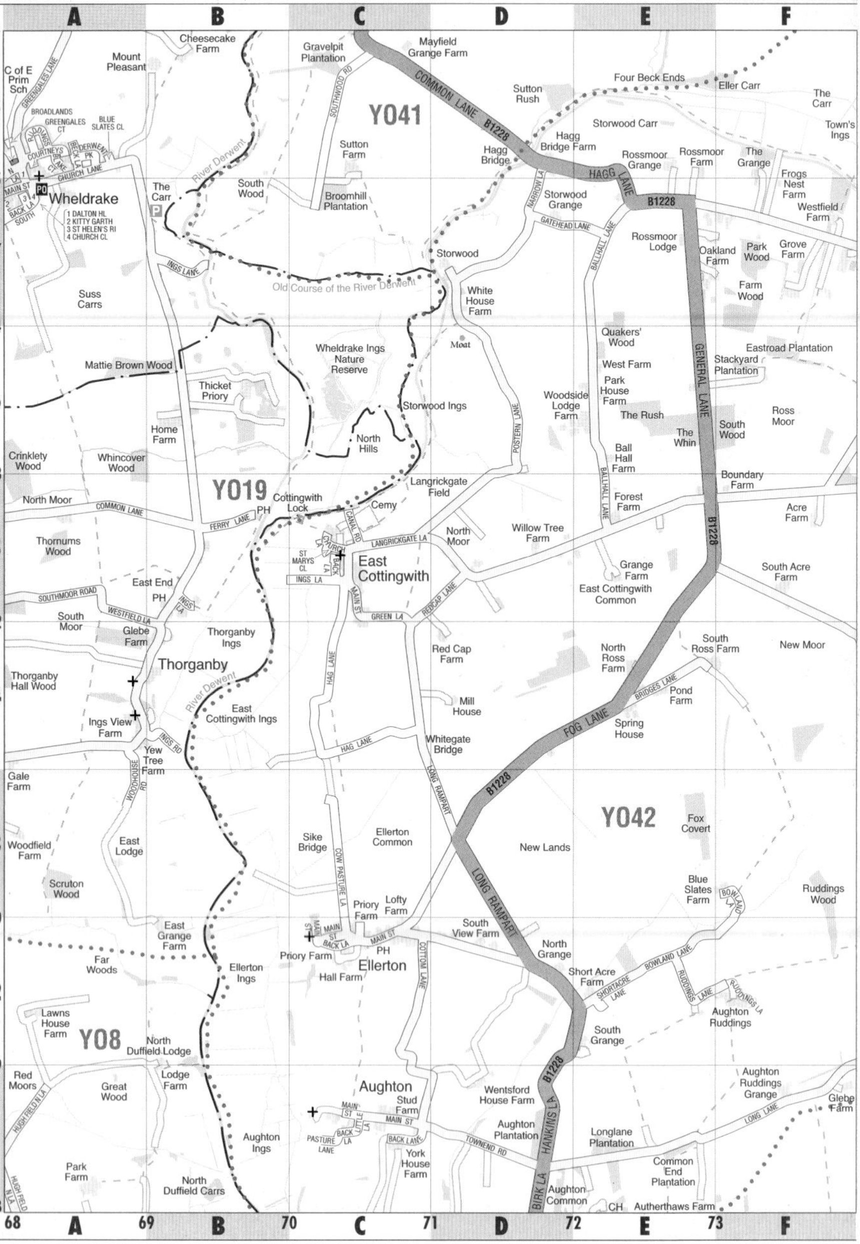

37
50

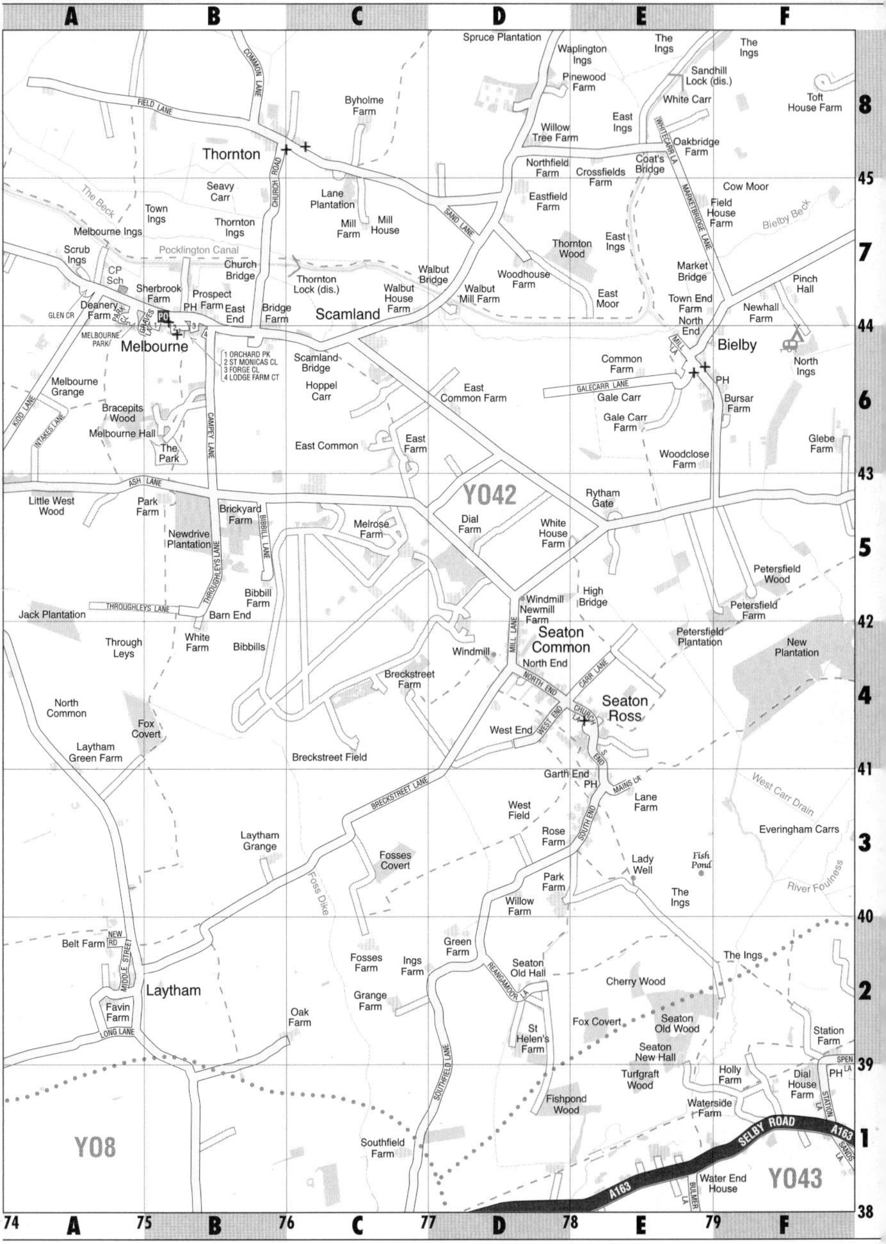
A
B
C
D
E
F
Spruce Plantation
Waplington Ings
The Ings
The Ings
Sandhill Lock (dis.)
Pinewood Farm
White Carr
Toft House Farm
COMMON LANE
FIELD LANE
Byholme Farm
East Ings
Willow Tree Farm
WHITECARR LA
Oakbridge Farm
Thornton
CHURCH ROAD
Northfield Farm
Crossfields Farm
Coat's Bridge
Cow Moor
The Beck
Seavy Carr
Lane Plantation
Eastfield Farm
MARKETBRIDGE LANE
Field House Farm
Bielby Beck
Town Ings
Thornton Ings
Mill Farm
Mill House
SAND LANE
East Ings
Melbourne Ings
Thornton Wood
Scrub Ings
Pocklington Canal
Church Bridge
Market Bridge
CP Sch
Thornton Lock (dis.)
Walbut Bridge
Woodhouse Farm
Pinch Hall
Sherbrook Farm
Prospect Farm
Walbut House Farm
Walbut Mill Farm
East Moor
Town End Farm
Newhall Farm
Deanery Farm
PH
East End
Bridge Farm
Scamland
North End
GLEN CR
PARK CL
GRAVES LA
PO
MELBOURNE PARK
Melbourne
1 ORCHARD PK
2 ST MONICAS CL
3 FORGE CL
4 LODGE FARM CT
Scamland Bridge
MILL LA
Bielby
Common Farm
North Ings
PH
Melbourne Grange
Hoppel Carr
East Common Farm
GALECARR LANE
Gale Carr
Bursar Farm
KIDD LANE
Bracepits Wood
Gale Carr Farm
INTAKES LANE
Melbourne Hall
CAMPEY LANE
East Farm
Glebe Farm
The Park
East Common
Woodclose Farm
ASH LANE
YO42
Rytham Gate
Little West Wood
Park Farm
Brickyard Farm
Dial Farm
Melrose Farm
White House Farm
Newdrive Plantation
BIBBILL LANE
THROUGHLEYS LANE
Petersfield Wood
Bibbill Farm
Windmill
High Bridge
Petersfield Farm
Newmill Farm
Jack Plantation
THROUGHLEYS LANE
Barn End
MILL LANE
Seaton Common
Petersfield Plantation
New Plantation
Through Leys
White Farm
Bibbills
Windmill
North End
CARR LANE
Breckstreet Farm
NORTH END
Seaton Ross
North Common
CHURCH LA
Fox Covert
WEST END
West End
Laytham Green Farm
Breckstreet Field
S END
Garth End
PH
MAINS LA
West Carr Drain
BRECKSTREET LANE
Lane Farm
West Field
Everingham Carrs
SOUTH END
Rose Farm
Laytham Grange
Fosses Covert
Lady Well
Fish Pond
Foss Dike
Park Farm
The Ings
River Foulness
Willow Farm
Belt Farm
NEW RD
Green Farm
The Ings
MIDDLE STREET
Fosses Farm
Ings Farm
Seaton Old Hall
Laytham
REANGAMOOR LA
Cherry Wood
Grange Farm
Favin Farm
St Helen's Farm
Fox Covert
Seaton Old Wood
Station Farm
Oak Farm
LONG LANE
Seaton New Hall
SPEN LA
PH
Turfgraft Wood
Holly Farm
Dial House Farm
SOUTHFIELD LANE
STATION LA
Fishpond Wood
Waterside Farm
SELBY ROAD
A163
Southfield Farm
YO8
SANDS LA
Water End House
YO43
A163
BULMER LA
8
45
7
44
6
43
5
42
4
41
3
40
2
39
1
38
74
75
76
77
78
79

39
29

Scale: 1¼ inches to 1 mile
0 ¼ ½ mile
0 250m 500m 750m 1 km

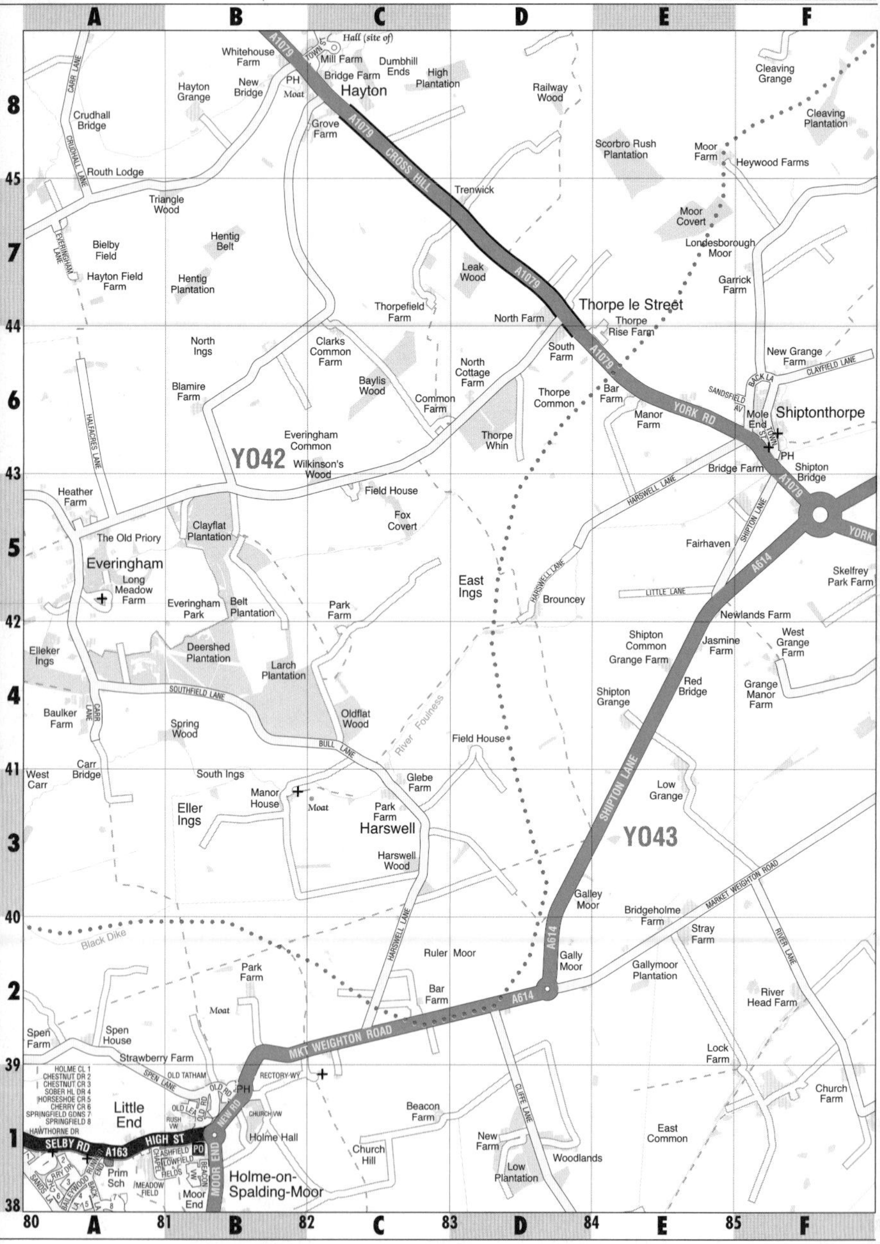

39
52

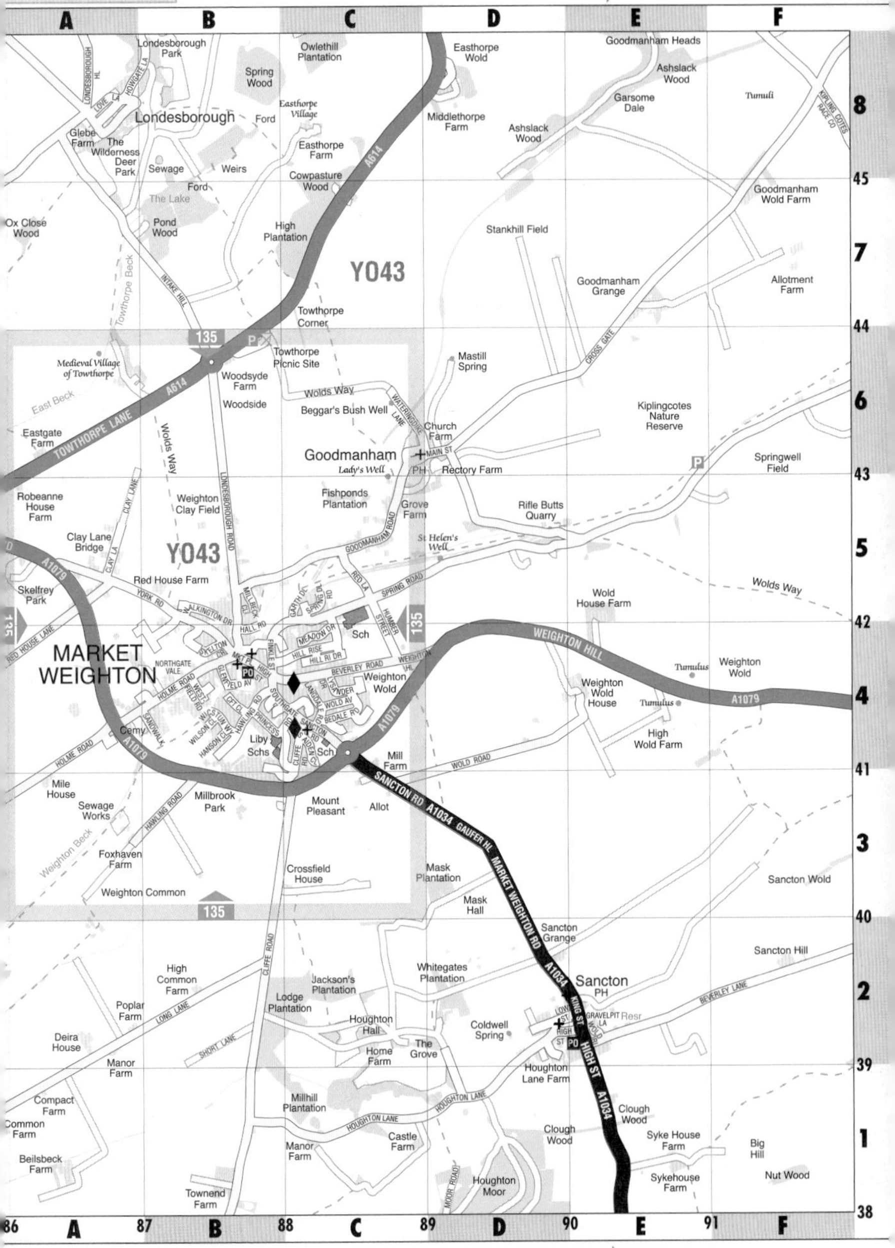

For full street detail of the highlighted area see page 135.

41
31
Scale: 1¼ inches to 1 mile
0 ¼ ½ mile
0 250m 500m 750m 1 km

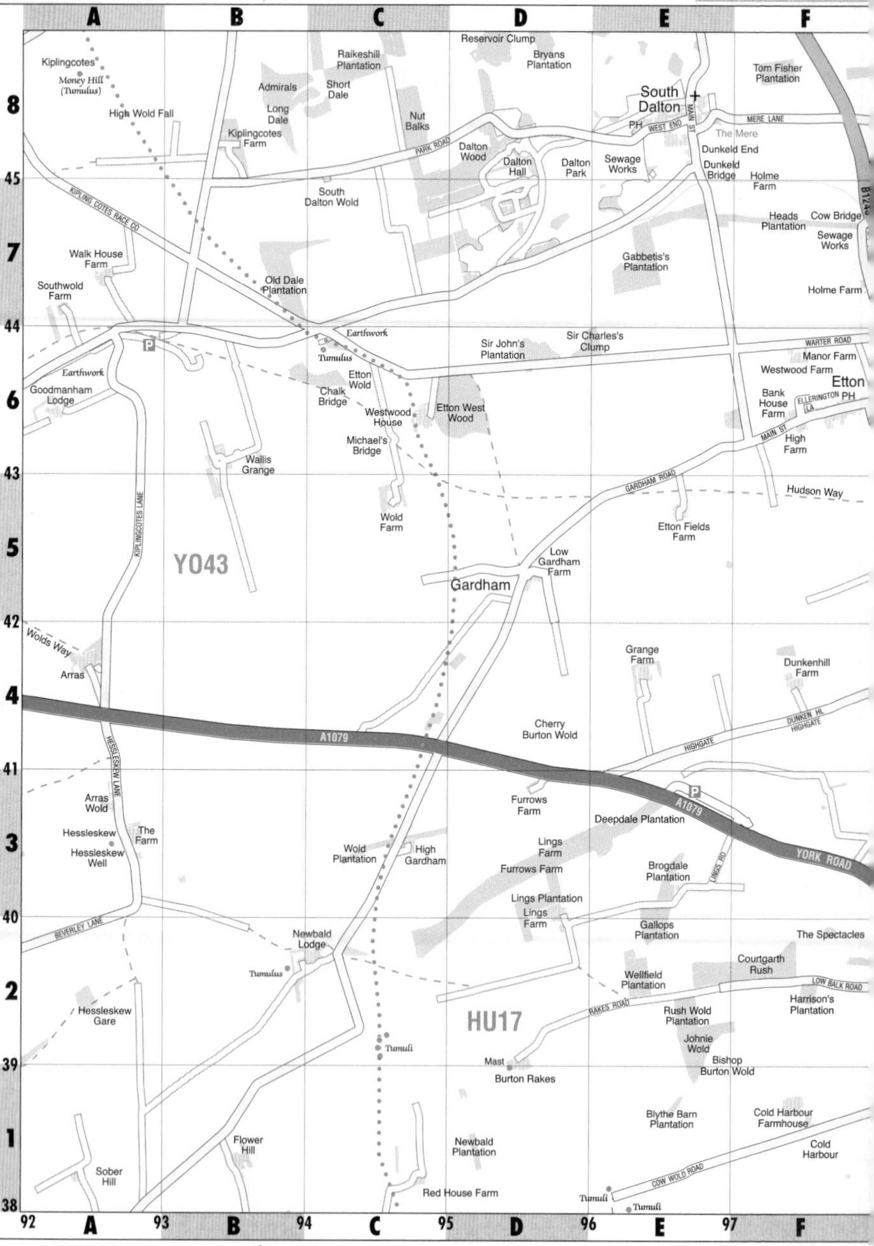

41
54

A
B
C
D
E
F
8
45
7
44
6
43
5
42
4
41
3
40
2
39
1
38
98
99
00
01
02
03
Lockington Wood
YO25
Moorfield Farm
Beverley's Lane
Scorborough Beck
Lakes Farm
White House Farm
Moat
Scorborough Lane
Park Farm
LC
Decoy Wood
Scorborough Ings
Minster Way
Arram Carrs
Lake's Wood
Ford
Scorborough
Great Heads Belt
Moat
Ella Dyke
Moat
Whipp's Whin
A164
Arram Green Farm
Arram Carrs
Catchwater Drain
Long Close Farm
Moor Plantation
Gommery Hall Farm
Sewage Works
New Arram
Croft Hill Farm
South Wolds School
Woodhouse Farm
Leconfield Grange
Station Farm
Arram
Old Wife Pit (dis)
Leman Wood
High Hall
Chantry Lane
Etton Dikes
Bygot Wood
Old Road
Ash Tree Dr
Arram Rd
Prim Sch
Grange Rd
Grange Road
Main St
Tower
A164 Main St
Hartill Av
Sellers Dr
Carnaby Cl
Lisset Cl
Leconfield
Airfield (dis)
Earthwork
Raventhorpe Nursery
Miles Lane
St Catherines Dr
PO
Bygot House Farm
HU17
Moat
Normandy Barracks
Butt Hill
Little Wood
B1248
New Road
Rootas La
Melbourne St
Windmill
Pump Bridge
Mill Farm
Rose Cottage Farm
Field House Farm
Etton Road
Rose La
Raventhorpe Village
Rufforth Dr
Elvington Cr
Dray Dr
Leaconfield Park House
Mast
Linton Garth
Canada Dr
Park House Farm
Cherry Burton
Catchwater Drain
Leconfield Low Parks
Gowlands Farm
PH
PO
Black Hill
Molescroft Carr
C of E Sch
Parkhouse
Moat
Fairy Ground
Molescroft Carr Farm
Thornleys Manor Farm
Highcroft
The MS
Main St
The Park
Moat
136
Driffield Rd
Carr Road
Carr Rd
Highgate
Two Riggs
Bishop Burton Road
Ings Rd
Ings Drain
Sewage Works
Minster Way
Grange Way
Long Plantation
Sewage Works
Dog Kennel Farm
Constitution Hill Farm
Woodhall Way
Hambling Dr
Lockwood Rd
B1248
Constitution Hl
Malton Rd
Driffield Rd
Lambfold Wood
Ashfield Farm
Dog Kennel Lane
Longcroft Lower Sch
Church Rd
Molescroft Rd
Prim Sch
PH
Scrubwood La
Thurlow Ave
Beverley Junction
Oaktree Wood
Scareman Pit (dis)
Froebel House Sch
Longcroft Sch
Cemy
Molescroft
Pool
Lane Side
154
Schs
High Sch
Norwood
Park Ends
Mount Pleasant Farm
New Wk
Bishop Burton Coll
North End Farm
136
College of F E
Hurn
PH
Race Course
HU17
East Lane End
York Rd
Inf Sch
A1079
Beverley Rd
Church La
A1079
PO
A1035
Stump Cross
New Walkergate
Beverley
Lairgate
154
Newbegin Pits
Westwood
PO
PO
Bishop Burton
West End
Garth Ends Road
Garth End
Mill Lane
The Grove
Killingwoldgraves
Killingwoldgraves Lane
Burton Bushes
Cobbler Well
Grange Farm
Westwood Pasture
Westwood
The Minster Sch
Blackmill Windmill
The Minster
Keldgate
Leisure Ctr
Minster Moorgate
Gategate
Cold Harbour Road
Finchcroft Lane
Dale Gate
Newbald Road
Walkington Rd
Keldgate Rd
Marsh Dr
Cold Harbour Plantation
A1079
Shorthill Hagg
Newbald Road
154
Windmill
CH
Grammar School
B1230
Crawberry Hill
Northlands
Burton Gates
Walkington Heads
Copplefat Lane
Blackmeredale Bottom
Swadgery Mere Wood
Cemy
Poplars Way
Victoria Rd
PO
Lincoln Wy
Ripon Av
Long Lane
Crawberry Dale
Chalk Pits
136

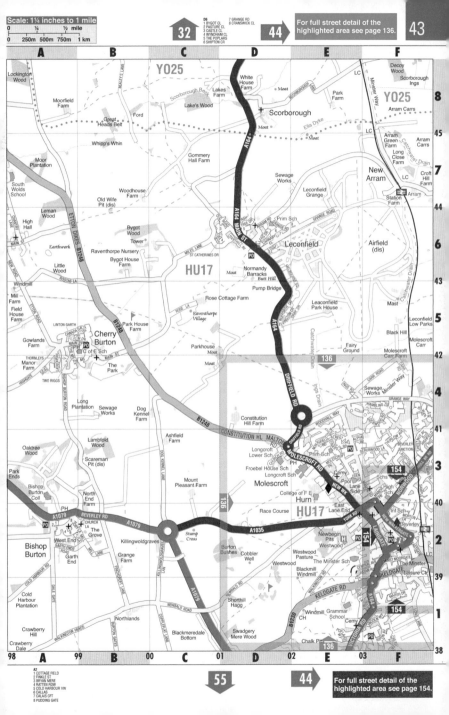

43
33

Scale: 1¼ inches to 1 mile
0 ¼ ½ mile
0 250m 500m 750m 1 km

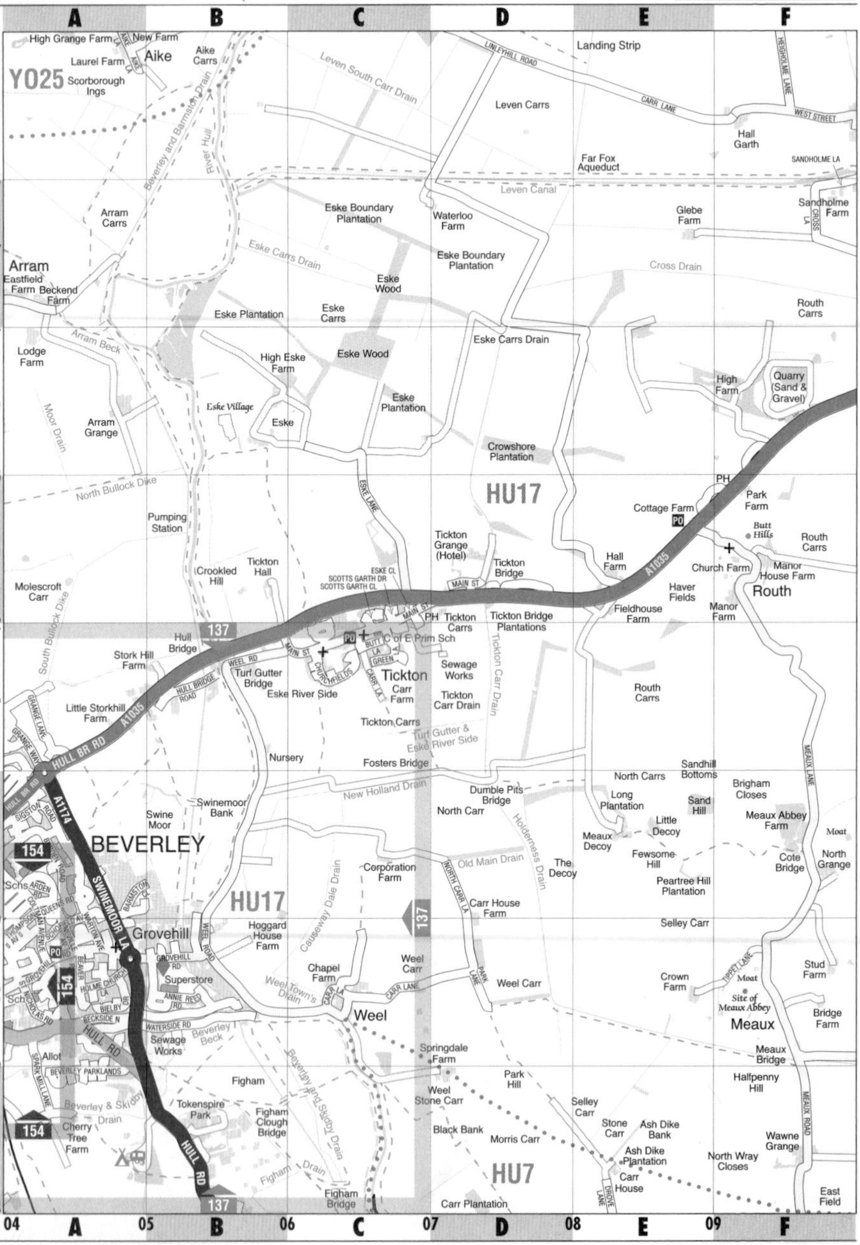

A B C D E F
8
45
7
44
6
43
5
42
4
41
3
40
2
39
1
38
04 05 06 07 08 09
High Grange Farm
New Farm
Aike
Aike Carrs
Laurel Farm
YO25
Scorborough Ings
Beverley and Barmston Drain
River Hull
Leven South Carr Drain
LINLEYHILL ROAD
Landing Strip
Leven Carrs
CARR LANE
HEIGHOLME LANE
WEST STREET
Hall Garth
Far Fox Aqueduct
SANDHOLME LA
Leven Canal
Sandholme Farm
CROSS LA
Glebe Farm
Arram Carrs
Eske Boundary Plantation
Waterloo Farm
Eske Carrs Drain
Eske Boundary Plantation
Cross Drain
Arram
Eastfield Farm
Beckend Farm
Eske Wood
Eske Plantation
Eske Carrs
Routh Carrs
Arram Beck
Lodge Farm
High Eske Farm
Eske Wood
Eske Carrs Drain
High Farm
Quarry (Sand & Gravel)
Moor Drain
Eske Village
Eske
Eske Plantation
Arram Grange
Crowshore Plantation
North Bullock Dike
ESKE LANE
HU17
PH
Park Farm
Cottage Farm
PO
Butt Hills
Routh Carrs
Pumping Station
Tickton Grange (Hotel)
Hall Farm
A1035
Church Farm
Manor House Farm
Molescroft Carr
Crookled Hill
Tickton Hall
ESKE CL
SCOTTS GARTH DR
SCOTTS GARTH CL
Tickton Bridge
MAIN ST
Haver Fields
Routh
Manor Farm
Fieldhouse Farm
South Bullock Dike
PH Tickton Carrs
Tickton Bridge Plantations
137
Hull Bridge
Stork Hill Farm
C of E Prim Sch
BUTT LA
GREEN
WEEL RD
MAIN ST
CHURCHFIELDS
CARR LA
Turf Gutter Bridge
Sewage Works
Tickton
Tickton Carr Drain
HULL BRIDGE ROAD
Eske River Side
Carr Farm
Tickton Carr Drain
Routh Carrs
Little Storkhill Farm
GRANGE LANE
Tickton Carrs
Turf Gutter & Eske River Side
GRANGE WAY
HULL BR RD
Nursery
Fosters Bridge
Sandhill Bottoms
North Carrs
Brigham Closes
MEAUX LANE
New Holland Drain
Dumble Pits Bridge
Long Plantation
Sand Hill
Meaux Abbey Farm
A1174
SIGSTON ROAD
Swine Moor
Swinemoor Bank
North Carr
Holderness Drain
Little Decoy
Moat
Meaux Decoy
154
BEVERLEY
Fewsome Hill
North Grange
Corporation Farm
Old Main Drain
The Decoy
Cote Bridge
Schs
ARDEN RD
SWINEMOOR LA
BARMSTON CL
Causeway Dale Drain
NORTH CARR LA
Peartree Hill Plantation
HU17
Carr House Farm
QUEENS RD
Grovehill
WEEL ROAD
Hoggard House Farm
Selley Carr
PO
GROVEHILL RD
Superstore
Chapel Farm
Weel Carr
PARK LANE
Crown Farm
TIPPET LANE
Stud Farm
HOLME CHURCH LA
Weel Carr
Weel Town's Drain
CARR LA
CARR LANE
Site of Meaux Abbey
Sch
ANNIE REED RD
BIELBY DR
Weel
Bridge Farm
BECKSIDE N
Meaux
WATERSIDE RD
Beverley Beck
HULL RD
Sewage Works
Springdale Farm
Meaux Bridge
Allot
BEVERLEY PARKLANDS
Beverley and Skidby Drain
Figham
Park Hill
Halfpenny Hill
SPARK MILL LANE
Weel Stone Carr
Beverley & Skidby Drain
Tokenspire Park
Figham Clough Bridge
Selley Carr
MEAUX ROAD
154
Cherry Tree Farm
Black Bank
Stone Carr
Ash Dike Bank
Morris Carr
Wawne Grange
Ash Dike Plantation
North Wray Closes
HULL RD
Figham Drain
HU7
Carr House
DROVE LANE
137
Figham Bridge
Carr Plantation
East Field

For full street detail of the highlighted area see page 154.

137

56

For full street detail of the highlighted area see page 137.

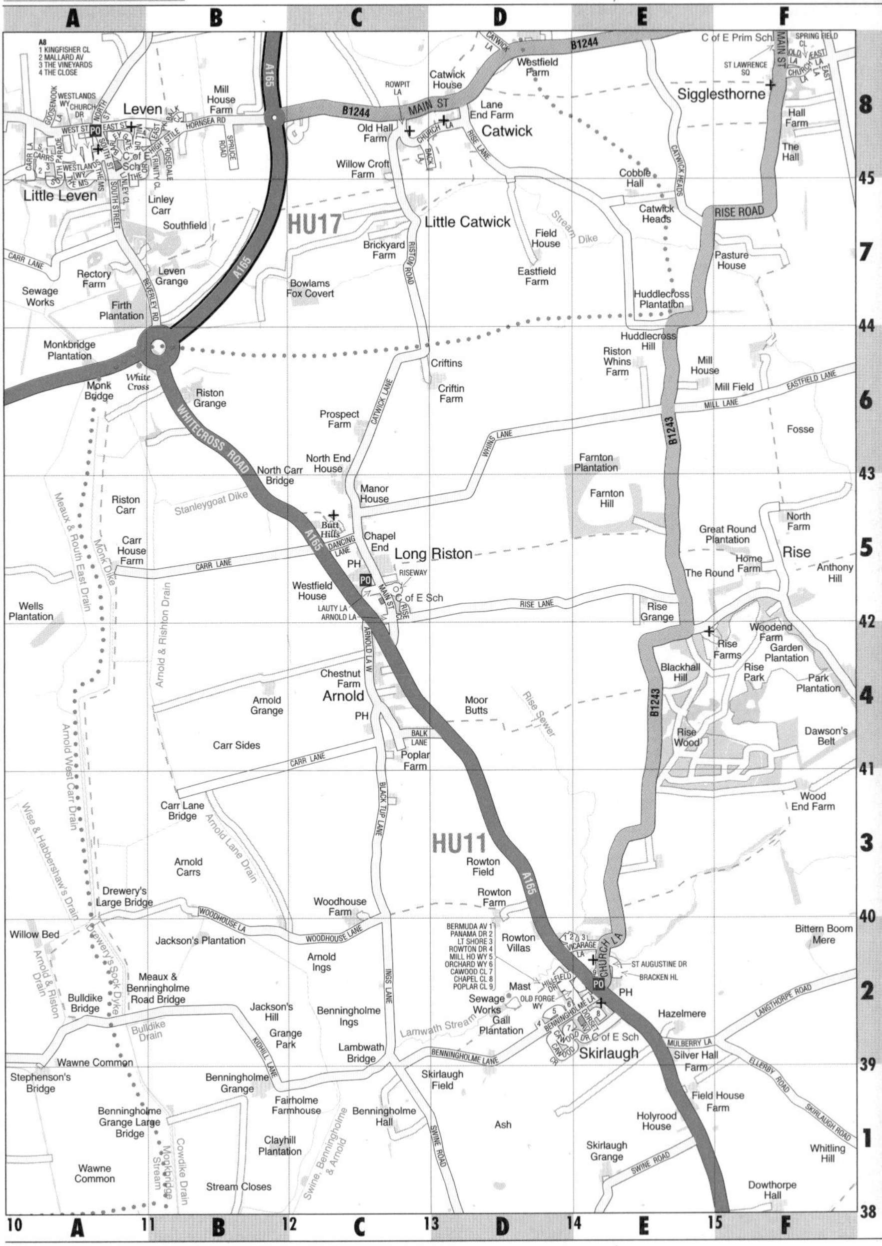
A
B
C
D
E
F
A8
1 KINGFISHER CL
2 MALLARD AV
3 THE VINEYARDS
4 THE CLOSE
Leven
Little Leven
Mill House Farm
HORNSEA RD
SPRUCE ROAD
A165
B1244
MAIN ST
Catwick House
Westfield Farm
C of E Prim Sch
Sigglesthorne
ST LAWRENCE SQ
SPRING FIELD CL
Hall Farm
The Hall
Old Hall Farm
Lane End Farm
Catwick
RISE LANE
Willow Croft Farm
Cobble Hall
CATWICK HEADS
Catwick Heads
RISE ROAD
Linley Carr
Southfield
HU17
Little Catwick
Field House
Stream Dike
Pasture House
CARR LANE
Rectory Farm
Leven Grange
Brickyard Farm
RISTON ROAD
Eastfield Farm
Sewage Works
Firth Plantation
BEVERLEY RD
Bowlams Fox Covert
Huddlecross Plantation
Huddlecross Hill
Monkbridge Plantation
White Cross
Monk Bridge
Criftins
Riston Whins Farm
Mill House
Mill Field
EASTFIELD LANE
Riston Grange
Criftin Farm
MILL LANE
WHITECROSS ROAD
Prospect Farm
CATWICK LANE
WHINS LANE
B1243
Fosse
North End House
North Carr Bridge
Farnton Plantation
Riston Carr
Manor House
Farnton Hill
Stanleygoat Dike
Butt Hills
North Farm
Carr House Farm
DANCING LANE
Chapel End
Long Riston
Great Round Plantation
Rise
CARR LANE
PH
RISEWAY
Home Farm
Anthony Hill
The Round
Meaux & Routh East Drain
Monk Dike
Arnold & Riston Drain
Westfield House
PO
MAIN ST
C of E Sch
RISE LANE
Wells Plantation
LAUTY LA
ARNOLD LA
Rise Grange
ARNOLD LA W
Woodend Farm
Rise Farms
Garden Plantation
Chestnut Farm
Blackhall Hill
Rise Park
Park Plantation
Arnold Grange
Arnold
Moor Butts
Rise Sewer
PH
BALK LANE
Rise Wood
Dawson's Belt
Carr Sides
CARR LANE
Poplar Farm
Arnold West Carr Drain
BLACK TUP LANE
Wood End Farm
Wise & Habbershaw's Drain
Carr Lane Bridge
Arnold Lane Drain
HU11
Arnold Carrs
Rowton Field
Drewery's Large Bridge
Rowton Farm
WOODHOUSE LA
Woodhouse Farm
Bittern Boom Mere
Willow Bed
Jackson's Plantation
WOODHOUSE LANE
BERMUDA AV 1
PANAMA DR 2
LT SHORE 3
ROWTON DR 4
MILL HO WY 5
ORCHARD WY 6
CAWOOD CL 7
CHAPEL CL 8
POPLAR CL 9
Rowton Villas
VICARAGE LA
CHURCH LA
ST AUGUSTINE DR
BRACKEN HL
Arnold & Riston Drain
Drewery's Sock Dyke
Meaux & Benningholme Road Bridge
Arnold Ings
Mast
HILLFIELD DR
OLD FORGE WY
PO
PH
Bulldike Bridge
Jackson's Hill
Benningholme Ings
INGS LANE
Sewage Works
Gall Plantation
BENNINGHOLME LA
DORSET
LANGTHORPE ROAD
Hazelmere
Bulldike Drain
Grange Park
Lamwath Stream
CAWOOD DR
C of E Sch
Skirlaugh
MULBERRY LA
Wawne Common
Lambwath Bridge
BENNINGHOLME LANE
Silver Hall Farm
ELLERBY ROAD
Stephenson's Bridge
KIDHILL LANE
Benningholme Grange
Skirlaugh Field
Field House Farm
Fairholme Farmhouse
Benningholme Hall
SKIRLAUGH ROAD
Benningholme Grange Large Bridge
Cowdike Drain
Swine, Benningholme & Arnold
Ash
Holyrood House
Clayhill Plantation
SWINE LANE
Skirlaugh Grange
Whitling Hill
Wawne Common
Mogbridge Stream
Stream Closes
SWINE ROAD
Dowthorpe Hall
8
45
7
44
6
43
5
42
4
41
3
40
2
39
1
38
10
11
12
13
14
15

45
35
134

Scale: 1¼ inches to 1 mile
0 ¼ ½ mile
0 250m 500m 750m 1 km

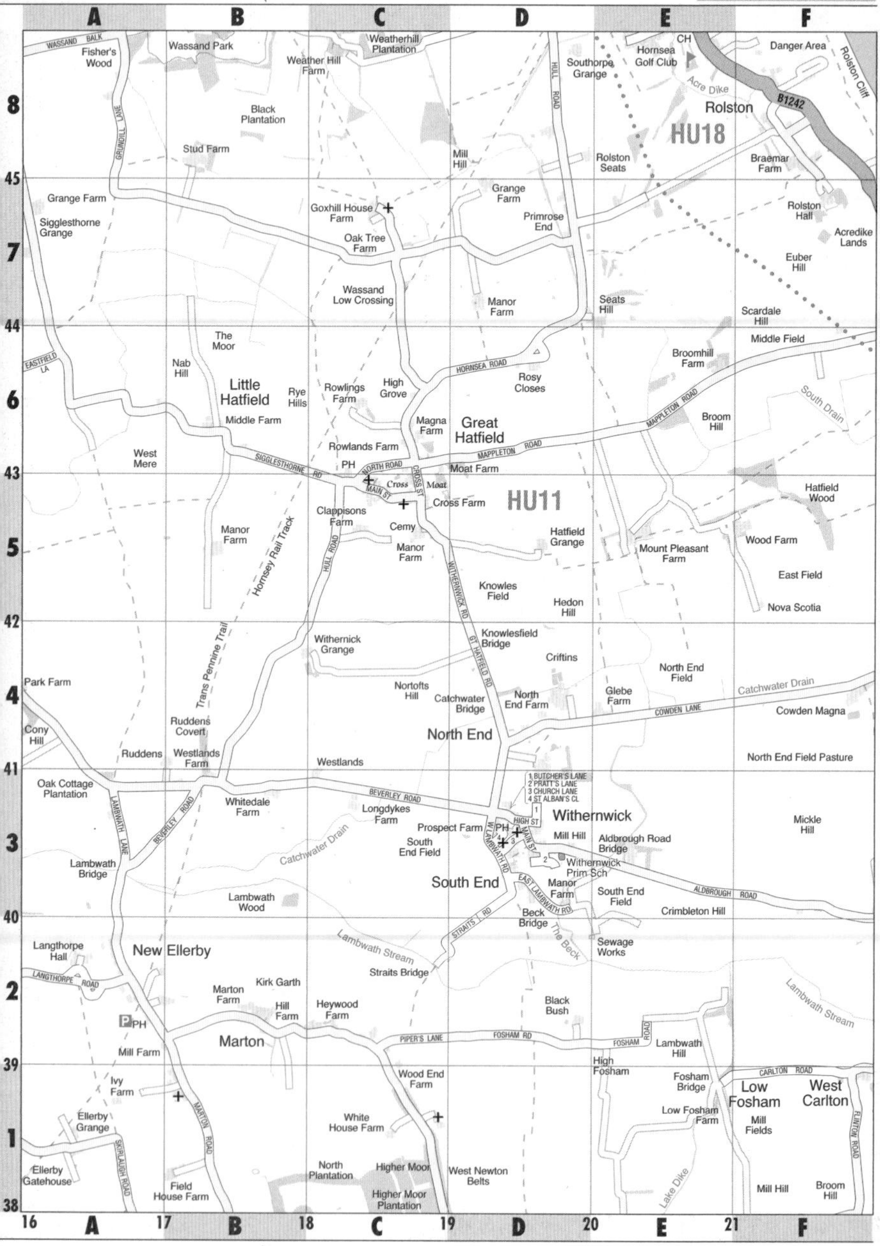

45
58

Scale: 1¼ inches to 1 mile
¼ ½ mile
250m 500m 750m 1 km

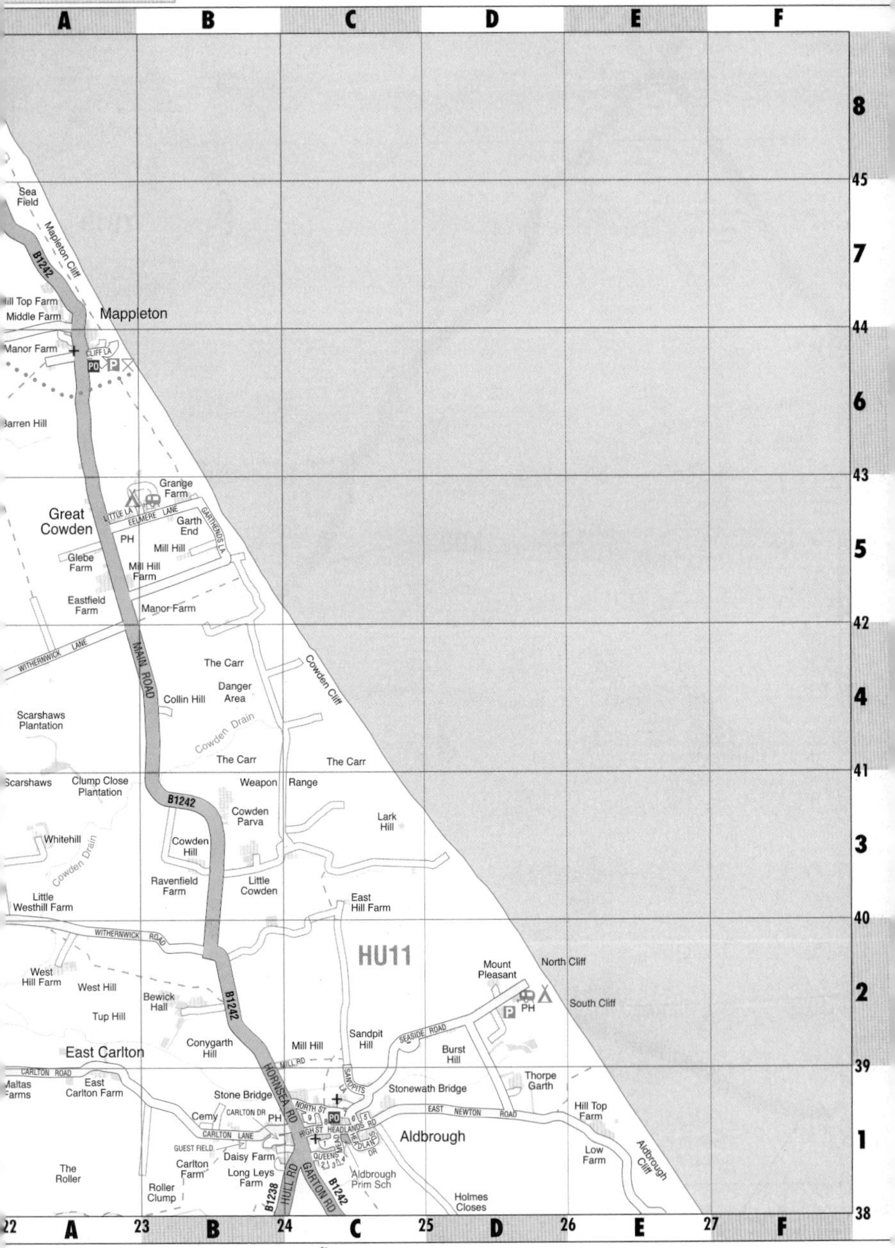
A
B
C
D
E
F
8
45
7
44
6
43
5
42
4
41
3
40
2
39
1
38
22
23
24
25
26
27
Sea Field
Mapleton Cliff
B1242
Hill Top Farm
Middle Farm
Mappleton
Manor Farm
CLIFF LA
PO
P
Barren Hill
Grange Farm
Great Cowden
LITTLE LA
EELMERE LANE
GARTHENDS LA
Garth End
PH
Mill Hill
Glebe Farm
Mill Hill Farm
Eastfield Farm
Manor Farm
WITHERNWICK LANE
MAIN ROAD
The Carr
Cowden Cliff
Danger Area
Collin Hill
Scarshaws Plantation
Cowden Drain
The Carr
The Carr
Scarshaws
Clump Close Plantation
Weapon
Range
B1242
Cowden Parva
Lark Hill
Whitehill
Cowden Drain
Cowden Hill
Ravenfield Farm
Little Cowden
East Hill Farm
Little Westhill Farm
WITHERNWICK ROAD
HU11
Mount Pleasant
North Cliff
West Hill Farm
West Hill
Bewick Hall
B1242
PH
South Cliff
P
Tup Hill
Conygarth Hill
Mill Hill
Sandpit Hill
SEASIDE ROAD
Burst Hill
East Carlton
MILL RD
CARLTON ROAD
HORNSEA RD
SANDPITS LA
Stonewath Bridge
Thorpe Garth
Maltas Farms
East Carlton Farm
Stone Bridge
NORTH ST
PO
EAST NEWTON ROAD
Hill Top Farm
Cemy
CARLTON DR
PH
HIGH ST
HEADLANDS RD
CARLTON LANE
Aldbrough
GUEST FIELD
Daisy Farm
QUEENS
HEADLANDS DR
Low Farm
Aldbrough Cliff
The Roller
Carlton Farm
Long Leys Farm
HULL RD
GARTON RD
B1242
Aldbrough Prim Sch
Roller Clump
B1238
Holmes Closes

C1
1 ELM GROVE
2 CEDAR GROVE
3 WILLOW GROVE
4 ASH GROVE
5 WENTWORTH GR
6 NOTTINGHAM RD
7 CHURCH ST
8 CROSS ST
9 CASTLE PARK

59

B8
1 SHERBURN ST
2 MARKET PL
3 CARDINALS CL
4 OLD BOYS SCHOOL LA
5 GOLD THREAD LA
6 KING ST
7 GEORGE ST
8 CHURCH HL
9 WOODALL CT

D6
1 GREENWAYS DR
2 GREEN WAYS
3 MOORFIELDS
4 HILL TOP RD
5 CHURCH WK
6 GARTH CL

36

F8
1 ASH GR
2 HAWTHORNS
3 CHURCH ST
4 HALL FARM CL
5 VIKING DR
6 THE CRESCENT
7 NORSEMAN CL
8 WEST CT
9 KELFIELD RD

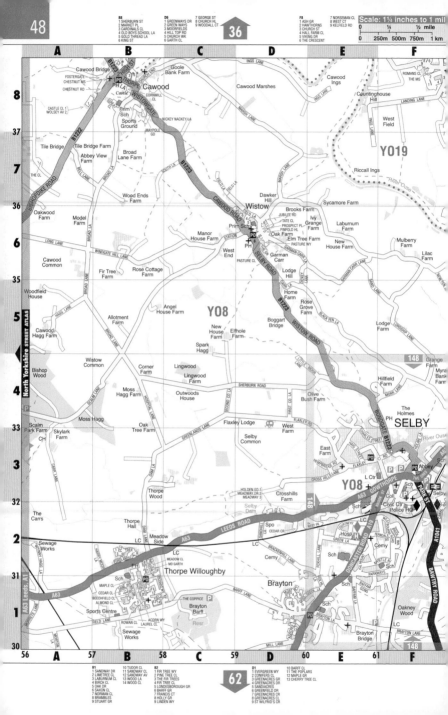

Scale: 1¼ inches to 1 mile
0 ¼ ½ mile
0 250m 500m 750m 1 km

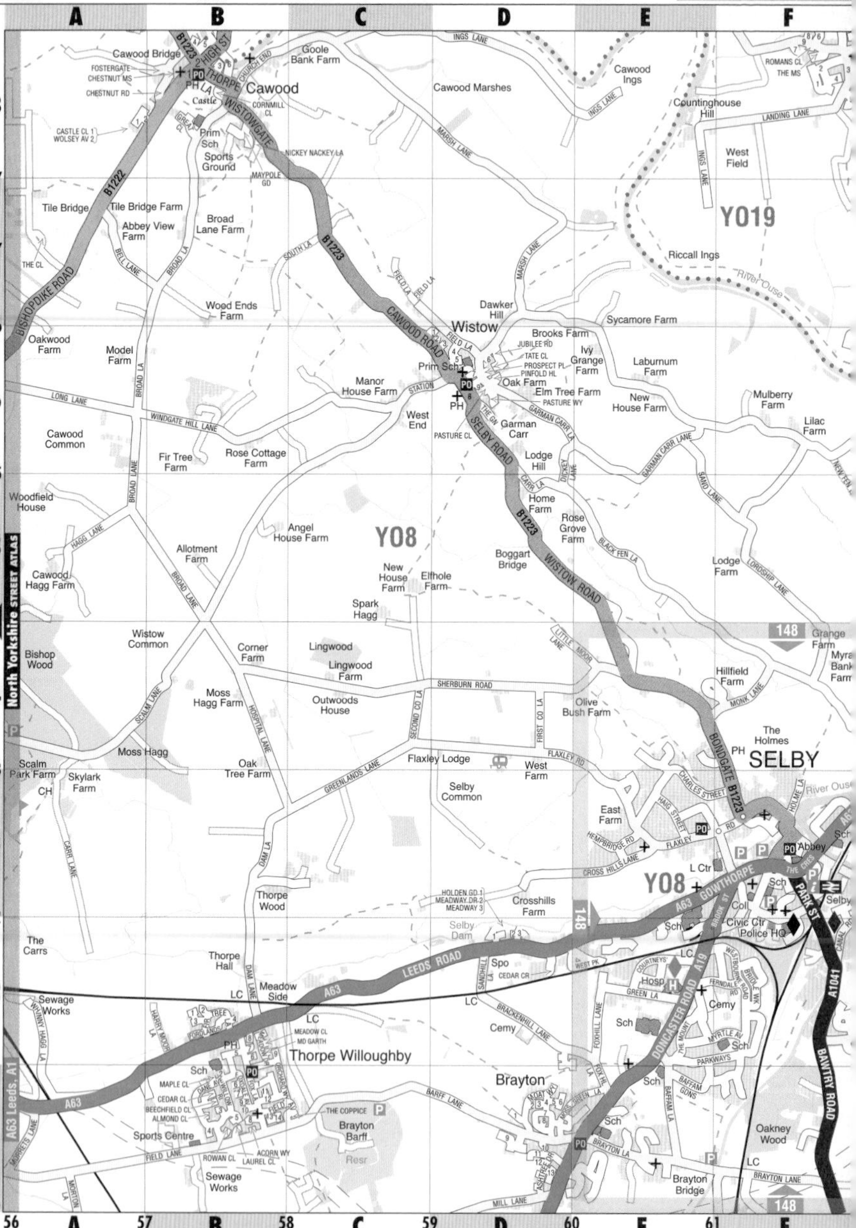

B1
1 SANDWAY DR
2 LIMETREE CL
3 LABURNUM CL
4 BIRCH CL
5 OAK DR
6 SAXON CL
7 NORMAN CL
8 BRAMBLES
9 STUART GR
10 TUDOR CL
11 SANDWAY CL
12 SANDWAY AV
13 WOOD LA
14 WOOD CL

B2
1 FIR TREE WY
2 PINE TREE CL
3 THE FIR TREES
4 FIR TREE CL
5 LONDESBOROUGH GR
6 BARFF GR
7 FRANCIS CT
8 HOLLY GR
9 LINDEN WY

62

D1
1 EVERGREEN WY
2 CONIFERS CL
3 GREENACRES GR
4 GREENACRES DR
5 SANDIACRES
6 GREENFIELD DR
7 GREENACRES CR
8 GREENACRES CL
9 ST WILFRID'S CR
10 BARFF CL
11 THE POPLARS
12 MAPLE GR
13 CHERRY TREE CL

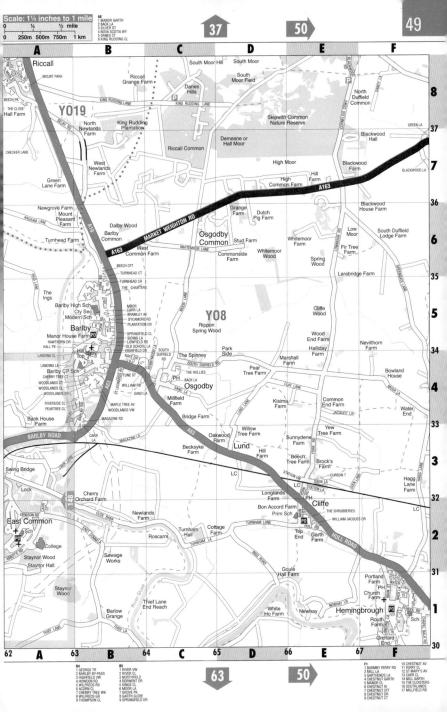

Scale: 1¼ inches to 1 mile
0 ¼ ½ mile
0 250m 500m 750m 1 km

A8
1 MANOR GARTH
2 BACK LA
3 SILVER ST
4 NOVA SCOTIA WY
5 DANES CT
6 KING RUDDING CL

37
50

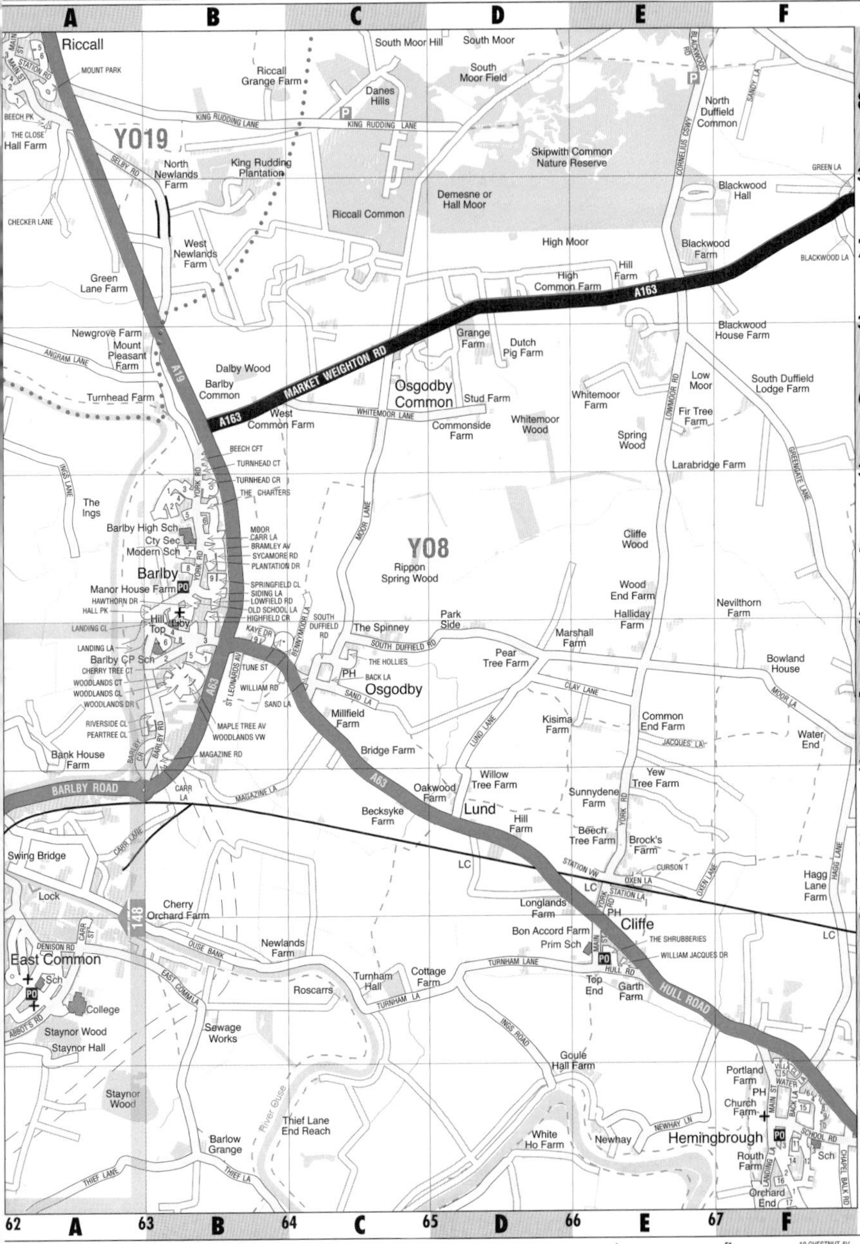

B4
1 GEORGE TR
2 BARLBY BY-PASS
3 HIGHFIELD VW
4 HOWDEN RD
5 WILFREDS RD
6 ACORN CL
7 CHERRY TREE WK
8 WILFREDS GR
9 THOMPSON CL

B5
1 RIVER VW
2 RIVER CL
3 NORTHFIELD
4 DERWENT DR
5 KINGS CL
6 MOOR LA
7 GROVE PK
8 GARTH GLEBE
9 SPRINGFIELD DR

63
50

F1
1 BARMBY FERRY RD
2 MILL LA
3 GARTHENDS LA
4 CHESTNUT GARTH
5 MANOR CL
6 CHESTNUT RI
7 CHESTNUT CFT
8 CHESTNUT DR
9 CHESTNUT CT
10 CHESTNUT AV
11 FERRY CL
12 ST MARY'S AV
13 CARR CL
14 MILL GARTH
15 THE CLOISTERS
16 SOUTHLANDS
17 MILLFIELD RD

49
38

Scale: 1¼ inches to 1 mile
0 ¼ ½ mile
0 250m 500m 750m 1 km

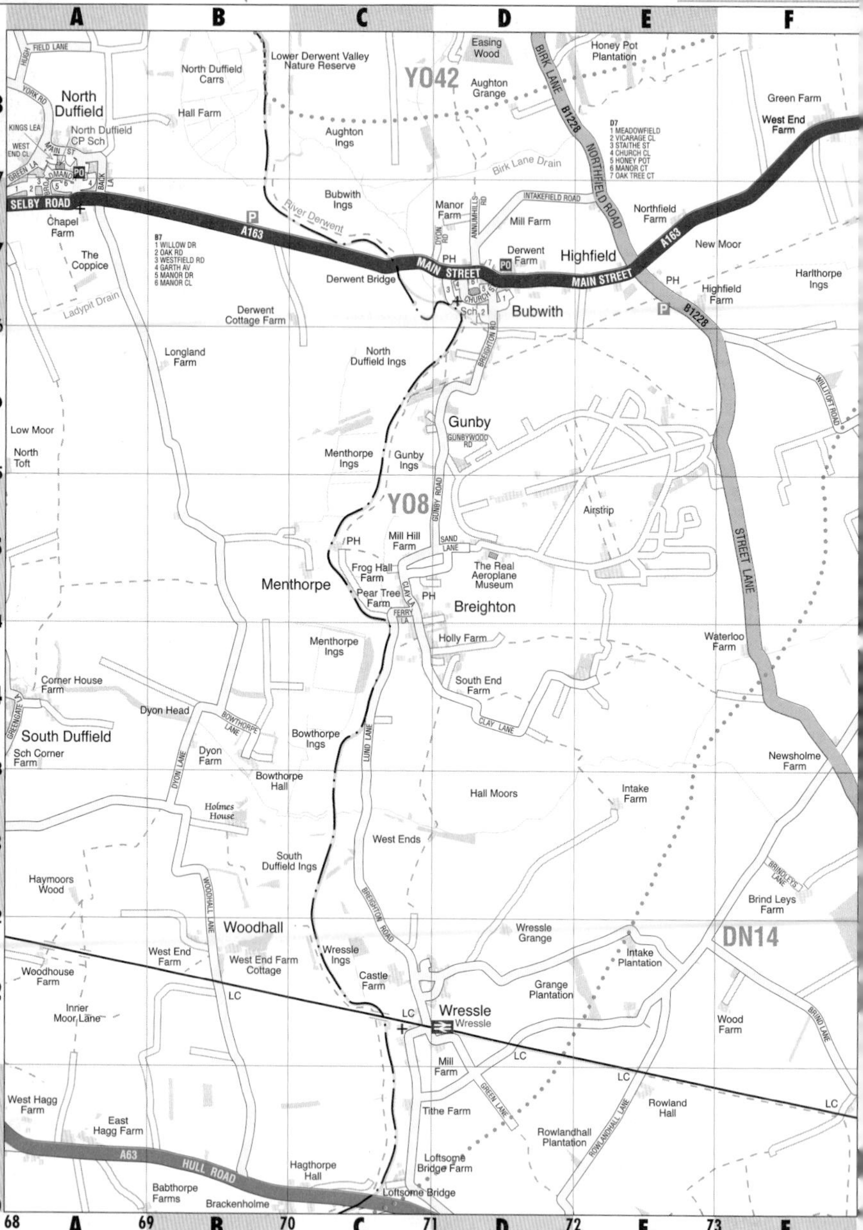

49
64

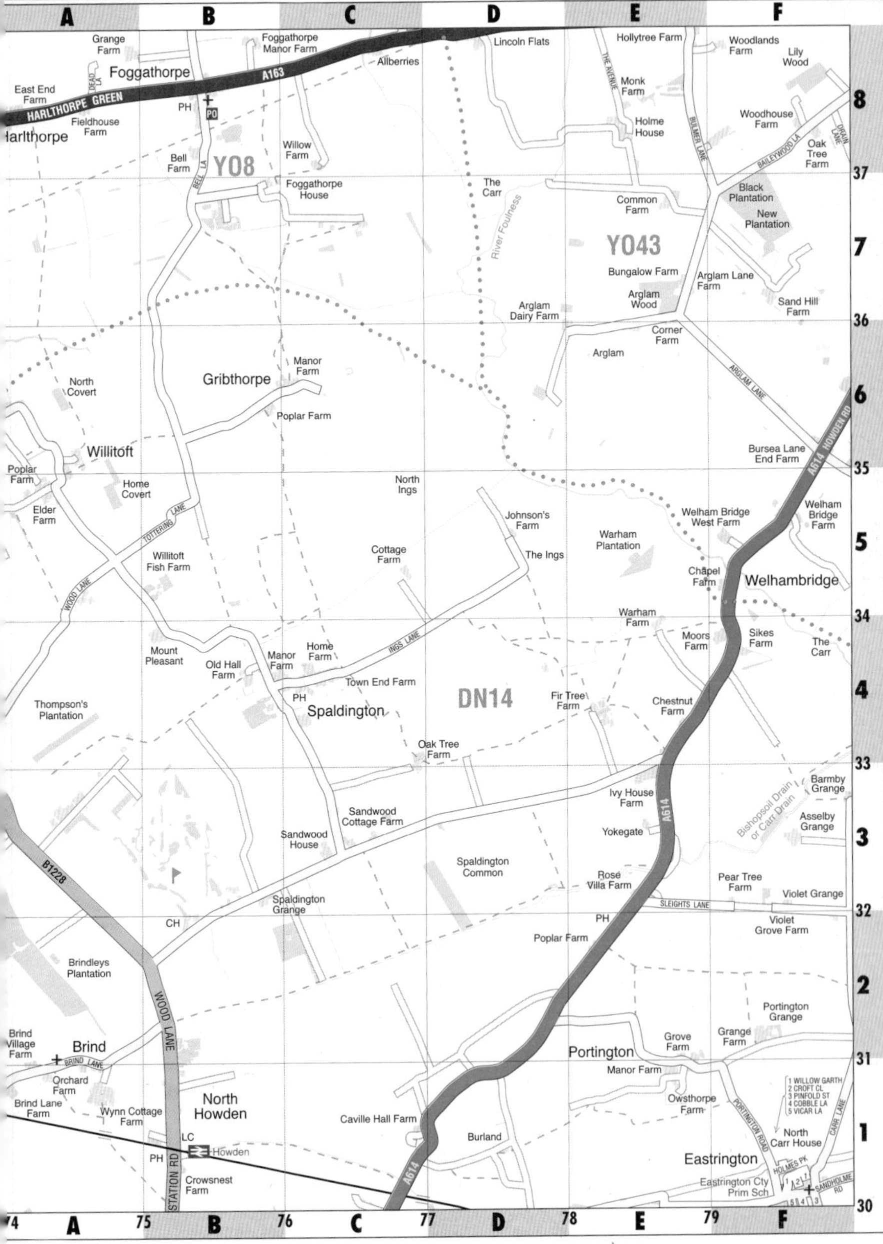
A
B
C
D
E
F
Grange Farm
Foggathorpe Manor Farm
Foggathorpe
A163
Allberries
Lincoln Flats
Hollytree Farm
Woodlands Farm
Lily Wood
East End Farm
HARLTHORPE GREEN
DEAD LA
PH
PO
Fieldhouse Farm
Harlthorpe
Willow Farm
Bell Farm
BELL LA
YO8
Foggathorpe House
THE AVENUE
Monk Farm
Holme House
BULMER LANE
Woodhouse Farm
DRAIN LANE
Oak Tree Farm
BAILEYWOOD LA
The Carr
River Foulness
Common Farm
Black Plantation
New Plantation
YO43
Bungalow Farm
Arglam Lane Farm
Arglam Wood
Sand Hill Farm
Arglam Dairy Farm
Corner Farm
Arglam
ARGLAM LANE
Manor Farm
North Covert
Gribthorpe
Poplar Farm
A614 HOWDEN RD
Willitoft
Bursea Lane End Farm
Poplar Farm
Home Covert
North Ings
Elder Farm
TOTTERING LANE
Johnson's Farm
Warham Plantation
Welham Bridge West Farm
Welham Bridge Farm
Willitoft Fish Farm
Cottage Farm
The Ings
Chapel Farm
Welhambridge
WOOD LANE
Warham Farm
INGS LANE
Moors Farm
Sikes Farm
The Carr
Mount Pleasant
Old Hall Farm
Manor Farm
Home Farm
Town End Farm
PH
Spaldington
DN14
Fir Tree Farm
Chestnut Farm
Thompson's Plantation
Oak Tree Farm
Barmby Grange
Ivy House Farm
A614
Bishopsoil Drain or Carr Drain
Asselby Grange
Sandwood Cottage Farm
Sandwood House
Yokegate
B1228
Spaldington Common
Rose Villa Farm
Pear Tree Farm
Violet Grange
Spaldington Grange
SLEIGHTS LANE
CH
PH
Poplar Farm
Violet Grove Farm
Brindleys Plantation
Portington Grange
WOOD LANE
Grove Farm
Grange Farm
Brind Village Farm
Brind
BRIND LANE
Portington
Manor Farm
Orchard Farm
1 WILLOW GARTH
2 CROFT CL
3 PINFOLD ST
4 COBBLE LA
5 VICAR LA
Brind Lane Farm
Wynn Cottage Farm
North Howden
Owsthorpe Farm
PORTINGTON ROAD
CARR LANE
Caville Hall Farm
North Carr House
LC
Burland
Howden
Eastrington
HOLMES PK
PH
STATION RD
Crowsnest Farm
A614
Eastrington Cty Prim Sch
SANDHOLME RD
8
37
7
36
6
35
5
34
4
33
3
32
2
31
1
30
74
75
76
77
78
79

51
40

Scale: 1¼ inches to 1 mile
0 ¼ ½ mile
0 250m 500m 750m 1 km

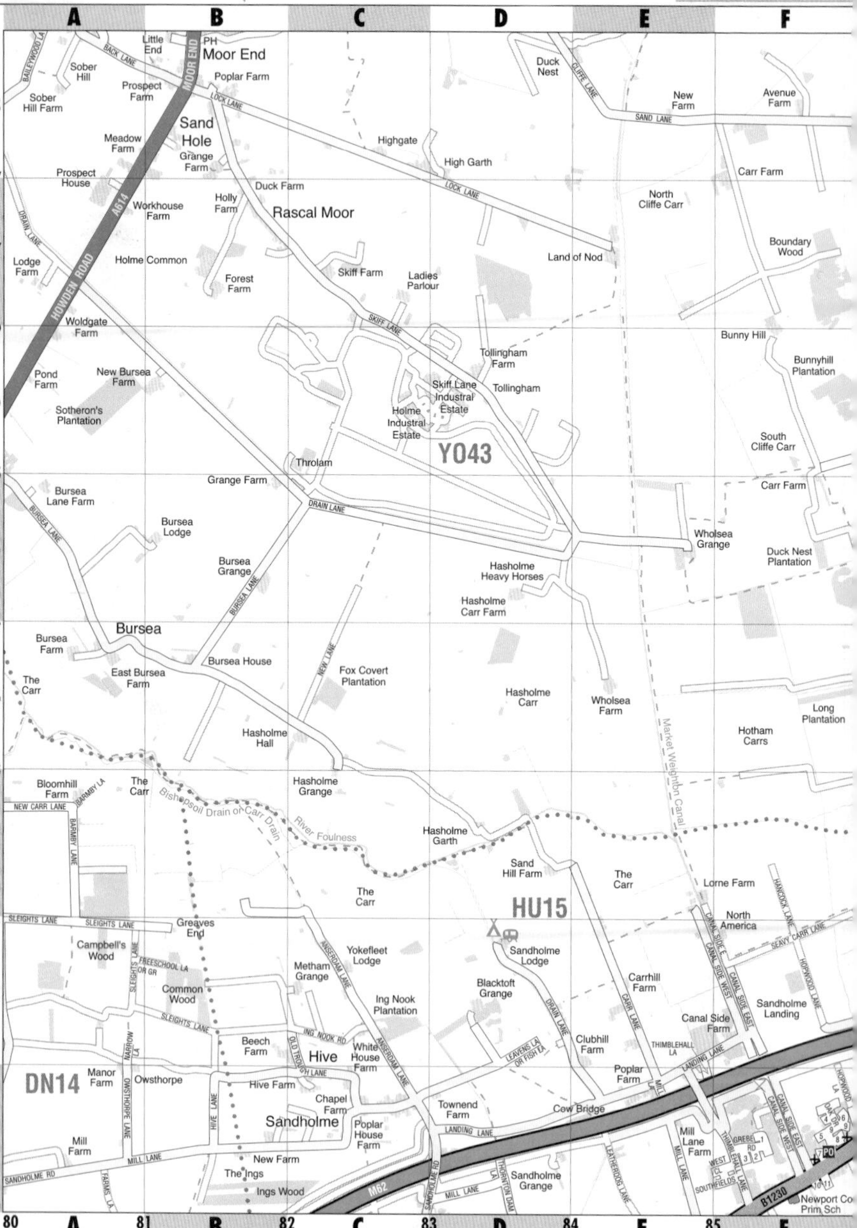

A B C D E F

51
66

F1
1 TEAL RD
2 GADWALL CL
3 POCHARD CL
4 BRIAR CL
5 HAWTHORN CL
6 THE SPINNEY
7 OCEAN DR
8 BLACKTHORN CL
9 MEADOW LA
10 TURKS HEAD GD
11 VILLAGE FARM CL

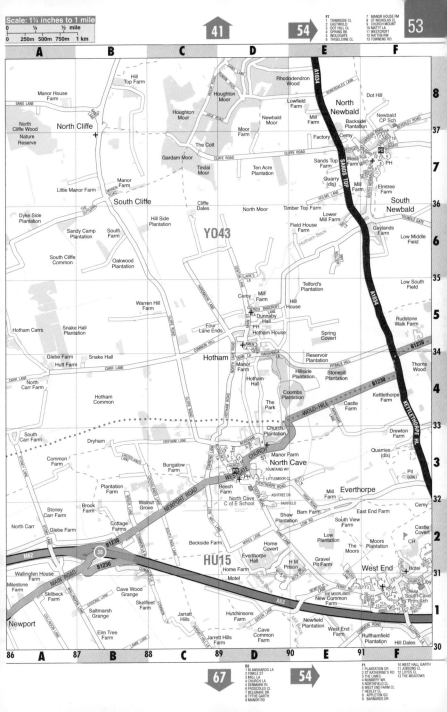

Scale: 1¼ inches to 1 mile
0 ¼ ½ mile
0 250m 500m 750m 1 km

41
54

F7
1 TOWNSIDE CL
2 EASTWOLD
3 DOT HILL CL
4 SPRING BK
5 WOLDGATE
6 THISELDINE CL
7 MANOR HOUSE FM
8 ST NICHOLAS CL
9 CHURCH MOUNT
10 MATTY LA
11 WESTCROFT
12 RATTEN RW
13 TOWNEND RD

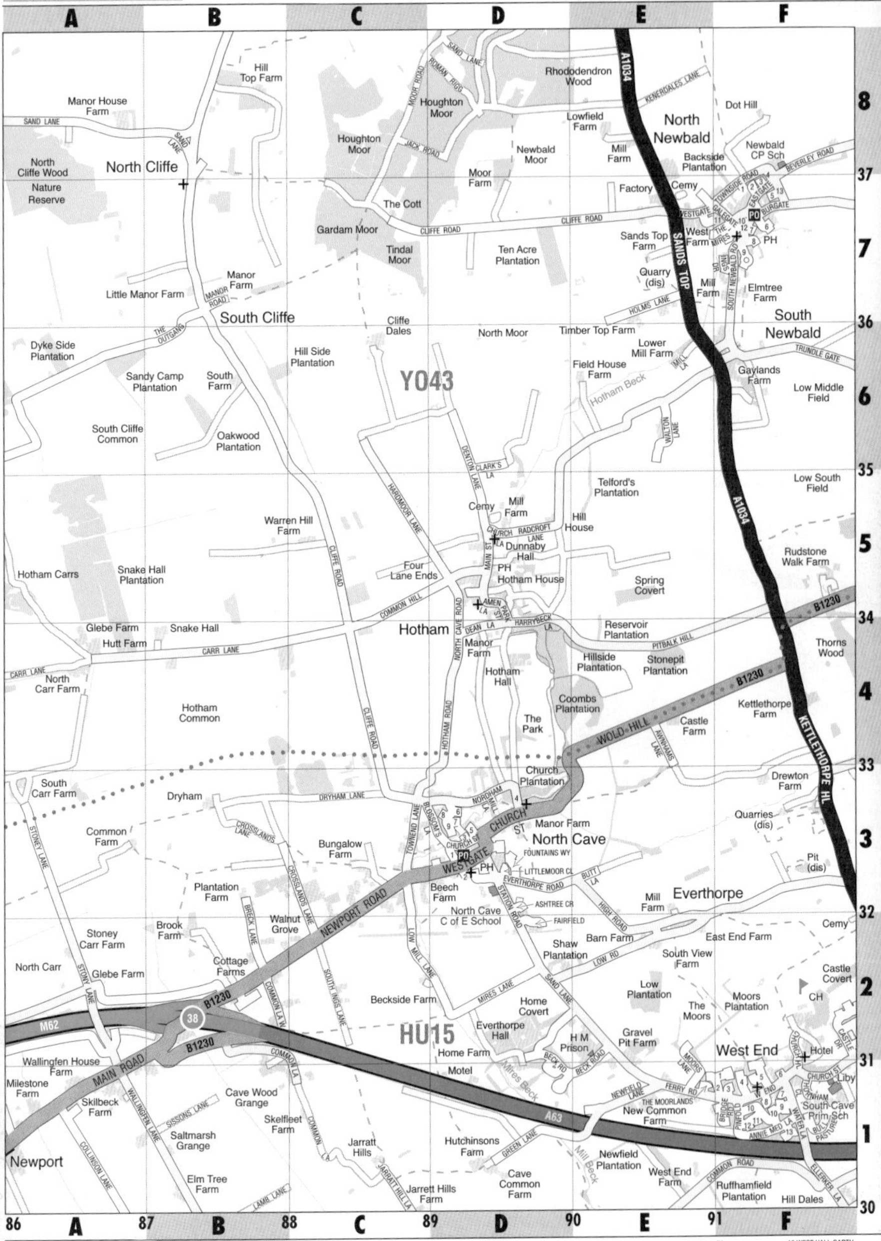

67
54

D3
1 BLANSHARDS LA
2 FINKLE ST
3 MILL LA
4 CHURCH LA
5 DENMARK RI
6 FROSCOLES CL
7 BELGRAVE DR
8 TYTHE GARTH
9 MANOR RD

F1
1 PLANTATION DR
2 ST KATHERINE'S RD
3 THE LIMES
4 NUNNERY WK
5 NORTHFIELD CL
6 WEST END FARM CL
7 HEDLEY CL
8 APPLETON GD
9 BARNARDS DR
10 WEST HALL GARTH
11 JOBSONS CL
12 LOYDS CL
13 THE MEADOWS

53
42

Scale: 1¼ inches to 1 mile
0 ¼ ½ mile
0 250m 500m 750m 1 km

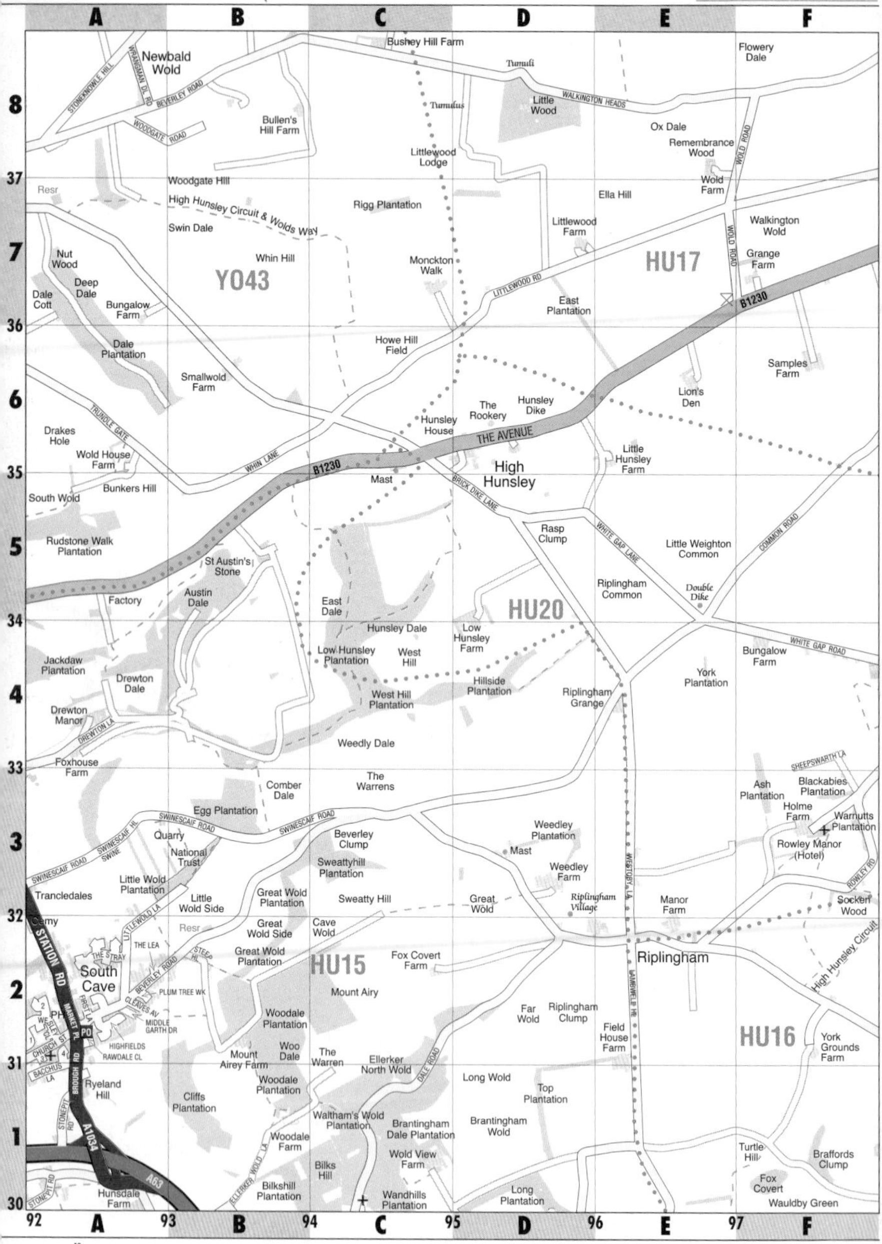

A2
1 CASTLE RISE
2 THE PARKLANDS
3 WOLD VW
4 SOUTHCOTE CL

53
68

For full street detail of the highlighted area see page 138.

F6
1 ARNCLIFFE CL
2 KETTLEWELL CL
3 WYTHERSTONE CL
4 KILKOY DR
5 SEDBURY CL
6 TRENT PK
7 KINGSBURY WY
8 RAINSWOOD CL
9 FRENSHAM CL
10 RAUCEBY CL
11 GRANTHAM AVE
12 EMBERTON PK
13 THURLSTONE CL

55

14 GREYGARTH CL
15 KINDERSCOUT CL
16 SAPPERTON CL
17 HYKEHAM CL
18 SEDGEBROOK GR
19 QUARRINGTON GR
20 WOOLSTHORPE GR

137

21 SLEIGHTHOLME CL
22 BRECON DR
23 SALCEY CL
24 BRANDON WY
25 LANGLEY PK
26 EMBERTON PK
27 BLACKWATER WY
28 FINDON CL
29 SALTWELL PK

44

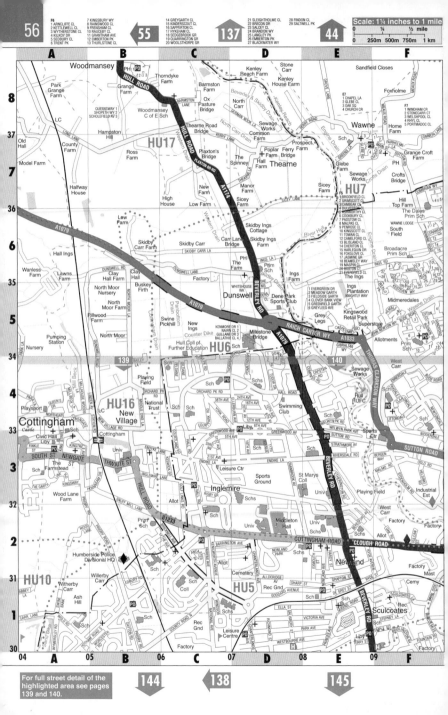

Scale: 1¼ inches to 1 mile
0 ¼ ½ mile
0 250m 500m 750m 1 km

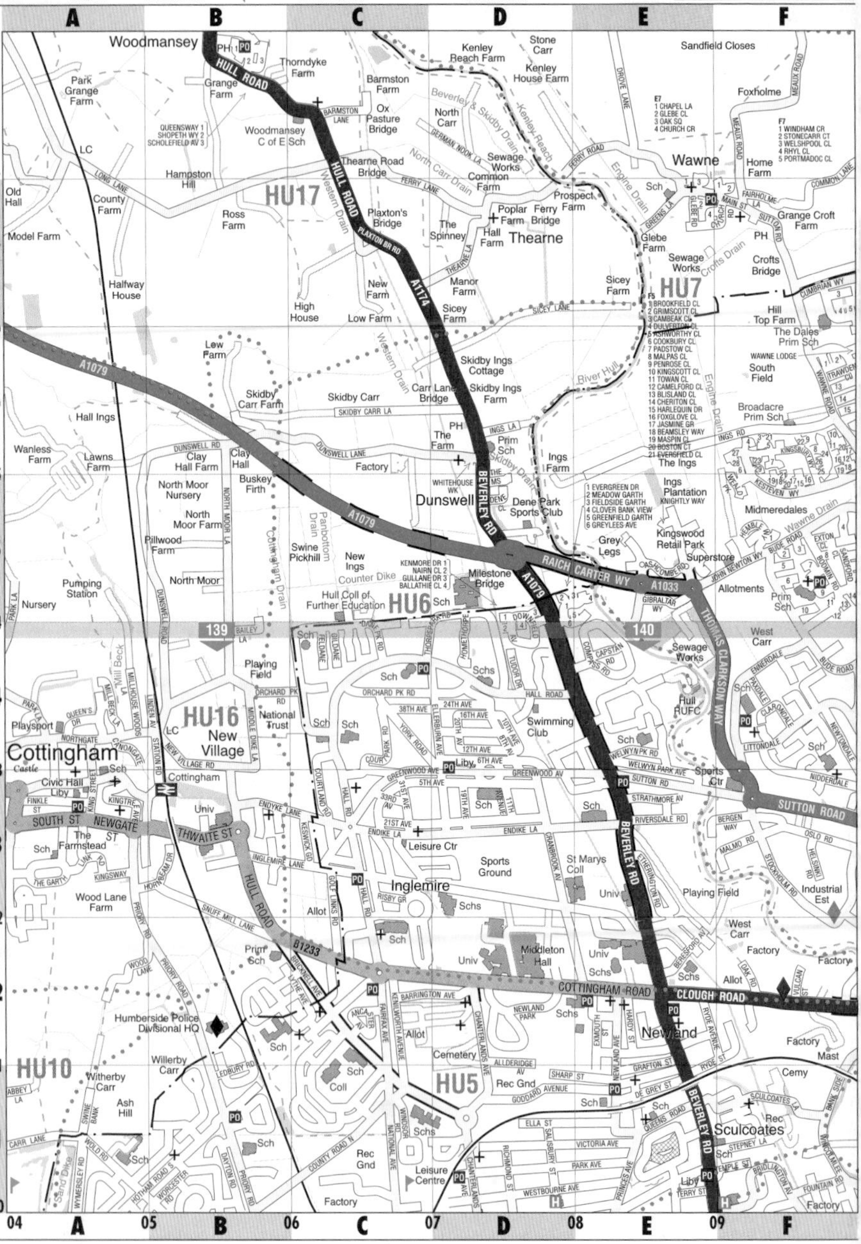

04 A 05 B 06 C 07 D 08 E 09 F

For full street detail of the highlighted area see pages 139 and 140.

Scale: 1¼ inches to 1 mile
0 ¼ ½ mile
0 250m 500m 750m 1 km

A6
1 HARLECH CL
2 LEITHOLM CL
3 BORTHWICK CL
4 SNOWHILL CL
5 RISHWORTH CL
6 RANNOCH CL
7 APPIN CL
8 MOORFOOT CL
9 RANGELEY CL
10 HELVELLYN CL
11 GRASSINGTON CL
12 WHERNSIDE CL
13 WHITEHOPE CL
14 BLACKHOPE CL
15 PYKESTONE CL
16 DALKEITH CL
17 LADYSIDE CL
18 PENDLE CL
19 SADDLEWORTH CL

45
58

A5
1 ABINGDON GARTH
2 BINBROOK GARTH
3 SELWORTHY CL
4 RINGSTEAD GARTH
5 COSFORD GARTH
6 HAYDOCK GARTH
7 SKILGATE CL
8 ALLERFORD DR
9 LYNMOUTH CL
10 BOSSINGTON CL
11 PITSFOLD CL
12 CLEEVE DR
13 MYLOR CL
14 FINNINGLEY GARTH
15 GATWICK GARTH
16 HUCKNALL GARTH
17 INNSWORTH GARTH
18 YATESBURY GARTH
19 SWINDERBY GARTH
20 ENSTONE GARTH

B5
1 JASON GARTH
2 KINLOSS GARTH
3 LEEMING GARTH
4 MANSTON GARTH
5 DRUMMOND CT
6 LEADHILLS WY
7 DOWNHILL DR
8 MAIDEN CT
9 NEATSHEAD GARTH

146
58
147

For full street detail of the highlighted area see pages 141 and 142.

57
46

Scale: 1¼ inches to 1 mile
0 ¼ ½ mile
0 250m 500m 750m 1 km

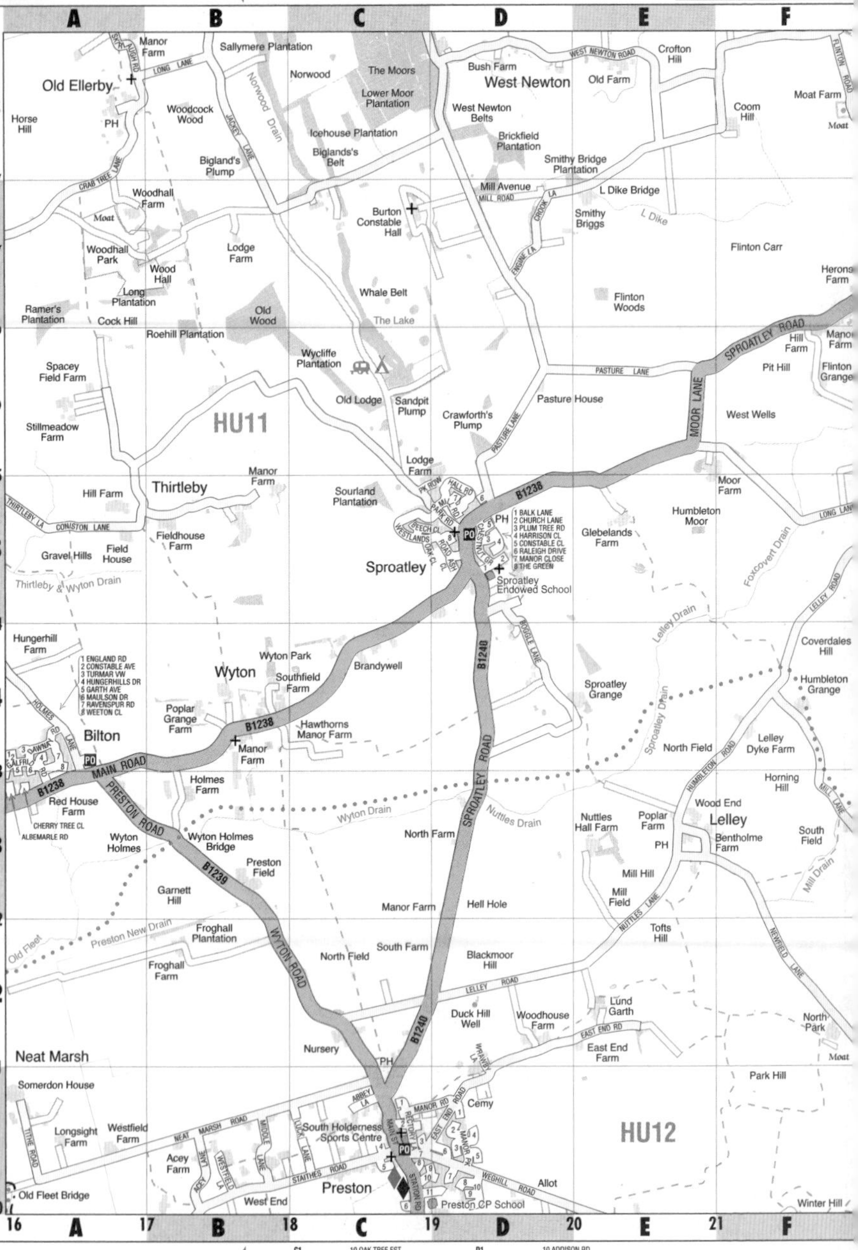

142
72

C1
1 NESS LA
2 KIRK RD
3 THORNTON GR
4 PINFOLD CT
5 VILLAGE FARM RD
6 HELMS AV
7 SCHOOL RD
8 SYCAMORE CL
9 BROCKLE BANK CT
10 OAK TREE EST
11 ELDON DR

D1
1 HIGHFIELD RI
2 GARBUTT CL
3 GRASSAM CL
4 ELLIS CL
5 HUNTER CL
6 PEACE WK
7 RANDS EST
8 WATKINSON CL
9 BARTLETT CL
10 ADDISON RD

Scale: 1¼ inches to 1 mile
0 ¼ ½ mile
0 250m 500m 750m 1 km

47
60

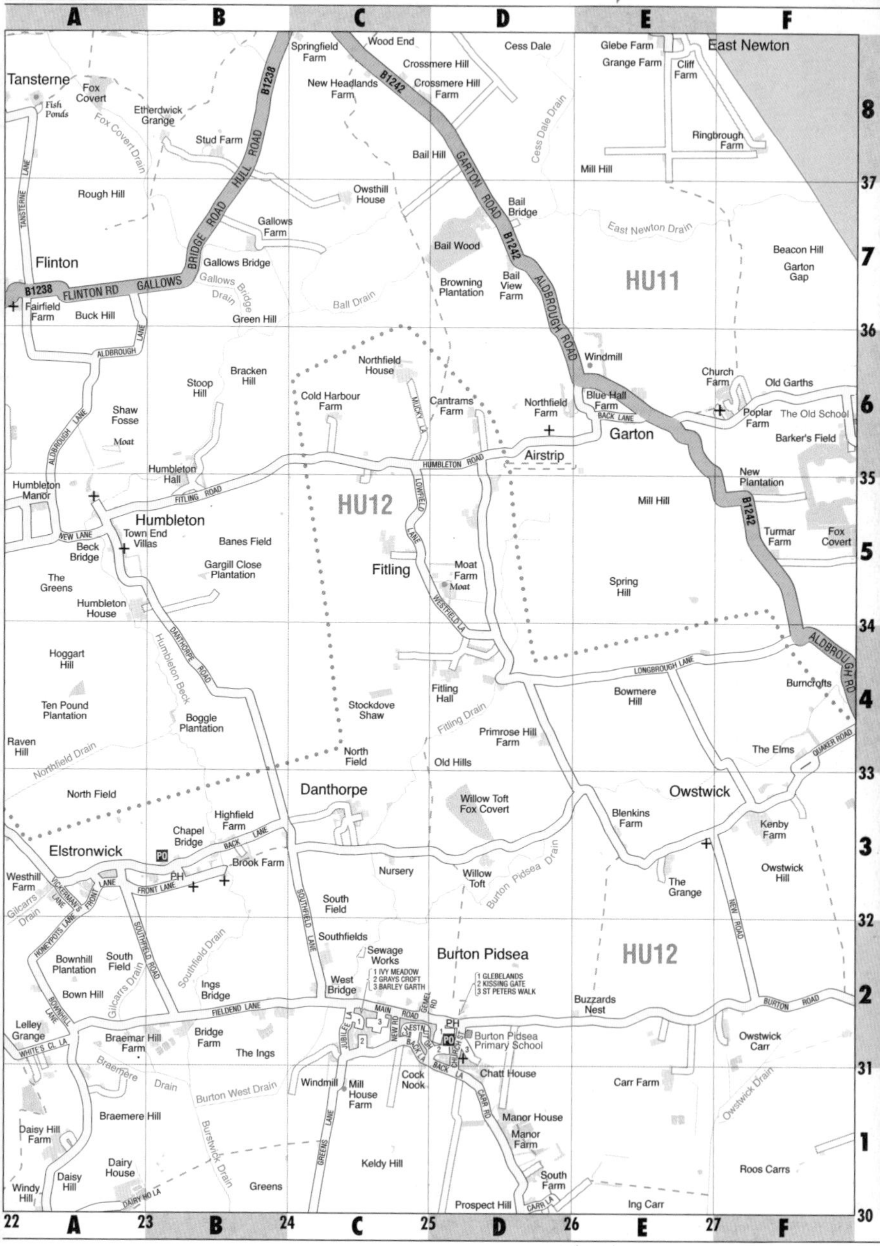

73
60

59

Scale: 1¼ inches to 1 mile
0 ¼ ½ mile
0 250m 500m 750m 1 km

A
B
C
D
E
F
8
37
7
36
6
35
5
34
4
33
3
32
2
31
1
30
28
29
30
31
32
33
Great Parks
The Mount
Moat Farm
Moat
Sewage Works
Grimston Garth
Grimston Park
Bracken Hill
Norwood Plantation
HU11
Admiral Storr's Tower
Glebe Farm
Tunstall Pastures
TOWER ROAD
Hilston
PASTURES LANE
Mayfield Farm
Mount Farm
Pit (dis)
HOGSEA LANE
QUAKER RD
Gills Mere
Monkwith
Roos Furze
East Furze
The Furze
North End Farm
Mill Hill
ALDBROUGH ROAD
West Furze
PASTURES LANE
RECTORY LA
Glebe Farm
HU12
Church Farm
FURZE ROAD
Westhill Farm
Manor Farm
Furze Farm
MAIN ST
SEASIDE LANE
Town Farm
Tunstall
Kiln House
B1242
Elmtree Farm
Allot
Carr Farm
KILNHOUSE LA
SEASIDE LANE
Kiln Well
PH
BURTON ROAD
Poplar Farm
ROSTUN ROAD
Cliff Farm
NORTH END RD
North End Villas
North End
East Field
Tunstall Hall
Sewage Works
PINFOLD LA
SOUTHFIELD LANE
Hill Top Farm
Cote Farm
Roos C of E School
1 HINCH GARTH
2 BEECHWOOD VIEWS
3 PILMAR LANE
Round Close Plantation
MAIN ST
Tunstall Drain
PILMAR LANE
B1242
INGLEPOOL CORNER
RECTORY RD
Roos
PD
B1242
Cherry Hill
HU19
Redhouse Farm
PH
EASTFIELD EST
Tedder Hill
WITHERNSEA RD
HODGSON LA
SOUTH PK
Broom Hill
Thirtle Bridge
Renish
CHESTNUT GARTH
ELM GARTH
SOUTH END RD
LAMB LA
THIRTLE BR LA
Burnham Carrs
Butcher Bridge

Scale: 1¼ inches to 1 mile
0 ¼ ½ mile
0 250m 500m 750m 1 km

A8
1 DEER PK CT
2 PRIORY PARK GR
3 PRIORY PARK CL
4 CHURCH LA
5 OLD VICARAGE LA
6 ORCHARD CL
7 THE MEADOWS
8 HILLCREST
9 HILLSIDE CL

A7
1 PINE TREE LA
2 ROSE LEA CL
3 HILLAM HALL VW
4 HILLAM HALL LA
5 HILLIAM HALL CL
6 BEDFORDS FOLD

62

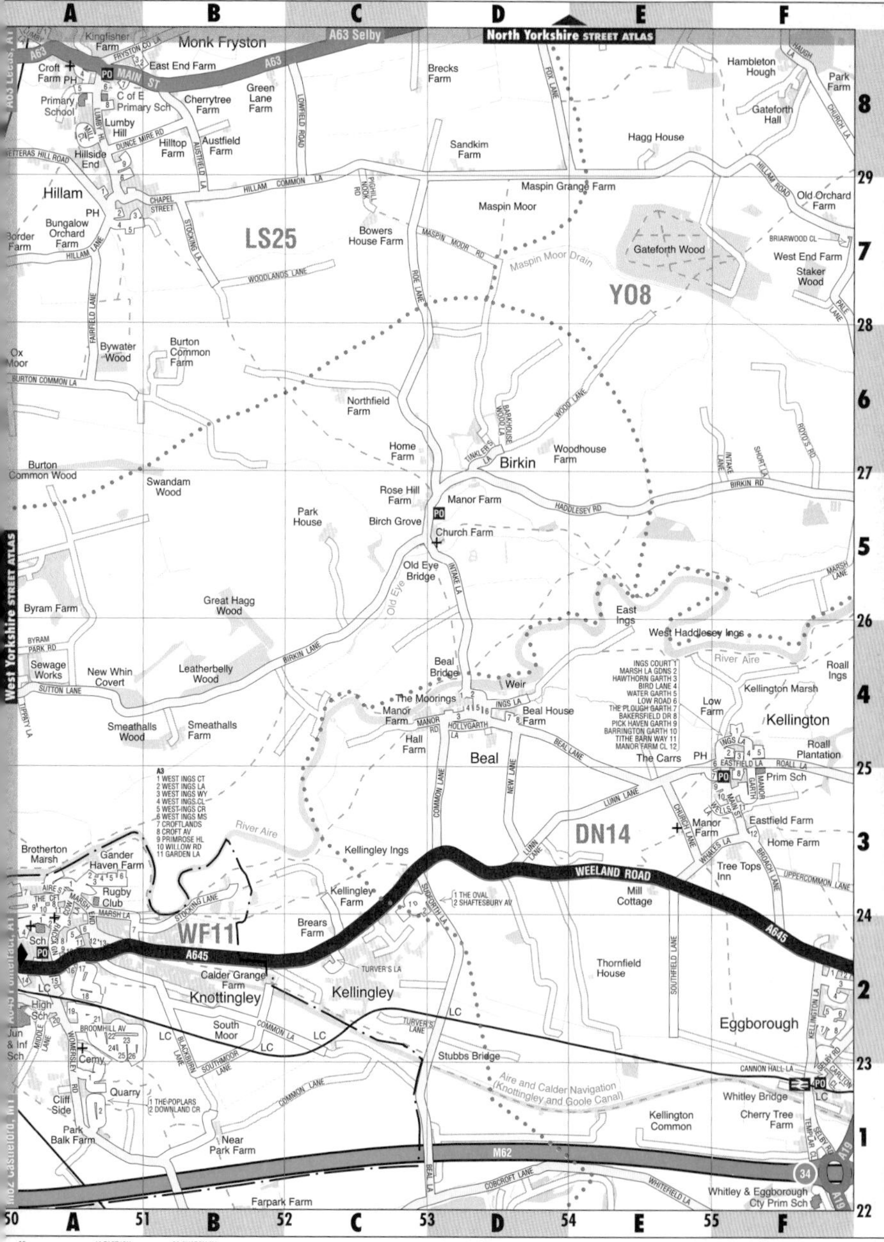

A2
1 PRIMROSE VALE
2 TITHE BARN RD
3 SUNNY BANK
4 ST BOLTOPHS CL
5 FOUNDRY LA
6 FERNLEY GREEN CL
7 TRUNDLES LA
8 GRENLEY ST
9 LAMB INN RD
10 EAST VW
11 RACCA AV
12 HARKER ST
13 LOW GN
14 MIDDLE LA
15 GILLANN ST
16 WEELAND CT
17 SPRINGFIELDS AV
18 SPRINGFIELDS
19 BROOMHILL GR
20 QUARRY AV
21 BROOMHILL WK
22 BROOMHILL PL
23 BROOMHILL CL
24 BROOMHILL SQ
25 BROOMHILL CR
26 BROOMHILL DR

76

D4
1 GARTH MILL
2 MARSH LA
3 MAIN ST
4 RIVERDALE
5 CRAVEN GARTH
6 BROAD LA
7 VILLAGE FARM CT
8 GABLES CL

62

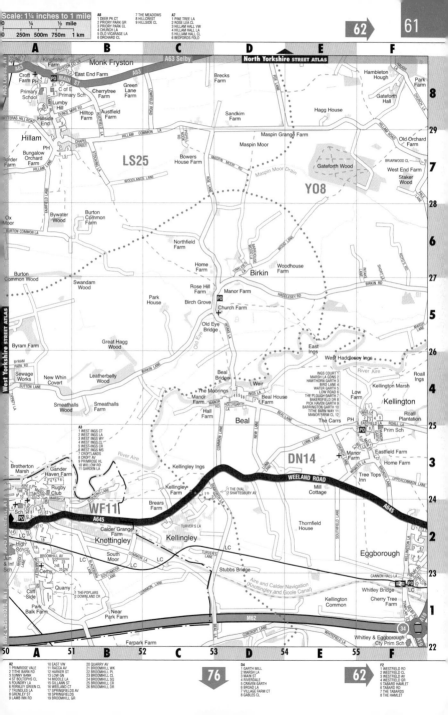

F2
1 WESTFIELD RD
2 WESTFIELD CL
3 WESTFIELD AV
4 WESTFIELD GR
5 TABARD HAMLET
6 TABARD RD
7 THE TABARDS
8 THE HAMLET

Scale: 1¼ inches to 1 mile
0 ¼ ½ mile
0 250m 500m 750m 1 km

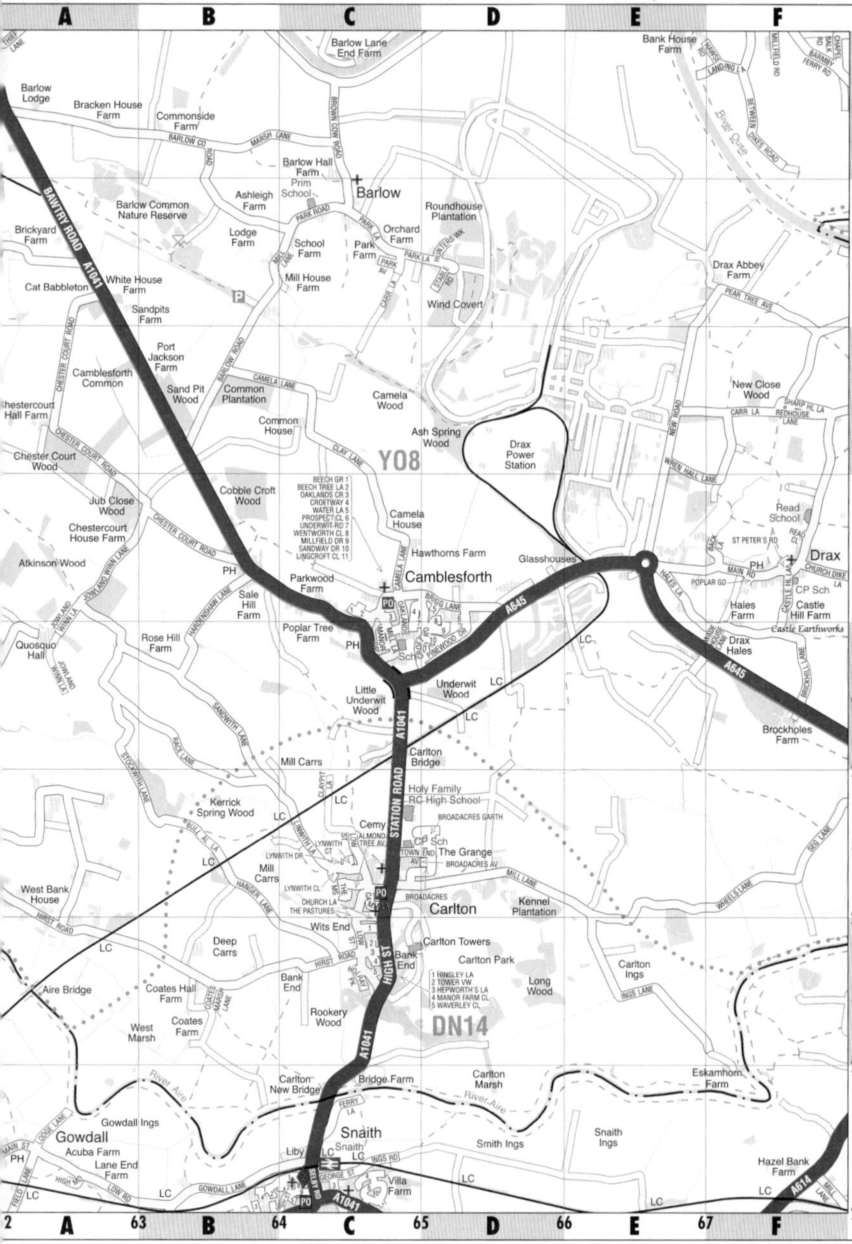

B1
1 PRIORY WAY
2 DAWNAY GARTH
3 MARINA AV
4 YARBURGH CL

C1
1 PRIORY LN
2 CHURCH LN
3 BUTTLE LA
4 VILLA FIELDS
5 LODGE GD
6 SAFFRON DR
7 LABURNUM CL
8 BUTTER MKT
9 MARKET PL
10 JASMINE CL

63
50

Scale: 1¼ inches to 1 mile
0 ¼ ½ mile
0 250m 500m 750m 1 km

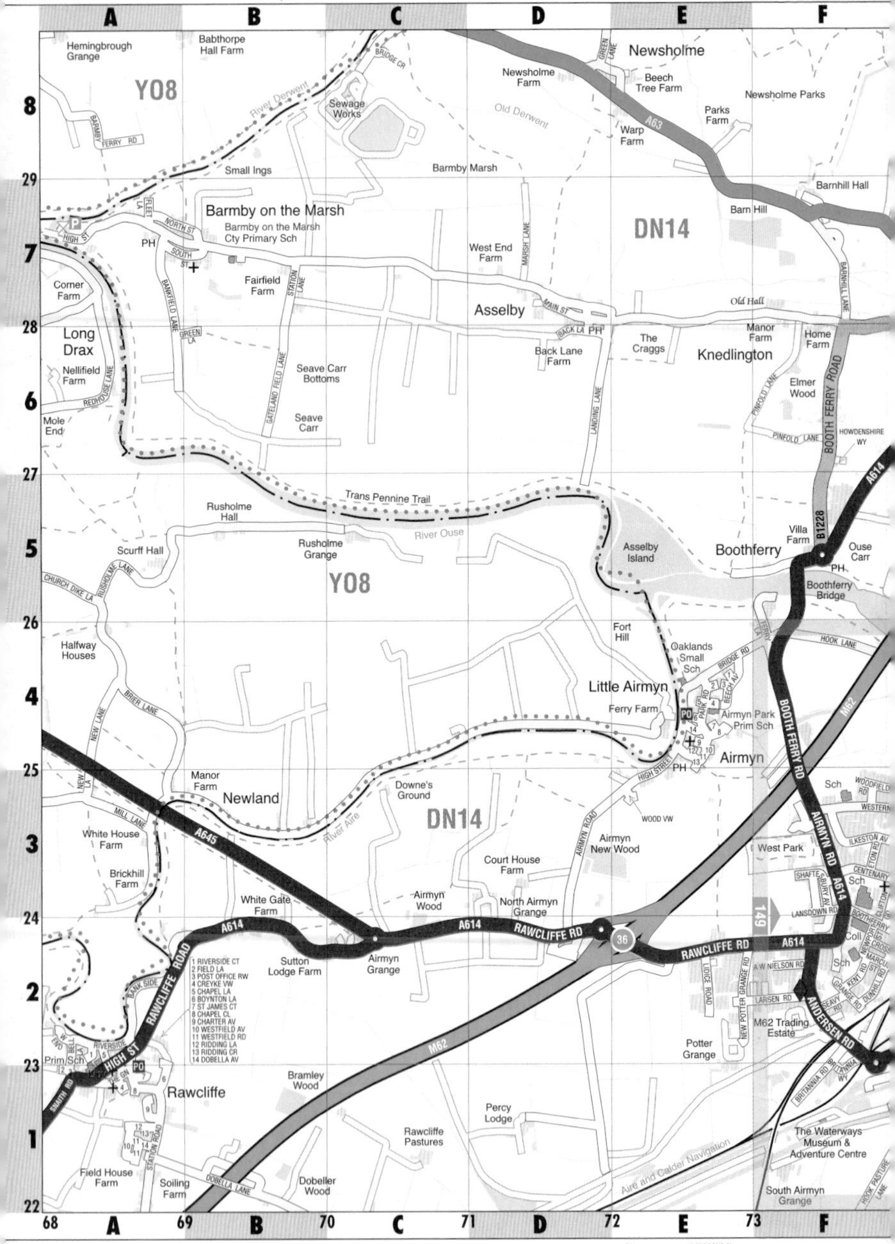

63
79

E4
1 BEECH GR
2 CHESTNUT AVE
3 BEECH AVE
4 PERCY DR
5 HALL CL
6 PARK CL
7 COURTS CL
8 WOODLAND WY
9 ST DAVID'S VW
10 PARSONS CL
11 PARSON'S WK
12 CHURCH VW
13 THE CROSSINGS
14 THE PADDOCK

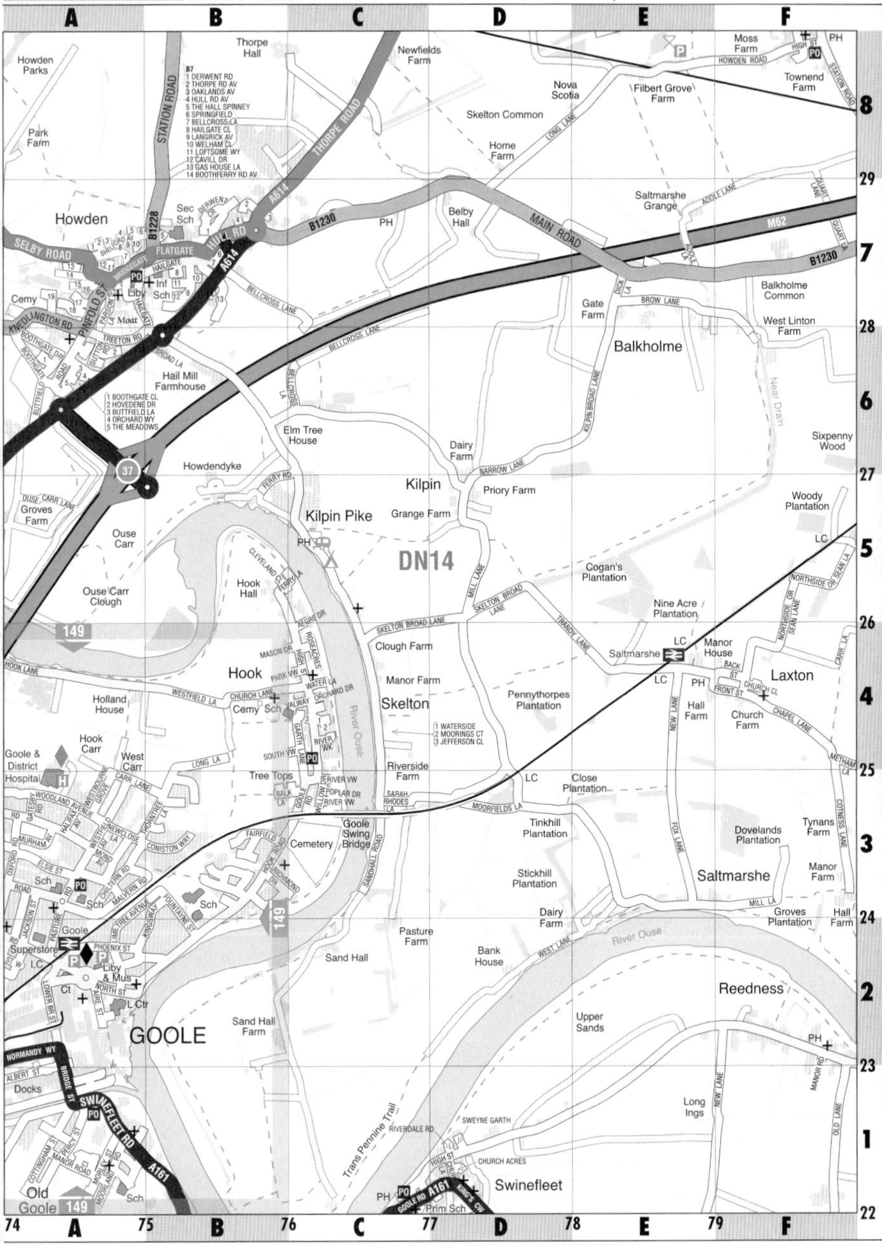
A B C D E F
8 29 7 28 6 27 5 26 4 25 3 24 2 23 1 22
74 75 76 77 78 79
Howden Parks
Park Farm
Thorpe Hall
STATION ROAD
THORPE ROAD
B7
1 DERWENT RD
2 THORPE RD AV
3 OAKLANDS AV
4 HULL RD AV
5 THE HALL SPINNEY
6 SPRINGFIELD
7 BELLCROSS LA
8 HAILGATE CL
9 LANGRICK AV
10 WELHAM CL
11 LOFTSOME WY
12 CAVILL DR
13 GAS HOUSE LA
14 BOOTHFERRY RD AV
Newfields Farm
Nova Scotia
Skelton Common
Home Farm
LONG LANE
Moss Farm
HOWDEN ROAD
HIGH ST
PH
PO
Townend Farm
STATION ROAD
Filbert Grove Farm
Howden
Sec Sch
B1228
A614
HULL RD
B1230
PH
Belby Hall
MAIN ROAD
Saltmarshe Grange
ADDLE LANE
QUART LANE
M62
SELBY ROAD
FLATGATE
BRIDGEGATE
HAILGATE
Inf Sch
Liby
Cemy
PINFOLD ST
KNEDLINGTON RD
Moat
BOOTHGATE DR
TREETON RD
BELLCROSS LANE
Gate Farm
DICK LA
BROW LANE
Balkholme Common
West Linton Farm
Balkholme
BROAD LA
Hail Mill Farmhouse
1 BOOTHGATE CL
2 HOVEDENE DR
3 BUTTFIELD LA
4 ORCHARD WY
5 THE MEADOWS
BELLCROSS LA
KILPIN BROAD LANE
Near Drain
Elm Tree House
Dairy Farm
NARROW LANE
Sixpenny Wood
37
Howdendyke
FERRY RD
Kilpin
Priory Farm
OUSE CARR LANE
Groves Farm
Kilpin Pike
Grange Farm
Woody Plantation
Ouse Carr
PH
DN14
LC
CLEVELAND CL
FERRY LA
MILL LANE
Cogan's Plantation
Hook Hall
Ouse Carr Clough
SKELTON BROAD LANE
Nine Acre Plantation
NORTHSIDE OR SEAN LA
149
TRANDY LANE
Clough Farm
HOOK LANE
MASON DR
HIGH ST
ROSEACRES
Saltmarshe
LC
Manor House
Hook
PARK VW ST
WATER LA
Manor Farm
LC
PH
BACK ST
Laxton
CARR LA
Holland House
WESTFIELD LA
CHURCH LANE
ORCHARD DR
Pennythorpes Plantation
FRONT ST
CHURCH CL
Cemy Sch
Skelton
Hall Farm
Church Farm
CHAPEL LANE
River Ouse
1 WATERSIDE
2 MOORINGS CT
3 JEFFERSON CL
NEW LANE
Hook Carr
Goole & District Hospital
West Carr
LONG LA
SOUTH VW
PO
Riverside Farm
LC
Close Plantation
METHAM LA
Tree Tops
CARR LANE
RIVER VW
POPLAR DR
SARAH RHODES LA
MOORFIELDS LA
WOODLAND AVENUE
Tinkhill Plantation
Tynans Farm
Goole Swing Bridge
FAIRFIELD
Cemetery
CONISTON WAY
FOX LANE
Dovelands Plantation
COTNESS LANE
Sch
Stickhill Plantation
Saltmarshe
Manor Farm
Sch
PO
MALVERN RD
HOOK ROAD
RICHMOND
SANDHALL ROAD
Sch
149
Dairy Farm
MILL LA
Groves Plantation
Hall Farm
Goole
Superstore
PHOENIX ST
LIME TREE AVENUE
KINGSWAY
Pasture Farm
River Ouse
LC
Liby & Mus
Sand Hall
Bank House
WEST LANE
Reedness
Ct
NORTH ST
L Ctr
GOOLE
Sand Hall Farm
Upper Sands
PH
NORMANDY WY
ALBERT ST
BRIDGE ST
Docks
SWINEFLEET RD
PO
Trans Pennine Trail
MANOR RD
Long Ings
NEW LANE
OLD LANE
RIVERDALE RD
SWEYNE GARTH
A161
COTTINGHAM ST
PERCY ST
MANOR ROAD
MORLEY ST
MOORLAND
Sch
HIGH ST
CHURCH ACRES
Swinefleet
Old Goole
149
PH
PO
GOOLE RD
A161
KING'S CW
Prim Sch

65
52

D8
1 SANDHOLME CL
2 THE PEPPERCORNS
3 VICTORIA DR
4 ST STEPHEN'S CR
5 HANSARD CR
6 HANSARD DR
7 WILLOW GN
8 CHAPEL MEADOWS
9 BISHOP CT
10 MANOR DR
11 CHAPEL GARTH
12 WESTBROOK RD
13 THE PADDOCK
14 SYCAMORE CL
15 CHESTNUT DR
16 CHERRY CT
17 LABURNUM WK

Scale: 1¼ inches to 1 mile
0 ¼ ½ mile
0 250m 500m 750m 1 km

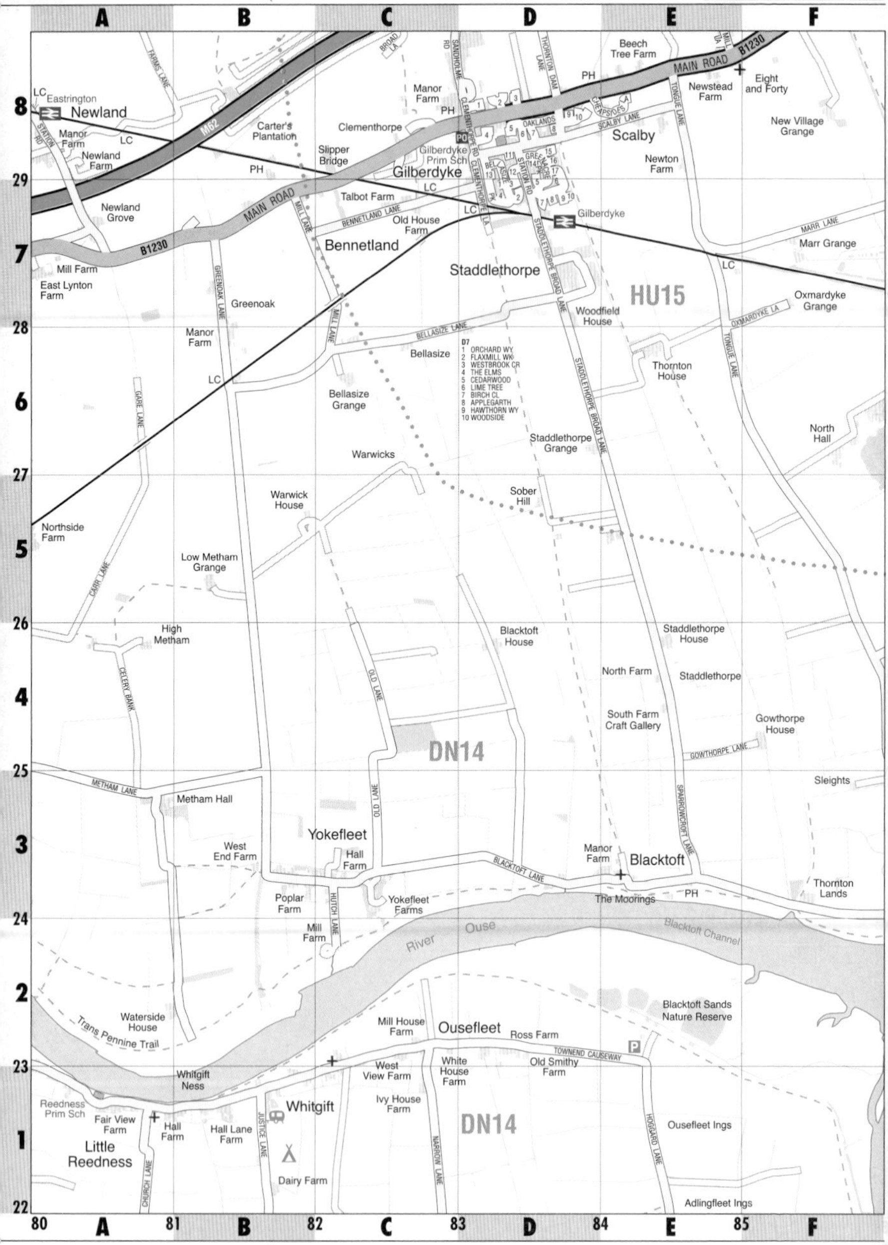
A B C D E F
8
29
7
28
6
27
5
26
4
25
3
24
2
23
1
22
80 81 82 83 84 85
Newland
Eastrington
LC
STATION RD
Manor Farm
Newland Farm
FARMS LANE
M62
Carter's Plantation
Clementhorpe
Slipper Bridge
Manor Farm
PH
BROAD LA
SANDHOLME RD
CLEMENTHORPE RD
PO
Gilberdyke Prim Sch
Gilberdyke
Talbot Farm
OAKLANDS
SCALBY LANE
Scalby
Beech Tree Farm
THORNTON DAM LANE
MAIN ROAD
B1230
Newstead Farm
Eight and Forty
MILL LA
New Village Grange
Newton Farm
TONGUE LANE
Newland Grove
MAIN ROAD
B1230
Mill Farm
East Lynton Farm
Greenoak
GREENOAK LANE
MILL LANE
BENNETLAND LANE
Old House Farm
Bennetland
Staddlethorpe
Gilberdyke
STADDLETHORPE BROAD LANE
MARR LANE
Marr Grange
HU15
Oxmardyke Grange
OXMARDYKE LA
Woodfield House
BELLASIZE LANE
Bellasize
Manor Farm
D7
1 ORCHARD WY
2 FLAXMILL WK
3 WESTBROOK CR
4 THE ELMS
5 CEDARWOOD
6 LIME TREE
7 BIRCH CL
8 APPLEGARTH
9 HAWTHORN WY
10 WOODSIDE
Thornton House
GARE LANE
Bellasize Grange
Staddlethorpe Grange
North Hall
Warwicks
Warwick House
Sober Hill
Northside Farm
Low Metham Grange
CARR LANE
High Metham
Blacktoft House
Staddlethorpe House
CELERY BANK
OLD LANE
North Farm
Staddlethorpe
South Farm Craft Gallery
Gowthorpe House
DN14
GOWTHORPE LANE
METHAM LANE
Metham Hall
Sleights
SPARROWCROFT LANE
Yokefleet
West End Farm
Hall Farm
Manor Farm
Blacktoft
BLACKTOFT LANE
Thornton Lands
Poplar Farm
HUTCH LANE
Yokefleet Farms
The Moorings
PH
Mill Farm
River Ouse
Blacktoft Channel
Waterside House
Trans Pennine Trail
Mill House Farm
Ousefleet
Ross Farm
Blacktoft Sands Nature Reserve
TOWNEND CAUSEWAY
West View Farm
White House Farm
Old Smithy Farm
Whitgift Ness
Reedness Prim Sch
Fair View Farm
Hall Farm
Hall Lane Farm
JUSTICE LANE
Whitgift
Ivy House Farm
DN14
HOGGARD LANE
Ousefleet Ings
Little Reedness
CHURCH LANE
Dairy Farm
NARROW LANE
Adlingfleet Ings

65
81

Scale: 1¼ inches to 1 mile
0 ¼ ½ mile
0 250m 500m 750m 1 km

53
68

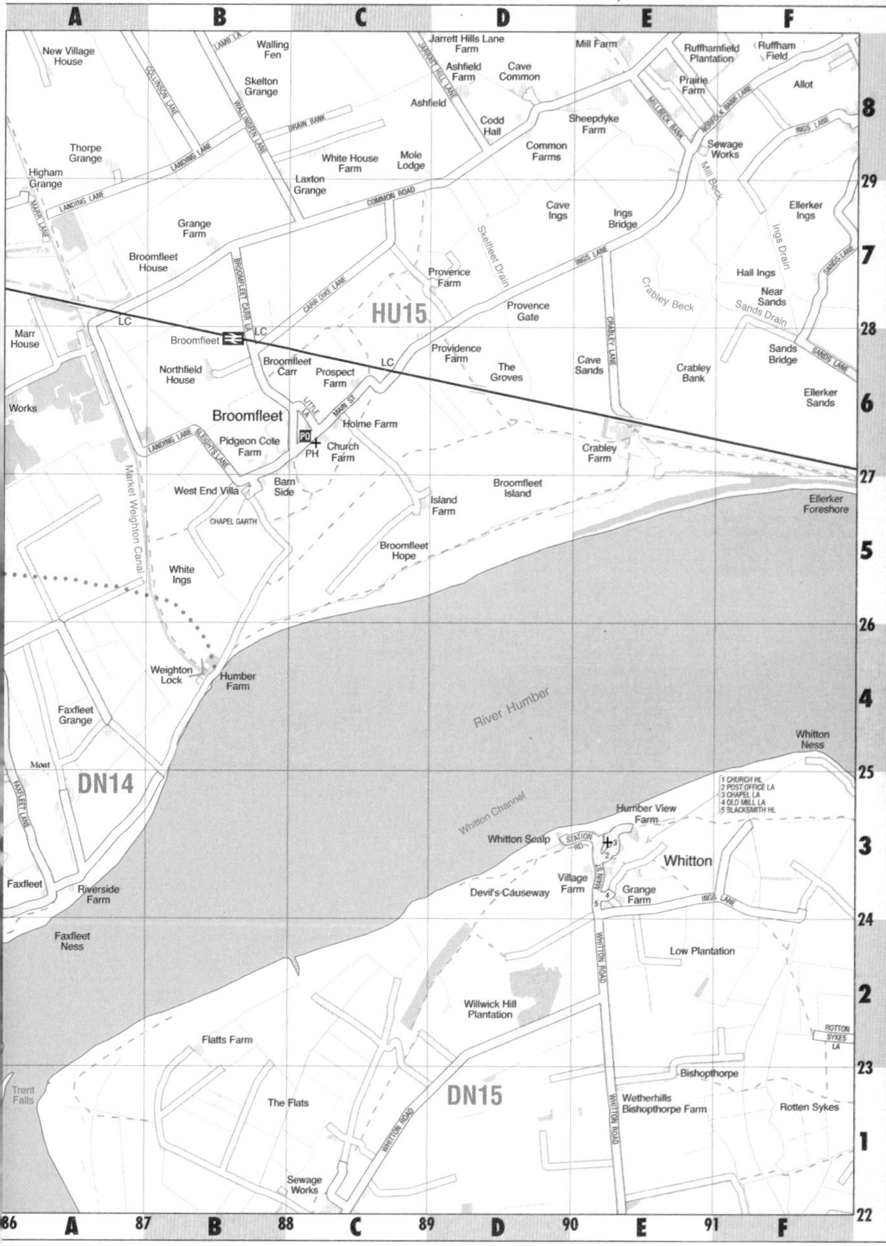

82
68

B5
1 HAVEN GARTH
2 HAVEN AV
3 GRASSDALE PK
4 KING EDWARDS TERR
5 ALBEMARLE CL
6 KINGSLEY CL

C7
1 SPINDLEWOOD
2 STOCKBRIDGE PK
3 CHURCH LA
4 CHURCH VIEW
5 DORSEY WY
6 THORNHAM'S WY

67

D5
1 BROADACRE PK
2 MEDLAR DR
3 BROADLEY CROFT
4 ASPEN WLK
5 FAIRFIELD VIEW

54

D6
1 HALL WK
2 BROOKSIDE
3 INGMIRES
4 BECKSIDE
5 THE GREEN
6 CHURCH ST
7 CREYKE LA
8 PARLIAMENT ST
9 ST ANNE'S WK
10 ST HELEN'S DR
11 MONKTON
12 RYEDALE
13 LOWERDALE

E6
1 CHAPEL HILL
2 TEMPLE WK
3 LADYWELL GATE

Scale: 1¼ inches to 1 mile
0 ¼ ½ mile
0 250m 500m 750m 1 km

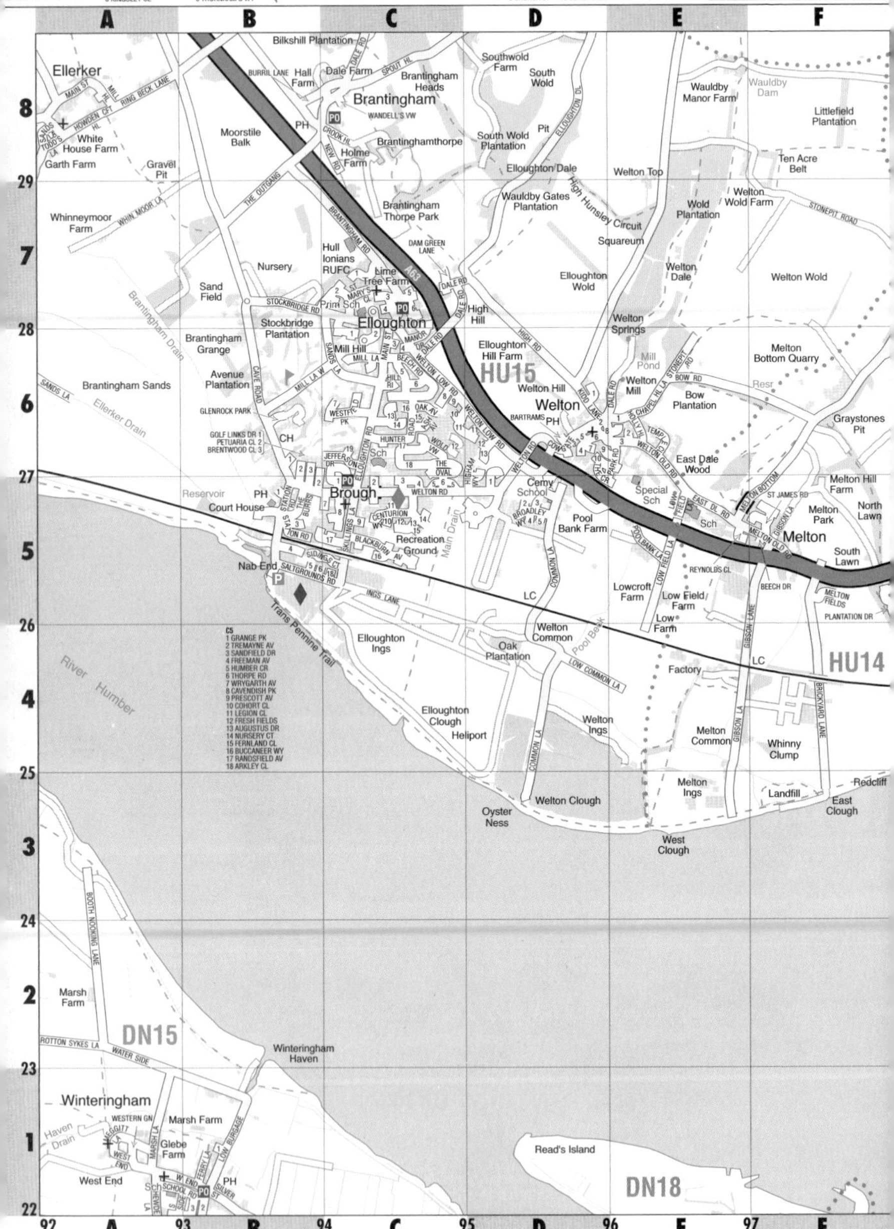

C5
1 GRANGE PK
2 TREMAYNE AV
3 SANDFIELD DR
4 FREEMAN AV
5 HUMBER CR
6 THORPE RD
7 WRYGARTH AV
8 CAVENDISH PK
9 PRESCOTT AV
10 COHORT CL
11 LEGION CL
12 FRESH FIELDS
13 AUGUSTUS DR
14 NURSERY CT
15 FERNLAND CL
16 BUCCANEER WY
17 RANDSFIELD AV
18 ARKLEY CL

B1
1 ORCHARD DR
2 HIGH BURGAGE
3 BACK LA

67

83

C6
1 DROVERS RISE
2 VICARAGE GD
3 CHAPEL MEWS
4 PINE WK
5 HOBSON RD
6 HARLAND RD
7 LARCHMONT CL
8 WOODLANDS LA
9 PLOVER DR
10 THORNTON
11 FRYSTON
12 LASTINGHAM
13 CHANTRYS DR
14 RANSOME WAY
15 ELM AV
16 LAMBERT AV
17 WOODLAND AV
18 SPRINGFIELD AV
19 ATKINSON DR

A B C D E F

98 A 99 B 00 C 01 D 02 E 03 F

139
143
140
For full street detail of the highlighted area see page 155.

Scale: 1¼ inches to 1 mile
0 ¼ ½ mile
0 250m 500m 750m 1 km

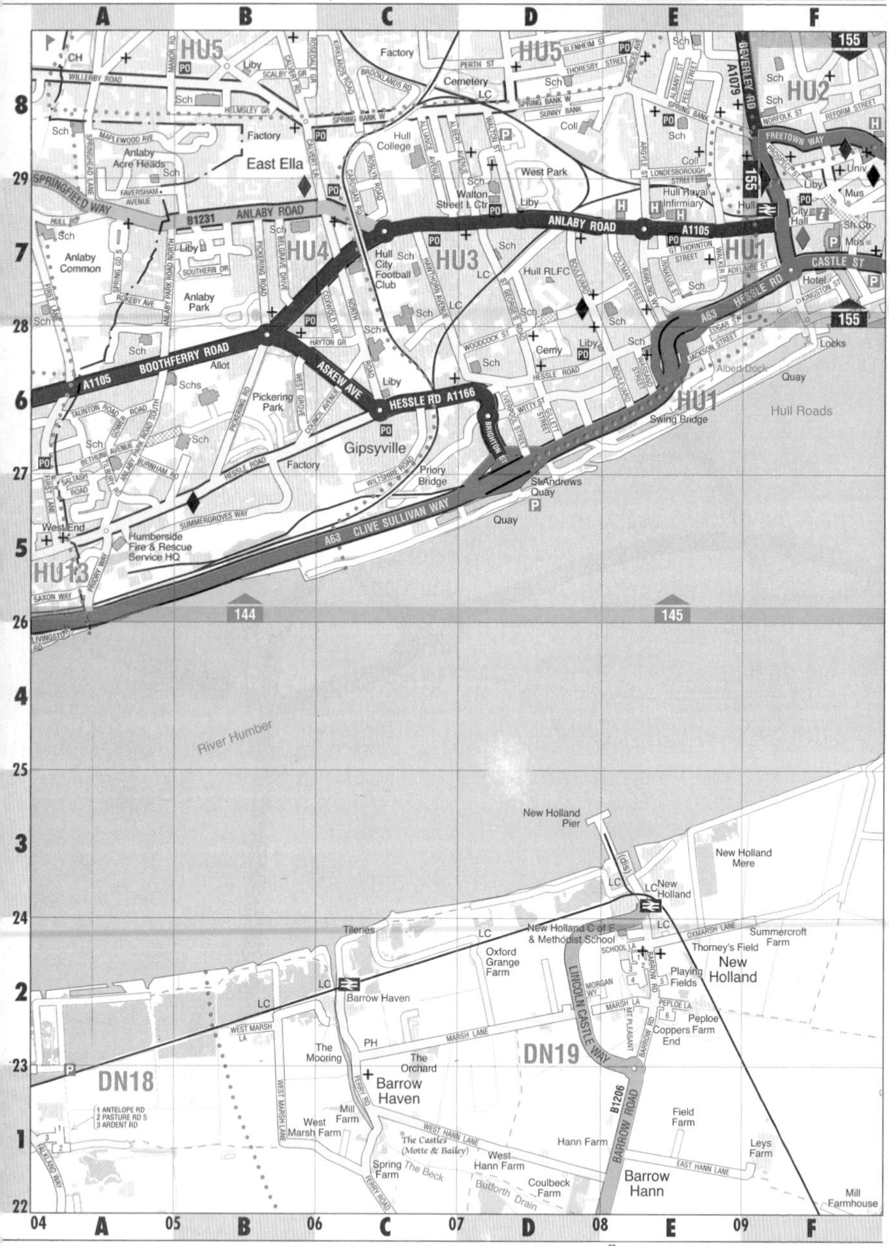

69
85

E2
1 WENTWORTH CRES
2 WESTBURN AV
3 FULFORD CRES
4 GLENEAGLES CRES
5 ALBERT ST
6 PEPLOE CRES

For full street detail of the highlighted area see pages 144 and 145.

A
B
C
D
E
F
8
29
7
28
6
27
5
26
4
25
3
24
2
23
1
22
10
11
12
13
14
15
CLEVELAND ST
Factory
MOUNT PLEASANT
VICTOR STREET
NEW BRI RD
Sch
ROSMEAD STREET
SOUTHCOATES LANE
BILSDALE GROVE
Factory
HU9
Factory
Marfleet
DODSWELL GROVE
Sch
GREAT FIELD LANE
Salt End
ST MARK ST
PO
HU8
DANSOM LA
SOUTH
A165
Liby
ELLIS ST
WYKE ST
HALLER ST
H.M. Prison
Cemy
Hull Maternity
Factory
MARFLEET AVENUE
Sch
MARFLEET LANE
CEYLON ST
Factory
VALLETTA STREET
Factory
SOMERDEN RD
Factory
WITHAM
WILLIAMSON ST
CHURCH STREET
155
HEDON ROAD
A1033
HULL ROAD
HEDON ROAD A1033
Coll
HEDON ROAD
GARRISON RD
Alexandra Dock
CORPORATION ROAD
Queen Elizabeth Dock
Fleet
Old
Ct
Mus
HIGH ST
TOWER ST
Sch
SOUTH BRIDGE ROAD
HARBOUR WAY
Locks
Factory
Wharf
Wharf
Locks
Factory
Lord's Clough
A63
Locks
CAMILLA CL
Victoria Dock Village
Hull Roads
HU12
Victoria Pier
KINGSTON UPON HULL
147
Quay
Quay
Salt End Jetties
River Humber
146
147
Skitter Ness
Haven Farm
Goxhill Haven
New Bank Farm
Chimney
New Green
New Green Farm
Factory
Regent House
Mast
NEATGANGS LANE
Neatgangs Farm
WEST MARSH LA
Salt Marsh Farm
DN19
East Marsh Farm
East Marsh
Salt Marsh
EAST MARSH ROAD
Ferry Farm
FERRY ROAD
HORSEGATE FIELD ROAD
Horsegate Farm
Fir Tree Farm
Glebe Farm
Spring Farm
SYKES LANE
Brook Hill
CHAPEL FIELD ROAD
East Halton Skitter
North End Farm
Brook Hill Farm
Cottage Farm
WINDSOR GR
Maydale Farm
Main Drain
Main Drain
SKITTER RD
Croft Side
THE CL
ELM LA
NORTH END
RUARDS LANE
Chapel Farm
MILL LA
North End
RUARD ROAD
SKITTER ROAD
DN40
Langmere Covert
The Grange

147

C7
1 PRINCES AV
2 SHIELDS RD
3 ANDREW LA
4 HARDYS RD
5 BURNSALLS RD
6 ROBSON WY
7 BEECH AV
8 CEDAR CT
9 OAK GR
10 POPLAR GR
11 FOTHERBIE GARTH
12 HALES CR
13 WESTLANDS CL
14 CLOEBERRY WY
15 GREEN RD
16 HERON CL
17 DRAPER'S LA
18 WARN AV
19 KETWELL LA
20 WAYFBAIN LA
21 CHURCH GA
22 SPENCER CL
23 LAMBERT PK RD
24 HAVEN STAITHES
25 WESTWICK
26 WOODMARKETGA
27 IVESON CL
28 GEORGE ST
29 KING'S PL
30 ST AUGUSTINE'S GA
31 MARKET PL

58

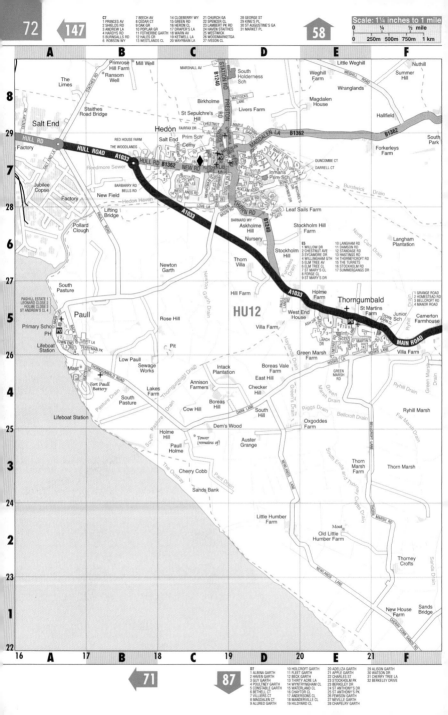

Scale: 1¼ inches to 1 mile
0 ¼ ½ mile
0 250m 500m 750m 1 km

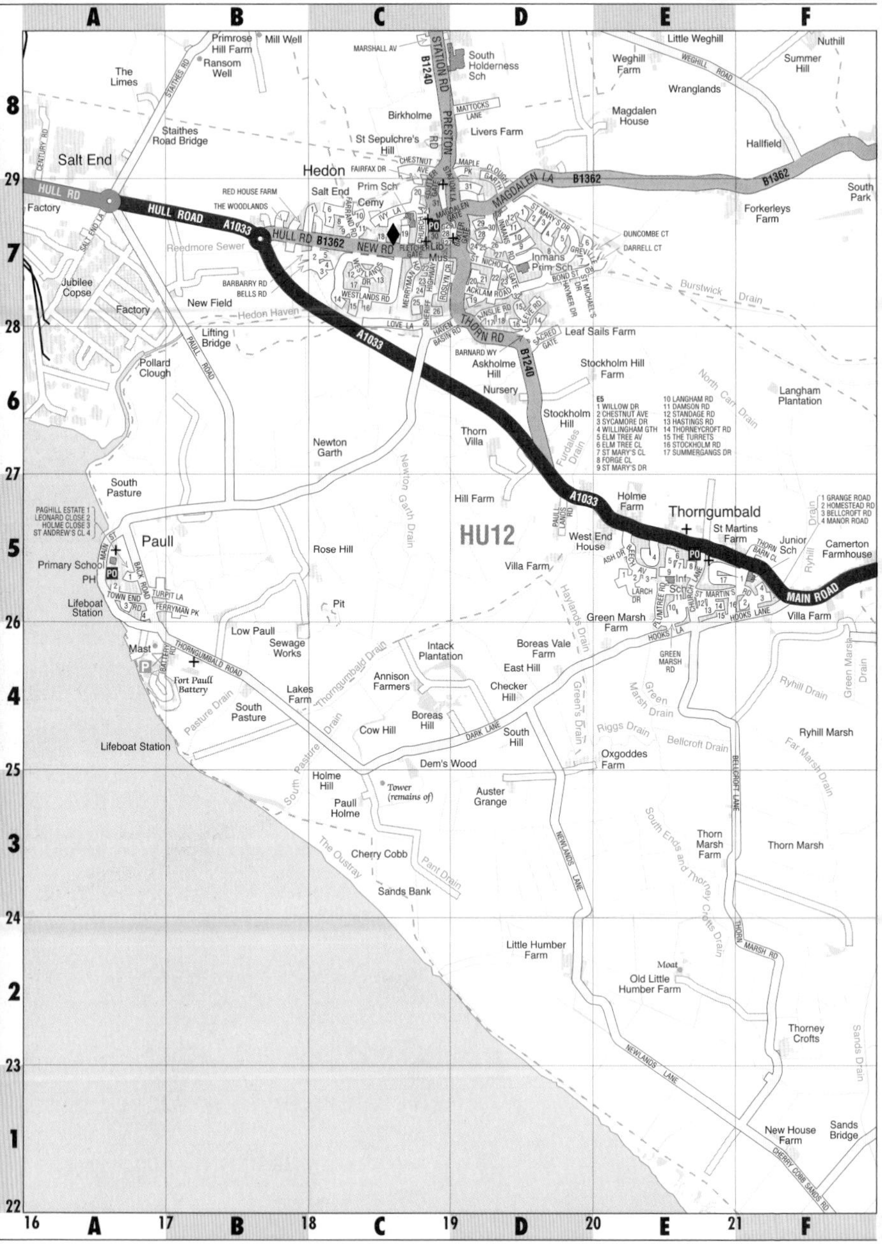

71

87

D7
1 ALBINA GARTH
2 HAVEN GARTH
3 GUY GARTH
4 POULTNEY GARTH
5 CONSTABLE GARTH
6 BETHELL CT
7 VILLIERS CT
8 MAGDALEN CT
9 ALURED GARTH
10 HOLCROFT GARTH
11 FLEET GARTH
12 BECK GARTH
13 THIRTY ACRE LA
14 WYNTRYNGHAM CL
15 WATERLAND CL
16 CHAYTOR CL
17 ANDERSONS CL
18 MANDERVILLE CL
19 HILDYARD CL
20 ADELIZA GARTH
21 APPLE GARTH
22 CHARLES ST
23 STOCKHOLM PK
23 BERKELEY DR
24 ST ANTHONY'S DR
25 ST ANTHONY'S PK
26 FEWSON GARTH
27 NEVILLE GARTH
28 CHAPELRY GARTH
29 ALISON GARTH
30 WATSON DR
31 CHERRY TREE LA
32 BERKELEY DRIVE

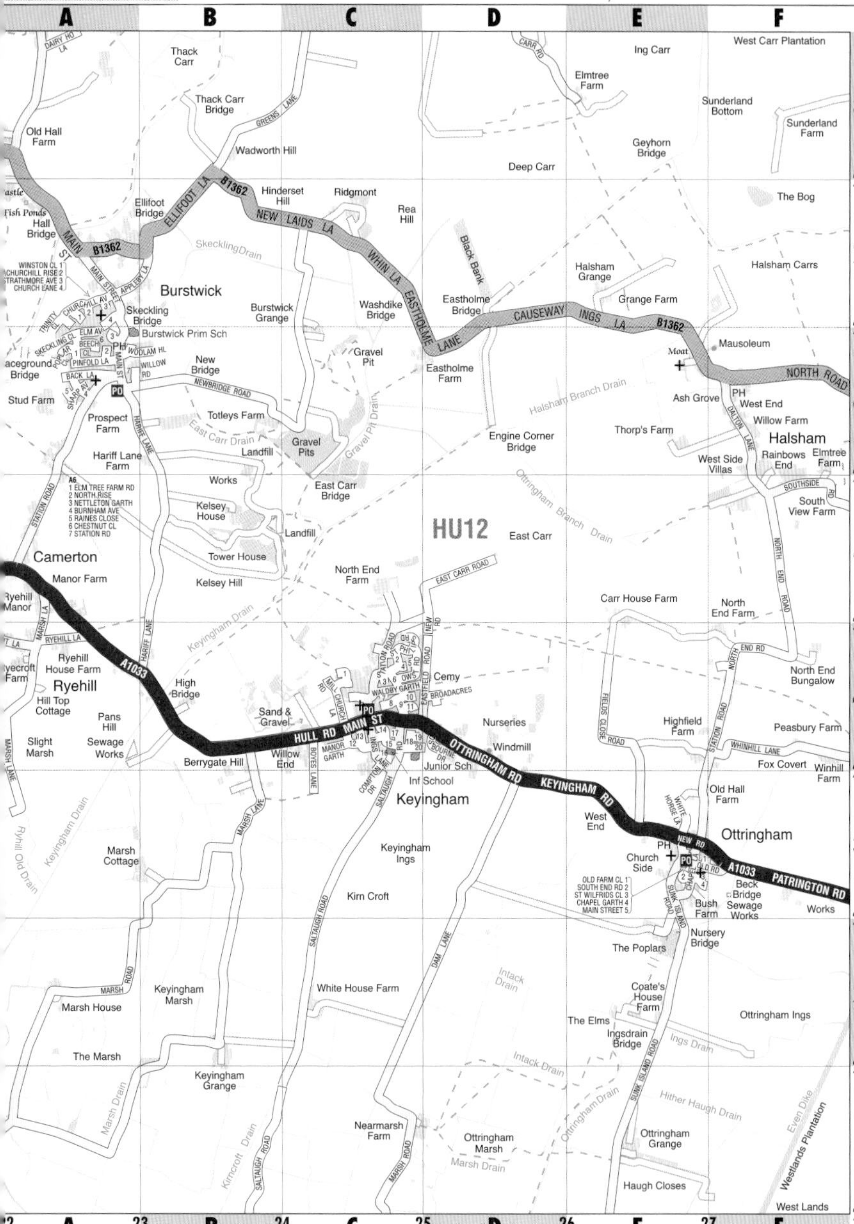

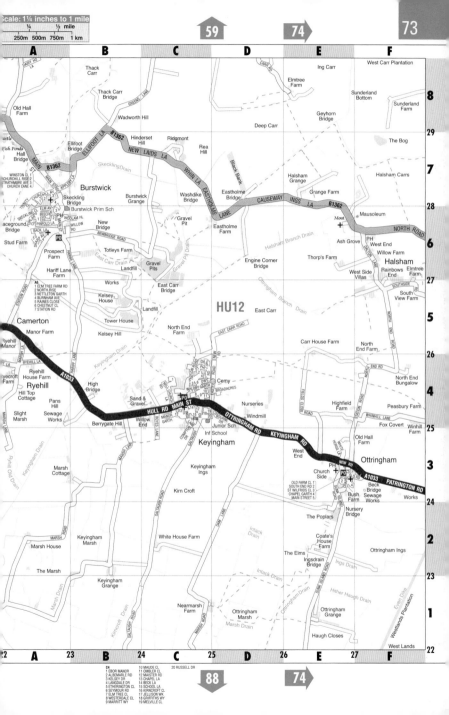

C4
1 EBOR MANOR
2 ALBEMARLE RD
3 KELSEY DR
4 LANGDALE DR
5 ETHERINGTON CL
6 SEYMOUR RD
7 ELM TREE CL
8 WESTERDALE CL
9 MARRITT WY
10 MAUDE CL
11 OMBLER CL
12 MAISTER RD
13 CHAPEL LA
14 BECK LA
15 SCHOOL LA
16 KIRNCROFT CL
17 JELLISON WK
18 GRIFFITHS WY
19 MELVILLE CL
20 RUSSELL DR

73
60

Scale: 1¼ inches to 1 mile
0 ¼ ½ mile
0 250m 500m 750m 1 km

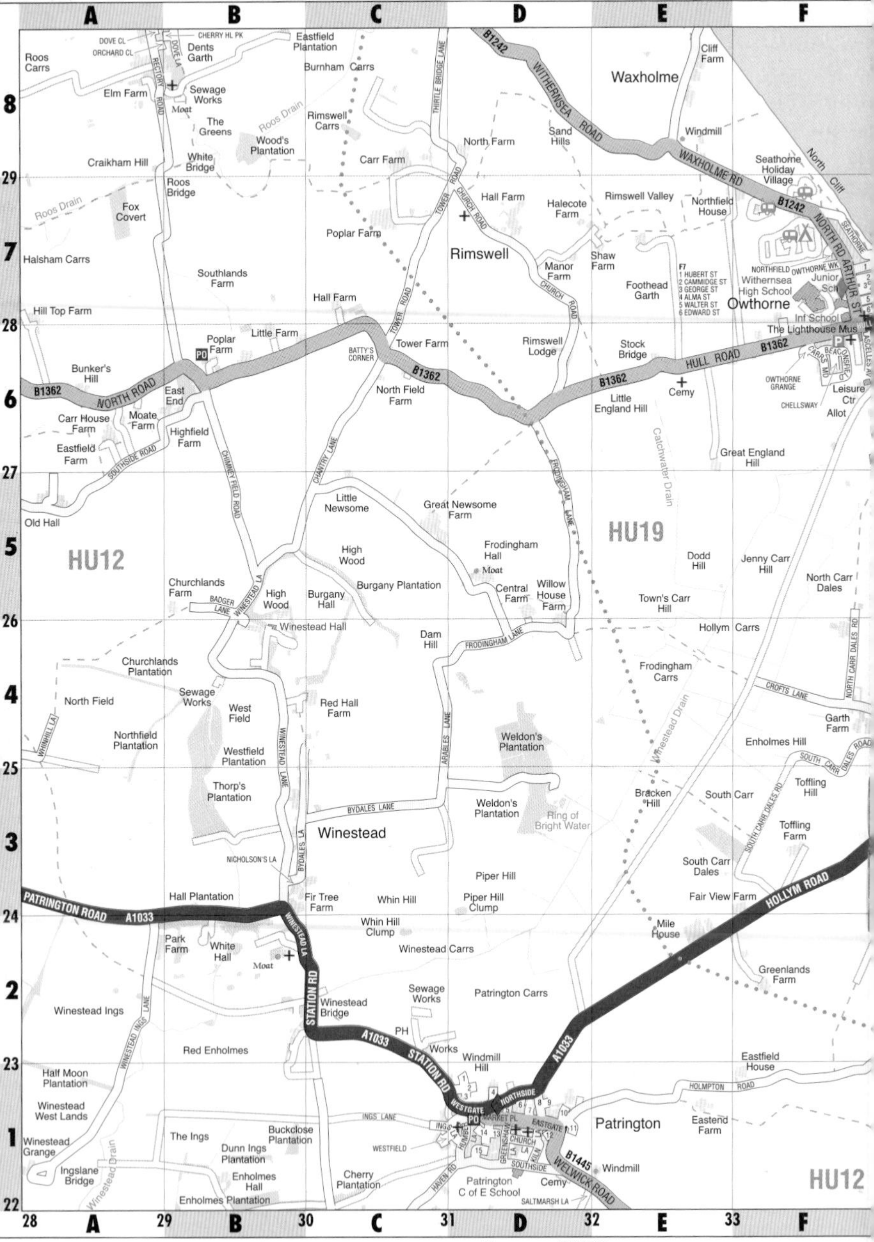

A B C D E F
Roos Carrs
DOVE CL
ORCHARD CL
CHERRY HL PK
DOVE LA
Dents Garth
Eastfield Plantation
Burnham Carrs
THIRTLE BRIDGE LANE
B1242
WITHERNSEA ROAD
Waxholme
Cliff Farm
Elm Farm
RECTORY ROAD
Sewage Works
Moat
The Greens
Roos Drain
Wood's Plantation
Rimswell Carrs
Carr Farm
North Farm
Sand Hills
Windmill
WAXHOLME RD
Seathorne Holiday Village
North Cliff
Craikham Hill
White Bridge
Roos Bridge
Roos Drain
Fox Covert
TOWER ROAD
CHURCH ROAD
Hall Farm
Halecote Farm
Rimswell Valley
Northfield House
B1242
NORTH RD
SEATHORNE
Poplar Farm
Rimswell
Halsham Carrs
Southlands Farm
Manor Farm
Shaw Farm
Foothead Garth
F7
1 HUBERT ST
2 CAMMIDGE ST
3 GEORGE ST
4 ALMA ST
5 WALTER ST
6 EDWARD ST
NORTHFIELD
OWTHORNE WK
Withernsea High School
Junior Sch
ARTHUR ST
Owthorne
Hall Farm
CHURCH ROAD
Hill Top Farm
Inf School
The Lighthouse Mus
Little Farm
Poplar Farm
PO
BATTY'S CORNER
Tower Farm
Rimswell Lodge
Stock Bridge
HULL ROAD
B1362
CARRS MD
BEACONSFIELD
LASCELLES AV
Bunker's Hill
B1362
NORTH ROAD
East End
B1362
North Field Farm
B1362
Cemy
Little England Hill
OWTHORNE GRANGE
CHELLSWAY
Leisure Ctr
Allot
Carr House Farm
Moate Farm
Highfield Farm
Eastfield Farm
SOUTHSIDE ROAD
CHIMNEY FIELD ROAD
CHANTRY LANE
FRODINGHAM LANE
Catchwater Drain
Great England Hill
Little Newsome
Great Newsome Farm
Old Hall
HU19
HU12
High Wood
Frodingham Hall
Moat
Dodd Hill
Jenny Carr Hill
North Carr Dales
Churchlands Farm
BADGER LANE
WINESTEAD LA
High Wood
Burgany Hall
Burgany Plantation
Central Farm
Willow House Farm
Town's Carr Hill
Winestead Hall
Dam Hill
FRODINGHAM LANE
Hollym Carrs
NORTH CARR DALES RD
Churchlands Plantation
Frodingham Carrs
CROFTS LANE
North Field
Sewage Works
West Field
Red Hall Farm
Garth Farm
Northfield Plantation
WHINHILL LA
Westfield Plantation
WINESTEAD LANE
ARABLES LANE
Weldon's Plantation
Winestead Drain
Enholmes Hill
SOUTH CARR DALES ROAD
Toffling Hill
Thorp's Plantation
BYDALES LANE
Weldon's Plantation
Ring of Bright Water
Bracken Hill
South Carr
SOUTH CARR DALES RD
Toffling Farm
Winestead
NICHOLSON'S LA
BYDALES LA
Piper Hill
South Carr Dales
HOLLYM ROAD
PATRINGTON ROAD
A1033
Hall Plantation
Fir Tree Farm
Whin Hill
Piper Hill Clump
Fair View Farm
WINESTEAD LA
Whin Hill Clump
Mile House
Park Farm
White Hall
Moat
Winestead Carrs
Greenlands Farm
STATION RD
Sewage Works
Patrington Carrs
Winestead Ings
WINESTEAD INGS LANE
Winestead Bridge
PH
A1033
A1033
Red Enholmes
Works
STATION RD
Windmill Hill
Eastfield House
Half Moon Plantation
NORTHSIDE
HOLMPTON ROAD
WESTGATE
Winestead West Lands
INGS LANE
INGS
MARKET PL
EASTGATE
Patrington
Eastend Farm
Winestead Grange
The Ings
Buckclose Plantation
Dunn Ings Plantation
WESTFIELD
HUMBER
GREENSHAW LA
CHURCH LA
KILN
B1445
WELWICK ROAD
Windmill
Ingslane Bridge
Winestead Drain
Enholmes Hall
Cherry Plantation
HAVEN RD
SOUTHSIDE
Patrington C of E School
Cemy
HU12
Enholmes Plantation
SALTMARSH LA
28 A 29 B 30 C 31 D 32 E 33 F

73
89

D1
1 HUNTER CL
2 GUARDIANS ROAD
3 FRANCIS WAY
4 WESTGATE MANOR
5 PUMP ROW
6 NORTHSIDE COURT
7 CHURCH VIEW
8 TITHE BARN LANE
9 TITHE BARN CL
10 CLARKS LANE
11 BEECH DRIVE
12 THE CLOSE
13 THE CRESCENT
14 ST PATRICK'S GN
15 SAFFRON GARTH

Scale: 1¼ inches to 1 mile

A
B
C
D
E
F
8
29
7
28
6
27
5
26
4
25
3
24
2
23
1
22
34
35
36
37
38
39
Noah's Wood
Submarine Forest
YOUNG ST
SEASIDE RD
WITHERNSEA
Withernsea
Liby
A1033
PO
QUEEN ST
Lifeboat
Station
A6
1 JAMES CL
2 RAILWAY CR
3 ROBERT CL
4 PIGGY LA
5 STATION RD
6 ST NICHOLAS PK
7 SCOTT GD
8 THE CL
9 CHERRY TREE AV
10 FRANCIS AV
11 WHITETHORN AV
12 VICTORIA AV
13 WESTFIELD RI
14 MEMORIAL AV
15 QUEEN ST SOUTH
16 KAY KENDALL CT
17 KING ST
18 HIGH BRIGHTON ST
19 CHEVERTON AV
PARK AVE
SOUTHCLIFF RD
PRINCE'S AV
SEACROFT RD
EGROM'S LA
CH
Withernsea
Golf Club
HAZEL AV 1
CHESTNUT AV 2
HOLMPTON RD 3
TURNER RD 4
NEWSHAM GD 5
HOLLYM RD
First
Farm
COLLEYS
KENWOOD
Holiday
Chalets
Red House
Valley
Farm
Smook
Hills
SMOOK
HILLS RD
Intack
Farm
HOLMPTON ROAD
Sewage
Works
Hollym
WITHERNSEA RD
PH
CHURCH
LA
NORTH LEYS ROAD
Nevilles
Farm
A1033
Bowmer
Hill
SOUTH LEYS ROAD
Manor
Farm
Eastfield
Farm
North Leys
The
Runnell
South Leys
WITHERNSEA ROAD
Scarborough Hill
HU19
Intack
Plantation
SEA RD
Nevills Drain
HOOKS LANE
Cliff House
Farm
SEASIDE ROAD
SCHOOL LANE
Holmpton
Brick Close
Plantation
PATRINGTON ROAD
MAIN ROAD
Cow Close
Plantation
Mill Hill
Old
Hive
PH
Manor
Farm
West Farm
WAKEFIELD LANE
Little
Plowland
Trinity House
Farm
OUT NEWTON ROAD
Long Close
Plantation
Old Hive Dike
RYSOME LANE
Woods
Plantation
Parker's Close
Plantation
Grass North
Field
NORTHFIELD LANE
Black Dike
Balk Hill
Cliff Farm
Beacon Hill
Rysome
Garth
Water Tower
Model Farm
North Farm

61

Scale: 1¼ inches to 1 mile
0 ¼ ½ mile
0 250m 500m 750m 1 km

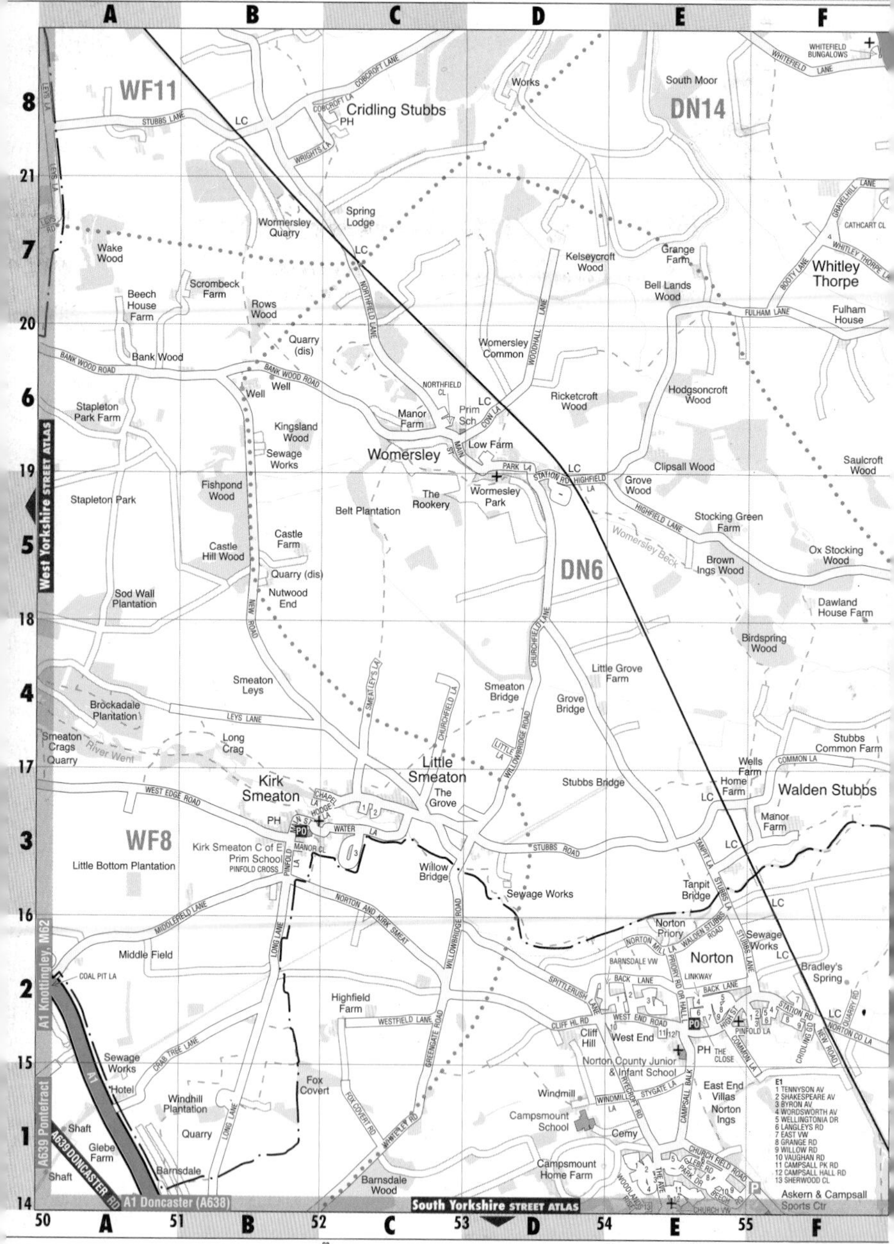

WF11
DN14
DN6
WF8
Cridling Stubbs
Womersley
Little Smeaton
Kirk Smeaton
Norton
Walden Stubbs
Whitley Thorpe
West End
South Moor
Works
Spring Lodge
Wormersley Quarry
Wake Wood
Beech House Farm
Scrombeck Farm
Rows Wood
Quarry (dis)
Bank Wood
Well
Stapleton Park Farm
Kingsland Wood
Sewage Works
Manor Farm
Prim Sch
Low Farm
Womersley Common
Ricketcroft Wood
Hodgsoncroft Wood
Kelseycroft Wood
Grange Farm
Bell Lands Wood
Fulham House
Clipsall Wood
Grove Wood
Saulcroft Wood
Stapleton Park
Fishpond Wood
The Rookery
Wormesley Park
Belt Plantation
Castle Farm
Castle Hill Wood
Nutwood End
Stocking Green Farm
Brown Ings Wood
Ox Stocking Wood
Womersley Beck
Sod Wall Plantation
Dawland House Farm
Birdspring Wood
Little Grove Farm
Smeaton Leys
Smeaton Bridge
Grove Bridge
Brockadale Plantation
Smeaton Crags
Quarry
River Went
Long Crag
Stubbs Common Farm
Stubbs Bridge
Wells Farm
Home Farm
Manor Farm
The Grove
Kirk Smeaton C of E Prim School
PINFOLD CROSS
Little Bottom Plantation
Willow Bridge
Sewage Works
Tanpit Bridge
Norton Priory
Middle Field
Bradley's Spring
Highfield Farm
Cliff Hill
Norton County Junior & Infant School
Sewage Works
Hotel
Windhill Plantation
Fox Covert
Windmill
Campsmount School
Cemy
East End Villas
Norton Ings
Shaft
Glebe Farm
Quarry
Barnsdale
Barnsdale Wood
Campsmount Home Farm
Askern & Campsall Sports Ctr
WHITEFIELD BUNGALOWS
WHITEFIELD LANE
CATHCART CL
GRAVELHILL LANE
WHITLEY THORPE LA
BOOTY LANE
FULHAM LANE
COBCROFT LANE
COBCROFT LA
WRIGHTS LA
STUBBS LANE
LEYS LA
NORTHFIELD LANE
NORTHFIELD CL
WOODHALL LANE
COW LA
MAIN ST
PARK LA
STATION RD
HIGHFIELD LA
HIGHFIELD LANE
BANK WOOD ROAD
NEW ROAD
CHURCHFIELD LANE
SMEATLEY'S LA
CHURCHFIELD LA
WILLOWBRIDGE ROAD
LITTLE LA
LEYS LANE
WEST EDGE ROAD
CHAPEL LA
HODGE LA
WATER LA
MANOR CL
PINFOLD LA
STUBBS ROAD
TANPIT LA
STUBBS LA
STUBBS LANE
COMMON LA
NORTON AND KIRK SMEAT
MIDDLEFIELD LANE
LONG LANE
COAL PIT LA
NORTON MILL LA
WALDEN STUBBS ROAD
BARNSDALE VW
BACK LANE
PRIORY RD
LINKWAY
SPITTLERUSH LANE
WEST END ROAD
CLIFF HL RD
WESTFIELD LANE
GREENGATE ROAD
CRAB TREE LANE
FOX COVERT RD
WHITLEY RD
WINDMILL LA
RYECROFT RD
STYGATE LA
CAMPSALL BALK
HIGH ST
THE CLOSE
PINFOLD LA
STATION RD
CRIDLING GD
NEW ROAD
NORTON CO LA
QUARRY RD
CHURCH FIELD ROAD
GLEBE RD
PARK DR
BEECH RD
CHURCH VW
THE AVE
WOODLANDS RISE
LC
PH
PO
A1 Knottingley, M62
A639 Pontefract
A639 DONCASTER RD
A1
A1 Doncaster (A638)
West Yorkshire STREET ATLAS
South Yorkshire STREET ATLAS
A B C D E F
8 21 7 20 6 19 5 18 4 17 3 16 2 15 1 14
50 51 52 53 54 55

E1
1 TENNYSON AV
2 SHAKESPEARE AV
3 BYRON AV
4 WORDSWORTH AV
5 WELLINGTONIA DR
6 LANGLEYS RD
7 EAST VW
8 GRANGE RD
9 WILLOW RD
10 VAUGHAN RD
11 CAMPSALL PK RD
12 CAMPSALL HALL RD
13 SHERWOOD CL

C3
1 WENTDALE
2 STAN VALLEY
3 SPRINGFIELD CR

E2
1 BROC-O-BANK
2 NEWTHORPE RD
3 FORRESTER'S CL
4 TRAFFORD RD
5 ARUNDEL RD
6 ADELAIDE RD
7 HEADINGLEY RD
8 ORCHARD DR
9 ORCHARD CL
10 RYECROFT AV
11 FIR TREE DR
12 MANOR CL

F2
1 LYNDHURST DR
2 LYNDHURST CL
3 LYNDHURST RI
4 ASHBURNHAM CL
5 ASHBURNHAM WK
6 DENVER RD
7 MANOR GARTH
8 SWAN SYKE DR
9 DRYHURST CL

Scale: 1¼ inches to 1 mile
¼ ½ mile
250m 500m 750m 1 km

62
78

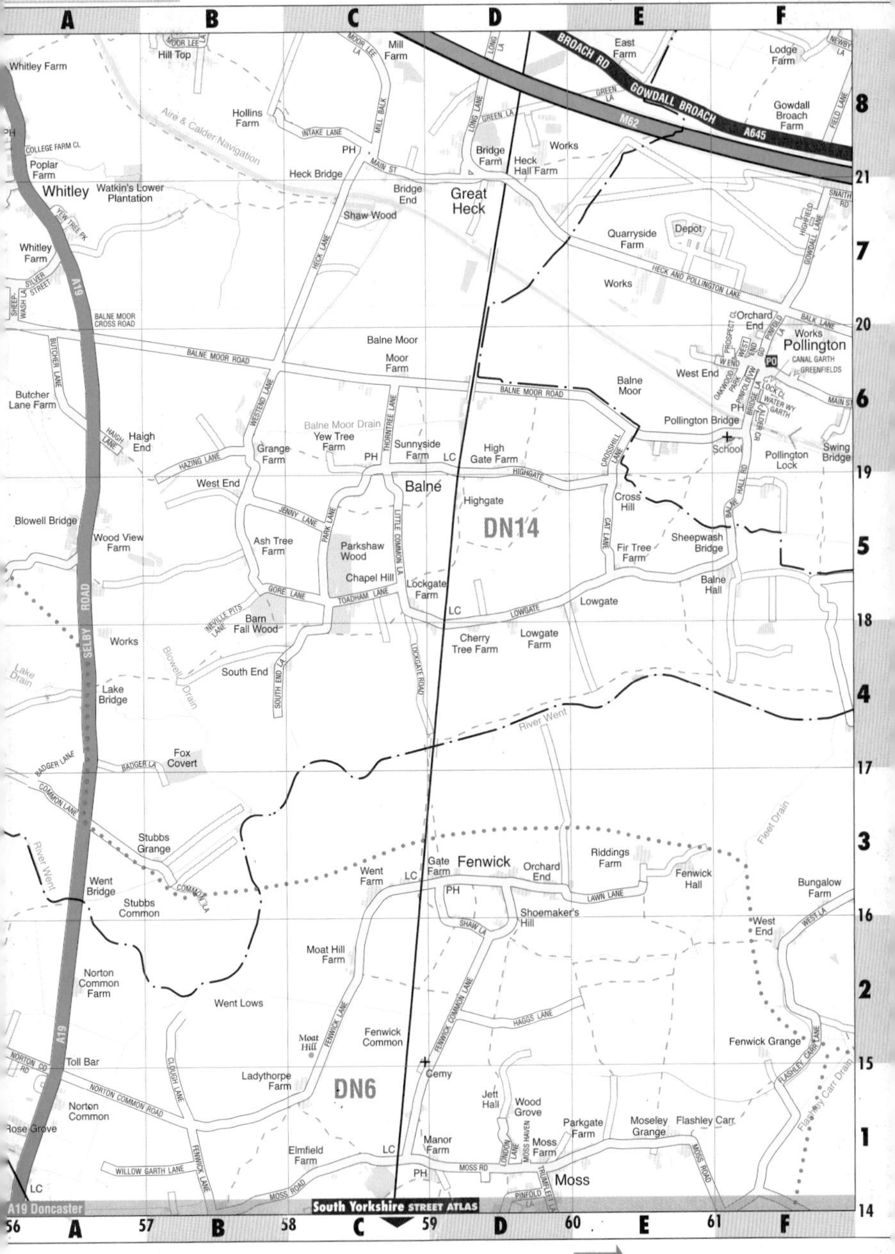

78

77
63

C8
1 ROLAND SIMPSON CL
2 THE CHASE
3 BEAN GDNS
4 SOUTH PARKWAY
5 PARK GDNS
6 OAKDALE CL
7 HALL CL
8 COURT GDNS
9 THE PARKWAY
10 MITTEN AVE
11 WALNUT CRES
12 SYCAMORE CL

Scale: 1¼ inches to 1 mile
0 ¼ ½ mile
0 250m 500m 750m 1 km

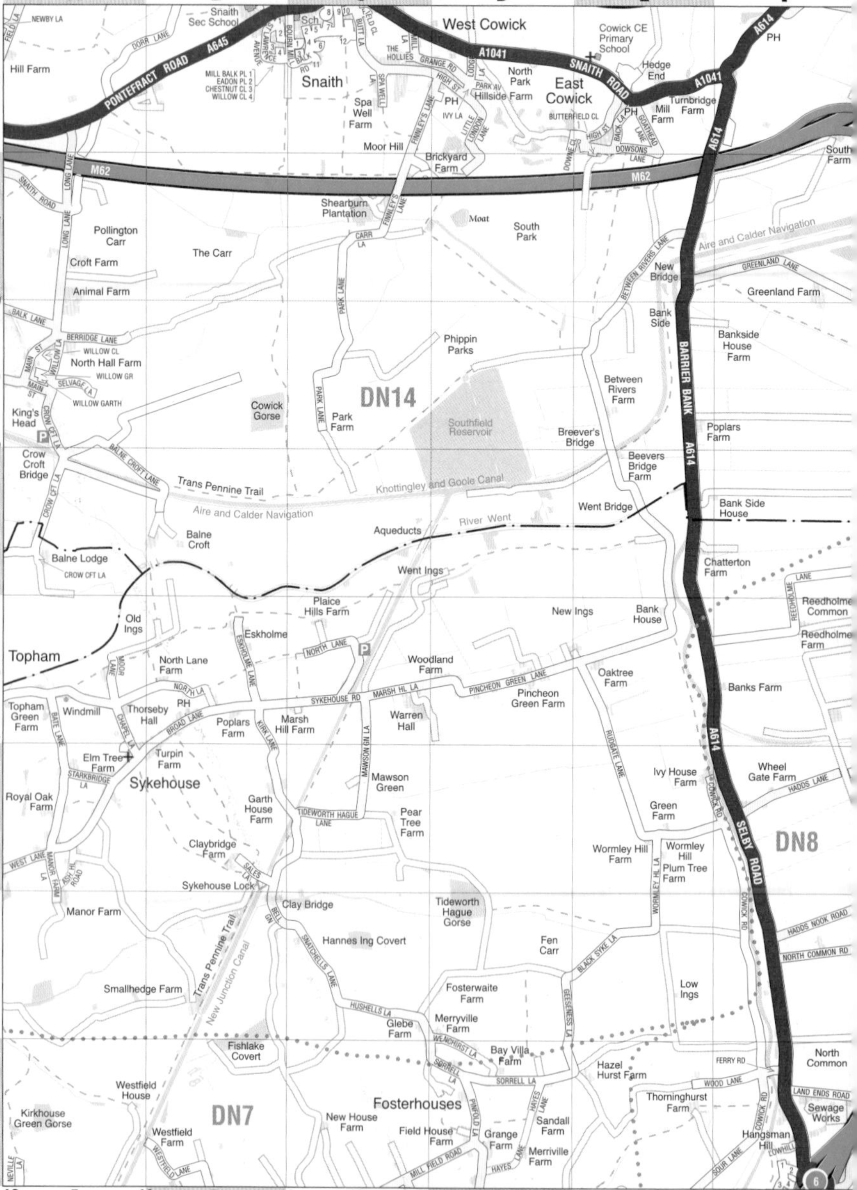

A B C D E F

F1
1 QUAYSIDE 1
2 WATERSIDE RD
3 WATERSIDE
4 QUAY RD

64 80 149

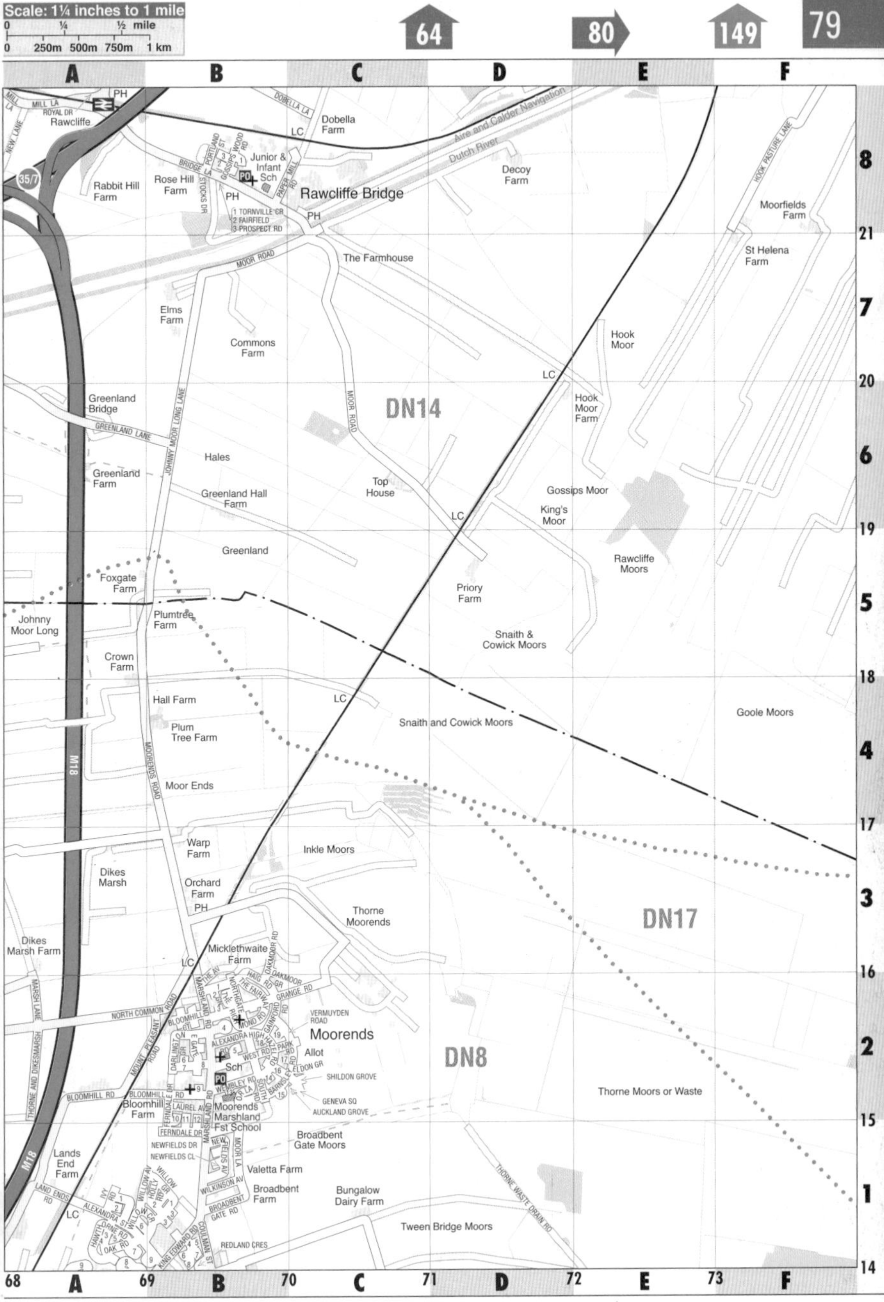

A1
1 WALNUT RD
2 BIRCHWOOD CL
3 CHERRY TREE DR
4 HAWTHORNE AV
5 HAWTHORNE GR
6 WILLOW RD
7 OAK CR
8 CORONA DR
9 HIGHFIELD CR

B1
1 MAPLE RD
2 CEDAR RD
3 WILLOW GR
4 KINGS CT RD
5 JAMES CT
6 EDWARD CT
7 CHARLES CT
8 HENRY CT
9 KING EDWARD CR

B2
1 MICKLETHWAITE RD
2 MICKLETHWAITE GR
3 GRANGE GR
4 BLOOMHILL CL
5 THE HERMITAGE
6 ALDER GR
7 BELVEDERE DR
8 NEWHOLME DR
9 BLOOM HL GR
10 ROWAN CL
11 LABURNUM AV
12 MULBERRY AV
13 DUNELM CR
14 KENTS GD
15 SILKSTONE OVAL
16 LOCARNO RD
17 WINDLESTONE SQ
18 GAINFORD SQ
19 THRISLINGTON SQ

93 80

149 79 65

Scale: 1¼ inches to 1 mile
0 ¼ ½ mile
0 250m 500m 750m 1 km

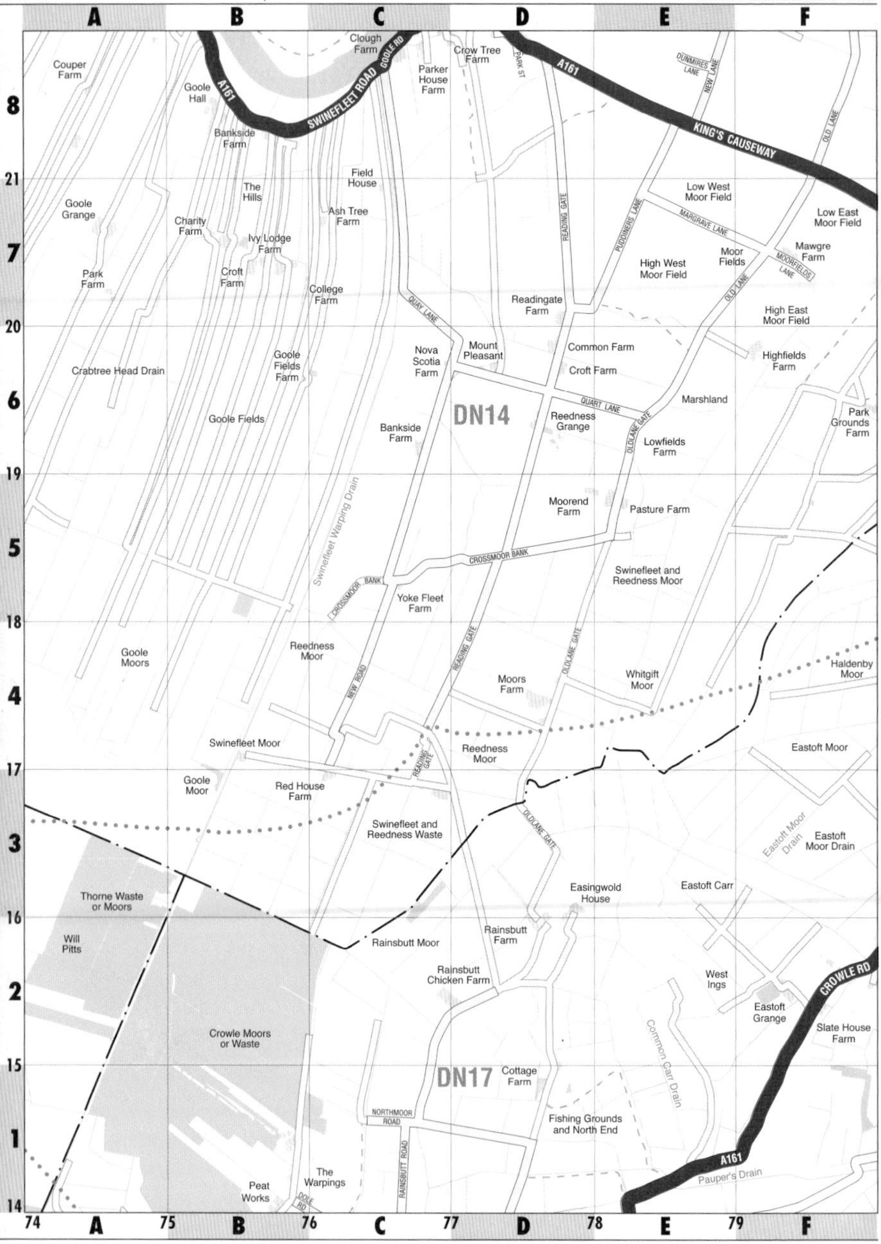
A B C D E F
8 21 7 20 6 19 5 18 4 17 3 16 2 15 1 14
74 75 76 77 78 79
Couper Farm
Clough Farm
GOOLE RD
Crow Tree Farm
Parker House Farm
PARK ST
A161
DUNMIRES LANE
NEW LANE
Goole Hall
SWINEFLEET ROAD
KING'S CAUSEWAY
OLD LANE
Bankside Farm
Field House
The Hills
Low West Moor Field
Goole Grange
Ash Tree Farm
Charity Farm
Ivy Lodge Farm
READING GATE
PUDDINERS LANE
MARGRAVE LANE
Low East Moor Field
Moor Fields
Mawgre Farm
MOORFIELDS LANE
High West Moor Field
Park Farm
Croft Farm
College Farm
Readingate Farm
High East Moor Field
QUAY LANE
Mount Pleasant
Common Farm
Goole Fields Farm
Nova Scotia Farm
Highfields Farm
Crabtree Head Drain
Croft Farm
Marshland
QUART LANE
Park Grounds Farm
DN14
Reedness Grange
Goole Fields
Bankside Farm
OLDLANE GATE
Lowfields Farm
Swinefleet Warping Drain
Moorend Farm
Pasture Farm
CROSSMOOR BANK
Swinefleet and Reedness Moor
Yoke Fleet Farm
Reedness Moor
Goole Moors
NEW ROAD
Moors Farm
Whitgift Moor
Haldenby Moor
Swinefleet Moor
Reedness Moor
Eastoft Moor
Goole Moor
Red House Farm
Swinefleet and Reedness Waste
Eastoft Moor Drain
Eastoft Moor Drain
Thorne Waste or Moors
Easingwold House
Eastoft Carr
Will Pitts
Rainsbutt Moor
Rainsbutt Farm
Rainsbutt Chicken Farm
West Ings
CROWLE RD
Eastoft Grange
Common Carr Drain
Crowle Moors or Waste
Slate House Farm
DN17
Cottage Farm
NORTHMOOR ROAD
Fishing Grounds and North End
RAINSBUTT ROAD
The Warpings
Peat Works
DOLE RD
Pauper's Drain

79 94

Scale: 1¼ inches to 1 mile
0 ¼ ½ mile
0 250m 500m 750m 1 km

66
82

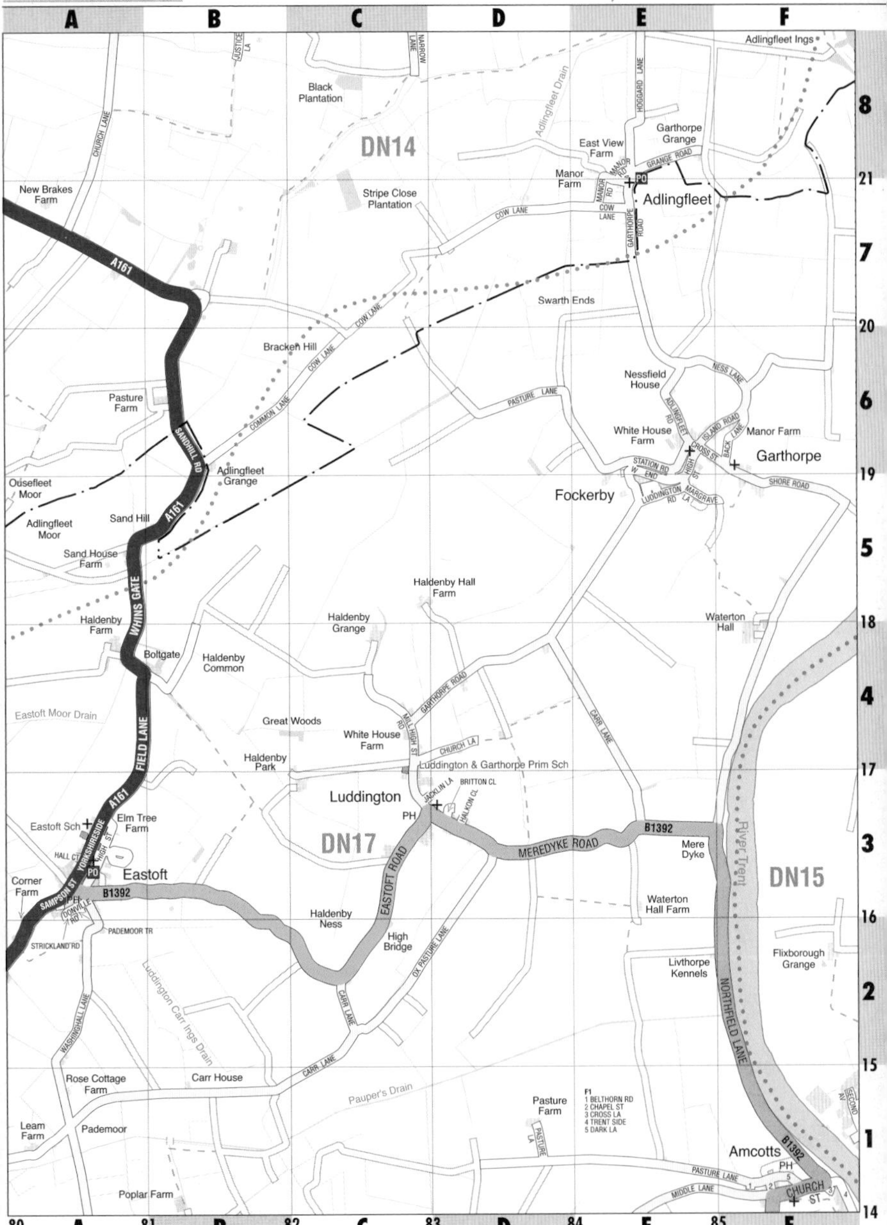

95
82

81
67

Scale: 1¼ inches to 1 mile

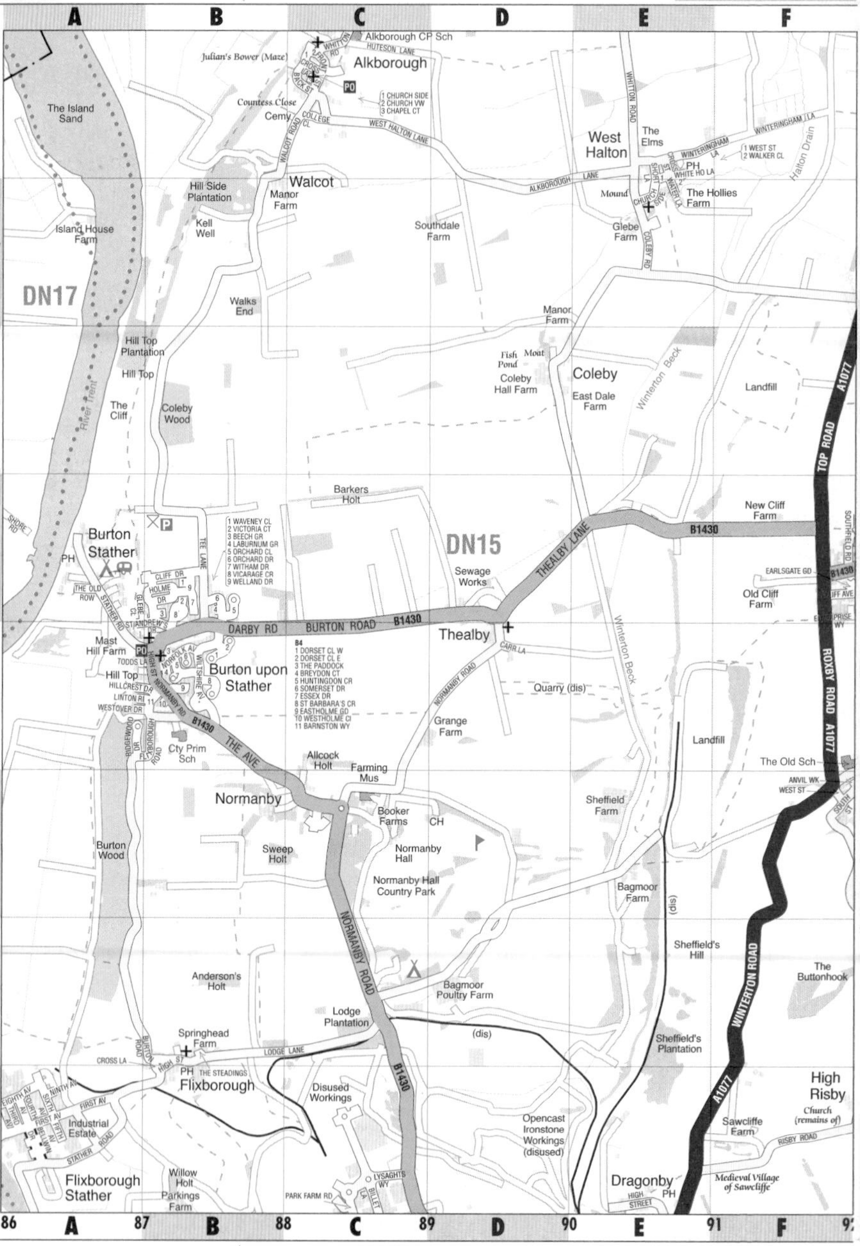

81
96

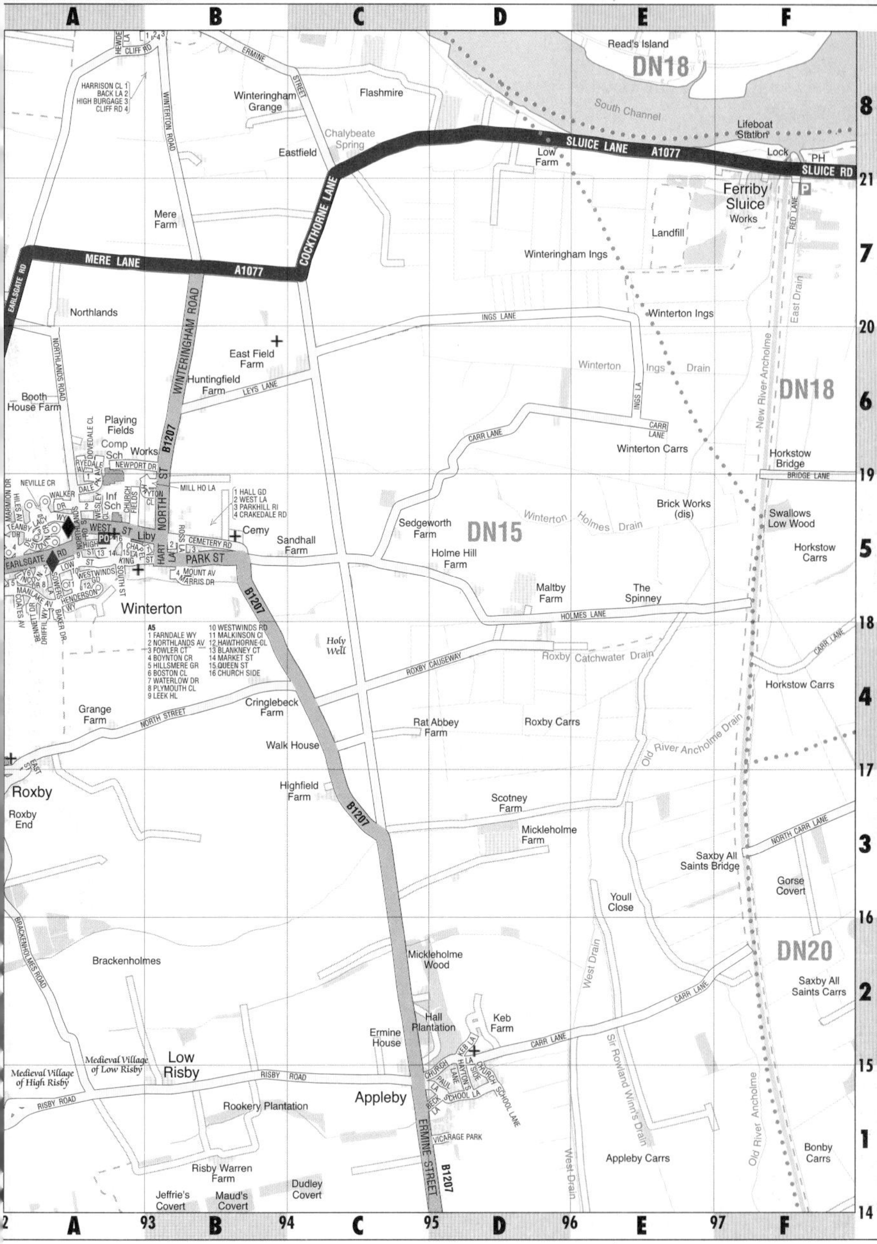
A B C D E F
8 7 6 5 4 3 2 1
21 20 19 18 17 16 15 14
Read's Island
DN18
South Channel
Lifeboat Station
Lock
PH
SLUICE LANE A1077
SLUICE RD
Ferriby Sluice
Works
Landfill
Low Farm
Flashmire
Winteringham Grange
Chalybeate Spring
Eastfield
COCKTHORNE LANE
MERE LANE A1077
Mere Farm
EARLSGATE RD
WINTERTON ROAD
WINTERINGHAM ROAD
ERMINE STREET
CLIFF RD
HEWDE LA
HARRISON CL 1
BACK LA 2
HIGH BURGAGE 3
CLIFF RD 4
Winteringham Ings
Winterton Ings
INGS LANE
INGS LA
Winterton Ings Drain
East Drain
New River Ancholme
RED LANE
DN18
Northlands
NORTHLANDS ROAD
East Field Farm
Huntingfield Farm
LEYS LANE
Booth House Farm
Playing Fields
Comp Sch
Works
B1207
NEWPORT DR
CARR LANE
Winterton Carrs
Horkstow Bridge
BRIDGE LANE
NEVILLE CR
MILL HO LA
1 HALL GD
2 WEST LA
3 PARKHILL RI
4 CRAKEDALE RD
Inf Sch
Liby
PO
WEST ST
NORTH ST
Cemy
CEMETERY RD
PARK ST
Sandhall Farm
Sedgeworth Farm
DN15
Winterton Holmes Drain
Brick Works (dis)
Swallows Low Wood
Horkstow Carrs
Holme Hill Farm
Maltby Farm
The Spinney
HOLMES LANE
MOUNT AV
MARRIS DR
Winterton
A5
1 FARNDALE WY
2 NORTHLANDS AV
3 FOWLER CT
4 BOYNTON CR
5 HILLSMERE GR
6 BOSTON CL
7 WATERLOW DR
8 PLYMOUTH CL
9 LEEK HL
10 WESTWINDS RD
11 MALKINSON CL
12 HAWTHORNE CL
13 BLANKNEY CT
14 MARKET ST
15 QUEEN ST
16 CHURCH SIDE
Holy Well
ROXBY CAUSEWAY
Roxby Catchwater Drain
CARR LANE
Horkstow Carrs
Grange Farm
NORTH STREET
Cringlebeck Farm
Rat Abbey Farm
Roxby Carrs
Walk House
Old River Ancholme Drain
Roxby
Roxby End
Highfield Farm
Scotney Farm
Mickleholme Farm
NORTH CARR LANE
Saxby All Saints Bridge
Gorse Covert
Youll Close
West Drain
DN20
BRACKENHOLMES ROAD
Brackenholmes
Mickleholme Wood
Saxby All Saints Carrs
Hall Plantation
Keb Farm
Ermine House
CARR LANE
Sir Rowland Winn's Drain
Medieval Village of Low Risby
Medieval Village of High Risby
Low Risby
RISBY ROAD
Appleby
Rookery Plantation
SCHOOL LANE
VICARAGE PARK
Old River Ancholme
Appleby Carrs
Bonby Carrs
Risby Warren Farm
Jeffrie's Covert
Maud's Covert
Dudley Covert
ERMINE STREET B1207
2 93 94 95 96 97

A7
1 BEAULAH VILLAS
2 BEAULAHLAND
3 SKINNERS LA
4 QUEEN ELIZABETH AVE
5 OLD POST OFFICE LA

83

69

E8
1 SUNNYBANK
2 TOFTS RD
3 BRADWELL CL
4 MILSON CL
5 PELHAM CL
6 MASONS CT
7 NICHOLAS CT
8 GEORGINA CT
9 GODDARD CL
10 HARROWDYKE
11 BERETUN GN
12 GRANGE AV
13 MOUNT AV
14 BEACON AV
15 PARKDALE
16 ELMDALE
17 WELTON CL
18 STEVENSON'S WY
19 HARVEST AV
20 SHARPE CL

Scale: 1¼ inches to 1 mile
0 ¼ ½ mile
0 250m 500m 750m 1 km

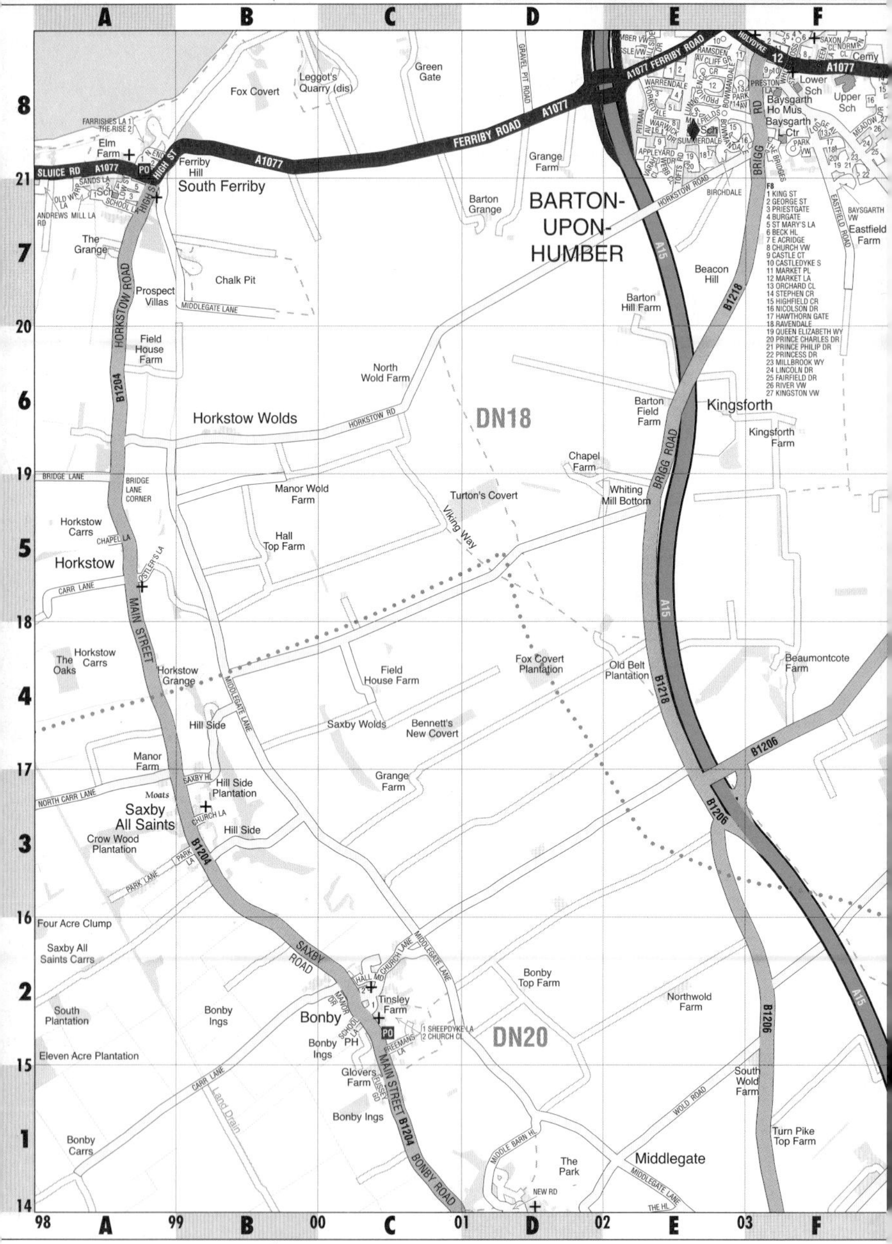

83

98

Scale: 1¼ inches to 1 mile
0 ¼ ½ mile
0 250m 500m 750m 1 km

70
86

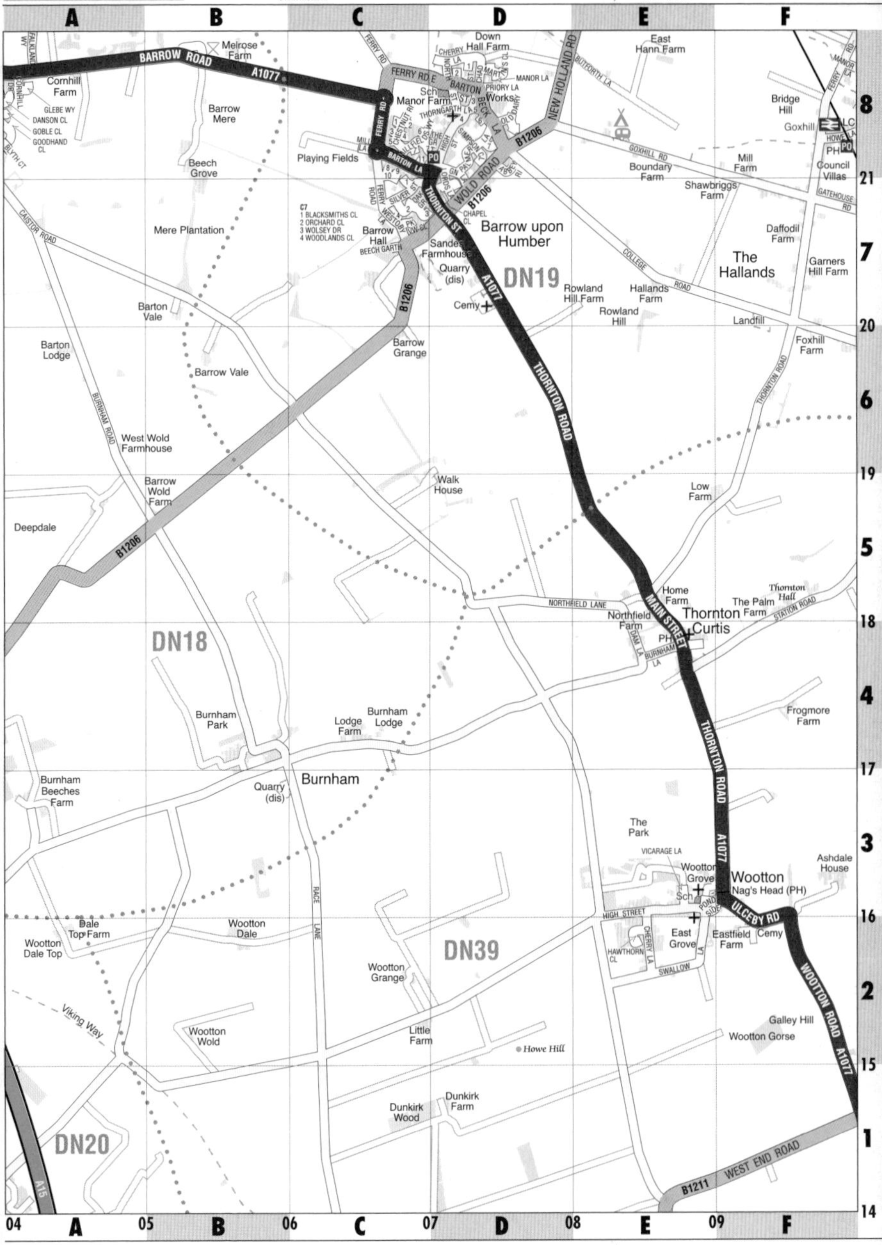

99
86

A8
1 STOTHARDS LA
2 GREENGATE LA
3 PIDGEON COTE LA
4 WESTFIELD RD
5 CHURCH ST

85
71

Scale: 1¼ inches to 1 mile
0 ¼ ½ mile
0 250m 500m 750m 1 km

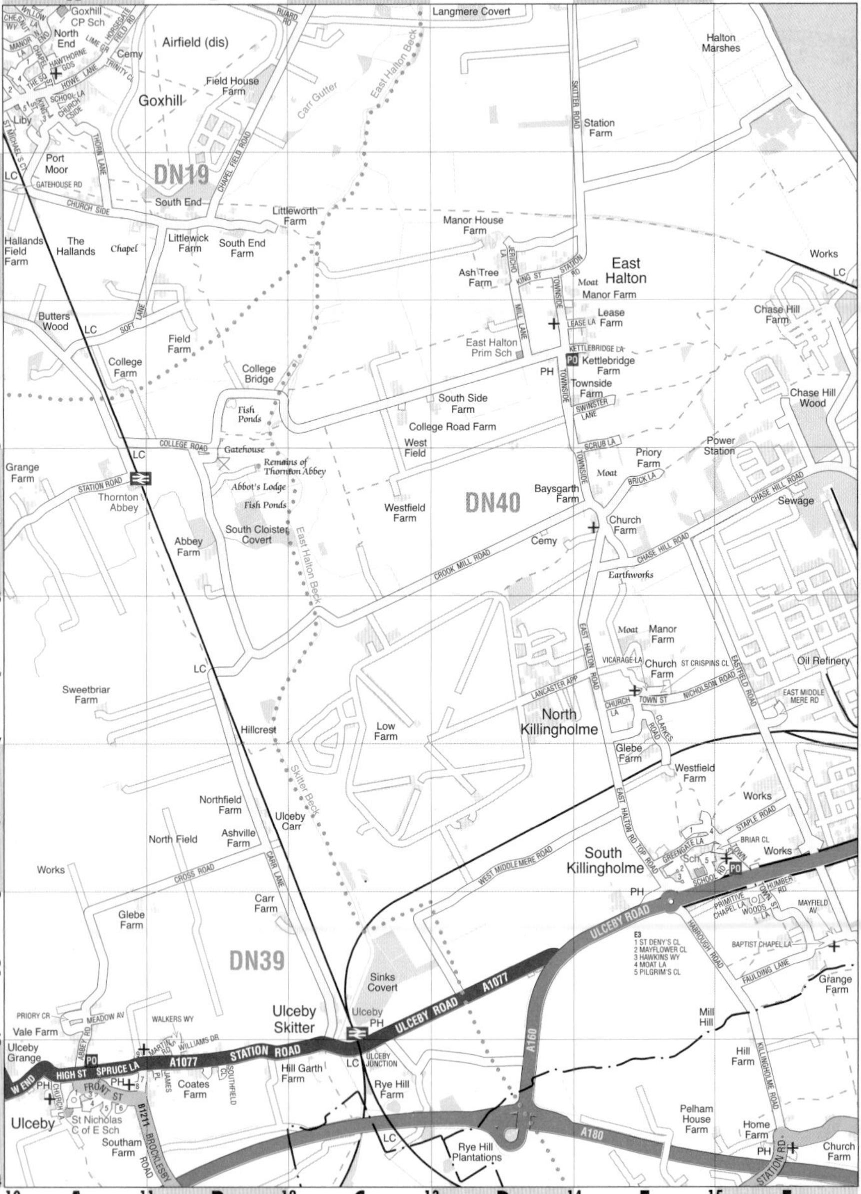

A1
1 HALLCROFT
2 STEPHEN CL
3 FORGE CR
4 MOUNT ROYALE CL
5 PITMOOR LA
6 NELTHORPE CL
7 CORONATION RD
8 PARKS CL
9 ADVENT CT

85
100

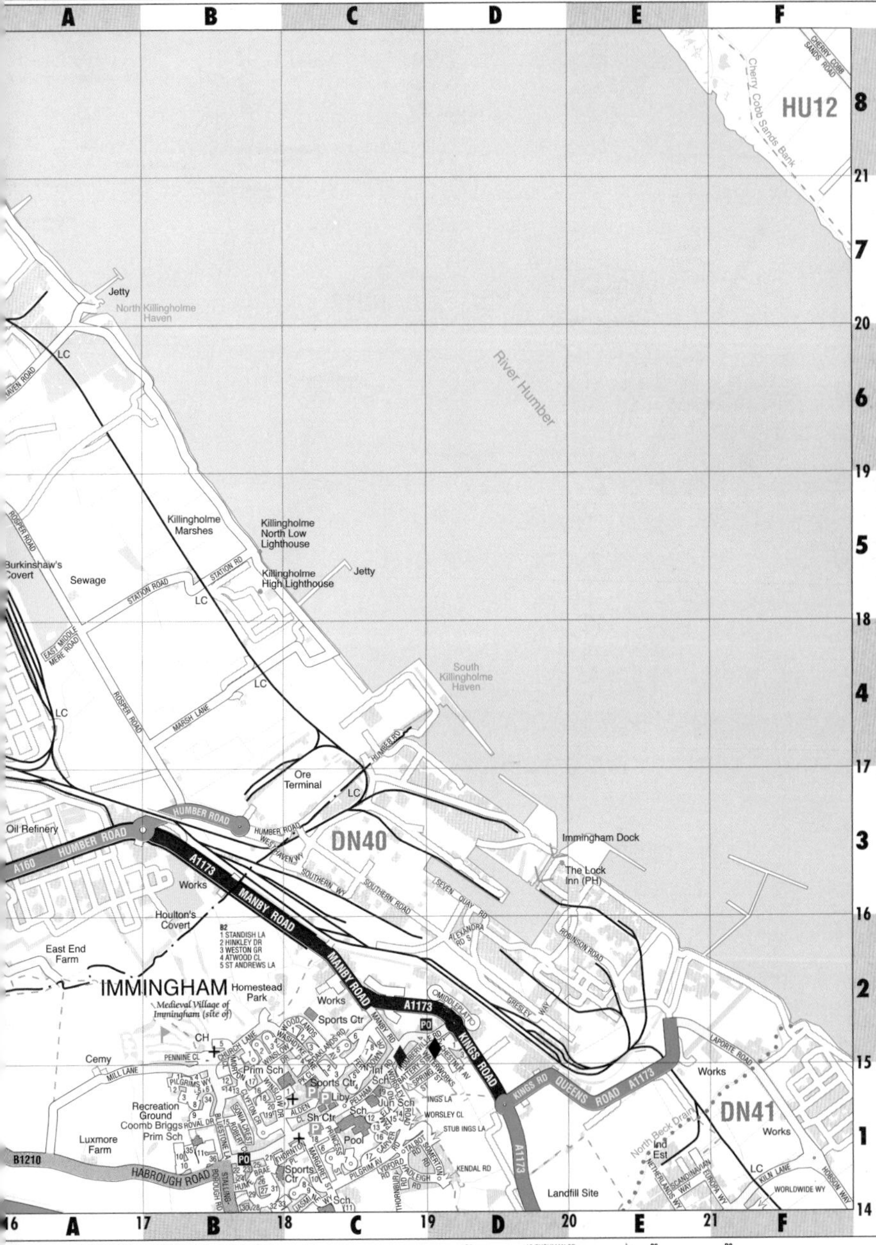
A
B
C
D
E
F
8
21
7
20
6
19
5
18
4
17
3
16
2
15
1
14
16
17
18
19
20
21
HU12
Cherry Cobb Sands Bank
CHERRY COBB SANDS ROAD
Jetty
North Killingholme Haven
River Humber
Killingholme Marshes
Killingholme North Low Lighthouse
Killingholme High Lighthouse
Jetty
Burkinshaw's Covert
Sewage
STATION ROAD
ROSPER ROAD
EAST MIDDLE MERE ROAD
MARSH LANE
South Killingholme Haven
Ore Terminal
HUMBER RD
HUMBER ROAD
Oil Refinery
A160
DN40
Immingham Dock
The Lock Inn (PH)
WEST HAVEN WY
SOUTHERN WY
SOUTHERN ROAD
SEVEN QUAY RD
ALEXANDRA RD S
ROBINSON ROAD
GRESLEY WAY
A1173
MANBY ROAD
Works
Houlton's Covert
B2
1 STANDISH LA
2 HINKLEY DR
3 WESTON GR
4 ATWOOD CL
5 ST ANDREWS LA
East End Farm
IMMINGHAM
Homestead Park
Medieval Village of Immingham (site of)
Works
Sports Ctr
MIDDLEPLATT RD
KINGS ROAD
QUEENS ROAD
KINGS RD
LAPORTE ROAD
Works
DN41
Works
CH
Cemy
PENNINE CL
MILL LANE
CHURCH LANE
Prim Sch
Sports Ctr
Inf Sch
Liby
Jun Sch
Sch
Pool
Sh Ctr
Recreation Ground
Coomb Briggs Prim Sch
Luxmore Farm
B1210
HABROUGH ROAD
ROYAL DR
INGS LA
WORSLEY CL
STUB INGS LA
KENDAL RD
North Beck Drain
Ind Est
Landfill Site
NETHERLANDS WY
SCANDINAVIAN WAY
EUROPA WY
KILN LANE
WORLDWIDE WY
HOBSON WAY
LC

B1
1 MAIDEN CL
2 VIKING CL
3 MILLHOUSE RI
4 CLEVELAND CL
5 HAZEL CFT
6 LYDIA CT
7 JACKSON MS
8 ST ANDREWS WY
9 HELEN CR
10 ANCHOLME AV
11 STEEPING DR
12 HOLLINGSWORTH AV
13 LANSDOWN RD
14 BALFOUR PL
15 STAINTON DR
16 AINSWORTH RD
17 HOLBECK PL
18 LEYDEN CL
19 CHILTON CL
20 BRADFORD RD
21 BLOSSOM WY
22 HIGHFIELD AV
23 LINDUM AV
24 MACKENZIE PL
25 CLARENCE CL
26 BOWMAN WY
27 HAMISH WK
28 KINLOCH WY
29 JAMES WY
30 KISHORN CT
31 HIGHLAND TARN
32 OBAN CT
33 PADDOCK CT
34 VALDA VALE
35 CALDER CL
36 AIRE CL

101

C1
1 ALLERTON DR
2 SPINNEY CL
3 BEECHWOOD AV
4 MUIRFIELD CFT
5 BERWICK CT
6 MAYFLOWER AV
7 ROUNDWAY
8 JAPONICA HL
9 MAGNOLIA RI
10 CUSHMAN CR
11 ORKNEY PL
12 DEANE RD
13 EATON RD
14 SACKVILLE CL
15 SACKVILLE RD
16 COLLIER RD
17 BREWSTER AV
18 CRAIK HILL AV
19 PAM CL

88

C2
1 COPSE CL
2 CEDAR DR
3 MAPLE GR
4 ROSE GD
5 ASH TREE CL
6 HOYLAKE DR
7 SUNNINGDALE DR
8 BIRKDALE DR

D2
1 HAWTHORN AV
2 LARCH CL
3 TRENCHARD CL

Scale: 1¼ inches to 1 mile
0 ¼ ½ mile
0 250m 500m 750m 1 km

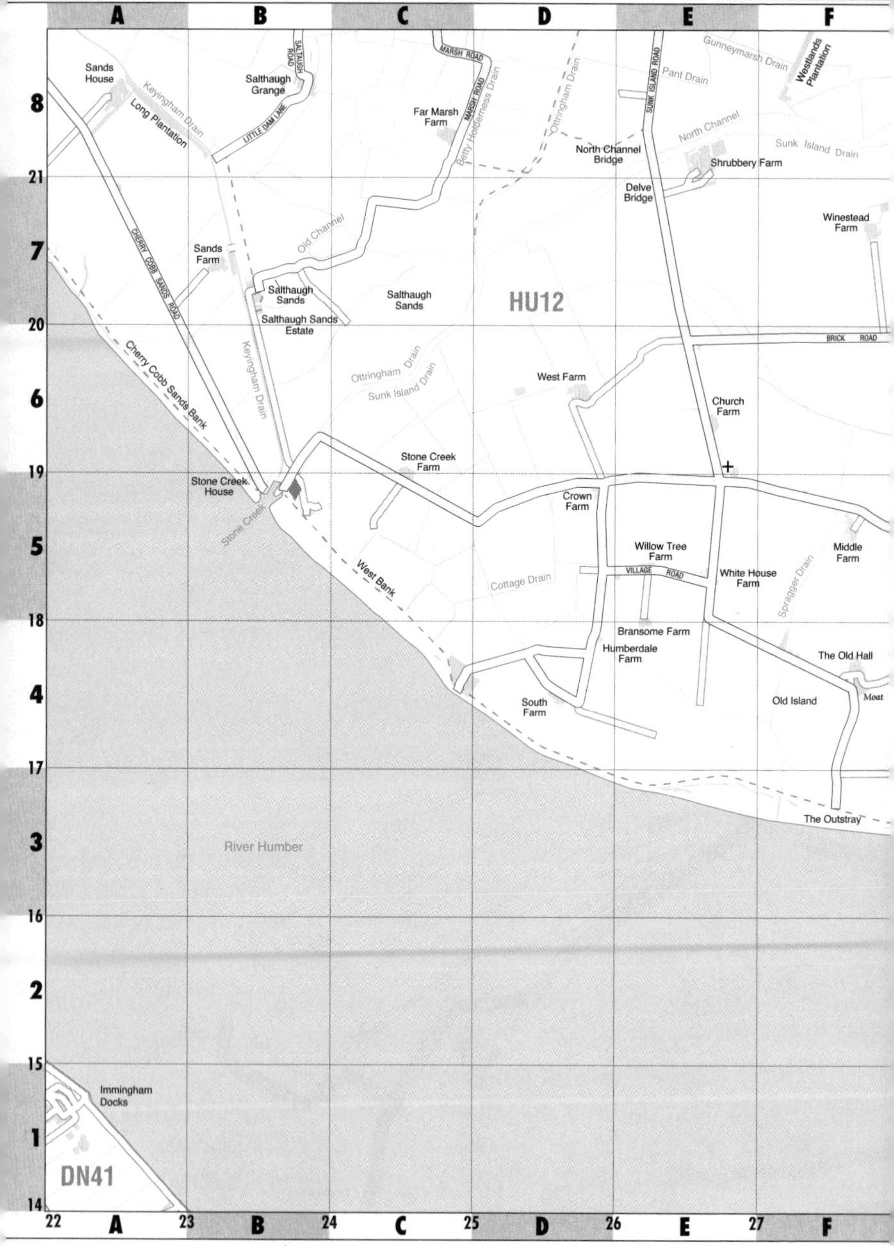

Scale: 1¼ inches to 1 mile
0 ¼ ½ mile
0 250m 500m 750m 1 km

74
90

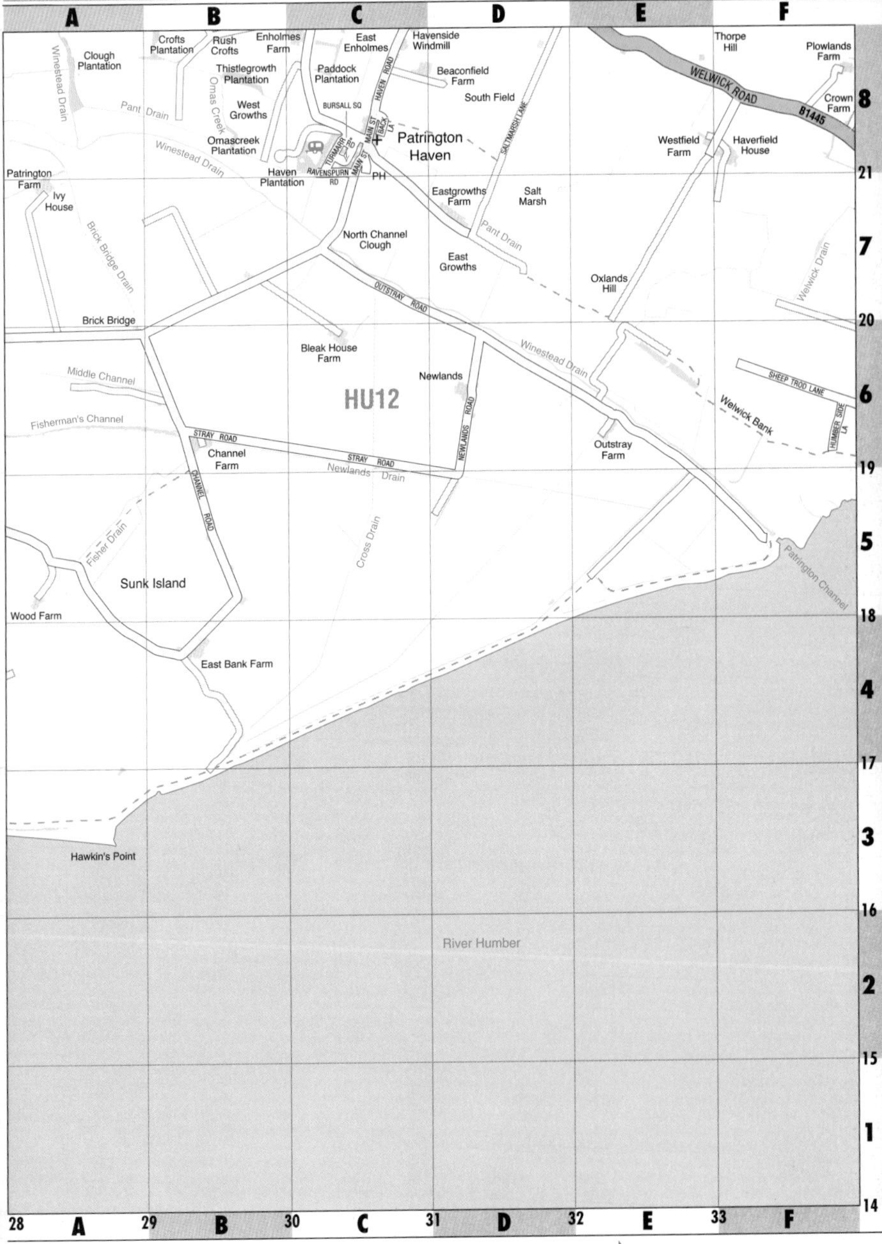
A
B
C
D
E
F
Clough Plantation
Crofts Plantation
Rush Crofts
Enholmes Farm
East Enholmes
Havenside Windmill
Thorpe Hill
Plowlands Farm
Winestead Drain
Thistlegrowth Plantation
Paddock Plantation
HAVEN ROAD
Beaconfield Farm
WELWICK ROAD
Pant Drain
Omas Creek
West Growths
BURSALL SQ
South Field
B1445
Crown Farm
MAIN ST
BACK LA
Patrington Haven
SALTMARSH LANE
Omascreek Plantation
TURMARR RD
Westfield Farm
Haverfield House
Winestead Drain
Haven Plantation
RAVENSPURN RD
PH
Patrington Farm
Ivy House
Eastgrowths Farm
Salt Marsh
Brick Bridge Drain
Pant Drain
North Channel Clough
East Growths
Welwick Drain
Oxlands Hill
OUTSTRAY ROAD
Brick Bridge
Bleak House Farm
Winestead Drain
Middle Channel
Newlands
SHEEP TROD LANE
HU12
Welwick Bank
Fisherman's Channel
NEWLANDS ROAD
HUMBER SIDE LA
STRAY ROAD
Outstray Farm
Channel Farm
STRAY ROAD
Newlands Drain
CHANNEL ROAD
Cross Drain
Fisher Drain
Patrington Channel
Sunk Island
Wood Farm
East Bank Farm
Hawkin's Point
River Humber
8
21
7
20
6
19
5
18
4
17
3
16
2
15
1
14
28
29
30
31
32
33

103
90

89
75

Scale: 1¼ inches to 1 mile
0 ¼ ½ mile
0 250m 500m 750m 1 km

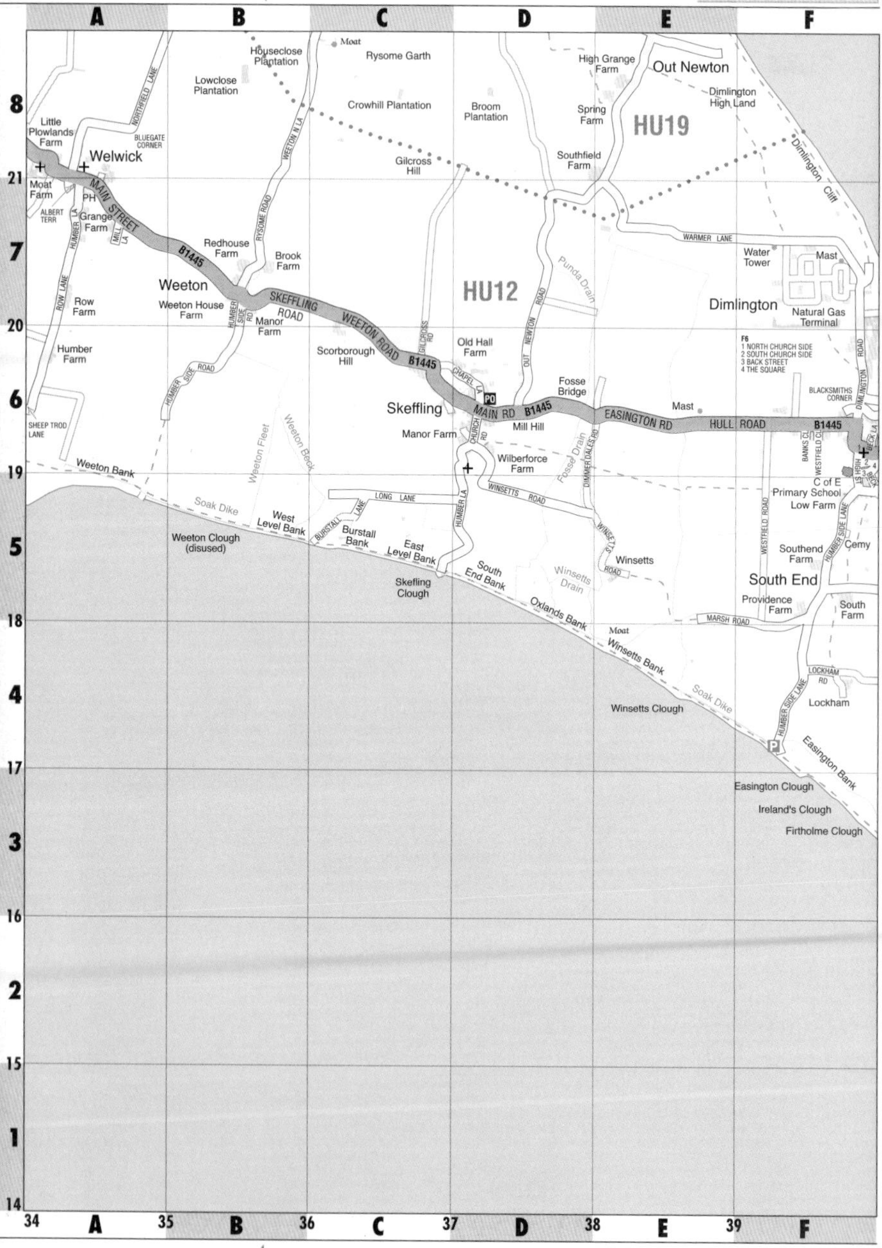
A
B
C
D
E
F
Houseclose Plantation
Moat
Rysome Garth
High Grange Farm
Out Newton
Lowclose Plantation
NORTHFIELD LANE
Crowhill Plantation
Broom Plantation
Spring Farm
Dimlington High Land
HU19
Little Plowlands Farm
BLUEGATE CORNER
WEETON N LA
Welwick
Gilcross Hill
Southfield Farm
Dimlington Cliff
Moat Farm
PH
MAIN STREET
ALBERT TERR
Grange Farm
MILL LA
HUMBER LA
RYSOME ROAD
Redhouse Farm
B1445
Brook Farm
WARMER LANE
Water Tower
Mast
Weeton
HU12
Punda Drain
ROW LANE
Row Farm
Weeton House Farm
HUMBER SIDE RD
Manor Farm
SKEFFLING ROAD
WEETON ROAD
OUT NEWTON ROAD
Dimlington
Natural Gas Terminal
Humber Farm
Scorborough Hill
GILCROSS RD
Old Hall Farm
F6
1 NORTH CHURCH SIDE
2 SOUTH CHURCH SIDE
3 BACK STREET
4 THE SQUARE
HUMBER SIDE ROAD
CHAPEL LA
DIMLINGTON ROAD
Fosse Bridge
BLACKSMITHS CORNER
PO
Mast
SHEEP TROD LANE
Skeffling
MAIN RD
EASINGTON RD
HULL ROAD
Mill Hill
Manor Farm
CHURCH RD
DIMMER DALES RD
BANKS CL
WESTFIELD CL
BECK LA
HIGH ST
Weeton Bank
Weeton Fleet
Weeton Beck
Wilberforce Farm
Fosse Drain
C of E Primary School
WINSETTS ROAD
LONG LANE
Low Farm
Soak Dike
West Level Bank
BURSTALL LANE
Burstall Bank
HUMBER LA
WESTFIELD ROAD
HUMBER SIDE LANE
Weeton Clough (disused)
East Level Bank
WINSETTS ROAD
Winsetts
Southend Farm
Cemy
Skeffling Clough
South End Bank
Winsetts Drain
South End
Providence Farm
South Farm
Oxlands Bank
MARSH ROAD
Moat
Winsetts Bank
LOCKHAM RD
Lockham
Soak Dike
Winsetts Clough
HUMBER SIDE LANE
P
Easington Bank
Easington Clough
Ireland's Clough
Firtholme Clough
8
21
7
20
6
19
5
18
4
17
3
16
2
15
1
14
34
35
36
37
38
39

89

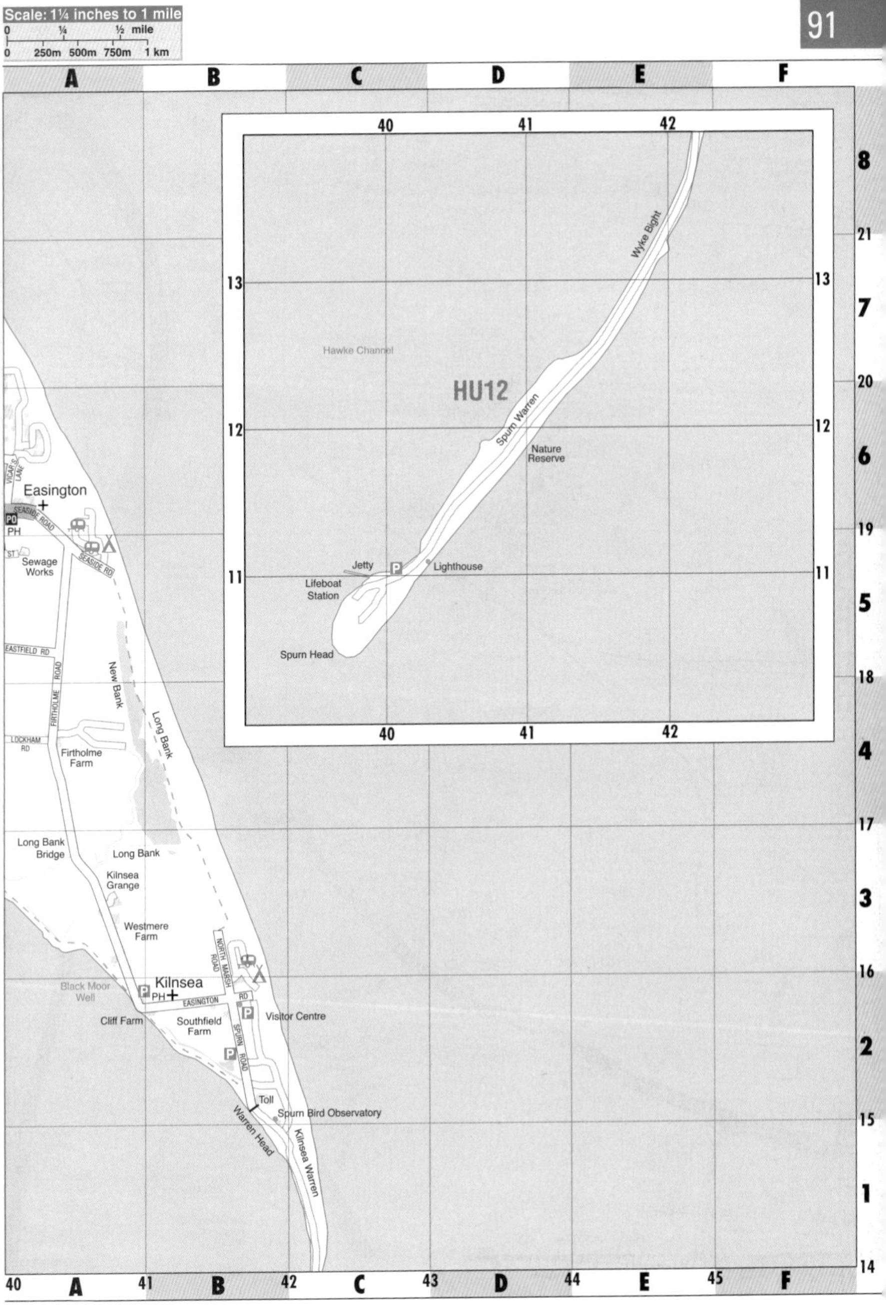
Scale: 1¼ inches to 1 mile
0 ¼ ½ mile
0 250m 500m 750m 1 km
A B C D E F
8 7 6 5 4 3 2 1
21 20 19 18 17 16 15 14
40 41 42 43 44 45
40 41 42
13 12 11
Wyke Bight
Hawke Channel
HU12
Spurn Warren
Nature Reserve
Jetty
Lighthouse
Lifeboat Station
Spurn Head
VICAR'S LANE
Easington
PO
PH
SEASIDE ROAD
SEASIDE RD
ST
Sewage Works
EASTFIELD RD
FIRTHOLME ROAD
New Bank
Long Bank
LOCKHAM RD
Firtholme Farm
Long Bank Bridge
Long Bank
Kilnsea Grange
Westmere Farm
NORTH MARSH ROAD
Black Moor Well
Kilnsea
PH
EASINGTON RD
Cliff Farm
Southfield Farm
Visitor Centre
SPURN ROAD
Toll
Spurn Bird Observatory
Warren Head
Kilnsea Warren

C6
1 SILVER ST
2 NEW GREEN
3 THORNE RD
4 BREEZEMOUNT CT
5 KENNETH AV
6 ASHFIELD GR
7 BEECH CR
8 NUTFIELDS GR
9 DR ANDERSON AV
10 CROSSWAYS
11 HOLME GD
12 BOOTHAM RD
13 DUKE ST
14 KINGSWAY
15 STANLEY GD
16 STANLEY RD
17 THOMAS RD

78

E4
1 AMBROSE AV
2 BRABBS AV
3 WESTFIELD VILLAS
4 WESTFIELD RD
5 SPRINGFIELD AV
6 LEYLAND AV
7 BROCKENHURST RD
8 MANOR GD
9 EPWORTH RD (WEST)

Scale: 1¼ inches to 1 mile
0 ¼ ½ mile
0 250m 500m 750m 1 km

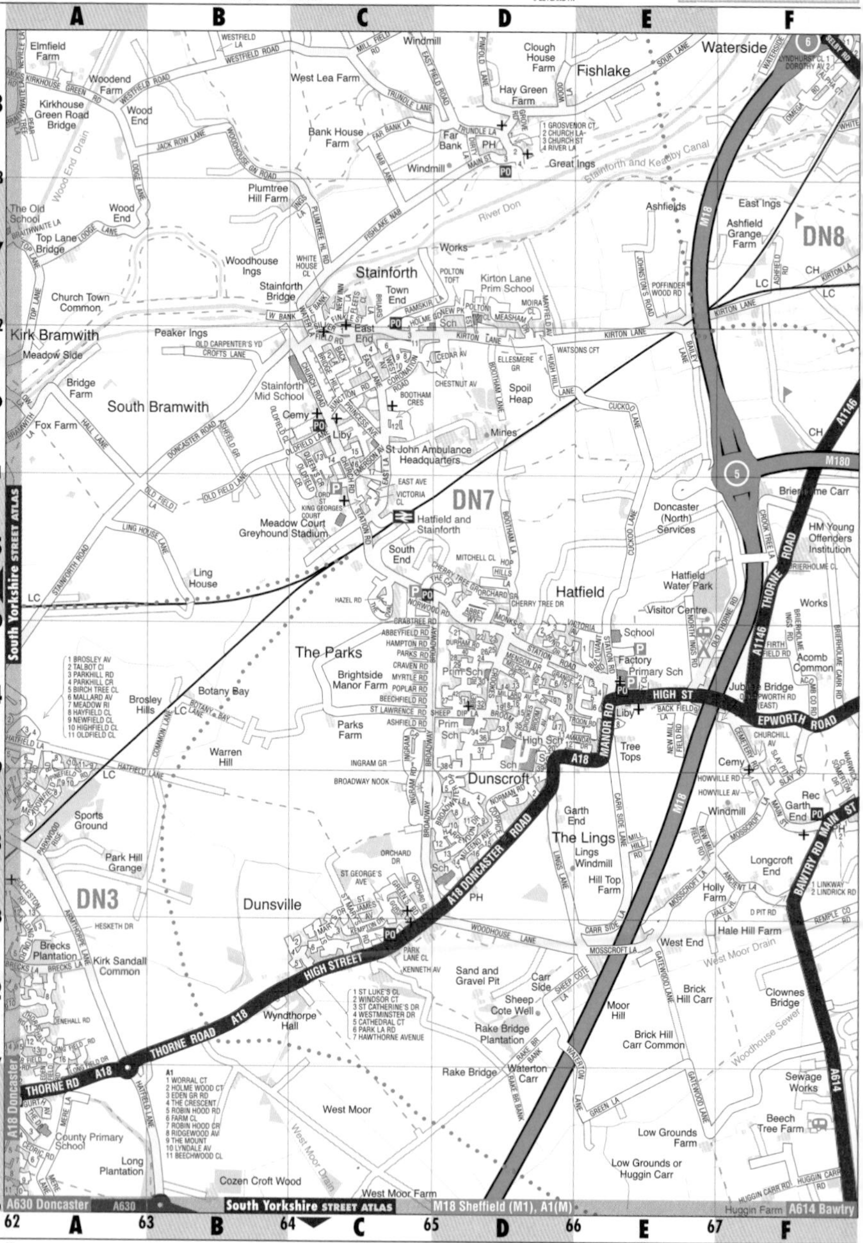

A2
1 TYNEDALE CT
2 GRANGE PK
3 TARLETON CL
4 HAREWOOD AV
5 CURZEN CR
6 ELIZABETH AV
7 REDHALL CL
8 NEWHALL RD
9 DERWENT DR
10 WINDERMERE CR
11 FERNHALL CL
12 EDEN FIELD RD
13 HARVEST CL
14 EDENCROFT DR
15 FAR FIELD CL
16 MEADOW CFT

A3
1 THE SPINNEY
2 ST ANDREW'S WY
3 LIMEDALE VW
4 PINEFIELD AV
5 MILL FIELD CT
6 GREENFIELD CL
7 HEATHFIELD CL
8 WHEATFIELD CL
9 LOWFIELD CL
10 THOROLD PL
11 SUTTON RD
12 LONGTON RD

D3
1 COPPICE LA
2 DANUM RD
3 NORMAN DR
4 ASTON GN
5 BRETTON CL
6 HARPENDON DR
7 WIDFORD GN
8 AMWELL GN
9 BARNET GN
10 AYOTS GN
11 SHENLEY CL
12 HARPENDEN CL
13 HODDESDON CR
14 NASEBY CL
15 BLENHEIM CL
16 BOSWORTH CL

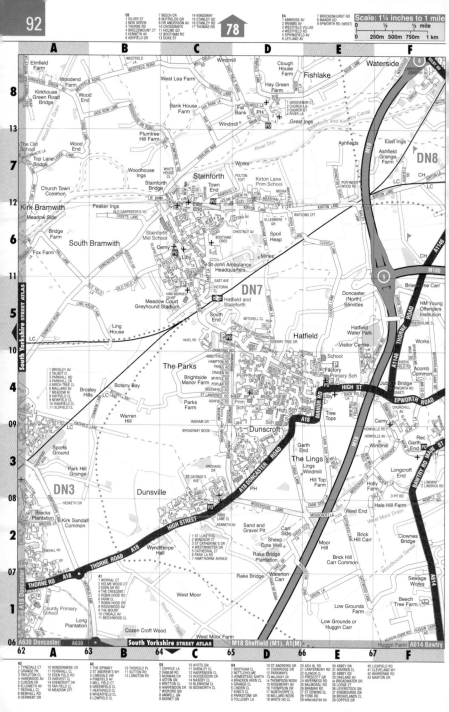

D4
1 BOOTHAM CL
2 NETTLEHOLME
3 HOMESTEAD GARTH
4 BRACKEN HEEN CL
5 GRANGE CL
6 LINDEN CL
7 KING'S CL
8 PARKSTONE GR
9 TOLLESBY LA
10 ST ANDREWS GR
11 COOKRIDGE DR
12 PARKWAYS
13 MILCROFT CR
14 THOMPSON NOOK
15 ROSEBERRY AV
16 THOMPSON DR
17 NUNTHORPE CL
18 MILLARD NOOK
19 WHITE HO CL
20 ASH HL RD
21 CANTERBURY RD
22 GLENCOE CL
23 PRESCOTT GR
24 INVERNESS RD
25 BALMORAL RD
26 BRAMAR RD
27 ST EDWINS CL
28 YORK RD
29 WINCHESTER RD
30 ABBEY GN
31 WARREN CL
32 ABBEY GD
33 OAKLAND AV
34 BROADWATER DR
35 LODGE CT
36 LEVERSTOCK GN
37 KINSBOURNE GN
38 BROADLANDS CL
39 COPPICE GR
40 LICHFIELD RD
41 CLEVELAND WY
42 WARRENNE RD
43 MARTON DR

Scale: 1¼ inches to 1 mile
0 ¼ ½ mile
0 250m 500m 750m 1 km

A8
1 CASSON'S RD
2 HIGHFIELD CR
3 MARSDEN G
4 LIME TREE GR
5 UPR KENYON ST
6 LWR KENYON ST
7 BELLWOOD CR
8 BROOKFIELD CL
9 FOSTER RD
10 DURHAM AV
11 GODFREY RD
12 BOATING DYKE WY
13 CAPSTAN WY
14 ASHBURNHAM RD
15 BROWNS LA
16 QUEEN ST
17 QUEEN'S CT
18 CHAPEL LA
19 BELLE VUE TR
20 THE GREEN
21 HORSE FAIR GN
22 FAIRTREE WK
23 MIDDLEBROOK LA
24 SILVER ST
25 PINFOLD LANE
26 DUNSTAN DR
27 CLIFTON CT

79

B8
1 INGLENOOK DR
2 REDLAND CR
3 ALBERT ST
4 COULMAN RD
5 COULMAN ST
6 LOCKWOOD CL
7 TENNYSON AV
8 CHURCH CL
9 HAYNES GN
10 HOUPS RD
11 LITTLEWOOD RD
12 COVENTRY RD
13 TITHE BARN LA
14 DANUM CL
15 HAYNES GD
16 TRAVIS CL
17 TRAVIS GR
18 TRAVIS AV
19 ALWYN RD

94

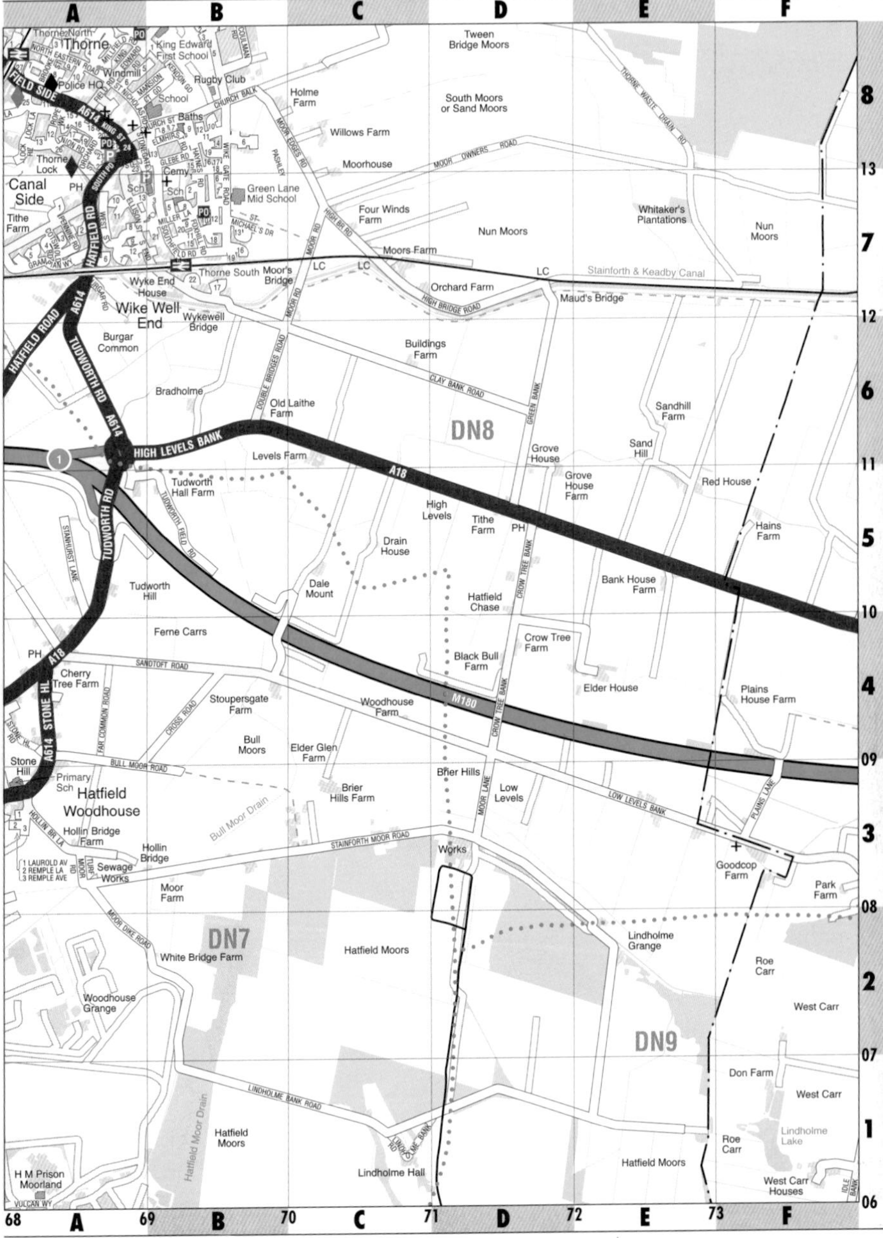

A7
1 ASHFIELD AV
2 CANAL VW
3 CHEVIOT CL
4 MALVERN CL
5 QUANTOCK CL
6 MARINA VW
7 WENDAN RD
8 WEST CT
9 PICKERING GR
10 PARK VIEW
11 PARK CRES
12 SOUTH WOOD DR
13 ASH TREE RD

B7
1 HAYNES GR
2 HAYNES CL
3 CHESTNUT AV
4 ELM TREE GR
5 PEEL HL RD
6 WIKE GATE GR
7 WIKE GATE CL
8 PEEL CASTLE RD
9 MARLBOROUGH RD
10 MILLER CL
11 OLDFIELD RD
12 FENLAND RD
13 ST MICHAEL'S CL
14 SOUTHFIELD CL
15 AXHOLME GN
16 ST GEORGES RD
17 SWANLAND CL
18 MOWBRAY ROAD
19 ST GEORGES CL
20 PASHLEY ROAD
21 BEECH TREE AVE
22 THE CROFT

104

94

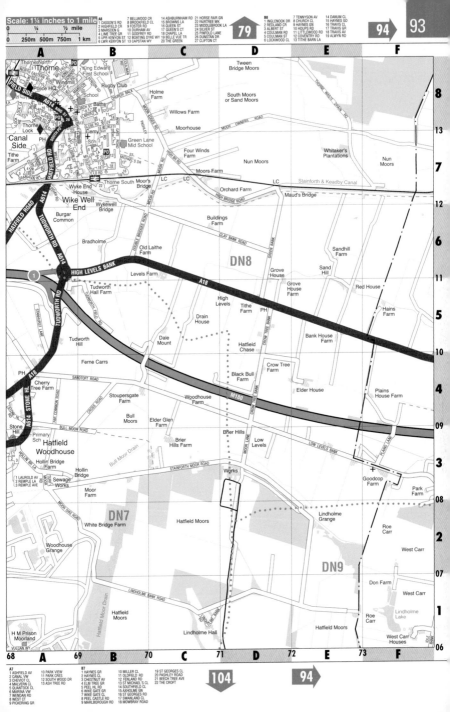

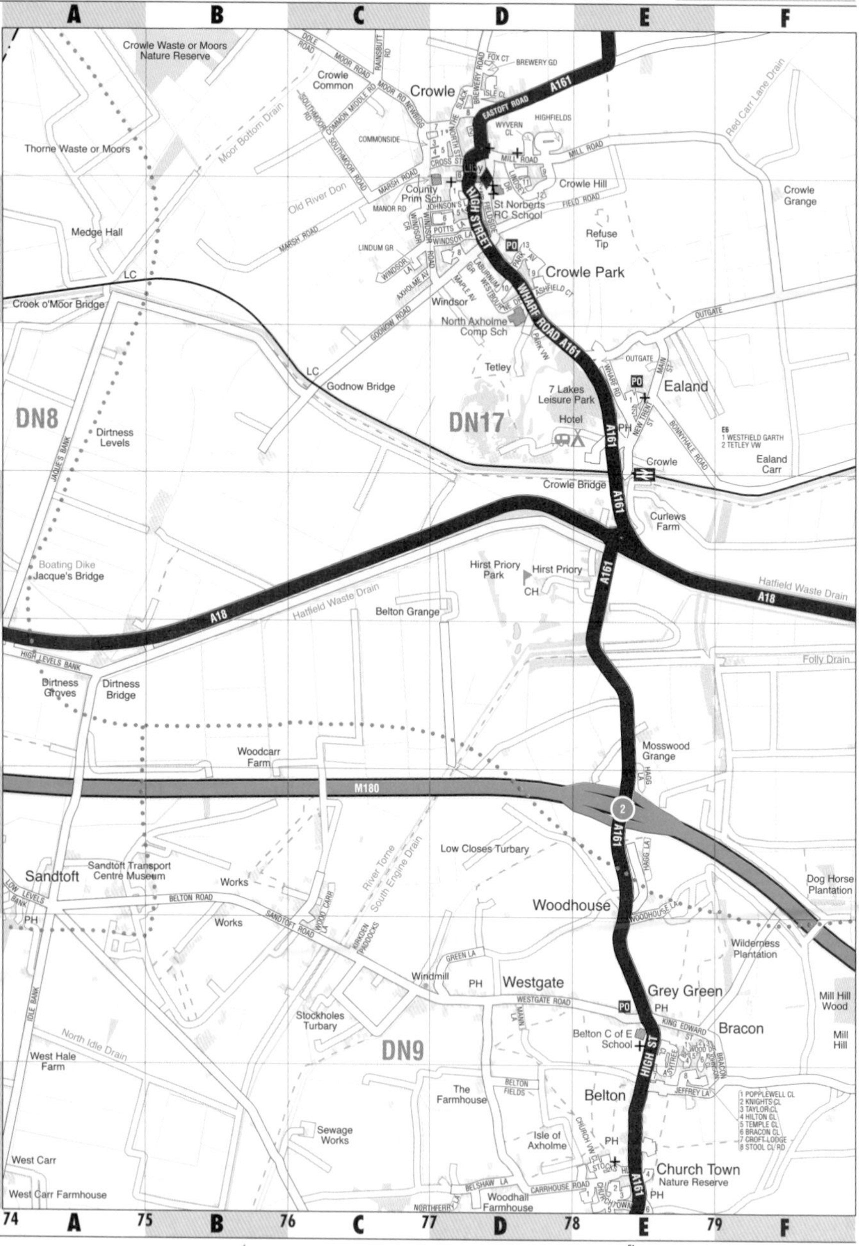
A B C D E F
8
13
7
12
6
11
5
10
4
09
3
08
2
07
1
06
74 75 76 77 78 79
Crowle Waste or Moors Nature Reserve
Crowle Common
Crowle
Thorne Waste or Moors
Moor Bottom Drain
Old River Don
Medge Hall
County Prim Sch
St Norberts RC School
Crowle Hill
Refuse Tip
Crowle Park
Crowle Grange
Red Carr Lane Drain
HIGH STREET
WHARF ROAD
A161
EASTOFT ROAD
MILL ROAD
FIELD ROAD
MARSH ROAD
MANOR RD
COMMONSIDE
HIGHFIELDS
Windsor
North Axholme Comp Sch
GODNOW ROAD
Croek o'Moor Bridge
LC
Godnow Bridge
Tetley
7 Lakes Leisure Park
Hotel
OUTGATE
Ealand
E6
1 WESTFIELD GARTH
2 TETLEY VW
Ealand Carr
Crowle
Crowle Bridge
Curlews Farm
DN8
DN17
Dirtness Levels
JACQUE'S BANK
Boating Dike
Jacque's Bridge
A18
Hatfield Waste Drain
Hirst Priory Park
Hirst Priory
CH
Belton Grange
Folly Drain
HIGH LEVELS BANK
Dirtness Groves
Dirtness Bridge
Woodcarr Farm
Mosswood Grange
M180
2
Low Closes Turbary
River Torne
South Engine Drain
Sandtoft
Sandtoft Transport Centre Museum
Works
BELTON ROAD
SANDTOFT ROAD
Woodhouse
WOODHOUSE LA
Dog Horse Plantation
Wilderness Plantation
Windmill
PH
Westgate
WESTGATE ROAD
Grey Green
KING EDWARD ST
Bracon
Mill Hill Wood
Mill Hill
Stockholes Turbary
North Idle Drain
IDLE BANK
West Hale Farm
DN9
Belton C of E School
HIGH ST
The Farmhouse
Belton
JEFFREY LA
1 POPPLEWELL CL
2 KNIGHTS CL
3 TAYLOR CL
4 HILTON CL
5 TEMPLE CL
6 BRACON CL
7 CROFT LODGE
8 STOOL CL RD
Sewage Works
Isle of Axholme
Church Town Nature Reserve
West Carr
West Carr Farmhouse
BELSHAW LA
CARRHOUSE ROAD
Woodhall Farmhouse

Scale: 1¼ inches to 1 mile

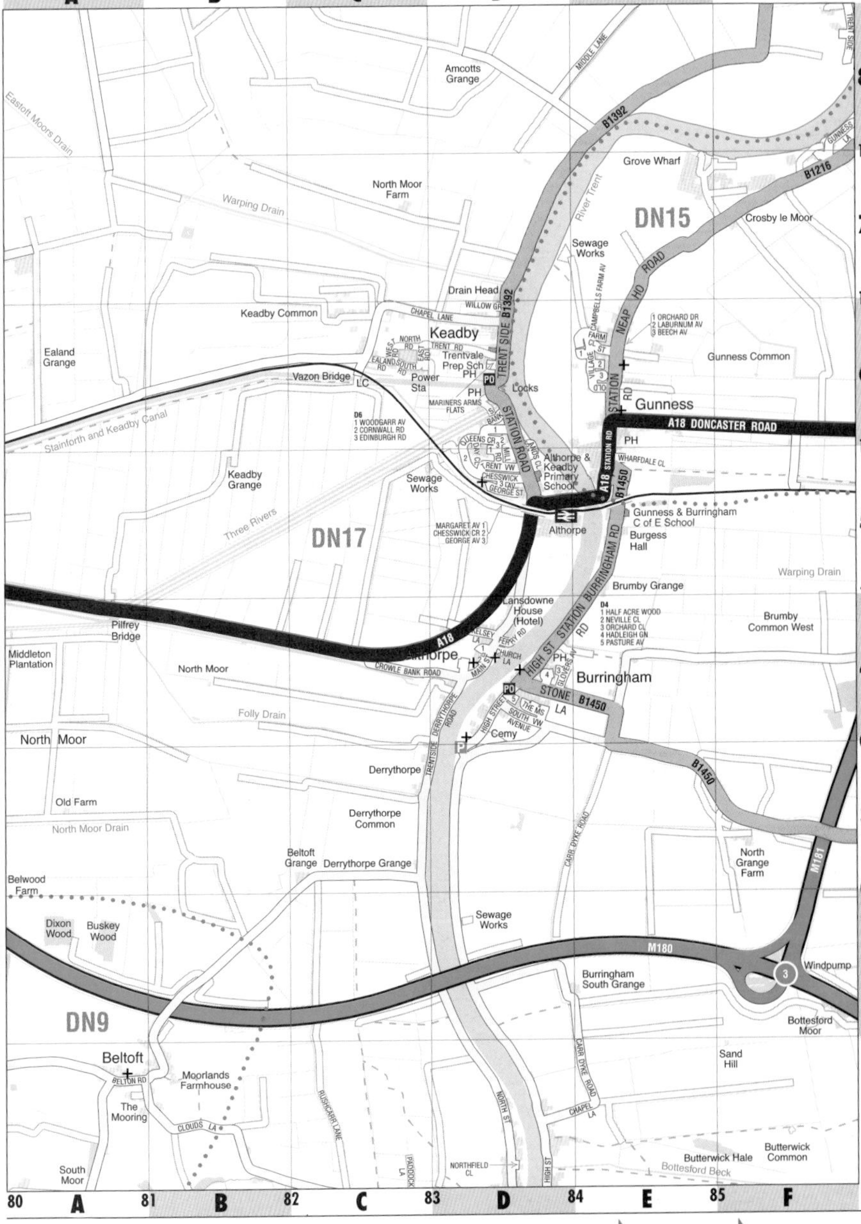

B7
1 PRIMROSE WY
2 POPPY CL
3 WOODALE CL
4 BETONY CL
5 COLTSFOOT CL
6 FLETCHER CL
7 BLACKTHORN CL
8 AVENSWOOD LA
9 ST MARY'S CT
10 HERON CL
11 PIPPIN CT
12 RUSSET CL
13 SEDGEWOOD WY
14 LUNEBURG PL
15 AV ROUEN
16 AV LOURDES
17 AV FONTENAY

95

82

Scale: 1¼ inches to 1 mile
0 ¼ ½ mile
0 250m 500m 750m 1 km

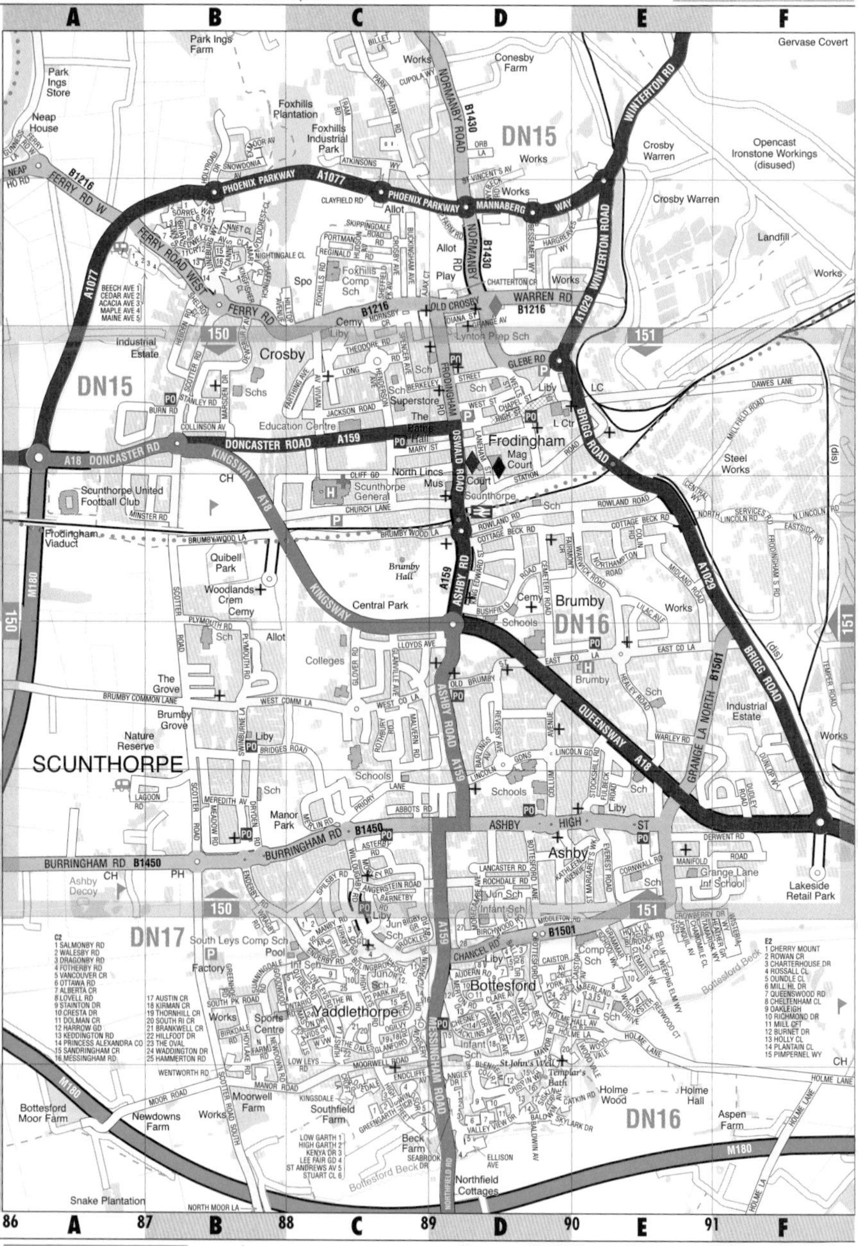

For full street detail of the highlighted area see pages 150 and 151.

95

107

D1
1 TYDEMAN CL
2 HOLSTEIN DR
3 HALES CL
4 HALLBROOK CT
5 LAXTON GR
6 TALISMAN DR
7 LAMBOURNE RI
8 BRAMLEY CR
9 RIBSTON CL
10 CONFERENCE CT
11 WORCESTER CL
12 RILESTON PL
13 MALLING WK
14 MERRYWEATHER CT
15 STURMER CT
16 PIPPIN DR
17 WREN CL

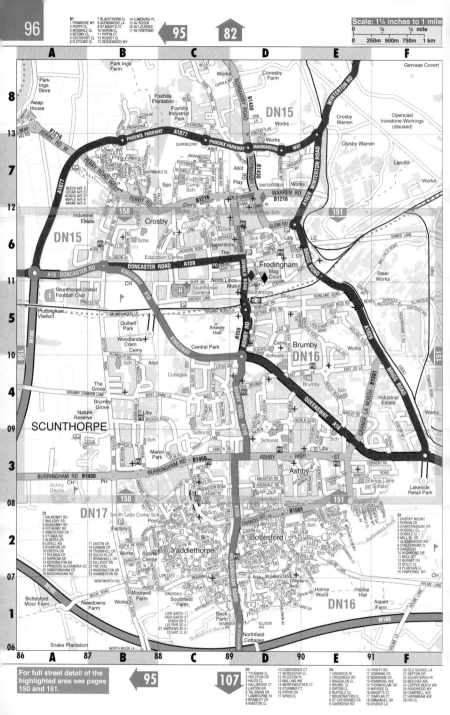

D2
1 OAKWOOD RI
2 CROSSBECK RD
3 MAGDALEN CL
4 BRUNEL CL
5 GIRTON CL
6 NUFFIELD CL
7 MOUNTBATTEN CL
8 ST CATHERINES CR
9 CAVENDISH RD
10 TRINITY RD
11 DOWNING CR
12 NEWNHAM CR
13 PEMBROKE AVE
14 THORNHOLME DR
15 WAYSIDE CL
16 KNIGHT'S CT
17 TEMPLAR CT
18 EMMANUEL DR
19 CHURCH LA
20 OLD SCHOOL LA
21 REPTON DR
22 SILVER BIRCH RI
23 BEECHES AVE
24 COPPER BEECH WK
25 ROSEWOOD WY
26 CAMPBELL AVE
27 HORNBEAM AVE
28 FIR CL

A B C D E F
8
13
7
12
6
11
5
10
4
09
3
08
2
07
1
06
2 A 93 B 94 C 95 D 96 E 97 F
Risby Warren
Rough Bottom Plantation
Padmoor Plantation
Scab Hill
Mill Farm
B1207 ERMINE STREET
Appleby Beck
Carrside Farm
Appleby Carrs
Weir Dyke
New River Ancholme
Bonby Carrs
Thornholme Plantation
North Side Plantation
Low Santon Farm
Santon Hill
Stone Pit Plantation
The Follies
High Santon Farm
LC
Haverholme House
Sandhouse Farm
Common Plantation
Keb Wood
Fishpond Plantation
DN15
Kebwood Farm
Santon
Old Broom Covert
Oak Tree Plantation
Works
(dis)
High Santon Farm
Clapgate Reservoir
Maud Hole
Broom Hill
Rowland Plantation
REDBOURNE RD
Sewage Works
New Enclosed Broom
Coronation Wood
Top Wood
Spring Wood
B1207
Lodge Farm
Old Decoy
Opencast Ironstone Workings (disused)
BURMA RD
Santon Wood
Broughton Decoy Farm
YARBOROUGH RD
Gokewell Priory Farm
B1208
Broughton Common
andfill
ORE BLENDING ROAD
DESPATCH RD
Far Wood
Broughton Grange
Common Farm
Heron Holt
Far Wood Farm
East Wood
BRIDGE ROAD
BOUNDARY ROAD
MILLS SERVICE ROAD
MEDIUM SECTION RD
DN20
Wressle Farm
Far Wood
Broughton
Wressle
DN16
Cemy
Wressle House
BILLET MILL APPROACH
THE SUBWAY
Steel Works
West Wood
APPLEBY LANE
BRIGG RD
HILLSIDE RD
COMMON RD
GREEN LA
Moor Beck
Millfield Plantation
James Farm
ANCHOR ROAD
CONCAST ROAD
S APPROACH ROAD
SCRAP BAY RD
(dis)
LIME AVE
D3
1 SOUTHFIELD RD
2 SYCAMORE CL
3 POPLAR DR
4 BEECH CL
5 CRAIG CL
6 BRUCE CL
7 STERNE AV
8 GREENHILL
9 STANIWELLS DR
P
CHAPTER WK
CLOISTER WK
BRIGG ROAD
HIGH ST
PO
Inf Sch
Liby
Bishop Burton Coll
Jun Sch
Allot
Broomfield Plantation
E3
1 BASSETT CL
2 BROOKLANDS
3 HARRYS DREAM
4 CORONATION GD
5 FAIRFIELD CL
6 CATHERINE GR
7 OLD MILL LA
8 CHANCEL WK
CARR LA
MMANUEL RD
SCRAP BAY ROAD
ANCHOR ROAD
Emanuel Bridge
Raventhorpe Farm
HOME BEAT DRIVE
LYCH GATE
CHURCH LA
GEORGE ST
ESTATE AV
WYATT AV
DIXON AV
Low Wood
Rose Cott
B1207
Broughton Vale
A18
Medieval Village of Raventhorpe
Gadbury Wood
Lundimore Wood
Vale Farm
Springfield Plantation
Sweeting Thorns
SCAWBY ROAD
KIRTON RD
Mendle Farm
Pinewood Farm
MORTAL ASH HL
HOLME LANE
Brick Hills
B1398
A18
CH
Hotel
olme
New Forest Plantation
North High Wood
A18
M180
Beckingham Shaw
Bracken Hill
Bow & Arrow Wood
Top Farm
Gray Yard
A18
Twigmoor Hall
Bog Plantation
Middleton Wood
4
Pond Head Wood
Warren Farm
Manton Warren
KIRTON RD
Beaulah Wood
A15
First Wood
VICARAGE LA
B1207
Scawby Park

D4
1 HERON HOLT
2 WESTMINSTER RD
3 THE BLACKTHORNS
4 WESTWOOD
5 TRINITY CT
6 YARBOROUGH CR

E4
1 BADGER WY
2 RUE DE NOZAY
3 BEECHWOOD CR
4 PINETREE CL
5 CHESTNUT GR
6 SCHOOL HOUSES
7 HUNTS CL
8 EASTWOOD DR
9 ST BERNARD'S CL
10 AIREDALE CL
11 LABRADOR DR
12 BEAGLE CL
13 DANE CL

97
84

F7
1 WOODLAND DR
2 DOLL LA
3 DUNNS PADDOCK
4 MALTKILN LA

Scale: 1¼ inches to 1 mile
0 ¼ ½ mile
0 250m 500m 750m 1 km

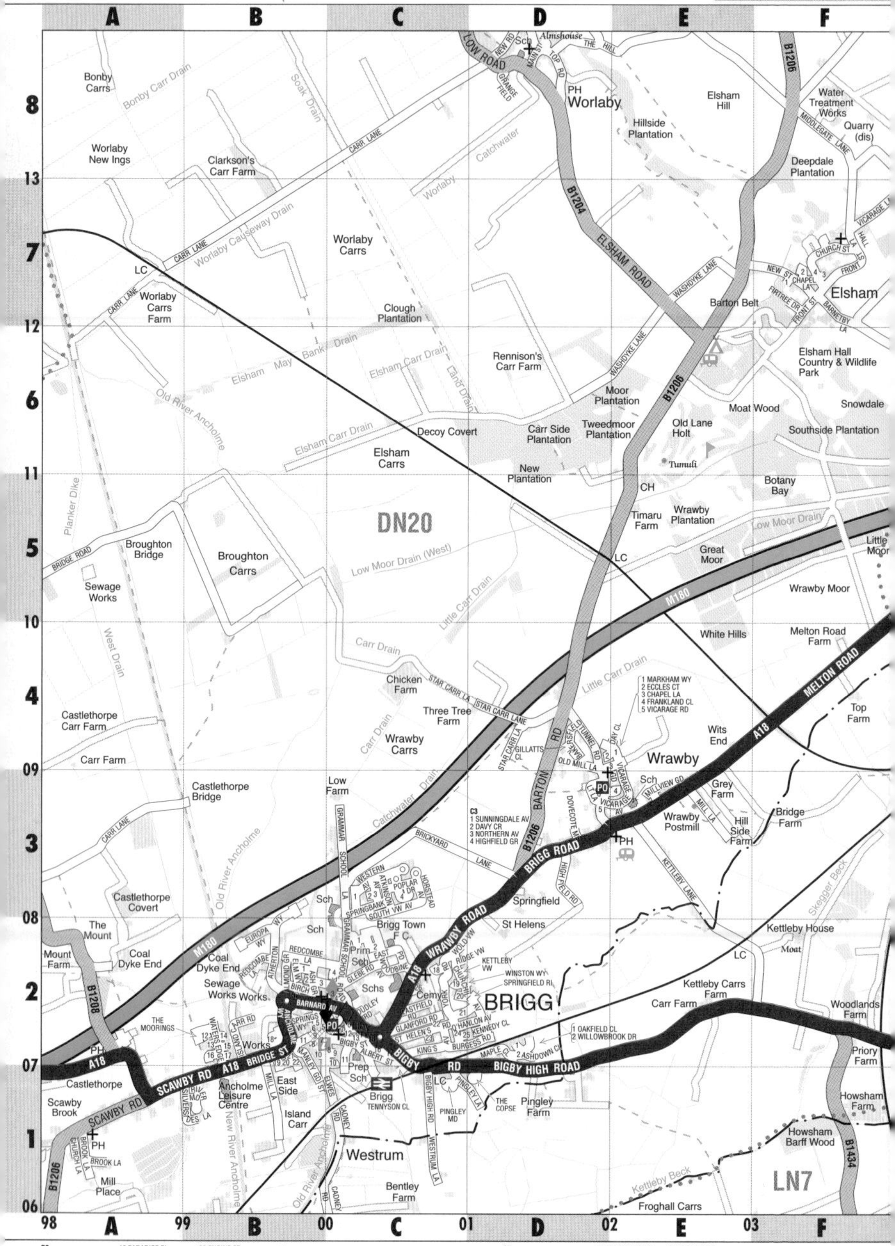

B2
1 CHERRY TREE AV
2 KINGSWAY
3 COLTON ST
4 DIXON CL
5 CARY LA
6 MARKET LA
7 EXCHANGE PL
8 ANCHORAGE ST
9 MARKET PL
10 PARADISE PL
11 BRIDGE ST
12 RIVERSIDE
13 TEAL CL
14 THE NARROW BOATS
15 MILLERS QUAY
16 MILL CL
17 ANCHORS WY
18 KILN LA
19 WEST TR
20 ENGINE ST
21 FORRESTER ST
22 JAMES ST

97
109

C2
1 PRESTON DR
2 HAWTHORN AV
3 MAGRATH CT
4 WESLEY RD
5 OLD COURTS RD
6 GRAMMAR SCHOOL RD S
7 WRAWBY ST
8 ELWES ST
9 THE BOTTLINGS
10 ANCHOLME GD
11 ST CLARES WK
12 CROSS ST
13 GARDEN ST
14 QUEEN ST
15 BIGBY RD
16 PRINCES ST
17 NEW ST
18 HOLME CL
19 WELLBECK CL
20 CHAPEL WY
21 ST JAMES RD
22 GLANFORD RD
23 HEDGEROW LA
24 YARBOROUGH RD
25 SPRINGFIELD RD
26 NICOLGATE LA

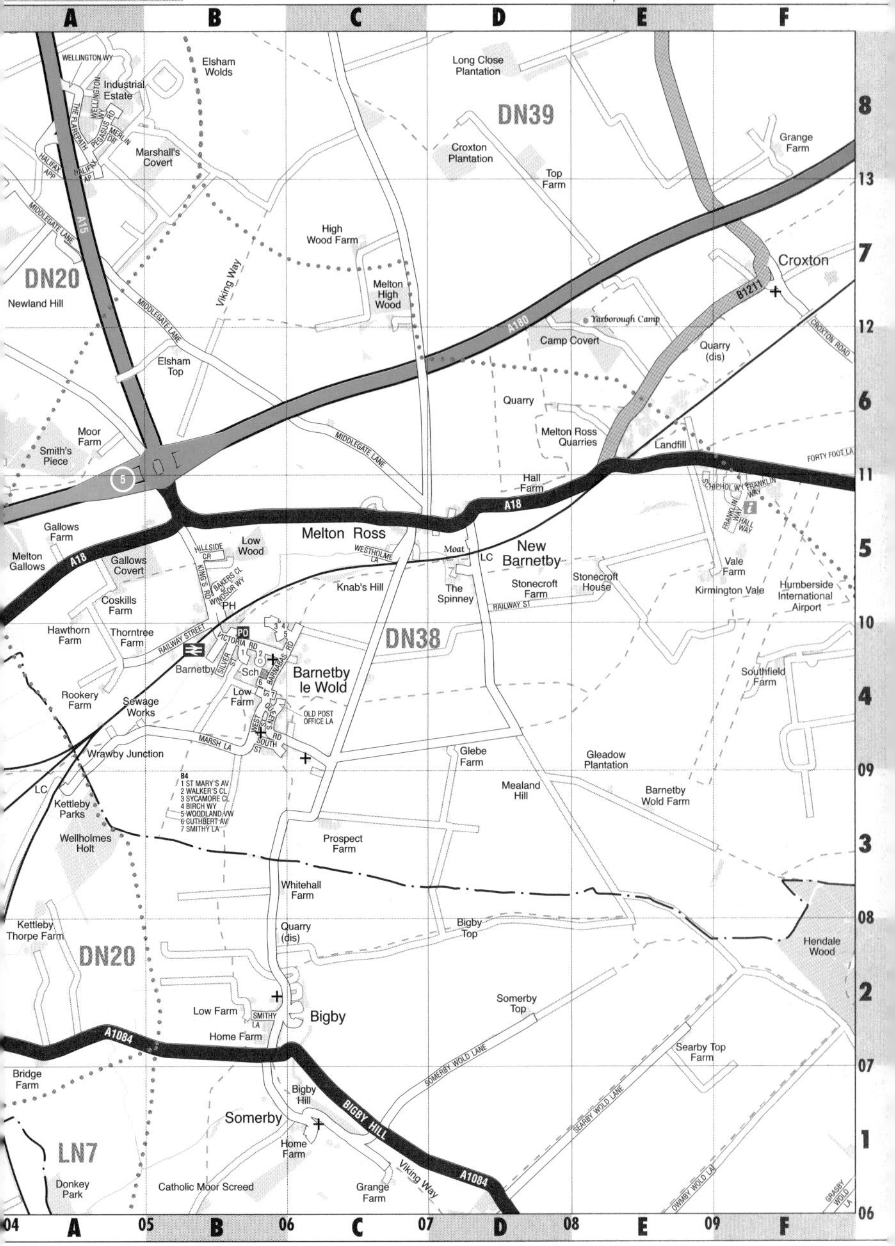

B4
1 ST MARY'S AV
2 WALKER'S CL
3 SYCAMORE CL
4 BIRCH WY
5 WOODLAND VW
6 CUTHBERT AV
7 SMITHY LA

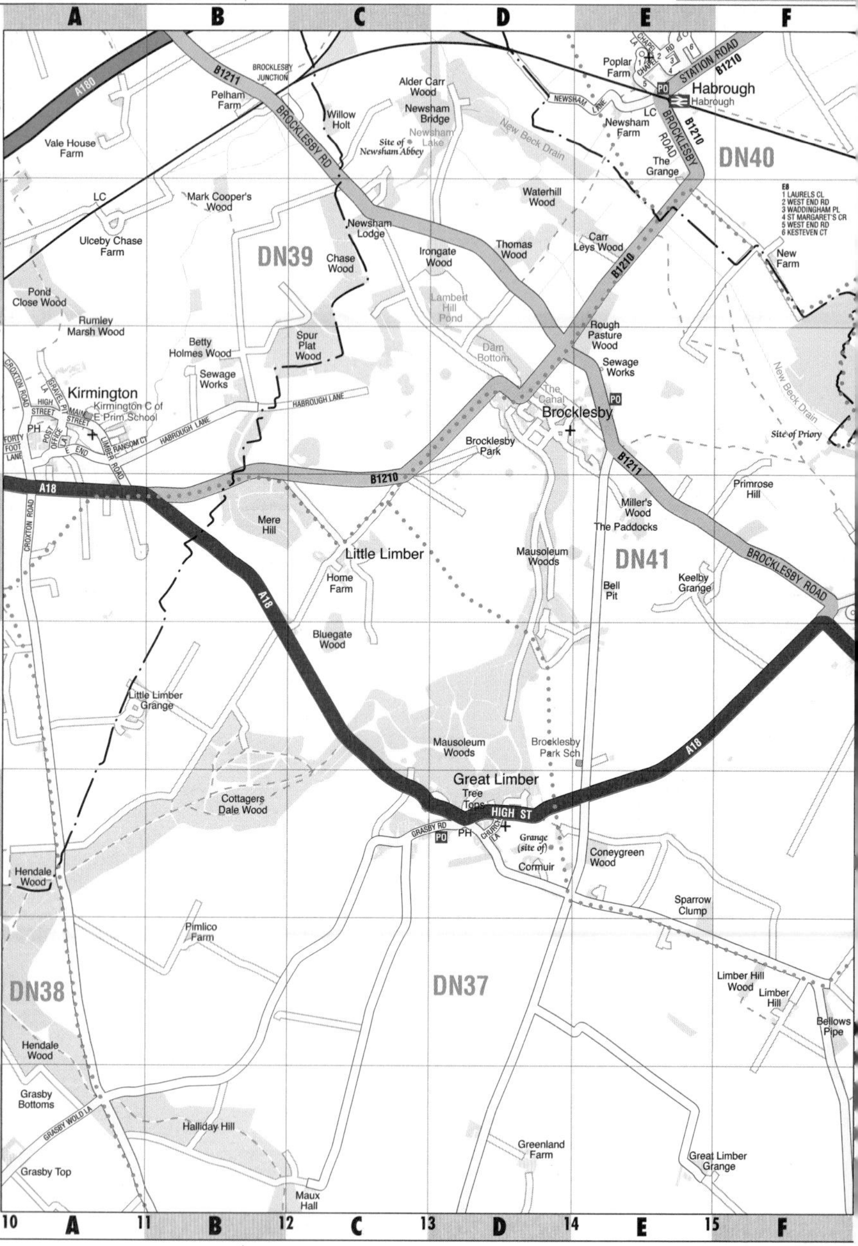
A
B
C
D
E
F
8
13
7
12
6
11
5
10
4
09
3
08
2
07
1
06
10
11
12
13
14
15
A180
B1211
BROCKLESBY JUNCTION
Pelham Farm
BROCKLESBY RD
Willow Holt
Alder Carr Wood
Newsham Bridge
Newsham Lake
Site of Newsham Abbey
New Beck Drain
NEWSHAM LANE
Poplar Farm
CHAPEL LA
CHAPEL RD
PO
STATION ROAD
B1210
Habrough
LC
Newsham Farm
BROCKLESBY ROAD
The Grange
DN40
E8
1 LAURELS CL
2 WEST END RD
3 WADDINGHAM PL
4 ST MARGARET'S CR
5 WEST END RD
6 KESTEVEN CT
Vale House Farm
LC
Mark Cooper's Wood
Ulceby Chase Farm
DN39
Newsham Lodge
Chase Wood
Irongate Wood
Thomas Wood
Waterhill Wood
Carr Leys Wood
New Farm
Pond Close Wood
Rumley Marsh Wood
Lambert Hill Pond
Spur Plat Wood
Betty Holmes Wood
Sewage Works
Dam Bottom
Rough Pasture Wood
Sewage Works
Kirmington
Kirmington C of E Prim School
CROXTON ROAD
GRAVEL PIT LA
HIGH STREET
MAIN STREET
PH
POST OFFICE LA
FORTY FOOT LANE
E END
LIMBER ROAD
RANSOM CT
HABROUGH LANE
HABROUGH LANE
The Canal
PO
Brocklesby
New Beck Drain
Site of Priory
Brocklesby Park
B1211
A18
B1210
Primrose Hill
Mere Hill
Miller's Wood
The Paddocks
CROXTON ROAD
Little Limber
Mausoleum Woods
DN41
Home Farm
Bell Pit
Keelby Grange
BROCKLESBY ROAD
A18
Bluegate Wood
Little Limber Grange
Mausoleum Woods
Brocklesby Park Sch
A18
Great Limber
Tree Tops
HIGH ST
Cottagers Dale Wood
GRASBY RD
PO
PH
CHURCH LA
Grange (site of)
Cormuir
Coneygreen Wood
Hendale Wood
Sparrow Clump
Pimlico Farm
DN38
DN37
Limber Hill Wood
Limber Hill
Bellows Pipe
Hendale Wood
Grasby Bottoms
GRASBY WOLD LA
Halliday Hill
Greenland Farm
Great Limber Grange
Grasby Top
Maux Hall

Scale: 1¼ inches to 1 mile
¼ ½ mile
250m 500m 750m 1 km

B8
1 KISHORN CT
2 KINLOCH WY
3 PERTH WY
4 TUMMEL CT
5 OBAN CT

C8
1 GUERNSEY GR
2 ALDERNEY WY
3 ORKNEY PL
4 SHETLAND WY
5 FAIRISLE RI

87
102

F5
1 APPLE TREE CT
2 MALLARD CL
3 SWALLOW DR
4 WREN CL
5 CARLTON RD
6 IVY FARM CT
7 PINNEY'S CT
8 MAPLE GR
9 FORD'S AV
10 MCVEIGH CT
11 BEVERLEY CT
12 WESTWOOD RD
13 ASHLEIGH CT

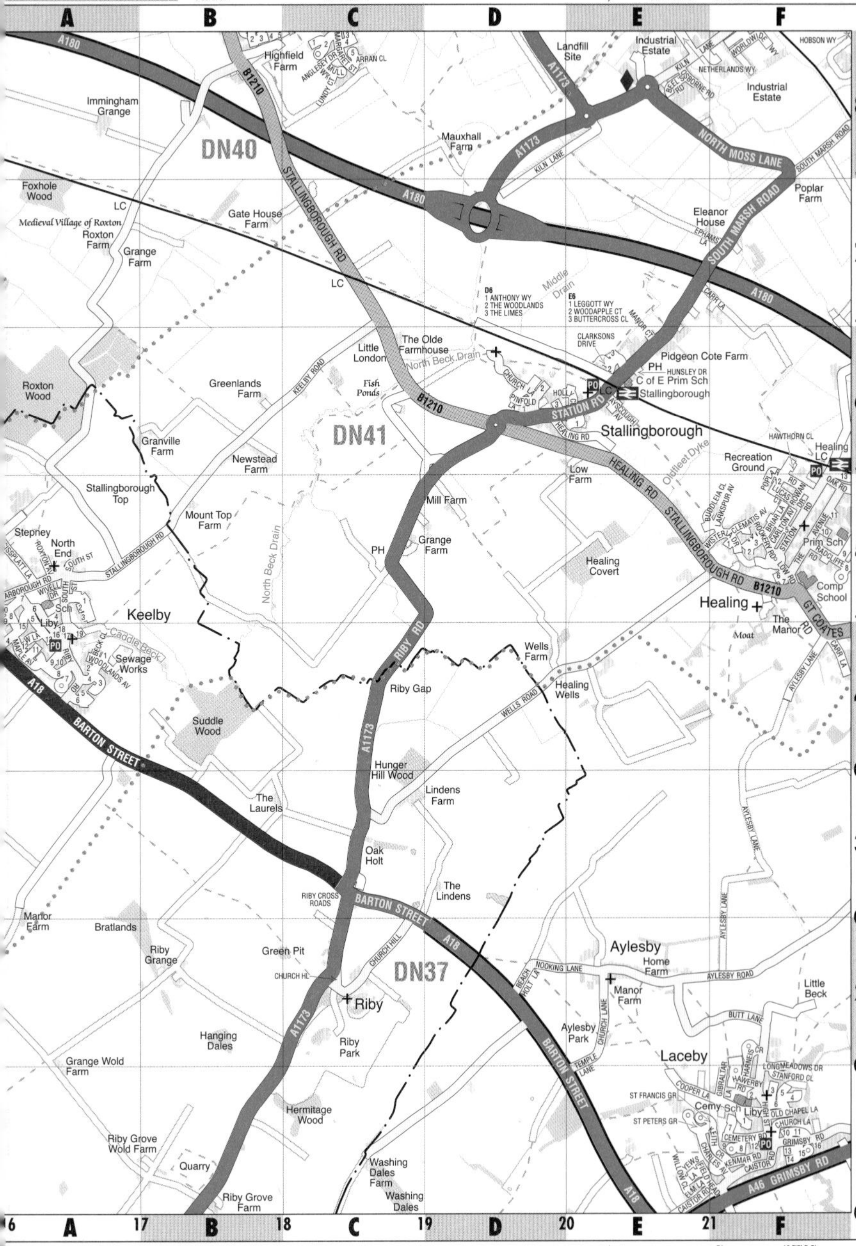

A4
1 MIDFIELD WY
2 ROWAN CLE
3 RAITHBY AV
4 SUDDLE WY
5 THORNTON GDN
6 COTHAM GDN
7 LONGMEADOW RI
8 MILSON RD
9 CADDLE RD
10 KAREN AV
11 HULBERRY CL
12 MAPLE CL
13 HALLS LA
14 MILL LA
15 PELHAM CR
16 ST MARTIN'S PL
17 ST BARTHOLOMEW'S CL
18 KING ST
19 CHURCH LA

A5
1 EASTFIELD RD
2 TOMLINE RD
3 WINDSOR CL
4 MANOR CL
5 VICTORIA RD
6 MANOR ST
7 BROADWAY
8 ST ANNE'S RD
9 WEST VIEW CL
10 CHURCHILL AV

112
102

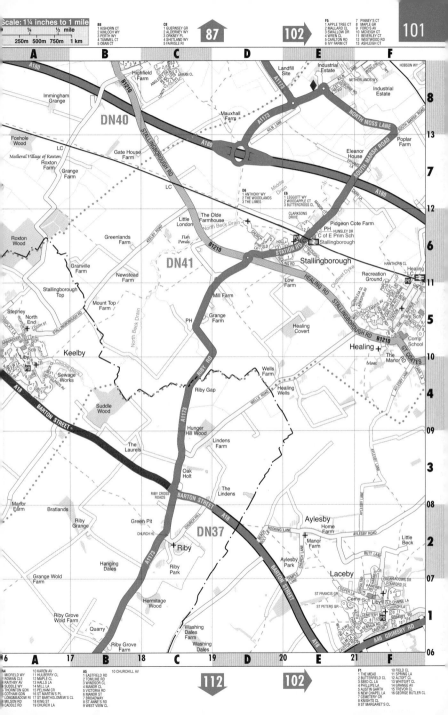

F1
1 THE MEAD
2 BUTTERFIELD CL
3 SEED CL LA
4 PHILLIPS LA
5 AUSTIN GARTH
6 NEW CHAPEL LA
7 CEMETERY CR
8 KNIGHTS CL
9 ST MARGARET'S CL
10 FIELD CL
11 SPRING LA
12 ALTOFT CL
13 WHITGIFT CL
14 GRANGE AV
15 TREVOR CL
16 GEORGE BUTLER CL

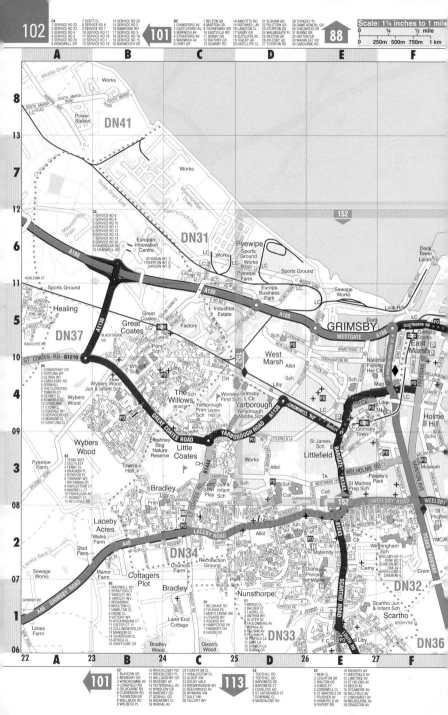

C4
1 SERVICE RD 22
2 SERVICE RD 23
3 SERVICE RD 4
4 SERVICE RD 5
5 SERVICE RD 25
6 HEMSWELL DR
7 SCOTT CL
8 SERVICE RD 6
9 SERVICE RD 7
10 SERVICE RD 17
11 SERVICE RD 18
12 SERVICE RD 1
13 SERVICE RD 19
14 SERVICE RD 20
15 SERVICE RD 2
16 BINBROOK WY
17 SERVICE RD 3
18 SERVICE RD 16
19 SERVICE RD 15
20 BARMOUTH DR

101

D2
1 CHINGFORD AV
2 CASTLEFORD AV
3 NORWICH AV
4 STRATFORD AV
5 WARWICK AV
6 ORBY GR
7 BELTON GR
8 MARTON GR
9 THORESWAY GR
10 EASTVILLE RD
11 BONBY GR
12 RAITHBY GR
13 SCAWBY RD
14 AMCOTTS RD
15 ROTHWELL AV
16 LANGTON CL
17 SAXBY GR
18 SUTCLIFFE AV
19 TEALBY GR
20 HATCLLFFE CL
21 ELSHAM GR
22 FULSTOW GR
23 STURTON GR
24 WALMSGATE PL
25 RESTON GR
26 AYLESBY GD
27 TOYNTON RD
28 TORKSEY PL
29 DAME KENDAL GR
30 CHELWOOD DR
31 BURNS GR
32 HATTON GR
33 WAINFLEET RD
34 CABOURNE RD

88

Scale: 1¼ inches to 1 mile
0 ¼ ½ mile
0 250m 500m 750m 1 km

A B C D E F
8
13
7
12
6
11
5
10
4
09
3
08
2
07
1
06
22 23 24 25 26 27
Middle Drain
Works
SOUTH MARSH ROAD
HOBSON WAY
Power Station
DN41
Oldfleet Drain
Three Drain End
Works
Mawmbridge Drain
Town's Croft Drain
152
C5
1 SERVICE RD 8
2 SERVICE RD 9
3 SERVICE RD 10
4 SERVICE RD 11
5 SERVICE RD 12
6 SERVICE RD 13
7 SERVICE RD 14
8 SERVICE RD 26
9 RAVENSCAR RD
10 CRANWELL DR
Europarc Innovation Centre
DN31
ATHENIAN WY 1
FISKERTON WY 2
SARGON WY 3
Pyewipe
Sports Ground
Works
Pyewipe Farm
Sports Ground
Dock Tower Locks
WESTSIDE ROAD
A180
ASHLEIGH CT
Sports Ground
Healing
Europa Business Park
Sewage Works
MOODY LANE
Industrial Estate
Great Coates
Factory
Lock Hill
GRIMSBY
WESTGATE
CLEETHORPE RD
Grimsby Docks
East Marsh
DN37
A1136
RADCLIFFE RD
GT COATES RD B1210
West Marsh
Allot
Sch
National Fishing Her Ctr
B4
1 CORMORANT DR
2 FORTUNA WY
3 GLORIA WY
4 CANDLESBY RD
5 FERNHILL
6 THE CLOISTERS
7 TIMBERLEY
8 GEDNEY CL
9 BOWFIELD CL
10 CROSLAND
11 STOW CL
12 ESKDALE WY
13 SERVICE RD 21
14 MINNOW CL
15 GRAYLING CL
Wybers Wood Jun & Infant Sch
Wybers Wood
The Willows
Worsley First Sch
Grimsby L Ctr
Yarborough
Yarborough Middle Sch
CROMWELL RD
Freshney Pl Sh Ctr
Grimsby Town
Holme Hill
Wybers Wood
GREAT COATES ROAD
YARBOROUGH ROAD
Freshney Bog Nature Reserve
Little Coates
St James Sch
Littlefield
BARGATE
A1243
People's Park
Museum
HAINTON AVE
Pyewipe Farm
B3
1 TEAM GATE
2 OLD FLEET
3 FENBY CL
4 BRACKEN PL
5 BYWOOD PL
6 TONNANT WY
7 BRITANNIA CR
8 HARLESTONE CT
9 MAXWELL CT
10 TRAFALGAR AV
11 ROMSEY CT
12 BELLEISLE RD
Town's Holt
Bradley
B1444
LT COATES RD
WELHOLME RD
St Martins Prep Sch
WEELSBY ROAD
Laceby Acres
Walks Farm
LACEBY ROAD
A46
DN34
Stud Farm
Recreation Ground
Council Farm
Maternity
Rec Ctr
Wintringham Sch
WEELSBY GR 1
DENE RD 2
QUINTON RD 3
OAK AV 4
MIRFIELD RD 5
DREW AV 6
St Hughs
YMCA
PEAKS PARKWAY
Sewage Works
Manor Farm
Cottagers Plot
B2
1 MAIDWELL WY
2 SPRATTON CT
3 YARDLEY WY
4 YARDLEY WY
5 BROADWAY
6 MOULTON CL
7 HAMILTON CL
8 DEENE CL
9 VICTORY WY
10 ROCKINGHAM CT
11 EXETER CT 11
12 COLLINGWOOD CR
13 MANSON CL
14 SOVEREIGN CL
15 AFRICA CL
16 SWIFTSURE CR
Bradley
Nunsthorpe
Diana Princess of Wales
Cemy
Crem
DN32
SCARTHO ROAD
Scartho Jun & Infant Sch
Scartho
GRIMSBY RD
A46 GRIMSBY ROAD
Limes Farm
NEW ROAD
D1
1 BELGRAVE RD
2 FULHAM PK
3 MARYLEBONE WK
4 UTGARD WY
5 ASGARD WY
6 HAMPSTEAD PK
7 FINSBURY DR
8 EASON RD
E1
1 BROCK CL
2 BALDER CT
3 LAUREL CL
4 ANTRIM WY
5 ULSTER AV
6 FAUCONBERG AV
7 SOPHIA AV
8 PELHAM AV
9 PELHAM PL
10 PINFOLD LA
11 GATE LA
12 CHURCH LA
13 SUNNY CR
Lane End Cottage
DN33
LOUTH RD
DN36
Bradley Wood
Dixon's Wood

C2
1 BLAYDON GR
2 NEWBURY GR
3 WINCHCOMBE AV
4 LONGFIELD RD
5 SELBOURNE RD
6 CLARENDON RD
7 THORNTON GR
8 WELLBECK RD
9 WELBECK PL
10 BROCKLESBY RD
11 BROCKLESBY PL
12 WILLOUGHBY GR
13 REVESBY AV
14 TATTERSHALL AV
15 WINSLOW GR
16 BARDNEY GD
17 GOXHILL GD
18 WICKENBY CL
19 WIRRAL AV
20 FISKERTON CL
21 HIBALDSTOW CL
22 ALDER VW
23 DOLBY VALE
24 BREMERHAVEN WY
25 BEECHWOOD AV
26 WYMARK VW
27 DALE VW
28 TALLERT WY

101

113

C3
1 TOOTHILL RD
2 TOOTHILL GD
3 BARONESS RD
4 BARONESS CT
5 FOXGLOVE GD
6 ST CATHERINES CT
7 DOWNING CL
8 MAGDALENE RD

E2
1 NEW CL
2 LEIGHTON GR
3 WALTON GR
4 KINGSLEY
5 CORNWELL CL
6 ST MARTIN'S CR
7 FRUSHER AV
8 HOMEFIELD AV
9 RUPERT RD
10 ROOKERY AV
11 WESTFIELD AV
12 LIMETREE AV
13 ST HELENS AV
14 BEECH AV
15 SYCAMORE AV
16 MILLFIELD AV
17 LYNDHURST AV
18 MELBOURNE AV
19 CRAGSTON AV

B2		C1			C2			D1		
1 CHATSWORTH PL	10 GREEN HL	1 PYTCHLEY WK	10 CONISTON CR	20 LALRGATE PL	1 PENSHURST RD	10 LYNTON RI	20 MARSHCHAPEL CL	1 CHELSEA WK	10 WESTBURY PK	20 CARRINGTON DR
2 BALMORAL RD	11 CHERRY DL	2 FITZWILLIAM MS	11 GRASMERE GR	21 ARDEN VILLAGE	2 THORESBY PL	11 CRAITHIE RD	21 LUDBOROUGH WY	2 ROCHESTER CT	11 GROVENOR CT	21 POPLAR DR
3 CURZON CT	12 MILL GARTH	3 WELLS CR	12 DERWENT DR	22 MARIGOLD WK	3 RUFFORD RD	12 MINSHULL RD	22 BEESBY DR	3 MAYFAIR CT	12 CUMBERLAND RD	22 CARLTON CL
4 TERRINGTON PL	13 BELMONT CL	4 BECKSIDE CL	13 ENNERDALE CL	23 CRANBOURNE CL	4 BLENHEIM PL	13 WEEKES RD	23 BUTTERWICK CL	4 FAIRFIELD CT	13 RUSSELL CT	23 NEWLANDS PK
5 CRIDLING PL	14 RAVENHILL CL	5 BULLFINCH LA	14 CHAFFINCH DR	24 DELAMERE CT	5 WOODSLEY AV	14 CAENBY RD	24 WALTHAM GR	5 WHITEHALL RD	14 CAVENDISH CL	24 FOREST WY
6 KENILWORTH RD	15 BRAMPTON WY	6 WOODLAND WK	15 BRAMBLE WY	25 LAMBOURN CT	6 WENDOVER RI	15 WESLEY CR	25 ALVINGHAM AV	6 SOUTH VW	15 BERNERS RD	25 ROYAL CT
7 HAVERSTOE PL		7 BECK WK	16 VIOLET CL	26 BURNHAM REACH	7 LINDSEY RD	16 BILLINGHAY CT	26 QUORN MS	7 FIELDHOUSE RD	16 CLEE NESS DR	
8 IRBY CT		8 GREENFINCH DR	17 HAREWOOD GR	27 WESTPORT RD	8 PARKER ST	17 LANSDOWN LINK		8 KINGSTON CL	17 ASHWOOD DR	
9 ORMSBY CL		9 WINDERMERE CR	18 HAMPTON CL	28 MEADOW VW	9 GUNBY PL	18 BURLEY AV		9 WEYFORD RD	18 SINDERSON RD	
			19 CONISTON CR	29 HAYLING MERE		19 ESKHAM CL			19 HURSTLEA DR	

A8
1 HAMPDEN CRES
2 LANCASTER DR
3 CUNNINGHAM RD
4 GIBSON RD
5 BLENHEIM RD
6 VARSITY CL

93

Scale: 1¼ inches to 1 mile
0 ¼ ½ mile
0 250m 500m 750m 1 km

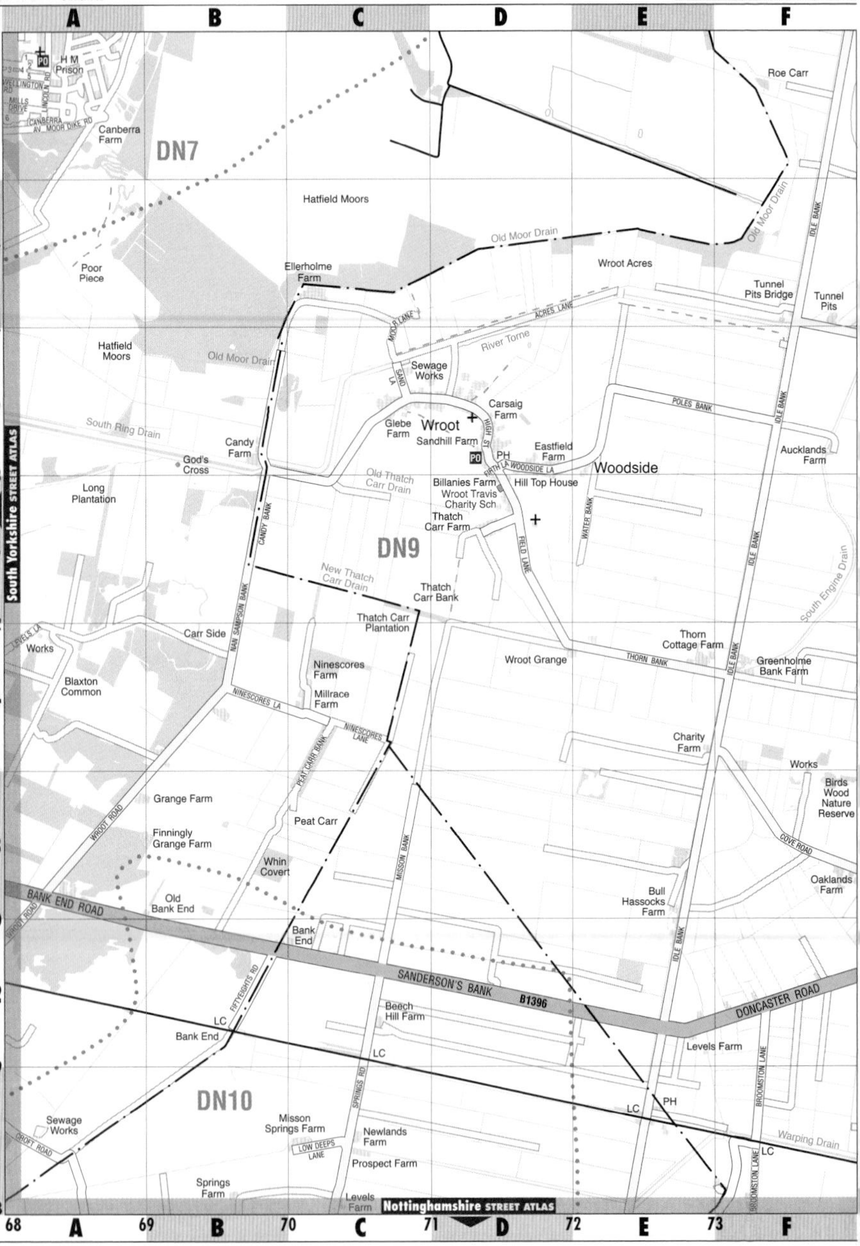

Scale: 1¼ inches to 1 mile
0 ¼ ½ mile
0 250m 500m 750m 1 km

94
106

D7
1 FERNBANK
2 FIELDS CL
3 ORCHARD CFT
4 SWALLOW CT
5 CARRSIDE
6 NICHOLSON WY

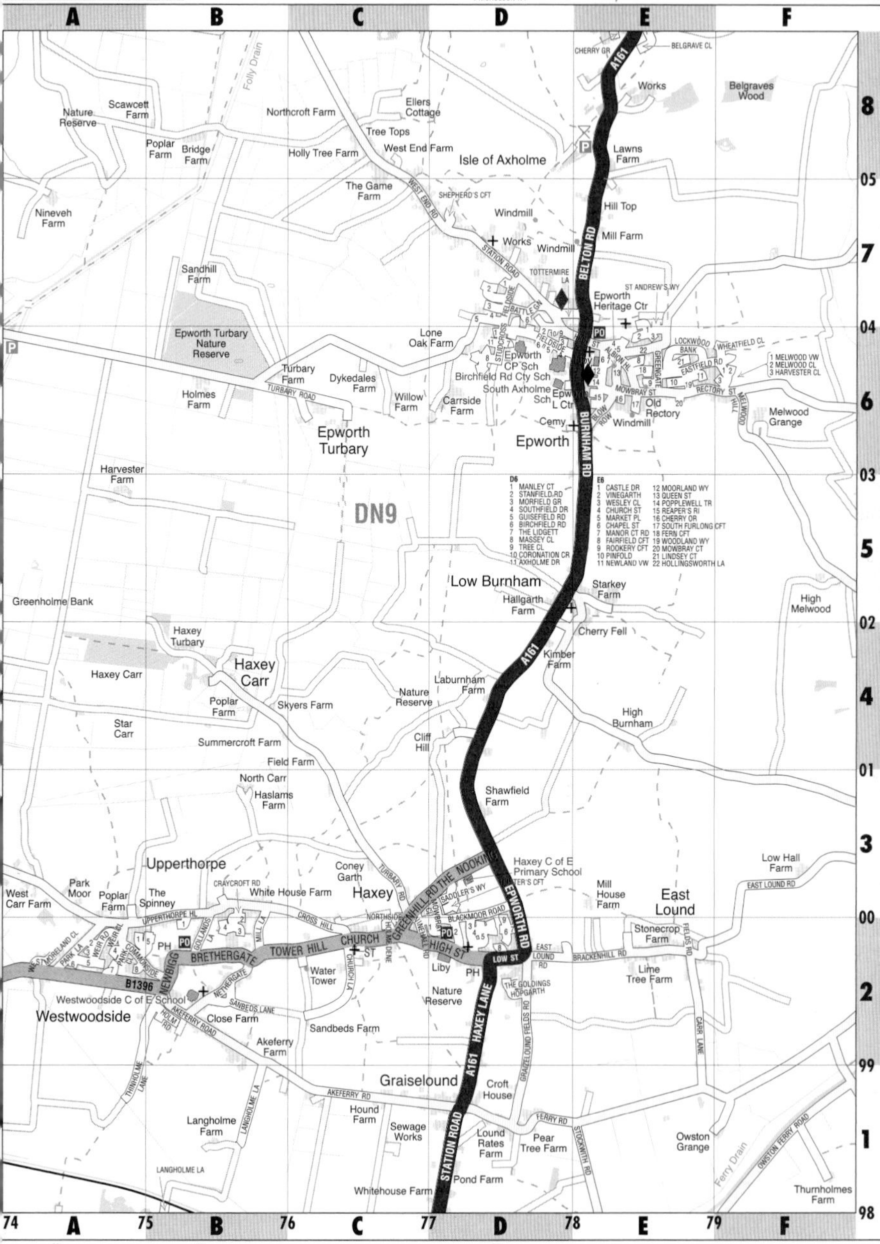

A2
1 THE ROWANS
2 AXHOLME RD
3 COLLEYWELL CL
4 PARK DR
5 THE MEADOWS
6 MOORLANDS
7 DREWRY LA
8 WEAVERS CFT

B2
1 TAVELLA CT
2 HIGHFIELD CR
3 WESTLAND RD
4 CHAPEL CL
5 THE BIRCHES

116
106

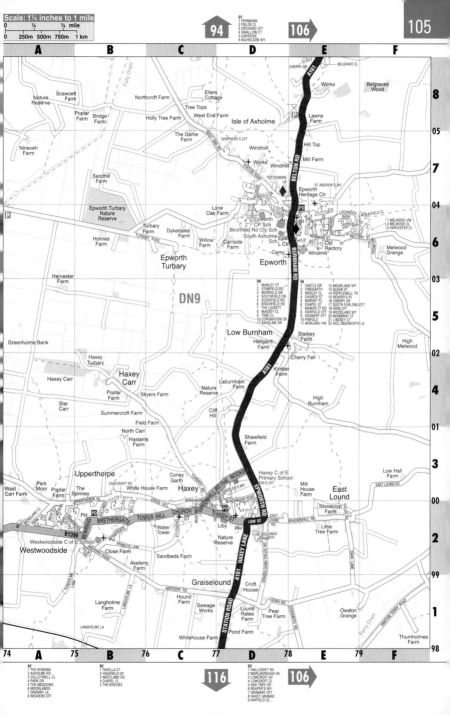

D2
1 HALLCROFT RD
2 MARLBOROUGH AV
3 LOWCROFT AV
4 LOWCROFT CL
5 ASH TREE DR
6 REAPER'S WY
7 GRANARY CFT
8 HAXEY GRANGE
9 HAYFIELD CL

105
95

D8
1 THE CROFT
2 FARM LA
3 PARKLANDS

Scale: 1¼ inches to 1 mile
0 ¼ ½ mile
0 250m 500m 750m 1 km

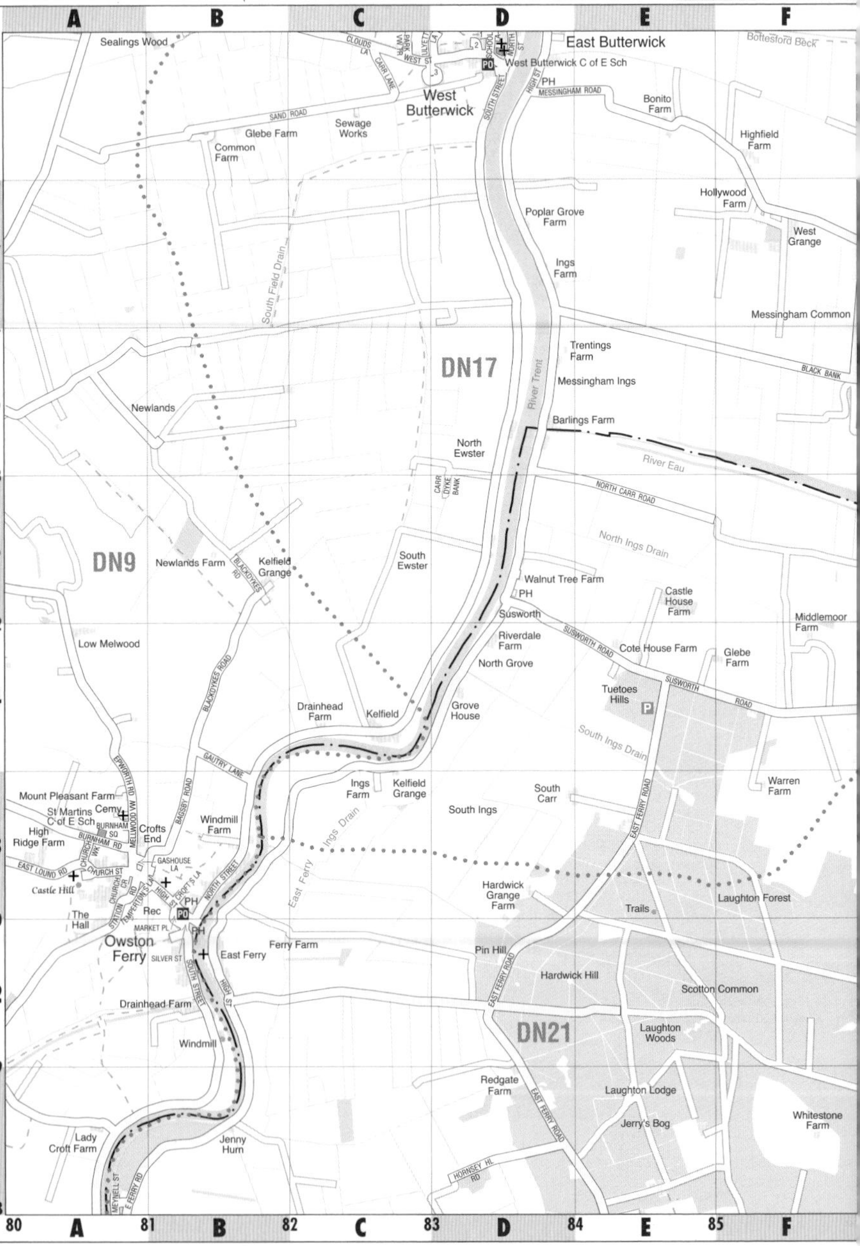
A B C D E F
8
05
7
04
6
03
5
02
4
01
3
00
2
99
1
98
80 81 82 83 84 85
Sealings Wood
East Butterwick
Bottesford Beck
West Butterwick C of E Sch
PH
MESSINGHAM ROAD
West Butterwick
SAND ROAD
Glebe Farm
Sewage Works
Common Farm
Bonito Farm
Highfield Farm
CLOUDS LA
WEST ST
CARR LANE
SCHOOL LA
SOUTH STREET
HIGH ST
Hollywood Farm
West Grange
Poplar Grove Farm
Ings Farm
South Field Drain
Messingham Common
Trentings Farm
Messingham Ings
DN17
BLACK BANK
River Trent
Newlands
Barlings Farm
North Ewster
River Eau
CARR DYKE BANK
NORTH CARR ROAD
North Ings Drain
DN9
Newlands Farm
BLACKDYKES RD
Kelfield Grange
South Ewster
Walnut Tree Farm
PH
Castle House Farm
Susworth
Middlemoor Farm
Low Melwood
Riverdale Farm
SUSWORTH ROAD
Cote House Farm
Glebe Farm
North Grove
Tuetoes Hills
BLACKDYKES ROAD
Drainhead Farm
Kelfield
Grove House
South Ings Drain
GAUTRY LANE
EPWORTH RD
Warren Farm
Ings Farm
Kelfield Grange
South Carr
Mount Pleasant Farm
St Martins C of E Sch
Cemy
BAGSBY ROAD
Windmill Farm
South Ings
EAST FERRY ROAD
High Ridge Farm
BURNHAM SQ
BURNHAM RD
Crofts End
Ings Drain
EAST LOUND RD
CHURCH WK
CHURCH ST
GASHOUSE LA
East Ferry
Castle Hill
NORTH STREET
Hardwick Grange Farm
Trails
Laughton Forest
CROFT'S LA
HIGH ST
PH
The Hall
Rec
STATION RD
MARKET PL
PH
Owston Ferry
SILVER ST
East Ferry
Ferry Farm
Pin Hill
Hardwick Hill
SOUTH STREET
HIGH ST
EAST FERRY ROAD
Scotton Common
Drainhead Farm
DN21
Laughton Woods
Windmill
Redgate Farm
Laughton Lodge
Jerry's Bog
Whitestone Farm
Lady Croft Farm
Jenny Hurn
HORNSEY HL RD
MEYNELL ST
E FERRY RD

105
117

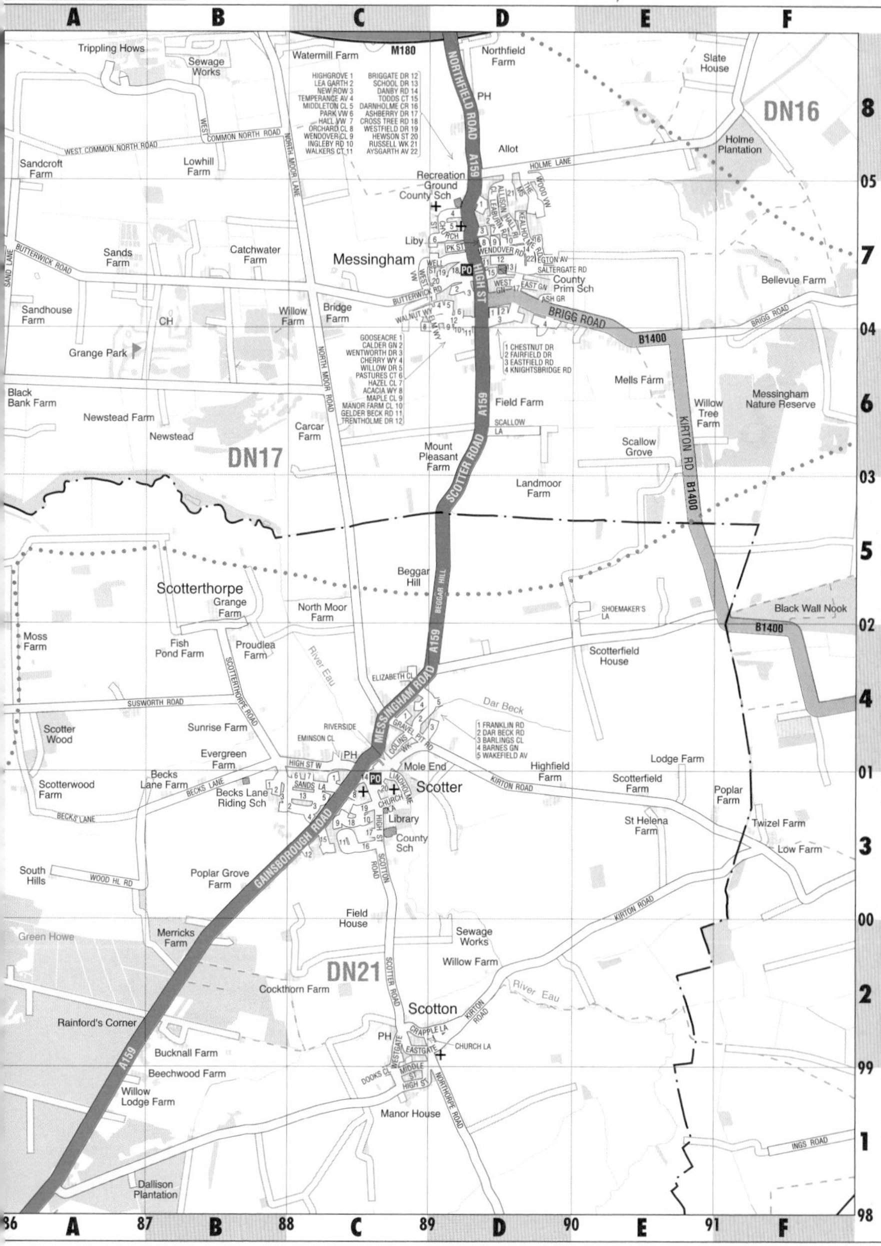

B3
1 BELLBUTTS VW
2 LARK RI
3 ASH GR

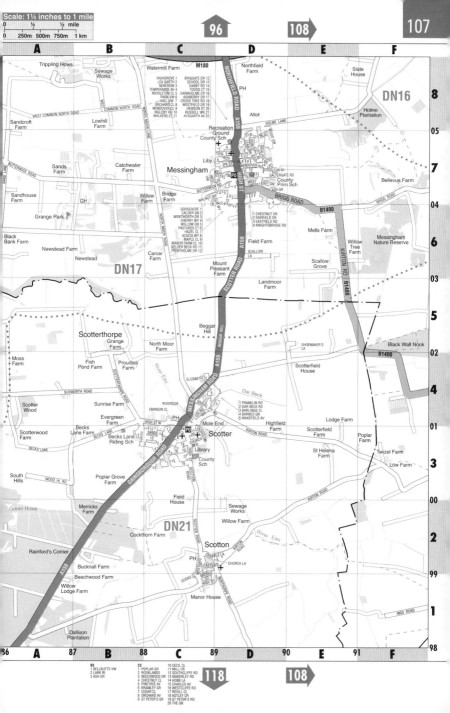

C3
1 POPLAR GR
2 ROOKLANDS
3 BEECHWOOD DR
4 CHESTNUT CL
5 PINETREE AV
6 BRAMLEY GR
7 CEDAR CL
8 ORCHARD AV
9 ST PETER'S GR
10 CECIL CL
11 MILL CR
12 SOUTHCLIFFE RD
13 WAKERLEY RD
14 HOBB LA
15 CHARLES AV
16 WESTCLIFFE RD
17 REVILL CL
18 ASTLEY CR
19 ST PETER'S RD
20 THE GN

107
97

Scale: 1¼ inches to 1 mile
0 ¼ ½ mile
0 250m 500m 750m 1 km

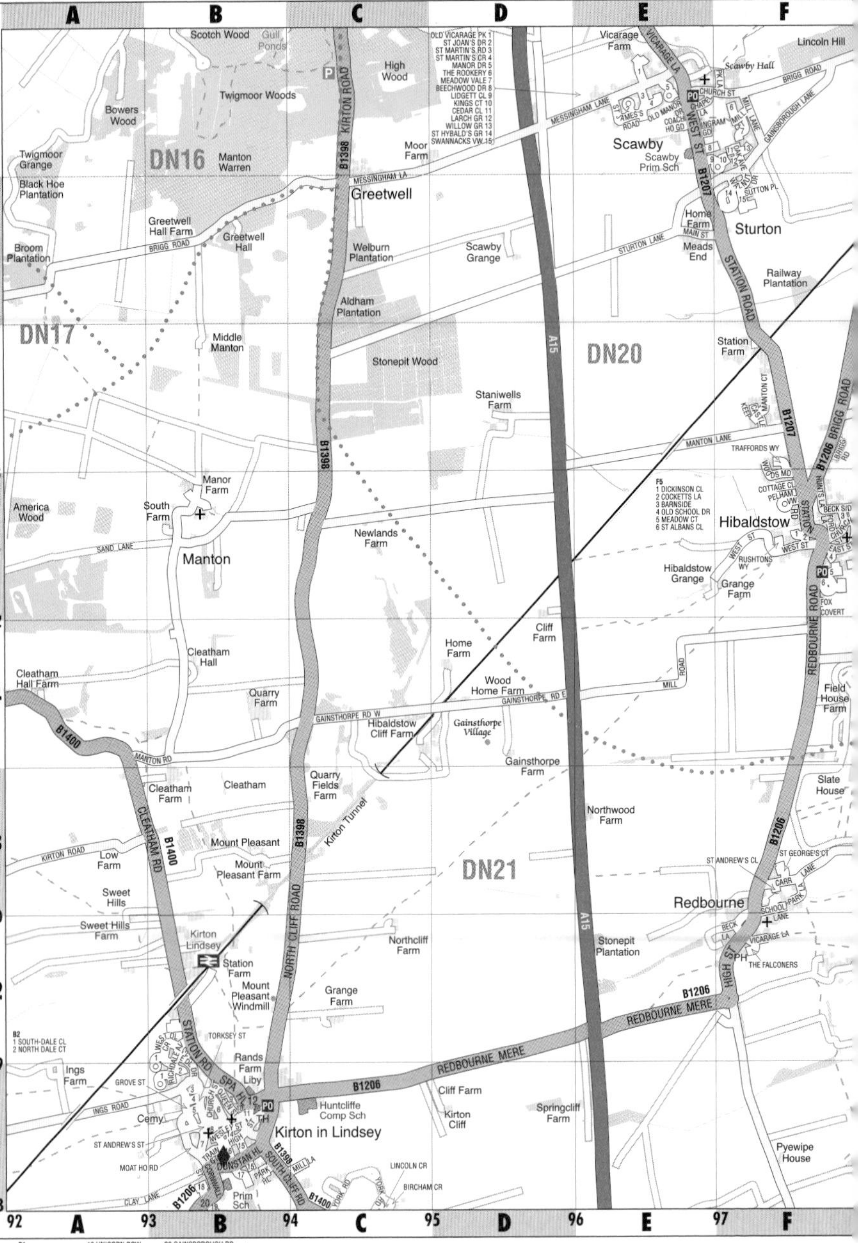

B1
1 HIGHFIELD DR
2 ORCHARD CL
3 WHITEWELL CL
4 DARWIN ST
5 TURNER ST
6 MARCH ST
7 CORNWALL ST
8 OLD SCHOOL YD
9 SUNNY HL
10 UNICORN ROW
11GEORGE ST
12 KING EDWARD ST
13 SYLVESTER ST
14 WRAY ST
15 EAST CROSS ST
16 WEST CROSS ST
17 DUNSTAN VILLAS
18 LOWFIELD CL
19 GRAYINGHAM RD
20 GAINSBOROUGH RD

107
119

Scale: 1¼ inches to 1 mile
0 ¼ ½ mile
0 250m 500m 750m 1 km

98
110

A B C D E F

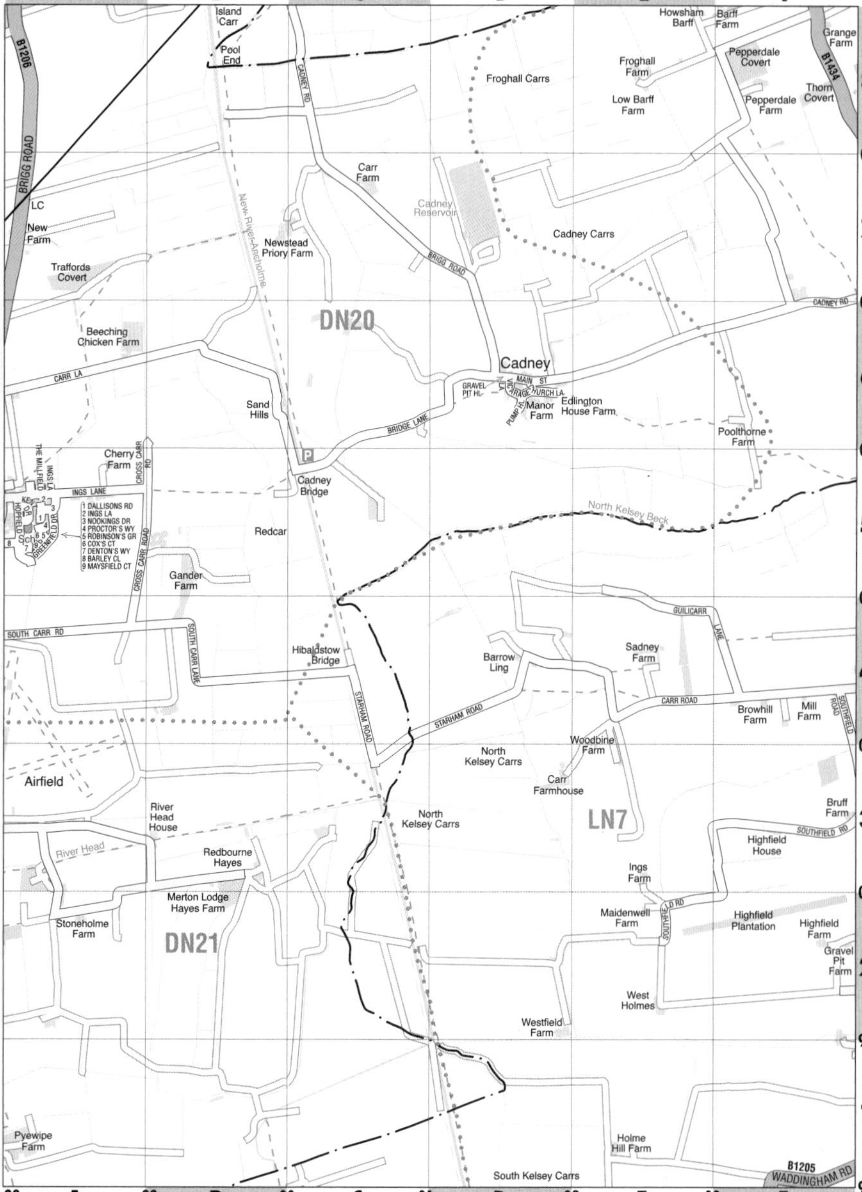

8 05 7 04 6 03 5 02 4 01 3 00 2 99 1 98

98 A 99 B 00 C 01 D 02 E 03 F

110

Scale: 1¼ inches to 1 mile
0 ¼ ½ mile
0 250m 500m 750m 1 km

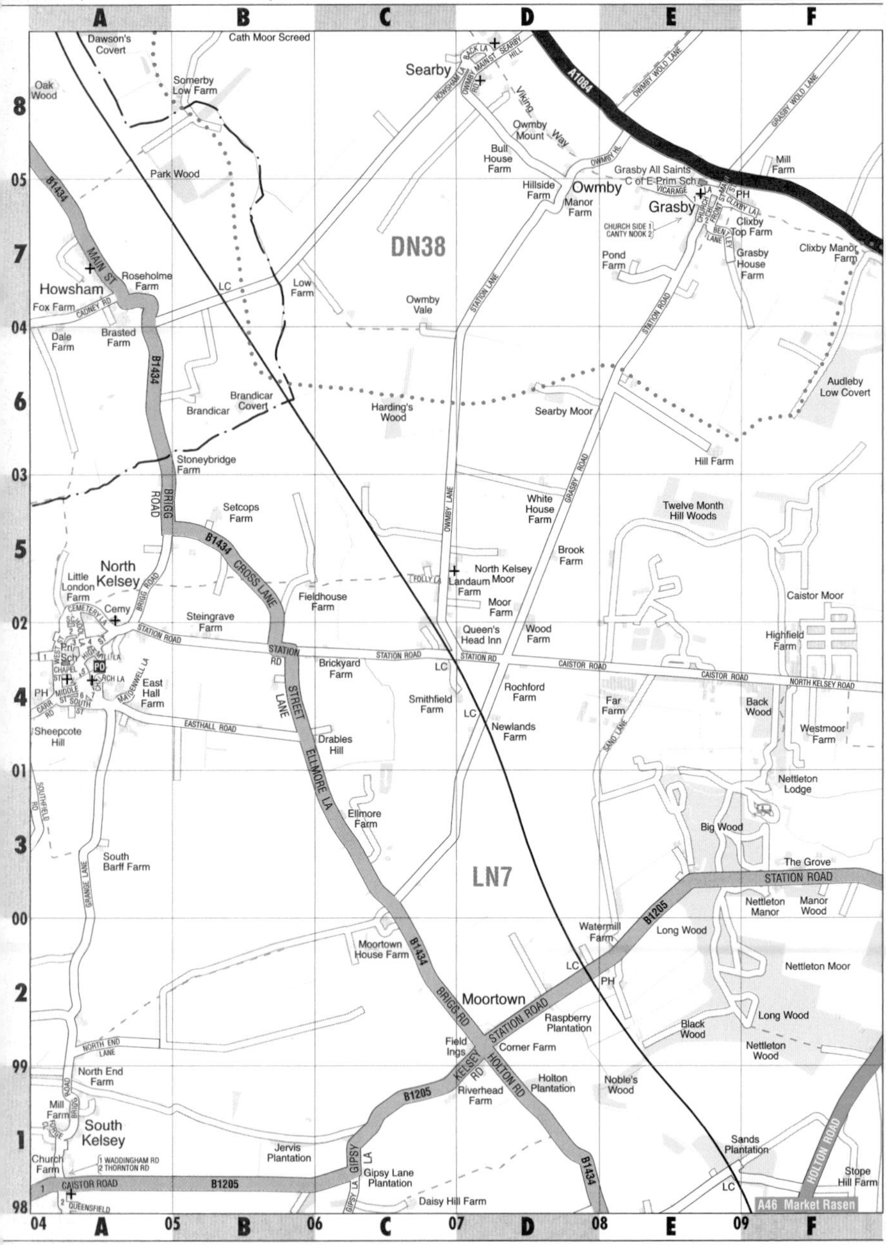

100
112

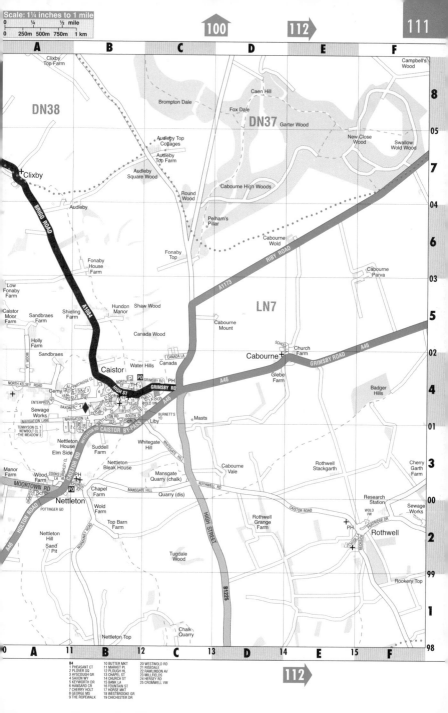

Scale: 1¼ inches to 1 mile

0 ¼ ½ mile

0 250m 500m 750m 1 km

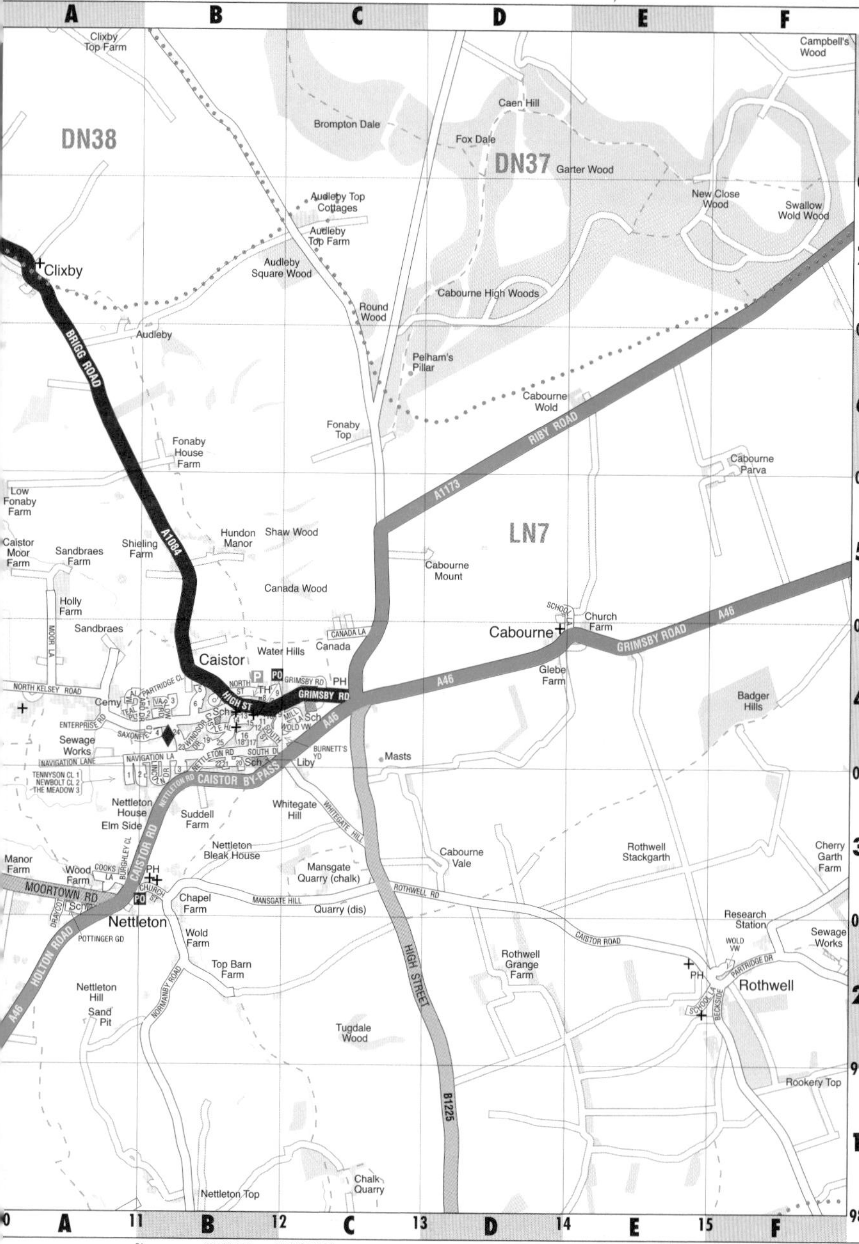

B4
1 PHEASANT CT
2 PLOVER SQ
3 AYSCOUGH GR
4 SAXON WY
5 KEYWORTH DR
6 HANSARD CR
7 CHERRY HOLT
8 GEORGE MS
9 THE ROPEWALK
10 BUTTER MKT
11 MARKET PL
12 PLOUGH HL
13 CHAPEL ST
14 CHURCH ST
15 BANK LA
16 FOUNTAIN ST
17 HORSE MKT
18 WESTBROOKE GR
19 CHICHESTER DR
20 WESTWOLD RD
21 RISEDALE
22 RAWLINSON AV
23 MILLFIELDS
24 HERSEY RD
25 CROMWELL VW

112

111

101

Scale: 1¼ inches to 1 mile
0 ¼ ½ mile
0 250m 500m 750m 1 km

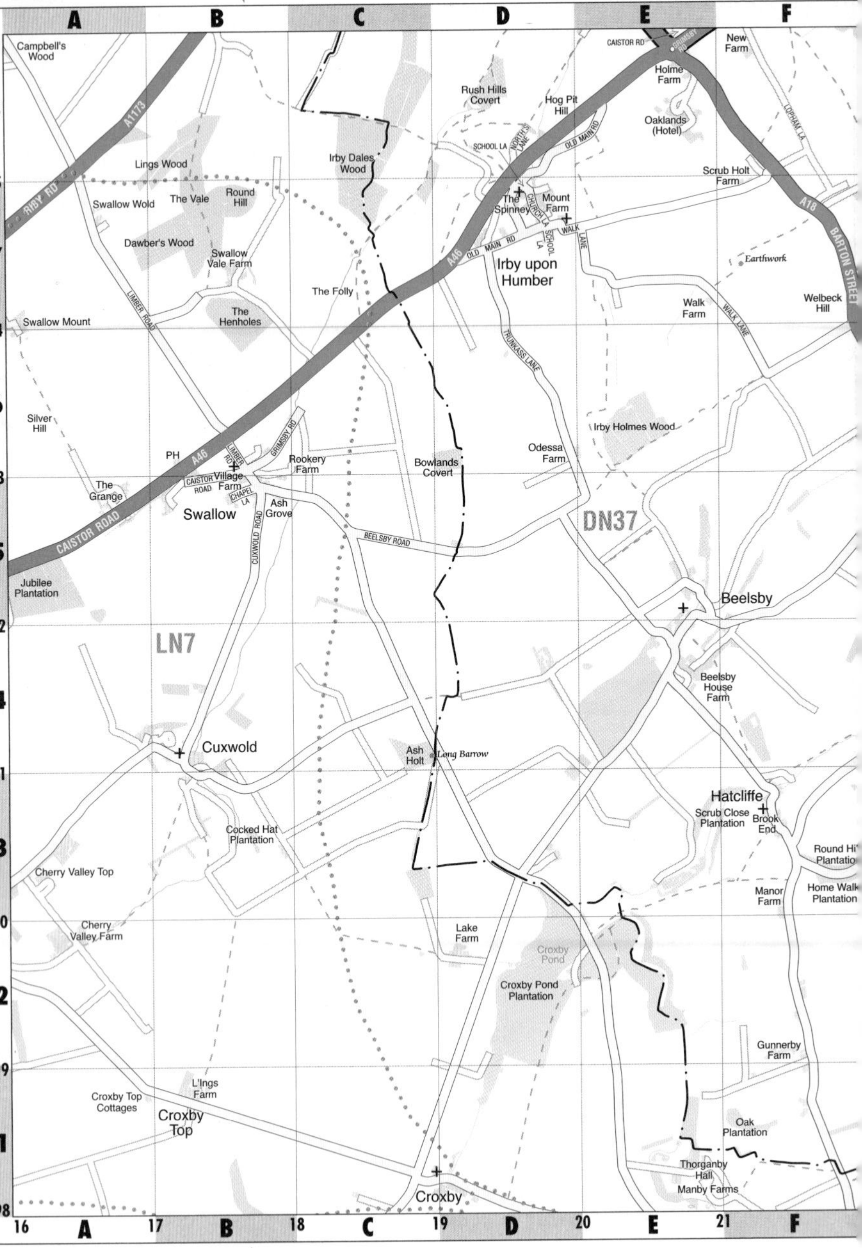
A
B
C
D
E
F
8
05
7
04
6
03
5
02
4
01
3
00
2
99
1
98
16
17
18
19
20
21
Campbell's Wood
A1173
RIBY RD
Lings Wood
Swallow Wold
The Vale
Round Hill
Dawber's Wood
Swallow Vale Farm
LIMBER ROAD
The Henholes
Swallow Mount
Silver Hill
The Grange
PH
A46
LIMBER RD
CAISTOR ROAD
Village Farm
CHAPEL LA
GRIMSBY RD
Rookery Farm
Swallow
Ash Grove
CUXWOLD ROAD
CAISTOR ROAD
Jubilee Plantation
LN7
Cuxwold
Cocked Hat Plantation
Cherry Valley Top
Cherry Valley Farm
Croxby Top Cottages
L'Ings Farm
Croxby Top
Croxby
Irby Dales Wood
The Folly
Bowlands Covert
BEELSBY ROAD
Ash Holt
Long Barrow
Lake Farm
Croxby Pond
Croxby Pond Plantation
Rush Hills Covert
Hog Pit Hill
SCHOOL LA
NORTH'S LANE
OLD MAIN RD
The Spinney
CHURCH LA
Mount Farm
SCHOOL LA
WALK
LANE
OLD MAIN RD
Irby upon Humber
TRUNKASS LANE
Odessa Farm
Irby Holmes Wood
DN37
CAISTOR RD
GRIMSBY RD
New Farm
Holme Farm
Oaklands (Hotel)
LOPHAM LA
Scrub Holt Farm
A18
BARTON STREET
Earthwork
Walk Farm
WALK LANE
Welbeck Hill
Beelsby
Beelsby House Farm
Hatcliffe
Scrub Close Plantation
Brook End
Round Hi' Plantatio
Manor Farm
Home Walk Plantation
Gunnerby Farm
Oak Plantation
Thorganby Hall
Manby Farms

111

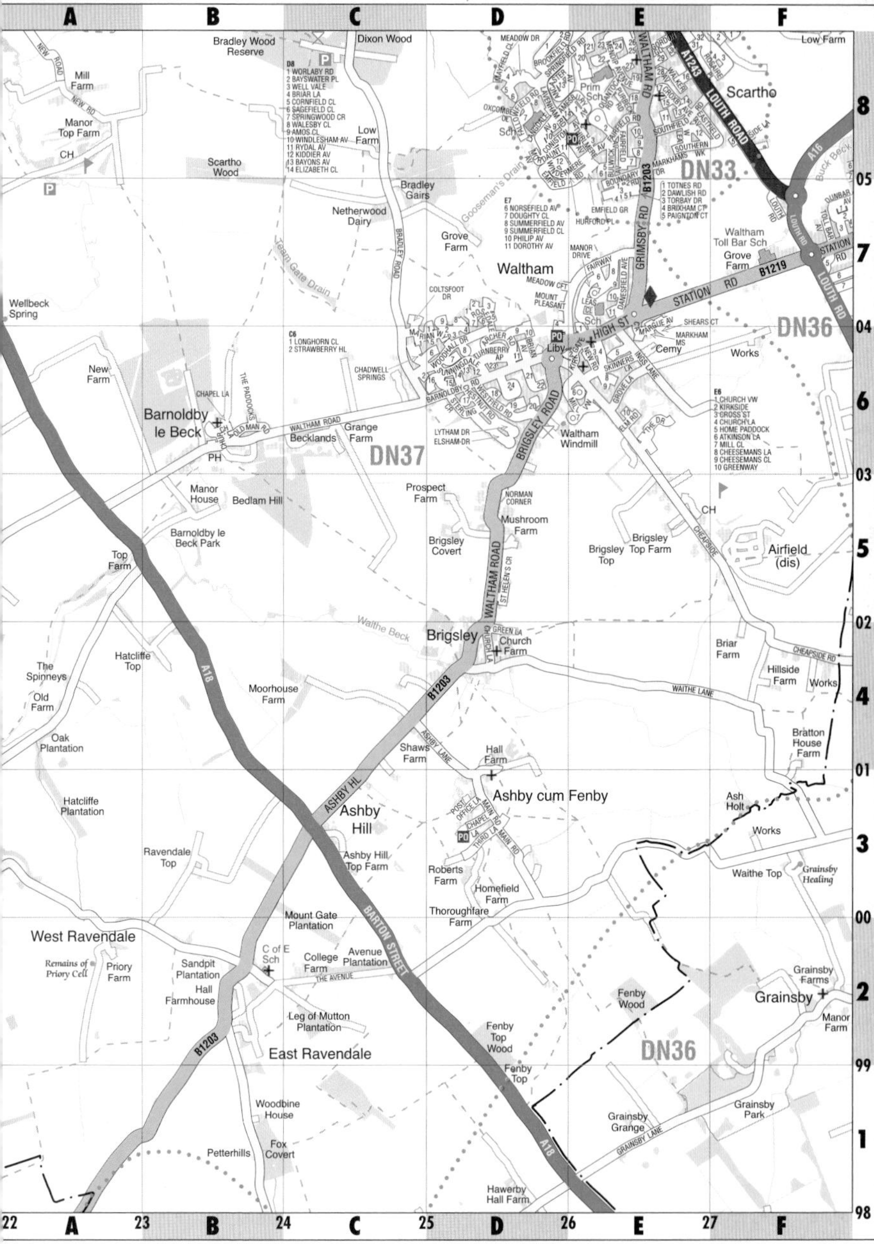
A B C D E F
8 05 7 04 6 03 5 02 4 01 3 00 2 99 1 98
22 23 24 25 26 27
Bradley Wood Reserve
Dixon Wood
Mill Farm
NEW ROAD
Manor Top Farm
CH
Scartho Wood
Low Farm
D8
1 WORLABY RD
2 BAYSWATER PL
3 WELL VALE
4 BRIAR LA
5 CORNFIELD CL
6 SAGEFIELD CL
7 SPRINGWOOD CR
8 WALESBY CL
9 AMOS CL
10 WINDLESHAM AV
11 RYDAL AV
12 KIDDIER AV
13 BAYONS AV
14 ELIZABETH CL
Bradley Gairs
Netherwood Dairy
Grove Farm
BRADLEY ROAD
Team Gate Drain
Gooseman's Drain
Scartho
LOUTH ROAD
A1243
A16
Buck Beck
DN33
WALTHAM RD
GRIMSBY RD
B1203
E7
6 NORSEFIELD AV
7 DOUGHTY CL
8 SUMMERFIELD AV
9 SUMMERFIELD CL
10 PHILIP AV
11 DOROTHY AV
1 TOTNES RD
2 DAWLISH RD
3 TORBAY DR
4 BRIXHAM CT
5 PAIGNTON CT
Waltham Toll Bar Sch
Grove Farm
STATION RD
B1219
Waltham
Wellbeck Spring
COLTSFOOT DR
C6
1 LONGHORN CL
2 STRAWBERRY HL
CHADWELL SPRINGS
HIGH ST
Cemy
Works
DN36
New Farm
Barnoldby le Beck
CHAPEL LA
THE PADDOCKS
WALTHAM ROAD
Grange Farm
Becklands
PH
DN37
BRIGSLEY ROAD
Waltham Windmill
E6
1 CHURCH VW
2 KIRKSIDE
3 CROSS ST
4 CHURCH LA
5 HOME PADDOCK
6 ATKINSON LA
7 MILL CL
8 CHEESEMANS LA
9 CHEESEMANS CL
10 GREENWAY
Manor House
Bedlam Hill
Prospect Farm
NORMAN CORNER
Mushroom Farm
Barnoldby le Beck Park
Brigsley Covert
Brigsley Top
Brigsley Top Farm
CHEAPSIDE
Airfield (dis)
Top Farm
WALTHAM ROAD
ST HELEN'S CR
Waithe Beck
Brigsley
Church Farm
Briar Farm
CHEAPSIDE RD
Hatcliffe Top
The Spinneys
Old Farm
A18
Moorhouse Farm
WAITHE LANE
Hillside Farm
Works
Oak Plantation
ASHBY LANE
Shaws Farm
Hall Farm
Bratton House Farm
Ashby cum Fenby
Ash Holt
Hatcliffe Plantation
ASHBY HL
Ashby Hill
Works
Ravendale Top
Ashby Hill Top Farm
Roberts Farm
Waithe Top
Grainsby Healing
Homefield Farm
Thoroughfare Farm
BARTON STREET
Mount Gate Plantation
West Ravendale
Remains of Priory Cell
Priory Farm
Sandpit Plantation
C of E Sch
College Farm
Avenue Plantation
THE AVENUE
Grainsby Farms
Hall Farmhouse
Fenby Wood
Grainsby
Manor Farm
Leg of Mutton Plantation
East Ravendale
Fenby Top Wood
DN36
Fenby Top
Woodbine House
Grainsby Park
Grainsby Grange
GRAINSBY LANE
Petterhills
Fox Covert
Hawerby Hall Farm

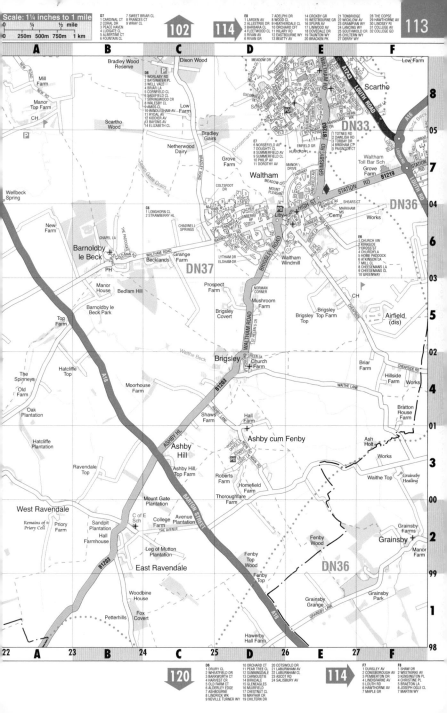

A7
1 SHAFTESBURY MS
2 CHANDLERS CL
3 DRURY LA
4 ADELPHI CT
5 DUNBAR AV
6 ALDWYCH CFT
7 BARBICAN WY
8 PICCADILLY
9 DOMINION CL
10 WYNDHAM RD
11 FARMHOUSE MS
12 SAVOY CT
13 GREENLANDS AV
14 THE ORCHARD
15 KAYMILE CL
16 RUTLAND DR
17 CHARLES AV
18 MARGARET PL
19 WADDINGHAM PL
20 GRANGE FARM LA

113

103

D8
1 STANILAND WY
2 CHIPPENDALE CL
3 SHERATON DR
4 WOODFIELD CL
5 EASTFIELD
6 ROWAN DR
7 BURCOM AV
8 COULAM PL
9 CHAPMAN CR
10 ASHWOOD DR
11 ANDREW RD
12 VISCOUNT WY
13 HUMBERSTON AV

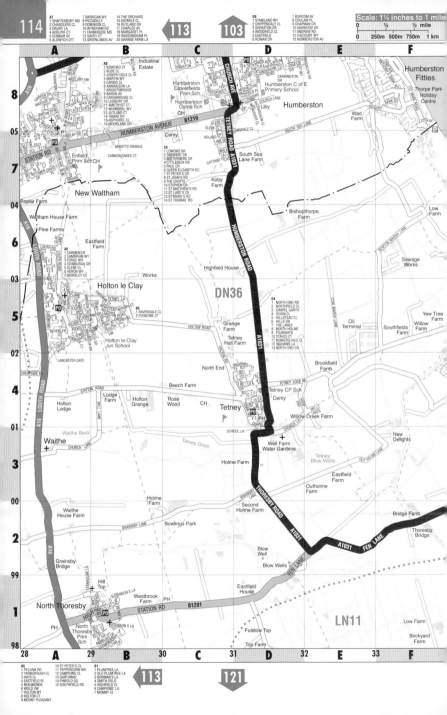

Scale: 1¼ inches to 1 mile
0 ¼ ½ mile
0 250m 500m 750m 1 km

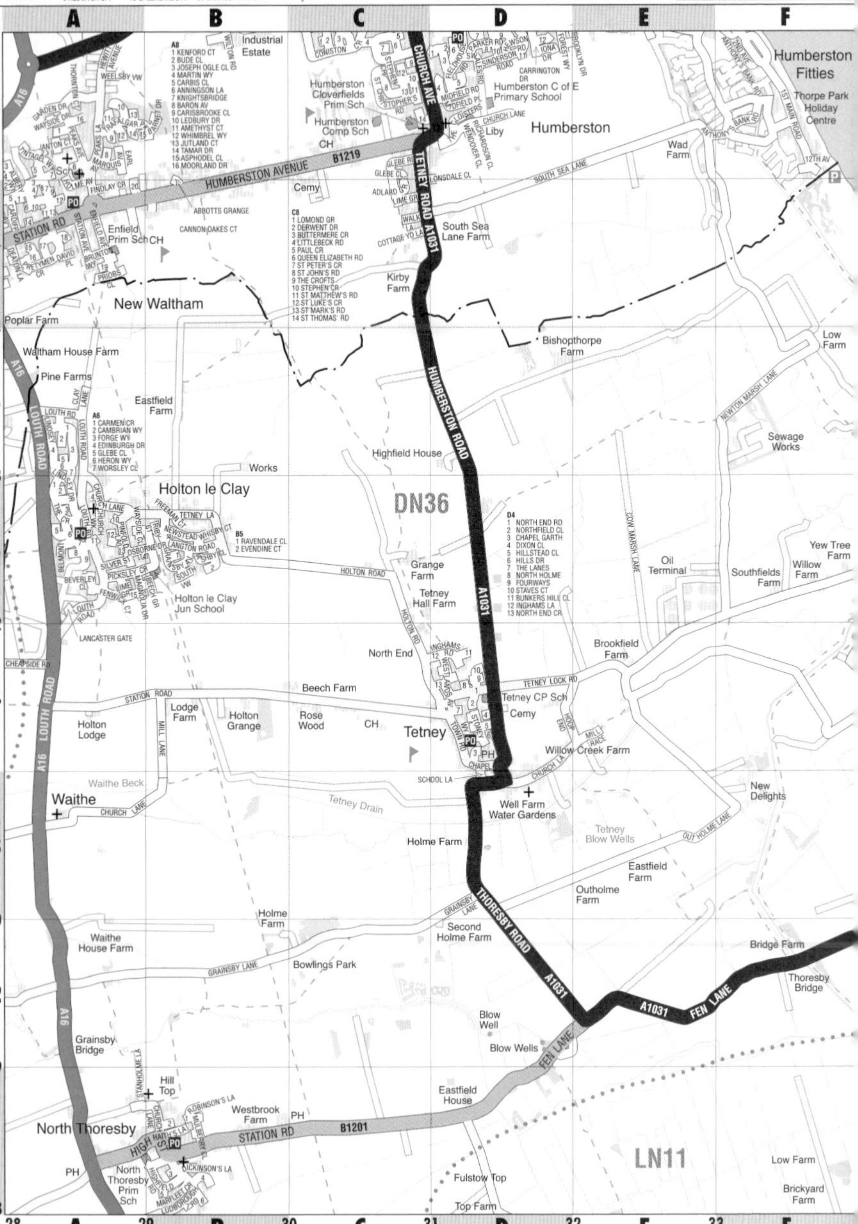

A5
1 PELHAM RD
2 YARBOROUGH CL
3 HAYS CL
4 EASTFIELD RI
5 BEAUMONDE
6 WOLD VW
7 HOLTON MT
8 HOLTON CT
9 MOUNT PLEASANT
10 ST PETER'S CL
11 PEPPERCORN WK
12 CAMPIONS CL
13 GARTHWAY
14 PINFOLD GD
15 SOUTHFIELD RD

B1
1 PLUMTREE LA
2 OLD PLUMTREE LA
3 BORMAN'S LA
4 SMITH FIELD
5 HIGHFIELD CL
6 CAMPIONS' LA
7 MUMBY CL

113

121

Scale: 1¼ inches to 1 mile
0 ¼ ½ mile
0 250m 500m 750m 1 km

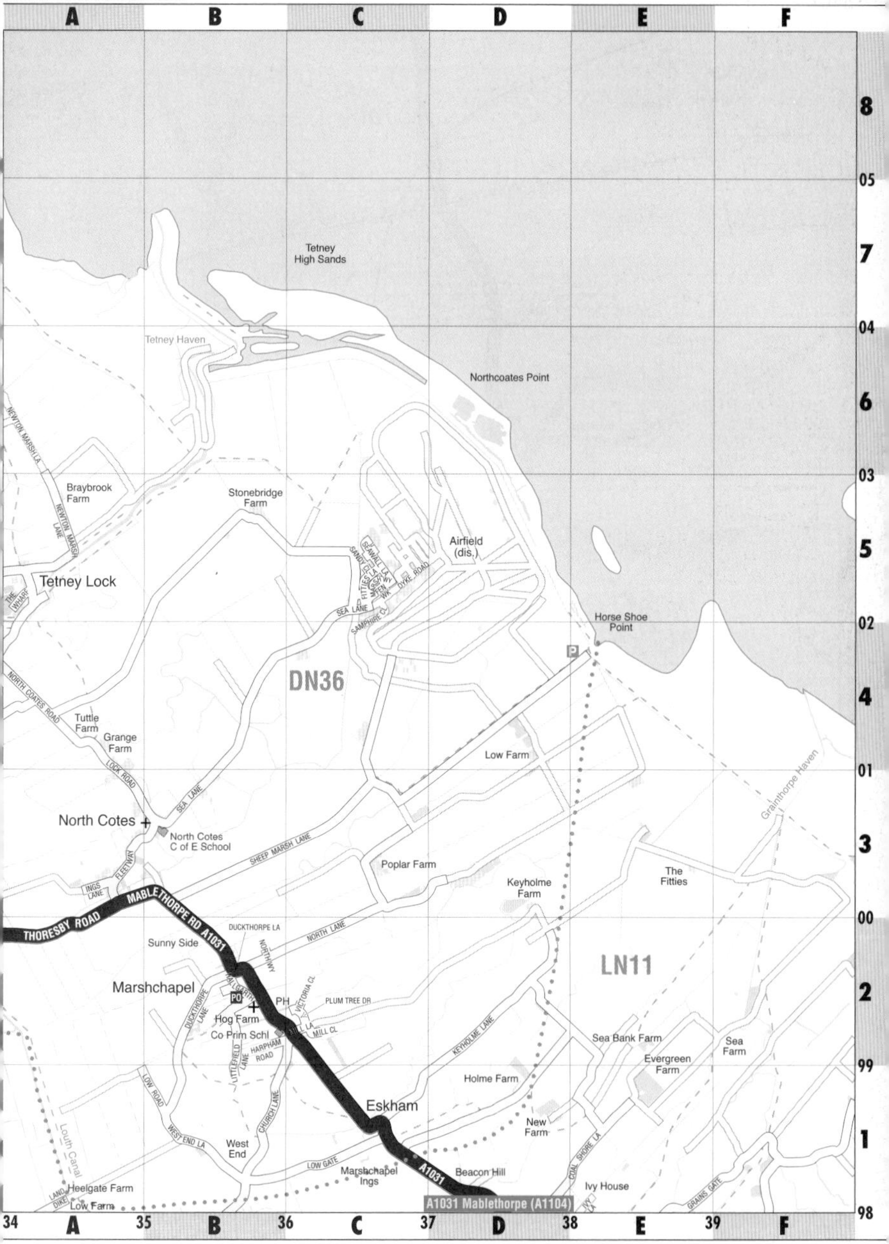
A
B
C
D
E
F
Tetney High Sands
Tetney Haven
Northcoates Point
Braybrook Farm
Stonebridge Farm
Airfield (dis.)
Tetney Lock
Horse Shoe Point
DN36
Tuttle Farm
Grange Farm
Low Farm
North Cotes
North Cotes C of E School
Poplar Farm
Keyholme Farm
The Fitties
Grainthorpe Haven
THORESBY ROAD
MABLETHORPE RD A1031
Sunny Side
Marshchapel
LN11
Hog Farm
Co Prim Schl
PH
Sea Bank Farm
Evergreen Farm
Sea Farm
Holme Farm
Eskham
New Farm
West End
Louth Canal
Heelgate Farm
Low Farm
Marshchapel Ings
Beacon Hill
Ivy House
A1031 Mablethorpe (A1104)
NEWTON MARSH LA
NEWTON MARSH LANE
THE WHARF
NORTH COATES ROAD
LOCK ROAD
SEA LANE
SHEEP MARSH LANE
FLEETWAY
INGS LANE
DUCKTHORPE LA
NORTHWAY
NORTH LANE
VICTORIA CL
PLUM TREE DR
MILL LA
MILL CL
KEYHOLME LANE
DUCKTHORPE LANE
LITTLEFIELD LANE
HARPHAM ROAD
CHURCH LANE
LOW ROAD
WEST END LA
LOW GATE
COAL SHORE LA
GRAINS GATE
LAND DIKE
SEA LANE
SAMPHIRE CL
DYKE ROAD
SEAWALL LA
SANDY CL
FITTIES LA
8
05
7
04
6
03
5
02
4
01
3
00
2
99
1
98
34
35
36
37
38
39

105

Scale: 1¼ inches to 1 mile
0 ¼ ½ mile
0 250m 500m 750m 1 km

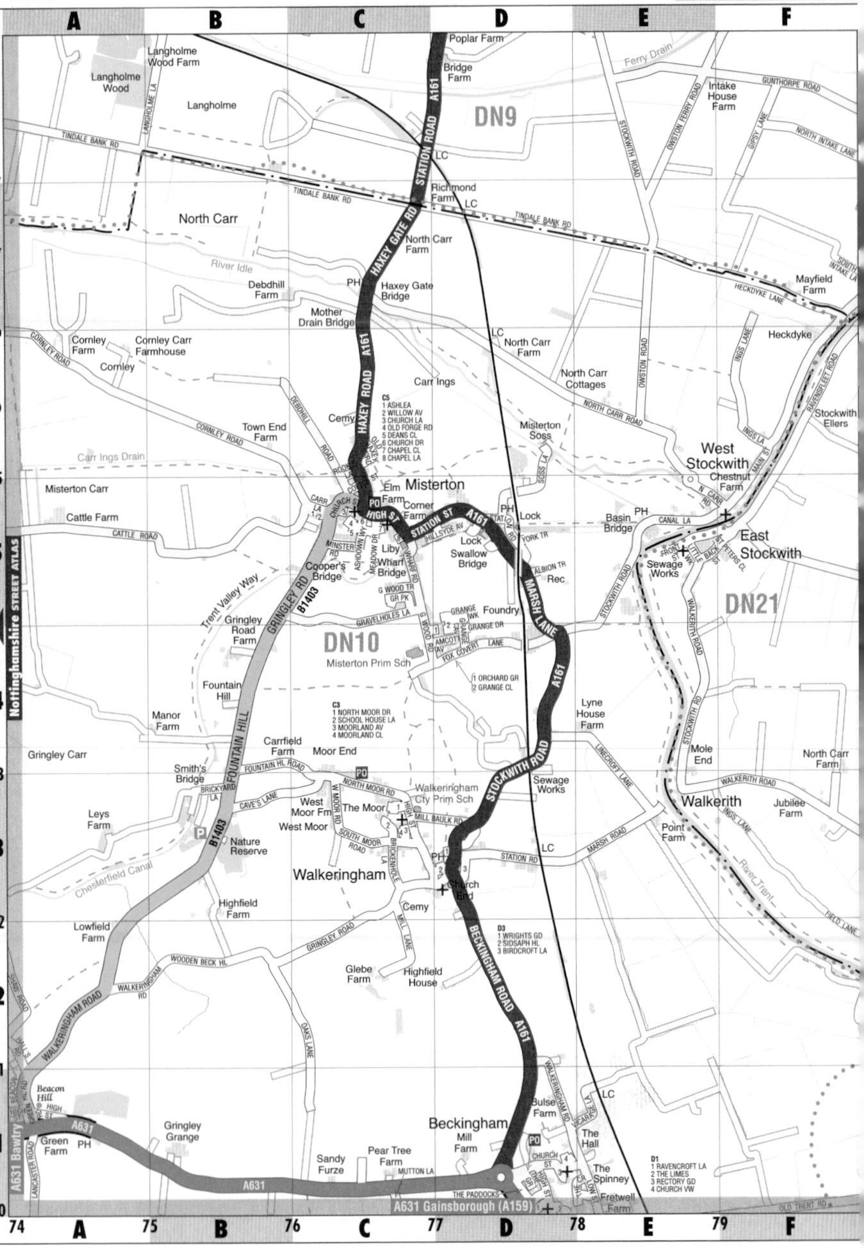

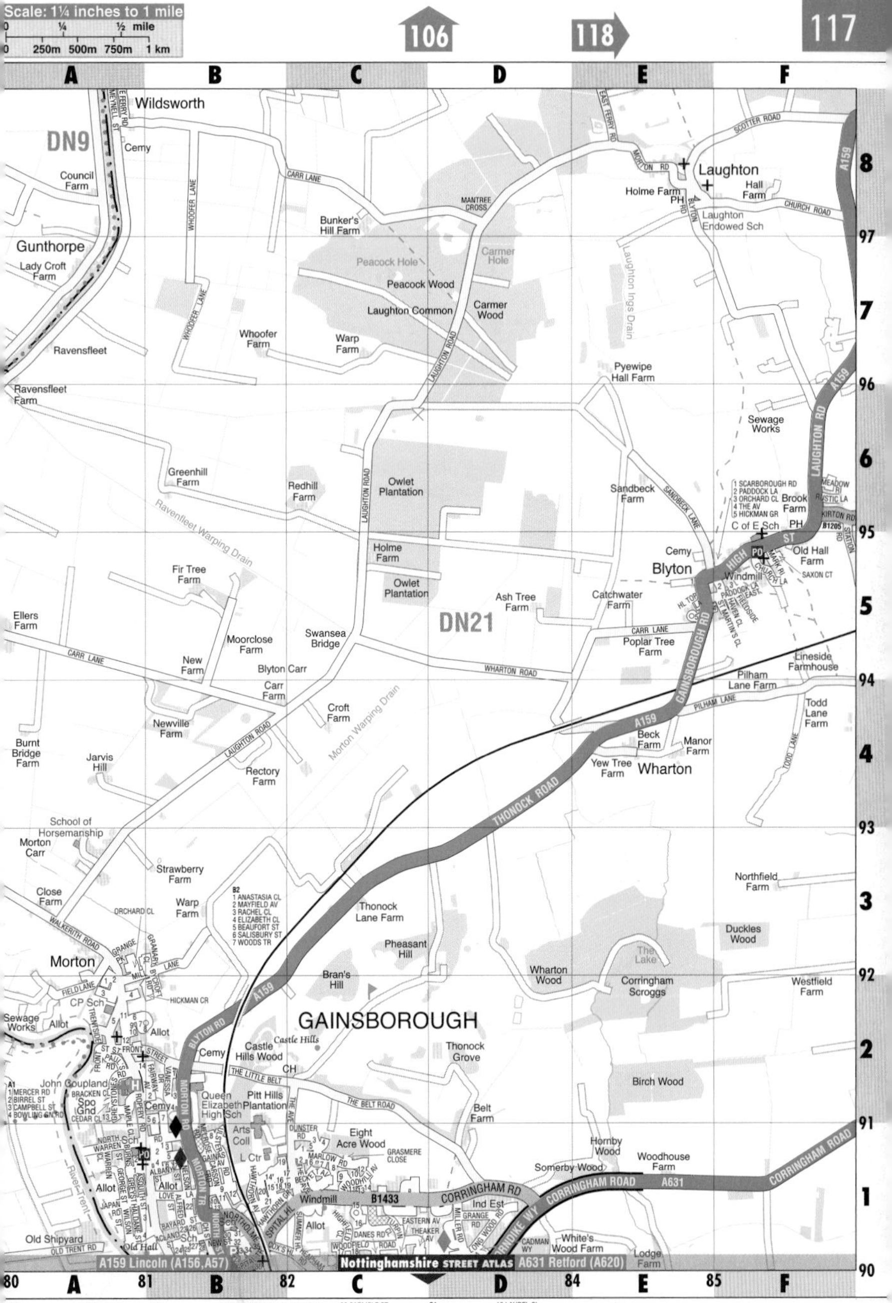

A2
1 SOUTHLANDS AV
2 SOUTHLANDS GD
3 SOUTHLANDS DR
4 MORTON CL
5 CROOKED BILLET ST
6 NORTH ST
7 CROSS ST
8 SOUTH ST
9 WEST ST
10 CHAPEL LA
11 WALKERITH RD
12 DOG AND DUCK LA
13 WILLOW CL
14 WOODLAND AV

B1
1 HOTSPUR RD
2 NOEL ST
3 MOWBRAY ST
4 CURZON ST
5 MELROSE RD
6 HENLEY CT
7 ROWSTON CL
8 OLD SHOWFIELDS
9 CONNAUGHT RD
10 ARKWRIGHT ST
11 EDWARD RD
12 ARTHUR RD
13 CROMFORD ST
14 BEECH AV
15 CHESTNUT AV
16 BIRCH GR
17 ASH GR
18 LABURNUM AV
19 THE AVE
20 ACACIA AV
21 LIME TREE AV
22 GARFIELD ST
23 LINCOLN ST
24 BALFOUR ST
25 CECIL ST
26 FORSTER ST
27 FAWCETT ST
28 SCOTT ST
29 DRILL HALL LA
30 CARLISLE ST
31 CHARLES ST
32 TOWER ST
33 TENNYSON ST
34 RECTORY AV
35 JUBILEE CRES
36 CROSS ST

C1
1 HAWTON CL
2 STIRLING CL
3 MILTON RD
4 ARUNDEL CL
5 MILTON CL
6 DUNBAR CL
7 PENDEEN CL
8 IONA CL
9 SYCAMORE DR
10 LAUREL CL
11 LARCH CT
12 HARROW CL
13 ASPEN CT
14 OAK TREE AV
15 REDMAN CL
16 BRAMLEY CT
17 NEWLANDS
18 CHERRY TREE RD

118

117

107

Scale: 1¼ inches to 1 mile
0 ¼ ½ mile
0 250m 500m 750m 1 km

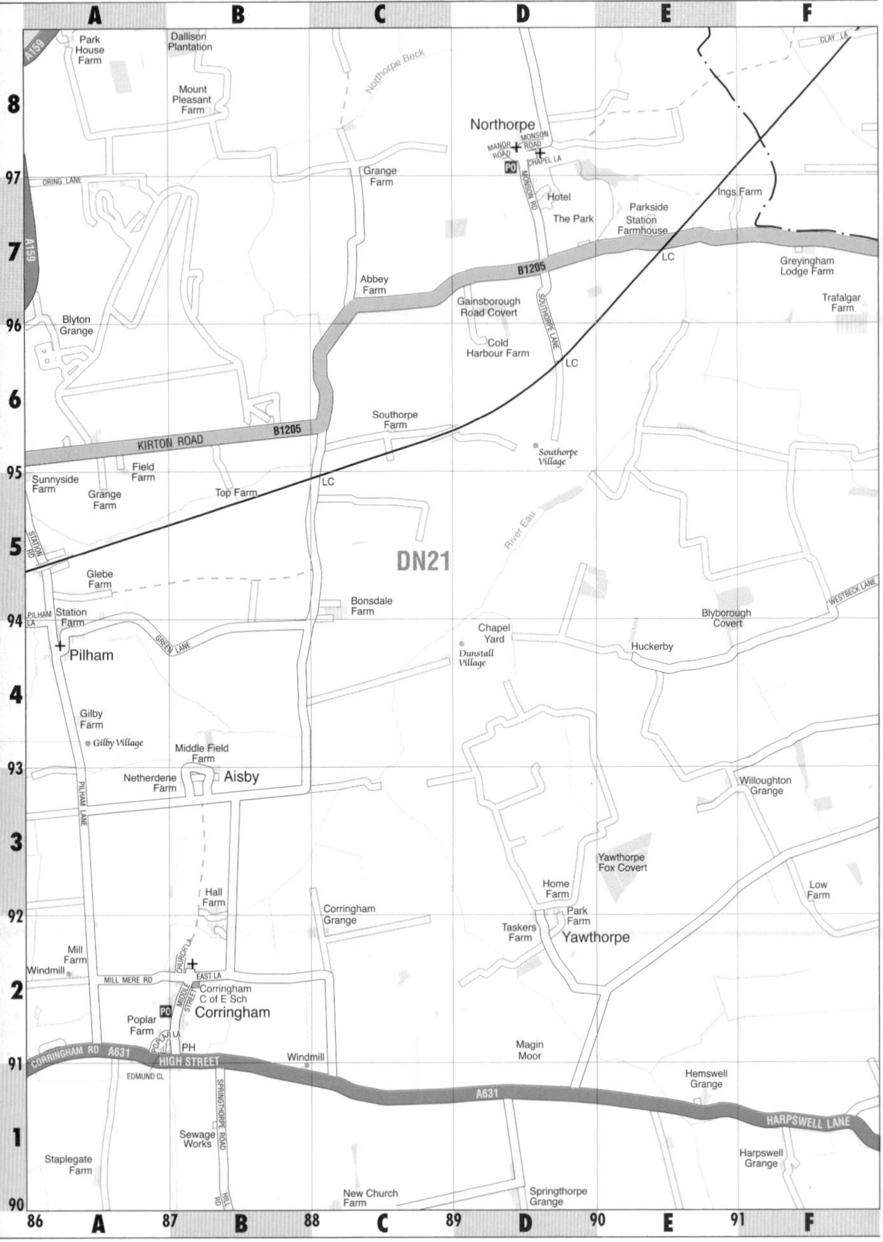

117

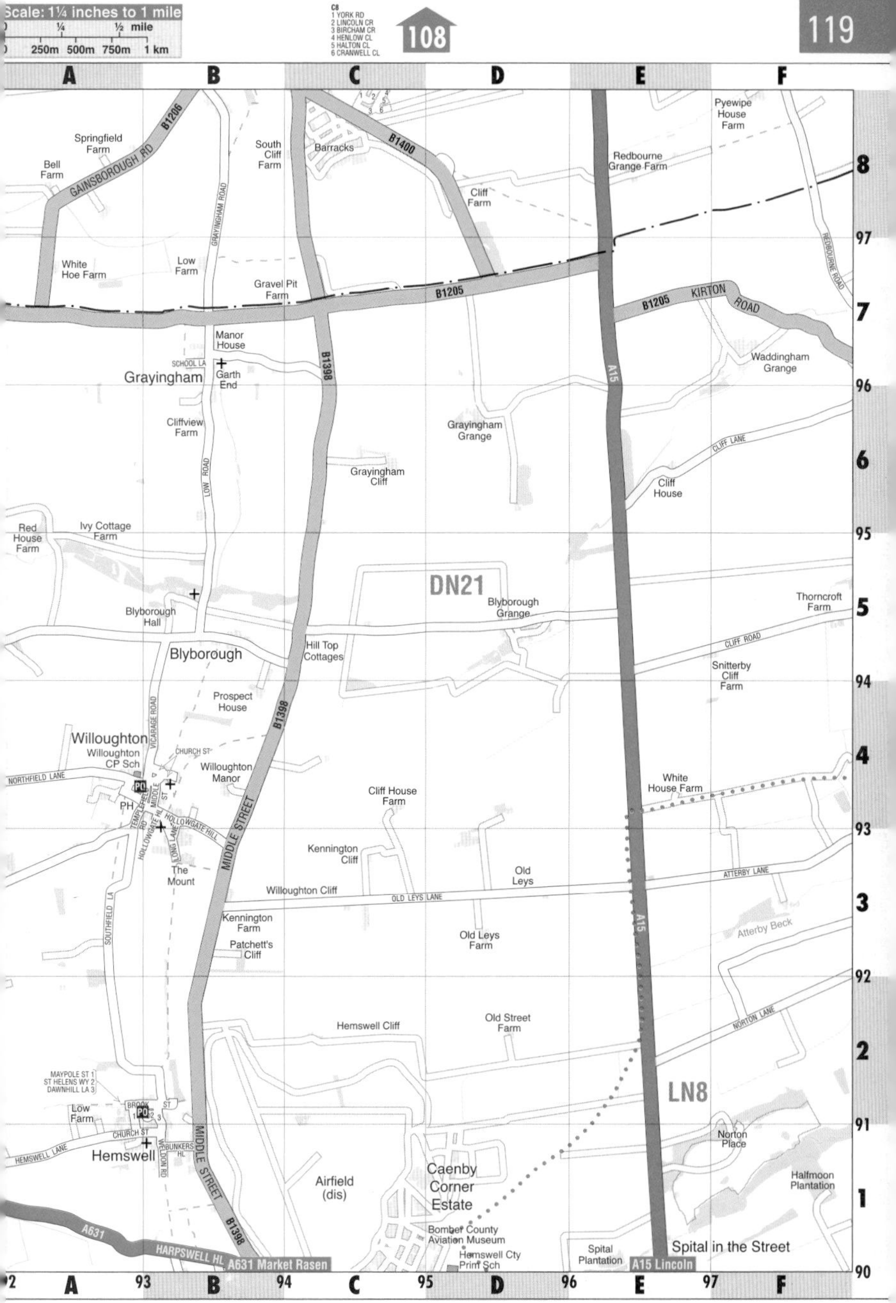
Scale: 1¼ inches to 1 mile
¼ ½ mile
250m 500m 750m 1 km
C8
1 YORK RD
2 LINCOLN CR
3 BIRCHAM CR
4 HENLOW CL
5 HALTON CL
6 CRANWELL CL
108
Springfield Farm
Bell Farm
GAINSBOROUGH RD
B1206
South Cliff Farm
Barracks
B1400
Pyewipe House Farm
Redbourne Grange Farm
Cliff Farm
REDBOURNE ROAD
White Hoe Farm
Low Farm
GRAYINGHAM ROAD
Gravel Pit Farm
B1205
KIRTON ROAD
Manor House
SCHOOL LA
Grayingham
Garth End
B1398
A15
Waddingham Grange
Cliffview Farm
Grayingham Grange
CLIFF LANE
Grayingham Cliff
LOW ROAD
Cliff House
Red House Farm
Ivy Cottage Farm
DN21
Blyborough Hall
Blyborough Grange
Thorncroft Farm
Blyborough
Hill Top Cottages
CLIFF ROAD
Snitterby Cliff Farm
Prospect House
VICARAGE ROAD
Willoughton
Willoughton CP Sch
CHURCH ST
Willoughton Manor
NORTHFIELD LANE
PO
PH
TEMPLEFIELD RD
MIDDLE ST
HOLLOWGATE HILL
HOLLOWGATE HL
LONG LANE
Cliff House Farm
White House Farm
Kennington Cliff
The Mount
MIDDLE STREET
Old Leys
ATTERBY LANE
Willoughton Cliff
OLD LEYS LANE
SOUTHFIELD LA
Kennington Farm
Patchett's Cliff
Old Leys Farm
Atterby Beck
Hemswell Cliff
Old Street Farm
NORTON LANE
MAYPOLE ST 1
ST HELENS WY 2
DAWNHILL LA 3
LN8
Low Farm
BROOK ST
CHURCH ST
HEMSWELL LANE
BUNKERS HL
WELDON RD
Hemswell
Norton Place
Caenby Corner Estate
Airfield (dis)
Halfmoon Plantation
Bomber County Aviation Museum
Hemswell Cty Prim Sch
A631
HARPSWELL HL
A631 Market Rasen
Spital Plantation
A15 Lincoln
Spital in the Street
A B C D E F
8 97 7 96 6 95 5 94 4 93 3 92 2 91 1 90
92 93 94 95 96 97

113

Scale: 1¼ inches to 1 mile
0 ¼ ½ mile
0 250m 500m 750m 1 km

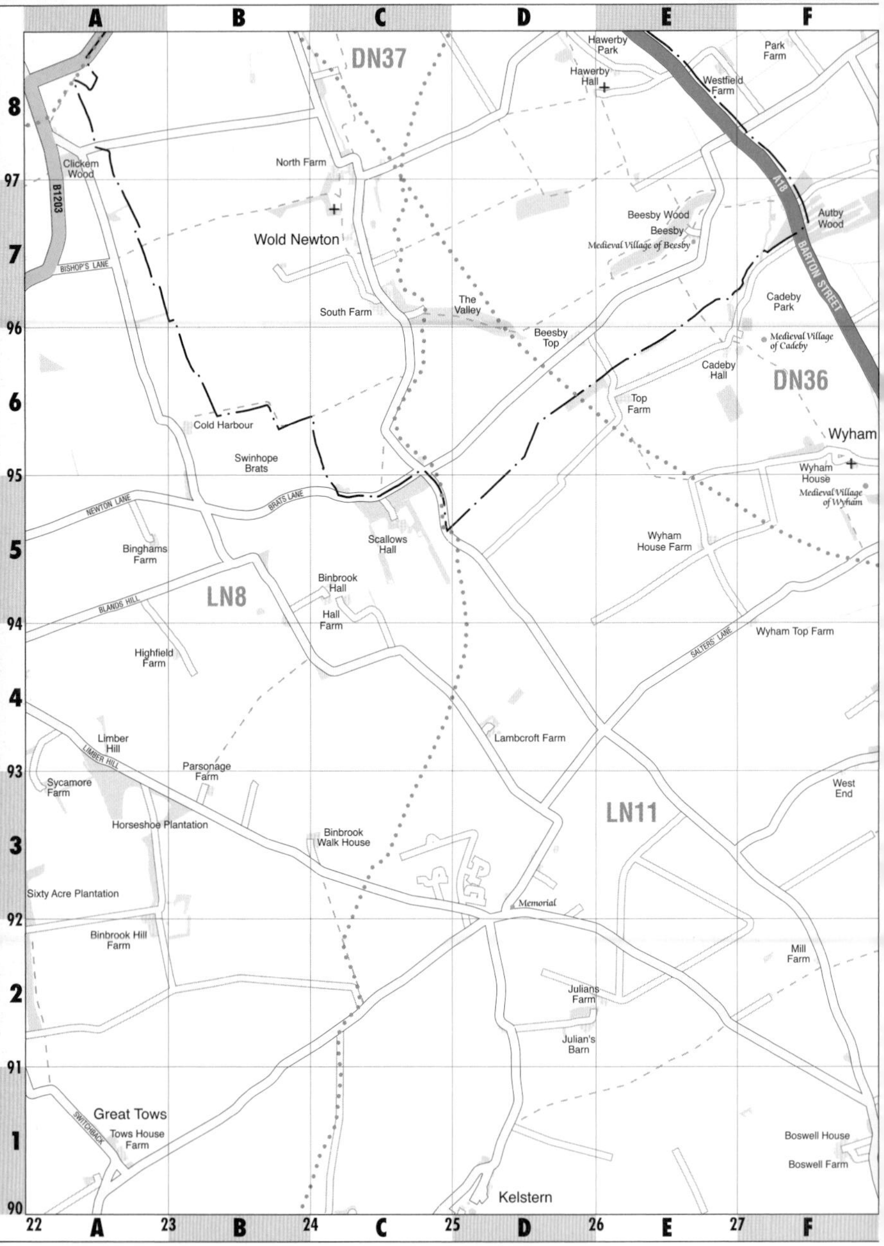
A
B
C
D
E
F
DN37
Hawerby Park
Hawerby Hall
Park Farm
Westfield Farm
Clickem Wood
B1203
North Farm
Wold Newton
A18
Beesby Wood
Beesby
Medieval Village of Beesby
Autby Wood
BISHOP'S LANE
BARTON STREET
South Farm
The Valley
Cadeby Park
Beesby Top
Medieval Village of Cadeby
Cadeby Hall
DN36
Top Farm
Cold Harbour
Wyham
Swinhope Brats
Wyham House
Medieval Village of Wyham
NEWTON LANE
BRATS LANE
Scallows Hall
Wyham House Farm
Binghams Farm
Binbrook Hall
LN8
BLANDS HILL
Hall Farm
Wyham Top Farm
SALTERS' LANE
Highfield Farm
Lambcroft Farm
Limber Hill
LIMBER HILL
Parsonage Farm
Sycamore Farm
West End
LN11
Horseshoe Plantation
Binbrook Walk House
Sixty Acre Plantation
Memorial
Binbrook Hill Farm
Mill Farm
Julians Farm
Julian's Barn
Great Tows
SWITCHBACK
Tows House Farm
Boswell House
Boswell Farm
Kelstern
8
97
7
96
6
95
5
94
4
93
3
92
2
91
1
90
22
23
24
25
26
27

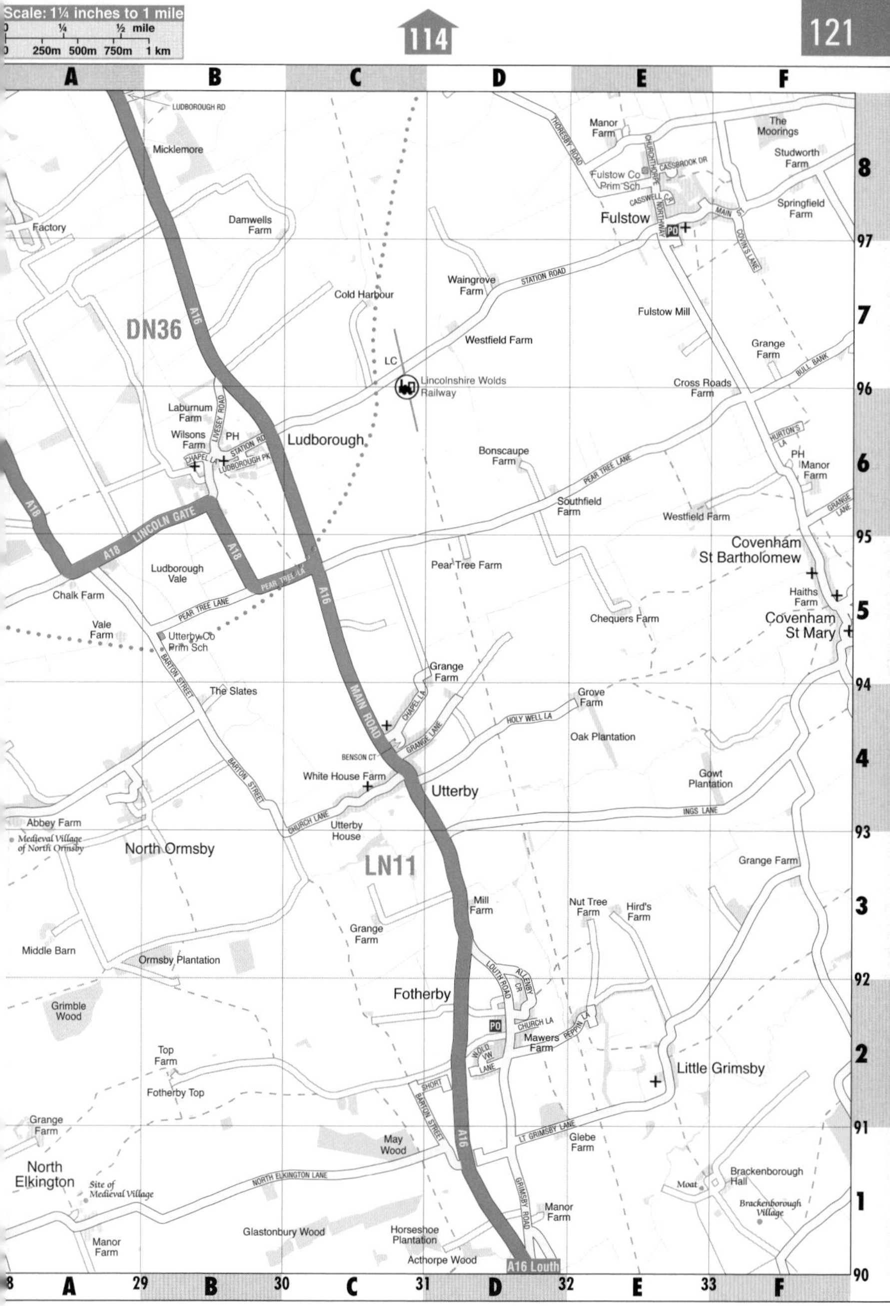
Scale: 1¼ inches to 1 mile
¼
½ mile
250m 500m 750m 1 km
A B C D E F
LUDBOROUGH RD
Micklemore
Factory
Damwells Farm
DN36
A16
Cold Harbour
Waingrove Farm
STATION ROAD
Westfield Farm
LC
Lincolnshire Wolds Railway
Laburnum Farm
LIVESEY ROAD
Wilsons Farm
PH
CHAPEL LA
STATION RD
LUDBOROUGH PK
Ludborough
A18
LINCOLN GATE
Ludborough Vale
PEAR TREE LA
PEAR TREE LANE
Chalk Farm
Vale Farm
Utterby Co Prim Sch
BARTON STREET
The Slates
MAIN ROAD
CHAPEL LA
GRANGE LANE
BENSON CT
White House Farm
Utterby
CHURCH LANE
Utterby House
Abbey Farm
Medieval Village of North Ormsby
North Ormsby
LN11
Manor Farm
THORESBY ROAD
CHURCHTHORPE
NORTHWAY
CASSBROOK DR
Fulstow Co Prim Sch
CASSWELL CR
Fulstow
PO
MAIN ST
COVIN'S LANE
The Moorings
Studworth Farm
Springfield Farm
Fulstow Mill
Grange Farm
BULL BANK
Cross Roads Farm
HURTON'S LA
PH
Manor Farm
Bonscaupe Farm
PEAR TREE LANE
Southfield Farm
Westfield Farm
GRANGE LANE
Covenham St Bartholomew
Pear Tree Farm
Haiths Farm
Chequers Farm
Covenham St Mary
Grange Farm
Grove Farm
HOLY WELL LA
Oak Plantation
Gowt Plantation
INGS LANE
Grange Farm
Mill Farm
Nut Tree Farm
Hird's Farm
Grange Farm
Middle Barn
Ormsby Plantation
LOUTH ROAD
ALLENBY CR
Fotherby
PO
CHURCH LA
PEPPIN LA
Mawers Farm
WOLD VW LANE
Little Grimsby
Grimble Wood
Top Farm
Fotherby Top
SHORT
BARTON STREET
LT GRIMSBY LANE
Glebe Farm
Grange Farm
May Wood
North Elkington
Site of Medieval Village
NORTH ELKINGTON LANE
Moat
Brackenborough Hall
Brackenborough Village
GRIMSBY ROAD
Manor Farm
Glastonbury Wood
Horseshoe Plantation
Manor Farm
Acthorpe Wood
A16 Louth
8 97 7 96 6 95 5 94 4 93 3 92 2 91 1 90
28 29 30 31 32 33

10
4

D6
1 TRENTHAM MS
2 N PINFOLD WY
3 PINFOLD CT
4 PINFOLD CL
5 CHATSWORTH CL
6 SANDRINGHAM CL
7 THORESBY MS
8 BALMORAL CL

10
11

C5
1 SEATHORNE RD
2 WYKENHAM CL
3 ELLERBURN DR
4 MILLFIELD RD
5 MILFORD CR
6 NEW PASTURE CL
7 SCARBOROUGH RD
8 SCARBOROUGH CR
9 THE HOLLOWS
10 MILL CT
11 MILLBANK
12 SHORT LA
13 STEPNEY AV

F2
1 CLARENCE RD
2 WESTMORLAND GR
3 WESTMORLAND AV
4 PRINCESS ST
5 PRINCESS TR
6 FORT TR
7 REGENT TR
8 MARLBOROUGH CRES
9 THE CRESCENT

F3
1 TRINITY GR
2 TRINITY MS
3 SWANLAND AV
4 ALEXANDRA CT
5 ALEXANDRA DR
6 GLADSTONE TR
7 BRIGHT CR
8 CARLISLE RD
9 LANSDOWNE CR
10 PROVIDENCE PL

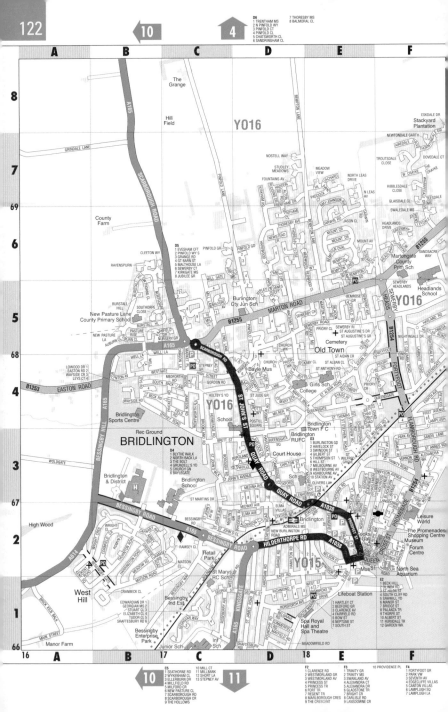

F4
1 FORTYFOOT GR
2 PARK VW
3 SEVENTH AV
4 EDGECLIFFE VILLAS
5 CANTON VILLAS
6 LAMPLUGH SQ
7 LAMPLUGH LA

A7
1 NIDDERDALE CL
2 CALDERDALE CL
3 YORDAS CT
4 CARROWAY CL
5 LYTH CL
6 MARTON CT

4

11

20
20

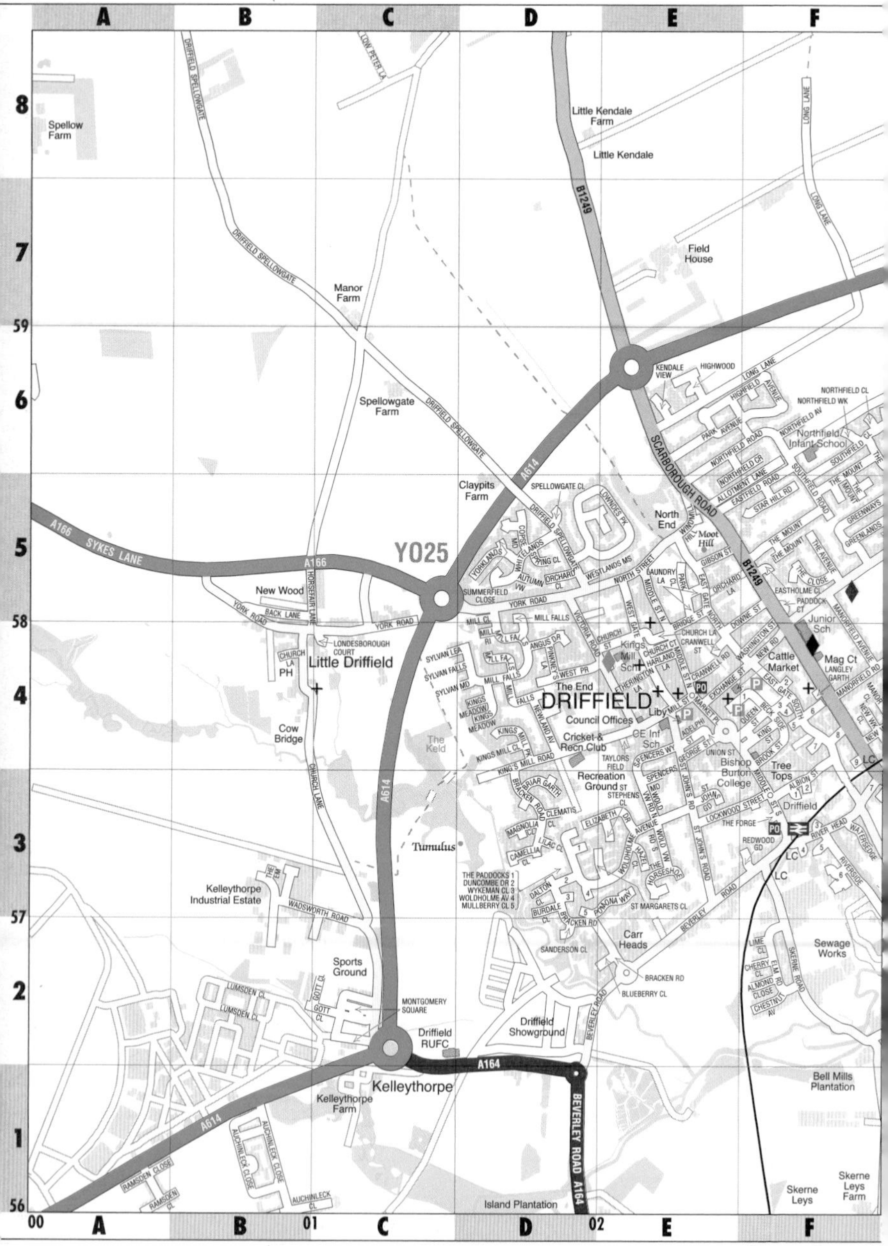
A
B
C
D
E
F
8
7
59
6
5
58
4
3
57
2
1
56
00
01
02
Spellow Farm
DRIFFIELD SPELLOWGATE
LOW PETER LA
Little Kendale Farm
Little Kendale
LONG LANE
B1249
Field House
Manor Farm
Spellowgate Farm
KENDALE VIEW
HIGHWOOD
LONG LANE
HIGHFIELD
AVENUE
NORTHFIELD CL
NORTHFIELD WK
NORTHFIELD AV
Northfield Infant School
PARK AVENUE
NORTHFIELD ROAD
NORTHFIELD CR
ALLOTMENT LANE
EASTFIELD ROAD
STAR HILL RD
SOUTHFIELD ROAD
SOUTHFIELD
THE MOUNT
GREENWAYS
GREENLANDS
SCARBOROUGH ROAD
A614
Claypits Farm
SPELLOWGATE CL
LOWNDES PK
North End
Moot Hill
A166
SYKES LANE
YO25
YORKLANDS
COPSE MD
WHITELANDS
SPRING CL
AUTUMN VW
ORCHARD CL
WESTLANDS MS
NORTH STREET
LAUNDRY LA
GIBSON ST
THE AVENUE
THE CLOSE
EASTHOLME CL
PADDOCK CT
MANORFIELD AVENUE
Junior Sch
Mag Ct
LANGLEY GARTH
New Wood
HORSEFAIR LANE
BACK LANE
YORK ROAD
SUMMERFIELD CLOSE
MILL CL
MILL FALLS
VICTORIA ROAD
WEST GATE
MIDDLE ST N
EAST GATE NORTH
BRIDGE ST
CHURCH LA
CRANWELL ST
DOWNE ST
WASHINGTON ST
NEW RD
Cattle Market
LONDESBOROUGH COURT
CHURCH LA
PH
Little Driffield
SYLVAN LEA
SYLVAN FALLS
SYLVAN MD
ANGUS DR
PINKNEY'S LA
WEST PR
Kings Mill Sch
HARLAND LA
ETHERINGTON LA
CRANWELL RD
EXCHANGE ST
EAST GATE SOUTH
The End
DRIFFIELD
Liby
MILL ST
MARKET PL
KINGS MEADOW
NEWLAND AV
Council Offices
Cow Bridge
The Keld
KINGS MILL PK
KINGS MILL CL
KING'S MILL ROAD
Cricket & Recn Club
CE Inf Sch
ADELPHI ST
QUEEN ST
KING ST
BECK SIDE
BROOK ST
UNION ST
Bishop Burton College
Tree Tops
TAYLORS FIELD
SPENCERS WY
GEORGE ST
Recreation Ground
ST STEPHENS CL
BRACKEN ROAD
BRIAR GARTH
CLEMATIS CL
MAGNOLIA CT
CAMELLIA CL
LILAC CL
ELIZABETH DR
WOLDHOLME AVENUE
WOLD VW RD N
WOLD VW RD S
HAZEL CL
THE HORSESHOE
ST JOHN'S RD
ST JOHN'S ROAD
ST JOHN GD
LOCKWOOD STREET
ALBION ST
MIDDLE ST S
Driffield
THE FORGE
PO
RIVER HEAD
WATERSEDGE
RIVERSIDE
REDWOOD GD
LC
Tumulus
CHURCH LANE
A614
THE PADDOCKS 1
DUNCOMBE DR 2
WYKEMAN CL 3
WOLDHOLME AV 4
MULLBERRY CL 5
DALTON CL
BURDALE CL
BRACKEN RD
POMONA WAY
ST MARGARETS CL
BEVERLEY ROAD
Kelleythorpe Industrial Estate
THE ELM
WADSWORTH ROAD
SANDERSON CL
Carr Heads
Sewage Works
LIME CL
CHERRY CL
ELM RD
ALMOND CLOSE
CHESTNUT AV
SKERNE ROAD
Sports Ground
GOTT CL
LUMSDEN CL
MONTGOMERY SQUARE
BRACKEN RD
BLUEBERRY CL
BEVERLEY ROAD
Driffield Showground
Driffield RUFC
A164
Kelleythorpe
Kelleythorpe Farm
Bell Mills Plantation
AUCHINLECK CLOSE
RAMSDEN CLOSE
RAMSDEN CL
AUCHINLECK CL
BEVERLEY ROAD A164
Island Plantation
Skerne Leys
Skerne Leys Farm

20
20

F3
1 ST JOHN'S WK
2 ST JOHN'S PL
3 RIVER HEAD DR
4 GEORGIAN MS
5 RIVERSIDE MS
6 RIVERSIDE CL
7 ANDERSON ST

F4
1 PROVIDENCE PL
2 JEVANS CT
3 GALLOWAY LA
4 GALLOWAY CT
5 BRIDGE LA
6 DUNN'S LA
7 NAYFIELD CL
8 HARPER ST
9 FAWCETT GDNS

20 21 21

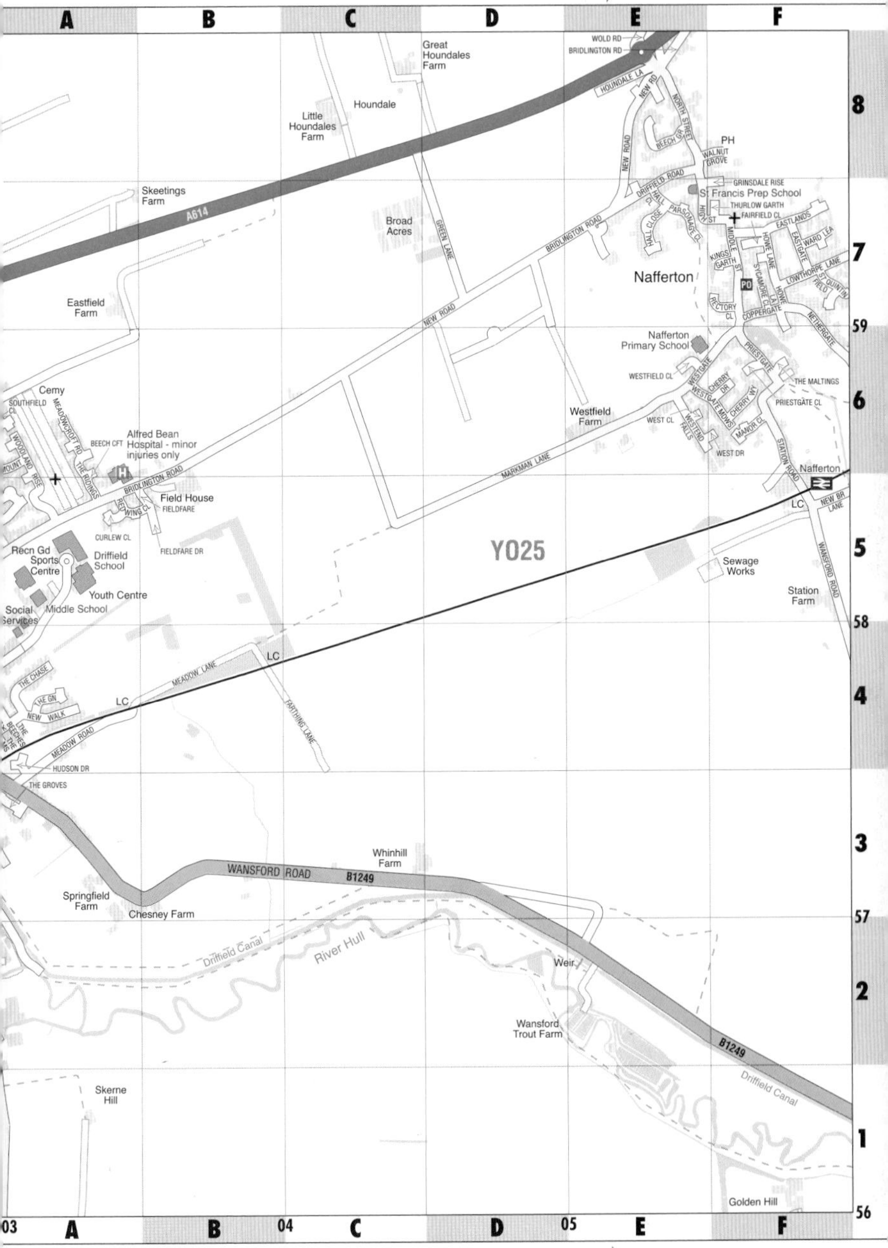
A
B
C
D
E
F
8
7
6
5
4
3
2
1
59
58
57
56
03
04
05
Great Houndales Farm
Houndale
Little Houndales Farm
WOLD RD
BRIDLINGTON RD
HOUNDALE LA
NEW RD
NEW ROAD
NORTH STREET
BEECH GR
PH
WALNUT GROVE
GRINSDALE RISE
St Francis Prep School
THURLOW GARTH
FAIRFIELD CL
DRIFFIELD ROAD
HALL CL
HALL CLOSE
PARSONAGE CL
HIGH ST
MIDDLE ST
EASTLANDS
EASTGATE
WARD LEA
HOWE LANE
KINGS GARTH
SYCAMORE CL
HOWE LA
LOWTHORPE LANE
ST QUINTIN FIELD
RECTORY CL
COPPERGATE
NETHERGATE
Nafferton
PO
Skeetings Farm
A614
Broad Acres
GREEN LANE
BRIDLINGTON ROAD
Eastfield Farm
NEW ROAD
Nafferton Primary School
WESTFIELD CL
WESTGATE
PRIESTGATE
CHERRY DR
WESTGATE MDWS
CHERRY WY
THE MALTINGS
PRIESTGATE CL
Westfield Farm
WEST CL
WESTEND FALLS
MANOR CL
WEST DR
STATION ROAD
Cemy
SOUTHFIELD CL
MEADOWCROFT RD
WOODLAND RISE
MOUNT
BEECH CFT
THE RIDINGS
Alfred Bean Hospital - minor injuries only
H
BRIDLINGTON ROAD
MARKMAN LANE
Nafferton
NEW BR LANE
LC
RED WING CL
Field House
FIELDFARE
CURLEW CL
FIELDFARE DR
Y025
WANSFORD ROAD
Recn Gd
Sports Centre
Driffield School
Sewage Works
Station Farm
Youth Centre
Social Services
Middle School
THE CHASE
THE GN
NEW WALK
LC
MEADOW LANE
LC
FARTHING LANE
MEADOW ROAD
HUDSON DR
THE GROVES
Whinhill Farm
WANSFORD ROAD
B1249
Springfield Farm
Chesney Farm
Driffield Canal
River Hull
Weir
Wansford Trout Farm
B1249
Driffield Canal
Skerne Hill
Golden Hill

20 21 21

12
13

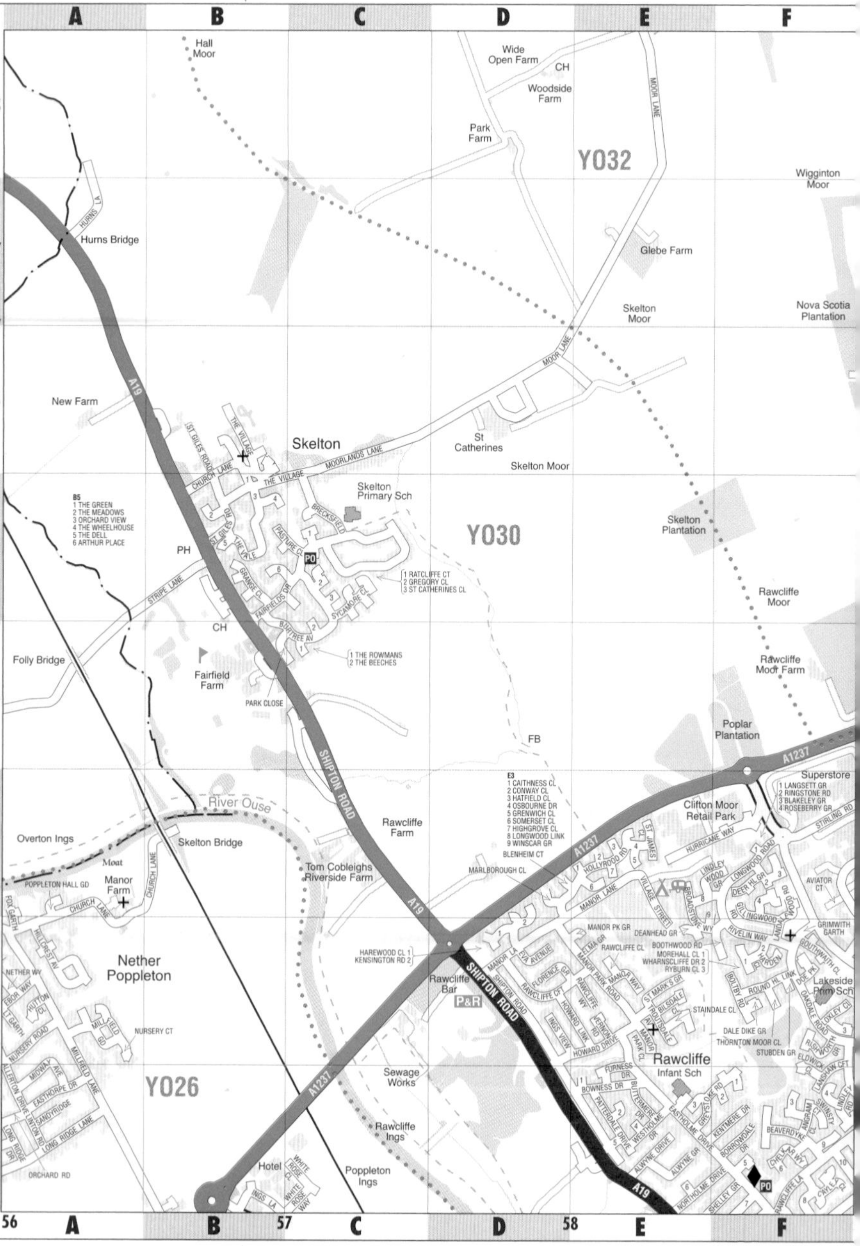

12
129

E1
1 CONISTON CL
2 WASDALE CL
3 GARBURN GR
4 SCAFELL CL
5 LOWESWATER RD
6 FYLINGDALES AV

F1
1 EMBLETON DR
2 COLEDALE CL
3 LEIGHTON CFT
4 BARMBY CL
5 GRASMERE GR
6 BARDEN CT
7 SOUTHOLME DR
8 MILTON CARR
9 FEWSTON DR
10 REIGHTON DR

C7
1 PLOUGHLANDS
2 THE GREENWAY
3 FOXCROFT

C8
1 DEALTRY AVE
2 ARENHALL CL
3 MINSTER CL
4 UPPERCROFT
5 BECKS CL
6 THE CHESTNUTS
7 COPWOOD GR
8 HESLIN CL
9 RUDDINGS CL
10 HUNTERS CL
11 CORNWOOD WY

13

D8
1 MEADOW LN
2 CHERRY OR
3 ORCHARD PADDOCK
4 CHERRY PADDOCK

128

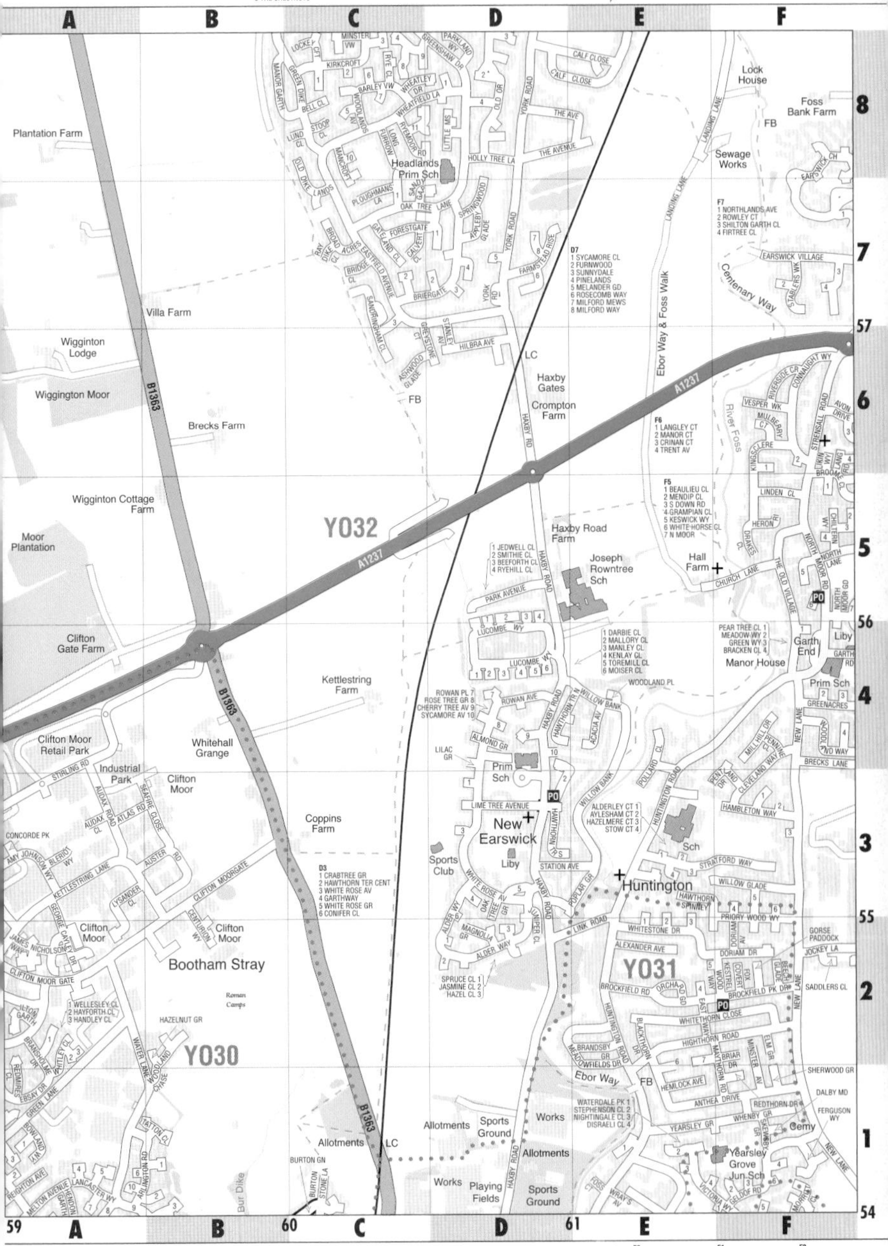
A
B
C
D
E
F
8
7
57
6
5
56
4
3
55
2
1
54
59
60
61
Plantation Farm
Villa Farm
Wigginton Lodge
Wiggington Moor
B1363
Brecks Farm
Wigginton Cottage Farm
Moor Plantation
Clifton Gate Farm
YO32
A1237
Kettlestring Farm
Clifton Moor Retail Park
Industrial Park
Whitehall Grange
Clifton Moor
Coppins Farm
Bootham Stray
Roman Camps
YO30
HAZELNUT GR
Allotments
LC
BURTON GN
Bur Dike
Headlands Prim Sch
Haxby Gates
Crompton Farm
FB
Haxby Road Farm
Joseph Rowntree Sch
New Earswick
Prim Sch
Sports Club
Liby
Huntington
Sch
YO31
Ebor Way
Works
Sports Ground
Allotments
Playing Fields
Lock House
Foss Bank Farm
Sewage Works
Centenary Way
Ebor Way & Foss Walk
River Foss
Hall Farm
Garth End
Manor House
Prim Sch
Cemy
Yearsley Grove Jun Sch
D7
1 SYCAMORE CL
2 FURNWOOD
3 SUNNYDALE
4 PINELANDS
5 MELANDER GD
6 ROSECOMB WAY
7 MILFORD MEWS
8 MILFORD WAY
F7
1 NORTHLANDS AVE
2 ROWLEY CT
3 SHILTON GARTH CL
4 FIRTREE CL
F6
1 LANGLEY CT
2 MANOR CT
3 CRINAN CT
4 TRENT AV
F5
1 BEAULIEU CL
2 MENDIP CL
3 S DOWN RD
4 GRAMPIAN CL
5 KESWICK WY
6 WHITE HORSE CL
7 N MOOR
1 JEDWELL CL
2 SMITHIE CL
3 BEEFORTH CL
4 RYEHILL CL
1 DARBIE CL
2 MALLORY CL
3 MANLEY CL
4 KENLAY CL
5 TOREMILL CL
6 MOISER CL
PEAR TREE CL 1
MEADOW WY 2
GREEN WY 3
BRACKEN CL 4
ROWAN PL 7
ROSE TREE GR 8
CHERRY TREE AV 9
SYCAMORE AV 10
ALDERLEY CT 1
AYLESHAM CT 2
HAZELMERE CT 3
STOW CT 4
D3
1 CRABTREE GR
2 HAWTHORN TER CENT
3 WHITE ROSE AV
4 GARTHWAY
5 WHITE ROSE GR
6 CONIFER CL
SPRUCE CL 1
JASMINE CL 2
HAZEL CL 3
1 WELLESLEY CL
2 HAYFORTH CL
3 HANDLEY CL
WATERDALE PK 1
STEPHENSON CL 2
NIGHTINGALE CL 3
DISRAELI CL 4
CONCORDE PK
SHERWOOD GR
DALBY MD
FERGUSON WY
SADDLERS CL
GORSE PADDOCK
WOODLAND PL
LILAC GR
HAXBY ROAD
YORK ROAD
HUNTINGTON ROAD
NEW LANE
LINK ROAD
STATION AVE
LIME TREE AVENUE
PARK AVENUE
LUCOMBE WY
CHURCH LANE
THE OLD VILLAGE
NORTH MOOR RD
STRENSALL ROAD
LANDING LANE
EARSWICK VILLAGE
CALF CLOSE
THE AVE
THE AVENUE
HOLLY TREE LA
OAK TREE LANE
BRIERGATE
HILBRA AVE
STIRLING RD
KETTLESTRING LANE
CLIFTON MOORGATE
CLIFTON MOOR GATE
WATER LANE
GREEN LANE
WHITESTONE DR
ALEXANDER AVE
BROCKFIELD RD
WHITETHORN CLOSE
HIGHTHORN ROAD
HEMLOCK AVE
ANTHEA DRIVE
YEARSLEY GR
STRATFORD WAY
WILLOW GLADE
PRIORY WOOD WY
BRECKS LANE
GREENACRES
HAMBLETON WAY
CLEVELAND WAY

A1
1 CALDBECK CL
2 STONELANDS CT
3 BELMONT CL
4 HASTINGS CL
5 HARROW GLADE
6 WIMPOLE CL
7 HALIFAX CT
8 WATER LA
9 TAMWORTH RD
10 LUNDY CL

B1
1 HERDWICK CL
2 HEADLEY CL
3 MINCHIN CL

130

128

E2
1 SCAWTON AV
2 GORMIRE AV
3 ROLSTON AV
4 HEATHER CFT
5 BADGER PADDOCK
6 PINEWOOD GR
7 THORNFIELD DR

F1
1 DICKENS CL
2 HOMESTEAD CL
3 CARRNOCK CT
4 ANDREW DR
5 MONKTON RD
6 THERESA CL

F3
1 CHEVIOT CL
2 CAMBRIAN CL
3 KENDREW CL
4 MERLIN COVERT
5 FIRWOOD WHIN
6 OAK GLADE

127 14 14

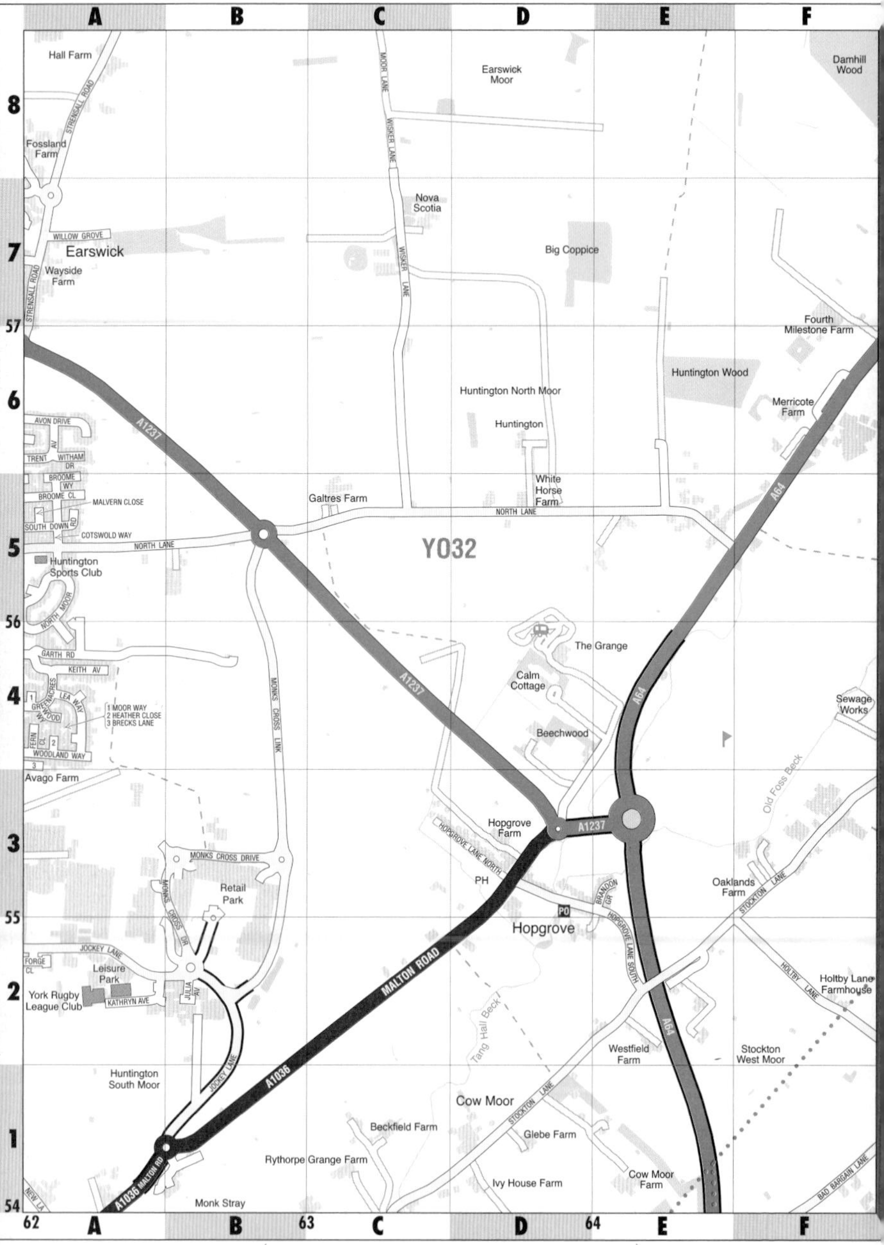

127 131 14

F5
1 CHUDLEIGH RD
2 BROMLEY ST
3 ALBANY ST
4 WALWORTH ST N
5 HANOVER ST E
6 UPR HANOVER ST
7 HANOVER ST W
8 STAMFORD ST W
9 WALWORTH ST S
10 STAMFORD ST E
11 KINGSLAND TR
12 BRUNNEL CT
13 ST BARNABAS CT
14 REGENTS CT
15 VICTORIA CT
16 CARLISLE ST
17 CARLETON ST

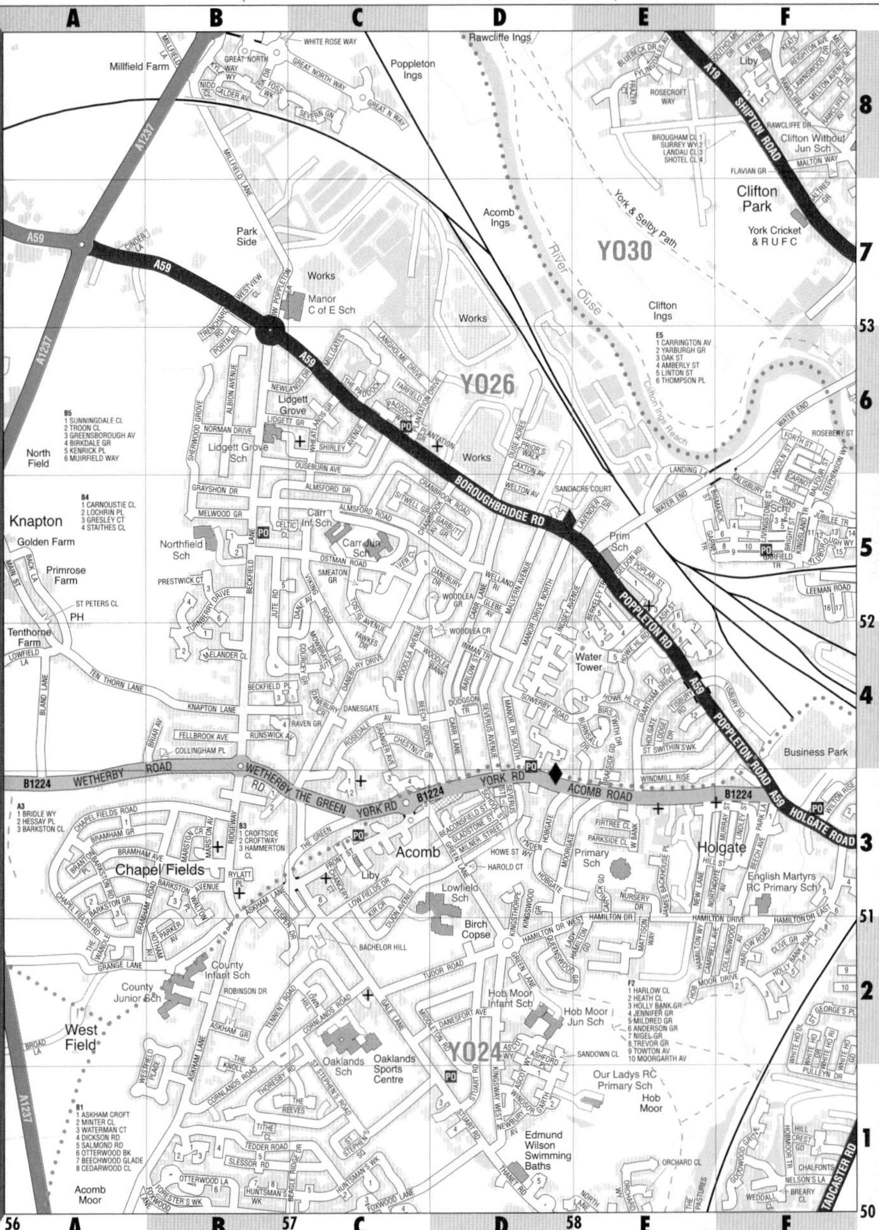

C1
1 THORNWOOD COVERT
2 MAPLEWOOD PADDOCK
3 FOXWOOD LANE
4 HERMAN WALK
5 FIR HEATH CL

C3
1 KIRK VIEW
2 CHURCH MEWS
3 ELMTREE GDNS
4 OAK RISE
5 CROSS ST
6 GALE FARM CT

D1
1 WOODFORD PL
2 KEMPTON C
3 CLAY PL
4 CHESNEY FIELDS
5 ST JAMES PLACE

D4
1 PATELY PL
2 HEBDON RISE
3 BAILDON CL

E4
1 WINCHESTER GR
2 GARLAND ST
3 WINCHESTER AV
4 CHATSWORTH TR
5 DILYS GR
6 PEPPERCORN CL
7 BONINGTON CT
8 RENSHAW GDNS
9 HILLARY GARTH
10 SEGRAVE WALK
11 MANTHORPE WK
12 CHELWOOD WK
13 BOUTHWAITE DR

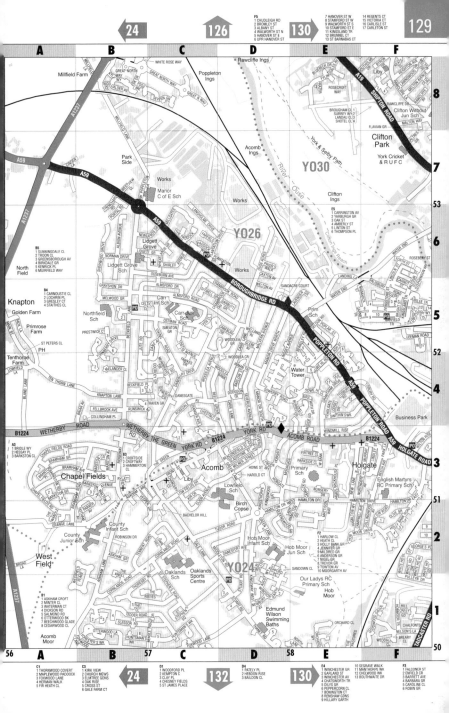

F3
1 FALCONER ST
2 ENFIELD CR
3 BARRETT AVE
4 BARBARA GR
5 CAROLINE CL
6 ROBIN GR

A8
1 LINDEN GROVE
2 MARTEN CLOSE
3 RAINSBOROUGH WAY

A7
1 BELCOMBE WAY
2 HUDSON CRESCENT
3 CLIFTON PLACE
4 PINFOLD COURT

129

C7
1 UPR NEWBOROUGH ST
2 ALLAN ST
3 MURROUGH WILSON PL
4 FEVERSHAM CR
5 HILLSBOROUGH TR
6 HUDSON ST

127

E8
1 KIRKHAM AV
2 THE CROSSWAY
3 LILLING AV

E5
1 HAWTHORN ST
2 EMMERSON ST
3 FLEMING AV
4 SCROPE AV

F8
1 ALBERT CL
2 VICTORIA WY
3 MORRITT CL
4 FOSTON GR
5 THORNFIELD AV
6 LABURNUM GARTH

For full street detail of the highlighted area see page 156.

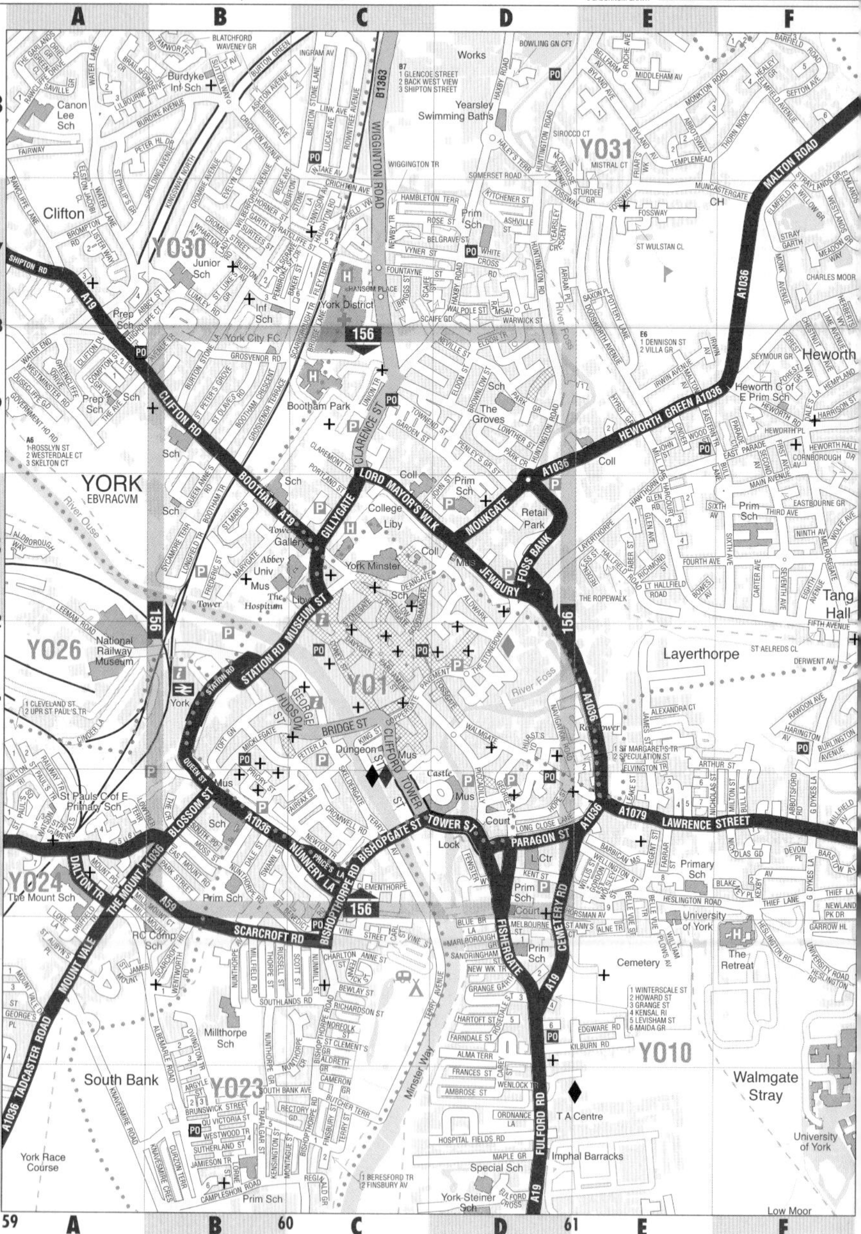

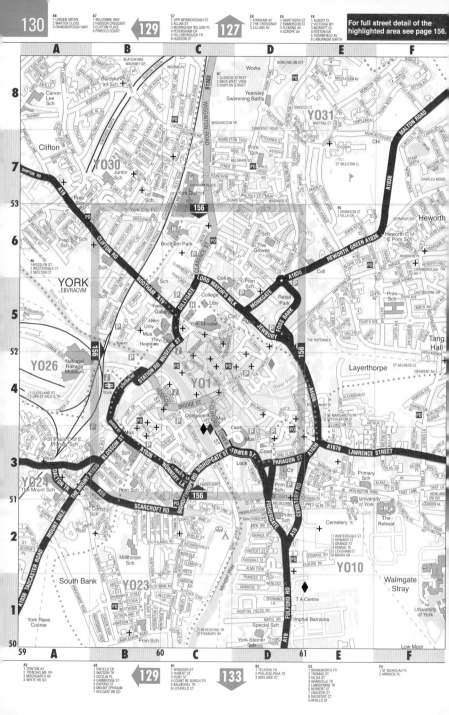

A5
1 MELROSE CL
2 APPLEBY PL
3 INGLETON WK
4 WOODHOUSE GR

128
26

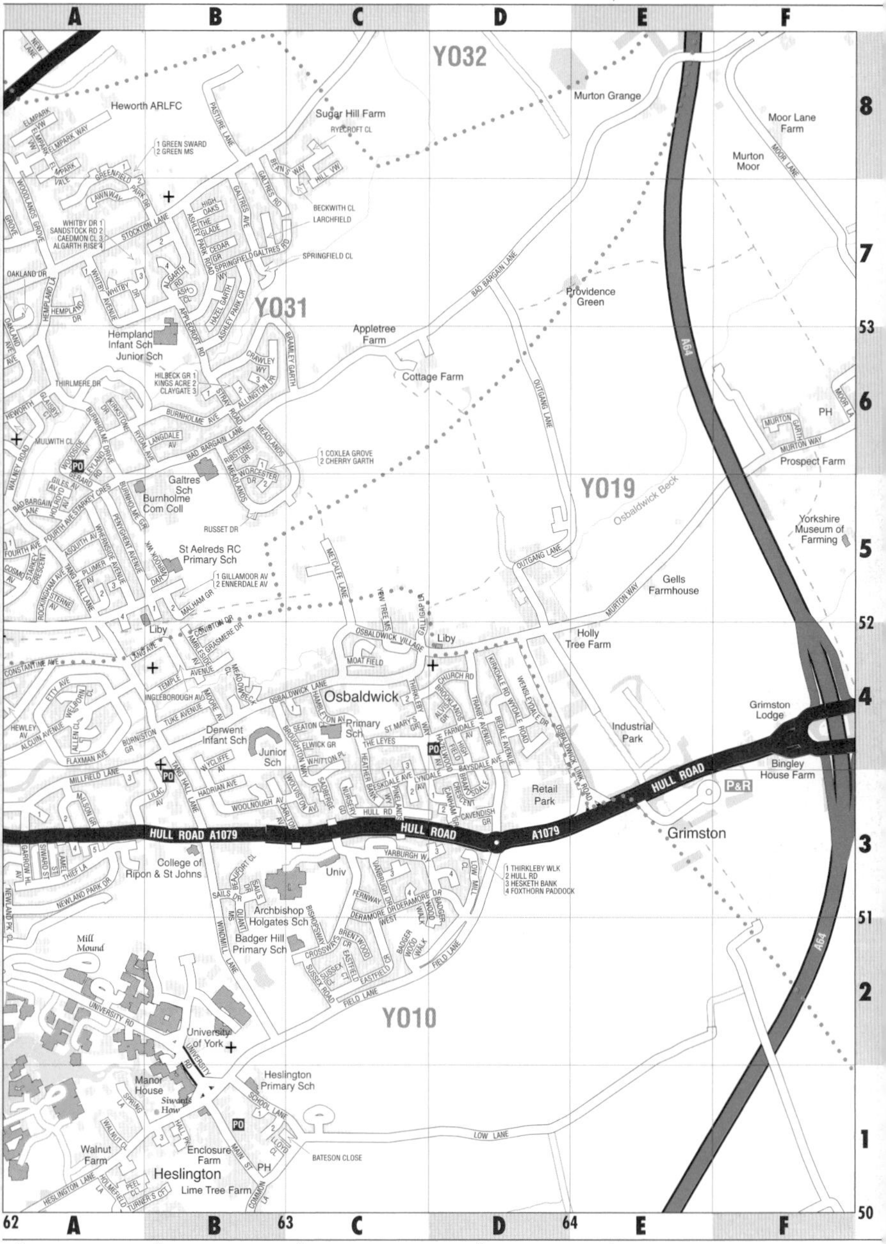
A
B
C
D
E
F
8
7
53
6
5
52
4
3
51
2
1
50
62
63
64
YO32
YO31
YO19
YO10
Heworth ARLFC
Sugar Hill Farm
RYECROFT CL
Murton Grange
Moor Lane Farm
Murton Moor
MOOR LANE
1 GREEN SWARD
2 GREEN MS
PASTURE LANE
GALTRES RD
BEAN'S WAY
HILL VW
BECKWITH CL
LARCHFIELD
SPRINGFIELD CL
WHITBY DR 1
SANDSTOCK RD 2
CAEDMON CL 3
ALGARTH RISE 4
OAKLAND DR
STOCKTON LANE
WOODLANDS GROVE
ELMPARK VW
ELMPARK WAY
GREENFIELD PARK DR
LAWNWAY
HIGH OAKS
THE GLADE
ASHLEY PARK ROAD
CEDAR GR
GALTRES AVE
SPRINGFIELD WY
HEMPLAND LA
HEMPLAND DR
WHITBY AVENUE
ALGARTH RD
APPLECROFT RD
HAZEL GARTH
ASHLEY PARK CR
BAD BARGAIN LANE
Providence Green
A64
Appletree Farm
Cottage Farm
Hempland Infant Sch
Junior Sch
BRAMLEY GARTH
CRAWLEY WY
ALLINGTON DR
HILBECK GR 1
KINGS ACRE 2
CLAYGATE 3
STRAY ROAD
THIRLMERE DR
BURNHOLME AVE
OUTGANG LANE
PH
MURTON GARTH
MURTON WAY
Prospect Farm
HEWORTH
MULWITH CL
LANGDALE AV
MEADLANDS
RIBSTONE GR
WORCESTER DR
1 COXLEA GROVE
2 CHERRY GARTH
Galtres Sch
Burnholme Com Coll
Osbaldwick Beck
Yorkshire Museum of Farming
RUSSET DR
St Aelreds RC Primary Sch
1 GILLAMOOR AV
2 ENNERDALE AV
METCALFE LANE
OUTGANG LANE
Gells Farmhouse
MURTON WAY
Liby
CONISTON DR
GRASMERE DR
OSBALDWICK VILLAGE
Holly Tree Farm
CONSTANTINE AVE
MOAT FIELD
TEMPLE AVENUE
CHURCH RD
Osbaldwick
INGLEBOROUGH AV
TUKE AVENUE
OSBALDWICK LANE
Primary Sch
Grimston Lodge
Industrial Park
HEWLEY AV
ALCUIN AVENUE
Derwent Infant Sch
Junior Sch
SEATON CL
ELWICK GR
THE LEYES
FARNDALE AV
BAYSDALE AVE
OSBALDWICK LINK ROAD
FLAXMAN AVE
MILLFIELD LANE
WYCLIFFE AV
HADRIAN AVE
WOOLNOUGH AV
HULL RD
Retail Park
HULL ROAD
P&R
Bingley House Farm
HULL ROAD A1079
HULL ROAD
A1079
Grimston
CAVENDISH GR
YARBURGH WY
1 THIRKLEBY WLK
2 HULL RD
3 HESKETH BANK
4 FOXTHORN PADDOCK
College of Ripon & St Johns
Univ
NEWLAND PARK DR
FERNWAY
DERAMORE DR WEST
BADGER WOOD WALK
Archbishop Holgates Sch
Badger Hill Primary Sch
Mill Mound
FIELD LANE
UNIVERSITY RD
CROSSWAYS
SUSSEX ROAD
EASTFIELD
WINDMILL LANE
University of York
Heslington Primary Sch
Manor House
Siwards How
SCHOOL LANE
LOW LANE
BATESON CLOSE
Walnut Farm
Enclosure Farm
Heslington
Lime Tree Farm
HESLINGTON LANE
MAIN ST
PH
COMMON LA

A3
1 HEATHFIELD RD
2 OWSTON AV
3 WAYNEFLEET GR
4 CYCLE ST
5 NORMAN ST

B1
1 ENCLOSURE GD
2 HESLINGTON CT
3 HOLBURNS CFT

C3
1 SHALLOWDALE GR
2 BRACKEN HILL
3 KIMBERLOWS WOOD HILL
4 PINEWOOD HILL

C4
1 VICARAGE GD
2 ST THOMAS'S CL
3 GIVENDALE GR

26
26

24
129

C8
1 HINTON AV
2 LYDHAM CT
3 MARTIN CHEESEMAN CT
4 CRANFIELD PL

D8
1 FARMLANDS RD
2 DRINGFIELD CL
3 HERDSMAN RD
4 SANDCROFT CL
5 DEEPDALE

E8
1 TURNMIRE RD
2 SOUTHFIELD CR
3 MEADOW CT
4 THE PASTURES
5 ST HELEN'S RD

F8
1 KENSINGTON CT
2 REGENCY MS

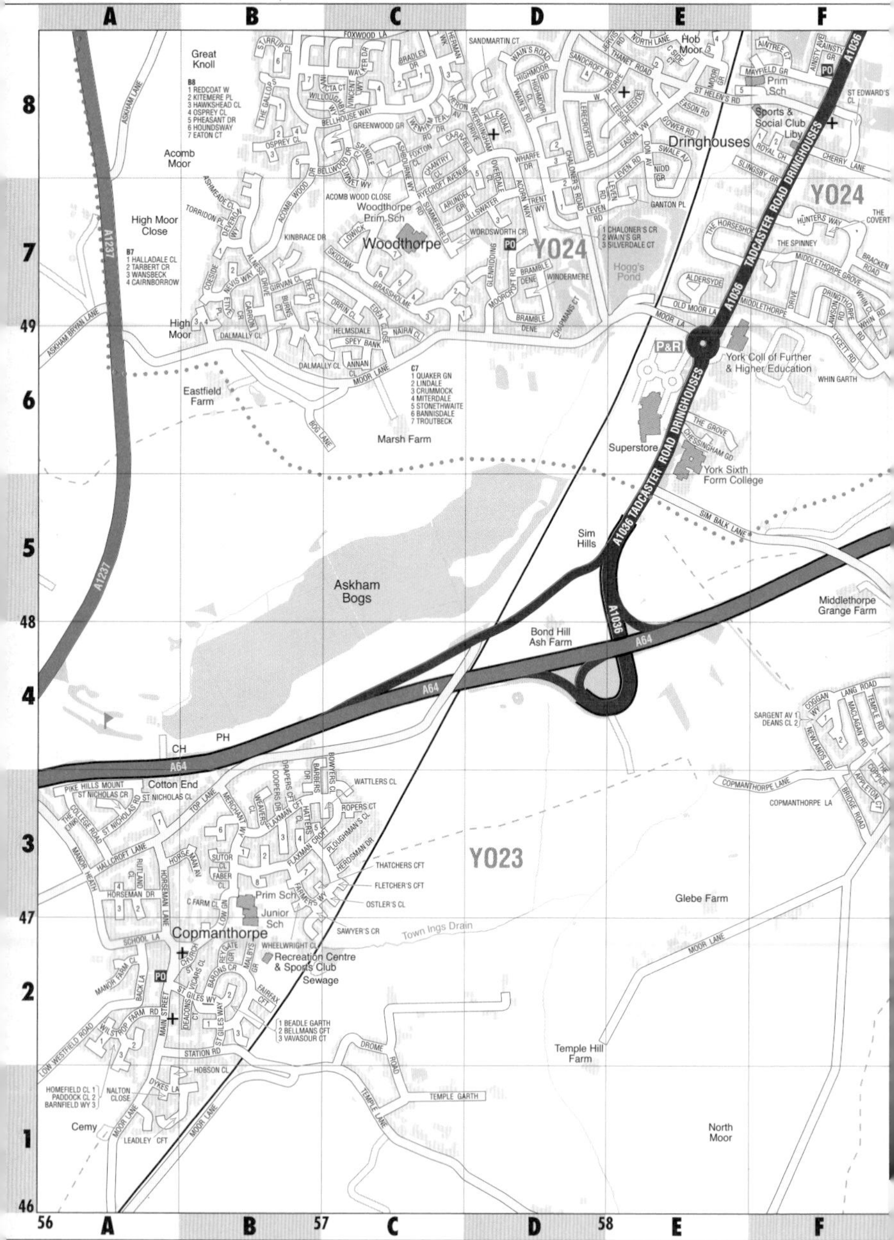

A3
1 LARKFIELD CL
2 HORSEMAN CL
3 LYNWOOD AV
4 LYNWOOD VW

B3
1 SADDLERS CL
2 FARRIERS CFT
3 WAGGONERS DR
4 POTTERS DR
5 WAINERS CL
6 MILLERS CFT
7 LORINERS DR
8 GARDENERS CL

24
36

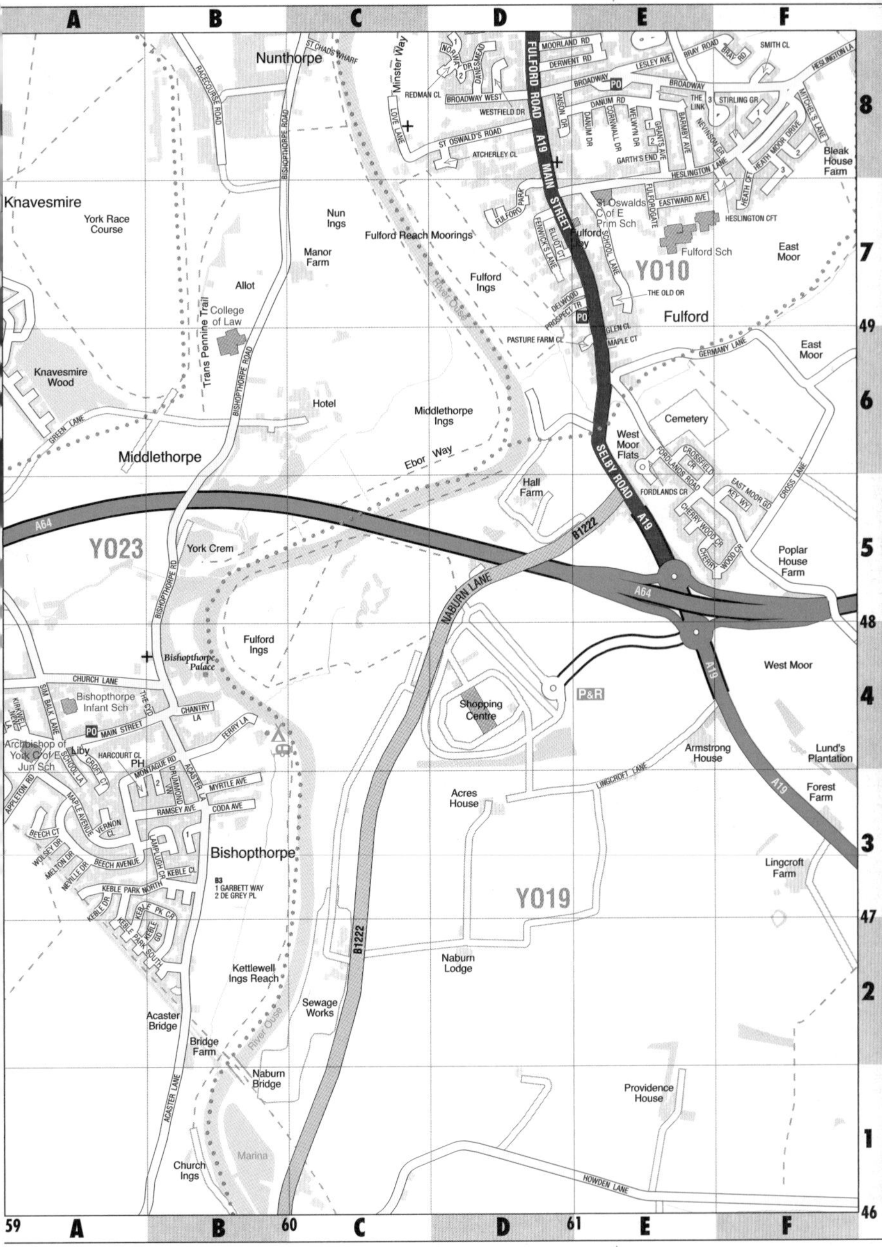
A
B
C
D
E
F
8
7
49
6
5
48
4
3
47
2
1
46
59
60
61
Nunthorpe
ST CHADS WHARF
RACECOURSE ROAD
BISHOPTHORPE ROAD
Minster Way
LOVE LANE
REDMAN CL
NORWAY DR
DANESMEAD
BROADWAY WEST
WESTFIELD DR
ST OSWALD'S ROAD
ATCHERLEY CL
FULFORD ROAD
A19
MAIN STREET
MOORLAND RD
DERWENT RD
LESLEY AVE
BRAY ROAD
BRAY RD
SMITH CL
HESLINGTON LA
BROADWAY
PO
THE LINK
STIRLING GR
MITCHEL'S LANE
ANSON DR
DANUM RD
DANUM DR
CORNWALL DR
WELWYN DR
GRANTS AVE
BARMBY AVE
NEVINSON GR
HEATH MOOR DRIVE
GARTH'S END
HESLINGTON LANE
HEATH CFT
Bleak House Farm
Knavesmire
York Race Course
Nun Ings
Manor Farm
Fulford Reach Moorings
FULFORD PARK
FENWICK'S LANE
ELLIOT CT
St Oswalds C of E Prim Sch
SCHOOL LANE
FULFORDGATE
EASTWARD AVE
HESLINGTON CFT
Fulford Liby
Fulford Sch
East Moor
YO10
Allot
College of Law
Trans Pennine Trail
River Ouse
Fulford Ings
THE OLD OR
DELWOOD
PROSPECT TR
Fulford
PASTURE FARM CL
GLEN CL
MAPLE CT
GERMANY LANE
East Moor
Knavesmire Wood
Hotel
Middlethorpe Ings
Cemetery
GREEN LANE
Middlethorpe
Ebor Way
West Moor Flats
CROSSFIELD CR
FORDLANDS ROAD
EAST MOOR GD
KEY WY
CROSS LANE
Hall Farm
SELBY ROAD
FORDLANDS CR
A64
YO23
York Crem
B1222
CHERRY WOOD CR
Poplar House Farm
NABURN LANE
A64
Fulford Ings
Bishopthorpe Palace
West Moor
CHURCH LANE
Bishopthorpe Infant Sch
THE CYD
CHANTRY LA
SIM BALK LANE
KIRKWELL
P&R
Shopping Centre
PO
MAIN STREET
FERRY LA
Archbishop of York C of E Jun Sch
Liby
SCHOOL LA
CROFT CT
HARCOURT CL
PH
MONTAGUE RD
DRUMMOND VW
ACASTER LA
MYRTLE AVE
Armstrong House
Lund's Plantation
LINGCROFT LANE
Acres House
Forest Farm
APPLETON RD
MAPLE AVENUE
VERNON CL
RAMSEY AVE
CODA AVE
BEECH CT
WOLSEY DR
MELTON DR
BEECH AVENUE
LAMPLUGH CR
Bishopthorpe
NEVILLE DR
KEBLE CL
B3
1 GARBETT WAY
2 DE GREY PL
Lingcroft Farm
KEBLE PARK NORTH
KEBLE DR
KEBLE PK CR
KEBLE GD
KEBLE PARK SOUTH
YO19
Kettlewell Ings Reach
Naburn Lodge
Acaster Bridge
Sewage Works
Bridge Farm
Naburn Bridge
ACASTER LANE
Providence House
Marina
Church Ings
HOWDEN LANE

35
35

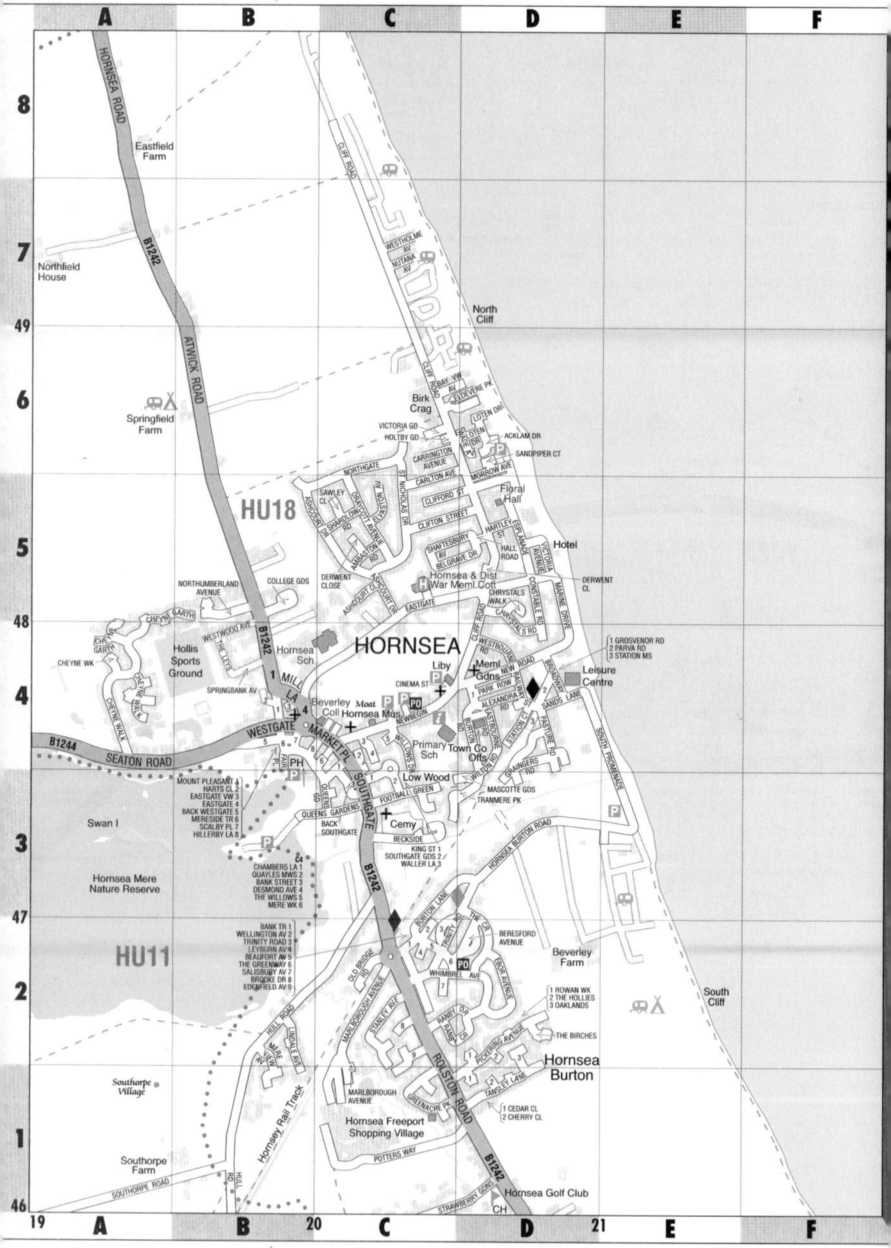
A
B
C
D
E
F
8
7
49
6
5
48
4
3
47
2
1
46
19
20
21
HORNSEA ROAD
Eastfield Farm
CLIFF ROAD
WESTHOLME AV
NUTANA AV
Northfield House
B1242
North Cliff
ATWICK ROAD
Springfield Farm
Birk Crag
BAY VW AV
BELVEDERE PK
LOTEN DR
VICTORIA GD
HOLTBY GD
ACKLAM DR
SANDPIPER CT
CARRINGTON AVENUE
NORTHGATE
MORROW AVE
CARLTON AVE
SAWLEY CL
Floral Hall
CLIFFORD ST
HU18
ASHCOURT DR
SHARDLOW RD
DRAYCOTT AVENUE
ELVASTON AV
ST NICHOLAS DR
CLIFTON STREET
HARTLEY ST
ESPLANADE
SHAFTESBURY AV
BELGRAVE DR
HALL ROAD
VICTORIA AVENUE
Hotel
AMBASTON RD
NORTHUMBERLAND AVENUE
COLLEGE GDS
DERWENT CLOSE
ASHCOURT CL
Hornsea & Dist War Meml Cott
DERWENT CL
EASTGATE
CHRYSTALS WALK
CONSTABLE RD
MARINE DRIVE
CHEYNE GARTH
WESTWOOD AVE
CHRYSTALS RD
HORNSEA
Hollis Sports Ground
Hornsea Sch
WESTBOURNE RD
1 GROSVENOR RD
2 PARVA RD
3 STATION MS
CHEYNE WK
THE LEYS
Liby
Meml Gdns
NEW ROAD
BROADWAY
Leisure Centre
MILL LA
CINEMA ST
PARK ROW
CHEYNE WALK
SPRINGBANK AV
Beverley Coll
Moat
Hornsea Mus
ALEXANDRA RD
RAILWAY ST
SANDS LANE
NEWBEGIN
WESTGATE
MARKET PL
EASTBOURNE RD
BURTON RD
STATION CT
PASTURE RD
SOUTH PROMENADE
B1244
SEATON ROAD
FAIR PL
PH
Primary Sch
Town Co Offs
WILLOWS DR
WILTON RD
GRAINGERS RD
MOUNT PLEASANT 1
HARTS CL 2
EASTGATE VW 3
EASTGATE 4
BACK WESTGATE 5
MERESIDE TR 6
SCALBY PL 7
HILLERBY LA 8
Low Wood
SOUTHGATE
QUEENS GD
FOOTBALL GREEN
MASCOTTE GDS
TRANMERE PK
Swan I
QUEENS GARDENS
BACK SOUTHGATE
Cemy
BECKSIDE
HORNSEA BURTON ROAD
C4
CHAMBERS LA 1
QUAYLES MWS 2
BANK STREET 3
DESMOND AVE 4
THE WILLOWS 5
MERE WK 6
KING ST 1
SOUTHGATE GDS 2
WALLER LA 3
Hornsea Mere Nature Reserve
BURTON LANE
TRINITY RD
THE CR
BERESFORD AVENUE
HU11
BANK TR 1
WELLINGTON AV 2
TRINITY ROAD 3
LEYBURN AV 4
BEAUFORT AV 5
THE GREENWAY 6
SALISBURY AV 7
BROOKE DR 8
EDENFIELD AV 9
Beverley Farm
OLD BRIDGE RD
PO
WHIMBREL AVE
EBOR AVENUE
MARLBOROUGH AVENUE
1 ROWAN WK
2 THE HOLLIES
3 OAKLANDS
South Cliff
STANLEY AVE
RANBY DR
RANBY CR
HULL ROAD
LINDALE AVE
MERE VIEW AV
THE BIRCHES
PICKERING AVENUE
Hornsea Burton
Southorpe Village
ROLSTON ROAD
TANSLEY LANE
MARLBOROUGH AVENUE
GREENACRE PK
1 CEDAR CL
2 CHERRY CL
Hornsey Rail Track
Hornsea Freeport Shopping Village
Southorpe Farm
POTTERS WAY
SOUTHORPE ROAD
HULL RD
STRAWBERRY GDNS
Hornsea Golf Club
CH

35
46

40 41 41

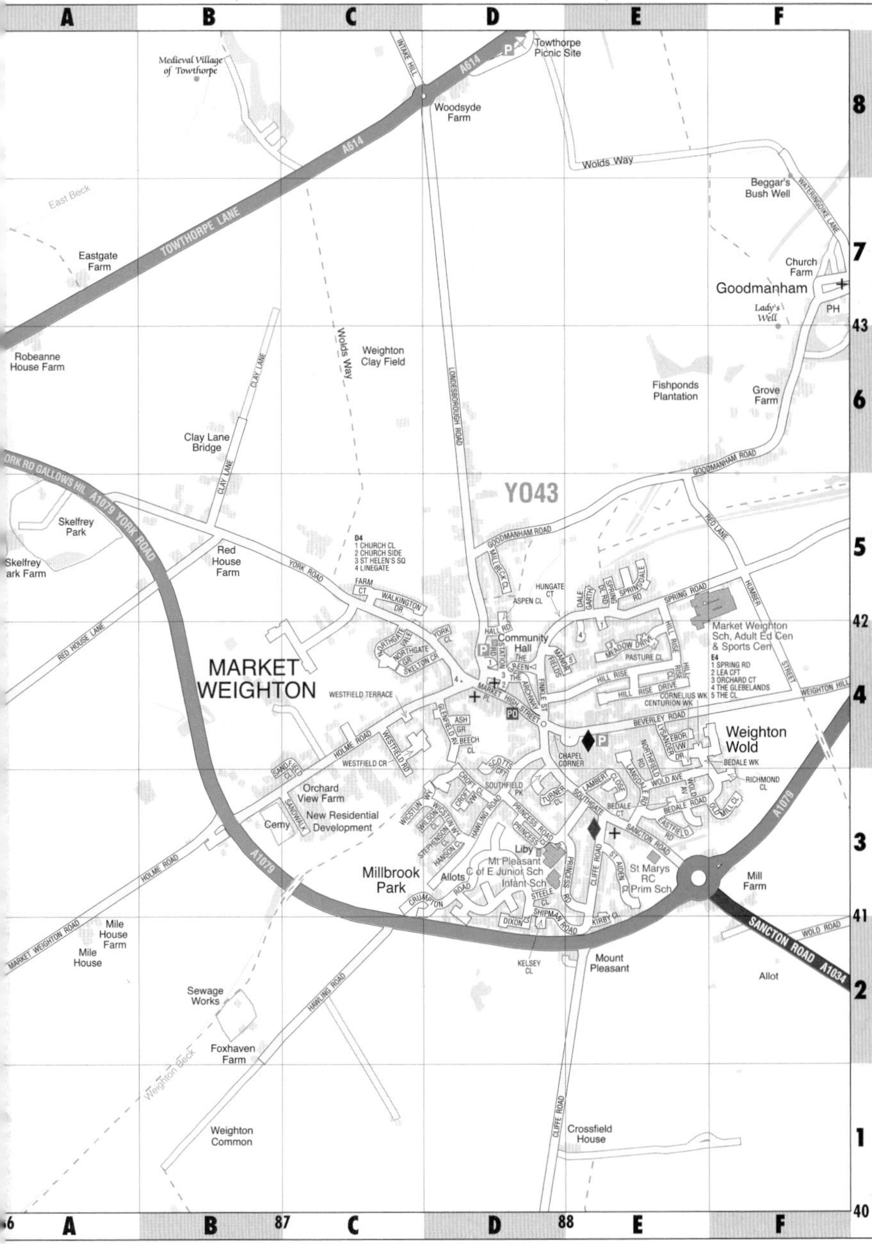

40 41 41

43
43

D6
1 WOODHALL DR
2 MOLESCROFT W CL
3 MOLESCROFT AV
4 MOLESCROFT PK

F7
1 WOODCOATES CL
2 MEADOW BANK
3 BEECH TREE CL
4 BRAMBLE GARTH
5 WILLOW TREE GARTH

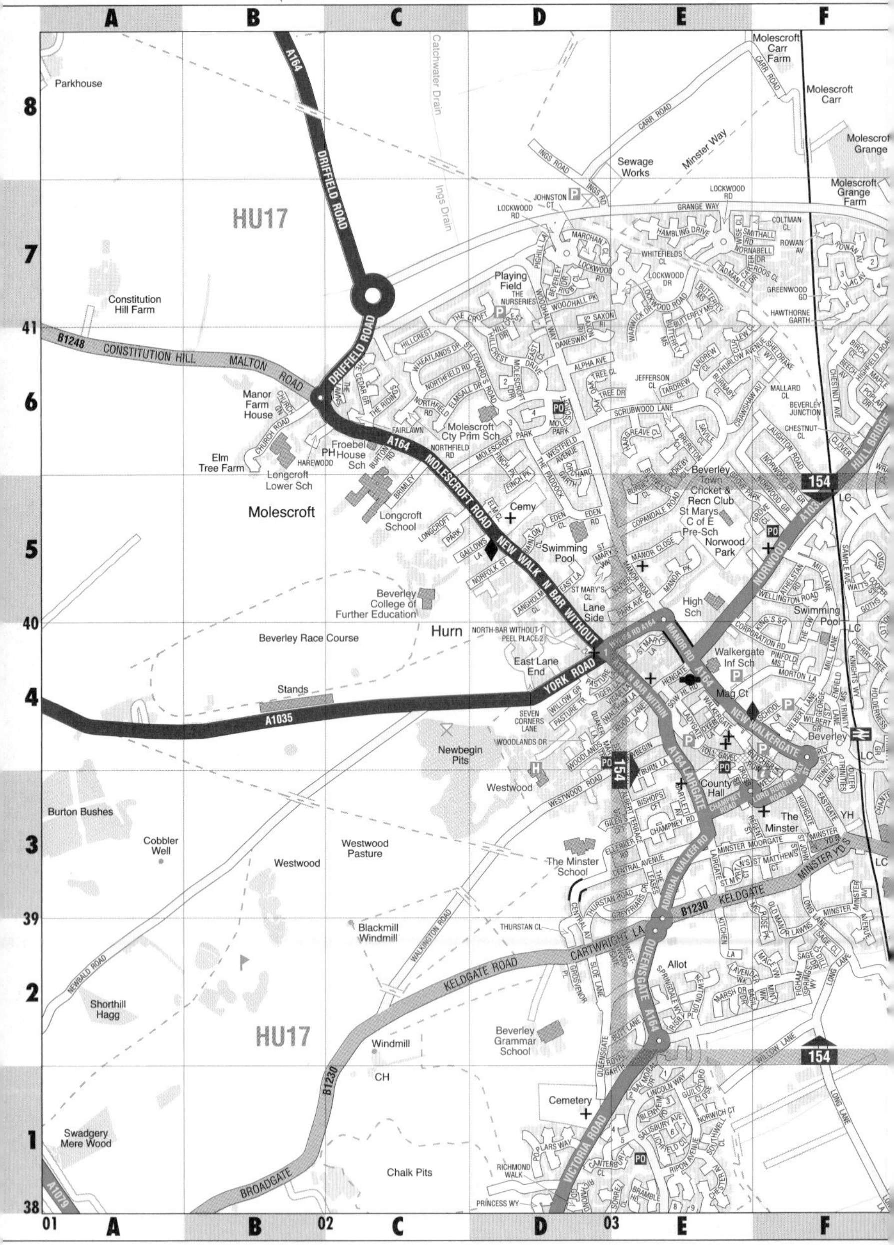

43
55

E1
1 LEATHLEY CL
2 CAVENDISH DR
3 BERKELEY DR
4 HEREFORD CL
5 WINCHESTER AV
6 OXFORD CL
7 ST ALBANS CL
8 CATHEDRAL CL
9 WELTON CL

For full street detail of the highlighted area see page 154.

A6
1 SOUTHFIELD DR
2 SIGSTON RD
3 EASTFIELD CL
4 SYMMONS CL

44
44

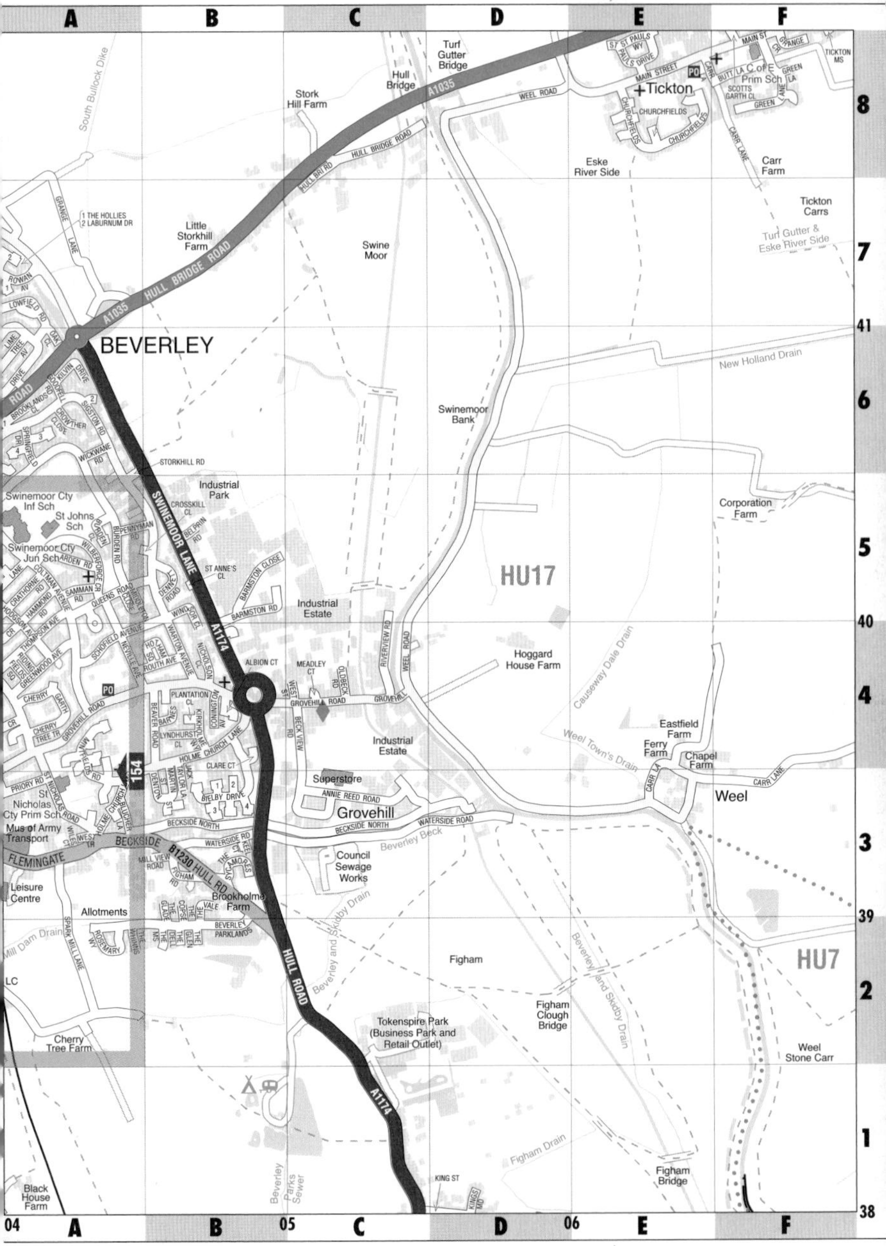

B3
1 TATTERSALL DR
2 HOLGATE CL
3 GILLYON CL
4 AKESTER CL

56
44

55
55

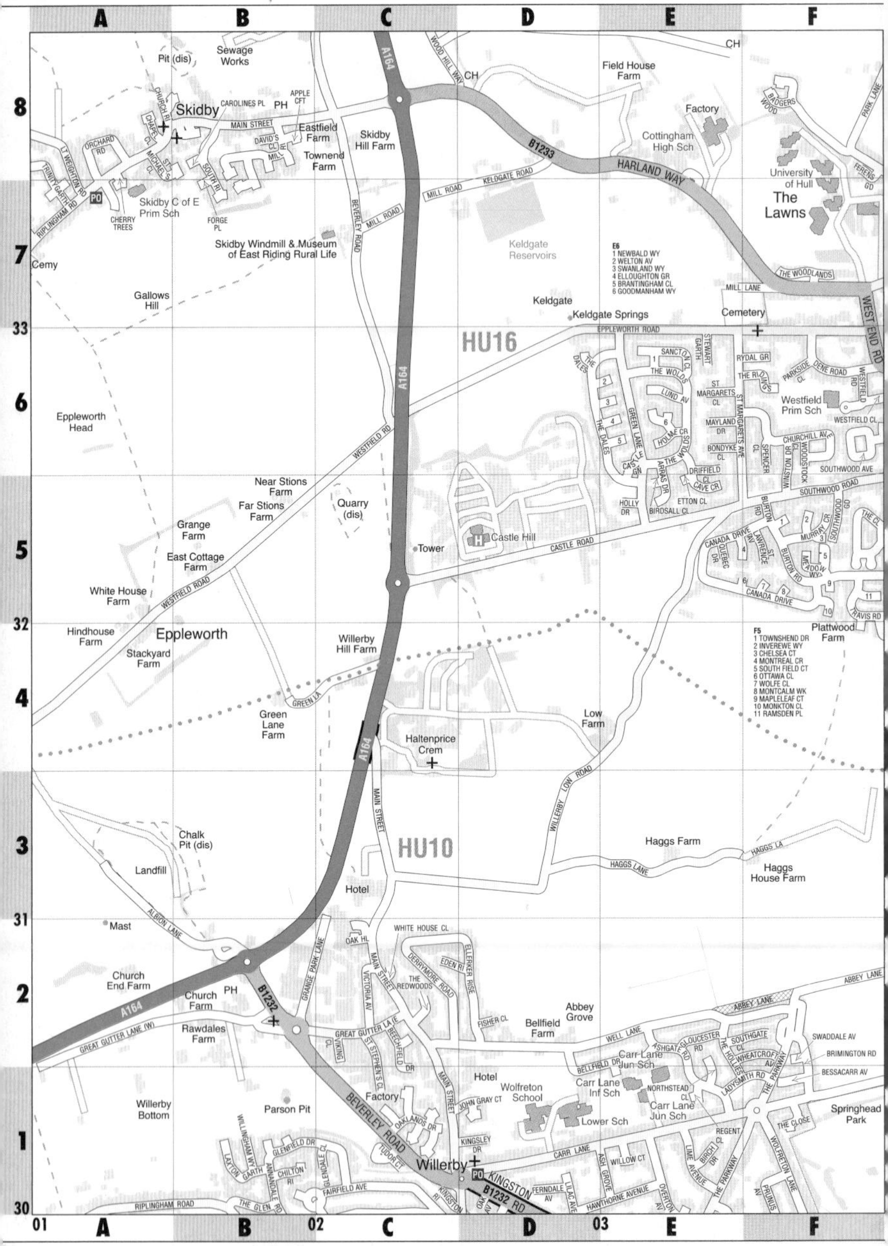
A
B
C
D
E
F
8
7
33
6
5
32
4
3
31
2
1
30
01
02
03
Pit (dis)
Sewage Works
Skidby
CHURCH RI
CHAPEL CL
CAROLINES PL
PH
APPLE CFT
MAIN STREET
DAVID'S CL
MILL RI
Eastfield Farm
Townend Farm
Skidby Hill Farm
ORCHARD RD
LT WEIGHTON RD
TRINITY GARTH
RIPLINGHAM RD
PO
ST MICHAEL'S CL
SOUTH RI
Skidby C of E Prim Sch
CHERRY TREES
FORGE PL
Skidby Windmill & Museum of East Riding Rural Life
BEVERLEY ROAD
MILL ROAD
Cemy
Gallows Hill
A164
WOOD HILL WAY
CH
B1233
HARLAND WAY
MILL ROAD
KELDGATE ROAD
Field House Farm
Factory
Cottingham High Sch
BADGERS WOOD
PARK LANE
University of Hull
FERENS GD
The Lawns
Keldgate Reservoirs
E6
1 NEWBALD WY
2 WELTON AV
3 SWANLAND WY
4 ELLOUGHTON GR
5 BRANTINGHAM CL
6 GOODMANHAM WY
THE WOODLANDS
MILL LANE
WEST END RD
Keldgate
Keldgate Springs
Cemetery
HU16
EPPLEWORTH ROAD
THE DALES
SANCTON CL
STEWART GARTH
THE WOLDS
LUND AV
GREEN LANE
RYDAL GR
THE RIDINGS
PARKSIDE CL
DENE ROAD
WESTFIELD RD
ST MARGARETS CL
ST MARGARETS AVE
Westfield Prim Sch
WESTFIELD CL
MAYLAND DR
BONDYKE CL
HOLME CR
CASTLE GN
ARRAS DR
DRIFFIELD CL
CAVE CR
SPENCER CL
WINSTON DR
CHURCHILL AVE
WOODSTOCK CL
SOUTHWOOD AVE
HOLLY DR
BIRDSALL CL
ETTON CL
SOUTHWOOD ROAD
Eppleworth Head
WESTFIELD RD
Near Stions Farm
Far Stions Farm
Quarry (dis)
Grange Farm
East Cottage Farm
Castle Hill
Tower
CASTLE ROAD
CANADA DRIVE
QUEBEC DR
BURTON RD
LAWRENCE AV
ST LAWRENCE
SOUTHWOOD GD
MURRAY CR
MEADOW WY
THE CL
RAVIS RD
White House Farm
WESTFIELD ROAD
Hindhouse Farm
Eppleworth
Stackyard Farm
Willerby Hill Farm
Plattwood Farm
F5
1 TOWNSHEND DR
2 INVEREWE WY
3 CHELSEA CT
4 MONTREAL CR
5 SOUTH FIELD CT
6 OTTAWA CL
7 WOLFE CL
8 MONTCALM WK
9 MAPLELEAF CT
10 MONKTON CL
11 RAMSDEN PL
GREEN LA
Green Lane Farm
Low Farm
Haltenprice Crem
WILLERBY LOW ROAD
MAIN STREET
Chalk Pit (dis)
HU10
Haggs Farm
HAGGS LA
HAGGS LANE
Haggs House Farm
Landfill
Hotel
Mast
ALBION LANE
WHITE HOUSE CL
OAK HL
GRANGE PARK LANE
VICTORIA AV
DERRYMORE ROAD
EDEN RI
ELLERKER RISE
THE REDWOODS
ABBEY LANE
Church End Farm
Church Farm
PH
B1232
Rawdales Farm
GREAT GUTTER LANE (W)
GREAT GUTTER LA (E)
VIKING CL
ST STEPHEN'S CL
BEECHFIELD DR
FISHER CL
Bellfield Farm
Abbey Grove
WELL LANE
ASHGATE RD
GLOUCESTER RD
SOUTHGATE CL
THE HOLLIES
WHEATCROFT AV
THE PARKWAY
SWADDALE AV
BRIMINGTON RD
BESSACARR AV
BELLFIELD DR
Carr Lane Jun Sch
Carr Lane Inf Sch
NORTHSTEAD CL
LADYSMITH RD
Hotel
Wolfreton School
Factory
Willerby Bottom
Parson Pit
BEVERLEY ROAD
JOHN GRAY CT
OAKLANDS DR
Lower Sch
Carr Lane Jun Sch
REGENT CL
Springhead Park
THE CLOSE
WILLINGHAM WY
GLENFIELD DR
LAYTON GARTH
ANNANDALE RD
CHILTON RI
GLENDALE CL
TUDOR CT
KINGSLEY DR
Willerby
CARR LANE
WILLOW CT
BIRCH DR
LIME AVENUE
THE PARKWAY
WOLFRETON LANE
PRUNUS AV
FAIRFIELD AVE
PO
KINGSTON RD
FERNDALE AV
LILAC AVE
ASH GROVE
HAWTHORNE AVENUE
OVERTON AV
RIPLINGHAM ROAD
THE GLEN
KINGSTON RI
OAK AV

55
143

56
140

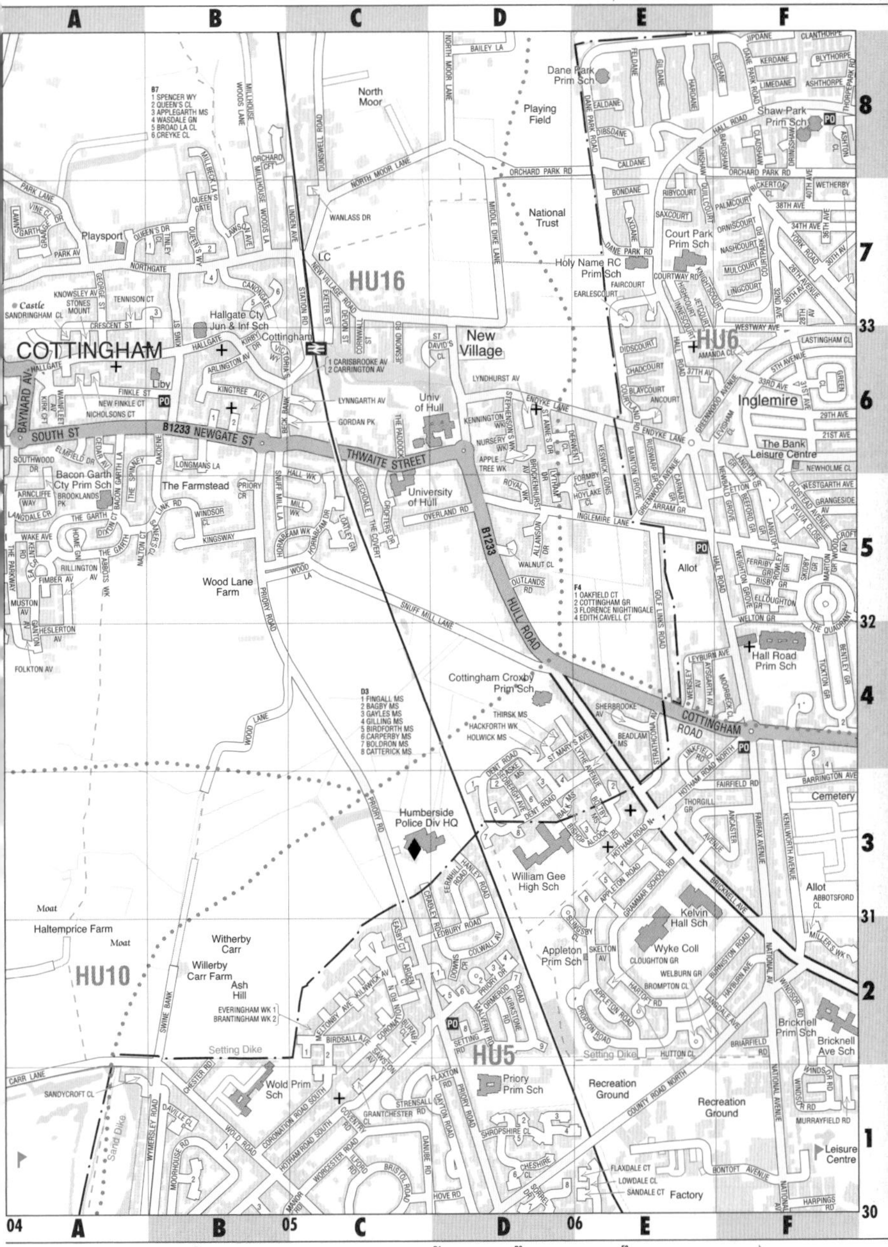

B1
1 MOORHOUSE RD
2 WILLERBY CARR CL
3 HUNSLEY AV

D1
1 WORCESTERSHIRE CL
2 HERTFORDSHIRE CL
3 YORKSHIRE CL
4 ERNEST KIRKWOOD CL
5 SUSSEX CL
6 WARWICKSHIRE CL
7 HEATHER CL
8 CELANDINE CL

D2
1 ST FRANCIS CT
2 ST THOMAS'S GRANGE
3 ST JUDE'S CT
4 ST EDMUNDS'S CT
5 ST OSWALD CT
6 ST HEDDA'S CT
7 ORMEROD CR
8 SETTING CR
9 MALVERN CR

E3
1 MARSKE WK
2 BURRILL MS
3 CALDBERG MS
4 SALTON AV
5 EBBERSTON GR
6 CASTLETON AV
7 KNAPTON AV

144
140

139

C8
1 FLAG WK
2 LARARD AV

C7
1 BEECHCLIFFE AV
2 CULLINGWORTH AV
3 DENHOLME AVE
4 STEETON AVE
5 SILSDEN AVE

56

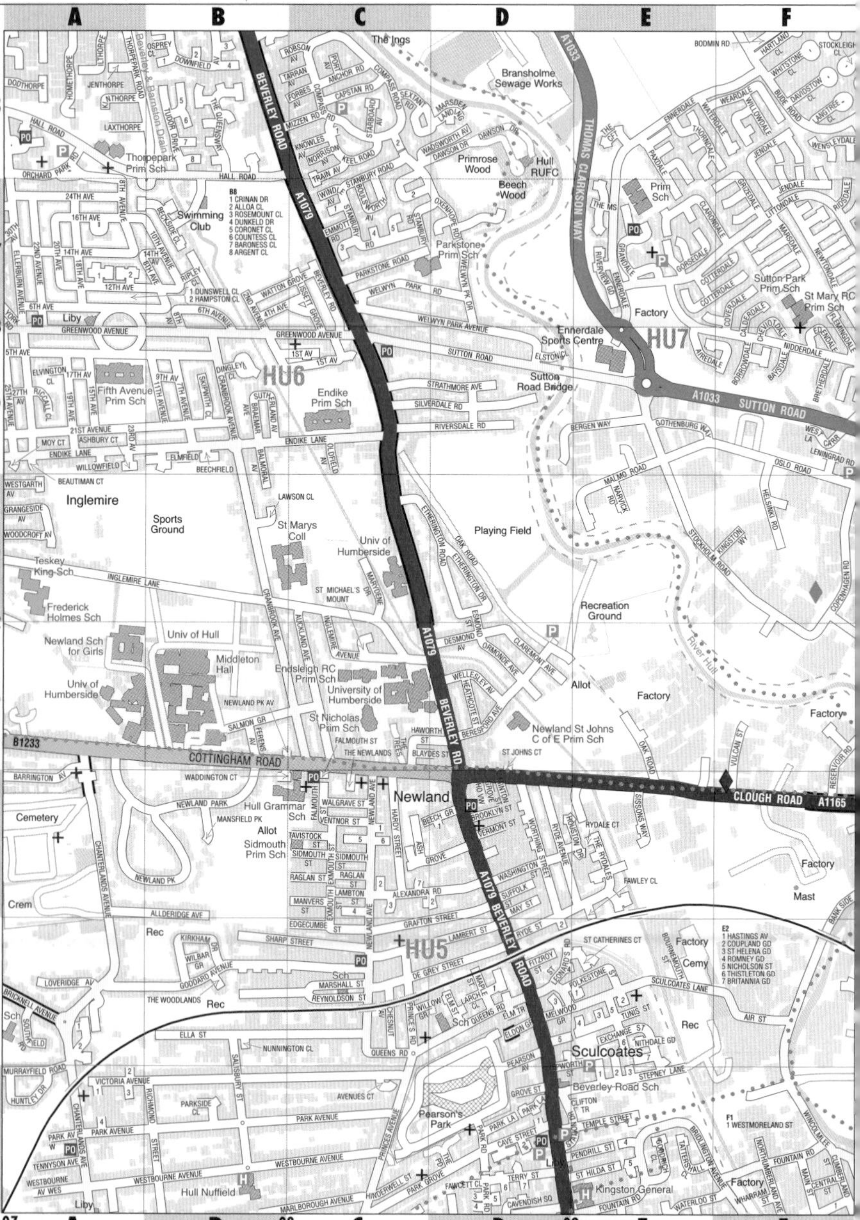

A1
1 VICTORIA GDNS
2 REGINA CR
3 WHITEHALL GDNS
4 MADISON GDNS

A2
1 ERNEST HL CT
2 RAINHILL RD

139

C3
1 NEWLAND GR
2 GOULDESBOROUGH CT
3 ST MONICA'S CT
4 MELBOURNE ST
5 TORRINGTON ST
6 WALTER'S TR
7 THEARNE CL

145

D1
1 CAVE TR
2 HUDSON GD
3 BARROW CT
4 BROMPTON CT
5 FRIARY CT
6 HAMPSTEAD CT
7 KNIGHTSBRIDGE CT

D2
1 BEACONSFIELD ST
2 SELSEY CL
3 BADEN CL
4 CROMER ST
5 ADDERBURY GR

D3
1 STRATHEARN ST
2 ST AUGUSTINE'S CT

E1
1 FENCHURCH ST
2 FARRINGDON ST
3 CLOVELLY GD
4 HADLEIGH CL
5 SCOTNEY CL

155

B7
1 PEVENSEY CLOSE
2 PEACEHAVEN CLOSE

57

D8
1 GOLDCREST CL
2 CORMORANT CL
3 LOWLAND CL
4 HOUSEMARTIN DR

142

F5
1 HAMMERSMITH RD
2 SHOREDITCH CL
3 TOTTENHAM CL
4 WILLESDEN CL

B1
1 CUDWORTH GR
2 OAKWELL GR
3 WOMBWELL GR
4 ALSTON AV

C1
1 DEARNE GR
2 AVON ST
3 DUNELM CL
4 BRANDON CT
5 BUCKINGHAM ST

D1
1 JAMES NIVEN COURT
2 FERENS CT

E1
1 ROTHESAY CL
2 ESKDALE AV

F1
1 EDGEWARE AV
2 N COUNTRY CT
3 TRINITY GR
4 WADHAM GR
5 MERTON GR

155
146
142

A5
1 PETERSHAM CL
2 TWICKENHAM CL
3 CHISWICK CL
4 WIMBLEDON CL
5 BELLFIELD AV

B5
1 ALWOODLEY CL
2 ATLANTA CT
3 GANTON CT
4 BELTON CL
5 HARLESTON CL

141

C5
1 DUNMOW CL
2 SHORWELL CL
3 ROOKLEY CL
4 COLDSTREAM CL
5 DRAYTON CL
6 FOYNES GN

57

C6
1 BICKLEIGH GR
2 HARLOW CL
3 ST MARGARETS CT
4 PARKHURST CL

58

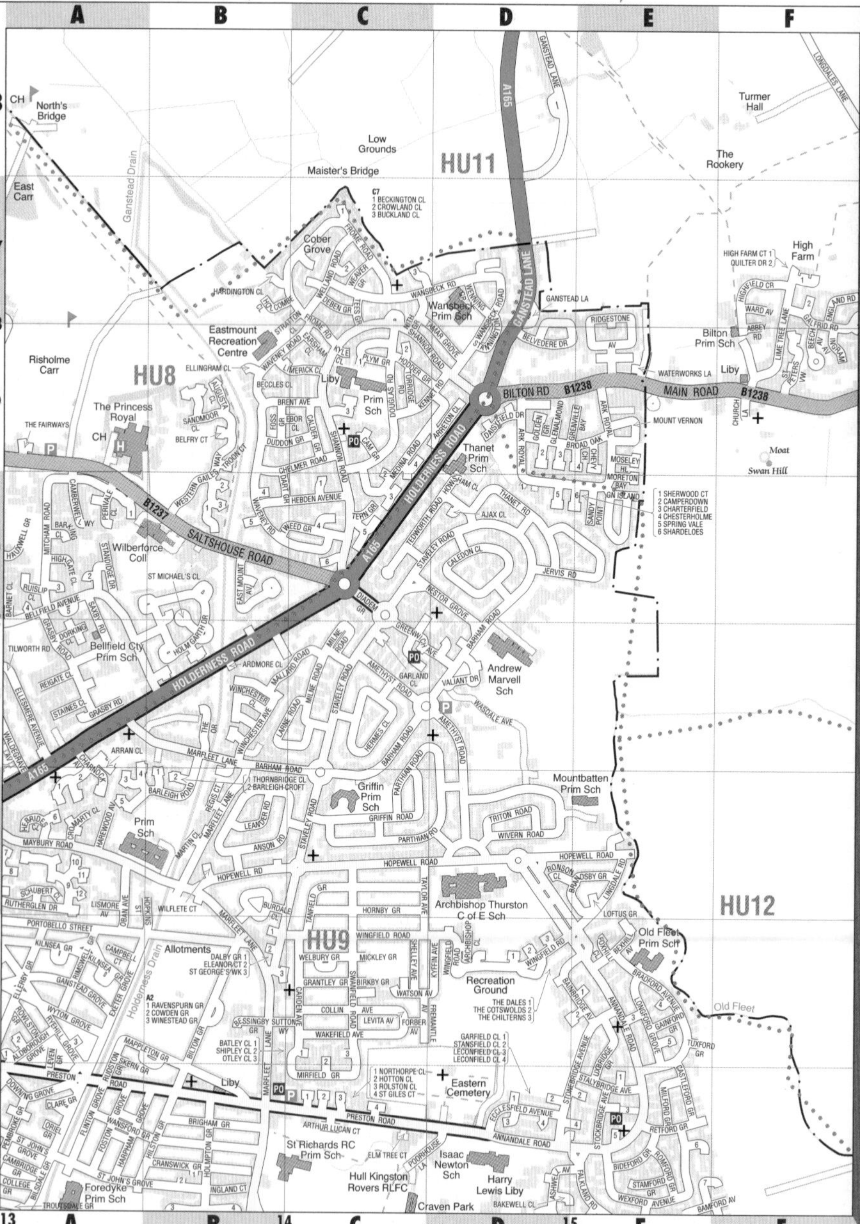

A3
1 FAROES CL
2 SPERRIN CL
3 BROUGHTON CL
4 BROADLAND DR
5 BEAULIEU CT
6 RONALDSWAY CL
7 MAJESTIC CT
8 THE BROADWAY
9 BROADWAY DR
10 GOLDEN CT
11 ZEIGFIELD CT
12 IMPERIAL CT

B1
1 ULROME CT
2 ATWICK CT
3 ENDEAVOUR CR
4 BEWHOLME GR

141

147

58

E1
1 STEMBRIDGE CL
2 CORBRIDGE CL
3 ELMBRIDGE PD
4 WADEBRIDGE GR
5 IVYBRIDGE WK
6 CHELMSFORD CL
7 CRAYFORD CL

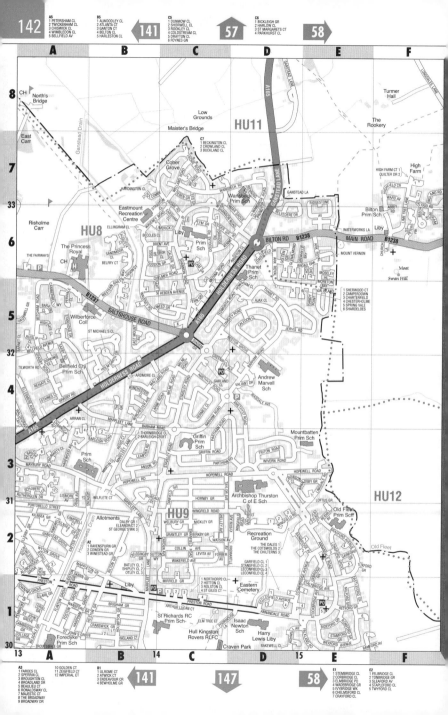

E2
1 FELBRIDGE CL
2 TONBRIDGE GR
3 SLEAFORD AV
4 STAPLEFORD CL
5 TWYFORD CL

69
138
144

E7
1 CROMWELL CT
2 WOODHILL CL
3 NORWOOD CL
4 WAULDBY CL
5 WEETON WY

E8
1 COLLYNSON CL
2 SETTERWOOD GARTH
3 OAKDALE AV

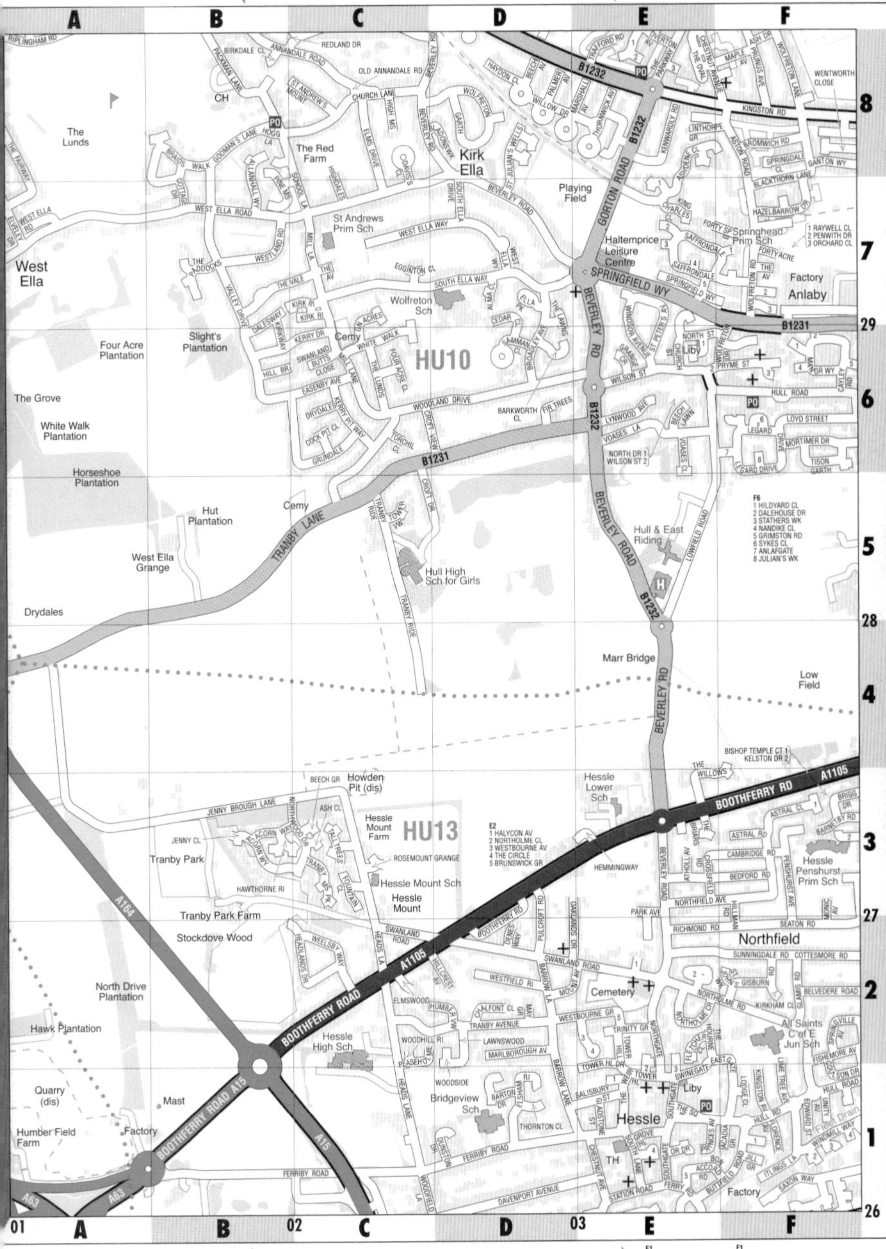
A
B
C
D
E
F
8
7
29
6
5
28
4
3
27
2
1
26
01
02
03
RIPLINGHAM RD
REDLAND DR
BIRKDALE CL
ANNANDALE ROAD
OLD ANNANDALE RD
PACKMAN LANE
CH
ST ANDREW'S MOUNT
CHURCH LANE
BEVERLEY RD
WOLFRETON GARTH
HAYDON CL
BEECH AV
PALMER AV
MARSHALL AV
WILLOW DR
THORNWICK AV
TRAFFORD RD
OVERTON AV
THE PARKWAY
B1232
PO
CHESTNUT AVENUE
THE OVAL
MAPLE AV
ASH DR
PRUNUS AVE
WOLFRETON LANE
WENTWORTH CLOSE
KINGSTON RD
The Lunds
The Red Farm
Kirk Ella
GODMAN'S LANE
HOGG LA
BRAIDS WALK
ALLANHALL WY
PINE MS
SCHOOL LA
COTTAGE DR
ELMS DRIVE
HIGH MS
HIGHDALES
DAVIS'S CL
GORTON ROAD
KENWARDLY RD
LINTHORPE GR
ASHDENE CL
ASTON ROAD
BROMWICH RD
SPRINGDALE CL
GANTON WY
BLACKTHORN LANE
HAZELBARROW DR
Playing Field
WEST ELLA ROAD
WEST ELLA RD
SOUTH ELLA DRIVE
BEVERLEY ROAD
ST JULIAN'S WELLS
KING CHARLES CL
FORTY SP
Springhead Prim Sch
1 RAYWELL CL
2 PENWITH DR
3 ORCHARD CL
St Andrews Prim Sch
WEST ELLA WAY
WESTLAND RD
MILL LA
Haltemprice Leisure Centre
SAFFRONDALE
FORTY ACRE
THE PADDOCKS
THE AV
EGGINTON CL
WEST ELLA WY
SPRINGFIELD WY
WOLFRETON RD
Factory
Anlaby
West Ella
THE VALE
VALLEY DRIVE
KIRK RI
SOUTH ELLA WAY
Wolfreton Sch
ALMA CL
ELLA PK
THE LAWNS
WINDSOR AVENUE
ST PETER'S AV
NORTH ST
Liby
B1231
DALESWAY
KIRKWAY
KERRY DR
Cemy
WHITE WALK
FOUR ACRES
CEDAR CL
SAMMAN CL
BROADLEY AVE
GRANGE CR
CHURCH ST
PRYME ST
MANOR WY
CAVLEY RD
Four Acre Plantation
Slight's Plantation
HU10
HILL BR
SWANLAND BUTTS CLOSE
MILL LANE
THE LUNDS
FOUR ACRE CL
WILSON ST
HULL ROAD
The Grove
EASENBY AVE
WOODLAND DRIVE
BARKWORTH CL
FIR TREES
LYNWOOD AVE
BEECH LAWN
LOYD STREET
LEGARD
White Walk Plantation
DRYDALES
KERRY PIT WAY
CROFT VIEW
VOASES LA
MORTIMER DR
COCK PIT CL
GRUNDALE
TORCHIL CL
NORTH DR 1
WILSON ST 2
VOASES CL
LEGARD DRIVE
TISON GARTH
Horseshoe Plantation
CROFT DR
F6
1 HILDYARD CL
2 DALEHOUSE DR
3 STATHERS WK
4 NANDIKE CL
5 GRIMSTON RD
6 SYKES CL
7 ANLAFGATE
8 JULIAN'S WK
Hut Plantation
Cemy
TRANBY RIDE
TOWER VW
LOWFIELD ROAD
Hull & East Riding
TRANBY LANE
West Ella Grange
Hull High Sch for Girls
H
Drydales
Marr Bridge
Low Field
BISHOP TEMPLE CT 1
KELSTON DR 2
THE WILLOWS
A1105
BOOTHFERRY RD
BRIGG DR
ASTRAL CL
BARNETBY RD
BEECH GR
Howden Pit (dis)
Hessle Lower Sch
JENNY BROUGH LANE
ASH CL
Hessle Mount Farm
HU13
ASTRAL RD
JENNY CL
ACORN WAY
NORTHWOOD DR
E2
1 HALYCON AV
2 NORTHOLME CL
3 WESTBOURNE AV
4 THE CIRCLE
5 BRUNSWICK GR
CAMBRIDGE RD
Hessle Penshurst Prim Sch
Tranby Park
TALL TREES
ROSEMOUNT GRANGE
HEMMINGWAY
ATHOLL AV
CROSSFIELD AV
BEDFORD RD
PENSHURST AVE
HAWTHORNE RI
FOUNTAIN CL
Hessle Mount Sch
Hessle Mount
NORTHFIELD AVE
MONIC AV
A164
Tranby Park Farm
PARK AVE
HILLMAN RD
RICHMOND RD
SEATON RD
Stockdove Wood
SWANLAND ROAD
BOOTHFERRY RD
DENES WAY
PULCROFT RD
OAKLANDS DR
Northfield
WEELSBY WAY
HEADLANDS DR
HEADS LA
SUNNINGDALE RD
COTTESMORE RD
HILLCREST AV
WESTFIELD RI
BARROW LA
MOUNT AV
Cemetery
GISBURN
BELVEDERE ROAD
North Drive Plantation
BOOTHFERRY ROAD
ELMSWOOD
HUMBER VW
CHALFONT CL
MAY GR
WESTBOURNE GR
NORTHOLME RD
KIRKHAM CL
All Saints C of E Jun Sch
Hawk Plantation
TRANBY AVENUE
TRINITY GR
TOWER HILL
NORTHGATE
FLETCHER CL
HOURNE CT
Hessle High Sch
WOODHILL RI
PEASEHOLME
LAWNSWOOD
MARLBOROUGH AV
TOWER HL DR
EAST GATE
FISHEMORE AV
WOODSIDE
BARTON DR
ELSHAM RI
BARROW LANE
SALISBURY ST
SWINEGATE
Liby
LODGE CL
KINGSTON AV
LIME TREE AVE
HULL ROAD
Quarry (dis)
Mast
A15
BOOTHFERRY ROAD A15
Bridgeview Sch
GLADSTONE ST
THE WEIR
SOUTHGATE
THE SQ
PO
Hessle
HULL RD
FLORENCE AV
EDWARD ST
Fleet Drain
WINDMILL WAY
Humber Field Farm
Factory
DUNSTON DR
THORNTON CL
SOUTH LANE
GROVE
ORCHARD
PRINCES AV
ACACIA GR
BUTTFIELD ROAD
JILL GR
ITLINGS LA
FERRIBY ROAD
TH
ACCORD RD
FERRY RD
Factory
SAXON WAY
A63
FERRIBY ROAD
WOODFIELD LA
DAVENPORT AVENUE
CHESTNUT AVE
STATION ROAD

69
69
144

E1
1 SPIRE VW
2 TOWER HL MS
3 VICARAGE LA
4 CLOWES CT
5 FISHWICK AV

F1
1 MARGARET GR
2 BISHOP BLUNT CL
3 BISHOP KEMPTHORNE CLO
4 BISHOP GURDON CL

A3
1 BARNETBY RD
2 KELSTON DR
3 YARMOUTH AV
4 WINTHORPE RD
5 BROCKLESBY CL
6 CORRAN GARTH

B7
1 LANGFORD WK
2 HOLLYTREE AV
3 LABURNUM DR
4 ROSEWOOD CL

143

C8
1 PRIMROSE DR
2 COUNTY RD S

139

D8
1 LOCKTON GR
2 HACKNESS GR
3 BARGATE GR
4 SNAINTON GR
5 SORREL DR

E6
1 AIRMYN AVE
2 ST MARTINS AVE

F6
1 HAWTHORN CT

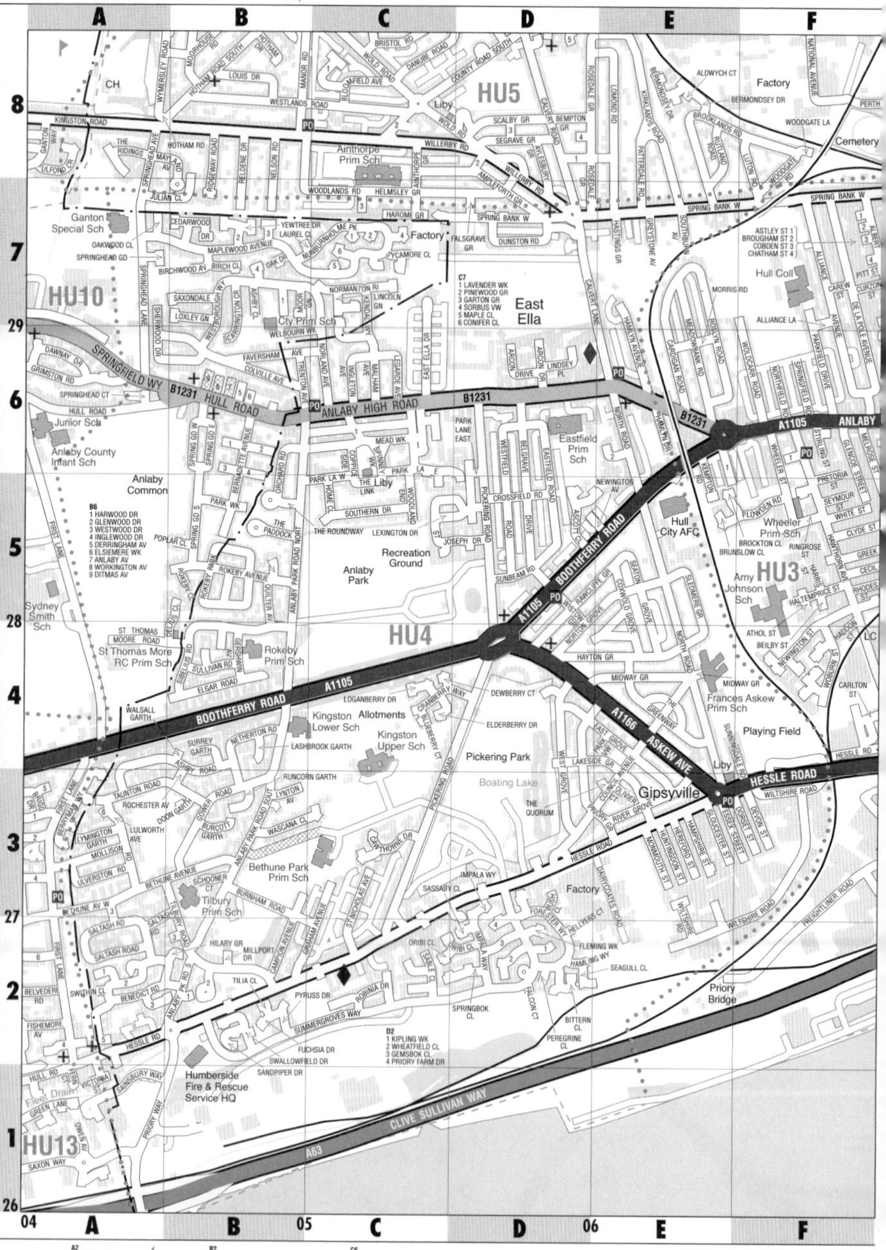

A2
1 VALENTINE CL
2 BENEDICT CL
3 VINCENT CL
4 NEWLYN CL
5 CRISPIN CL
6 COTTESMORE RD

143

B2
1 AVONDALE
2 WOOLWICH DR
3 DATCHET GARTH

C6
1 THE GREENWAY

70

For full street detail of the highlighted area see page 155.

A6
1 GRANVILLE ST
2 SANDRINGHAM ST
3 COULTAS CT
4 ACLAND ST
5 LONSDALE ST
6 CARNEGIE ST

B8
1 ROXBURGH ST
2 RICHMOND ST
3 LANARK ST

C6
1 KINGS LEIGH
2 KING'S CROSS CL
3 THORN LEIGH

D8
1 BERKELEY ST
2 CROMWELL CL
3 BROWNING CL
4 LEONARD ST
5 TRAFALGAR ST
6 SHAKESPEARE CL

140
146

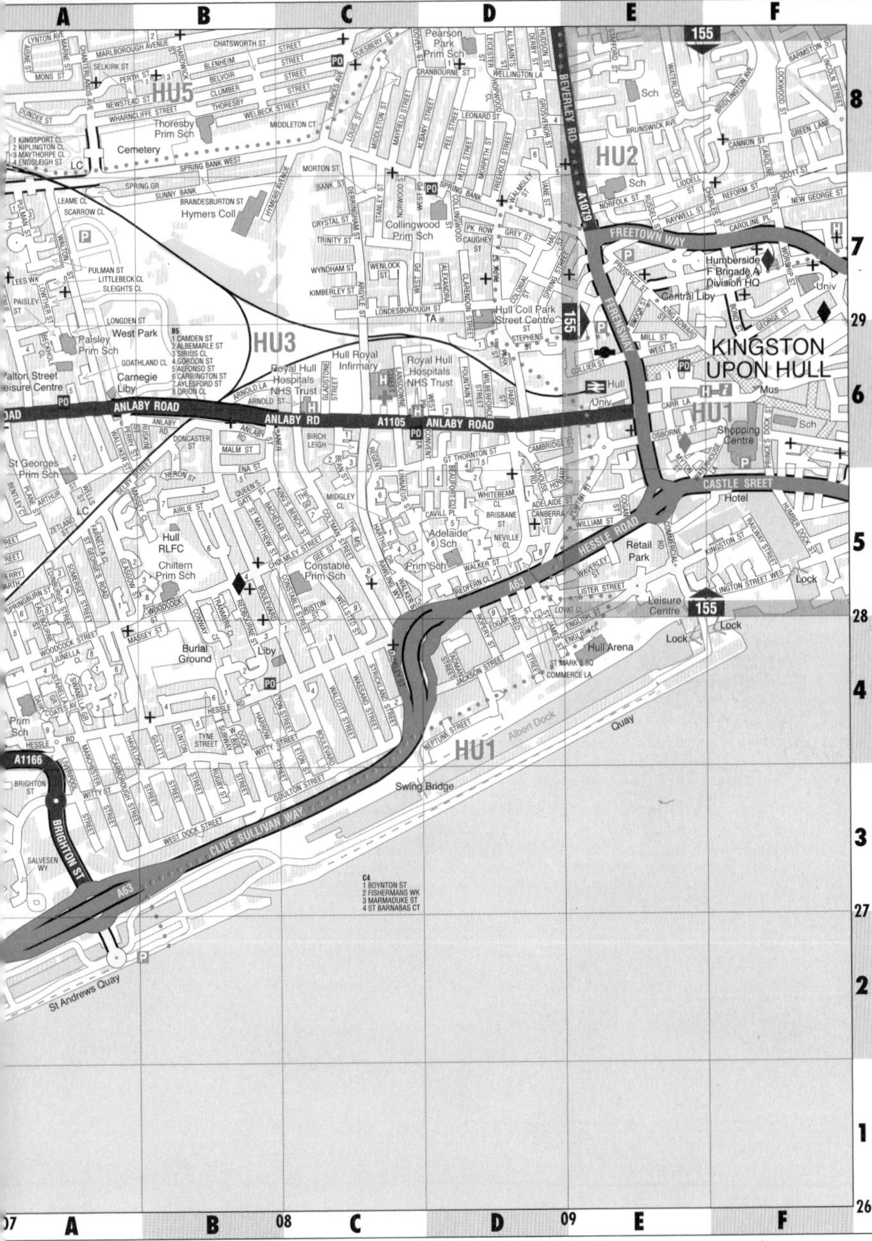

A4
1 JADE GR
2 ONYX GR
3 TOPAZ GR
4 CORSAIR GR
5 WESTBOURNE ST
6 GARNET GR
7 SAPPHIRE GR
8 EMERALD GR
9 ST NECTAN CL

A5
1 CORDELLA CL
2 DORADO CL
3 SANDLEMERE CL
4 DARRISMERE VILLAS
5 BRIXHAM CT
6 OTTERBURN ST

B4
1 DIVISION RD
2 SEFTON ST
3 NEWTON ST
4 RIBBLE ST
5 RUGBY ST
6 DEE ST
7 ROSAMOND ST

70

C5
1 LYRIC CL
2 THORNWICK CL
3 BARBERRY CT
4 WINSHIP CL
5 EVER THORPE CL
6 TICHBOURNE CL
7 WESLEY CT
8 BEECH CL
9 CAROL DICKSON CT

D5
1 GOODWIN PD
2 HAZEL GR
3 FIRETHORN CL
4 NEWPORT CL
5 PEACH TREE CT
6 ELDERWOOD CT
7 QUANTOCK CL
8 BATHURST ST
9 MECHANIC LA

D6
1 BLOOMSBURY CT
2 ARLINGTON ST
3 ALMOND GR
4 BLACKTHORN CT
5 SORBUS CT

146

155

B7
1 PEMBERTON ST
2 BLYTH ST
3 NAYLOR'S ROW
4 WILSON ST
5 EAST ST
6 ALMA ST

C7
1 PELHAM DR
2 EDWARD COLLINS SQ
3 HODGE CT
4 ROSEY ROW
5 ALDERSON MS
6 BROADLEY CL
7 DENMARK CT
8 EMILY ST

141

C8
1 NORNABELL ST
2 VICTOR ST
3 BALFOUR ST
4 ARUNDEL ST
5 HORNSEA PD
6 ST QUINTINS CL

D7
1 BUTTERCUP CL
2 PENISTONE CT
3 BEAUMONT CT
4 BRUMBY'S TR
5 EMPRINGHAM ST

E8
1 DOVEDALE GR
2 DEEPDALE GR
3 MIDDLEHAM CL
4 BYLAND CT

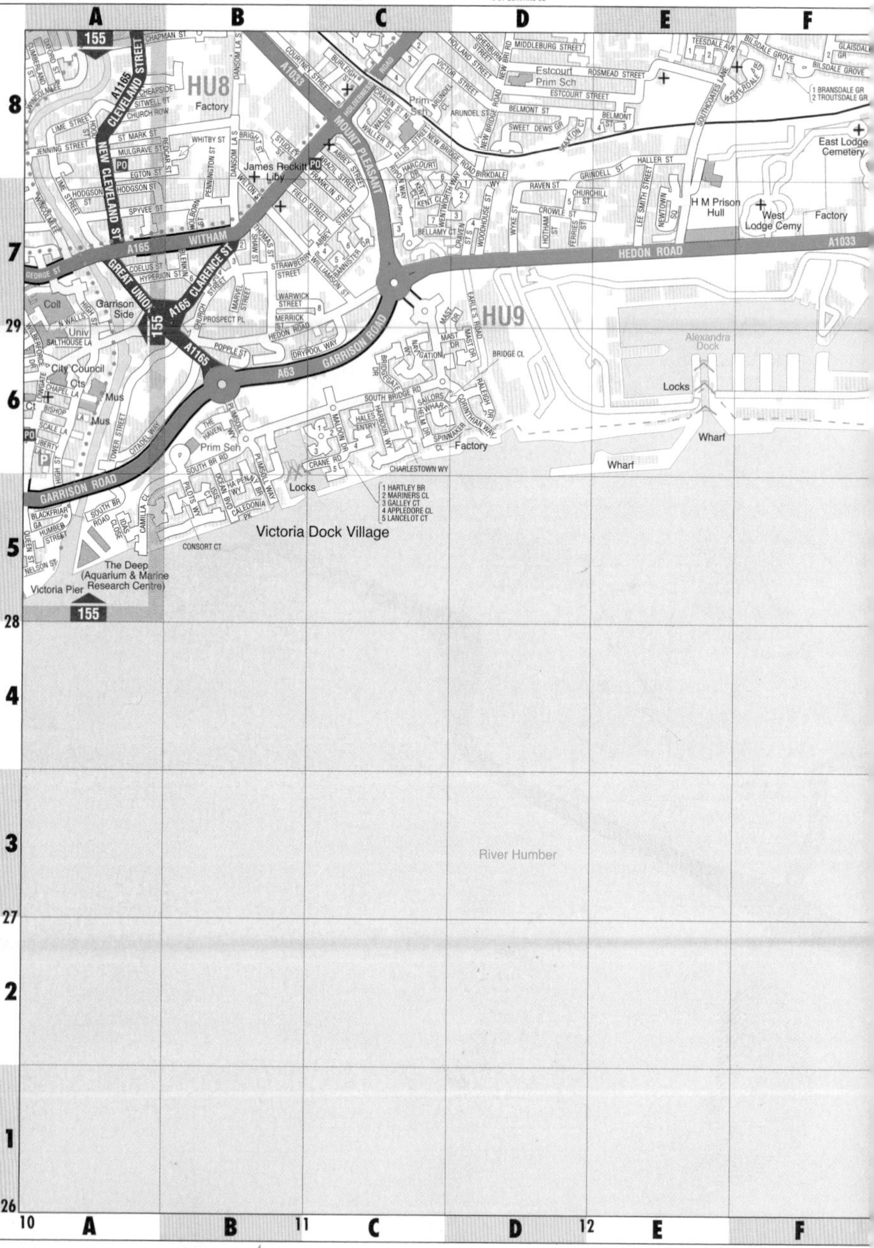

For full street detail of the highlighted area see page 155.

145

71

A
B
C
D
E
F
8
7
29
6
5
28
4
3
27
2
1
26
Holderness Drain
Hull Maternity
BEWHOLME GR
Factory
BURMA DRIVE
MARFLEET LA
MARFLEET AVENUE
MARFLEET LANE
GT FIELD LA
Factory
Marfleet
Marfleet Prim Sch
Factory
CYPRUS ST
FRODSHAM ST
EGYPT ST
DELHI ST
LITTLEFAIR ROAD
CEYLON ST
CHURCH LANE
ELBA ST
Factory
A1033
HEDON ROAD
HU9
CORPORATION ROAD
CORPORATION RD
King George Dock
Lock
Lock
Lock
Queen Elizabeth Dock
ASHWELL AV
BOTHWELL GR
HEMSWELL
AVENUE
FALKLAND ROAD
DODSWELL GROVE
STOCKWELL GR
Stockwell Prim Sch
1 SOUTHWELL AV
2 BAMFORD AV
3 SALTFORD AV
4 HALLIWELL CL
GREAT FIELD LANE
VALLETTA STREET
SOMERDEN ROAD
Factory
Factory
TOWER HO LA
A1033
HULL RD
Old Fleet
Factory
Lord's Clough
HU12
Salt End
Quay
Quay
Salt End
River Humber
Salt End Jetties No 1
Salt End Jetties No 3
3
14
15

C5
1 YORK ST
2 HARPER ST
3 DOUGLAS ST
4 RAINCLIFFE ST
5 LONDESBOROUGH ST
6 HILDA ST
7 PORTHOLME CR
8 SOUTH PAR
9 TURNERS SQ
10 AUDUS ST
11 MARKET PL

48

D5
1 MICKLEGATE
2 WREN LA
3 CHURCH HL
4 CHURCH LA

49 49

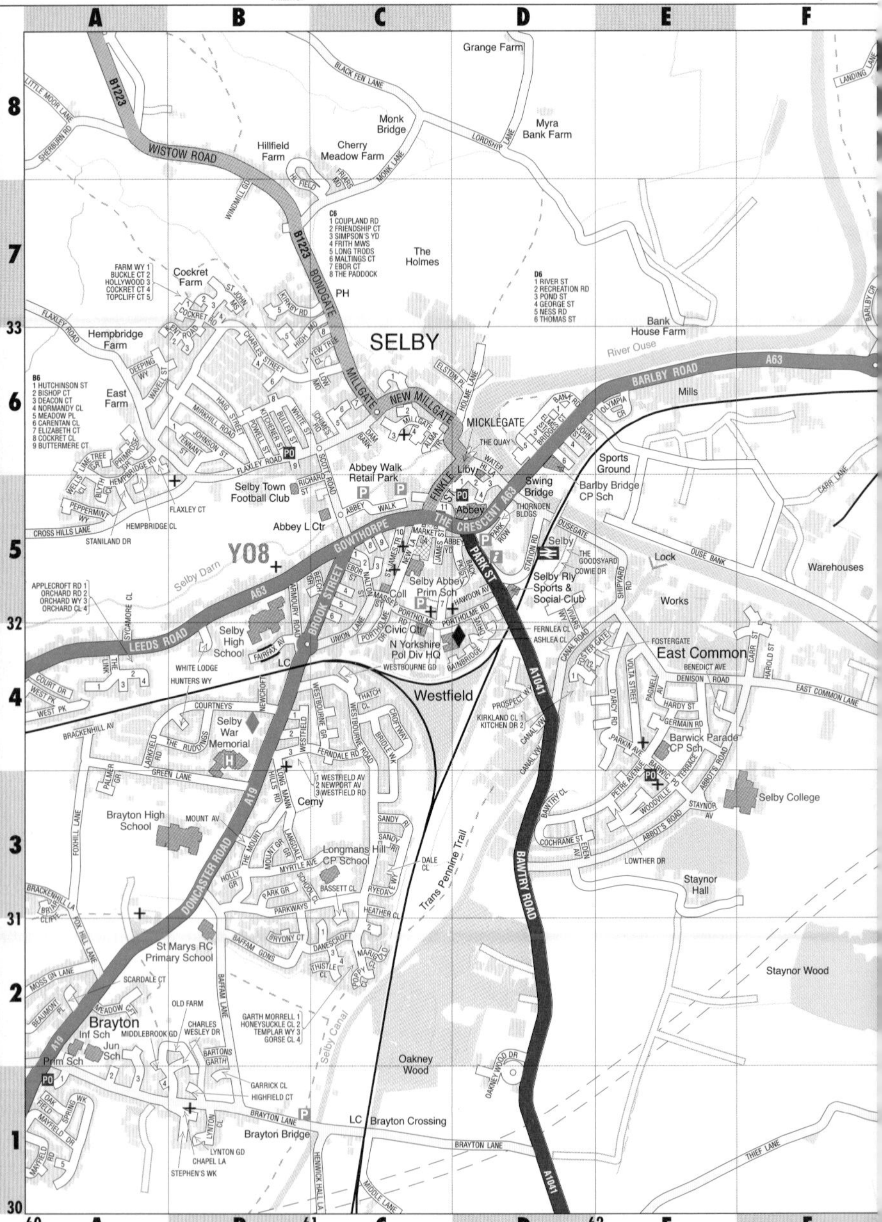

A1
1 MANOR FARM CL
2 HOLMEFIELD CT
3 HOLMEFIELD CL
4 CHILVERS CT
5 MAYFIELD DR

62 63 49

64 65 65

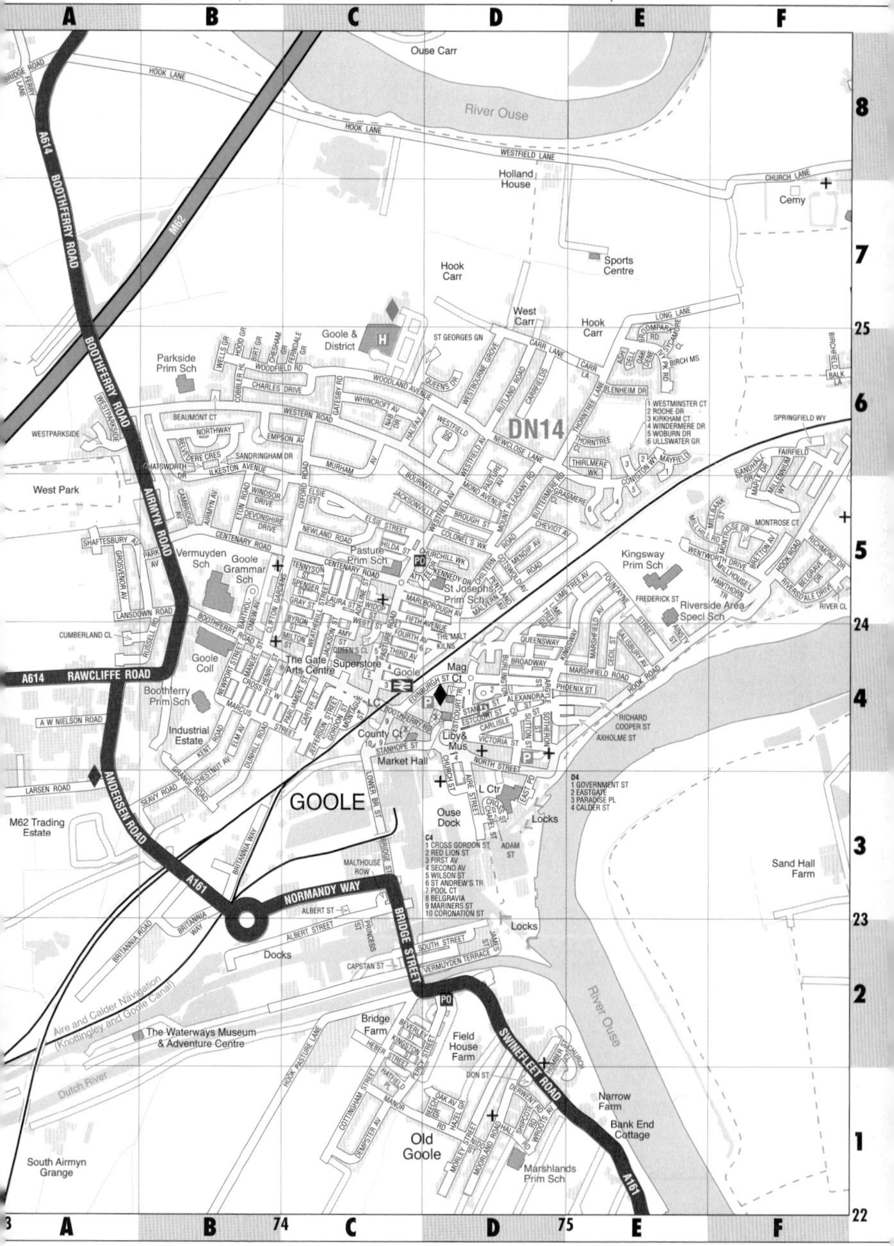

A
B
C
D
E
F
8
7
25
6
5
24
4
3
23
2
1
22
74
75
Ouse Carr
River Ouse
HOOK LANE
WESTFIELD LANE
BRIDGE ROAD
FERRY LANE
A614
BOOTHFERRY ROAD
M62
Holland House
CHURCH LANE
Cemy
Hook Carr
Sports Centre
West Carr
Hook Carr
LONG LANE
Goole & District
H
ST GEORGES GN
CARR LANE
Parkside Prim Sch
WOODFIELD RD
CHARLES DRIVE
WOODLAND AVENUE
QUEENS DR
WESTBOURNE GROVE
RUTLAND ROAD
CARRFIELDS
BLENHEIM DR
BIRCH MS
BALK LA
1 WESTMINSTER CT
2 ROCHE DR
3 KIRKHAM CT
4 WINDERMERE DR
5 WOBURN DR
6 ULLSWATER GR
DN14
SPRINGFIELD WY
WESTERN ROAD
WHINCROFT AV
HALIFAX AV
WESTFIELD
NEWCLOSE LANE
THORNTREE CL
THORNTREE LANE
THIRLMERE WK
CONISTON WY
MAYFIELD
FAIRFIELD
BEAUMONT CT
NORTHWAY
EMPSON AV
WESTPARKSIDE
BELVEDERE CRES
SANDRINGHAM DR
CHATSWORTH DR
ILKESTON AVENUE
MURHAM AV
BOURNVILLE
MOND AVENUE
MOUNT PLEASANT RD
BUTTERMERE RD
GRASMERE CL
SANDHALL DR
MAPLE DR
MILLENNIUM WY
West Park
CAMBRIDGE AV
AIRMYN AV
ETON ROAD
WINDSOR DRIVE
DEVONSHIRE DRIVE
OXFORD ROAD
ELSIE ST
ELSIE STREET
JACKSONVILLE
WESTFIELD AV
BROUGH ST
CHEVIOT AV
MILLBANK ST
MILLHILL RD
MONTROSE DR
MONTROSE CT
SHAFTESBURY AV
CENTENARY ROAD
NEWLAND ROAD
HILDA ST
COLONEL'S WK
MENDIP AV
WENTWORTH DRIVE
BRETTON AV
HOOK ROAD
RICHMOND DR
GROSVENOR AV
PARK AV
Vermuyden Sch
Goole Grammar Sch
AIRMYN ROAD
Pasture Prim Sch
PO
CHURCHILL WK
KENNEDY DR
St Josephs Prim Sch
CHILTERN
COTSWOLD AV
PENTLAND
Kingsway Prim Sch
MILLHOUSE L
HAWTHORN TR
BELGRAVE DR
RIVERSDALE DRIVE
RIVER CL
LIME TREE AV
FOUNTAYNE
FREDERICK ST
Riverside Area Specl Sch
LANSDOWN ROAD
TENNYSON ST
SPENSER ST
GRAY ST
BYRON ST
MILTON ST
LAURA ST
WIDOP ST
MARLBOROUGH AV
FIFTH AVENUE
FOURTH AV
THIRD AV
THE MALT KILNS
QUEENSWAY
KINGSWAY
MARSHFIELD AV
CECIL ST
SALISBURY AV
AINSTY ST
CUMBERLAND CL
RUSSELL RD
BOOTHFERRY ROAD
CLIFTON GARDENS
WEATHERILL STREET
JACKSON STREET
PASTURE ROAD
QUEEN'S CL
Superstore
Goole
The Gate Arts Centre
BROADWAY
MARSHFIELD ROAD
A614
RAWCLIFFE ROAD
Goole Coll
Mag Ct
BURLINGTON CR
PHOENIX ST
ALEXANDRA
EDINBURGH ST
ESTCOURT TR
STANLEY ST
ESTCOURT ST
CARLISLE
VICTORIA ST
SUTTON ST
SOTHERON ST
HOOK ROAD
RICHARD COOPER ST
AXHOLME ST
Boothferry Prim Sch
NEWPORT STREET
MANUEL ST
CROSS ST
HENRY ST
PARLIAMENT ST
CARTER ST
LC
A W NIELSON ROAD
MARCUS
KENT ROAD
ELM AV
DUNHILL ROAD
Industrial Estate
JEFFERSON STREET
GORDON ST
MONTAGUE ST
BOOTHFERRY RD
County Ct
STANHOPE ST
Liby & Mus
NORTH STREET
Market Hall
P
D4
1 GOVERNMENT ST
2 EASTGATE
3 PARADISE PL
4 CALDER ST
LARSEN ROAD
ANDERSEN ROAD
GRANGE RD
CHESTNUT AV
SEAVY ROAD
GOOLE
LOWER BR ST
CHURCH ST
AIRE STREET
L Ctr
EAST PD
CROSS ST
CHAPEL ST
Locks
M62 Trading Estate
Ouse Dock
C4
1 CROSS GORDON ST
2 RED LION ST
3 FIRST AV
4 SECOND AV
5 WILSON ST
6 ST ANDREW'S TR
7 POOL CT
8 BELGRAVIA
9 MARINERS ST
10 CORONATION ST
ADAM ST
Sand Hall Farm
BRITANNIA WAY
A161
MALTHOUSE ROW
BRIDGE ST
NORMANDY WAY
ALBERT ST
ALBERT STREET
PRINCESS ST
BRIDGE STREET
Locks
BRITANNIA ROAD
BRITANNIA WAY
SOUTH STREET
JAMES ST
Docks
CAPSTAN ST
VERMUYDEN TERRACE
PO
Aire and Calder Navigation
(Knottingley and Goole Canal)
The Waterways Museum & Adventure Centre
River Ouse
Bridge Farm
BEVERLEY ST
KINGSTON ST
HEBER STREET
PERCY STREET
Field House Farm
SWINEFLEET ROAD
HUMBER ST
CHURCH
Dutch River
HOOK PASTURE LANE
COTTINGHAM STREET
HATFIELD PL
DON ST
MANOR RD
OAK AV
BEECH GR
HAZEL GR
DERWENT RD
Narrow Farm
DEMPSTER AV
Old Goole
MORLEY STREET
SNIDD ST
MOORLAND ROAD
HALL RD
SHIPCOTE RD
WROOTS AV
Bank End Cottage
Marshlands Prim Sch
South Airmyn Grange
A161

64 80 65

95
96

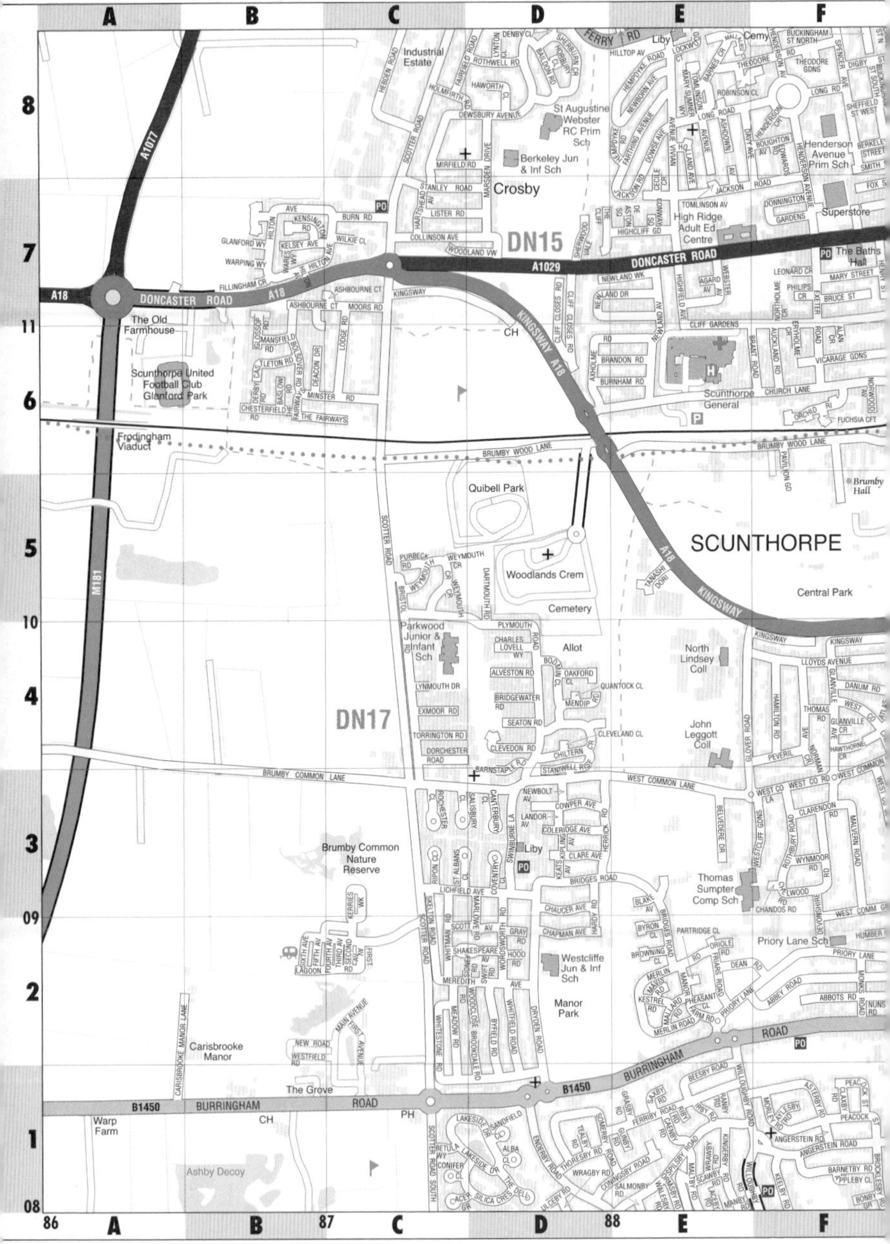
A
B
C
D
E
F
8
7
6
5
4
3
2
1
11
10
09
08
86
87
88
A1077
A18
DONCASTER ROAD
A1029
DONCASTER ROAD
KINGSWAY
A18
M181
B1450
BURRINGHAM
ROAD
B1450
BURRINGHAM ROAD
Industrial Estate
Crosby
DN15
St Augustine Webster RC Prim Sch
Berkeley Jun & Inf Sch
High Ridge Adult Ed Centre
Henderson Avenue Prim Sch
Superstore
The Baths Hall
Cemy
Liby
The Old Farmhouse
Scunthorpe United Football Club Glanford Park
Scunthorpe General
Frodingham Viaduct
BRUMBY WOOD LANE
Quibell Park
Brumby Hall
SCUNTHORPE
Woodlands Crem
Cemetery
Central Park
Parkwood Junior & Infant Sch
Allot
North Lindsey Coll
John Leggott Coll
DN17
BRUMBY COMMON LANE
WEST COMMON LANE
Brumby Common Nature Reserve
Thomas Sumpter Comp Sch
Priory Lane Sch
Westcliffe Jun & Inf Sch
Manor Park
Carisbrooke Manor
CARISBROOKE MANOR LANE
The Grove
Warp Farm
CH
PH
Ashby Decoy
SCOTTER ROAD
SCOTTER ROAD SOUTH

95
96

B7
1 BELGRAVE SQ
2 FRODINGHAM FOOTPATH
3 CHURCH SQ

96
97

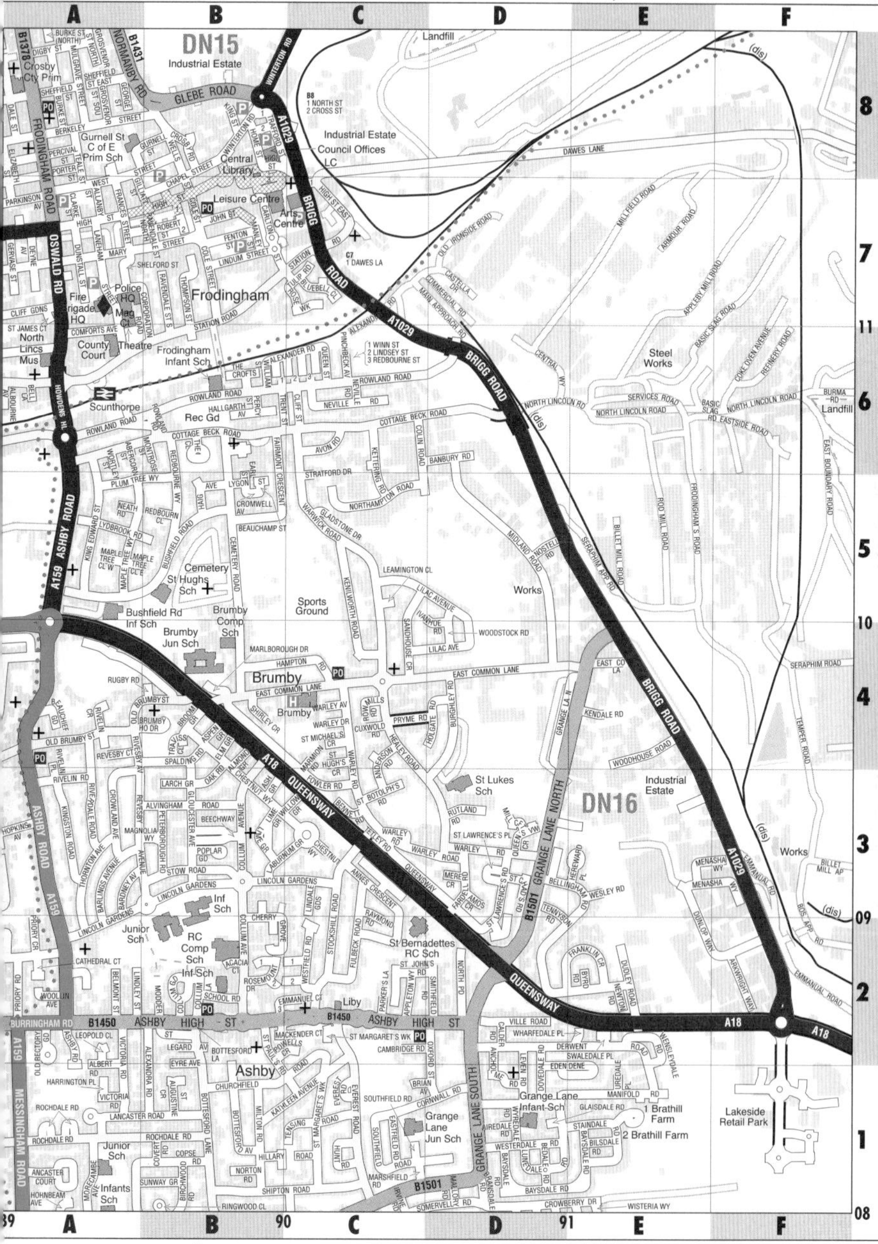
DN15
Industrial Estate
Landfill
Industrial Estate
Council Offices
LC
Crosby
Cty Prim
Gurnell St
C of E
Prim Sch
Central
Library
Leisure Centre
Arts
Centre
Police
HQ
Fire
Brigade
HQ
Mag
Ct
Frodingham
North
Lincs
Mus
County
Court
Theatre
Frodingham
Infant Sch
Scunthorpe
Rec Gd
Steel
Works
Landfill
Works
Cemetery
St Hughs
Sch
Sports
Ground
Bushfield Rd
Inf Sch
Brumby
Comp
Sch
Brumby
Jun Sch
Brumby
DN16
Industrial
Estate
St Lukes
Sch
Works
Inf
Sch
Junior
Sch
RC
Comp
Sch
Inf Sch
St Bernadettes
RC Sch
Liby
Ashby
Junior
Sch
Infants
Sch
Grange
Lane
Jun Sch
Grange Lane
Infant Sch
1 Brathill
Farm
2 Brathill Farm
Lakeside
Retail Park
GLEBE ROAD
BRIGG ROAD
A1029
OSWALD RD
FRODINGHAM ROAD
ASHBY ROAD
A159
QUEENSWAY
A18
GRANGE LANE NORTH
GRANGE LANE SOUTH
B1501
B1450
ASHBY HIGH ST
MESSINGHAM ROAD
BURRINGHAM RD
DAWES LANE
NORTH LINCOLN RD
EAST COMMON LANE
ROWLAND ROAD
COTTAGE BECK ROAD
LINCOLN GARDENS
B8
1 NORTH ST
2 CROSS ST
C7
1 DAWES LA
1 WINN ST
2 LINDSEY ST
3 REDBOURNE ST
A
B
C
D
E
F
8
7
6
5
4
3
2
1
11
10
09
08
89
90
91

B2
1 ASHBERRY DR
2 ORCHARD CL
3 MACKENDER CT

C2
1 NORTHFIELD CL
2 SPRINGFIELD CL

96
97

102
102

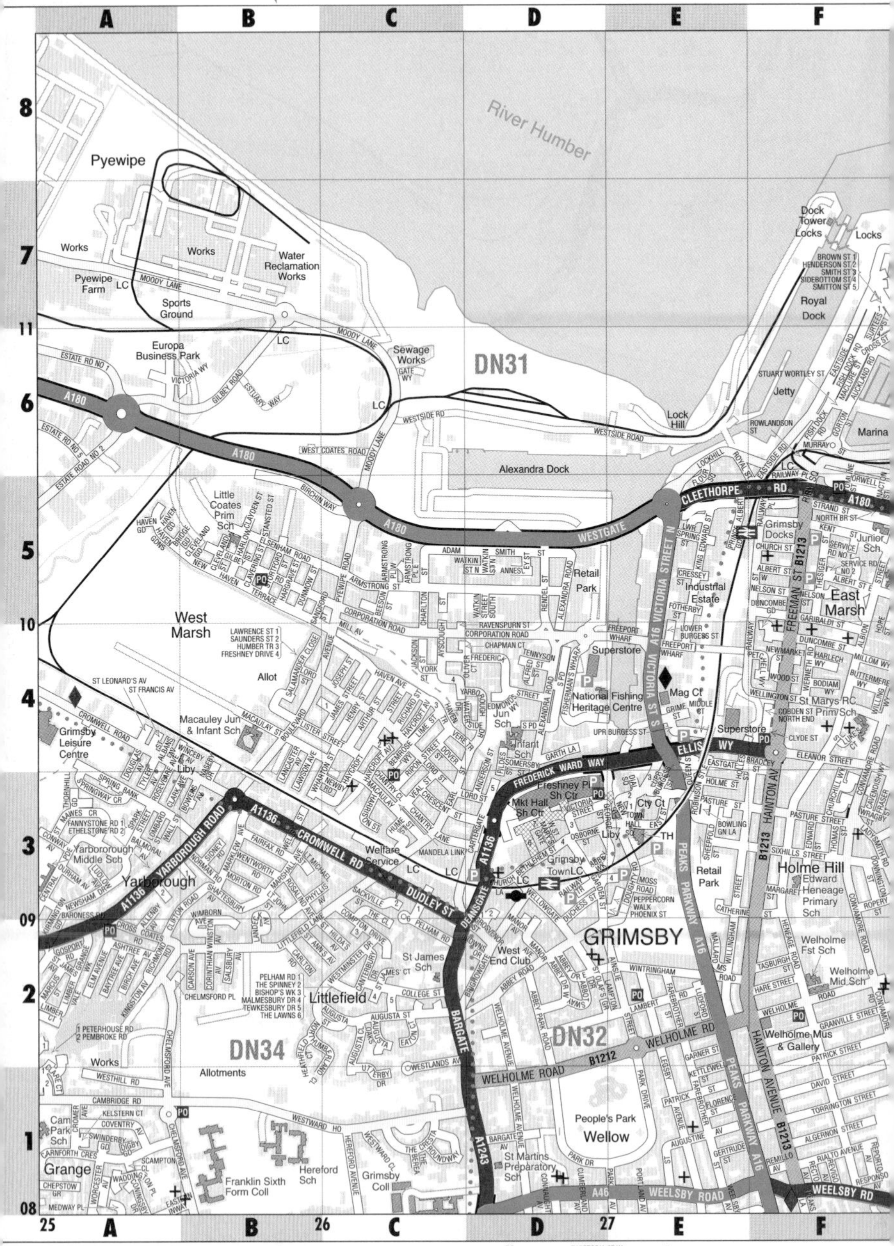
A
B
C
D
E
F
8
7
11
6
5
10
4
3
09
2
1
08
25
26
27
River Humber
Pyewipe
Works
Works
Water
Reclamation
Works
Pyewipe
Farm
LC
MOODY LANE
Sports
Ground
LC
MOODY LANE
Europa
Business Park
ESTATE RD NO 1
VICTORIA WY
GILBEY ROAD
ESTUARY WAY
Sewage
Works
GATE WY
DN31
LC
WESTSIDE RD
WESTSIDE ROAD
Lock
Hill
A180
A180
ESTATE RD NO 5
ESTATE ROAD NO 2
WEST COATES ROAD
MOODY LANE
Alexandra Dock
BIRCHIN WAY
A180
WESTGATE
CLEETHORPE RD
A180
Little
Coates
Prim
Sch
HAVEN GD
HAVEN GDNS
CLEVELAND GD
SENHAM ROAD
NEW HAVEN TERRACE
PO
STANSTED ST
CLAYDEN ST
ARMSTRONG ST
ARMSTRONG PL W
ARMSTRONG PL E
PYEWIPE ROAD
DUNMOW ST
ADAM
WATKIN
SMITH
ST N
ANNESLEY ST
Retail
Park
ALEXANDRA ROAD
RENDEL ST
CORPORATION ROAD
RAVENSPURN ST
MILL AV
West
Marsh
LAWRENCE ST 1
SAUNDERS ST 2
HUMBER TR 3
FRESHNEY DRIVE 4
CHAPMAN CT
TENNYSON
FREDERICK
FREEPORT WHARF
Superstore
A16 VICTORIA STREET N
VICTORIA ST S
Allot
ST LEONARD'S AV
ST FRANCIS AV
CROMWELL ROAD
Grimsby
Leisure
Centre
Macauley Jun
& Infant Sch
MACAULAY ST
BOULEVARD
LISTER STREET
HAVEN AVE
National Fishing
Heritage Centre
Mag Ct
FISHERMAN'S WHARF
UPR BURGESS ST
Jun
Sch
Infant
Sch
GARTH LA
FREDERICK WARD WAY
ELLIS WY
Superstore
Freshney Pl
Sh Ctr
Mkt Hall
Sh Ctr
Cty Ct
TH
Liby
Liby
DOUGLAS
SPRING BANK
SPRINGWAY CR
YARBOROUGH ROAD
A1136
A1136
CROMWELL RD
A1136
FANNYSTONE RD 1
ETHELSTONE RD 2
Yarborough
Middle Sch
Yarborough
Welfare
Service
LC
LC
MANDELA LINK
CARTERGATE
DUDLEY ST
DEANSGATE
Grimsby
Town
LC
PEAKS PARKWAY
Retail
Park
PO
BARONESS RD
NEWSHAM DRIVE
ASHTREE AV
CLIFTON ROAD
WIMBORN AVE
PELHAM RD
COMPTON DRIVE
ST HILDA'S AV
CARLTON
WESTMINSTER DR
St James
Sch
GRIMSBY
West
End Club
MOSS ROAD
PEPPERCORN WALK
PHOENIX ST
WINTRINGHAM ROAD
PELHAM RD 1
THE SPINNEY 2
BISHOP'S WK 3
MALMESBURY DR 4
TEWKESBURY DR 5
THE LAWNS 6
Littlefield
CHELMSFORD PL
COLLEGE ST
AUGUSTA ST
BARGATE
DN34
DN32
1 PETERHOUSE RD
2 PEMBROKE RD
Works
Allotments
WESTHILL RD
WESTLANDS AV
WELHOLME ROAD
B1212
WELHOLME RD
CAMBRIDGE RD
KELSTERN CT
COVENTRY AV
CHELMSFORD AVE
PO
WESTWARD HO
People's Park
Wellow
Cam
Park
Sch
SWINDERBY
CARNFORTH CRES
Grange
CHEPSTOW GR
MEDWAY PL
SCAMPTON
Franklin Sixth
Form Coll
Hereford
Sch
Grimsby
Coll
HEREFORD AVENUE
THE CRESTA
ROUNDWAY
A1243
St Martins
Preparatory
Sch
PARK DR
A46
WEELSBY ROAD
WEELSBY RD
HAINTON AVENUE
B1213
PEAKS PARKWAY
A16
Dock
Tower
Locks
Locks
BROWN ST 1
HENDERSON ST 2
SMITH ST 3
SIDEBOTTOM ST 4
SMITTON ST 5
Royal
Dock
STUART WORTLEY ST
Jetty
ROWLANDSON ST
Marina
Grimsby
Docks
Junior
Sch
FREEMAN ST B1213
CHURCH ST
ALBERT ST
Industrial
Estate
East
Marsh
LOWER BURGESS ST
DUNCOMBE ST
MILLOM WY
BUTTERMERE WY
St Marys RC
Prim Sch
COBDEN ST
NORTH END
CLYDE ST
ELEANOR STREET
HAINTON AV
B1213
PASTURE STREET
SIXHILLS STREET
Holme Hill
Edward
Heneage
Primary
Sch
Welholme
Fst Sch
Welholme
Mid Sch
TASBURGH ST
HARE STREET
WELHOLME
PO
Welholme Mus
& Gallery
GRANVILLE STREET
PATRICK STREET
DAVID STREET
TORRINGTON STREET
ALGERNON STREET
RIALTO AVENUE

102
102

A5
1 SALACON WY
2 CALVI CT
3 BRADMAN CT
4 CASSWELL CL

103 103

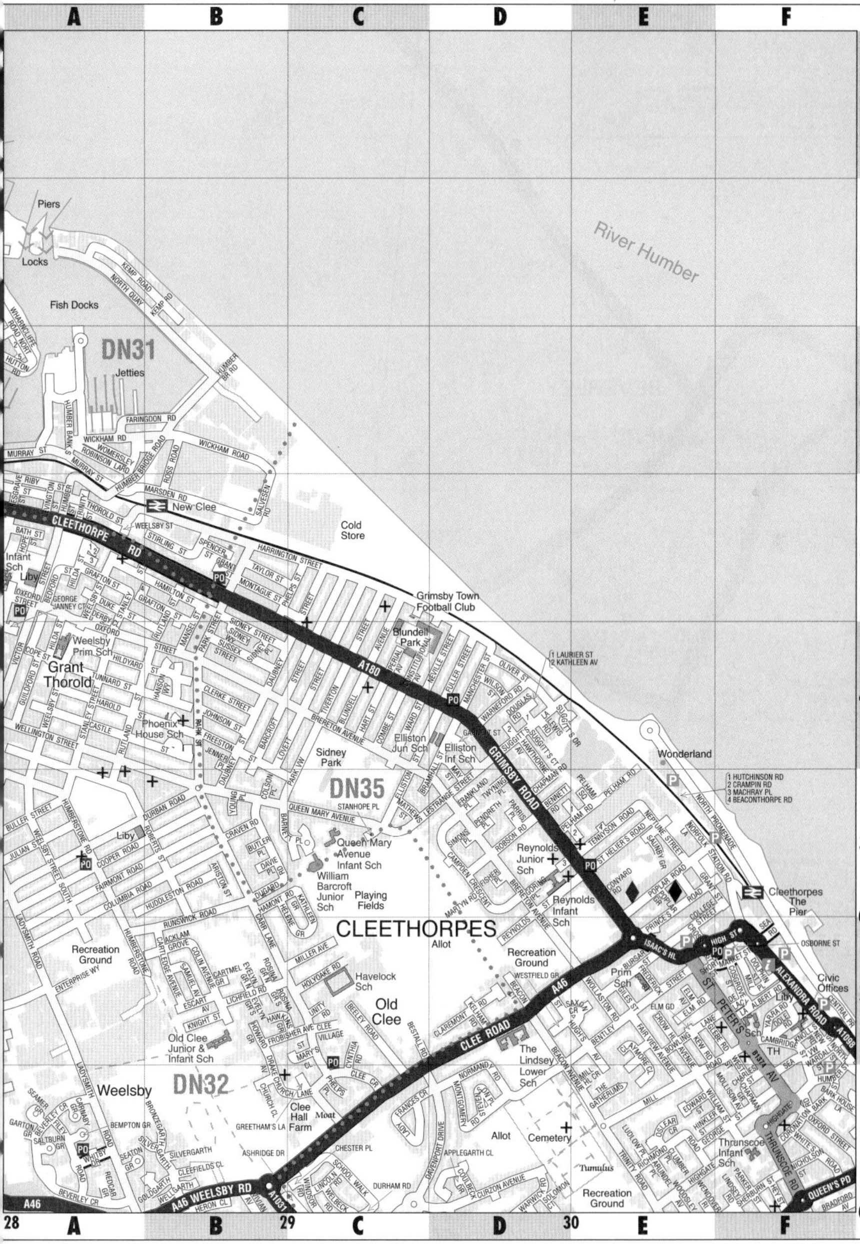

103 103

One-way streets

136 136 137

House numbers
1 59
HIGH ST

Scale: 7 inches to 1 mile
0 110 yards 220 yards
0 125 m 250 m

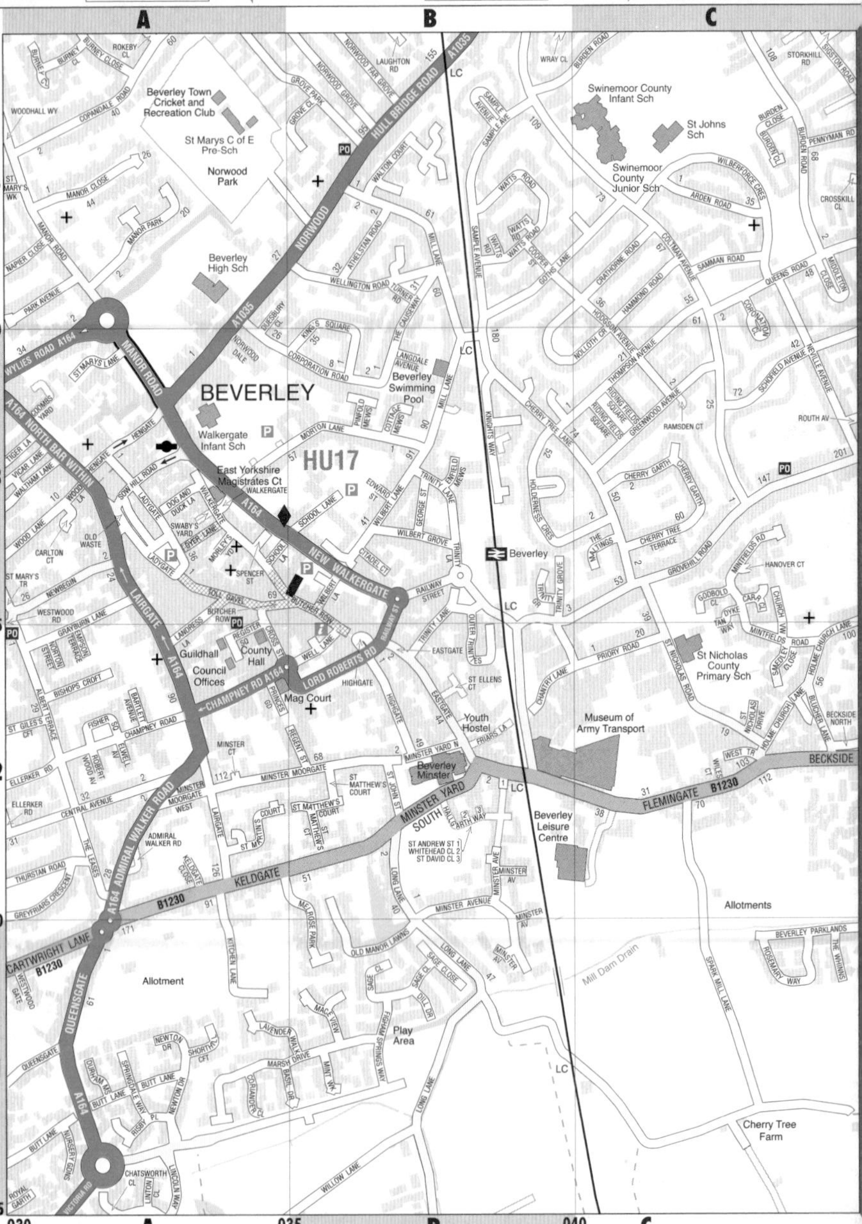

136 136 137

A B C

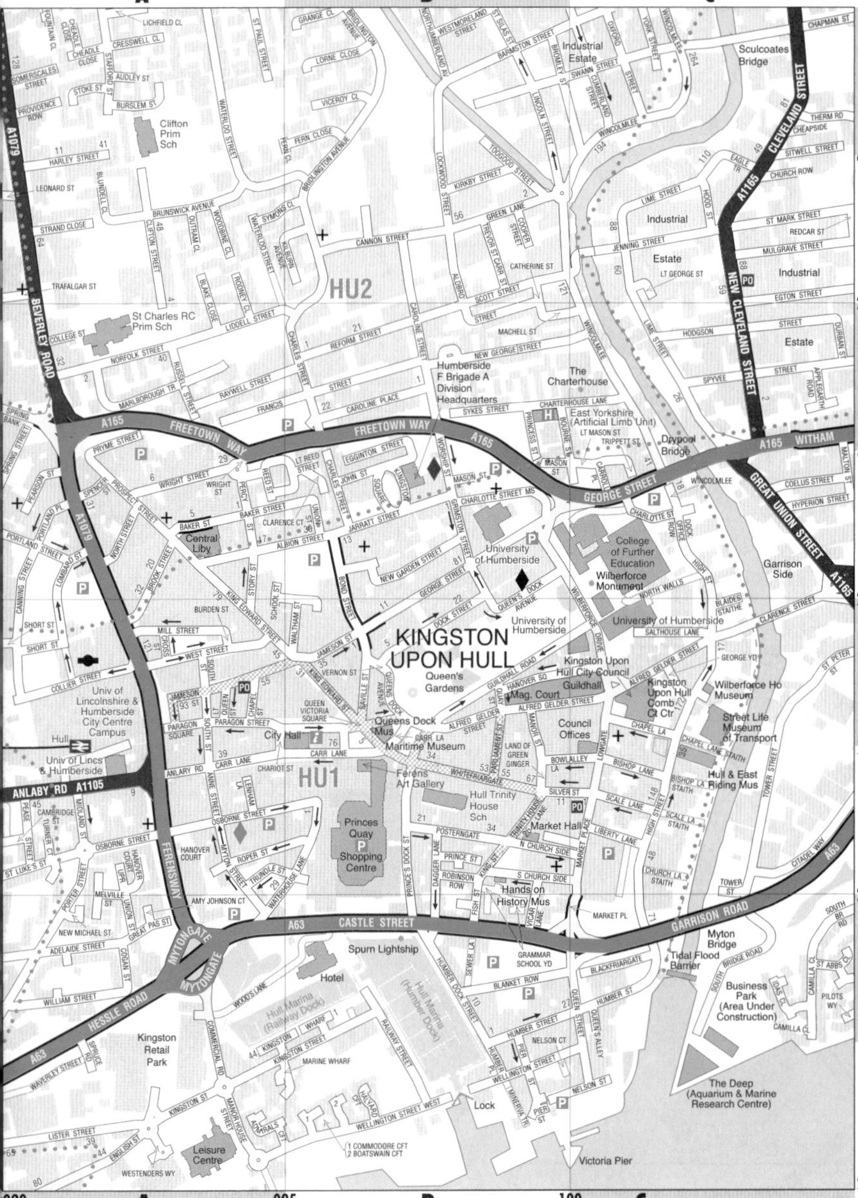

090 095 100
4 295 3 290 2 285 1 280

One-way streets

House numbers
1 59
HIGH ST

130 130 130

Scale: 7 inches to 1 mile
0 110 yards 220 yards
0 125 m 250 m

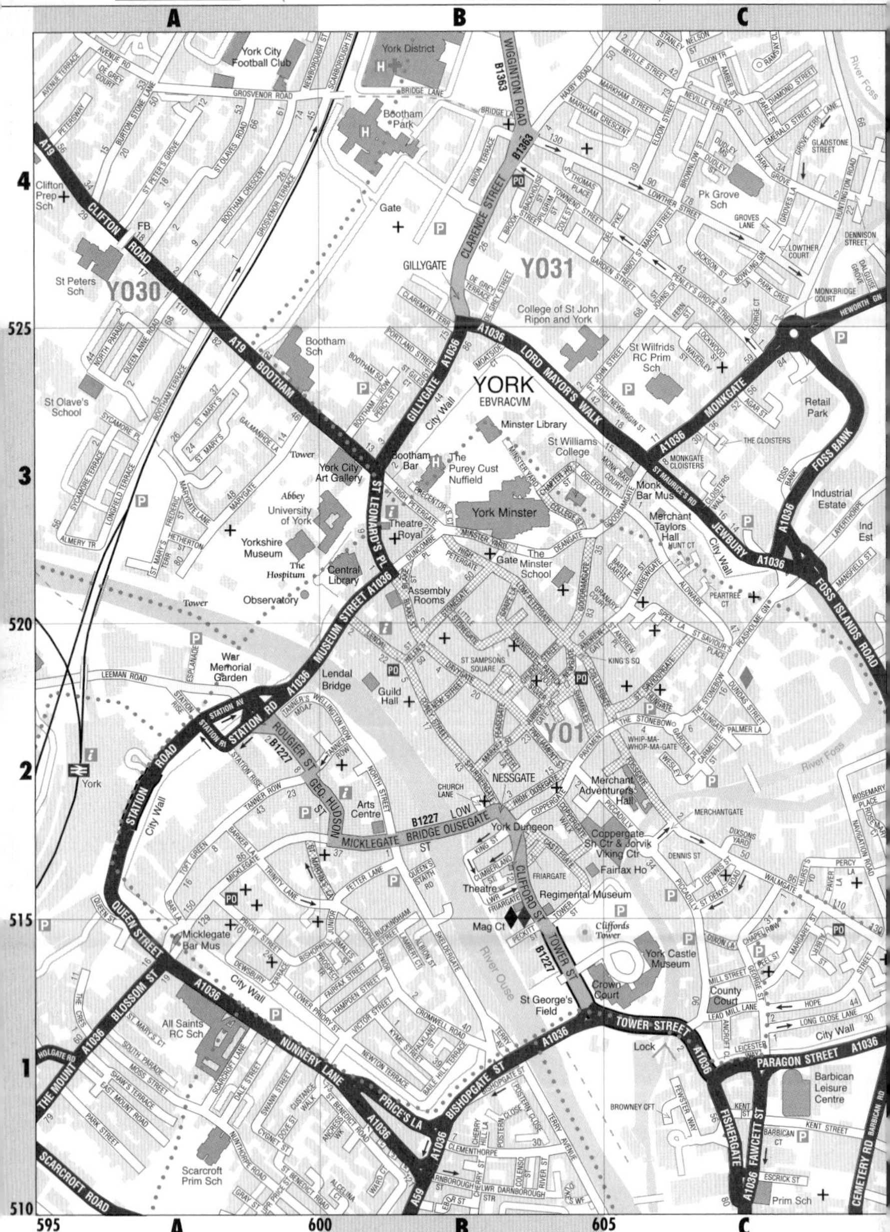

130 130 130

B1
1 VICTORIA ST
2 DRAKE ST
3 SPENCER ST
4 CLEMENT ST

Scarborough

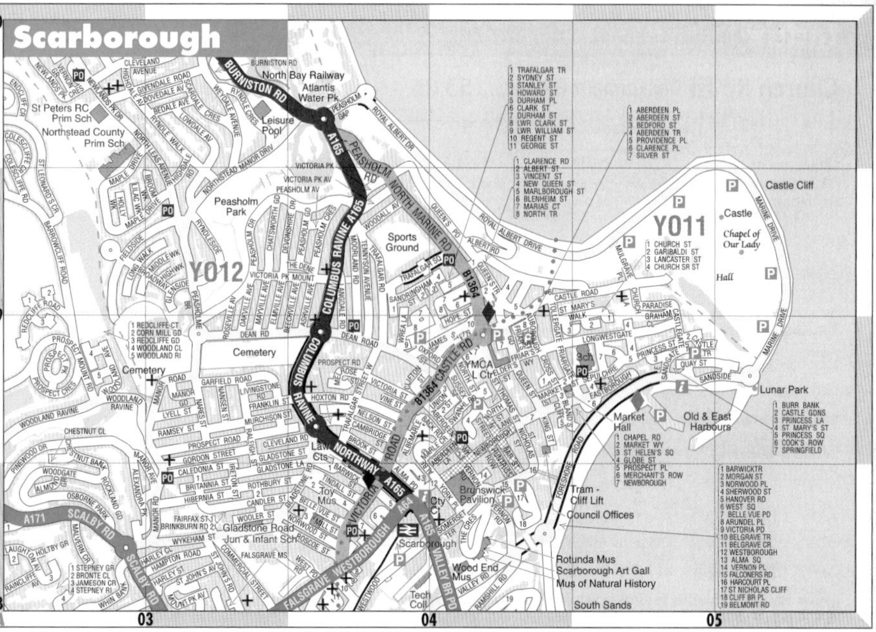

Doncaster

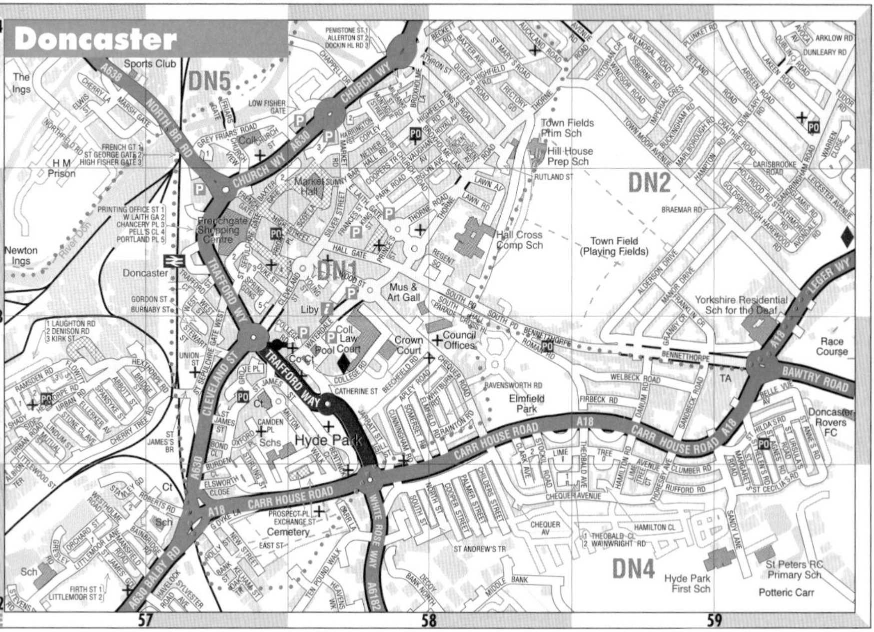

Index

Church Rd **6** Beckenham BR2..........**53** C6

Place name
May be abbreviated on the map

Location number
Present when a number indicates the place's position in a crowded area of mapping

Locality, town or village
Shown when more than one place has the same name

Postcode district
District for the indexed place

Page and grid square
Page number and grid reference for the standard mapping

Public and commercial buildings are highlighted in magenta. Places of interest are highlighted in blue with a star★

Abbreviations used in the index

Acad	**Academy**	Comm	**Common**	Gd	**Ground**	L	**Leisure**	Prom	**Prom**
App	**Approach**	Cott	**Cottage**	Gdn	**Garden**	La	**Lane**	Rd	**Road**
Arc	**Arcade**	Cres	**Crescent**	Gn	**Green**	Liby	**Library**	Recn	**Recreation**
Ave	**Avenue**	Cswy	**Causeway**	Gr	**Grove**	Mdw	**Meadow**	Ret	**Retail**
Bglw	**Bungalow**	Ct	**Court**	H	**Hall**	Meml	**Memorial**	Sh	**Shopping**
Bldg	**Building**	Ctr	**Centre**	Ho	**House**	Mkt	**Market**	Sq	**Square**
Bsns, Bus	**Business**	Ctry	**Country**	Hospl	**Hospital**	Mus	**Museum**	St	**Street**
Bvd	**Boulevard**	Cty	**County**	HQ	**Headquarters**	Orch	**Orchard**	Sta	**Station**
Cath	**Cathedral**	Dr	**Drive**	Hts	**Heights**	Pal	**Palace**	Terr	**Terrace**
Cir	**Circus**	Dro	**Drove**	Ind	**Industrial**	Par	**Parade**	TH	**Town Hall**
Cl	**Close**	Ed	**Education**	Inst	**Institute**	Pas	**Passage**	Univ	**University**
Cnr	**Corner**	Emb	**Embankment**	Int	**International**	Pk	**Park**	Wk, Wlk	**Walk**
Coll	**College**	Est	**Estate**	Intc	**Interchange**	Pl	**Place**	Wr	**Water**
Com	**Community**	Ex	**Exhibition**	Junc	**Junction**	Prec	**Precinct**	Yd	**Yard**

Index of localities, towns and villages

A

Acaster Malbis 36 D8
Acaster Selby 36 B4
Acklam 16 E8
Acomb 129 C3
Adlingfleet 81 E7
Aike 44 A8
Airmyn 64 E4
Aisby 118 B3
Aldbrough 47 C1
Alkborough 82 C8
Allerthorpe 28 E2
Althorpe 95 D4
Amcotts 81 F1
Angram 24 C3
Anlaby 143 F7
Appleby 83 C1
Arnold 45 C4
Arram 44 A7
Ashby 151 B1
Ashby cum Fenby 113 D3
Ashby Hill 113 C3
Askham Bryan 24 F3
Askham Richard 24 D3
Asselby 64 D7
Atwick 35 C5
Aughton 38 C1
Aylesby 101 E2

B

Bainton 31 E7
Balkholme 65 E6
Balne 77 C5
Barlby 49 B5
Barlow 63 C7
Barmby Moor 28 E3
Barmby on the Marsh 64 B7
Barmston 23 A6
Barnetby le Wold 99 C4
Barnoldby le Beck 113 B6
Barrow Hann 70 E1
Barrow Haven 70 C1
Barrow upon Humber 85 D7
Barton Waterside 69 F2
Barton-upon-Humber 84 D7
Beal 61 D4
Beckingham 116 D1
Beeford 22 C1
Beelsby 112 F5
Beltoft 95 A1
Belton 94 E1
Bempton 4 D4
Beningbrough 12 D4
Bennetland 66 C7
Bentley 55 D7
Bessingby 10 F4
Beswick 32 D3
Beverley 154 A3
Bewholme 35 A5
Bielby 39 F6
Bigby 99 C2
Bilbrough 24 D1
Bilton 58 A4
Birkin 61 D6
Bishop Burton 43 A2
Bishop Wilton 16 F2
Bishopthorpe 133 B3
Blacktoft 66 E3
Blyborough 119 B5
Blyton 117 E5
Bolton 28 D7
Bonby 84 C2
Bootham Stray 127 B2
Boothferry 64 E5
Bossall 15 D7
Bottesford 96 D2
Boynton 10 D7
Bracon 94 F2
Bradley 102 B3
Bradley 102 C1
Brandesburton 34 C2
Bransholme 141 A8
Brantingham 68 C8
Brayton 148 A2
Breighton 50 D5
Bridlington 122 B3
Brigg 98 D2
Brigham 33 E8
Brigsley 113 D4
Brind 51 A2
Brockfield 14 E2
Brocklesby 100 D6
Broomfleet 67 B6
Brough 68 C5
Broughton 97 E4
Brumby 151 B4
Bubwith 50 D7
Buckton 4 C4
Bugthorpe 16 D4
Burn 62 D7
Burnby 29 D1
Burnham 85 C3
Burringham 95 E4
Bursea 52 A4
Burstwick 73 B7
Burton Agnes 10 A1
Burton Fleming 2 E3
Burton Pidsea 59 D2
Burton Stather 82 A5
Burton upon Stather 82 B4
Buttercrambe 15 E5
Butterwick 1 B2

C

Cabourne 111 D4
Cadney 109 D6
Caenby Corner Estate 119 D1
Caistor 111 B4
Camblesforth 63 D5
Camerton 73 A5
Canal Side 93 A7
Carlton 63 D3
Carnaby 10 E4
Catwick 45 D8
Cawkeld 32 B5
Cawood 48 B8
Chapel Fields 129 B3
Chapel Haddlesey 62 C5
Cherry Burton 43 B5
Church End 33 F8
Church Town 94 E1
Claxton 15 B7
Cleethorpes 153 C2
Cliffe 49 E2
Clifton 130 A7
Clifton Park 129 F7
Clixby 111 A7
Cock Hill 12 B2
Coleby 82 E6
Coniston 57 F6
Copmanthorpe 132 B2
Corringham 118 B2
Cottagers Plot 102 B2
Cottingham 139 A6
Covenham St Bartholomew 121 F5
Covenham St Mary 121 F5
Cridling Stubbs 76 C8
Crockey Hill 26 A1
Crosby 150 D7
Crowle 94 D8
Crowle Park 94 D7
Croxby 112 C1
Croxby Top 112 B1
Croxton 99 F7
Cuxwold 112 B4

D

Danthorpe 59 C3
Deighton 37 A7
Dimlington 90 F7
Dragonby 82 E1
Drax 63 F5
Driffield 124 D4
Dringhouses 132 E8
Duggleby 6 B6
Dunnington 26 F7
Dunnington 34 F7
Dunscroft 92 D3
Dunsville 92 B3
Dunswell 56 D5

E

Ealand 94 E6
Earswick 128 A7
Easington 91 A6
East Butterwick 106 E8
East Carlton 47 A2
East Common 148 E4
East Cottingwith 38 C5
East Cowick 78 D8
East Ella 144 D7
East Halton 86 E7
East Lound 105 E3
East Lutton 7 C8
East Marsh 152 F5
East Newton 59 F8
East Ravendale 113 C2
East Stockwith 116 F5
Eastburn 20 B2
Eastoft 81 A3
Eastrington 51 F1
Eggborough 61 F2
Ellerker 68 A8
Ellerton 38 C2
Elloughton 68 C7
Elmswell 20 B5
Elsham 98 F7
Elstronwick 59 A3
Elvington 27 B2
Eppleworth 138 A4
Epworth 105 D6
Epworth Turbary 105 C6
Escrick 37 B5
Eskham 115 C1
Etton 42 F6
Everingham 40 A5
Everthorpe 53 E3

F

Fangfoss 28 C7
Fenwick 77 D3
Ferriby Sluice 83 F7
Fimber 18 D7
Fishlake 92 E8
Fitling 59 C5
Flamborough 5 B2
Flinton 59 A7
Flixborough 82 B1
Flixborough Stather 82 A1
Fockerby 81 E5
Foggathorpe 51 B8
Fordon 2 A6
Fosterhouses 78 C1
Foston on the Wolds 22 A2
Fotherby 121 C2
Foxholes 1 D3
Fraisthorpe 22 F8
Fridaythorpe 18 B6
Frodingham 151 B7
Fulford 133 E7
Full Sutton 16 A2
Fulstow 121 E8

G

Gainsborough 117 C2
Ganstead 57 F5
Ganton 1 A8
Gardham 42 D5
Garthorpe 81 F6
Garton 59 E6
Garton-on-the-Wolds 20 A6
Gate Helmsley 15 B2
Gateforth 62 A7
Gembling 22 A3
Gilberdyke 66 C8
Gipsyville 144 E3
Goodmanham 135 F7
Goole 149 C3
Gowdall 63 A1
Gowthorpe 16 C1
Goxhill 86 B8
Grainsby 113 F2
Graiselound 105 C1
Grange 152 A1
Gransmoor 22 C6
Grant Thorold 153 A4
Grasby 110 E7
Grayingham 119 B7
Great Coates 102 B5

Great Cowden 47 A5
Great Givendale 29 B8
Great Hatfield 46 D6
Great Heck 77 D7
Great Kelk 22 A5
Great Kendale 20 D7
Great Limber 100 D3
Great Tows 120 A1
Greetwell 108 C7
Grey Green 94 E2
Gribthorpe 51 B6
Grimsby 152 E2
Grimston 131 E3
Grindale 3 D2
Grovehill 137 C3
Gunby 50 D6
Gunness 95 E6
Gunthorpe 117 A7

H

Habrough 100 E8
Haisthorpe 10 C3
Hall Garth 26 F6
Halsham 73 F6
Harlthorpe 51 A8
Harpham 21 F8
Harswell 40 C3
Harton 15 C8
Hatcliffe 112 F3
Hatfield 92 D5
Hatfield Woodhouse 93 A3
Haxey 105 C3
Haxey Carr 105 B4
Hayton 40 C8
Healing 102 A5
Hedon 72 C8
Hemingbrough 49 F1
Hemswell 119 A1
Hensall 62 D2
Heslington 131 B1
Hessay 24 C8
Hessle 143 E1
Heworth 130 F6
Hibaldstow 108 F5
High Catton 27 D8
High Hunsley 54 D6
High Mowthorpe 6 D7
High Risby 82 F1
Highfield 50 E7
Hilderthorpe 11 B4
Hillam 61 A7
Hilston 60 B4
Hirst Courtney 62 F3
Hive 52 C2
Holgate 129 F3
Hollym 75 A4
Holme 97 A1
Holme Hill 152 F3
Holme on the Wolds 31 E1
Holme-on-Spalding-Moor 40 B1
Holmpton 75 C2
Holtby 14 F1
Holton le Clay 114 B5
Hopgrove 128 D2
Horkstow 84 A5
Horkstow Wolds 84 B6
Hornsea 134 C4
Hornsea Burton 134 D2
Hotham 53 D4
Howden 65 A7
Howsham 110 A7
Huggate 18 B2
Humberston 114 E8
Humberston Fitties 114 F8
Humbleton 59 B5
Hunmanby 2 F8
Huntington 127 E3
Hurn 136 C4
Hut Green 62 A2
Hutton 32 E8
Hutton Cranswick 32 D7
Hutton Wandesley 24 A5

I

Immingham 87 B2
Inglemire 139 F6
Irby upon Humber 112 D7

K

Keadby 95 D6
Keelby 101 B5
Kelfield 36 D1
Kelleythorpe 124 C1
Kellingley 61 C2
Kellington 61 F4
Kelstern 120 D1
Kexby 27 C6
Keyingham 73 D3
Kilham 9 C3
Kilnsea 91 B2
Kilnwick 32 B4
Kilnwick Percy 29 C5
Kilpin 65 D5
Kilpin Pike 65 C5
Kingsforth 84 E6
Kingston upon Hull 155 B2
Kirby Grindalythe 6 E6
Kirby Underdale 17 A5
Kirk Bramwith 92 A6
Kirk Ella 143 D8
Kirk Smeaton 76 B3
Kirkburn 20 A2
Kirmington 100 A6
Kirton in Lindsey 108 B1
Knapton 129 A5
Knavesmire 133 A7
Knedlington 64 E6
Knottingley 61 B2

L

Laceby 101 E2
Laceby Acres 102 B2
Langtoft 8 D5
Laughton 117 F8
Laxton 65 F4
Layerthorpe 130 E4
Laytham 39 B2
Leconfield 43 D6
Lelley 58 F3
Leppington 16 C8
Leven 45 A8
Lissett 22 E4
Little Airmyn 64 E4
Little Burton 34 B2
Little Catwick 45 D7
Little Coates 102 C3
Little Driffield 124 C4
Little End 40 A1
Little Grimsby 121 E2
Little Hatfield 46 B6
Little Heck 62 D1
Little Leven 45 A7
Little Limber 100 C5
Little Reedness 66 A1
Little Skipwith 37 D1
Little Smeaton 76 C3
Little Weighton 55 A4
Littlefield 152 C2
Lockington 32 B2
Londesborough 41 B8
Long Drax 64 A6
Long Marston 24 A6
Long Riston 45 C5
Low Burnham 105 D5
Low Catton 27 C8
Low Fosham 46 F1
Low Risby 83 B1
Lowthorpe 21 E7
Ludborough 121 C6
Luddington 81 C3
Lund 31 F3
Lund 49 D3

M

Manton 108 B5
Mappleton 47 A7
Marfleet 147 C8
Market Weighton 135 B4
Marshchapel 115 B2
Marton 46 B2
Marton 123 D8
Meaux 44 F2
Melbourne 39 B6
Melton 68 F5
Melton Ross 99 C5
Meltonby 28 F7
Menthorpe 50 C5
Messingham 107 C7
Middlegate 84 E1
Middlethorpe 133 B6
Middleton-on-the-Wolds 31 B4
Millbrook Park 135 C3
Millington 29 C6
Misterton 116 C5
Molescroft 136 B5
Monk Fryston 61 B8
Moor End 52 B8
Moor Monkton 12 A3
Moorends 79 C2
Moortown 110 D2
Morton 117 A3
Moss 77 D1
Murton 26 D7

N

Naburn 36 D8
Nafferton 125 E7
Neat Marsh 58 A2
Nether Poppleton 126 A2
Nettleton 111 A2
New Arram 43 F7
New Barnetby 99 D5
New Earswick 127 D3
New Ellerby 46 A2
New Holland 70 E2
New Village 139 D6
New Waltham 114 A7
Newland 64 B3
Newland 66 A8
Newland 140 C3
Newport 53 A1
Newsholme 64 E8
Newton upon Derwent 27 E4
Newton-on-Ouse 12 B6
Normanby 82 B3
North Cave 53 D3
North Cliffe 53 B8
North Cotes 115 A3
North Dalton 31 B7
North Duffield 50 A8
North Elkington 121 A1
North End 46 D4
North End 71 A1
North Ferriby 69 B4
North Frodingham 34 A8
North Howden 51 B1
North Kelsey 110 A5
North Killingholme 86 D4
North Newbald 53 E8
North Ormsby 121 B3
North Thoresby 114 A1
Northfield 143 F2
Northorpe 118 D8
Norton 76 E2
Nun Monkton 12 A4
Nunburnholme 29 E3
Nunsthorpe 102 D1
Nunthorpe 133 C8

O

Octon 8 F8
Old Clee 153 C2
Old Ellerby 58 A8
Old Goole 149 C1
Old Town 122 E5
Osbaldwick 131 C4
Osgodby 49 C4
Osgodby Common 49 C6
Ottringham 73 F3
Ousefleet 66 D2
Out Newton 90 E8
Overton 12 F2
Owmby 110 D7
Owston Ferry 106 A2
Owstwick 59 E3
Owthorne 74 F7

P

Painsthorpe 17 B5
Patrington 74 E1
Patrington Haven 89 C8
Paull 72 A5
Pilham 118 A4
Pocklington 29 A4
Pollington 77 F6
Portington 51 E2
Preston 58 C1
Pyewipe 152 A8

R

Rascal Moor 52 B7
Rawcliffe 64 A1
Rawcliffe 126 E2
Rawcliffe Bridge 79 C8
Redbourne 108 F3
Reedness 65 F2
Reighton 3 D6
Riby 101 C2
Riccall 49 A8
Rimswell 74 D7
Riplingham 54 E2
Risby 55 C5
Rise 45 F5
Rolston 46 E8
Roos 60 A1
Rothwell 111 F2
Routh 44 F5
Roxby 83 A3
Rudston 9 F6
Rufforth 24 C6
Ruston Parva 21 C8
Ryehill 73 A4

S

Salt End 72 A8
Saltmarshe 65 F3
Sancton 41 E2
Sand Hole 52 B8
Sand Hutton 15 B5
Sandholme 52 C1
Sandtoft 94 A3
Santon 97 B7
Saxby All Saints 84 A3
Scalby 66 E8
Scamland 39 C7
Scartho 102 F1
Scawby 108 E8
Scorborough 43 D8
Scotter 107 D3
Scotterthorpe 107 B5
Scotton 107 D2
Scrayingham 15 F7
Sculcoates 140 E2
Scunthorpe 150 F5
Searby 110 C8
Seaton 35 A1
Seaton Common 39 D4
Seaton Ross 39 E4
Selby 148 C6
Sewerby 123 A5
Shipton 12 F5
Shiptonthorpe 40 F6
Sigglesthorne 45 F8
Skeffling 90 C6
Skelton 65 C4
Skelton 126 C6
Skerne 21 A2
Skidby 138 B8
Skipsea 23 B2
Skipwith 37 E1
Skirlaugh 45 E2
Skirpenbeck 16 A4
Sledmere 7 B3
Snaith 63 C1
Somerby 99 B1
South Bank 130 A1
South Bramwith 92 B6
South Cave 54 A2
South Cliffe 53 B7
South Dalton 42 E8
South Duffield 50 A4
South End 46 D3
South End 90 F5
South Ferriby 84 B7
South Field 69 E4
South Kelsey 110 A1
South Killingholme 86 E3
South Newbald 53 F6
Southburn 20 B1
Spaldington 51 C4
Speeton 3 F5
Spital in the Street 119 E1
Sproatley 58 C5
Staddlethorpe 66 D7
Stainforth 92 C7
Stallingborough 101 E6
Stamford Bridge 15 E2
Stillingfleet 36 C3
Stockton on the Forest 14 D3
Stoneferry 141 B3
Strensall 14 A7
Strensall Camp 14 B6
Sturton 108 F7
Summergangs 141 C2
Sutton Ings 141 F4
Sutton upon Derwent 27 C1
Sutton-on-Hull 141 D6
Swallow 112 B5
Swanland 69 B6
Swine 57 D6
Swinefleet 65 D1
Sykehouse 78 B3

T

Tang Hall 130 F5
Tansterne 59 A8
Temple Hirst 62 E4
Tetney 114 D4
Tetney Lock 115 A5
The Hallands 85 F7
The Lawns 138 F7
The Lings 92 D3
The Parks 92 C4
The Willows 102 C4
Thealby 82 D4
Thearne 56 D7
Thirtleby 58 B5
Thixendale 17 E7
Thorganby 38 B4
Thorne 93 A8
Thorngumbald 72 E5
Thornholme 10 B2
Thornton 39 B8
Thornton Curtis 85 E5
Thorpe 32 B1
Thorpe le Street 40 D7
Thorpe Willoughby 48 C2
Thwing 2 B1
Tibthorpe 19 D2
Tickton 137 E8
Topham 78 A4
Towthorpe 6 D1
Towthorpe 14 B5
Tunstall 60 C2

U

Ulceby 86 A1
Ulceby Skitter 86 C2
Ulrome 23 A3
Upper Helmsley 15 B3
Upper Poppleton 12 F1
Upperthorpe 105 B3
Upton 22 E1
Utterby 121 D4

V

Victoria Dock Village 146 B5

W

Waithe 114 A3
Walcot 82 C7
Walden Stubbs 76 F3
Walkeringham 116 C3
Walkerith 116 E3
Walkington 55 B8
Walmgate Stray 130 F1
Waltham 113 D7
Wansford 21 C3
Warter 30 A5
Warthill 14 F2
Waterside 92 F8
Watton 32 D5
Wawne 56 E8
Waxholme 74 E8
Weel 137 F3
Weelsby 153 A1
Weeton 90 B7
Weighton Wold 135 F4
Welhambridge 51 F5
Wellow 152 D1
Welton 68 D6
Welwick 90 A8
West Butterwick 106 D8
West Carlton 46 F1
West Cowick 78 D8
West Ella 143 A7
West End 53 F2
West Field 129 A2
West Haddlesey 62 A5
West Halton 82 E8
West Hill 122 A1
West Lutton 7 B8
West Marsh 152 B5
West Newton 58 D8
West Ravendale 113 A2
West Stockwith 116 F6
Westfield 148 C4
Westgate 94 D2
Westrum 98 C1
Westwoodside 105 A2
Wetwang 19 B6
Wharram le Street 6 A4
Wharton 117 E4
Wheldrake 38 A7
Whitgift 66 B1
Whitley 77 A7
Whitley Thorpe 76 F7
Whitton 67 E3
Wigginton 13 D5
Wike Well End 93 B7
Wilberfoss 27 F5
Wildsworth 117 A8
Willerby 138 C1
Willitoft 51 A6
Willoughton 119 A4
Wilsthorpe 11 A2
Winestead 74 C3
Winteringham 68 A1
Winterton 83 A5
Wistow 48 D6
Withernsea 75 A6
Withernwick 46 D3
Wold Haven 29 B3
Wold Newton 2 A3
Wold Newton 120 B7
Womersley 76 C6
Woodhall 50 B2
Woodhouse 94 E3
Woodmansey 56 B8
Woodside 104 E6
Woodthorpe 132 C7
Wootton 85 F3
Worlaby 98 D8
Wrawby 98 E4
Wressle 50 D2
Wressle 97 F4
Wroot 104 D6
Wybers Wood 102 A3
Wyham 120 F6
Wyton 58 B4

Y

Yaddlethorpe 96 C2
Yapham 28 E1
Yarborough 152 A3
Yawthorpe 118 D2
Yokefleet 66 C3
York 156 B3
Youlthorpe 16 C2

1

1st Ave HU6 140 C6
1st Main Rd DN36 114 F8
10th Ave HU6 140 B7
11th Ave HU6 140 B6
12th Ave
Humberston DN36 114 F8
Kingston upon Hull HU6 140 A7
14th Ave HU6 140 A7
15th Ave HU6 140 A6
16th Ave HU6 140 A7
17th Ave HU6 140 A6
18th Ave HU6 140 A7
19th Ave HU6 140 A6

2

2nd Ave
Humberston DN36 114 F8
Kingston upon Hull HU6 140 B7
20-21 Visual Arts Ctr
DN15 151 C7
20th Ave HU6 140 A7
21st Ave HU6 139 F6
22nd Ave HU6 140 A7
23rd Ave HU6 140 A6
24th Ave HU6 140 A7
25th Ave HU6 140 A6
26th Ave HU6 139 F7
27th Ave HU6 140 A6
28th Ave HU6 139 F7
29th Ave HU6 139 F6

3

30th Ave HU6 139 F7
31st Ave HU6 139 F6
32nd Ave HU6 139 F7
33rd Ave HU6 139 F6
34th Ave HU6 139 F7
36th Ave HU6 139 F7
37th Ave HU6 139 E6
38th Ave HU6 139 F7

4

4th Ave HU6 140 B7
40th Ave HU6 139 F7

5

5th Ave HU6 139 F6

6

6th Ave HU6 140 A7

7

7 Lakes L Pk* DN17 94 D6
7th Ave HU6 140 B6

8

8th Ave HU6 140 A7

9

9th Ave HU6 140 B6

A

A W Nielson Rd DN14 149 A4
Abber La LS24 24 A2
Abbey Dr E DN32 152 D2
Abbey Dr W DN32 152 D2
Abbey Gdns 32 DN7 92 D4
Abbey Gn 30 DN7 92 D4
Abbey La
Kingston upon Hull
HU10 138 E2
Preston HU12 58 C1
Abbey Leisure Ctr
YO8 148 C5
Abbey Pk Rd DN32 152 D2
Abbey Rd
Bridlington YO16 122 B2
Grimsby DN32 152 D2
Hatfield DN7 92 D4
Kingston upon Hull
HU11 142 F6
Scunthorpe DN17 150 F2
Ulceby DN39 86 A1
Abbey Rise DN19 85 D8
Abbey St
Kingston upon Hull HU9 146 C7
York YO30 130 A7
Abbey Walk Ret Pk
YO8 148 C6
Abbey Way DN7 92 D5
Abbey Wlk
Grimsby DN32 152 D3
Selby YO8 148 C5
Abbey Yd YO8 148 C5
Abbeyfield Rd DN7 92 C4
Abbot St YO31 156 C4
Abbots Cl HU8 141 E5
Abbot's Lodge* DN39 86 B5
Abbots Rd DN17 150 F2
Abbot's Rd YO8 148 E3
Abbots Wlk HU16 139 A5
Abbotsford Cl HU5 139 F3
Abbotsford Rd YO10 130 F3
Abbotsway
Grimsby DN32 152 D2
York YO31 130 E8
Abbotts Grange DN36 114 B7
Abbotts Way YO16 122 D4
Abelton Gr 33 YO32 13 E5
Abercorn St DN16 151 A6
Aberdeen St HU9 141 F3
Aberdovey Cl 3 HU7 57 A7
Abingdon Garth 1 HU7 57 A5
Acacia Ave
Flixborough DN15 96 B7
Gainsborough DN21 117 B1
York YO32 127 E4
Acacia Ct DN16 151 B2
Acacia Dr HU8 141 D2
Acacia Way DN17 107 C6
Acadia Gr HU13 143 F1
Acaster Ave YO23 36 A3
Acaster La
Acaster Malbis YO23 133 B1
Acaster Selby YO23 36 A4
Accommodation Rd
YO25 8 D6
Acer Gr DN17 150 C1
Acey La HU12 58 B1
Achille Rd DN34 102 B3
Acklam Dr HU18 134 D6
Acklam Gr DN32 153 B2
Acklam Rd HU12 72 D7
Ackworth St HU8 141 C1
Acland St
Gainsborough DN21 117 B1
4 Kingston upon Hull
HU3 145 A6
Acomb Comm Rd DN7 92 F4
Acomb Prim Sch
YO24 129 E3
Acomb Rd YO24 129 D3
Acomb Wood Cl YO24 132 C7
Acomb Wood Dr YO24 132 B7
Acorn Cl 6 Barlby YO8 49 B4
Bridlington YO16 123 B7
Acorn Gr HU8 141 E7
Acorn Way
Gateforth YO8 48 B1
Hessle HU13 143 B3
York YO24 132 D7
Acredykes 7 YO15 4 D3
Acres La
Scrayingham YO41 16 B8
Wroot DN9 104 D7
Acton Cl HU8 141 F5
Adam Smith St DN31 152 C5
Adam St DN14 149 D3
Adderbury Gr 5 HU5 140 D2
Addison Gdns HU8 141 D3
Addison Rd 10 HU12 58 D1
Addle La DN14 65 E7
Addlekeld YO42 30 A5
Adelaide Prim Sch
HU3 145 D5
Adelaide Rd 6 DN6 76 E2
Adelaide Sch HU3 145 D5
Adelaide St
Kingston upon Hull HU3 145 D5
Kingston upon Hull HU1 155 A1
3 York YO23 130 B2
Adeline St DN14 149 C5
Adeliza Garth 20 HU12 72 D7
Adelphi Cl HU8 141 F4
Adelphi Ct 4 DN36 114 A7
Adelphi Dr 7 DN33 113 E8
Adelphi St YO25 124 E4
Adlard Gr DN36 114 C7
Adlingfleet Rd DN17 81 E6
Adlington Cl 8 YO32 14 A7
Admiral Storr's Twr*
HU11 60 A4
Admiral Walker Rd
HU17 154 A2
Admirals Croft HU1 155 A1
Admirals Mews YO15 122 D2
Advent Ct 9 DN39 86 A1
Aegre Dr DN14 65 C4
Africa Cl 15 DN34 102 B2
Agar St YO31 156 C3
Agard Ave DN15 150 E7
Aike La YO25 33 A1
Ainshaw HU6 139 E8
Ainslie Rd HU12 72 D7
Ainslie St DN32 152 E2
Ainsty Ave YO24 132 F8
Ainsty Gr YO24 132 F8
Ainsty St DN14 149 E4
Ainsty View YO17 16 E8
Ainsworth Rd 16 DN40 87 B1
Ainthorpe Gr HU5 144 C7
Ainthorpe Prim Sch
HU5 144 C8
Aintree Ct YO24 132 F8
Air St HU5 140 F2
Aire Cl 36 DN40 87 B1
Aire St Goole DN14 149 D3
Knottingley WF11 61 A3
Airedale HU7 140 E6
Airedale Cl 10 DN20 97 E4
Airedale Dr YO16 122 F7
Airedale Rd DN16 151 D1
Airlie St HU3 145 B5
Airmyn Ave
Goole DN14 149 B5
1 Kingston upon Hull
HU3 144 E6
Airmyn Park Prim Sch
DN14 64 E4
Airmyn Rd Airmyn DN14 64 D3
Goole DN14 149 B5
Aisne St HU5 145 A8
Ajax Cl Grimsby DN34 102 B2
Kingston upon Hull HU9 142 D5
Ajax Ct DN15 96 C7
Akeferry Rd
Haxey DN9 105 C1
Westwoodside DN9 105 B2
Akester Cl 4 HU17 137 B3
Alan Cres DN15 150 F6
Alaska St HU8 141 B1
Alba Cl DN17 150 D1
Albany St
Gainsborough DN21 117 B1
Kingston upon Hull HU3 145 D8
3 York YO26 129 F5
Albatross Dr DN37 102 A4
Albemarle Cl 5 HU15 68 B5
Albemarle Rd
Bilton HU11 58 A3
2 Keyingham HU12 73 C4
York YO23 130 B2
Albemarle St 2 HU3 145 B5
Albert Ave HU3 145 A7
Albert Cl 1 YO32 130 F8
Albert Rd
Cleethorpes DN35 153 F2
Scunthorpe DN16 151 A1
Albert St
10 Bridlington YO15 122 E2
Brigg DN20 98 C2
Goole DN14 149 C2
5 New Holland DN19 70 E2
3 Thorne/Moorends DN8 93 B8
York YO10 156 C1
Albert St E DN32 152 F5
Albert St W DN32 152 F5
Albert Terr
Beverley HU17 154 A2
Kingston upon Hull HU7 141 D6
Welwick HU12 90 A7
Alberta Cres 7 DN17 96 C2
Albertine Ct 5 DN37 113 D7
Albery Way DN36 114 A8
Albina Garth 1 HU12 72 D7
Albion Ave YO26 129 B6
Albion Ct HU17 137 B4
Albion Hill DN9 105 E6
Albion La HU10 138 A3
Albion St
Great Driffield YO25 124 F3
Grimsby DN32 152 F4
Kingston upon Hull HU1 155 A3
York YO1 156 B1
Albion Terr
Bridlington YO15 122 F3
Misterton DN10 116 D5
Albourne Ave DN15 151 A6
Alcelina Ct YO23 156 B1
Alcuin Ave YO10 131 A4
Aldborough Gr HU9 142 A2
Aldborough Way YO26 129 F5
Aldbro' St HU2 155 B4
Aldbrough La HU11 59 A6
Aldbrough Prim Sch
HU11 47 C1
Aldbrough Rd
East Garton HU11 59 D7
Withernwick HU11 46 E3
Alden Cl DN40 87 C1
Alder Gr 6 DN8 79 B2
Alder View 22 DN33 102 C2
Alder Way YO32 127 D2
Alderley Ct YO32 127 E3
Alderley Edge 6 DN37 113 D6
Alderman Cogans C of E Prim
Sch HU9 141 F2
Aldermans Way 10 YO25 34 B2
Alderney Way 2 DN40 101 C8
Alderson Ct YO16 122 D2
Alderson Mews 5 HU9 146 C7
Aldersyde YO24 132 E7
Aldreth Gr YO23 130 C2
Aldrich Rd DN35 103 C2
Aldwark YO1 156 C3
Aldwych Croft 6 DN36 114 A7
Aldwych Ct HU5 144 E8
Alexander Ave YO31 127 E2
Alexander Rd DN16 151 B6
Alexandra Ct
4 Bridlington YO15 122 F3
York YO10 130 E4
Alexandra Dock DN31 152 D6
Alexandra Dr
1 Beverley HU17 55 E8
5 Bridlington YO15 122 F3
Alexandra Prom YO15 123 A3
Alexandra Rd
Cleethorpes DN35 153 F2
Grimsby DN31 152 D4
Hornsea HU18 134 D4
Kingston upon Hull HU5 140 C3
Scunthorpe DN16 151 B2
Strensall YO32 14 A6
Thorne/Moorends DN8 79 B2
Alexandra Rd S DN40 87 D2
Alexandra St
Goole DN14 149 D4
Kingston upon Hull HU3 145 D7
Alexandra St *continued*
Thorne DN8 79 A1
Alexandra Wlk YO15 122 F3
Alfonso St 5 HU3 145 B5
Alfred Bean Hospl
YO25 125 A6
Alfred Gelder St HU1 155 B2
Alfred St
Gainsborough DN21 117 B1
Grimsby DN31 152 D4
Kingston upon Hull HU3 145 D5
Alfriston Cl HU7 141 B6
Algarth Rd
Pocklington YO42 29 A4
York YO31 131 B7
Algarth Rise
Pocklington YO42 28 F4
York YO31 131 B7
Algernon St DN32 152 F1
Alison Garth 29 HU12 72 D7
Alkborough CP Sch
DN15 82 C8
Alkborough La DN15 82 D7
All Hallows Rd 3 HU17 55 B7
All Saints C of E Jun Sch
HU13 143 F2
All Saints Cl 4 HU13 69 F4
All Saints RC Comp Sch
YO24 156 A1
All Saints' St HU3 145 D8
Allan St 2 YO30 130 C7
Allanby St DN15 151 A7
Allanhall Way HU10 143 B8
Allanson Dr HU16 139 D5
Allderidge Ave HU5 140 B3
Allen Cl YO10 131 A4
Allenby Ave DN34 152 A2
Allenby Cres LN11 121 D3
Allendale YO24 132 D8
Allerford Dr 8 HU7 57 A5
Allerthorpe Common Nature
Reserve* YO42 28 C2
Allerton Dr
1 Immingham DN40 87 C1
22 Poppleton YO26 12 F1
Poppleton YO26 126 A1
Allerton Prim Sch
DN40 87 B1
Allestree Dr 2 DN33 113 E8
Alliance Ave HU3 144 F7
Alliance La HU3 144 F7
Allington Dr YO31 131 B6
Allison Cl DN17 107 D7
Allison La
14 Flamborough YO15 5 A2
Ulrome YO25 22 F4
Alloa Cl 2 HU6 140 B8
Allotment La YO25 124 E5
Alma Cl HU10 143 D7
Alma St
6 Kingston upon Hull
HU9 146 B7
4 Withernsea HU19 74 F7
Alma Terr Selby YO8 148 C6
York YO10 130 D2
Almery Terr YO30 156 A3
Almond Cl
Great Driffield YO25 124 F2
Hambleton YO8 48 B1
Almond Gr Brigg DN20 98 B2
3 Kingston upon Hull
HU3 145 D6
Scunthorpe DN16 151 B4
York YO32 127 D4
Almond Tree Ave DN14 63 C3
Almsford Dr YO26 129 C5
Almsford Rd YO26 129 C5
Alne Terr YO10 130 E2
Alness Dr YO24 132 B7
Alpha Ave HU17 136 D6
Alpha Ct DN8 92 F8
Alston Ave 4 HU8 141 B1
Althorpe & Keadby Prim Sch
DN17 95 D5
Althorpe Sta DN17 95 D5
Altoft Cl
2 Brandesburton YO25 34 B2
12 Laceby DN37 101 F1
Alton Pk YO25 22 C1
Alton Rd YO16 122 D7
Altyre Way DN36 103 B1
Alured Garth 9 HU12 72 D7
Alveston Rd DN17 150 D4
Alvin Wlk 9 YO41 27 B2
Alvingham Ave 25 DN35 103 C2
Alvingham Rd DN16 151 B3
Alvis Gr YO10 131 D4
Alwoodley Cl 1 HU8 142 B5
Alwyn Rd 19 DN8 93 B8
Alwyne Dr YO30 126 E1
Alwyne Gr YO30 126 E1
Amanda Cl HU6 139 E6
Amanda Dr DN7 92 D4
Ambaston Rd HU18 134 C5
Amber St YO31 156 C4
Amberley Cl HU7 141 B6
Amberly St 4 YO26 129 E5
Ambler's La YO30 12 F7
Ambleside Ave YO10 131 B4
Ambrey Cl 16 YO14 2 F8
Ambrose Ave 1 DN7 92 E4
Ambrose St YO10 130 D1
Amcott Ave DN10 116 D4
Amcotts Rd 14 DN33 102 D1
Amen La YO43 53 D5
Amesbury Ave DN33 113 D8
Amethyst Ct 11 DN36 114 A8
Amethyst Rd HU9 142 C4
Amos Cl 9 DN33 113 D8
Amos Cres DN16 151 D3
Ampleforth Gr HU5 144 D8
Amsterdam Rd HU7 141 A5
Amwell Gn 8 DN7 92 D3
Amy Johnson Ave
YO16 122 E6
Amy Johnson Ct HU1 155 A1
Amy Johnson Sch
HU3 144 F5
Amy Johnson Way
YO30 127 A3
Amy St DN14 149 C4
Anastasia Cl 1 DN21 117 B2
Ancaster Ave
Grimsby DN33 113 D8
Kingston upon Hull HU5 139 F3
Ancaster Ct DN16 151 A1
Ancholme Ave 10 DN40 87 B1
Ancholme Gdns 10 DN20 98 C2
Ancholme Rd DN16 151 D2
Ancholme Way DN20 98 B2
Anchor Rd
Kingston upon Hull HU6 140 C8
Scunthorpe DN16 97 A3
Anchorage St 8 DN20 98 B2
Anchors Way 17 DN20 98 B2
Ancient La DN7 92 F3
Ancourt HU6 139 E6
Ancress Wlk YO23 156 B1
Ancroft Cl YO1 156 C1
Anderby Dr DN37 102 B4
Andersen Rd DN14 149 A3
Anderson Gr 6 YO24 129 F2
Anderson Rd DN16 151 C3
Anderson St
7 Great Driffield YO25 124 F3
Grimsby DN31 152 D3
Andersons Cl 17 HU12 72 D7
Andrew Dr 4 YO32 127 F1
Andrew La 3 HU12 72 C7
Andrew Marvell Sch
HU9 142 D4
Andrew Rd 11 DN36 114 D8
Andrew's Ct 15 YO42 28 F4
Andrews Rd DN18 84 A7
Andrews Way 8 DN40 87 B1
Angerstein Rd DN17 150 F1
Anglesey Dr DN40 101 C8
Angram Cl YO30 126 F1
Angram La YO19 49 A6
Angram Rd YO26 24 A5
Angus Dr YO25 124 D4
Anlaby Acre Head Cty Prim
Sch HU4 144 B7
Anlaby Ave 7 HU4 144 B6
Anlaby Cty Inf Sch
HU10 144 A6
Anlaby Cty Jun Sch
HU10 144 A6
Anlaby High Rd HU4 144 C6
Anlaby Park Rd N
HU4 144 B5
Anlaby Park Rd S HU4 144 B2
Anlaby Rd HU3 155 A2
Anlafgate 7 HU10 143 F6
Anlary Rd HU1 155 A2
Ann Gr DN35 103 B2
Ann Watson St HU7 141 A4
Annan Cl YO24 132 C6
Annandale Rd
Kingston upon Hull
HU10 138 B1
Kingston upon Hull HU9 142 E2
Anne St
Kingston upon Hull HU1 155 A2
York YO23 130 C2
Annerley Dr YO16 123 A7
Annes Cres DN16 151 C3
Annesley St DN31 152 D5
Annie Med La HU15 53 F1
Annie Reed Rd HU17 137 C3
Anningson La 6 DN36 114 A8
Annumhills Rd YO8 50 D7
Anserdam La HU15 52 C2
Anson Dr YO10 133 D8
Anson Rd HU9 142 B3
Antelope Rd DN18 70 A1
Anthea Dr YO31 127 E1
Antholme Cl HU7 141 C6
Anthony Way 1 DN41 101 D6
Anthony's Bank Rd
DN36 103 E1
Antrim Way 4 DN33 102 E1
Antwerp Rd HU7 141 A5
Anvil Wlk DN15 82 F3
Apollo St 9 YO10 130 E3
Appin Cl 7 HU7 57 A6
Apple Croft HU16 138 B8
Apple Garth
21 Hedon HU12 72 D7
15 Poppleton YO26 12 F1
Apple Tree Cl HU8 141 D4
Apple Tree Ct 1 DN41 101 F5
Apple Tree Wlk HU16 139 D6
Appleby Cl DN17 150 F1
Appleby Gdns DN20 97 D4
Appleby Glade YO32 127 D7
Appleby La
Broughton DN20 97 D4
Burstwick HU12 73 A7
Appleby Mill Rd DN16 151 E7
Appleby Pl 2 YO31 131 A5
Applecroft Rd
Selby YO8 148 A4
York YO31 131 B7
Appledore Cl HU9 146 C6
Applegarth 8 HU15 66 D7

Applegarth Cl DN35 153 D1
Applegarth La
Bainton YO25 31 E7
Bridlington YO16 122 D4
Applegarth Mews 3 HU16 139 B7
Applegarth Rd HU8 155 C3
Appleton Ct YO23 132 F3
Appleton Gdns 8 HU15 53 F1
Appleton Prim Sch HU5 139 E2
Appleton Rd
Bishopthorpe YO23 133 A3
Kingston upon Hull HU5 139 E3
Appleton Way DN16 151 C2
Appleyard Dr DN18 84 E8
Arables La HU12 74 C4
Archbishop Cl HU9 142 D2
Archbishop Holgates Sch YO10 131 B3
Archbishop of York C of E Jun Sch YO23 133 A4
Archbishop Thurston C of E Sch HU9 142 D3
Archer Rd DN37 113 D6
Archway The YO43 135 D4
Arcon Dr HU4 144 D6
Arden Ct HU5 139 C2
Arden Rd HU17 154 C4
Arden Village 21 DN35 103 C1
Ardent Rd DN18 70 A1
Ardmore Cl HU9 142 B4
Arenhall Cl 2 YO32 127 C8
Argam Dikes*
Grindale YO25 3 B2
Rudston YO25 10 A7
Argam La YO25 2 F1
Argent Cl 8 HU6 140 B8
Argiam La YO43 51 F6
Argyle St Goole DN14 149 D4
Kingston upon Hull HU3 145 C7
York YO23 130 B1
Ariston St DN32 153 B3
Ark Royal HU11 142 E6
Arkley Cl 18 HU15 68 C5
Arkwright St 10 DN21 117 B1
Arkwright Way DN16 151 F2
Arlington Ave HU16 139 B6
Arlington Rd YO30 127 A1
Arlington St 2 HU3 145 D6
Armour Rd DN16 151 E7
Armoury Rd YO8 148 B5
Armstrong Pl E DN31 152 C5
Armstrong Pl W DN31 152 C5
Armstrong St DN31 152 C5
Armthorpe La DN3 92 A3
Arncliffe Cl 1 HU7 56 F6
Arncliffe Way HU16 139 A5
Arnold La
Kingston upon Hull HU3 145 B6
Riston HU11 45 C5
Arnold La W HU11 45 C4
Arnold St HU3 145 B6
Arnside Pl 2 YO10 130 F3
Arram Gr HU6 139 E5
Arram Rd HU17 43 D6
Arram Sta HU17 43 F7
Arran Cl
Immingham DN40 101 C8
Kingston upon Hull HU9 142 A4
Arran Pl YO31 130 D7
Arras Dr HU16 138 E6
Arreton Cl HU8 142 D6
Arthur Lucan Ct HU9 142 C1
Arthur Pl 6 YO30 126 B5
Arthur Rd 12 DN21 117 B1
Arthur St
Grimsby DN31 152 C4
Kingston upon Hull HU3 145 A5
Withernsea HU19 74 F7
York YO10 130 E4
Arundel Cl
4 Gainsborough DN21 117 C1
Kingston upon Hull HU9 146 C8
Arundel Gr YO24 132 C7
Arundel Pl DN35 153 E1
Arundel Rd 5 DN6 76 E2
Arundel St 4 HU9 146 C8
Ascot Rd 23 DN37 113 D6
Ascot Way YO24 129 D1
Ascott Cl HU4 144 D5
Asgard Way 5 DN33 102 D1
Ash Ave HU15 68 C6
Ash Cl Hessle HU13 143 C3
Newton on Derwent YO41 27 E4
Sproatley HU11 58 D5
York YO31 131 B7
Ash Ct 13 DN35 103 B1
Ash Dell DN14 149 E6
Ash Dene 7 HU17 55 D8
Ash Dr
Kingston upon Hull HU10 143 F8
Thorngumbald HU12 72 E5
Ash Gr 4 Aldbrough HU11 47 C1
Brigg DN20 98 B2
17 Gainsborough DN21 117 B1
Hutton Cranswick YO25 32 E6
Kingston upon Hull HU10 138 D1
Kingston upon Hull HU5 140 C3
Market Weighton YO43 135 D4
Messingham DN17 107 D7
1 Riccall YO19 48 F8
3 Scotter DN21 107 B3
Scunthorpe DN16 151 B3
Ash Hill Cres DN7 92 D4
Ash Hill Mid Sch DN7 92 D4
Ash Hill Rd
20 Hatfield DN7 92 D4
Sykehouse DN14 78 A3
Ash La 8 Haxby YO32 13 E5
Melbourne YO42 39 A5
Ash St YO26 129 E4
Ash Tree Cl 5 DN40 87 C2
Ash Tree Dr
5 Haxey DN9 105 D2
Leconfield HU17 43 D6
Ash Tree Rd 18 DN8 93 A7
Ashberry Dr
Messingham DN17 107 D7
1 Scunthorpe DN16 151 B2
Ashbourne 7 DN37 113 D6
Ashbourne Ct DN15 150 B7
Ashbourne Way YO24 132 C8
Ashburnham Cl 4 DN6 76 F2
Ashburnham Rd 14 DN8 93 A8
Ashburnham Wlk 5 DN6 76 F2
Ashbury Ct HU6 140 A6
Ashby Cl Grimsby DN37 102 B4
Holton le Clay DN36 114 B5
Kingston upon Hull HU4 144 B7
Ashby High St DN16 151 A2
Ashby Hill DN37 113 C3
Ashby Inf Sch DN16 151 B2
Ashby La DN37 113 C4
Ashby Rd
Cleethorpes DN35 103 B2
Kingston upon Hull HU4 144 B4
Scunthorpe DN16 151 A2
Ashcombe Rd HU7 56 E5
Ashcourt Cl HU18 134 C5
Ashcourt Dr HU18 134 B5
Ashdale Pk 14 HU14 69 A5
Ashdale Rd 19 YO19 26 F7
Ashdene Cl HU10 143 E7
Ashdown Ave DN15 150 E8
Ashdown Cl DN20 98 D2
Ashdown Way DN10 116 C5
Ashendon Dr HU8 141 A2
Ashfield YO43 40 A1
Ashfield Ave 1 DN8 93 A7
Ashfield Ct DN17 94 D7
Ashfield Gr 6 DN7 92 C6
Ashfield Rd Hatfield DN7 92 C4
Thorne DN8 92 F7
Ashford Pl YO24 129 D2
Ashgate Rd HU10 138 E2
Ashlea 1 DN10 116 C5
Ashlea Cl YO8 148 D4
Ashleigh Ct 13 DN41 101 F5
Ashleigh Dr 6 YO25 22 D1
Ashley Park Cres YO31 131 B6
Ashley Park Rd YO31 131 B7
Ashmeade Cl YO24 132 B8
Ashridge Dr DN32 153 B1
Ashthorpe HU6 139 F8
Ashton Ave YO30 130 B8
Ashton Cl HU6 139 F8
Ashtree Ave DN34 152 A2
Ashtree Cl DN9 94 E1
Ashtree Cres HU15 53 D3
Ashtree Dr YO8 48 D1
Ashville St
Bridlington YO16 122 D3
York YO31 130 D7
Ashwell Ave HU9 142 D1
Ashwood Dr
17 Humberston DN36 103 D1
10 Humberston DN36 114 D8
Ashwood Glade YO32 127 C6
Ashworthy Cl 5 HU7 56 F5
Aske Mews HU5 139 D3
Askern & Campsall Sports Ctr DN6 76 F1
Askew Ave HU4 144 E4
Askham Bryan Coll YO23 24 F2
Askham Bryan La YO23 132 A6
Askham Croft 1 YO24 129 B1
Askham Fields La YO23 24 F2
Askham Gr YO24 129 B2
Askham La
Askham Bryan YO24 132 A8
York YO24 129 B1
Aspen Cl
3 Dunnington YO19 26 F7
Market Weighton YO43 135 D5
Aspen Ct
15 Cleethorpes DN35 103 B1
13 Gainsborough DN21 117 C1
Aspen Gr DN16 151 B4
Aspen Wlk 4 HU15 68 D5
Asphodel Cl 15 DN36 114 B8
Asquith Ave YO31 131 A5
Asquith St DN21 117 A1
Asterby Rd DN17 150 F1
Astley Cres 18 DN21 107 C3
Astley St HU3 144 F7
Aston Gn 4 DN7 92 D3
Aston Hall Dr 11 HU14 69 A5
Aston Rd HU10 143 F8
Astoria Cres HU8 141 F4
Astral Cl
Kingston upon Hull HU7 141 D7
Kingston upon Hull HU13 143 F3
Astral Rd HU13 143 F3
Astral Way HU7 141 C7
Astral Way Gdns HU7 141 C7
Atcherley Cl YO10 133 D8
Athelstan Rd HU17 154 B4
Athenian Way DN37 102 C6
Atherton Way DN20 98 B2
Athol St HU3 144 F4
Atholl Ave HU13 143 E3
Atkinson Ave DN20 98 C3
Atkinson Dr 19 HU15 68 C6
Atkinson La 6 DN37 113 E6
Atkinsons Way DN15 96 C8
Atlanta Cl 2 HU8 142 B5
Atlas Rd
Scunthorpe DN17 150 F4
York YO30 127 A3
Atterby La LN8 119 F3
Atterwith La YO26 24 A7
Attlee Dr DN14 149 C5
Atwick Ct 2 HU9 142 B1
Atwick Rd
Bewholme YO25 35 A4
Hornsea HU18 134 B6
Atwood Cl 4 DN40 87 B2
Auburn Cl YO16 122 B5
Auchinleck Cl
Kelleythorpe YO25 124 B1
Kirkburn YO25 124 B1
Auckland Ave HU6 140 C5
Auckland Gr DN8 79 C2
Auckland Rd
Grimsby DN31 152 F6
Scunthorpe DN15 150 F6
Audax Cl YO30 127 A3
Audax Rd YO30 127 A3
Audern Rd DN16 96 D2
Audley St HU2 155 A4
Audus St 10 YO8 148 C5
Augusta Cl
Grimsby DN34 152 C2
Kingston upon Hull HU8 142 B6
Augusta Oaks DN34 152 C2
Augusta St DN34 152 B2
Augustinian Priory (site of)* YO42 30 B5
Augustus Dr 13 HU15 68 C5
Auster Rd YO30 127 B3
Austfield La LS25 61 B8
Austin Cres 17 DN17 96 C2
Austin Garth 5 DN37 101 F1
Autherd Garth 1 HU17 55 C8
Autumn View YO25 124 D5
Avenswood La 8 DN15 96 B7
Avenue Cannes DN15 96 B7
Avenue Clamart DN15 96 B7
Avenue Fontenay 17 DN15 96 B7
Avenue Lourdes 16 DN15 96 B7
Avenue Nozay DN20 97 E4
Avenue Rd YO30 156 A4
Avenue Rouen 15 DN15 96 B7
Avenue Terr YO30 156 A4
Avenue The
Blyton DN21 117 E5
Burton upon Stather DN15 82 B4
Campsall DN6 76 E1
East Ravendale DN37 113 C2
19 Gainsborough DN21 117 B1
Great Driffield YO25 124 F5
Grimsby DN37 102 B4
5 Haxby YO32 13 E5
Haxby YO32 127 D8
Healing DN41 101 F5
Holme-on-Spalding-Moor YO43 51 E8
Kingston upon Hull HU7 141 E6
Kingston upon Hull HU10 143 C7
Kingston upon Hull HU10 143 F7
Nun Monkton YO26 12 A4
11 Pocklington YO42 29 A4
Rowley HU20 54 D6
Rufforth YO23 24 C6
Thorne/Moorends DN8 79 B3
Watton YO25 32 D4
York YO30 130 A6
Avenue Vivian DN15 150 E8
Avenues Ct HU5 140 C1
Aviator Ct YO30 126 F3
Avon Dr YO32 127 F6
Avon Rd DN16 151 C6
Avon St 2 HU8 141 C1
Avondale 1 HU4 144 B2
Awnhams La
Bishop Wilton YO42 16 D2
North Cave HU15 53 E4
Axdane HU6 139 E7
Axholme Ave DN17 94 C7
Axholme Dr 11 DN9 105 D6
Axholme Gn 15 DN8 93 B7
Axholme Rd
Scunthorpe DN15 150 D6
2 Westwoodside DN9 105 A2
Axholme St DN14 149 E4
Axminster Cl HU7 141 A8
Aylesbury Gr HU5 144 D8
Aylesby Gdns 26 DN33 102 D2
Aylesby La
Aylesby DN37 101 F2
Healing DN41 101 F4
Aylesby Rd
Aylesby DN37 101 E2
Scunthorpe DN17 150 F1
Aylesford St 7 HU3 145 B5
Aylesham Ct YO32 127 E3
Ayots Gn 10 DN7 92 D3
Ayscough Ave DN41 101 E6
Ayscough Gr 3 LN7 111 B4
Ayscough St DN31 152 C4
Aysgarth Ave
Kingston upon Hull HU6 139 E4
Messingham DN17 107 D7
Aysgarth Rise YO16 122 E6

B

Bacchus La HU15 54 A1
Bacheler St HU3 145 B5
Bachelor Hill YO24 129 C2
Back Field La DN7 92 E4
Back La
Acaster Selby YO23 36 B3
Allerthorpe YO42 28 E2
Appleton Roebuck YO23 36 A5
Asselby DN14 64 D6
Barlby with Osgodby YO8 49 C4
Bilbrough YO23 24 D1
Burstwick HU12 73 A6
Burton Agnes YO25 10 A2
Burton Pidsea HU12 59 C2
Catwick HU17 45 C8
Copmanthorpe YO23 132 A2
Cottingwith YO42 38 C5
Drax YO8 63 F5
Driffield YO25 124 B5
East Garton HU11 59 E6
Ellerton YO42 38 C1
Elstronwick HU12 59 B3
Fangfoss YO41 28 C8
Garthorpe & Fockerby DN17 81 F6
11 Haxby YO32 13 D5
Hayton YO42 29 C1
Hemingbrough YO8 49 F1
Hirst Courtney YO8 62 F3
Holme-on-Spalding-Moor YO43 40 A1
Holtby YO19 26 E8
Kilham YO25 9 B3
Luttons YO17 7 B8
Newton-on-Ouse YO30 12 B6
North Duffield YO8 50 A7
Norton DN6 76 E2
Nunburnholme YO42 29 F3
Patrington Haven HU12 89 C8
2 Riccall YO19 49 A8
Searby cum Owmby DN38 110 D8
3 Seaton HU11 35 A1
Shiptonthorpe YO43 40 F6
Snaith & Cowick DN14 78 E8
Stainforth DN7 92 C6
Wilberfoss YO41 27 F5
3 Winteringham DN15 68 B1
Winteringham DN15 83 B8
Wold Newton YO25 2 A4
York YO26 129 A5
Back La S YO19 37 F7
Back O' Newton YO41 27 E3
Back Park St YO8 148 D5
Back Rd HU12 72 A5
Back Side YO17 6 B5
Back Southgate HU18 134 C3
Back St Alkborough DN15 82 C8
Bainton YO25 31 E7
Burton Fleming YO25 2 E3
3 Easington HU12 90 F6
East/West Stockwith DN21 116 E5
Fridaythorpe YO25 18 B6
Langtoft YO25 8 D5
Laxton DN14 65 F4
Skerne & Wansford YO25 21 A2
Skipsea YO25 23 A2
Wold Newton YO25 2 A4
Back West View 2 YO30 130 B7
Back Westgate HU18 134 B4
Backcarr La YO25 21 C5
Backhouse St YO31 156 B4
Bacon Garth Cty Prim Sch HU16 139 A5
Bacon Garth La HU16 139 A5
Bad Bargain La YO31 131 A5
Baden Cl 3 HU5 140 D2
Badger Hill Prim Sch YO10 131 B2
Badger La
Halsham HU12 74 B5
Walden Stubbs DN6 77 A3
Badger Paddock 5 YO31 127 E2
Badger Way 1 DN20 97 E4
Badger Wood Wlk YO10 131 D3
Badgers Wood HU16 138 F8
Baffam Gdns YO8 148 B2
Baffam La YO8 148 B2
Bagby Mews 2 HU5 139 D3
Baggaby Hill YO42 29 E4
Bagsby Rd DN9 106 B3
Baildon Cl 3 YO26 129 D4
Baildon Rd DN15 150 D8
Baile Hill Terr YO1 156 B1
Bailey La Hatfield DN7 92 E6
Kingston upon Hull HU16 139 D8
Warter YO42 30 B5
Baileywood La YO43 51 F8
Bainbridge Ave HU9 142 D2
Bainbridge Dr YO8 148 C4
Bainton Cl HU17 136 D5
Bainton Gr HU6 139 E6
Bainton Infant Sch YO25 31 E7
Bainton Rd YO25 19 E2
Bakehouse La 5 YO25 9 C3
Baker Dr DN15 83 A5
Baker St
Kingston upon Hull HU2 155 A3
York YO30 130 C7
Bakers Cl DN38 99 B5
Bakersfield DN20 98 D4
Bakersfield Dr DN14 61 F3
Bakewell Cl HU9 142 D1
Balder Ct 2 DN33 102 E1
Baldwin Ave DN16 96 D1
Balfour Pl 14 DN40 87 B1
Balfour St
24 Gainsborough DN21 117 B1
3 Kingston upon Hull HU9 146 C8
York YO26 129 F5
Balfour Way YO32 14 A6
Balham Ave HU8 141 E6
Balk Cl HU17 45 B8
Balk La Hook DN14 149 F6
Pollington DN14 77 F7
Riston HU11 45 C4
Sproatley HU11 58 D5
Balk Mews HU5 139 D3
Balk The
Bishop Wilton YO41 16 C2
Millington YO42 29 C7
Pocklington YO42 29 A3
Ballantyne Cl HU7 141 C4
Ballhall La YO42 38 E6
Balliol Dr DN16 96 D2
Balmoral Ave
Grimsby DN34 152 A3
Kingston upon Hull HU6 140 B6
Balmoral Cl 8 YO16 122 D6
Balmoral Dr HU17 136 E1
Balmoral Rd
2 Cleethorpes DN35 103 B2
25 Hatfield DN7 92 D4
Balmoral Terr 5 YO23 130 B1
Balne Croft La DN14 78 A6
Balne Hall Rd DN14 77 F5
Balne Moor Rd DN14 77 B6
Bamford Ave HU9 142 E1
Banbury Rd DN16 151 D6
Bank End Rd DN9 104 A3
Bank L Ctr The HU6 139 F6
Bank La 15 LN7 111 B4
Bank Rd YO8 148 D6
Bank Side
Kingston upon Hull HU5 140 F2
Rawcliffe DN14 64 A2
Bank St
3 Hornsea HU18 134 C4
Kingston upon Hull HU3 145 C7
Bank Terr HU18 134 C2
Bank Wood Rd WF8 76 A6
Bankfield La DN14 64 A7
Banks Cl HU12 90 F6
Bankside Cl 3 YO26 12 F1
Bannisdale 6 YO24 132 C7
Bannister Cl 3 HU13 69 F4
Bannister Dr HU9 146 C7
Bannister St HU19 75 A7
Baptist Chapel La DN40 86 F2
Baptist Pl YO16 122 D4
Bar La YO1 156 A2
Barbara Cl 3 DN33 113 E8
Barbara Gr 4 YO24 129 F3
Barbarry Rd HU12 72 B7
Barberry Ct 3 HU3 145 C5
Barbers Dr YO23 132 B4
Barbican Ct YO10 156 C1
Barbican L Ctr YO10 156 C1
Barbican Mews YO10 130 E3
Barbican Rd YO10 156 C1
Barbican Way 7 DN36 114 A7
Barbriggs La YO25 22 E2
Barcroft St DN35 153 B4
Barden Ct 6 YO30 126 F1
Bardney Ave DN16 151 A3
Bardney Gdns 16 DN34 102 C2
Bardney Rd 14 YO14 2 F8
Bardshaw HU6 139 F8
Barf La YO41 16 D4
Barff Cl 10 YO8 48 D1
Barff Gr 6 YO8 48 B2
Barff La YO8 48 C1
Barff View YO8 62 D7
Barfhill Cswy YO25 32 F2
Barfield Rd YO31 130 F8
Bargate DN34 152 C2
Bargate Ave DN32 152 D1
Bargate Gr 3 HU5 144 D8
Barham Rd HU9 142 B4
Bark House La DN35 153 F1
Bark St DN35 153 F1
Barker La YO1 156 A2
Barkhouse La DN35 153 F1
Barkhouse Wood La WF11 61 D6
Barking Cl HU8 142 A5
Barkston Ave YO26 129 B3
Barkston Cl 3 YO26 129 A3
Barkston Gr YO26 129 A3
Barkston Rd YO26 129 A3
Barkworth Cl HU10 143 D6
Barkworth Ct 3 DN37 113 D6
Barlby Bridge CP Sch YO8 148 D5
Barlby By-Pass 2 YO8 49 B4
Barlby CP Sch YO8 49 B4
Barlby Cres YO8 148 F7
Barlby High Sch YO8 49 B5
Barlby Rd YO8 148 E6
Barleigh Croft HU9 142 B3

Barleigh Rd HU9 142 B3
Barley Cl DN20 109 A5
Barley Garth
14 Brandesburton YO25 34 B2
Burton Pidsea HU12 59 C2
Barley Gate HU17 45 A8
Barley Rise
Bridlington YO16 123 A6
Strensall YO32 14 A6
Barley View YO32 127 C8
Barlings Ave DN16 151 A3
Barlings Cl DN21 107 D4
Barlow C of E Prim Sch YO8 63 C7
Barlow Comm Nature Reserve* YO8 63 B7
Barlow Comm Rd YO8 63 B8
Barlow Rd YO8 63 B6
Barlow St YO26 129 D4
Barmby Ave YO10 133 E8
Barmby Cl 4 YO30 126 F1
Barmby Ferry Rd 1 YO8 49 F1
Barmby La DN14 52 A3
Barmby Moor C of E Sch YO42 28 D4
Barmby on the Marsh Cty Prim Sch DN14 64 B7
Barmby Rd YO42 28 E4
Barmouth Cl 4 HU7 57 A7
Barmouth Dr 20 DN37 102 C4
Barmston Cl HU17 137 B5
Barmston La HU17 56 C8
Barmston Rd HU17 137 B5
Barmston St HU2 155 B4
Barnard Ave DN20 98 B2
Barnard Way HU12 72 D6
Barnards Dr 9 HU15 53 F1
Barnes Cl HU17 137 B4
Barnes Cres DN15 150 E8
Barnes Gn DN21 107 C4
Barnet Cl HU8 142 A5
Barnet Dr DN36 114 B8
Barnet Gn 9 DN7 92 D3
Barnetby C of E Sch DN38 99 B4
Barnetby La DN20 98 F7
Barnetby Rd
1 Kingston upon Hull HU13 144 A3
Scunthorpe DN17 150 F1
Barnetby Sta DN38 99 B4
Barnett Pl DN35 153 B3
Barnfield Way YO23 132 A2
Barnhill La DN14 64 F7
Barnoldby Rd DN37 113 D6
Barnsdale View DN6 76 E2
Barnside DN20 108 F5
Barnsley Rd DN8 79 B2
Barnsley St HU8 141 B1
Barnstaple Rd
Kingston upon Hull HU7 141 B7
Scunthorpe DN17 150 D3
Barnston Way 11 DN15 82 B4
Baron Ave 8 DN36 114 A8
Baroness Cl 7 HU6 140 B8
Baroness Ct 4 DN34 102 C3
Baroness Rd
3 Grimsby DN34 102 C3
Grimsby DN34 152 A3
Barons Cres YO23 132 B2
Baronwood Cres 7 YO25 22 D1
Barr La YO32 14 D4
Barra Cl HU8 141 F6
Barraclough's La DN18 69 E2
Barrett Ave 3 YO24 129 F3
Barrick Cl 7 DN19 85 D8
Barrier Bank DN14 78 E6
Barrington Ave HU5 139 F3
Barrington Garth DN14 61 F3
Barrow Ct 3 HU3 140 D1
Barrow Haven Sta DN19 70 C2
Barrow La HU13 143 D2
Barrow Rd
Barrow upon Humber DN19 70 E1
Barton-upon-Humber DN18 85 A8
New Holland DN19 70 E2
Barry Ave DN34 102 C2
Barstow Ave YO10 130 F3
Bartholomew Ave DN14 149 B5
Bartindale Rd YO14 3 A5
Bartle Garth YO1 156 C3
Bartlett Ave HU17 154 A2
Bartlett Cl 9 HU12 58 D1
Barton Dr HU13 143 D1
Barton La DN19 85 C8
Barton Rd DN20 98 D3
Barton St
Barrow upon Humber DN19 85 D8
Irby DN37 112 F7
Keelby DN41 101 A4
Wyham cum Cadeby DN36 120 F7
Barton St Peters C of E Prim Sch DN18 69 F1
Barton-on-Humber Sta DN18 69 F1
Bartons Garth YO8 148 B2
Bartrams HU15 68 D6
Barwic Par YO8 148 E4
Barwick Parade CP Sch YO8 148 E4
Basic Slag Rd DN16 151 E6
Basil Dr HU17 154 A1
Baslow Rd DN15 150 B6
Bassett Cl
1 Broughton DN20 97 E3
Selby YO8 148 C3
Bassett Rd 2 DN35 103 D2
Bate La DN14 78 A4
Bateson Cl YO10 131 C1
Bath St DN32 153 A5
Baths Hall The DN15 150 F7
Bathurst St 8 HU3 145 D5
Batley Cl HU9 142 C2
Battersea Cl HU8 141 F5
Battery Rd HU12 72 A4
Battery St DN40 87 C1
Battle Gn DN9 105 D7
Battleflats Way YO41 15 D2
Batty La 7 DN14 65 A7
Bawtry Cl YO8 148 D3
Bawtry Rd Hatfield DN7 92 F3
Selby YO8 148 D3
Baxter Gate HU12 72 D7
Bay View Ave HU18 134 C6
Bayard St DN21 117 B1
Bayle Mus* YO16 122 D4
Baylegate 6 YO16 122 D4
Baynard Ave HU16 139 A6
Bayons Ave 13 DN33 113 D8
Baysdale HU7 140 F6
Baysdale Ave YO10 131 D3
Baysdale Rd DN16 151 D1
Baysgarth L Ctr DN18 84 F8
Baysgarth Lower Sch DN18 84 F8
Baysgarth Mus* DN18 84 F8
Baysgarth Upper Sch DN18 84 F8
Baysgarth View DN18 84 F7
Bayswater Ct HU8 141 E5
Bayswater Pl 2 DN33 113 D8
Baytree Ave DN34 152 A2
Beach Holt La DN37 101 D2
Beacon Ave
14 Barton-upon-Humber DN18 84 E8
Cleethorpes DN35 153 D2
Beacon Ct DN35 153 D2
Beacon Hill* DN10 116 A1
Beacon Hill Rd DN10 116 A1
Beacon La YO25 21 B8
Beacon Rd
Bridlington YO16 123 A6
Millington YO42 17 B1
Beacon View YO43 40 B1
Beaconsfield HU19 74 F6
Beaconsfield St
1 Kingston upon Hull HU5 140 D2
York YO24 129 D3
Beaconthorpe Rd DN35 153 E3
Beadlam Mews HU5 139 E4
Beadle Garth YO23 132 B2
Beagle Cl 12 DN20 97 E4
Beagle Croft YO41 15 C1
Beagle Ridge Dr YO24 129 C1
Beagle Spinney YO41 15 C1
Beal La Beal DN14 61 D4
Cridling Stubbs WF11 61 C1
Bealey's La YO25 32 B1
Beamsley Way 18 HU7 56 F5
Bean Gdns 3 DN14 78 C8
Bean St HU3 145 C6
Beanland La YO32 14 D2
Bean's Way YO31 131 B8
Beatty Ave 18 DN33 113 E8
Beauchamp St DN16 151 B5
Beauchief Gdns DN16 151 A4
Beaufort Ave HU18 134 C2
Beaufort Cl
Kingston upon Hull HU3 145 D6
York YO10 131 B3
Beaufort Cres 5 DN35 103 B1
Beaufort St 5 DN21 117 B2
Beaulah Villas 1 DN18 84 A7
Beaulahland 2 DN18 84 A7
Beaulieu Cl 1 YO32 127 F5
Beaulieu Ct 5 HU9 142 A3
Beaumonde 5 DN36 114 A5
Beaumont Ct
Goole DN14 149 B6
3 Kingston upon Hull HU9 146 D7
Beaumont Pl YO8 148 A2
Beautiman Ct HU6 140 A5
Beaver Rd HU17 137 B4
Beaverdyke YO30 126 F1
Beccles Cl HU8 142 B6
Beck Bank HU16 139 C6
Beck Cl 6 Elvington YO41 27 B2
Keelby DN41 101 A4
Beck Garth 12 HU12 72 D7
Beck Hill
6 Barton-upon-Humber DN18 84 F8
1 Bridlington YO15 122 E2
Beck La Appleby DN15 83 D1
5 Barrow upon Humber DN19 85 D8
Broughton DN20 97 E3
Easington HU12 90 F6
Redbourne DN21 108 F2
Scunthorpe DN16 96 D2
Wheldrake YO19 38 A8
Beck Rd HU15 53 D2
Beck Row YO41 16 D5
Beck Side
Barmby Moor YO42 28 D3
Great Driffield YO25 124 F4
Hibaldstow DN20 108 F5
Beck St HU12 90 F6
Beck View 14 YO42 29 A3
Beck View Rd HU17 137 C4
Beck Wlk 7 DN35 103 C1
Beckdale 4 HU7 141 A6
Beckett Ave DN21 117 C1
Beckfield La YO26 129 B5
Beckfield Pl YO26 129 B4
Beckhole Cl HU3 145 A6
Beckhythe Cl DN33 102 F1
Beckingham Rd DN10 116 D2
Beckington Cl 1 HU8 142 C7
Becks Cl 5 YO32 127 C8
Becks La DN21 107 A3
Becks La Riding Sch DN21 107 B3
Beckside
Beverley HU17 154 C2
4 Brough HU15 68 D6
7 Elvington YO41 27 B2
Hornsea HU18 134 C3
Rothwell LN7 111 F2
Wilberfoss YO41 27 F6
Beckside Cl
4 Humberston DN35 103 C1
Kingston upon Hull HU6 140 B7
Beckside N HU17 154 C2
Beckwith Cl YO31 131 C7
Bedale Ave
Kingston upon Hull HU9 141 E1
York YO10 131 D4
Bedale Ct YO43 135 E3
Bedale Rd
Market Weighton YO43 135 E3
Scunthorpe DN16 151 D1
Bedale Wlk YO43 135 F4
Bede Ave YO30 130 B7
Bedford Gr YO15 122 D1
Bedford Rd
Humberston DN35 103 D1
Kingston upon Hull HU13 143 F3
Bedford St
Grimsby DN32 153 A5
Kingston upon Hull HU8 141 A1
Bedfords Fold 6 LS25 61 A7
Beech Ave
3 Airmyn DN14 64 E4
Beverley HU17 136 F6
Bishopthorpe YO23 133 A3
3 Flamborough YO15 5 A2
Flixborough DN15 96 A7
14 Gainsborough DN21 117 B1
14 Grimsby DN33 102 E2
Gunness DN15 95 E6
Kingston upon Hull HU8 141 C2
Kingston upon Hull HU11 142 F6
Kingston upon Hull HU10 143 D8
7 Preston HU12 72 C7
Thorngumbald HU12 72 E5
York YO24 129 F3
Beech Cl
4 Broughton DN20 97 D3
Burstwick HU12 73 A6
2 Elvington YO41 27 B2
Kilham YO25 9 B3
8 Kingston upon Hull HU3 145 C5
Market Weighton YO43 135 D4
Sproatley HU11 58 C5
Beech Cres 7 DN7 92 C6
Beech Croft
Barlby with Osgodby YO8 49 B6
Driffield YO25 125 A6
Beech Ct
Bishopthorpe YO23 133 A3
6 Pocklington YO42 29 A4
Beech Dr
Bridlington YO16 123 A6
2 North Ferriby HU14 69 A4
11 Patrington HU12 74 D1
Beech Garth DN19 85 C7
Beech Glade YO31 127 F2
Beech Gr 1 Airmyn DN14 64 E4
Burton upon Stather DN15 82 B5
Camblesforth YO8 63 C5
2 Flamborough YO15 5 A2
Goole DN14 149 D1
Holton le Clay DN36 114 B5
Kingston upon Hull HU5 140 C3
Kingston upon Hull HU13 143 C3
Nafferton YO25 125 E8
Selby YO8 148 C5
1 Swanland HU14 69 C7
York YO26 129 C4
Beech Hill Rd HU14 69 C7
Beech Lawn HU10 143 E6
Beech Pk YO19 49 A8
Beech Pl 5 YO32 14 A6
Beech Rd Brough HU15 68 C6
Campsall DN6 76 E1
Beech Tree Ave 21 DN8 93 B7
Beech Tree Cl 3 HU17 136 F7
Beech Tree La YO8 63 C5
Beech View
Hutton Cranswick YO25 32 E6
Walkington HU17 55 C8
Beech Way 10 DN36 103 B1
Beechcliffe Ave 1 HU6 140 C7
Beechdale HU16 139 C5
Beeches Ave 23 DN16 96 D2
Beeches The
Great Driffield YO25 125 A4
Pocklington YO42 29 A4
Skelton YO30 126 C4
Beechfield
Kingston upon Hull HU6 140 B6
Newton-on-Ouse YO30 12 B6
Beechfield Cl YO8 48 B1
Beechfield Dr HU10 138 C2
Beechfield Rd DN7 92 C4
Beechway DN16 151 B3
Beechwood Ave
25 Grimsby DN33 102 C2
3 Immingham DN40 87 C1
Beechwood Cl 11 DN3 92 A1
Beechwood Cres 3 DN20 97 E4
Beechwood Dr
Scawby DN20 108 E8
3 Scotter DN21 107 C3
Beechwood Glade 7 YO24 129 B1
Beechwood Views HU12 60 B1
Beeford C of E Sch YO25 22 C1
Beeford Gr HU6 139 F5
Beeford Rd YO25 22 F1
Beeforth Cl YO32 127 D5
Beeley Rd DN32 153 C2
Beel's Rd DN41 101 E8
Beelsby Rd DN37 112 C5
Beesby Dr 22 DN35 103 C2
Beesby Medieval Village* DN36 120 E7
Beesby Rd DN17 150 E1
Beeson St DN31 152 C5
Beggar Hill DN21 107 D5
Beilby St HU3 144 F4
Belcombe Way 1 YO30 130 A7
Beldevere Pk HU18 134 C6
Belfry Ct HU8 142 B6
Belgrave Cl 6 Belton DN9 94 E1
Belton DN9 105 E8
Belgrave Dr
Goole DN14 149 F5
Hornsea HU18 134 C5
Kingston upon Hull HU4 144 D5
7 North Cave HU15 53 D3
Belgrave Rd
Bridlington YO15 122 D1
1 Grimsby DN33 102 D1
Belgrave Sq 1 DN15 151 B7
Belgrave St YO31 130 C7
Belgravia 8 DN14 149 C4
Bell Cl Haxby YO32 127 C8
Kingston upon Hull HU7 141 D5
Bell Gn DN14 78 B2
Bell Hall* YO19 36 E6
Bell La Cawood YO8 48 A7
Foggathorpe YO8 51 B7
Rawcliffe DN14 64 A2
Scunthorpe DN15 151 A6
Bellamy Ct HU9 146 C7
Bellasize La HU15 66 C6
Bellasize Pk HU15 66 D8
Bellbutts View 1 DN21 107 B3
Bellcroft La HU12 72 E4
Bellcroft Rd HU12 72 F5
Bellcross La
7 Howden DN14 65 B7
Kilpin DN14 65 C6
Belle Vue St YO10 130 E3
Belle Vue Terr
19 Thorne/Moorends DN8 93 A8
York YO10 130 E3
Belleisle Rd 12 DN34 102 B3
Bellfarm Ave YO31 130 E8
Bellfield Ave 5 HU8 142 A5
Bellfield Cty Prim Sch HU8 142 A4
Bellfield Dr HU10 138 D1
Bellground La YO30 12 D4
Bellguy Springs* YO25 8 F8
Bellhouse Way YO24 132 B8
Bellingham Rd DN16 151 D3
Bellmans Croft YO23 132 B2
Bells Rd HU12 72 B7
Bellwin Dr DN15 82 A1
Bellwood Cres 7 DN8 93 A8
Bellwood Dr YO24 132 B8
Belmont DN36 114 A5
Belmont Cl
13 Cleethorpes DN35 103 B2
3 York YO30 127 A1
Belmont St
Kingston upon Hull HU9 146 D8
Scunthorpe DN16 151 A2
Belprin Rd HU17 137 B5
Belshaw La DN9 94 D1
Belt Rd The DN21 117 C2
Belthorn Rd 1 DN17 81 F1
Belthorpe La YO42 16 E1
Belton C of E Sch DN9 94 E2
Belton Cl 4 HU8 142 B5
Belton Fields DN9 94 D1
Belton Gr 7 DN33 102 D2
Belton Rd Belton DN9 95 A1
Epworth DN9 105 E7
Sandtoft DN9 94 B3
Belvedere Cres DN14 149 B6
Belvedere Dr
Kingston upon Hull HU11 142 D6
Scunthorpe DN17 150 E3
7 Thorne/Moorends DN8 79 B2
Belvedere Par YO15 11 B4
Belvedere Rd
Bridlington YO15 11 B4
Kingston upon Hull HU13 143 F2
Belvoir Ave 8 YO41 27 B2
Belvoir Rd DN35 103 B1
Belvoir St HU5 145 C8
Belwood Dr DN9 94 E2
Bempton Cl YO16 122 E6
Bempton Cliffs Nature Reserve* YO15 4 D4
Bempton Cres YO16 122 E6
Bempton Cty Prim Sch YO15 4 C3
Bempton Dr YO16 122 E6
Bempton Gdns YO16 122 E6
Bempton Gr
Grimsby DN32 153 A1
Kingston upon Hull HU5 144 D8
Bempton La
Bempton YO16 4 B1
Bridlington YO16 122 D8
Bempton Oval YO16 122 E6
Bempton Sta YO16 4 C2
Bemrose Gr YO16 122 E5
Bemrose Way DN31 152 C4
Bence The YO42 17 C3
Benedict Ave YO8 148 E4
Benedict Cl 2 HU4 144 A2
Benedict Rd HU4 144 A2
Beningbrough La YO30 12 D5
Benjy La YO19 37 E7
Bennetland La HU15 66 C7
Bennett Dr DN15 83 A4
Bennett Rd
Cleethorpes DN35 153 D3
Scunthorpe DN16 151 C3
Benningholme La HU11 45 D2
Bennymoor La YO8 49 C4
Benson Ct LN11 121 C4
Bentley Ct HU3 145 A5
Bentley Gr HU6 139 F4
Bentley La DN38 110 E7
Bentley St DN35 153 E2
Berea The DN34 152 C1
Beresford Ave
Hornsea HU18 134 D2
Kingston upon Hull HU6 140 D4
Beresford Terr YO23 130 C1
Beretun Gn 11 DN18 84 E8
Bergen Way HU7 140 D6
Berkeley Dr
3 Beverley HU17 136 E1
32 Hedon HU12 72 D7
Berkeley Jun & Inf Sch DN15 150 D8
Berkeley Rd DN35 103 D1
Berkeley St
1 Kingston upon Hull HU3 145 D8
Scunthorpe DN15 150 F8
Berkeley Terr YO26 129 E5
Berkshire Cl 4 HU17 55 F8
Berkshire St HU8 141 C1
Bermondsey Dr HU5 144 E8
Bermuda Ave HU11 45 D2
Bernadette Ave HU4 144 B5
Berners Rd 15 DN35 103 D1
Berridge La DN14 78 A6
Berriman's La YO25 9 B3
Berryman Way HU13 144 A3
Berwick Ct 5 DN40 87 C1
Bessacarr Ave HU10 138 F1
Bessemer Way DN15 96 D7
Bessingby Gate YO16 122 A2
Bessingby Gr HU9 142 B2
Bessingby Hill YO16 122 B3
Bessingby Rd YO16 122 C2
Bessingby Way YO16 122 C1
Bestall Rd DN32 153 C2
Beswick C of E Sch YO25 32 D3
Beswick Hall* YO25 32 D3
Beswick Heads YO25 32 C3
Beswick Rd YO25 32 E2
Bethell Ct 6 HU12 72 D7
Bethlehem St DN32 152 D3
Bethune Ave HU4 144 A3
Bethune Ave W HU13 144 A3
Bethune Park Prim Sch HU4 144 C3
Betony Cl 4 DN15 96 B7
Betteras Hill Rd LS25 61 A8
Betula Way DN17 150 C1
Between Dikes Rd YO8 63 F8
Between Rivers La DN14 78 E7
Beverley Balk YO41 15 B2
Beverley Cl DN36 114 A5
Beverley Coll HU18 134 C4
Beverley Coll of F Ed HU17 136 C5
Beverley Cres DN32 153 A1
Beverley Ct 11 DN41 101 F5
Beverley Dr HU17 136 D7
Beverley Gram Sch HU17 136 D2
Beverley High Sch HU17 154 A4
Beverley L Ctr HU17 154 C2
Beverley La YO43 41 E2
Beverley Minster* HU17 154 B2
Beverley Parklands HU17 154 C1

Beverley Race Course HU17 136 B4
Beverley Rd
Beeford YO25 22 D1
Bishop Burton HU17 43 B2
Great Driffield YO25 124 E2
Hutton Cranswick YO25 20 E1
Kingston upon Hull HU6 140 B8
Kingston upon Hull HU13 143 E3
Kingston upon Hull HU3 155 A4
Kirkburn YO25 124 D1
Leven HU17 45 A7
Market Weighton YO43 135 E4
Middleton YO25 31 D4
Newbald YO43 53 F8
Skidby HU16 138 C7
South Cave HU15 54 A2
Watton YO25 32 D5
Withernwick HU11 46 A3
Beverley Road Sch HU5 140 E1
Beverley St DN14 149 C2
Beverley Sta HU17 154 B3
Beverley Swimming Pool HU17 154 B4
Beverley Town Cricket & Recn Club HU17 154 A4
Bewholme Gr
4 Kingston upon Hull HU9 142 B1
Kingston upon Hull HU9 147 B8
Bewholme La
Bewholme YO25 35 A8
Seaton HU11 35 A2
Skipsea YO25 23 A1
Bewholme Rd YO25 35 C5
Bewlay St YO23 130 C2
Bexhill Ave HU9 142 E2
Bibbill La YO42 39 B5
Bibury Cl HU8 141 B2
Bickerton Cl HU6 139 F7
Bickleigh Gr 1 HU8 142 C6
Bideford Gr HU9 142 E1
Bielby Dr HU17 137 B3
Bigby Gr DN17 96 C2
Bigby High Rd DN20 99 C1
Bigby Hill DN38 99 C1
Bigby Rd 15 DN20 98 C2
Bigby St DN20 98 C2
Biggin Ave HU7 141 C8
Biggin Hill Prim Sch HU7 141 C8
Billet La DN15 96 C8
Billet Mill App DN16 151 F3
Billet Mill Rd DN16 151 E5
Billinghay Ct 16 DN35 103 C2
Billings La YO25 34 E5
Bilsdale Cl YO30 126 E2
Bilsdale Gr HU9 146 F8
Bilsdale Rd DN16 151 E1
Bilton Gr HU9 142 B2
Bilton Prim Sch HU11 142 E6
Bilton Rd HU11 142 D6
Binbrook Garth 2 HU7 57 A5
Binbrook Way 16 DN37 102 C4
Birch Ave Brigg DN20 98 B2
Grimsby DN34 152 A2
Birch Cl Beverley HU17 136 F6
5 Bridlington YO16 123 A6
7 Gilberdyke HU15 66 D7
Kingston upon Hull HU4 144 B7
4 Thorpe Willoughby YO8 48 B1
Birch Dr HU10 138 E1
Birch Gr 18 DN21 117 B1
Birch La 13 YO32 13 E5
Birch Lea 3 HU17 55 B8
Birch Leigh HU3 145 C6
Birch Mews DN14 149 E6
Birch Tree Cl DN3 92 A4
Birch Way 4 DN38 99 B4
Bircham Cres 3 DN21 119 C8
Birchdale DN18 84 E7
Birches The
5 Haxey DN9 105 B2
Hornsea HU18 134 D2
Birchfield DN14 149 F6
Birchfield Rd 6 DN9 105 D6
Birchfield Road Cty Sch DN9 105 D6
Birchin Way DN31 152 B5
Birchwood Ave HU4 144 B7
Birchwood Cl 2 DN8 79 A1
Birchwood Rd DN16 151 B1
Bird La Hensall DN14 62 D2
Kellington DN14 61 F4
Birdcroft La 3 DN10 116 D3
Birdforth Mews 5 HU5 139 D3
Birds Wood Nature Reserve* DN9 104 F3
Birdsall Ave HU5 139 C2
Birdsall Cl HU16 138 E5
Birk La YO42 50 D8
Birkby Gr HU9 142 C2
Birkdale 14 DN37 113 D6
Birkdale Cl HU10 143 B8
Birkdale Dr 8 DN40 87 C2
Birkdale Gr 4 YO26 129 B5
Birkdale Rd DN17 96 B2
Birkdale Way HU9 146 D8
Birker La
Newton on Derwent YO41 27 D4
Wilberfoss YO41 27 F6
Birkin La WF11 61 B4
Birkin Rd YO8 61 F5
Birklands Dr HU8 141 E4
Birrel St 2 DN21 117 A1
Birstwith Dr YO26 129 E4
Birt Gr DN14 149 B6
Bishop Alcock Rd HU5 139 D3
Bishop Blunt Cl 2 HU13 143 F1
Bishop Burton Coll
Bishop Burton HU17 43 A3
Broughton DN20 97 E3
Great Driffield YO25 124 F4
Bishop Burton Rd HU17 43 A4
Bishop Ct
9 Gilberdyke HU15 66 D8
2 Selby YO8 148 B6
Bishop Gurdon Cl 4 HU13 143 F1
Bishop Kempthorne Clo 3 HU13 143 F1
Bishop La HU1 155 C2
Bishop La Staith HU1 155 C2
Bishop Temple Ct HU13 143 F3
Bishop Witton Sch YO42 16 F2
Bishopdike Rd YO8 48 A6
Bishopgate St YO23 156 B1
Bishophill Jun YO1 156 A1
Bishophill Senior YO1 156 B1
Bishops Croft HU17 154 A2
Bishop's La LN8 120 A7
Bishop's Wlk DN34 152 C2
Bishopsway YO10 131 C3
Bishopthorpe Inf Sch YO23 133 A4
Bishopthorpe Palace* YO23 133 B4
Bishopthorpe Rd
Bishopthorpe YO23 133 B5
Cleethorpes DN35 103 C2
Bisley Gr HU7 141 A7
Bismarck St YO26 129 E5
Bittern Cl HU4 144 D2
Black Bank DN17 106 F6
Black Dike La YO26 24 F8
Black Fen La YO8 148 C8
Black Syke La DN14 78 E2
Black Tup La HU11 45 C3
Blackburn Ave
Bridlington YO15 122 F3
Brough HU15 68 C5
Blackburn La WF11 61 B2
Blackdykes Rd DN9 106 B4
Blackfriargate HU1 155 C1
Blackhope Cl 14 HU7 57 A6
Blacklee Cl 4 YO32 14 B8
Blackmoor Rd DN9 105 D2
Blacksmith Hill DN15 67 E3
Blacksmiths Cl 1 DN19 85 C7
Blackthorn Cl
8 Newport HU15 52 F1
7 Scunthorpe DN15 96 B7
Blackthorn Ct 4 HU3 145 D6
Blackthorn Dr
Healing DN37 102 B5
York YO31 127 E2
Blackthorn La HU10 143 F7
Blackthorns The 3 DN20 97 D4
Blacktoft La DN14 66 D3
Blackwater Way 27 HU7 56 F6
Blackwood La YO8 49 F7
Blackwood Rd YO8 49 E8
Bladon Rd YO16 122 E5
Bladons Wlk HU10 143 C8
Blaides Staithe HU1 155 C2
Blake Ave DN17 150 E3
Blake Cl HU2 155 A4
Blake Ct YO19 38 A8
Blake St YO1 156 B3
Blakeley Gr YO30 126 F3
Blakeney Lea DN35 103 C1
Blakeney Pl YO10 130 F3
Bland La YO26 129 A4
Blandford Cl HU7 141 B6
Blands Hill LN8 120 A5
Blanket Row HU1 155 B1
Blankney Ct 13 DN15 83 A5
Blanshards La 1 HU15 53 D3
Blatchford YO30 130 B8
Blaycourt HU6 139 E6
Blaydes St HU6 140 C4
Blaydon Gr 1 DN34 102 C2
Bleaberry La YO41 16 B5
Blenheim Cl 15 DN7 92 D3
Blenheim Ct
Rawcliffe YO30 126 D3
Scunthorpe DN16 96 D1
Blenheim Dr DN14 149 E6
Blenheim Pl 4 DN35 103 C2
Blenheim Rd
Beverley HU17 136 E1
Bridlington YO16 122 E3
5 Moorland Prison DN7 104 A8
Blenheim St HU5 145 C8
Blenkin St HU9 146 B7
Bleriot Way YO30 127 A3
Blisland Cl 13 HU7 56 F5
Bloom Hill Gr
18 Thorne/Moorends DN8 79 B2
9 Thorne/Moorends DN8 79 B2
Bloom Mill App Rd DN16 97 A4
Bloomfield Ave HU5 144 C8
Bloomhill Cl 4 DN8 79 B2
Bloomhill Ct DN8 79 B2
Bloomhill Rd DN8 79 A2
Bloomsbury Ct 1 HU3 145 D6
Blossom Gr HU8 141 D8
Blossom St YO24 156 A1
Blossom Way 21 DN40 87 B1
Blossom's La HU15 53 C3
Blow Row DN9 105 E6
Blucher La HU17 154 C2
Blue Bridge La YO10 130 D2
Blue Slates Cl YO19 38 A8
Bluebeck Dr YO30 129 E8
Bluebell Cl DN15 151 C7
Blueberry Cl YO25 124 E2
Blueberry Ct HU4 144 C4
Bluestone Bottoms HU17 55 A6
Bluestone La DN40 87 B1
Blundell Ave DN35 153 C4
Blundell Cl HU2 155 A4
Blyth Cl YO8 148 A5
Blyth Ct DN18 85 A8
Blyth St 2 HU9 146 B7
Blythe Wlk 1 YO16 122 D4
Blythorpe HU6 139 F8
Blyton C of E Sch DN21 117 F6
Blyton Rd
Gainsborough DN21 117 B2
Laughton DN21 117 E8
Boardman La 6 YO25 34 B2
Boardman Pk 7 YO25 34 B2
Boatcliffe Rd YO14 3 D7
Boating Dyke Way 12 DN8 93 A8
Boatswain Croft HU1 155 B1
Bodiam Way DN32 152 F4
Bodmin Cl DN17 150 D4
Bodmin Rd HU7 140 E8
Bog La YO24 132 B6
Boggle La HU11 58 D5
Bolam La YO16 4 C2
Boldron Mews 7 HU5 139 D3
Bolingbroke Rd
Cleethorpes DN35 103 D2
Scunthorpe DN17 96 C2
Bolsover Rd DN15 150 B6
Bolt The 3 YO16 122 D4
Boltby Mews HU5 139 E3
Boltby Rd YO30 126 F2
Bolton La
Bishop Wilton YO42 16 E1
Wilberfoss YO41 28 A5
Bomber Cty Aviation Mus* DN21 119 D1
Bon Accord Rd HU13 143 E1
Bonby Gr
11 Grimsby DN33 102 D2
Scunthorpe DN17 150 F1
Bonby La YO8 37 E2
Bonby Rd DN20 84 C1
Bond St Hedon HU12 72 D7
Kingston upon Hull HU1 155 B3
Bondane HU6 139 E7
Bondgate YO8 148 B7
Bondsville Model Village* YO15 123 B6
Bondyke Cl HU16 138 E6
Bonington Ct 7 YO26 129 E4
Bonnyhale Rd DN17 94 E6
Bontoft Ave HU5 139 E1
Booth Ferry Rd DN14 64 F6
Booth Nooking La DN15 68 A3
Bootham YO30 156 A3
Bootham Bar* YO31 156 B3
Bootham Cl 1 DN7 92 D4
Bootham Cres
Stainforth DN7 92 C6
York YO30 156 A4
Bootham La
Hatfield DN7 92 D5
Stainforth DN7 92 D6
Bootham Park Hospl YO31 156 B4
Bootham Rd 12 DN7 92 C6
Bootham Row YO31 156 B3
Bootham Sch YO31 156 A3
Bootham Sq YO31 156 B3
Bootham Terr YO30 156 A3
Boothferry Prim Sch DN14 149 B4
Boothferry Rd
Airmyn DN14 149 A8
Hessle HU13 143 B2
Boothferry Rd Ave 14 DN14 65 B7
Boothgate DN14 65 A6
Boothgate Cl DN14 65 A6
Boothgate Dr DN14 65 A6
Boothwood Rd YO30 126 E2
Booty La DN14 76 F7
Bore Tree Baulk YO19 26 D6
Borman's La 3 DN36 114 B1
Borough Rd YO16 122 C3
Boroughbridge Rd YO26 129 D5
Borrowdale HU7 140 F6
Borrowdale Dr YO30 126 F1
Borthwick Cl 3 HU7 57 A6
Bos App Rd DN16 151 F3
Bossall Hall* YO60 15 D7
Bossington Cl 10 HU7 57 A5
Boston Cl 6 DN15 83 A5
Boston Ct 20 HU7 56 F5
Bosworth Cl 16 DN7 92 D3
Botany Bay DN3 92 B4
Botany Bay La DN3 92 B4
Bothwell Gr HU9 147 D8
Bottesford Ave DN16 151 B1
Bottesford Inf Sch DN16 96 D2
Bottesford La DN16 151 B1
Bottesford Town Football & Cricket Club DN17 96 B2
Bottlings The 9 DN20 98 C2
Boughton Ave DN15 150 F8
Boulevard HU3 145 B5
Boulevard Ave DN31 152 B4
Boulsworth Ave HU6 140 C7
Boulton Gr HU9 141 E2
Boundary Rd
Bridlington YO15 122 C1
Grimsby DN33 113 E7
Bourn Mill Balk Rd DN14 78 B8
Bourne St HU2 155 B3
Bournemouth St HU5 140 E2
Bournville DN14 149 C5
Bouthwaite Dr 13 YO26 129 E4
Bow Rd HU15 68 E6
Bow St YO15 122 D1
Bowers Ave DN34 152 B3
Bowes Ave YO31 130 E5
Bowfield Cl 9 DN37 102 B4
Bowlalley La HU1 155 B2
Bowland La YO42 38 E2
Bowland Way YO30 127 A1
Bowling Green Ct YO31 130 D8
Bowling Green La
4 Crowle DN17 94 D8
Grimsby DN32 152 E3
9 Hunmanby YO14 2 F8
York YO31 156 C4
Bowling Green Rd 4 DN21 117 A1
Bowling La DN35 153 E2
Bowman Way 26 DN40 87 B1
Bowmandale DN18 84 E8
Bowmandale Prim Sch DN18 84 E8
Bowness Dr YO30 126 E1
Bownhill La HU12 59 A2
Bowthorpe La YO8 50 B4
Bowyers Cl YO23 132 C4
Boyes La HU12 73 C4
Boynton Ave YO16 122 B4
Boynton Cres 4 DN15 83 A5
Boynton La DN14 64 A1
Boynton Sch YO16 10 E7
Boynton St 1 HU3 145 C4
Brabbs Ave 2 DN7 92 E4
Bracken Cl
Gainsborough DN21 117 A2
York YO32 127 F4
Bracken Heen Cl 4 DN7 92 D4
Bracken Hill
Skirlaugh HU11 45 E2
2 York YO10 131 C3
Bracken La YO25 32 A5
Bracken Pk 20 DN33 113 E8
Bracken Pl 4 DN37 102 B3
Bracken Rd
Great Driffield YO25 124 D3
York YO24 132 F7
Brackendale Cl 1 HU7 141 B4
Brackenhill Ave YO8 148 A4
Brackenhill La YO8 148 A3
Brackenhill Rd DN9 105 E2
Brackenhills YO26 12 F1
Brackenholmes Rd DN15 83 A2
Brackley Cl HU8 141 B2
Bracon DN9 94 F2
Bracon Cl DN9 94 E2
Bradford Ave
Cleethorpes DN35 103 C2
Kingston upon Hull HU9 142 E2
Bradford Rd 20 DN40 87 B1
Bradley Cres YO23 24 D6
Bradley Dr YO24 132 C8
Bradley La YO23 24 C5
Bradley Rd DN37 102 C1
Bradley St DN32 152 E4
Bradman Ct 3 DN32 153 A5
Bradwell Cl 3 DN18 84 E8
Braemar Ave HU6 140 B6
Braemar Ct YO25 34 C8
Braemar Rd DN35 103 C2
Braeside Gdns YO24 129 E3
Braeton La 5 DN33 113 F8
Braids Wlk HU10 143 B8
Brailsford Cres YO30 130 A8
Braithegayte YO19 37 F8
Braithwaite La DN7 92 A7
Bramar Rd 26 DN7 92 D4
Bramble Dene YO24 132 D7
Bramble Garth 4 HU17 136 F7
Bramble Hill HU17 136 E1
Bramble Way 15 DN35 103 C1
Brambles 8 YO8 48 B1
Brambles The 2 DN19 85 C8
Bramhall St DN35 153 C3
Bramham Ave YO26 129 A3
Bramham Gr YO26 129 A3
Bramham Rd YO26 129 A2
Bramley Ave YO8 49 B5
Bramley Cres 8 DN16 96 D1
Bramley Ct 10 DN21 117 C1
Bramley Garth YO31 131 B6
Bramley Gr 6 DN21 107 C3
Brampton Way DN35 103 B2
Bramwith La DN7 92 A6
Brandesburton CP Sch YO25 34 B2
Brandesburton Hospl YO25 34 B2
Brandesburton St HU3 145 B7
Brandon Ct 4 HU8 141 C1
Brandon Gr YO32 128 E3
Brandon Rd DN15 150 D6
Brandon Way 24 HU7 56 F6
Brandsby Gr
Kingston upon Hull HU9 142 E3
York YO31 127 E2
Brandsdale Cres YO10 131 D3
Brankwell Cres 21 DN17 96 C2
Bransdale Gr HU9 146 F8
Bransdale Rd DN16 151 D1
Bransholme Dr YO30 127 A2
Bransholme Rd HU7 57 B5
Brant Rd DN15 150 E6
Brantingham Cl 5 HU16 138 E6
Brantingham Rd HU15 68 C7
Brantingham Wlk HU5 139 C2
Branton Pl YO26 129 A3
Brats La LN8 120 B5
Bratt La YO42 29 E3
Bravener Ct YO30 12 B6
Bray Gate YO42 16 E2
Bray Rd YO10 133 F8
Brayton C of E Prim Sch YO8 148 A2
Brayton Cty Inf Sch YO8 148 A2
Brayton Cty Jun Sch YO8 148 A2
Brayton High Sch YO8 148 A3
Brayton La YO8 148 B1
Brazil St HU9 146 C8
Breamer La HU11 35 A2
Breary Cl YO24 129 F1
Breck La HU15 53 B3
Brecks La
Kirk Sandall DN3 92 A2
Strensall YO32 14 B7
York YO32 127 F4
Brecksfield YO30 126 C5
Breckstreet La YO42 39 C3
Brecon Dr 22 HU7 56 F6
Brecon St HU8 141 B1
Breeze La YO25 22 D1
Breezemount Ct 4 DN7 92 C6
Breighton Rd
Bubwith YO8 50 D6
Wressle YO8 50 C3
Bremerhaven Way 24 DN33 102 C2
Brendon Ave HU8 141 B3
Brent Ave HU8 142 B6
Brentwood Cl HU15 68 B6
Brentwood Cres YO10 131 C2
Brereton Ave DN35 153 C4
Brereton Cl HU17 136 E6
Bretherdale HU7 140 F6
Brethergate DN9 105 B2
Brett St YO16 122 C3
Bretton Ave DN14 149 F5
Bretton Cl 5 DN7 92 D3
Brewery Gdns DN17 94 D8
Brewery Rd DN17 94 D8
Brewster Ave 17 DN40 87 C1
Breydon Ct 4 DN15 82 B4
Brian Ave
Cleethorpes DN35 103 B2
Scunthorpe DN16 151 C1
Waltham DN37 113 D6
Briar Ave YO26 129 B4
Briar Cl 4 Newport HU15 52 F1
South Killingholme DN40 86 F3
Briar Cliffe YO8 148 A3
Briar Dr YO31 127 F2
Briar Garth YO25 124 D3
Briar La
4 Grimsby DN33 113 D8
Healing DN41 101 F5
Briar Way DN15 96 B7
Briarfield Rd HU5 139 F2
Briars La DN7 92 C7
Briars The HU13 143 E3
Briarsfield YO42 28 D4
Briarwood Cl YO8 61 F7
Brick Dike La HU20 54 C5
Brick Kiln Balk YO16 122 A1
Brick Kiln La YO8 62 D6
Brick La DN40 86 E5
Brick Lands La YO8 62 F4
Brick Rd HU12 88 F6
Brickenhole La DN10 116 C3
Brickhill La YO8 63 F4
Bricknell Ave HU5 139 E3
Bricknell Ave Sch HU5 139 F2
Bricknell Prim Sch HU5 139 F2
Brickyard La
Melton HU14 68 F4
Walkeringham DN10 116 B3
Wrawby DN20 98 C3
Bridge Cl Haxby YO32 127 C7
Kingston upon Hull HU9 146 D6
Bridge Cres DN14 64 C8
Bridge Gdns DN31 152 A5
Bridge Hill DN7 92 C6
Bridge La Cadney DN20 109 C6
5 Great Driffield YO25 124 F4
Horkstow DN18 83 F5
Pollington DN14 77 F6
Rawcliffe DN14 79 B8

Bridge La *continued*
York YO30 156 B4
Bridge Rd
Airmyn DN14 149 A8
Bishopthorpe YO23 132 F3
Broughton DN20 97 F5
South Cave HU15 53 F1
Bridge St
7 Bridlington YO15 122 E2
11 Brigg DN20 98 B2
Goole DN14 149 C3
Great Driffield YO25 124 E4
Pocklington YO42 29 A4
Thorne/Moorends DN8 93 A8
York YO1 156 B2
Bridgegate DN14 65 A7
Bridgegate Dr HU9 146 C6
Bridges Ct YO8 148 D6
Bridges La YO42 38 E4
Bridges Rd DN17 150 E3
Bridges The DN18 84 F8
Bridgeview Sch HU13 143 D1
Bridgewater Rd DN17 150 D4
Bridle Way 1 YO26 129 A3
Bridle Wlk YO8 148 C4
Bridlington & District Hospl YO16 122 B3
Bridlington Ave HU2 155 B4
Bridlington Balk YO25 34 A8
Bridlington Bay Rd YO16 10 E4
Bridlington Harbour Museum* YO15 122 F2
Bridlington Leisure World* YO15 122 F2
Bridlington New Pasture Lane Prim Sch YO16 122 B5
Bridlington Rd
Barmston YO25 22 F6
Brandesburton YO25 34 C3
Driffield YO25 125 A5
Flamborough YO15 4 F1
Hunmanby YO14 3 A7
Sledmere YO25 7 C4
1 Stamford Bridge YO41 15 D2
Ulrome YO25 23 A2
Wold Newton YO25 2 A4
Bridlington RUFC YO16 122 D3
Bridlington Sch YO16 122 C3
Bridlington Sports Ctr YO16 122 B4
Bridlington St YO14 2 F8
Bridlington Sta YO15 122 D2
Bridlington Town Football Club YO16 122 E4
Bridport Cl HU7 141 C7
Brier La YO8 64 A4
Briergate YO32 127 C7
Brierholme Carr Rd DN7 92 F5
Brierholme Cl DN7 92 F5
Brierholme Ings Rd DN7 92 F5
Brierley Cl 10 DN14 65 A7
Brigg Cty Prim Sch DN20 98 C2
Brigg Dr HU13 143 F3
Brigg La YO8 63 D5
Brigg Prep Sch DN20 98 C1
Brigg Rd
Barton-upon-Humber DN18 84 E5
Broughton DN20 97 F3
Cadney DN20 109 C7
Grasby LN7 111 A6
Hibaldstow DN20 108 F6
Messingham DN17 107 D7
North Kelsey LN7 110 A5
Scunthorpe DN15 151 C7
South Kelsey LN7 110 A1
Wrawby DN20 98 D3
Brigg Sta DN20 98 C1
Brigg Town Football Club DN20 98 C2
Briggate Dr DN17 107 D7
Briggs St YO31 130 C7
Brigham Gr HU9 142 B1
Brigham La YO25 21 E1
Brighowgate DN34 152 D2
Bright Cres 7 YO15 122 F3
Bright St
Kingston upon Hull HU8 146 B8
York YO26 129 F5
Brighton St HU3 145 A3
Brigsley Rd DN37 113 D6
Brimington Rd HU10 138 F2
Brimley HU17 136 C5
Brind La DN14 50 F2
Brindlegate 4 YO42 29 A4
Brindley St HU9 141 E2
Brindleys La DN14 50 F3
Brinkworth Terr 1 YO10 130 E3
Brisbane St HU3 145 D5
Bristol Rd
Kingston upon Hull HU5 144 C8
Scunthorpe DN17 150 C5
Britannia Cres 7 DN34 102 B3
Britannia Gdns 7 HU5 140 E2
Britannia Rd DN14 149 A2
Britannia Way DN14 149 B3
Britton Cl DN17 81 D3
Brixham Ct
5 Kingston upon Hull HU3 145 A5
Waltham DN33 113 E7
Brixton Cl HU8 141 E5
Broach La Heck DN14 62 D1
Kellington DN14 61 F3
Broach Rd Heck DN14 77 D8
Hensall DN14 62 C1
Broad Acres YO32 127 C7
Broad Balk YO17 6 A5
Broad Highway YO19 37 F8
Broad La
Appleton Roebuck YO23 36 A6
6 Beal DN14 61 D4
Catton YO41 27 C7
Cawood YO8 48 A6
Gilberdyke HU15 66 C8
Howden DN14 65 B6
Rufforth YO23 129 A2
Sykehouse DN14 78 B4
Wistow YO8 48 A5
Broad La Cl 5 HU16 139 B7
Broad Manor YO42 29 A3
Broad Oak
Kingston upon Hull HU11 142 D6
Sutton-on-the-Forest YO61 13 D8
Broad Oak La 18 YO32 13 E5
Broadacre Pk 1 HU15 68 D5
Broadacre Prim Sch HU7 56 F6
Broadacres
Carlton DN14 63 D3
Keyingham HU12 73 D4
Broadacres Ave DN14 63 D3
Broadacres Garth DN14 63 D3
Broadbent Gate Rd DN8 79 B1
Broadgate HU17 136 B1
Broadland Dr 4 HU9 142 A3
Broadlands YO19 38 A8
Broadlands Cl 38 DN7 92 D4
Broadley Ave HU10 143 D6
Broadley Cl 6 HU9 146 C7
Broadley Croft 3 HU15 68 D5
Broadley Way HU15 68 D5
Broadmanor
North Duffield YO8 50 A7
Pocklington YO42 29 A3
Broadstairs Cl 1 HU8 141 E7
Broadstone Cl HU7 141 C6
Broadstone Way YO30 126 E3
Broadwater Dr 34 DN7 92 D4
Broadway Goole DN14 149 D4
5 Grimsby DN34 102 B2
Hatfield DN7 92 C3
Hornsea HU18 134 D4
7 Keelby DN41 101 A5
York YO10 133 E8
Broadway Dr 9 HU9 142 A3
Broadway Gr 3 YO10 133 E8
Broadway Nook DN7 92 C3
Broadway The 8 HU9 142 A3
Broadway W YO10 133 D8
Brock Cl 1 DN33 102 E1
Brockenhurst Ave HU16 139 D6
Brockenhurst Rd 7 DN7 92 E4
Brockfield Pk Dr YO31 127 F2
Brockfield Rd YO31 127 E2
Brockle Bank Ct 9 HU12 58 C1
Brocklesby Cl 5 HU13 144 A3
Brocklesby Park Sch DN41 100 E4
Brocklesby Pl 11 DN34 102 C2
Brocklesby Rd
10 Grimsby DN34 102 C2
Scunthorpe DN17 150 F1
Ulceby DN39 100 B8
Brockley Cl HU8 141 E6
Brockton Cl HU3 144 F5
Broc-o-Bank 1 DN6 76 E2
Bromley St
Kingston upon Hull HU2 155 B4
2 York YO26 129 F5
Brompton Cl HU5 139 E2
Brompton Ct 4 HU3 140 D1
Brompton Rd YO30 130 A7
Bromwich Rd HU10 143 F8
Bronzegarth DN32 153 B1
Brook La DN20 98 A1
Brook St
Great Driffield YO25 124 F4
Hemswell DN21 119 A2
Kingston upon Hull HU2 155 A3
Selby YO8 148 C4
York YO31 156 B4
Brookdale Rd DN17 150 D2
Brooke Dr HU18 134 C2
Brooke St DN8 93 A8
Brookfield Cl
Carnaby YO16 10 E4
1 Kingston upon Hull HU7 56 F5
8 Thorne/Moorends DN8 93 A8
Brookfield Rd DN33 102 D1
Brookland Rd YO16 122 C4
Brooklands
2 Broughton DN20 97 E3
York YO10 131 D4
Brooklands Ave
Broughton DN20 97 D4
Cleethorpes DN35 103 D3
Brooklands Cl HU17 137 A6
Brooklands Pk HU16 139 A5
Brooklands Rd HU5 144 E8
Brooklyn Dr DN36 114 D8
Brooklyn St HU5 140 D3
Brookside 2 HU15 68 D6
Brookside Cl YO42 28 D3
Broom Gr DN16 151 B4
Broome Cl YO32 127 F5
Broome Way YO32 128 A5
Broomfield Way YO25 23 A6
Broomfleet Carr La HU15 67 B7
Broomfleet Sta HU15 67 B6
Broomhead Cl 5 HU7 141 E7
Broomhill Cl 23 WF11 61 A2
Broomhill Cres 25 WF11 61 A2
Broomhill Dr 26 WF11 61 A2
Broomhill Gr 19 WF11 61 A2
Broomhill Pl 22 WF11 61 A2
Broomhill Sq 24 WF11 61 A2
Broomhill Wlk 21 WF11 61 A2
Broompark Rd DN14 149 E6
Broomston La DN9 104 F1
Brosley Ave DN3 92 A4
Brough County Prim Sch HU15 68 C7
Brough Cty Prim Sch HU15 68 C6
Brough Rd HU15 54 A1
Brough St DN14 149 D5
Brougham Cl YO30 129 F8
Brougham St HU3 144 F7
Broughton Cl 3 HU9 142 A3
Broughton Inf Sch DN20 97 E3
Broughton Jun Sch DN20 97 E3
Broughton Way YO10 131 B4
Brow La DN14 65 E7
Brown Cow Rd YO8 63 C8
Brown Moor 22 YO41 15 D2
Brown St DN31 152 F7
Browney Croft YO10 156 C1
Browning Cl
3 Kingston upon Hull HU3 145 D8
Scunthorpe DN17 150 E2
Browning Rd 20 YO42 29 A3
Brownlow St YO31 156 C4
Brownmoor La YO61 13 B8
Browns La 15 DN8 93 A8
Browns Orch DN32 152 D2
Bruce Cl 6 DN20 97 D3
Bruce St DN15 150 F7
Brumby Comm La DN17 150 C3
Brumby Common Nature Reserve* DN17 150 C3
Brumby Comp Sch DN16 151 B5
Brumby Hall* DN17 150 F5
Brumby Hospl DN16 151 C4
Brumby House Dr DN16 151 A4
Brumby Jun Sch DN16 151 B4
Brumby Wood La DN15 150 D6
Brumby's Terr 4 HU9 146 D7
Brunel Cl 4 DN16 96 D2
Brunel Ct 12 YO26 129 F5
Brunslow Cl HU3 144 E5
Brunswick Ave HU2 155 A4
Brunswick Cl 2 YO32 14 C8
Brunswick Gr 5 HU13 143 E2
Brunswick St YO23 130 B1
Brunton Way DN36 114 A7
Bryan Mere 3 HU17 43 A2
Bryony Ct YO8 148 B2
Bubwith Cty Prim Sch YO8 50 D7
Buccaneer Way 16 HU15 68 C5
Buck Beck Way 12 DN36 103 B1
Buckingham Ave DN15 96 C7
Buckingham Prim Sch HU8 141 C1
Buckingham St
5 Kingston upon Hull HU8 141 C1
York YO1 156 B1
Buckingham St N DN15 150 F8
Buckingham St S DN15 150 F8
Buckland Cl 3 HU8 142 C7
Buckle Ct YO8 148 B7
Buckton Gate YO15 4 C3
Buddleia Cl DN41 101 F5
Bude Cl 2 DN36 114 A8
Bude Park Prim Sch HU7 56 F5
Bude Rd HU7 140 F8
Bugthorpe La
Bugthorpe YO41 16 D5
Kirby Underdale YO41 16 F5
Bugthorpe La Town E YO41 16 E5
Bull Alley La DN14 63 B3
Bull Balk YO41 27 E4
Bull Bank LN11 121 F7
Bull La Everingham YO42 40 C4
Huby YO61 13 B7
York YO10 130 F3
Bull Moor La YO60 15 A8
Bull Moor Rd DN7 93 A4
Bull Pasture HU15 53 F1
Buller St Grimsby DN32 153 A3
Selby YO8 148 B6
Bullfinch La 5 DN35 103 C1
Bullivant Rd DN7 92 E4
Bulmer La YO43 51 E8
Bulwick Ave DN33 113 E8
Bunkers Hill DN21 119 B1
Bunkers Hill Cl 11 DN36 114 D4
Burbage Ave HU8 141 C4
Burcom Ave 7 DN36 114 D8
Burcott Garth HU4 144 B3
Burdale Cl
Great Driffield YO25 124 D3
Kingston upon Hull HU9 142 B3
Burden Cl HU17 154 C4
Burden Rd HU17 154 C4
Burden St HU1 155 A2
Burdike Ave YO30 130 A8
Burdock Rd DN16 96 E2
Burdyke Inf Sch YO30 130 B8
Burgar Rd DN8 93 A7
Burgate
4 Barton-upon-Humber DN18 84 F8
North Newbald YO43 53 F7
Burgess Rd DN20 98 C2
Burghley Cl LN7 111 A3
Burghley Rd DN16 151 D4
Burke St DN15 151 A8
Burke St N DN15 151 A8
Burlands La YO26 24 F7
Burleigh St HU8 146 C8
Burley Ave 18 DN35 103 C2
Burlington Ave YO10 130 F4
Burlington Cres DN14 149 D4
Burlington Cty Jun Sch YO16 122 D5
Burlington Gdns YO16 122 D3
Burlington Rd HU8 141 D5
Burlyn Rd 3 YO14 3 A8
Burma Dr HU9 147 B8
Burma Rd DN16 151 F6
Burn Hall Cl YO8 62 D7
Burn La YO8 62 D6
Burn Rd DN15 150 C7
Burnaby Cl HU17 136 E6
Burnbutts La
Hutton Cranswick YO25 32 C7
Watton YO25 32 B6
Burnby Cl HU5 139 C2
Burnby Hall Gdns* YO42 29 A3
Burnby La YO42 29 A3
Burnet Dr 12 DN16 96 E2
Burnett's Yd LN7 111 C4
Burney Cl HU17 154 A4
Burnham Ave 4 HU12 73 A6
Burnham La DN39 85 E4
Burnham Rd
Barton-upon-Humber DN18 85 A6
Epworth DN9 105 E6
Kingston upon Hull HU4 144 B3
Owston Ferry DN9 106 A3
Scunthorpe DN15 150 D6
Burnham Reach 26 DN35 103 C1
Burnham Sq DN9 106 A3
Burnholme Ave YO31 131 B6
Burnholme Com Coll YO31 131 A5
Burnholme Dr YO31 131 A6
Burnholme Gr YO31 131 A5
Burniston Gr YO10 131 A4
Burniston Rd HU5 139 E2
Burns Cl 2 YO42 28 F4
Burns Ct YO24 132 B7
Burns Gr 31 DN33 102 D2
Burns St DN21 117 A1
Burnsall Dr YO26 129 E4
Burnsalls Rd 5 HU12 72 C7
Burnside DN20 97 D3
Burrill Ave YO30 130 B8
Burrill Dr 13 YO32 13 D5
Burrill La HU15 68 B8
Burrill Mews 2 HU5 139 E3
Burringham Rd DN17 150 B1
Burrs The HU15 68 B5
Bursall Sq HU12 89 C8
Bursar Prim Sch DN35 153 E2
Bursar St DN35 153 E2
Bursea La YO43 52 A5
Burslem St HU2 155 A4
Burstall Hill YO16 122 B5
Burstall La HU12 90 C5
Burstwick Prim Sch HU12 73 B6
Burton Agnes Balk YO25 9 F5
Burton Agnes Hall* YO25 10 A2
Burton Agnes Sch YO25 10 A1
Burton Ave YO30 130 B7
Burton Comm La LS25 61 A6
Burton Constable Hall* HU11 58 C7
Burton Fields Cl 12 YO41 15 D2
Burton Fields Rd 4 YO41 15 D2
Burton Fleming Rd
Rudston YO25 9 F8
Wold Newton YO25 2 B3
Burton Gates HU17 55 B8
Burton Gn YO30 130 B8
Burton La HU18 134 C2
Burton Pidsea Prim Sch HU12 59 D2
Burton Rd
Beverley HU17 136 C6
Flixborough DN15 82 B2
Burton Rd *continued*
Hornsea HU18 134 D4
Kilham YO25 9 C3
Kingston upon Hull HU16 138 F5
Roos HU12 59 F2
Burton Stone La YO30 156 A4
Burton upon Stather Cty Prim Sch DN15 82 B4
Burtree Ave YO30 126 B4
Burwell Dr DN33 102 D2
Bush Cl HU4 144 D3
Bushfield Rd DN16 151 B5
Bushfield Rd Inf Sch DN16 151 A5
Butcher La DN14 77 A6
Butcher Row HU17 154 A3
Butcher Terr YO23 130 C1
Butcher's La
Burton Fleming YO25 2 E3
Withernwick HU11 46 D3
Butchers Row HU11 35 A1
Butforth La DN19 85 E8
Butler Pl DN35 153 B3
Butlers La 23 YO15 5 A2
Butt Balk YO25 9 E1
Butt Fields La DN14 62 F1
Butt Hedge YO26 24 A5
Butt Hill 22 Haxby YO32 13 D5
Leconfield HU17 43 D6
Butt Hills* Riston HU11 45 C5
Routh HU17 44 F5
Wold Newton YO25 2 A3
Butt La Beverley HU17 154 A1
Laceby DN37 101 F2
North Cave HU15 53 E3
Nunburnholme YO42 29 E3
Snaith DN14 78 C8
Thwing YO25 9 A8
Tickton HU17 137 F8
Warter YO42 30 A5
Wold Newton YO25 2 A3
Buttacre La YO23 24 D2
Butter Mkt
10 Caistor LN7 111 B4
8 Snaith DN14 63 C1
Buttercrambe Rd YO41 15 C3
Buttercross Cl 3 DN41 101 E6
Buttercup Cl 1 HU9 146 D7
Butterfield Cl
2 Laceby DN37 101 F1
Snaith DN14 78 D8
Butterfly Gdns* DN35 103 D2
Butterfly La YO16 10 F5
Butterfly Mdws HU17 136 E6
Buttermere Cres 3 DN36 114 C8
Buttermere Ct 9 YO8 148 B6
Buttermere Dr YO30 126 E1
Buttermere Rd DN14 149 D5
Buttermere Way DN32 152 F4
Butters Cl 20 YO32 13 D5
Butterwick Cl 23 DN35 103 C2
Butterwick Rd
Foxholes YO17 1 B1
Langtoft YO25 8 C7
Messingham DN17 107 A7
Buttfield La DN14 65 A6
Buttfield Rd
Howden DN14 65 A6
Kingston upon Hull HU13 143 E1
Buttle La 3 DN14 63 C1
Butts Cl
Bridlington YO16 122 D4
19 Stamford Bridge YO41 15 D2
Butts Hill YO14 3 C6
Butts La YO25 19 E2
Butts Rd DN18 69 F1
Butts The HU20 55 A4
Byass Ave YO16 122 E4
Bycroft Rd DN21 117 B3
Bydales La HU12 74 B3
Byedales 4 YO15 4 D3
Byfield Rd DN17 150 D2
Bygot Cl 1 HU17 43 D6
Byland Ave YO31 130 E8
Byland Ct 4 HU9 146 E8
Byram Park Rd WF11 61 A4
Byrd Rd DN16 151 E2
Byron Ave 3 DN6 76 E1
Byron Cl DN17 150 E2
Byron Dr YO30 129 F8
Byron Gr DN33 102 E2
Byron St Goole DN14 149 C5
Kingston upon Hull HU8 141 D2
Bywood Pl 5 DN37 102 B3

C

Cabourne Rd 34 DN33 102 D2
Caddle Rd 9 DN41 101 A4
Cadeby Medieval Village* DN36 120 F6
Cadeleigh Cl HU7 141 A8
Cadman Rd YO16 123 A7
Cadney Rd Bigby DN20 98 C1
Cadney DN20 109 C8
Cadney LN7 109 F6
Caedmon Cl YO31 131 A7
Caenby Rd
14 Cleethorpes DN35 103 C2
Scunthorpe DN17 150 E1
Cairnborrow 4 YO24 132 B7
Caistor Ave DN16 96 D2
Caistor By-Pass LN7 111 B3

Caistor Dr DN33 102 D2
Caistor Joint C of E & Methodist Prim Sch LN7 111 B4
Caistor Rd
Barton-upon-Humber DN18 85 A7
Laceby DN37 112 E8
Nettleton LN7 111 A3
North Kelsey LN7 110 D4
Rothwell LN7 111 E2
South Kelsey LN7 110 A1
Swallow LN7 112 A5
Caistor Yarborough Sch LN7 111 C4
Caithness Cl 1 YO30 126 E3
Calais Croft 7 HU17 43 A2
Calam Villas YO25 35 C5
Caldane HU6 139 E8
Caldbeck Cl 1 YO30 127 A1
Caldberg Mews 3 HU5 139 E3
Calder Ave YO26 129 B8
Calder Cl 35 DN40 87 B1
Calder Cres DN14 77 F6
Calder Gn DN17 107 D7
Calder Gr HU8 142 C6
Calder Rd DN16 151 D2
Calder St 4 DN14 149 D4
Calderdale HU7 140 F6
Calderdale Cl 2 YO16 123 A7
Caledon Cl HU9 142 D5
Caledonia Pk HU9 146 B5
Calf Cl YO32 127 D8
Callas 6 HU17 43 A2
Calver Cres DN37 102 B4
Calvert Cl YO32 127 C7
Calvert La HU4 144 D7
Calvert Rd HU5 144 D8
Calvi Ct 2 DN32 153 A5
Cam Gr HU8 142 C6
Camargue Ave DN37 113 E7
Cambeak Cl 3 HU7 56 F5
Camberwell Way HU8 142 A5
Camblesforth CP Sch YO8 63 C4
Camborne Gr HU8 141 B3
Cambrian Cl 2 YO32 127 F3
Cambrian Way 2 DN36 114 A6
Cambridge Ave
Goole DN14 149 B5
Scunthorpe DN16 96 D2
Cambridge Gr HU9 141 F1
Cambridge Park Sch DN34 152 A1
Cambridge Rd
Grimsby DN34 152 A1
Kingston upon Hull HU13 143 F3
Scunthorpe DN16 151 C2
Cambridge St
Bridlington YO16 122 D3
Cleethorpes DN35 153 F2
Kingston upon Hull HU1 155 A2
4 York YO24 130 A3
Camden St 1 HU3 145 B5
Camela La YO8 63 B6
Camelford Cl 12 HU7 56 F5
Camellia Cl YO25 124 D3
Cameron Gr YO23 130 C1
Camerton Gr HU9 141 F2
Camilla Cl HU9 155 C1
Camm La DN14 63 C3
Cammidge St 2 HU19 74 F7
Camp The (Earthworks)* YO11 2 C7
Campbell Ave
26 Scunthorpe DN16 96 D2
York YO24 129 E2
Campbell Ct HU9 142 A2
Campbell St 3 DN21 117 A1
Campbells Farm Ave DN15 95 E6
Campden Cres DN35 153 D3
Camperdown HU11 142 D6
Campey La YO42 39 B6
Campion Ave HU4 144 B2
Campions Cl 12 DN36 114 A5
Campions' La 6 DN36 114 B1
Campleshon Rd YO23 130 B1
Campsall Balk DN6 76 E1
Campsall Hall Rd 12 DN6 76 E1
Campsall Park Rd 11 DN6 76 E1
Campsmount Sch DN6 76 D1
Canada Dr
Cherry Burton HU17 43 A5
Kingston upon Hull HU16 138 E5
Canada La LN7 111 C4
Canal Garth DN14 77 F6
Canal La
Barmby Moor YO42 28 F3
West Stockwith DN10 116 E5
Canal Rd
Cottingwith YO42 38 C5
Selby YO8 148 D4
Canal Side E HU15 52 E3
Canal Side W HU15 52 E2
Canal View Selby YO8 148 D3
2 Thorne/Moorends DN8 93 A7
Canberra Ave DN7 104 A8
Canberra St HU3 145 D5
Candlesby Rd 4 DN37 102 B4
Candy Bank DN9 104 B5
Canham Gr YO10 131 D3
Canham La YO25 35 C5
Canning St HU1 155 A2
Cannon Hall La DN14 61 F1
Cannon Oakes Ct DN36 114 B7
Cannon St HU2 155 B4
Canon Lee Sch YO30 130 A8
Canongate HU16 139 B7
Canterbury Cl
Beverley HU17 136 D1
9 Haxby YO32 13 D5
Scunthorpe DN17 150 D3
Canterbury Dr
Grimsby DN34 152 C2
2 Kingston upon Hull HU8 141 E7
Canterbury Rd 21 DN7 92 D4
Canton Villas 5 YO15 122 F4
Canty Nook DN38 110 E7
Capstan Rd HU6 140 C8
Capstan St DN14 149 C2
Capstan Way 13 DN8 93 A8
Carbis Cl 5 DN36 114 A8
Carden Ave HU9 142 C2
Cardiff Ave DN36 114 A7
Cardigan Rd
Bridlington YO15 122 D1
Kingston upon Hull HU3 144 E6
Cardinal Ct 1 DN37 113 D7
Cardinals Cl 3 YO8 48 B8
Carentan Cl 6 YO8 148 B6
Carew St HU3 144 F7
Carey St YO10 130 D1
Carisbrooke Ave HU16 139 B6
Carisbrooke Cl 9 DN36 114 A8
Carisbrooke Manor La DN17 150 A1
Carl St YO23 130 C2
Carlam La HU7 57 A7
Carleton St 17 YO26 129 F5
Carlisle Rd 8 YO15 122 F3
Carlisle St
30 Gainsborough DN21 117 B1
Goole DN14 149 D4
16 York YO26 129 F5
Carlton Ave
Healing DN41 101 F5
Hornsea HU18 134 C5
York YO10 131 B3
Carlton Cl
Eggborough DN14 61 F1
22 Humberston DN35 103 D1
Carlton Ct HU17 154 A3
Carlton Dr HU11 47 B1
Carlton La HU11 47 B1
Carlton Rd
Aldbrough HU11 46 F1
Grimsby DN34 152 B2
5 Healing DN41 101 F5
Sutton upon Derwent YO41 27 C1
Carlton Rise 2 HU17 55 F8
Carlton St
Bridlington YO16 122 D3
Kingston upon Hull HU3 144 F4
Scunthorpe DN15 151 B7
Carlton Twrs* DN14 63 D2
Carlton-in-Snaith CP Sch DN14 63 C3
Carmelite St YO1 156 C2
Carmen Cres 1 DN36 114 A6
Carmires Ave YO32 13 F5
Carnaby Ave YO16 122 B2
Carnaby Cl HU17 43 D6
Carnaby Gr
Grimsby DN32 153 A1
Kingston upon Hull HU6 139 E5
Carnaby Ind Est YO15 10 E3
Carnegie St 6 HU3 145 A6
Carnforth Cres DN34 152 A1
Carnot St YO26 129 F5
Carnoustie 13 DN37 113 D6
Carnoustie Cl
Kingston upon Hull HU8 141 C3
1 York YO26 129 B4
Carol Dickson Ct 9 HU3 145 C5
Caroline Cl 5 YO24 129 F3
Caroline Pl HU2 155 B3
Caroline St HU2 155 B4
Carolines Pl HU16 138 B8
Carperby Mews 6 HU5 139 D3
Carr Cl Beverley HU17 154 C3
13 Hemingbrough YO8 49 F1
Carr Dike La HU15 67 C7
Carr Dyke Bank DN17 106 D5
Carr Dyke Rd DN17 95 D3
Carr Inf Sch YO26 129 C5
Carr Jun Sch YO26 129 C5
Carr La Appleby DN15 83 D2
Barlby with Osgodby YO8 148 F5
Barlow YO8 63 C7
Blyton DN21 117 A5
Bonby DN20 84 B1
Broughton DN20 97 F3
Burton Pidsea HU12 59 D1
Burton upon Stather DN15 82 D4
Eastrington DN14 51 F1
Escrick YO19 37 B5
Everingham YO42 40 A4
Garthorpe & Fockerby DN17 81 E4
Goole DN14 149 D6
Grimsby DN32 153 B3
Haxey DN9 105 E2
Healing DN41 101 F4
Hibaldstow DN20 109 A6
Horkstow DN18 83 F4
Carr La *continued*
Hotham YO43 53 A4
Kingston upon Hull HU10 138 D1
Kingston upon Hull HU1 155 A2
Laxton DN14 65 F4
Leven HU17 44 E8
Long Drax YO8 63 F6
Luddington & Haldenby DN17 81 C1
Misterton DN10 116 C5
Nafferton YO25 21 C4
Newport HU15 52 E2
Newton on Derwent YO41 27 F4
Pocklington YO42 40 A8
Redbourne DN21 108 F3
Riston HU11 45 B5
Seaton Ross YO42 39 E4
Snaith & Cowick DN14 78 C7
Stallingborough DN41 101 E7
Tickton HU17 137 E3
Tickton HU17 137 E8
Ulceby DN39 86 B3
Watton YO25 33 A4
West Butterwick DN17 106 C8
Wildsworth DN21 117 C8
Winterton DN15 83 D6
Wistow YO8 48 A3
Worlaby DN20 98 A7
York YO26 129 D5
Carr Lane Infants Sch HU10 138 E1
Carr Lane Jun Sch HU10 138 E1
Carr Rd
Burton Pidsea HU12 59 D1
Molescroft HU17 136 E8
North Kelsey LN7 109 E4
Carr Side La DN7 92 E2
Carr St
Kingston upon Hull HU2 155 B4
Selby YO8 148 F4
Carrbank La YO32 14 E3
Carrfield YO24 132 C8
Carrfields DN14 149 D6
Carrhouse Rd DN9 94 D1
Carrick Gdns YO24 129 E3
Carrington Ave
Hornsea HU18 134 C6
Kingston upon Hull HU16 139 B6
1 York YO26 129 E5
Carrington Dr
20 Humberston DN36 103 D1
Humberston DN36 114 D8
Carrington St 6 HU3 145 B5
Carrnock Ct 3 YO32 127 F1
Carroll Pl HU1 155 C3
Carron Cres YO24 132 B7
Carroway Cl 4 YO16 123 A7
Carrs Mdw Escrick YO19 37 B5
Withernsea HU19 74 F6
Carrside 5 DN9 105 D7
Carson Ave DN34 152 B2
Carson Rd DN21 117 B1
Carter Ave YO31 130 F5
Carter Dr HU17 136 E7
Carter La YO15 5 A2
Carter St DN14 149 C4
Cartergate DN31 152 D3
Cartledge Ave DN32 153 B2
Cartmel Gr DN32 153 B2
Cartwright La HU17 154 A1
Carver Rd DN40 87 C1
Cary La 5 DN20 98 B2
Cassbrook Dr LN11 121 E8
Casson's Rd 1 DN8 93 A8
Casswell Cl 4 DN32 153 A5
Casswell Cres LN11 121 E8
Castella Dr DN16 151 D7
Castle Cl Cawood YO8 48 A8
1 Haxby YO32 13 D5
3 Leconfield HU17 43 D6
Castle Cres 16 YO15 5 A2
Castle Ct 9 DN18 84 F8
Castle Dr
1 Epworth DN9 105 E6
South Cave HU15 53 F2
Castle Earthworks* YO8 63 F4
Castle Gn HU16 138 E6
Castle Hill Caistor LN7 111 B4
8 Hunmanby YO14 2 F8
Owston Ferry DN9 106 A3
Castle Hill Hospl HU16 138 D5
Castle Hill La YO8 63 F5
Castle Hills* DN21 117 C2
Castle Keep DN20 108 F6
Castle Pk 9 HU11 47 C1
Castle Rd HU16 138 D5
Castle Rise 1 HU15 54 A2
Castle St Grimsby DN32 153 A4
Kingston upon Hull HU1 155 A1
Castle View YO25 23 A1
Castle Way HU13 69 F4
Castledyke Prim Sch DN18 69 E1
Castledyke S 10 DN18 84 F8
Castledyke W 10 DN18 69 E1
Castleford Ave 2 DN34 102 D2
Castleford Gr HU9 142 E2
Castlegate YO1 156 B2
Castlehill Rd HU7 141 D8
Castlehills Com Arts Coll DN21 117 B1
Castleton Ave 6 HU5 139 E3
Castleton Rd DN15 150 B6
Cat La Balne DN14 77 E5
Bilbrough YO23 24 D1
Upper Poppleton YO26 24 D8
Catford Cl HU8 141 E5
Catfoss Rd YO25 35 A4
Cathcart Cl DN14 76 F7
Cathedral Cl 8 HU17 136 E1
Cathedral Ct
Hatfield DN7 92 C2
Scunthorpe DN16 151 A2
Catherine Gr 6 DN20 97 E3
Catherine St
13 Barton-upon-Humber DN18 69 F1
Grimsby DN32 152 E3
Kingston upon Hull HU2 155 B4
Catkin Rd DN16 96 D1
Catterick Mews 8 HU5 139 D3
Catterton La LS24 24 A1
Cattle Rd DN10 116 A5
Catton La YO42 28 F4
Catwick Heads HU11 45 E8
Catwick La
Brandesburton YO25 34 C2
Catwick HU17 45 D8
Riston HU11 45 C6
Caughey St HU3 145 D7
Causeway Ings La HU12 73 E7
Causewy The HU17 154 B3
Cave Cres HU16 138 E5
Cave Rd HU15 68 B6
Cave St HU5 140 D1
Cave Terr 1 HU5 140 D1
Cavendish Cl 14 DN35 103 D1
Cavendish Dr 2 HU17 136 E1
Cavendish Gr YO10 131 D3
Cavendish Pk 8 HU15 68 C5
Cavendish Prim Sch HU8 141 E4
Cavendish Rd
Kingston upon Hull HU8 141 D5
9 Scunthorpe DN16 96 D2
Cavendish Sq HU3 140 D1
Cavendish Way DN32 152 F3
Cave's La DN10 116 B3
Cavill Dr 12 DN14 65 B7
Cavill Pl HU3 145 D5
Cawood C of E Prim Sch YO8 48 B8
Cawood Cl HU11 45 D2
Cawood Cres HU11 45 D2
Cawood Dr HU11 45 D2
Cawood Rd
Stillingfleet YO19 36 D3
Wistow YO8 48 C7
Cawthorne Dr HU4 144 C3
Caxton Ave YO26 129 D6
Cayley Cl YO30 126 F1
Cayley Rd HU10 143 F6
Cayton Rd HU8 141 D4
Cecil Cl 10 DN21 107 C3
Cecil Rd 7 YO14 3 A8
Cecil St
25 Gainsborough DN21 117 B1
Goole DN14 149 E4
Kingston upon Hull HU3 144 F5
Cecile Cres DN15 150 E7
Cecilia Pl 3 YO24 130 A3
Cedar Ave
Flixborough DN15 96 A7
Kingston upon Hull HU16 139 A6
Stainforth DN7 92 D6
Cedar Cl
11 Cleethorpes DN35 103 B1
Gainsborough DN21 117 A2
Hambleton YO8 48 B1
Hornsea HU18 134 D1
Kingston upon Hull HU10 143 D7
Scawby DN20 108 F8
7 Scotter DN21 107 C3
Cedar Cres YO8 48 D2
Cedar Ct
Bridlington YO16 123 A8
8 Hedon HU12 72 C7
Cedar Dr 2 DN40 87 C2
Cedar Glade YO19 26 E7
Cedar Gr
2 Aldbrough HU11 47 C1
York YO31 131 B7
Cedar Gr The HU17 136 C6
Cedar Rd 2 DN8 79 B1
Cedarwood 5 HU15 66 D7
Cedarwood Cl 8 YO24 129 B1
Cedarwood Dr HU4 144 B7
Cedric Rd DN3 92 A1
Celandine Cl 8 HU5 139 D1
Celery Bank DN14 66 A4
Celtic Cl YO26 129 B5
Cemetery Cres 7 DN37 101 F1
Cemetery La
North Kelsey LN7 110 A5
Pocklington YO42 29 A3
Cemetery Rd
Hatfield DN7 92 F4
Laceby DN37 101 F1
Scunthorpe DN16 151 B5
Winterton DN15 83 B5
York YO10 156 C1
Centenary Rd DN14 149 B5
Central Ave
Beverley HU17 154 A2
Ulrome YO25 23 B3
Central Par DN34 152 A3
Central Prom DN35 153 F2
Central St HU2 140 F1
Central Way DN16 151 D6
Centurion Way
Brough HU15 68 C5
Clifton YO30 127 B3
Centurion Wlk YO43 135 E4
Century Rd HU12 72 A8
Ceylon St HU9 147 C7
Chadcourt HU6 139 E6
Chadwell Springs DN37 113 C6
Chaffinch Cl DN15 96 B7
Chaffinch Dr 14 DN35 103 C1
Chaldon Cl 4 YO32 14 A6
Chalfont Cl HU13 143 D2
Chalfonts YO24 129 F1
Chaloner's Cres YO24 132 D7
Chaloner's Rd YO24 132 D8
Chamberlain Cl HU7 141 D6
Chamberlain Ct HU7 141 D7
Chamberlain Gdns HU8 141 C3
Chamberlain Rd HU8 141 B3
Chamberlain St HU7 141 D6
Chambers La 1 HU18 134 C4
Chamomile Cl DN16 96 E2
Champney Rd HU17 154 A2
Chancel Rd DN16 96 D2
Chancel Wlk 8 DN20 97 E3
Chancery Ct YO24 129 C3
Chancery La 2 DN17 94 D7
Chandlers Cl 2 DN36 114 A7
Chandos Rd DN17 150 F3
Channel Rd HU12 89 B6
Chanterlands Ave HU5 140 A1
Chantreys Dr 13 HU15 68 C6
Chantry Ave 14 YO26 12 F1
Chantry Cl
Grimsby DN31 152 C3
York YO24 132 C8
Chantry Gap 11 YO26 12 F1
Chantry Gr 13 YO26 12 F1
Chantry La
Beverley HU17 154 B2
Bishopthorpe YO23 133 B4
Etton HU17 43 A6
Grimsby DN31 152 C3
Rimswell HU12 74 C5
Chantry Mdws 1 YO25 9 C3
Chantry Way 13 HU14 69 B7
Chantry Way E 9 HU14 69 B7
Chapel Balk Rd YO8 49 F1
Chapel Cl
Barrow upon Humber DN19 85 D7
7 Misterton DN10 116 C5
Rawcliffe DN14 64 A1
Skidby HU16 138 A8
Skirlaugh HU11 45 E2
4 Westwoodside DN9 105 B2
Chapel Cnr YO43 135 D4
Chapel Ct DN15 82 C8
Chapel Field Rd DN19 86 B7
Chapel Fields YO43 40 A1
Chapel Fields Rd YO26 129 A3
Chapel Garth
Broomfleet HU15 67 B5
11 Gilberdyke HU15 66 D8
Ottringham HU12 73 E3
Skipsea YO25 23 A1
3 Tetney DN36 114 D4
Chapel Haddlesey C of E Prim Sch YO8 62 B5
Chapel Hill 1 HU15 68 E6
Chapel Hill La HU15 68 E6
Chapel Hill Rd YO42 29 A4
Chapel La
Ashby cum Fenby DN37 113 D3
Askham Bryan YO23 24 F3
Barmston YO25 23 A6
Barnoldby le Beck DN37 113 B6
14 Barton-upon-Humber DN18 69 E1
Brayton YO8 148 B1
Broughton DN20 97 E3
Elsham DN20 98 F7
10 Gainsborough DN21 117 A2
Habrough DN40 100 E8
Horkstow DN18 84 A5
Keadby with Althorpe DN17 95 C6
13 Keyingham HU12 73 C4
Kilham YO25 9 B3
Kingston upon Hull HU10 69 C8
Kingston upon Hull HU1 155 C2
Langtoft YO25 8 D5
Laxton DN14 65 F4
Little Smeaton WF8 76 B3
Ludborough DN36 121 B6
Middleton YO25 31 C4
8 Misterton DN10 116 C5
Northorpe DN21 118 D8
Ottringham HU12 73 E3
Rawcliffe DN14 64 A2
Reighton YO14 3 E5
3 Riccall YO19 37 A1
Scawby DN20 108 E8
Skeffling HU12 90 C6
Swallow LN7 112 B5
Sykehouse DN14 78 A4
18 Thorne/Moorends DN8 93 A8
Utterby LN11 121 C4
1 Wawne HU7 56 E7

Chapel La *continued*
West/East Butterwick DN17 95 D1
Whitton DN15 67 E3
Winterton DN15 83 A5
Wrawby DN20 98 D4
Chapel La Staith HU1 155 C2
Chapel Mdws 8 HU15 66 D8
Chapel Mews 3 HU15 68 C6
Chapel Rd
Broughton DN20 97 E3
Habrough DN40 100 E8
Tetney DN36 114 D4
Chapel Row YO10 156 C1
Chapel St
2 Amcotts DN17 81 F1
Barmby Moor YO42 28 D3
Bridlington YO15 122 E2
13 Caistor LN7 111 B4
5 Crowle DN17 94 D8
6 Epworth DN9 105 E6
6 Flamborough YO15 5 A2
Goole DN14 149 D3
Goxhill DN19 86 A8
Hillam LS25 61 B7
Kingston upon Hull HU1 155 A2
Lockington YO25 32 B2
North Kelsey LN7 110 A4
Scunthorpe DN15 151 B7
Chapel Way 20 DN20 98 C2
Chapel Wlk 4 YO19 37 A1
Chapelry Garth 28 HU12 72 D7
Chapman Ave DN17 150 D2
Chapman Cl 1 YO32 14 C8
Chapman Ct DN31 152 D4
Chapman Gr DN35 153 F1
Chapman Rd DN35 153 D3
Chapman St HU8 155 C4
Chapmans Ct YO24 132 D6
Chapman's La YO30 12 E7
Chapter House St YO1 156 B3
Chapter Wk DN20 97 E3
Chariot St HU1 155 A2
Charles Ave
Grimsby DN33 102 E1
Laceby DN37 101 E1
17 New Waltham DN36 114 A7
11 Scotter DN21 107 C3
Charles Ct 7 DN8 79 B1
Charles Dr DN14 149 B6
Charles Lovell Way DN17 150 D4
Charles Moor YO31 130 F7
Charles St
Cleethorpes DN35 153 F1
31 Gainsborough DN21 117 B1
22 Hedon HU12 72 D7
Kingston upon Hull HU2 155 B3
Selby YO8 148 B6
Charles Wesley Dr YO8 148 B2
Charlestown Way HU9 146 C6
Charlotte St HU1 155 C3
Charlotte St Mews HU1 155 B3
Charlton St
Grimsby DN31 152 C4
York YO23 130 C2
Charnock Ave HU9 142 A4
Charter Ave DN14 64 A1
Charterfield HU11 142 D6
Charterhouse Dr 3 DN16 96 E2
Charterhouse La HU2 155 B3
Charterhouse The* HU2 155 C3
Charter's La 4 YO25 34 B2
Charters The YO8 49 B5
Chase Hill Rd DN40 86 E5
Chase Side Ct YO24 132 E8
Chase The
Driffield YO25 125 A4
2 Snaith DN14 78 C8
Chatham St HU3 144 F7
Chatsworth Cl
Beverley HU17 154 A1
5 Bridlington YO16 122 D6
Chatsworth Dr
Goole DN14 149 B6
16 Haxby YO32 13 F5
Chatsworth Pl 1 DN35 103 B2
Chatsworth St HU5 145 B8
Chatsworth Terr 4 YO26 129 E4
Chatterton Cres DN15 96 D7
Chaucer Ave DN17 150 D3
Chaucer St
Kingston upon Hull HU8 141 C2
7 York YO10 130 E3
Chaumont Way 1 YO32 14 D2
Chaytor Cl 16 HU12 72 D6
Cheadle Cl HU2 155 A4
Cheapside
Kingston upon Hull HU8 155 C4
Waltham DN37 113 E5
Cheapside Rd DN37 113 F4
Cheapsides La HU15 66 D8
Checker La YO19 49 A7
Cheesemans Cl 9 DN37 113 E6
Cheesemans La 8 DN37 113 E6
Chelkar Way YO30 126 F1
Chellsway HU19 74 F6
Chelmer Rd HU8 142 B5
Chelmsford Ave DN34 152 A1
Chelmsford Cl 6 HU9 142 E1
Chelmsford Pl DN34 152 B2
Chelsea Cl HU8 141 F5
Chelsea Ct 3 HU16 138 F5
Chelsea Wlk 1 DN35 103 D1
Cheltenham Ave HU7 141 A8
Cheltenham Cl 8 DN16 96 E2
Cheltenham Way DN35 103 C1
Chelwood Dr 30 DN33 102 D2
Chelwood Rd DN17 150 F3
Chelwood Wlk 12 YO26 129 E4
Chepstow Gr DN34 152 A1
Cheriton Cl 14 HU7 56 F5
Cherry Burton C of E Sch HU17 43 B5
Cherry Cl
Great Driffield YO25 124 F2
Hornsea HU18 134 D1
Cherry Cobb Sands Rd HU12 87 F8
Cherry Cres YO43 40 A1
Cherry Ct 16 HU15 66 D8
Cherry Dale 11 DN35 103 B2
Cherry Dr
Holme-on-Spalding-Moor YO43 40 A1
Nafferton YO25 125 F6
Cherry Garth
Beverley HU17 154 C3
Kingston upon Hull HU3 145 A5
Lund YO25 31 F2
York YO31 131 B5
Cherry Gr 5 Belton DN9 94 E1
Belton DN9 105 E8
10 Poppleton YO26 12 F1
Scunthorpe DN16 151 B2
Cherry Hill La YO23 156 B1
Cherry Hill Pk HU12 74 B8
Cherry Holt 7 LN7 111 B4
Cherry La
Barrow upon Humber DN19 85 D8
Kingston upon Hull HU8 141 C4
Wootton DN39 85 E2
York YO24 132 F8
Cherry Mount 1 DN16 96 E2
Cherry Orch
10 Epworth DN9 105 E6
2 Haxby YO32 127 D8
Cherry Orch Mews 12 YO42 29 A4
Cherry Paddock
4 Haxby YO32 127 D8
Kexby YO41 15 C2
Cherry Rd 4 YO14 3 A8
Cherry St YO23 156 B1
Cherry Tree Ave
1 Brigg DN20 98 B2
Kingston upon Hull HU8 141 C2
Newton-on-Ouse YO30 12 B6
9 Withernsea HU19 75 A6
York YO32 127 D4
Cherry Tree Cl
Bilton HU11 58 A3
18 Brayton YO8 48 D1
Cherry Tree Cres DN34 102 C4
Cherry Tree Dr
Hatfield DN7 92 D5
3 Thorne/Moorends DN8 79 A1
Cherry Tree Gr DN7 92 C5
Cherry Tree La
Beverley HU17 154 B3
31 Hedon HU12 72 D7
Cherry Tree Rd 18 DN21 117 C1
Cherry Tree Terr HU17 154 C3
Cherry Tree Wlk 7 YO8 49 B4
Cherry Trees HU16 138 A7
Cherry Way Messingham DN17 107 D7
Nafferton YO25 125 F6
Cherry Wood Cres YO19 133 E5
Chesham Gr DN14 149 B6
Cheshire Ave YO32 14 A6
Cheshire Cl HU5 139 D1
Chesney Dr DN16 96 D2
Chesney Fields 4 YO24 129 D1
Chesnut Ave HU5 140 C2
Chesnut Way DN19 86 A8
Chessingham Gdns YO24 132 E6
Chessingham Pk YO19 26 F6
Chesswick Ave DN17 95 D5
Chesswick Cres DN17 95 D5
Chester Ave
3 Beverley HU17 55 F8
Beverley HU17 136 E1
Chester Ct Rd YO8 63 A6
Chester Grange DN33 102 F1
Chester Pl DN35 153 C1
Chester Rd HU5 139 B1
Chesterfield Rd DN15 150 B6
Chesterholme HU11 142 E6
Chestnut Ave
2 Airmyn DN14 64 E4
Beverley HU17 136 F6
15 Gainsborough DN21 117 B1
Goole DN14 149 B3
Great Driffield YO25 124 F2
Hedon HU12 72 C8
10 Hemingbrough YO8 49 F1
Immingham DN40 87 D2
Chestnut Ave *continued*
Kingston upon Hull HU13 143 E1
Kingston upon Hull HU10 143 E8
Stainforth DN7 92 D6
5 Thorne/Moorends DN8 93 B7
2 Thorngumbald HU12 72 E5
Withernsea HU19 75 A5
York YO31 130 F6
Chestnut Cl
Beverley HU17 136 F6
Bridlington YO15 123 B7
6 Burstwick HU12 73 A6
4 Scotter DN21 107 C3
Snaith DN14 78 B8
17 Waltham DN37 113 D6
Chestnut Cres YO43 40 A1
Chestnut Croft 7 YO8 49 F1
Chestnut Ct 9 YO8 49 F1
Chestnut Dr
15 Gilberdyke HU15 66 D8
8 Hemingbrough YO8 49 F1
Holme-on-Spalding-Moor YO43 40 A1
Messingham DN17 107 D7
Chestnut Garth
Burton Pidsea HU12 59 C2
4 Hemingbrough YO8 49 F1
Roos HU12 60 A1
Chestnut Gr
5 Broughton DN20 97 E4
Kingston upon Hull HU8 141 B2
Sproatley HU11 58 D5
York YO26 129 C4
Chestnut Mews YO8 48 A8
Chestnut Pk YO41 28 C8
Chestnut Rd
Cawood YO8 48 A8
Waltham DN37 113 D6
Chestnut Rise
Barrow upon Humber DN19 85 C8
6 Hemingbrough YO8 49 F1
Chestnut View YO42 29 B3
Chestnut Way DN16 151 B3
Chestnut Wlk DN41 102 A5
Chestnuts The
6 Haxby YO32 127 C8
Hensall DN14 62 D2
Cheverton Ave 15 HU19 75 A6
Cheviot Ave DN14 149 D5
Cheviot Cl
3 Thorne/Moorends DN8 93 A7
1 York YO32 127 F3
Cheviotdale HU7 140 F6
Chevy Chase HU11 142 E6
Cheyne Garth HU18 134 A4
Cheyne Wlk HU18 134 A4
Chichester Dr 19 LN7 111 B4
Chichester Rd DN35 103 C2
Chiltern Cres DN17 150 D4
Chiltern Dr 19 DN37 113 D6
Chiltern Prim Sch HU3 145 B5
Chiltern Rd DN14 149 D5
Chiltern Way
26 Grimsby DN33 113 E8
York YO32 127 F5
Chilterns The HU9 142 D2
Chilton Cl 19 DN40 87 B1
Chilton Rise HU10 138 B1
Chilvers Ct 4 YO8 148 A1
Chimes Rd YO8 148 C6
Chimney Field Rd HU12 74 B6
Chingford Ave 1 DN34 102 D2
Chippendale Cl 2 DN36 114 D8
Chiswick Cl 3 HU8 142 A5
Cholmley St HU3 145 B5
Christine Pl 4 DN33 113 F8
Chrystals Rd HU18 134 D5
Chrystals Wlk HU18 134 D5
Chudleigh Rd 1 YO26 129 F5
Church Acres DN14 65 D1
Church Ave
Humberston DN36 114 C8
6 North Ferriby HU14 69 A4
Church Balk
Dunnington YO19 26 E7
Thorne/Moorends DN8 93 B8
Church Cl
Askham Bryan YO23 24 F3
Bonby DN20 84 C2
Bridlington YO16 122 D4
4 Bubwith YO8 50 D7
25 Flamborough YO15 5 A2
Goole DN14 149 E2
Grimsby DN32 153 B1
Kingston upon Hull HU7 141 D6
Laxton DN14 65 F4
1 Market Weighton YO43 135 D4
8 Thorne/Moorends DN8 93 B8
Wheldrake YO19 38 A7
Church Cres
Owston Ferry DN9 106 A3
4 Wawne HU7 56 E7
Church Ct YO25 124 E4
Church Dike La YO8 63 F5
Church Dr Leven HU17 45 A8
6 Misterton DN10 116 C5
Church End YO8 48 B8
Church Farm Cl YO23 24 C6
Church Field Rd DN6 76 E1
Church Fields DN15 83 A5
Church Gate 21 HU12 72 C7
Church Gn
Beverley HU17 136 B6
5 Bridlington YO16 122 D4
3 Elvington YO41 27 C2
Church Hill
Grasby DN38 110 E7
10 Hunmanby YO14 2 F8
Reighton YO14 3 C6
Riby DN37 101 B2
3 Selby YO8 148 D5
South Cave HU15 53 F2
Stillingfleet YO19 36 D3
Whitton DN15 67 E3
8 Wistow YO8 48 D6
Church Hill Rd YO25 31 C4
Church La Appleby DN15 83 C1
Atwick YO25 35 C5
Aylesby DN37 101 E2
Barnetby Le Beck DN37 113 B6
1 Beeford YO25 22 D1
Beswick YO25 32 B4
Bilton HU11 142 F6
Bishop Burton HU17 43 B2
Bishopthorpe YO23 133 A4
Blyton DN21 117 F5
Bonby DN20 84 C2
Bradley DN37 102 C1
Brandesburton YO25 34 B2
Bridlington YO15 123 B7
Brigsley DN37 113 D4
3 Brough HU15 68 C7
Broughton DN20 97 E3
6 Buckton/Bempton YO15 4 D3
Burstwick HU12 73 A7
Cadney DN20 109 D6
Carlton DN14 63 C3
Carnaby YO16 10 D5
Catton YO41 27 D8
Catwick HU17 45 C8
Corringham DN21 118 B2
Driffield YO25 124 B4
Dunnington YO19 26 E7
4 Elvington YO41 27 C2
Fishlake DN7 92 D8
24 Flamborough YO15 5 A2
Fotherby LN11 121 D2
Fridaythorpe YO25 18 B7
Garton YO25 124 B4
Gateforth YO8 61 F8
Great Driffield YO25 124 E4
Great Limber DN37 100 D3
12 Grimsby DN33 102 E1
Grimsby DN32 152 D3
Grimsby DN32 153 B1
17 Haxby YO32 13 E5
Haxey DN9 105 C2
Hedon HU12 72 C7
Hensall DN14 62 C1
Hollym HU19 75 A4
Holton le Clay DN36 114 A5
Hook DN14 149 F7
Hotham YO43 53 D5
Humberston DN36 114 D8
Hutton Cranswick YO25 32 E8
Immingham DN40 86 E4
Immingham DN40 87 B2
Irby DN37 112 D7
Keadby with Althorpe DN17 95 D4
Kellington DN14 61 E3
Keyingham HU12 73 C4
2 Kilham YO25 9 C3
Kingston upon Hull HU10 143 C8
Kingston upon Hull HU9 147 C8
Laceby DN37 101 F1
Langtoft YO25 8 C5
Lockington YO25 32 B1
Luddington & Haldenby DN17 81 D4
Marsh Chapel DN36 115 B1
Millington YO42 29 D6
3 Misterton DN10 116 C5
4 Monk Fryston LS25 61 A8
Moor Monkton YO26 12 B2
Nether Poppleton YO26 126 B3
New Earswick YO32 127 F5
4 North Cave HU15 53 D3
North Frodingham YO25 33 F8
North Kelsey LN7 110 A4
North Thoresby DN36 114 B1
Nunburnholme YO42 29 E2
Patrington HU12 74 D1
Poppleton YO26 126 A3
Rudston YO25 9 F6
Saxby All Saints DN20 84 B3
Scawby DN20 98 A1
Scotter DN21 107 C3
19 Scunthorpe DN16 96 D2
Scunthorpe DN15 150 F6
Seaton Ross YO42 39 E4
4 Selby YO8 148 D5
Sigglesthorne HU11 45 F8
Skelton YO30 126 B5
Skirlaugh HU11 45 E2
2 Snaith DN14 63 C1
Sproatley HU11 58 D5
Stallingborough DN41 101 D6
10 Stamford Bridge YO41 15 D2
Strensall YO32 14 A7
Swinefleet DN14 65 D1
Tetney DN36 114 D3
Thorngumbald HU12 72 E5
Thwing YO25 2 A1
Twin Rivers DN14 81 A8
Ulceby DN39 86 A1
Utterby LN11 121 C3
Waithe DN36 114 A3
Church La *continued*
4 Waltham DN37 113 E6
Watton YO25 32 D4
Wetwang YO25 19 B6
Wheldrake YO19 38 A7
Withernwick HU11 46 D3
York YO1 156 B2
Church La Staith HU1 155 C2
Church Mews 2 YO26 129 C3
Church Mount 9 YO43 53 F7
Church Rd
Beverley HU17 136 B6
Laughton DN21 117 F8
North Ferriby HU14 69 A4
Rimswell HU19 74 D7
Skeffling HU12 90 D6
Stainforth DN7 92 C6
Stamford Bridge YO41 15 D2
Thornton YO42 39 B7
Wawne HU7 56 E7
York YO10 131 D4
Church Rise Holtby YO19 14 F1
Skidby HU16 138 A8
Church Row HU8 155 C4
Church Side
Alkborough DN15 82 C8
Appleby DN15 83 D2
Goxhill DN19 86 A7
Grasby DN38 110 E7
2 Market Weighton YO43 135 D4
West Halton DN15 82 E7
16 Winterton DN15 83 A5
Church Sq 3 DN15 151 B7
Church St
7 Aldbrough HU11 47 C1
Amcotts DN17 81 F1
Bainton YO25 31 E7
Beckingham DN10 116 D1
6 Brough HU15 68 D6
Bubwith YO8 50 D7
Burton Pidsea HU12 59 D1
14 Caistor LN7 111 B4
Copmanthorpe YO23 132 B2
Dunnington YO19 26 E7
Elsham DN20 98 F7
4 Epworth DN9 105 E6
Fishlake DN7 92 D8
19 Flamborough YO15 5 A2
Gainsborough DN21 117 B1
Goole DN14 149 D4
5 Goxhill DN19 86 A8
Great Driffield YO25 124 D4
Grimsby DN32 152 F5
Haxey DN9 105 C2
Hemswell DN21 119 A1
Hibaldstow DN20 108 F5
Huggate YO42 18 C2
Hutton Cranswick YO25 32 E8
4 Kilham YO25 9 C3
Kingston upon Hull HU7 141 E6
Kingston upon Hull HU10 143 E6
Kingston upon Hull HU9 146 B6
Kirton in Lindsey DN21 108 B1
Messingham DN17 107 D7
Misterton DN10 116 C5
Nettleton LN7 111 B3
North Cave HU15 53 D3
North Kelsey LN7 110 A4
Owston Ferry DN9 106 A3
Scawby DN20 108 E8
South Cave HU15 53 F1
Thorne/Moorends DN8 93 A8
Willoughton DN21 119 B4
York YO1 156 B2
Church View
12 Airmyn DN14 64 E4
Alkborough DN15 82 C8
8 Barton-upon-Humber DN18 84 F8
4 Beckingham DN10 116 D1
Beverley HU17 154 C3
4 Brough HU15 68 C7
Grimsby DN34 102 C4
Norton DN6 76 E1
7 Patrington HU12 74 D1
1 Waltham DN37 113 E6
Church View Cl DN9 94 E1
Church Wlk
Bridlington YO16 122 D5
Holton le Clay DN36 114 A5
Owston Ferry DN9 106 A3
5 Wistow YO8 48 D6
Churchfield Dr 28 YO32 13 E5
Churchfield La
Little Smeaton DN6 76 C4
Womersley DN6 76 D4
Churchfield Rd DN16 151 B1
Churchfields HU17 137 E8
Churchill Ave
Brigg DN20 98 C2
Burstwick HU12 73 A7
Hatfield DN7 92 F4
Hutton Cranswick YO25 32 E7
10 Keelby DN41 101 A5
Kingston upon Hull HU16 138 F6
Churchill Rise HU12 73 A7
Churchill St HU9 146 D7
Churchill Way DN32 152 F3
Churchill Wlk DN14 149 C5
Churchside 4 DN19 85 D8
Churchthorpe LN11 121 E8
Churchtown DN9 94 E1
Cinder La
Upper Poppleton YO26 12 F1
Upper Poppleton YO26 129 A7

Cinder La *continued*
York YO26 130 A4
York YO31 130 E6
Cinema St HU18 134 C4
Circle The 4 HU13 143 E2
Cissplatt La DN41 101 A5
Citadel Ct HU17 154 B3
Citadel Way HU9 155 C2
Cladshaw HU6 139 F8
Clanthorpe HU6 139 F8
Clapham Ave HU8 141 E5
Clare Ave DN17 150 D3
Clare Ct Beverley HU17 137 B4
Grimsby DN34 152 A1
Clare Gr HU9 142 A1
Claremont Ave HU6 140 D4
Claremont Rd DN32 153 D2
Claremont Terr YO31 156 B4
Clarence Ave
Bridlington YO15 122 D1
Kingston upon Hull HU8 141 E4
Clarence Cl 25 DN40 87 B1
Clarence Ct HU2 155 A3
Clarence Rd 1 YO15 122 F2
Clarence St
Kingston upon Hull HU9 155 C2
York YO31 156 B4
Clarendon Rd
6 Grimsby DN34 102 C2
Scunthorpe DN17 150 F3
Clarendon St HU3 145 D7
Clark Ave DN34 152 A3
Clarke Cres 9 YO15 4 D3
Clarke St DN15 151 A7
Clarkes Rd DN40 86 E4
Clark's La YO43 53 D6
Clarks La 10 HU12 74 D1
Clarksons Dr DN41 101 E6
Clarondale HU7 140 E7
Clavering St DN31 152 B5
Claxby Rd DN17 150 F1
Clay Bank Rd DN8 93 C6
Clay Hill YO41 16 C3
Clay La Bubwith YO8 50 C5
Camblesforth YO8 63 C6
Cliffe YO8 49 D4
Holton le Clay DN36 114 A6
Kirton in Lindsey DN21 118 F8
Market Weighton YO43 135 B5
Millington YO42 29 C6
Clay Pl 3 YO24 129 D1
Clay St HU8 141 A3
Clayden St DN31 152 B5
Clayfield Cl 18 YO42 29 A3
Clayfield La
Pocklington YO42 29 A4
Shipton Thorpe YO43 40 F6
Clayfield Rd
Pocklington YO42 29 A3
Scunthorpe DN15 96 C7
Claygate YO31 131 B6
Claymore Cl DN35 153 E2
Claypit La DN14 63 C3
Cleatham Rd DN21 108 A3
Cleaves Ave HU15 54 A2
Clee Cres DN32 153 C1
Clee Ness Dr 16 DN36 103 D1
Clee Rd DN35 153 D2
Clee Village DN32 153 C2
Cleefields Cl DN32 153 B1
Cleethorpe Rd DN32 153 A5
Cleethorpes Ctry Pk*
DN35 103 C1
Cleethorpes L Ctr
DN35 103 D2
Cleethorpes Miniature Rly*
DN35 103 E2
Cleethorpes Sta DN35 153 F3
Cleeton La YO25 23 A2
Cleeton Way YO16 122 B6
Cleeve Dr 12 HU7 57 A5
Cleeve Prim Sch HU7 57 A5
Cleeve Rd HU12 72 D6
Clematis Ave DN41 101 F5
Clematis Cl YO25 124 D3
Clematis Way DN16 96 E2
Clement St 4 YO23 156 B1
Clementhorpe YO23 156 B1
Clementhorpe La HU15 66 D8
Clementhorpe Rd
HU15 66 D8
Clerke St DN35 153 B4
Clevedon Rd DN17 150 D4
Cleveland Cl Hook DN14 65 B5
4 Immingham DN40 87 B1
Scunthorpe DN17 150 D4
Cleveland Gdns DN31 152 B5
Cleveland St
Grimsby DN31 152 B5
Kingston upon Hull HU8 141 A1
Kingston upon Hull HU8 155 C4
York YO24 130 A4
Cleveland Way
41 Hatfield DN7 92 D4
York YO32 127 F3
Cliff Ave DN15 82 F5
Cliff Closes Rd DN15 150 D6
Cliff Dr
Burton upon Stather
DN15 82 B5
3 Kingston upon Hull HU13 69 E4
Cliff Gdns DN15 150 E6
Cliff Gr DN18 84 E8
Cliff Hill Rd DN6 76 D2
Cliff La Bempton YO15 4 D4
Mappleton HU18 47 A6
Waddingham DN21 119 F6
Cliff Rd Atwick YO25 35 D5

Cliff Rd *continued*
Bridlington YO15 123 B6
Hessle HU13 69 E4
Hornsea HU18 134 C6
Snitterby DN21 119 F5
Winteringham DN15 83 A8
Cliff St Bridlington YO15 122 F2
Scunthorpe DN16 151 C6
Cliff The DN15 150 D7
Cliff Top La 2 HU13 69 E4
Cliff Wlk YO15 123 C6
Cliffe La YO43 52 D8
Cliffe Prim Sch YO8 49 E2
Cliffe Rd
Market Weighton YO43 135 D1
Newbald YO43 53 C7
North Cave YO43 53 C4
Clifford Ave HU8 141 E4
Clifford St
Hornsea HU18 134 C5
York YO1 156 B2
Cliffords Twr* YO1 156 B1
Clifton Ct 27 DN8 93 A8
Clifton Dale YO30 130 A6
Clifton Gdns DN14 149 B4
Clifton Moor Gate
YO30 127 A2
Clifton Moor Ret Pk
YO30 126 E3
Clifton Moorgate
YO30 127 B3
Clifton Pl 3 YO30 130 A7
Clifton Prep Sch
YO30 156 A4
Clifton Prim Sch HU2 155 A4
Clifton Rd
Grimsby DN34 152 A2
York YO30 156 A4
Clifton St
Hornsea HU18 134 C5
Kingston upon Hull HU2 155 A4
Clifton Terr HU5 140 E1
Clifton Without Jun Sch
YO30 129 F8
Clive Gr YO24 129 F2
Clive Sullivan Way
HU4 144 C1
Clixby Cl DN35 103 D2
Clixby La DN38 110 E7
Clockmill La YO42 29 A4
Cloeberry Way 14 HU12 72 C7
Cloister Wk DN20 97 E3
Cloisters The
6 Grimsby DN37 102 B4
15 Hemingbrough YO8 49 F1
Humberston DN36 114 D8
Wilberfoss YO41 27 F6
York YO31 156 C3
Cloisters Wlk YO31 156 C3
Close The Cawood YO8 48 A7
Goxhill DN19 71 A1
Great Driffield YO25 124 F5
Grimsby DN34 152 C3
Kingston upon Hull
HU10 138 F1
Kingston upon Hull
HU16 138 F5
Kingston upon Hull HU7 141 D6
4 Leven HU17 45 A8
5 Market Weighton YO43 135 E4
Norton DN6 76 E2
12 Patrington HU12 74 D1
Riccall YO19 49 A8
Scunthorpe DN16 151 B6
8 Withernsea HU19 75 A6
York YO30 129 F8
Clouds La Belton DN9 95 B1
West Butterwick DN17 106 C8
Clough Garth HU12 72 D8
Clough La DN6 77 B2
Clough Rd HU5 140 F3
Cloughton Gr HU5 139 E2
Clovelly Gdns 3 HU5 140 E1
Clover Bank View HU6 56 E5
Cloverley Cl YO41 15 C2
Cloverley Rd 6 YO16 123 A6
Clowes Ct 4 HU13 143 E1
Clumber Pl DN35 153 E1
Clumber St HU5 145 C8
Clyde St Grimsby DN32 152 F4
Kingston upon Hull HU3 144 F5
Clyfton Cres DN40 87 B1
Coach House Garth
YO42 28 D3
Coach House Gdns
DN20 108 E8
Coachings The 4 HU13 69 E4
Coal Pit La WF8 76 A2
Coal Shore La LN11 115 E1
Coastguard Hill YO14 3 E5
Coates Ave DN15 83 A5
Coates Marsh La DN14 63 B2
Cobble La DN14 51 F1
Cobbler Hill DN14 149 B6
Cobcroft La WF11 76 B8
Cobdale La YO42 29 F7
Cobden St HU3 144 F7
Cobden St North End
DN32 152 F4
Cochrane St YO8 148 D3
Cock Pit Cl HU10 143 C6
Cockerell La YO25 22 B4
Cocketts La DN20 108 F5
Cockret Cl 8 YO8 148 B6
Cockret Ct YO8 148 B7
Cockret Rd YO8 148 B7
Cockthorne La DN15 83 C7
Coda Ave YO23 133 B3

Coelus St HU9 155 C3
Coeside YO24 132 B7
Cogan St HU1 155 A1
Coggan Way YO23 132 F4
Cohort Cl 10 HU15 68 C5
Coke Oven Ave DN16 151 F6
Cold Harbour Rd HU17 43 A1
Cold Harbour View 5
HU17 43 A2
Coldstream Cl 4 HU8 142 C5
Cole St
Scunthorpe DN15 151 B7
York YO31 156 B4
Coleby Rd DN15 82 E7
Coledale Cl 2 YO30 126 F1
Coleford Gr HU7 141 A7
Coleford Prim Sch
HU7 141 A7
Colenso St YO23 156 B1
Coleridge Ave DN17 150 D3
Coleridge St HU8 141 D2
Colin Ave DN32 153 B2
Colin Rd DN16 151 C6
Colins Wlk DN21 107 C4
Coll of St John The
YO31 156 B3
College Ave 31 DN33 113 E8
College Cl DN15 82 C8
College Farm Cl DN14 77 A8
College Gdns
32 Grimsby DN33 113 E8
Hornsea HU18 134 B5
College Gr HU9 141 F1
College of Law YO23 133 B7
College of Ripon & St Johns
YO10 131 B3
College of Ripon & York St
Johns YO31 156 B3
College Rd
Barrow upon Humber
DN19 85 E7
Copmanthorpe YO23 132 A3
Thornton Curtis DN39 86 B6
College St
Cleethorpes DN35 153 E2
Grimsby DN34 152 C2
Kingston upon Hull HU7 141 D6
Kingston upon Hull HU2 155 A3
York YO1 156 B3
Colleridge Gr 4 HU17 55 E8
Colleys HU19 75 A5
Colleywell Cl 3 DN9 105 A2
Collier Cl 10 HU14 69 A4
Collier Hag La YO23 24 B3
Collier Rd 16 DN40 87 C1
Collier St HU1 155 A2
Colliergate YO1 156 B2
Collin Ave HU9 142 C2
Collingwood Ave
YO24 129 F2
Collingwood Cres 12
DN34 102 B2
Collingwood Prim Sch
HU3 145 C7
Collingwood Rd 3 YO15 4 C3
Collingwood St HU3 145 D7
Collinson Ave DN15 150 C7
Collinson La HU15 67 A8
Collum Ave DN16 151 B3
Collum Gdns DN16 151 B2
Collum La DN16 151 B2
Collynson Cl 1 HU10 143 E8
Colonel's Wlk DN14 149 D5
Colonial St HU2 145 D7
Colson Pl DN35 153 B3
Coltman Ave HU17 154 C4
Coltman Cl HU17 136 F7
Coltman St HU3 145 C5
Colton St 3 Brigg DN20 98 B2
Misterton DN10 116 C5
Coltsfoot Cl 5 DN15 96 B7
Coltsfoot Dr DN37 113 D7
Columbia Rd DN32 153 A3
Columbus Way DN33 102 C2
Colville Ave HU4 144 B6
Colwall Ave HU5 139 D2
Colwyn Cl 5 HU7 57 A7
Combe St DN35 153 C4
Comforts Ave DN15 151 A6
Commerce La HU1 145 D4
Commercial Rd
Kingston upon Hull HU1 155 A1
Scunthorpe DN16 151 C7
Commodore Croft
HU1 155 B1
Common Croft La YO26 12 E1
Common Hill YO43 53 C5
Common La
Barnby Dun with Kirk Sandall
DN3 92 B4
Beal DN14 61 D3
Burn YO8 62 E7
Catton YO41 27 E8
Dunnington YO19 26 F5
Fangfoss YO41 16 B1
Knottingley WF11 61 B1
North Cave HU15 53 B2
Norton DN6 76 E2
1 Seaton HU11 35 A1
Sutton upon Derwent
YO41 38 C8
Temple Hirst YO8 62 F4
Thorganby YO19 37 F5
Thornton YO42 39 B8
Twin Rivers DN17 81 B6
Walden Stubbs DN6 76 F4
Warthill YO19 14 F2
Wawne HU7 56 F7

Common La *continued*
Welton HU15 68 D4
York YO10 131 B1
Common La W HU15 53 B2
Common Mid Rd DN17 94 C8
Common Rd
Broughton DN20 97 E4
Dunnington YO19 26 F7
Rowley HU20 54 F5
Skipwith YO8 37 E1
South Cave HU15 67 C7
Commonside
Crowle DN17 94 C8
Westwoodside DN9 105 A2
Compass Rd HU6 140 C8
Compton Dr
Grimsby DN34 152 C3
Keyingham HU12 73 C3
Compton St YO30 130 A6
Comrie Dr 16 YO42 29 A3
Concast Rd DN16 97 A3
Concorde Pk YO30 127 A3
Coney St YO1 156 B2
Coneycroft 10 YO19 26 F7
Coneygarth La YO19 26 E5
Conference Ct 10 DN16 96 D1
Conifer Cl
6 Kingston upon Hull
HU4 144 C7
Scunthorpe DN17 150 C1
6 York YO32 127 D3
Conifers Cl 2 YO8 48 D1
Coningsby Dr DN34 152 A1
Coningsby Rd DN17 150 D1
Conington Ave HU17 137 B4
Conisborough Ave 2
DN36 113 F7
Coniston Ave DN33 113 D8
Coniston Cl 1 YO30 126 E1
Coniston Cres
19 Humberston DN36 103 C1
10 Humberston DN36 103 C1
Humberston DN36 114 C8
Coniston Dr YO10 131 B4
Coniston La
Coniston HU11 58 A5
Swine HU11 57 E6
Coniston Way DN14 149 E5
Connaught Ave DN32 152 D1
Connaught Rd 9 DN21 117 B1
Connaught Way YO32 127 F6
Consort Ct HU9 146 B5
Constable Ave HU11 58 A4
Constable Cl
18 Flamborough YO15 5 A2
Sproatley HU11 58 D5
Constable Garth 5 HU12 72 D7
Constable Prim Sch
HU3 145 C5
Constable Rd
Flamborough YO15 5 A2
Hornsea HU18 134 D5
Hunmanby YO14 3 A8
Constable St HU3 145 C5
Constantine Ave YO10 131 A4
Constitution Hill
HU17 136 A6
Constitutional Ave
DN35 153 C4
Convamore Rd DN32 152 F2
Convent La HU3 145 D6
Conway Ave DN34 152 A3
Conway Cl
Kingston upon Hull HU3 145 B5
2 York YO30 126 E3
Conway Sq DN15 150 E7
Conyard Rd DN35 153 E3
Conyers Ave DN33 102 E1
Cookbury Cl 6 HU7 56 F5
Cookridge Dr 11 DN7 92 D4
Cooks La Grimsby DN37 102 B5
Nettleton LN7 111 A3
Coomb Briggs Prim Sch
DN40 87 B1
Coombs Yd HU17 154 A3
Cooper La DN37 101 E1
Cooper Rd DN32 153 A3
Cooper St
Beverley HU17 154 B4
Kingston upon Hull HU2 155 B4
Coopers Dr YO23 132 B3
Copandale Rd HU17 154 A4
Cope St DN32 153 A4
Copenhagen Rd HU7 140 F5
Copmanthorpe Jun Sch
YO23 132 B3
Copmanthorpe La
YO23 132 E3
Copmanthorpe Prim Sch
YO23 132 B3
Copmanthorpe Recn Ctr &
Sports Club YO23 132 B2
Copper Beech Cl 6
HU14 69 B6
Copper Beech Wlk 24
DN16 96 D2
Copper Beeches The 2
YO19 26 E7
Coppergate
Nafferton YO25 125 F7
1 Riccall YO19 36 F1
York YO1 156 B2
Coppergate Wlk YO1 156 B2
Coppice Ave DN7 92 D3
Coppice Cl 10 YO32 13 E5
Coppice Gr 39 DN7 92 D3
Coppice La 1 DN7 92 D3
Coppice Side HU4 144 C6

Coppice The
Bishopthorpe YO23 132 F4
Brayton YO8 48 C1
Coppleflat La
Rowley HU17 55 D6
Walkington HU17 43 C1
Copse Cl 1 DN40 87 C2
Copse Mead YO25 124 D5
Copse Rd DN16 151 B1
Copse The
Beverley HU17 137 B3
Bigby DN20 98 D1
28 Grimsby DN33 113 E8
Copwood Gr 7 YO32 127 C8
Coral Dr 2 DN37 113 D7
Corban La YO32 13 B6
Corban Way 21 YO32 13 D5
Corbridge Cl 2 HU9 142 E1
Corby Pk HU14 69 A5
Cordella Cl 1 HU3 145 A5
Coriander Cl HU17 154 A1
Corinthian Ave DN34 152 B2
Corinthian Way HU9 146 D6
Cormorant Cl 2 HU7 141 D8
Cormorant Dr 1 DN37 102 B4
Cornborough Av YO31 130 F6
Cornelius Cswy YO8 49 E8
Cornelius Wlk YO43 135 E4
Corner Cl 17 YO32 13 D5
Cornfield Cl 5 DN33 113 D8
Cornfield Cres YO16 122 B2
Cornhill Dr DN18 85 A8
Cornlands Rd YO24 129 B1
Cornley Rd DN10 116 A6
Cornmill Cl YO8 48 B8
Cornwall Dr YO10 133 E8
Cornwall Rd
2 Keadby DN17 95 D6
Scunthorpe DN16 151 C1
Cornwall St
Kingston upon Hull
HU16 139 C6
Kingston upon Hull HU8 141 A1
7 Kirton in Lindsey DN21 108 B1
Cornwell Cl 5 DN33 102 E2
Cornwood Way 11 YO32 127 C8
Corona Dr
Kingston upon Hull HU8 141 C4
8 Thorne/Moorends DN8 79 A1
Coronation Cl HU17 154 C3
Coronation Cres 10
DN9 105 D6
Coronation Gdns 4
DN20 97 E3
Coronation Rd
Cleethorpes DN35 153 F1
Stainforth DN7 92 C6
7 Ulceby DN39 86 A1
Coronation Rd N HU5 139 C2
Coronation Rd S HU5 139 B1
Coronation St 10 DN14 149 C4
Coronet Cl 5 HU6 140 B8
Corporation Rd
Beverley HU17 154 A3
Grimsby DN31 152 C5
Kingston upon Hull HU9 147 A7
Scunthorpe DN15 151 A7
Corpslanding Rd YO25 33 A7
Corran Garth 6 HU4 144 A3
Corringham C of E Sch
DN21 118 B2
Corringham Rd
Corringham DN21 117 D1
Gainsborough DN21 117 D1
Corsair Gr 4 HU3 145 A4
Cosford Garth 5 HU7 57 A5
Cosgrove St DN35 153 F2
Cosmo Ave YO31 131 A5
Cotham Gdns 6 DN41 101 A4
Cotness La DN14 65 F3
Cotswold Ave DN14 149 D5
Cotswold Dr 20 DN37 113 D6
Cotswold Rd DN8 93 A7
Cotswold Way YO32 128 A5
Cotswolds The HU9 142 D2
Cottage Beck Rd
DN16 151 B6
Cottage Cl DN20 108 F5
Cottage Dr HU10 143 B8
Cottage Field 1 HU17 43 A2
Cottage Mews HU17 154 B3
Cottage Yard La DN36 114 C7
Cottam La YO25 8 C5
Cotterdale HU7 140 E7
Cottesmore Rd
Cleethorpes DN35 103 C1
6 Kingston upon Hull
HU13 144 A2
Cottingham Croxby Prim Sch
HU5 139 D4
Cottingham Gr 2 HU6 139 F4
Cottingham High Sch
HU16 138 E8
Cottingham Playsport
HU16 139 A7
Cottingham Rd HU5 139 E4
Cottingham St DN14 149 C1
Cottingham Sta HU16 139 B6
Cottom La YO42 38 C2
Coulam Pl 8 DN36 114 D8
Coulbeck Dr DN35 153 D1
Coulman Rd 4 DN8 93 B8
Coulman St 5 DN8 93 B8
Coulson Cl 5 YO32 14 C8
Coulson Dr HU13 143 F2

Coultas Ct 3 HU3 ....145 A6
Council Ave HU4 ....144 E3
Council Terr 9 DN18 ....69 E1
Council Villas DN19 ....85 F8
Count De Burgh Terr 4 YO23 ....130 B1
Countess Cl* Alkborough DN15 ....82 B8
6 Kingston upon Hull HU6 ....140 B8
County Rd N HU5 ....139 E1
County Rd S 2 HU5 ....144 C8
Coupland Gdns 2 HU5 ....140 E2
Coupland Rd 1 YO8 ....148 C6
Courcey Gr YO26 ....129 C4
Court Dr YO8 ....148 A4
Court Gdns 8 DN14 ....78 C8
Court Park Prim Sch HU6 ....139 E7
Courtland Rd HU6 ....139 E6
Courtney St HU8 ....146 B8
Courtneys Selby YO8 ....148 B4
Wheldrake YO19 ....38 A8
Courtpark Rd HU6 ....139 F7
Courts Cl 7 DN14 ....64 E4
Courtway Rd HU6 ....139 E7
Courtyard The YO23 ....133 B4
Cove Rd DN9 ....104 F3
Coventry Ave DN34 ....152 A1
Coventry Cl DN17 ....150 D3
Coventry Rd
Kingston upon Hull HU5 ....139 C1
12 Thorne/Moorends DN8 ....93 B8
Coverdale HU7 ....140 F7
Covert Rd DN16 ....151 B1
Covert The
Kingston upon Hull HU16 ....139 C5
York YO24 ....132 F7
Covin's La LN11 ....121 F8
Cow La Knottingley WF11 ....61 A2
Twin Rivers DN17 ....81 C6
Womersley DN6 ....76 D6
Cow Marsh La DN36 ....114 E5
Cow Pasture La YO42 ....38 C3
Cow Wold Rd HU17 ....42 E1
Cowden Gr 2 HU9 ....142 A2
Cowden La HU11 ....46 E4
Cowgate HU15 ....68 D6
Cowick C of E Prim Sch DN14 ....78 E8
Cowick Rd Fishlake DN8 ....78 F1
Sykehouse DN14 ....78 E3
Cowie Dr YO8 ....148 D5
Cowlings Cl 16 YO14 ....3 A8
Cowper Ave DN17 ....150 D3
Cowper La YO23 ....36 C8
Cowslams La YO25 ....21 E1
Cowton La YO14 ....3 C6
Cox La 1 DN17 ....94 D8
Coxlea Gr YO31 ....131 B6
Cox's Ct DN20 ....109 A5
Cox's Hill DN21 ....117 B1
Coxwold Gr HU4 ....144 E5
Crab Tree La
Coniston HU11 ....57 F7
Kirk Smeaton WF8 ....76 A1
Crabley La HU15 ....67 E7
Crabtree Gr 1 YO32 ....127 D3
Crabtree La YO25 ....32 B4
Crabtree Rd DN7 ....92 C4
Cradley Rd HU5 ....139 C3
Cragston Ave 19 DN33 ....102 E2
Craig Cl 5 DN20 ....97 D3
Craik Hill Ave 18 DN40 ....87 C1
Craithie Rd 11 DN35 ....103 C2
Crake Ave DN33 ....102 E1
Crake Wells HU17 ....55 C8
Crakedale Rd DN15 ....83 B5
Crampin Rd DN35 ....153 E3
Cranbeck Cl YO16 ....122 B1
Cranberry Way HU4 ....144 C4
Cranbourne Cl 23 DN35 ....103 C1
Cranbourne St HU3 ....145 C8
Cranbrook Ave
Kingston upon Hull HU6 ....140 B6
York YO26 ....129 C5
Cranbrook Rd YO26 ....129 C5
Cranbrooks The YO19 ....37 F8
Crane Rd HU9 ....146 C6
Cranfield Pl 4 YO24 ....132 C8
Cranham Gr HU7 ....141 A7
Cranidge Cl 2 DN17 ....94 D8
Cranswick Cl 8 HU17 ....43 E6
Cranswick Gr HU9 ....142 B1
Cranwell Cl 6 DN21 ....119 C8
Cranwell Dr 10 DN37 ....102 C5
Cranwell Rd YO25 ....124 E4
Cranwell St YO25 ....124 E4
Crapple La DN21 ....107 C2
Crathorne Rd HU17 ....154 C4
Craven Garth 5 DN14 ....61 D4
Craven Prim Sch HU9 ....146 C8
Craven Rd
Cleethorpes DN35 ....153 B3
Hatfield DN7 ....92 C4
Craven St N HU9 ....146 C8
Craven St S HU9 ....146 D7
Crawley Way YO31 ....131 B6
Crawshaw Ave HU17 ....136 E6
Craycroft Rd DN9 ....105 B3
Crayford Cl 7 HU9 ....142 E1
Crayke The YO16 ....122 F7
Crescent St
Grimsby DN31 ....152 C3
Crescent St *continued*
Kingston upon Hull HU16 ....139 A6
Crescent The
Beckingham DN10 ....116 E1
9 Bridlington YO15 ....122 F2
Brough HU15 ....68 D6
Burton Fleming YO25 ....2 E3
Hatfield DN7 ....92 C5
Holton le Clay DN36 ....114 A5
Hornsea HU18 ....134 D3
Huggate YO42 ....18 C2
Kelfield YO19 ....36 D1
Kexby YO41 ....27 C5
4 Kirk Sandall DN3 ....92 A1
13 Patrington HU12 ....74 D1
6 Riccall YO19 ....48 F8
Stamford Bridge YO41 ....15 D2
York YO24 ....156 A1
Cressey St DN31 ....152 E5
Cresswell Cl HU2 ....155 A4
Cresta Dr 10 DN17 ....96 C2
Cresta The DN34 ....152 C1
Creyke Cl 6 HU16 ....139 B7
Creyke La 7 HU15 ....68 D6
Creyke View DN14 ....64 A1
Crichton Ave YO30 ....130 B8
Cridling Gdns DN6 ....76 F2
Cridling Pl 5 DN35 ....103 B2
Crinan Ct 3 YO32 ....127 F6
Crinan Dr 1 HU6 ....140 B8
Crispin Cl 5 HU4 ....144 A2
Crispin Way DN16 ....96 D1
Croft Ave 8 WF11 ....61 A3
Croft Cl
Eastrington DN14 ....51 F1
Market Weighton YO43 ....135 D3
Croft Ct YO23 ....133 A4
Croft Dr HU10 ....143 C5
Croft Farm Cl YO23 ....132 B3
Croft La DN17 ....96 C1
Croft Lodge DN9 ....94 E1
Croft Pk HU14 ....69 A5
Croft Rd
Camblesforth YO8 ....63 D4
Finningley DN10 ....104 A1
Croft The
Beverley HU17 ....136 C7
Kingston upon Hull HU7 ....140 E8
Knottingley WF11 ....61 A3
22 Thorne/Moorends DN8 ....93 B7
1 West/East Butterwick DN17 ....106 D8
Croft View
Kingston upon Hull HU7 ....141 C7
Kingston upon Hull HU10 ....143 C6
Market Weighton YO43 ....135 D3
Crofters Dr HU16 ....139 C5
Croftlands 7 WF11 ....61 A3
Crofts La HU19 ....74 F4
Croft's La DN9 ....106 B3
Crofts La DN7 ....92 B6
Crofts The
9 Humberston DN36 ....114 C8
Scunthorpe DN16 ....151 B6
Croftside 1 YO26 ....129 B3
Croftway
Camblesforth YO8 ....63 C5
Selby YO8 ....148 C4
2 York YO26 ....129 B3
Cromarty Cl HU9 ....142 A3
Crombie Ave YO30 ....130 B7
Cromer Ave DN34 ....152 A1
Cromer St
4 Kingston upon Hull HU5 ....140 D2
York YO30 ....130 B7
Cromford St 13 DN21 ....117 B1
Cromwell Ave DN16 ....151 B5
Cromwell Cl 2 HU3 ....145 D8
Cromwell Ct 1 HU10 ....143 E7
Cromwell Rd
Cleethorpes DN35 ....103 D2
Grimsby DN31 ....152 A4
York YO1 ....156 B1
Cromwell View 25 LN7 ....111 B4
Crook Hill HU15 ....68 C8
Crook La HU11 ....58 D7
Crook Mill Rd DN40 ....86 D5
Crook Tree La DN7 ....92 F5
Crooked Billet St 5 DN21 ....117 A2
Crookes Broom Ave DN7 ....92 D4
Crookes Broom La DN7 ....92 D4
Crookland La YO32 ....13 F5
Croom Medieval Village* YO25 ....7 B4
Croome Dale La YO17 ....7 C6
Croome Rd YO25 ....7 B4
Cropton Rd HU5 ....139 E2
Crosby Ave DN15 ....96 C7
Crosby Inf & Jun Sch DN15 ....151 A8
Crosby Rd
Grimsby DN33 ....102 D1
Scunthorpe DN15 ....151 B8
Crosland Rd DN37 ....102 B4
Cross Carr Rd DN20 ....109 A5
Cross Coates Rd DN34 ....152 A2
Cross Gate YO43 ....41 E6
Cross Gates YO25 ....21 F8
Cross Gordon St 1 DN14 ....149 C4
Cross Hill
5 Brandesburton YO25 ....34 B2
Haxey DN9 ....105 C3
Hayton YO42 ....40 C8
Cross Hills La YO8 ....148 A5
Cross La
Alkborough DN15 ....82 C8
3 Amcotts DN17 ....81 F1
Flaxton YO60 ....14 E8
Flixborough DN15 ....82 A2
Fulford YO19 ....133 F5
Hutton Cranswick YO25 ....32 F6
Leven HU17 ....44 F7
North Frodingham YO25 ....33 F7
North Kelsey LN7 ....110 B5
Cross Rd Hatfield DN7 ....93 B4
North Frodingham YO25 ....33 F7
Ulceby DN39 ....86 B3
Cross Slack 8 DN17 ....94 D8
Cross St
8 Aldbrough HU11 ....47 C1
3 Barrow upon Humber DN19 ....85 D8
Beverley HU17 ....154 A2
Bridlington YO15 ....122 F2
12 Brigg DN20 ....98 C2
Cleethorpes DN35 ....153 E2
Crowle DN17 ....94 D8
7 Gainsborough DN21 ....117 A2
36 Gainsborough DN21 ....117 B1
Garthorpe & Fockerby DN17 ....81 E6
Goole DN14 ....149 D3
Grimsby DN31 ....152 F6
Hatfield HU11 ....46 C6
Kingston upon Hull HU1 ....155 A2
2 Scunthorpe DN15 ....151 B8
Skipsea YO25 ....23 A2
3 Waltham DN37 ....113 E6
West Halton DN15 ....82 E8
5 York YO24 ....129 C3
Cross St W DN14 ....149 B4
Cross Tree Rd DN17 ....107 D7
Crossbeck Rd 2 DN16 ....96 D2
Crossfield Cres YO19 ....133 E6
Crossfield Rd
Kingston upon Hull HU13 ....143 E3
Kingston upon Hull HU4 ....144 D5
Crosshill La DN14 ....77 E6
Crossings The 13 DN14 ....64 E4
Crosskill Cl HU17 ....154 C4
Crosslands La HU15 ....53 B3
Crosslands Rd 2 YO10 ....133 E8
Crossmoor Bank DN14 ....80 C5
Crossmoor La YO32 ....13 E6
Crossway The
Grimsby DN34 ....102 B2
2 York YO31 ....130 E8
Crossways
10 Stainforth DN7 ....92 C6
York YO10 ....131 C2
Crosswood Cl 6 HU7 ....57 A7
Crow Croft La
Balne DN14 ....78 A5
Pollington DN14 ....78 A5
Crow Hill Ave DN35 ....153 E2
Crow Tree Bank DN8 ....93 D4
Crowberry Dr DN16 ....151 D1
Crowland Ave
Grimsby DN34 ....102 C2
Scunthorpe DN16 ....151 A3
Crowland Cl 2 HU8 ....142 C7
Crowland Rd 8 DN17 ....94 D7
Crowle Bank Rd DN17 ....95 C4
Crowle County Prim Sch DN17 ....94 C7
Crowle Dr DN33 ....102 D2
Crowle Rd DN17 ....80 F2
Crowle St HU9 ....146 D7
Crowle Sta DN17 ....94 E6
Crowle Waste or Moors Nature Reserve* DN17 ....94 B8
Crowther Cl HU17 ....137 A6
Crowther Way 5 HU14 ....69 B7
Croxby Ave DN33 ....113 E8
Croxby Gr 14 DN33 ....113 E8
Croxton Rd
Croxton DN39 ....99 F7
Kirmington DN39 ....100 A5
Cruckley La YO25 ....21 E1
Crudhall La YO42 ....40 A8
Crummock 3 YO24 ....132 C7
Crumpton Rd YO43 ....135 C3
Crystal St HU3 ....145 C7
Cuckoo La DN7 ....92 E6
Cudworth Gr 1 HU8 ....141 B1
Cullen Cl HU8 ....141 C5
Cullingworth Ave 2 HU6 ....140 C7
Cumberland Ave DN32 ....152 D1
Cumberland Cl
Goole DN14 ....149 A4
6 Strensall YO32 ....14 B6
Cumberland Rd DN35 ....103 D1
Cumberland St
Kingston upon Hull HU2 ....155 C4
York YO1 ....156 B2
Cumbrian Ave 4 YO32 ....14 B6
Cumbrian Way HU7 ....56 F7
Cundall Cl
Kingston upon Hull HU9 ....141 E1
6 Strensall YO32 ....14 C8
Cunningham Rd 3 DN7 ....104 A8
Cupid's Alley YO17 ....6 B6
Cupola Way DN15 ....96 C8
Curlew Cl
Beverley HU17 ....136 E6
Driffield YO25 ....125 A5
Kingston upon Hull HU7 ....141 D8
Curlew Glebe 8 YO19 ....26 E7
Curry Rd DN34 ....102 C4
Curson Terr YO8 ....49 E3
Curzen Cres 5 DN3 ....92 A2
Curzon Ave DN35 ....153 D1
Curzon Ct 3 DN35 ....103 B2
Curzon St
4 Gainsborough DN21 ....117 B1
Kingston upon Hull HU3 ....144 F7
Curzon Terr YO23 ....130 B1
Cushman Cres 10 DN40 ....87 C1
Custance Wlk YO23 ....156 A1
Cuthbert Ave 6 DN38 ....99 B4
Cuxwold Rd
Scunthorpe DN16 ....151 C4
Swallow LN7 ....112 B5
Cycle St 4 YO10 ....131 A3
Cygnet St YO23 ....156 A1
Cynthia Rd DN32 ....153 C1
Cyprus St HU9 ....147 B8
Cyrano Way DN37 ....102 B4

D

Dacre Lakeside Pk* YO25 ....34 B1
Dagger La HU1 ....155 B2
Daggett La YO25 ....21 F8
Daggett Rd DN35 ....103 D2
Dairy House La HU12 ....73 A8
Dairycoates Ave HU3 ....145 A4
Dairycoates Rd HU4 ....144 E3
Daisyfield Dr HU9 ....142 D6
Dalby Gr HU9 ....142 B2
Dalby Mead YO32 ....127 F1
Dale Cl Selby YO8 ....148 C3
8 Swanland HU14 ....69 B7
Dale Dike Gr YO30 ....126 F2
Dale Garth YO43 ....135 E5
Dale Gate HU17 ....43 A1
Dale Pit Rd DN7 ....92 F3
Dale Pk Ave DN15 ....83 A5
Dale Rd
Brantingham HU15 ....68 C8
Bridlington YO16 ....122 D4
Elloughton-cum-Brough HU15 ....68 C6
Swanland HU14 ....69 B7
Welton HU15 ....68 E6
Dale St
Scunthorpe DN15 ....151 A8
York YO23 ....156 A1
Dale St N DN15 ....150 F8
Dale View 27 DN33 ....102 C2
Dalehouse Dr 2 HU10 ....143 F6
Dale's La YO31 ....130 F6
Dales Prim Sch The HU7 ....56 F6
Dales The
Kingston upon Hull HU16 ....138 D6
Kingston upon Hull HU9 ....142 D2
Scunthorpe DN17 ....96 C2
Dalesway HU10 ....143 B6
Dalguise Gr YO31 ....156 C4
Dalkeith Cl 16 HU7 ....57 A6
Dallisons Rd DN20 ....109 A5
Dalmais Cl 1 YO42 ....28 F4
Dalmally Cl YO24 ....132 B6
Dalmatian Way DN20 ....97 E4
Dalsetter Rise HU8 ....141 F6
Dalton Cl YO25 ....124 D3
Dalton Hill YO19 ....38 A8
Dalton La HU12 ....73 F6
Dalton St HU8 ....141 A1
Dalton Terr YO24 ....130 A3
Dalwood Cl HU7 ....141 B8
Dam Bank YO8 ....148 C6
Dam Green La HU15 ....68 C7
Dam Hill YO23 ....24 B4
Dam La Ottringham HU12 ....73 D2
Selby YO8 ....48 B3
Thornton Curtis DN39 ....85 E4
Dam Rd DN18 ....69 E1
Dame Kendal Gr 29 DN33 ....102 D2
Damson Garth YO25 ....31 F2
Danby Cl HU8 ....141 E7
Danby Rd DN17 ....107 D7
Dancing La Riston HU11 ....45 C5
Swine HU11 ....57 D7
Dane Ave
Thorpe Willoughby YO8 ....48 B1
York YO26 ....129 C5
Dane Cl 18 DN20 ....97 E4
Dane Park Prim Sch HU6 ....139 E8
Dane Park Rd HU6 ....139 E7
Danebury Cres YO26 ....129 C4
Danebury Dr YO26 ....129 C4
Danes Croft
Bridlington YO16 ....122 D5
2 York YO10 ....133 D8
Danes Ct 5 YO19 ....49 A8
Danes Dr HU13 ....69 F4
Danes' Dyke* YO15 ....4 F2
Dane's Graves (Tumuli)* YO25 ....8 D2
Danes Hills (Tumuli)* YO8 ....37 E2
Danes Rd DN21 ....117 C1
Danescroft YO8 ....148 C2
Danesfield Ave DN37 ....113 E7
Danesfort Ave YO24 ....129 D2
Danesgate YO26 ....129 C4
Danesmead YO10 ....133 D8
Danesway HU17 ....136 D6
Daneswell Cl 3 YO41 ....15 D2
Dansom La HU8 ....141 B1
Dansom La S HU8 ....146 B8
Danson Cl DN18 ....85 A8
Danthorpe Rd HU11 ....59 B4
Danube Rd HU5 ....144 C8
Danum Cl 14 DN8 ....93 B8
Danum Dr YO10 ....133 E8
Danum Rd
2 Hatfield DN7 ....92 D3
Scunthorpe DN17 ....150 F4
York YO10 ....133 E8
Dar Beck Rd DN21 ....107 C4
Darbie Cl YO32 ....127 D4
Darby Rd DN15 ....82 B4
D'arcy Rd YO8 ....148 E4
Dark La 5 Amcotts DN17 ....81 F1
Paull HU12 ....72 D4
Darley Cl Kilham YO25 ....9 B3
7 Stamford Bridge YO41 ....15 D2
Darling La YO23 ....36 C8
Darlington Gr DN8 ....79 B2
Darnborough St YO23 ....156 B1
Darnbrook Wlk YO31 ....131 B5
Darnholm Ct 14 HU8 ....141 E7
Darnholme Cres DN17 ....107 D7
Darrismere Villas 4 HU3 ....145 A5
Dart Gr HU8 ....142 B5
Dartmouth Rd DN17 ....150 D5
Darwin Rd YO16 ....122 E6
Darwin St 4 DN21 ....108 B1
Datchet Garth 3 HU4 ....144 B2
Daubney St DN35 ....153 B4
Dauby La YO41 ....27 B3
Davenport Ave HU13 ....143 D1
Davenport Dr DN35 ....153 D1
David Lister High Sch HU9 ....141 E1
David Pl DN36 ....114 A7
David St DN32 ....152 F1
David's Cl HU16 ....138 B8
Davidstow Cl HU7 ....140 F8
Davie Pl DN35 ....153 B3
Daville Cl HU5 ....139 B1
Davis's Cl HU10 ....143 C8
Davy Ave DN15 ....150 E8
Davy Cres 2 DN20 ....98 C3
Davygate YO1 ....156 B2
Daw La YO23 ....36 A5
Dawes La 1 DN15 ....151 C7
Dawlish Rd DN33 ....113 E7
Dawnay Dr HU10 ....144 A6
Dawnay Garth
Shipton YO30 ....12 E5
2 Snaith DN14 ....63 B1
Dawnay Rd HU11 ....58 A4
Dawnhill La DN21 ....119 B2
Dawson Dr HU6 ....140 D8
Day Cl Keadby DN17 ....95 D6
Wrawby DN20 ....98 E4
Daysfoot Ct 8 YO10 ....130 E3
Dayton Rd HU5 ....139 D1
De Aston Sq DN15 ....150 E7
De Grey Ct YO30 ....156 A4
De Grey Pl 2 YO23 ....133 B3
De Grey St
Kingston upon Hull HU5 ....140 C2
York YO31 ....156 B4
De Grey Terr YO31 ....156 B4
De La Pole Ave HU3 ....144 F7
De Lacy La DN35 ....153 F2
De Lacy Way DN15 ....83 A5
De Mowbray Ct YO23 ....24 D3
Deacon Ct 3 YO8 ....148 B6
Deacon Dr DN15 ....150 B6
Deacons Ct YO23 ....132 B2
Dead La Bainton YO25 ....31 E7
Foggathorpe YO8 ....51 A8
Kirkburn YO25 ....20 A2
Lockington YO25 ....32 B2
Deal Cl HU8 ....141 E8
Dealtry Ave 1 YO32 ....127 C8
Dean La YO43 ....53 D4
Dean Rd DN17 ....150 E2
Deane Rd 12 DN40 ....87 C1
Deangate YO1 ....156 B3
Deanhead Gr YO30 ....126 E2
Deans Cl
Bishopthorpe YO23 ....132 F4
5 Misterton DN10 ....116 C5
Dean's La 7 YO42 ....29 A3
Deansgate DN34 ....152 C2
Dearne Gr 1 HU8 ....141 C1
Deaton La DN36 ....114 A7
Debdhill Rd DN10 ....116 C6
Deben Gr HU8 ....142 C7
Dee Cl YO24 ....132 B7
Dee St 6 HU3 ....145 B4
Deene Cl 8 DN34 ....102 B2
Deep The (Aquarium & Marine Research Ctr)* HU9 ....155 C1
Deepdale 5 YO24 ....132 D8
Deepdale Gr 2 HU9 ....146 E8
Deepfurrows La YO41 ....27 D3
Deeping Way YO8 ....148 A6
Deer Hill Gr YO30 ....126 F3
Deer Park Ct 1 LS25 ....61 A8
Deer Park Way 6 HU17 ....55 F8
Deerhurst Gr HU7 ....141 A7
Deerstone Way 22 YO19 ....26 F7
Defender Dr DN37 ....102 A4

Del Pyke YO31 156 C4
Delamere Cl 6 YO32 13 D5
Delamere Ct 24 DN35 103 C1
Delhi St HU9 147 B7
Delius Cl HU4 144 B4
Dell The Beverley HU17 137 B2
Scunthorpe DN17 150 D1
5 Skelton YO30 126 B5
Delwood YO10 133 D7
Dempster Ave DN14 149 C1
Denby Cl DN15 150 D8
Denby Dr DN36 103 B2
Dene Cl Dunswell HU6 56 D5
Hensall DN14 62 C2
Dene Park Sports Club HU6 56 D5
Dene Rd Grimsby DN32 102 F2
Kingston upon Hull HU16 138 F6
Dene St HU9 141 D1
Denehall Rd DN3 92 A2
Denesway HU13 143 D2
Denholme Ave 3 HU6 140 C7
Denison Rd
Pocklington YO42 29 A4
Selby YO8 148 E4
Denmark Ct 7 HU9 146 C7
Denmark Rise 5 HU15 53 D3
Dennett Rd HU17 137 B5
Dennis St YO1 156 C2
Dennison St
1 York YO31 130 E6
York YO31 156 C4
Dent Rd HU5 139 D3
Denton La YO43 53 D6
Denton St HU17 137 B3
Denton's Way DN20 109 A5
Denver Rd 6 DN6 76 F2
Deramore Dr YO10 131 C3
Deramore Dr W YO10 131 C3
Derby Cl DN32 153 A5
Derby Rd DN15 150 B6
Derby St HU3 145 D8
Derringham Ave 5 HU4 144 B6
Derringham St HU3 145 C7
Derry Way 27 DN33 113 E8
Derrymore Rd HU10 138 C2
Derrythorpe Rd DN17 95 D4
Derwent Ave
18 North Ferriby HU14 69 A4
York YO31 130 F4
Derwent Cl
Elvington YO41 27 B3
Hornsea HU18 134 C5
Kingston upon Hull HU6 139 D6
2 Stamford Bridge YO41 15 D2
Derwent Cres DN14 65 B7
Derwent Ct YO41 27 C2
Derwent Dr 4 Barlby YO8 49 B5
12 Humberston DN36 103 C1
2 Humberston DN36 114 C8
9 Kirk Sandall DN3 92 A2
Wheldrake YO19 37 F7
Derwent Est YO19 26 E7
Derwent Inf Sch YO10 131 B4
Derwent Jun Sch YO10 131 B4
Derwent Pk YO19 38 A8
Derwent Rd
Goole DN14 149 D1
1 Howden DN14 65 B7
Scunthorpe DN16 151 D2
York YO10 133 D8
Derwent St HU8 141 B1
Desmond Ave
4 Hornsea HU18 134 C4
Kingston upon Hull HU6 140 D4
Despatch Rd DN16 97 A5
Detuyll St W DN15 96 C7
Deveron Way YO24 132 B7
Devon Pl YO10 130 F3
Devon St
Kingston upon Hull HU16 139 C7
Kingston upon Hull HU4 144 F3
Devonshire Ave DN32 102 E2
Devonshire Dr DN14 149 B5
Devonshire Rd DN17 150 F2
Dewberry Ct HU4 144 D4
Dewsbury Ave DN15 150 C8
Dewsbury Terr YO1 156 A1
Deyne Ave DN15 151 A7
Diadem Gr HU9 142 C5
Dial Sq DN31 152 E3
Diamond St YO31 156 C4
Diana Princess of Wales Hospl DN33 102 E2
Diana St DN15 96 D7
Dibsdane HU6 139 E8
Dick La DN14 65 E7
Dickens Cl 1 YO32 127 F1
Dickey La YO8 48 D5
Dickinson Cl DN20 108 F5
Dickinson's La DN36 114 B1
Dickson Rd 4 YO24 129 B1
Didscourt HU6 139 E6
Digby Garth HU7 57 A5
Digby Gdns DN34 152 A1
Digby St DN15 150 F8
Dijon Ave YO24 129 C2
Dikelands Cl 19 YO26 12 F1
Dikelands La YO26 12 F1
Dill Dr HU17 154 B1
Dilys Gr 5 YO26 129 E4
Dimlington Rd HU12 90 F6
Dimmer Dales Rd HU12 90 D5
Dingley Cl HU6 140 B6
Dirty La DN7 92 D8
Discovery Ctr* DN35 103 D2
Disraeli Cl YO32 127 E1
Ditmas Ave 9 HU4 144 B6
Division Rd 1 HU3 145 B4
Dixon Ave
Broughton DN20 97 D3
Grimsby DN32 102 F2
Dixon Cl 4 Brigg DN20 98 C2
Market Weighton YO43 135 D2
4 Tetney DN36 114 D4
Dixon Ct HU16 139 A5
Dixon La YO1 156 C1
Dixsons Yd YO1 156 C2
Dobella Ave DN14 64 A1
Dobella La DN14 79 B8
Dock Office Row HU1 155 C3
Dock St HU1 155 B2
Dodgson Terr YO26 129 D4
Dodswell Gr HU9 147 E8
Dodsworth Ave YO31 130 E7
Dodthorpe HU6 140 A8
Doe Park La YO41 16 B4
Doe Pk YO30 126 F2
Dog & Duck La
Beverley HU17 154 A3
12 Gainsborough DN21 117 A2
Dog & Duck Sq 13 YO15 5 A2
Dog Kennel La HU17 43 C3
Dolby Vale 23 DN34 102 C2
Dole Rd DN17 80 B1
Dolegate YO41 15 F4
Doll La 2 DN20 98 F7
Dollyth Howe* YO17 6 F6
Dolman Cres 11 DN17 96 C2
Dolphin St DN35 153 F2
Dominion Cl 9 DN36 114 A7
Don Ave YO24 132 E8
Don St DN14 149 D1
Doncaster Rd
Brayton YO8 148 B3
Gunness DN15 95 E6
Hatfield DN7 92 D3
Haxey DN9 104 F2
North Elmsall WF8 76 A1
Scunthorpe DN15 150 A7
Stainforth DN7 92 B6
Doncaster St HU3 145 B6
Donna Fields YO25 9 F6
Donnington Gdns DN15 150 F7
Donnington St DN32 152 F3
Donville Rd DN17 81 A3
Dooks Cl DN21 107 C1
Doon Garth HU4 144 A3
Dorado Cl 2 HU3 145 A5
Dorchester Prim Sch HU7 141 B6
Dorchester Rd
Kingston upon Hull HU7 141 B7
Scunthorpe DN17 150 C4
Doriam Ave YO31 127 F2
Doriam Dr YO31 127 F2
Dorking Cl HU8 142 A4
Dornoch Dr HU8 141 C3
Dorothy Ave
Thorne/Moorends DN8 92 F8
6 Waltham DN37 113 E7
Dorr La DN14 78 A8
Dorrington Cl 23 YO42 29 A3
Dorset Ave HU11 45 E2
Dorset Cl E 2 DN15 82 B4
Dorset Cl W 1 DN15 82 B4
Dorset St HU4 144 F3
Dorsey Way 5 HU15 68 C7
Dot Hill Cl 3 YO43 53 F7
Double Bridges Rd DN8 93 B6
Double Dike* HU20 54 E5
Doughty Cl 2 DN37 113 E7
Doughty Rd DN32 152 E3
Douglas Ave DN34 152 A4
Douglas Rd
Cleethorpes DN35 153 D4
Kingston upon Hull HU8 142 C6
Douglas St 3 YO8 148 C5
Dove Cl HU12 74 A8
Dove Cote Gdns DN14 62 D2
Dove La HU12 74 B8
Dove St YO23 156 A1
Dovecote Garth 5 YO41 27 B2
Dovecote Mdws DN20 98 D3
Dovedale Cl DN15 83 A6
Dovedale Ct YO16 122 F7
Dovedale Dr 18 DN33 113 E8
Dovedale Gr 1 HU9 146 E8
Dovedale Rd DN16 151 D1
Dover St Grimsby DN31 152 C4
Kingston upon Hull HU3 145 C8
Dower Chase YO19 37 A6
Dower Pk YO19 37 B6
Dower Rise 11 HU14 69 B7
Downe Cl DN14 78 D7
Downe St YO25 124 E4
Downfield Ave HU6 140 B8
Downhill Dr 7 HU7 57 B5
Downing Cl 7 DN34 102 C3
Downing Cres 11 DN16 96 D2
Downing Gr HU9 142 A1
Downland Cres WF11 61 A1
Downs Cres HU5 139 D2
Dowse Ave DN15 150 E8
Dowsons La DN14 78 E8
Dr Anderson Ave 9 DN7 92 C6
Dragon La YO16 122 C5
Dragonby Rd 3 DN17 96 C2
Drain Bank HU15 67 B8
Drain La
Gilberdyke HU15 52 D2
Holme-on-Spalding-Moor YO43 51 F8
Drake Ave DN32 153 B2
Drake St 2 YO23 156 B1
Drakes Cl YO32 127 F5
Drapers Croft YO23 132 B4
Draper's La 17 HU12 72 C7
Drax CP Sch YO8 63 F5
Dray Dr HU17 43 E5
Draycot LN7 111 A2
Draycott Ave HU18 134 C5
Drayton Cl 5 HU8 142 C5
Dressay Gr HU8 141 F7
Drew Ave DN32 102 F2
Drewry La 7 DN9 105 A2
Drewton Ct 8 DN14 65 A7
Drewton La HU15 54 A4
Driffield C of E VC Inf Sch YO25 124 E4
Driffield Cl HU16 138 E6
Driffield Cricket & Recn Club YO25 124 D4
Driffield Cty Jun Sch YO25 124 F5
Driffield Rd
Beverley HU17 136 C6
Huggate YO42 18 C1
Kilham YO25 9 C2
Langtoft YO25 8 C4
Molescroft HU17 136 B8
Nafferton YO25 125 E7
Skerne & Wansford YO25 21 A2
Driffield RUFC YO25 124 C2
Driffield Sch YO25 125 A5
Driffield Showground* YO25 124 D2
Driffield Spellowgate YO25 124 B7
Driffield Sports Ctr YO25 125 A5
Driffield Sta YO25 124 F3
Driffield Terr YO24 130 A2
Driffil Way DN15 83 A4
Drill Hall La 29 DN21 117 B1
Dring La DN21 118 A7
Dringfield Cl 2 YO24 132 D8
Dringhouses Prim Sch YO24 132 F8
Dringhouses Sports & Social Club YO24 132 F8
Dringshaw HU6 139 F8
Dringthorpe Rd YO24 132 F7
Drive The
Cherry Burton HU17 43 A4
Kirk Sandall DN3 92 A1
Waltham DN37 113 E6
Drome Rd YO23 132 C2
Drove La HU7 44 E1
Drovers Rise 1 HU15 68 C6
Drummer's Well* YO25 21 F8
Drummond Ct 5 HU7 57 B5
Drummond View YO23 133 B4
Drury Cl 1 DN37 113 D6
Drury La 3 DN36 114 A7
Drydales HU10 143 C6
Dryden Rd DN17 150 D2
Dryden St HU8 141 C2
Dryham La HU15 53 C3
Dryhurst Cl 9 DN6 76 F2
Drypool Way HU9 146 B6
Duchess St DN32 152 D2
Duck La YO12 1 A8
Duckthorpe La DN36 115 B2
Duddon Gr HU8 142 B6
Dudley Mews YO31 156 C4
Dudley Pl DN35 103 B2
Dudley Rd Brigg DN20 98 C2
Scunthorpe DN16 151 E2
Dudley St
Grimsby DN34 152 C3
York YO31 156 C4
Duesbery St HU5 145 C8
Duesbury Cl HU17 154 A3
Dugard Rd DN32 153 B3
Duggleby Howe* YO17 6 C5
Duke St Grimsby DN32 153 A5
13 Stainforth DN7 92 C6
Duke's La YO25 2 A1
Dukes Wharf YO23 156 B1
Dulverton Cl 4 HU7 56 F5
Dunbar Ave 5 DN36 114 A7
Dunbar Cl 6 DN21 117 C1
Dunce Mire Rd LS25 61 A8
Duncombe Ct HU12 72 E7
Duncombe Dr YO25 124 D3
Duncombe Gdns DN32 152 F5
Duncombe La YO32 14 B8
Duncombe Pl YO1 156 B3
Duncombe St DN32 152 F4
Dundas St YO1 156 C2
Dundee St HU5 145 A8
Dunelm Cl 3 HU8 141 C1
Dunelm Cres 13 DN8 79 B2
Dunflat Gate HU17 55 D6
Dunflat La HU20 55 B5
Dunflat Rd HU17 55 D6
Dunhill Rd DN14 149 B4
Dunkeld Dr 4 HU6 140 B8
Dunken Hill Highgate HU17 42 F4
Dunlin Cl HU7 141 D8
Dunlop Way DN16 151 E3
Dunmires La DN14 80 E8
Dunmow Cl 1 HU8 142 C5
Dunmow St DN31 152 B5
Dunnington C of E Prim Sch YO19 26 E7
Dunnington La
Beeford YO25 34 D7
Skipsea YO25 22 F1
Dunnock Cl 7 HU8 141 D7
Dunn's La 6 YO25 124 F4
Dunns Paddock 3 DN20 98 F7
Dunscombe Pk HU8 141 B2
Dunstall St DN15 151 A7
Dunstan Dr 26 DN8 93 A8
Dunstan Hill DN21 108 B1
Dunstan Villas 17 DN21 108 B1
Dunster Rd DN21 117 C1
Dunston Dr HU13 143 D1
Dunston Rd HU4 144 D7
Dunswell Cl HU6 140 A7
Dunswell La HU6 56 C6
Dunswell Prim Sch HU6 56 D6
Dunswell Rd
Cottingham HU16 56 B6
Kingston upon Hull HU16 139 C8
Dunvegan Rd HU8 141 F6
Durban Rd DN32 153 B3
Durban St HU8 155 C3
Durham Ave
Grimsby DN34 152 A3
10 Thorne/Moorends DN8 93 A8
Durham Mews HU17 154 A1
Durham Rd
Cleethorpes DN35 153 C1
Hatfield DN7 92 D4
Durham St HU8 141 C1
Durlston Dr YO32 14 A7
Dursley Ave 1 DN36 113 F7
Dyer La HU17 154 A3
Dyke Cl 2 HU13 69 F4
Dyke Rd DN36 115 C5
Dykelands Cl YO19 37 F7
Dykes La YO23 132 A1
Dymoke Dr DN37 102 B3
Dyon La YO8 50 B3
Dyon Rd YO8 50 D7

E

Eadon Pl DN14 78 B8
Eagle Terr HU8 155 C4
Ealand Rd DN17 95 C6
Ealdane HU6 139 E8
Ealing Cl HU8 141 F5
Earfit La YO23 36 A8
Earl Ave DN36 114 A8
Earl St Grimsby DN31 152 C3
Scunthorpe DN16 151 B6
Earle St YO31 156 C4
Earle's Rd HU9 146 D7
Earlescourt HU6 139 E7
Earlsgate Gdns DN15 82 F5
Earlsgate Rd DN15 83 A5
Earsham Cl HU8 142 C6
Earswick Chase YO32 127 F7
Earswick Village YO32 127 F7
Easby Ct HU5 139 C2
Easenby Ave HU10 143 C6
Easenby Cl 3 HU14 69 C7
Easington C of E Prim Sch HU12 90 F5
Easington Rd
Easington HU12 91 B2
Skeffling HU12 90 E6
Eason Rd
8 Grimsby DN33 102 D1
York YO24 132 E8
Eason View YO24 132 E8
East Acridge 7 DN18 84 F8
East Back Side YO25 10 C3
East Bank DN7 92 C7
East Boundary Rd DN16 151 F6
East Carr Rd
Keyingham HU12 73 D5
Kingston upon Hull HU8 141 F7
East Cl HU17 136 D6
East Comm La
Scunthorpe DN16 151 B4
Selby YO8 148 F4
East Cross St 15 DN21 108 B1
East Dale Dr DN21 108 B2
East Dale Rd HU14 68 E5
East Ella Dr HU4 144 C6
East End
Humberside Airport DN39 100 A6
Walkington HU17 55 C8
East End Cl DN33 102 E1
East End Rd HU12 58 D1
East Ferry Rd
Laughton DN21 106 D1
Wildsworth DN21 117 A8
East Field Rd DN7 92 C8
East Gate Rudston YO25 9 F6
Thorne/Moorends DN8 79 B2
East Gate N YO25 124 E5
East Gate S YO25 124 F4
East Gn DN17 107 D7
East Gr
Barton-upon-Humber DN18 69 F1
Kingston upon Hull HU4 144 D4
East Halton Prim Sch DN40 86 D6
East Halton Rd DN40 86 E3
East Hann La DN19 70 E1
East La Beverley HU17 136 D5
Corringham DN21 118 B2
Sigglesthorne HU11 45 F8
Stainforth DN7 92 C6
East Lambwath Rd HU11 46 D3
East Lound Rd
Haxey DN9 105 D2
Owston Ferry DN9 106 A3
East Marsh Rd DN19 71 C3
East Mid Mere Rd DN40 86 F4
East Moor Gdns YO19 133 F5
East Mount 8 HU14 69 A4
East Mount Ave HU8 142 B5
East Mount Rd YO24 156 A1
East Newton Rd HU11 47 D1
East Par Brigg DN20 98 C2
Goole DN14 149 D3
York YO31 130 F6
East Park Ave HU8 141 E3
East Pk HU17 45 B8
East Ravendale C of E Sch DN37 113 B2
East Rd
Bridlington YO15 122 D1
Keadby with Althorpe DN17 95 C6
East St
Dalton Holme HU17 31 E1
Grimsby DN32 152 E3
Hibaldstow DN20 108 F5
Kilham YO25 9 C3
5 Kingston upon Hull HU9 146 B7
Leven HU17 45 A8
Roxby cum Risby DN15 83 A4
East St Mary's Gate 3 DN31 152 D3
East View
7 Campsall DN6 76 E1
10 Knottingley WF11 61 A2
East Way YO31 127 E2
East Yorkshire Coll YO16 122 D4
East Yorkshire Hospl (Artificial Limb Unit) HU2 155 C3
Eastbourne Gr YO31 130 F5
Eastbourne Rd HU18 134 D4
Eastbourne St HU3 145 A5
Eastbourne Way 12 DN33 113 E8
Eastern Ave DN21 117 C1
Eastern Inway DN34 152 A1
Eastern Terr YO31 130 E6
Eastfield 5 DN36 114 D8
Eastfield Ave
Grimsby DN33 113 E8
Haxby YO32 127 C7
Eastfield Cl
3 Beverley HU17 137 A6
North Frodingham YO25 34 A8
Eastfield Cres YO10 131 C2
Eastfield Ct YO10 131 C2
Eastfield Cty Inf Sch DN40 87 C1
Eastfield Est HU12 60 B1
Eastfield La
Dunnington YO19 26 F8
Kellington DN14 61 F4
Rise HU11 45 F6
Eastfield Prim Sch HU4 144 D6
Eastfield Rd
Barton-upon-Humber DN18 84 F7
Brandesburton YO25 34 C2
Bridlington YO16 122 E5
Brigg DN20 98 C2
Easington HU12 91 A5
Epworth DN9 105 E6
Fangfoss YO41 28 D7
Great Driffield YO25 124 E5
1 Keelby DN41 101 A5
Keyingham HU12 73 D4
Kingston upon Hull HU4 144 D6
Market Weighton YO43 135 E3
Messingham DN17 107 D7
North Killingholme DN40 86 F4
Scunthorpe DN16 151 C1
Eastfield Rise 4 DN36 114 A5
Eastgate Beverley HU17 154 B2
2 Goole DN14 149 D4
Grimsby DN32 152 E4
4 Hornsea HU18 134 B4
Kingston upon Hull HU13 143 E2
Lund YO25 31 F2
Nafferton YO25 125 F7
North Newbald YO43 53 F7
Patrington HU12 74 D1
Scotton DN21 107 C2
Eastgate View HU18 134 B4
Easthall Rd LN7 110 B4
Eastholme Cl YO25 124 F5
Eastholme Dr YO30 126 E1
Eastholme Gdns 9 DN15 82 B4
Eastholme La HU12 73 C7
Easthorpe Dr YO26 126 A1
Eastlands YO25 125 F7
Eastlands Rd YO25 19 E2
Eastmount Recn Ctr HU8 142 B6
Eastoft Rd Crowle DN17 94 D8

Eastoft Rd *continued*
Luddington & Haldenby DN17 81 C3
Eastoft Sch DN17 81 A3
Easton Ave HU8 141 A2
Easton Rd YO16 122 A4
Eastrington Cty Prim Sch DN14 51 F1
Eastrington Sta DN14 66 A8
Eastside Rd
Grimsby DN31 152 F5
Scunthorpe DN16 151 F6
Eastville Rd 10 DN33 102 D2
Eastward Ave YO10 133 E7
Eastwold 2 YO43 53 F7
Eastwood Ave DN32 102 E2
Eastwood Dr 8 DN20 97 E4
Eaton Ct Grimsby DN34 152 C2
7 York YO24 132 B8
Eaton Rd 13 DN40 87 C1
Ebberston Gr 5 HU5 139 E3
Ebor Ave HU18 134 D2
Ebor Cl HU8 142 B6
Ebor Ct 7 YO8 148 C6
Ebor Manor 1 HU12 73 C4
Ebor Prep Sch YO30 130 A7
Ebor St Selby YO8 148 C5
York YO23 156 B1
Ebor View YO43 135 E4
Ebor Way
7 Poppleton YO26 12 F1
Poppleton YO26 126 A2
Ebsay Dr YO30 127 A1
Eccles Ct DN20 98 D4
Ecclesfield Ave HU9 142 D1
Eccleston Rd DN3 92 A3
Eddlemere La YO25 32 E7
Eden Ave YO8 148 D3
Eden Cl Beverley HU17 136 D5
York YO24 132 C7
Eden Dene DN16 151 D1
Eden Dr HU8 141 C3
Eden Field Rd 12 DN3 92 A2
Eden Gdns YO15 4 D2
Eden Gr Rd 3 DN3 92 A1
Eden Rd HU17 136 D5
Eden Rise HU10 138 C2
Edencroft Dr 14 DN3 92 A2
Edendale HU7 140 F6
Edenfield Ave HU18 134 C2
Edenthorpe Hall Prim Sch DN3 92 A1
Edgar St HU3 145 D5
Edge Ave DN33 102 E1
Edgecliffe Villas 4 YO15 122 F4
Edgecumbe St HU5 140 C2
Edgeware Ave 1 HU9 141 F1
Edgware Rd YO10 130 E2
Edinburgh Dr 4 DN36 114 A6
Edinburgh Rd 3 DN17 95 D6
Edinburgh St
Goole DN14 149 C4
Kingston upon Hull HU3 145 A5
Edison Gr HU9 141 E2
Edith Cavell Ct 4 HU5 139 F4
Edmonds Way DN31 152 D4
Edmund Cl DN21 118 A1
Edmund Wilson Swimming Baths YO24 129 D1
Edward Collins Sq 2 HU9 146 C7
Edward Ct 6 DN8 79 B1
Edward Heneage Prim Sch DN32 152 F3
Edward Rd 11 DN21 117 B1
Edward St
Beverley HU17 154 B3
Cleethorpes DN35 153 E1
Grimsby DN32 152 F3
Kingston upon Hull HU13 143 F1
1 Pocklington YO42 29 A4
6 Withernsea HU19 74 F7
Edwardian Dr YO15 122 C1
Edwards Rd DN15 150 F8
Eelmere La HU11 47 A5
Egginton Cl HU10 143 C7
Egginton St HU2 155 B3
Eglinton Ave HU8 141 F3
Egremont Cl 11 YO41 15 D2
Egrom's La HU19 75 A5
Egton Ave DN17 107 D7
Egton St HU8 155 C4
Egypt St HU9 147 B7
Eighth Ave
Bridlington YO15 122 F4
Fixborough Ind Est. DN15 82 A1
York YO31 130 F5
Elba St HU9 147 C7
Elderberry Dr HU4 144 D4
Elderberry Way 4 DN35 103 B1
Elderwood Ct 6 HU3 145 D5
Eldon Dr 11 HU12 58 C1
Eldon Gr
Kingston upon Hull HU5 140 D2
Thorne/Moorends DN8 79 C2
Eldon St YO31 156 C4
Eldon Terr YO31 156 C4
Eldwick Cl YO30 126 F2
Eleanor Ct HU9 142 B2
Eleanor St DN32 152 F4
Elgar Rd HU4 144 B4
Elizabeth Ave 6 DN3 92 A2
Elizabeth Cl
Bridlington YO15 122 C1
4 Gainsborough DN21 117 B2
14 Grimsby DN33 113 D8
Scotter DN21 107 C4
Elizabeth Ct 7 YO8 148 B6
Elizabeth Dr YO25 124 D3
Elizabeth St DN15 151 A8
Ella Pk HU10 143 D7
Ella St HU5 140 B2
Ellerburn Ave HU6 140 A7
Ellerburn Dr 3 YO16 122 C5
Ellerby Gatehouse* HU11 46 A1
Ellerby Gr HU9 141 F2
Ellerby Rd HU11 45 F2
Ellerington La HU17 42 F6
Ellerker La HU15 53 F1
Ellerker Rd HU17 154 A2
Ellerker Rise HU10 138 D2
Ellerker Wold La HU15 54 B1
Ellesmere Ave HU8 142 A4
Ellesmere Gr DN7 92 D6
Ellesmere Rise DN34 102 B2
Ellifoot La HU12 73 B7
Ellingham Cl HU8 142 B6
Elliot Ct YO10 133 D7
Ellis Cl 4 HU12 58 D1
Ellis St HU9 146 C8
Ellis Way DN31 152 E4
Ellison Ave DN16 96 D1
Ellison St DN8 93 A7
Elliston Inf Sch DN35 153 D4
Elliston Jun Sch DN35 153 C4
Elliston St DN35 153 C3
Ellmore La LN7 110 B4
Elloughton Dale HU15 68 D8
Elloughton Gr 4 HU16 138 E6
Elloughton Rd HU15 68 C5
Elm Ave 15 Brough HU15 68 C6
Burstwick HU12 73 A6
Cleethorpes DN35 153 E2
Goole DN14 149 B4
Grimsby DN34 152 A2
Kingston upon Hull HU8 141 C2
Elm Cl HU17 136 D5
Elm Dr HU17 43 A5
Elm End 9 YO32 13 E5
Elm Garth HU12 60 B1
Elm Gdns DN35 153 E2
Elm Gr 1 Aldbrough HU11 47 C1
Healing DN41 102 A5
Scunthorpe DN16 151 B4
York YO31 127 F2
Elm La Goxhill DN19 71 A1
Laceby DN37 101 E1
Elm Rd
Cleethorpes DN35 153 E2
Great Driffield YO25 124 F2
Waltham DN37 113 E6
Elm St
Kingston upon Hull HU5 140 D2
Selby YO8 148 D6
Elm Terr HU5 140 D2
Elm Tree Ave
9 Poppleton YO26 12 F1
5 Thorngumbald HU12 72 E5
Elm Tree Cl
Keyingham HU12 73 C4
6 Thorngumbald HU12 72 E5
Elm Tree Ct HU9 142 C1
Elm Tree Farm Rd 1 HU12 73 A6
Elm Tree Gr 4 DN8 93 B7
Elm Way Brigg DN20 98 B2
Messingham DN17 107 C7
Elma Ave YO16 122 D2
Elma Gr YO30 126 E2
Elma Villas YO16 122 D2
Elmbridge Par 3 HU9 142 E1
Elmdale 16 DN18 84 E8
Elmfield HU6 140 B6
Elmfield Ave YO31 130 F8
Elmfield Dr
16 Brandesburton YO25 34 B2
Kingston upon Hull HU16 139 A6
Elmfield Terr YO31 130 F7
Elmhirst Rd DN8 93 B8
Elmlands Gr YO31 130 F8
Elmpark Vale YO31 131 A8
Elmpark View YO31 131 A8
Elmpark Way YO31 131 A8
Elms Cl 2 YO19 36 F1
Elms Dr HU10 143 C8
Elms The 4 HU15 66 D7
Elmsall Dr HU17 136 C6
Elmswell Spellowgate YO25 20 B6
Elmswood HU13 143 C2
Elmtree Ave 9 HU14 69 A4
Elmtree Gdns 3 YO26 129 C3
Elsenham Rd DN31 152 B5
Elsham Dr DN37 113 D6
Elsham Gr 21 DN33 102 D2
Elsham Hall Ctry & Wildlife Pk* DN20 98 F6
Elsham Rd DN20 98 D7
Elsham Rise HU13 143 D1
Elsie St DN14 149 C5
Elsiemere Wlk 6 HU4 144 B6
Elsternwick Ave HU8 141 B2
Elston Cl
Kingston upon Hull HU6 140 D6
York YO30 130 A8
Elston Pl YO8 148 C6
Elvaston Ave HU18 134 C5
Elveley Dr HU10 143 A7
Elvington C of E Prim Sch YO41 27 B3
Elvington Cl HU6 140 A6
Elvington Cres HU17 43 D5
Elvington Ind Est YO41 27 A3
Elvington La YO19 26 E5
Elvington Pk YO41 27 A3
Elvington Terr YO10 130 E4
Elwell Ave HU17 154 A2
Elwes St 8 DN20 98 C2
Elwick Gr YO10 131 C4
Elwyn Pl 2 DN35 103 B1
Embankment The YO25 124 B3
Emberton Pk
26 Kingston upon Hull HU7 56 F6
12 Kingston upon Hull HU7 56 F6
Embleton Dr 1 YO30 126 F1
Emerald Gr 8 HU3 145 A4
Emerald St YO31 156 C4
Emerson Ave DN7 92 C5
Emfield Gr DN33 113 E7
Emfield Rd DN33 113 D8
Emily St 8 HU9 146 C7
Eminson Cl DN21 107 C4
Emmanual Rd DN16 151 F2
Emmanuel Ct DN16 151 B2
Emmanuel Dr 18 DN16 96 D2
Emmerson St 2 YO31 130 E5
Emmery Cl DN20 97 D4
Emmott Rd HU6 140 C7
Empringham St 5 HU9 146 D7
Empson Ave DN14 149 B6
Empson Terr HU17 154 A2
Ena St HU3 145 B6
Enclosure Gdns 1 YO10 131 B1
Endcliffe Ave DN17 96 C1
Endeavour Cres 3 HU9 142 B1
Enderby Rd DN17 150 D1
Enderby Rd Inf Sch DN17 96 C2
Endfields Rd 1 YO10 133 E8
Endike La HU6 140 A6
Endike Prim Sch HU6 140 C6
Endsleigh RC Prim Sch HU6 140 C4
Endsleigh St HU3 145 A7
Endyke La HU16 139 D6
Endymion St HU8 141 B1
Enfield Ave DN36 114 A7
Enfield Cres
2 York YO24 129 F3
1 York YO24 130 A3
Enfield Mews HU17 154 B3
Enfield Prim Sch DN36 114 A7
Engine La HU11 58 D7
Engine St 20 DN20 98 B2
England Rd HU11 142 F7
English Cl HU3 145 E4
English Martyrs RC Prim Sch YO24 129 F3
English St HU1 155 A1
Ennerdale HU7 140 E7
Ennerdale Ave YO31 131 B5
Ennerdale Cl 13 DN36 103 C1
Ennerdale Sports Ctr HU7 140 E6
Enstone Garth 20 HU7 57 A5
Enterprise Rd LN7 111 A4
Enterprise Way
Grimsby DN32 153 A2
Winterton DN15 82 F5
Ephams La DN41 101 E7
Epping Cl HU8 141 E6
Eppleworth Rd HU16 138 D6
Epworth Cty Prim Sch DN9 105 D6
Epworth Heritage Ctr* DN9 105 E7
Epworth L Ctr DN9 105 D6
Epworth Rd Hatfield DN7 92 F4
Haxey DN9 105 D3
Owston Ferry DN9 106 A4
Epworth Rd W 9 DN7 92 E4
Epworth St HU5 140 D1
Epworth Turbarg Nature Reserve* DN9 105 B6
Ermine St Appleby DN15 97 D8
Winteringham DN15 83 B8
Ernest Hill Ct 11 HU5 140 A2
Ernest Kirkwood Cl 4 HU5 139 D1
Eryholme Cres DN15 150 F7
Escart Ave DN32 153 B2
Escrick C of E Prim Sch YO19 37 A5
Escrick Ct YO19 37 B5
Escrick Park Gdns YO19 37 B5
Escrick St YO10 156 C1
Esk Dr YO26 129 B8
Eskdale Ave
2 Kingston upon Hull HU9 141 E1
York YO10 131 C3
Eskdale Dr YO16 122 F8
Eskdale Way 12 DN37 102 B4
Eske Cl HU17 44 C5
Eske La HU17 44 C5
Eskham Cl 19 DN35 103 C2
Eskholme La DN14 78 B4
Esmond St HU6 140 D5
Esplanade
Hornsea HU18 134 D5
York YO26 156 A2
Essex Dr 7 DN15 82 B4
Essex St HU4 144 E3
Estate Ave DN20 97 D3
Estate Rd No 1 DN31 152 A6
Estate Rd No 2 DN31 152 A5
Estate Rd No 3 DN31 102 C5
Estate Rd No 4 DN31 102 C5
Estate Rd No 5 DN31 152 A6
Estate Rd No 6 DN37 102 C5
Estate Rd No 7 DN37 102 C5
Estate Rd No 8 DN37 102 C5
Estcourt Prim Sch HU9 146 D8
Estcourt St
Goole DN14 149 D4
Kingston upon Hull HU9 146 D8
Estcourt Terr DN14 149 D4
Estuary Way DN31 152 B6
Ethelstone Rd DN34 152 A3
Etherington Cl 5 HU12 73 C4
Etherington Dr HU6 140 D5
Etherington La YO25 124 E4
Etherington Rd HU6 140 C5
Etive Pl YO24 132 B7
Eton Dr 7 Haxby YO32 13 D5
Scunthorpe DN17 96 C2
Eton Rd DN14 149 B5
Eton St HU3 145 C4
Etton Cl HU16 138 E5
Etton Dikes HU17 43 A6
Etton Gr HU6 139 F5
Etton Rd HU17 43 A5
Etty Ave YO10 131 A4
Europa Bsns Pk DN31 152 A6
Europa Way Brigg DN20 98 B2
Immingham DN41 87 E1
Europarc Innovation Ctr DN37 102 B6
Eva Ave YO30 126 D2
Evelyn Cres YO30 130 B7
Evelyn Gr N DN32 153 B2
Evelyn Gr S DN32 153 B2
Evendine Ct 2 DN36 114 B5
Ever Thorpe Cl 5 HU3 145 C5
Everest Rd DN16 151 C1
Evergreen Dr HU6 56 D5
Evergreen Way 1 YO8 48 D1
Everingham La YO42 40 A7
Everingham Wlk HU5 139 C2
Eversfield Cl 21 HU7 56 F5
Everthorpe Rd HU15 53 D3
Evesham Ave DN34 102 C3
Evesham Croft 1 YO16 122 D5
Exchange Pl 7 DN20 98 B2
Exchange St
Great Driffield YO25 124 E4
Kingston upon Hull HU5 140 E2
Exeter Ct 11 DN34 102 B2
Exeter Gr HU9 142 A2
Exeter Rd DN15 150 F7
Exeter St HU16 139 C7
Exmoor Ave DN15 96 B8
Exmoor Rd DN17 150 C4
Exmouth St HU5 140 C3
Exton Cl HU7 56 F5
Eyre Ave DN16 151 B1

F

Faber Cl YO23 132 B3
Faber St YO31 130 E5
Fair Pl HU18 134 B4
Fair View Ave DN35 153 E2
Fairbourne Cl 1 HU7 57 A7
Faircourt HU6 139 E7
Fairfax 15 YO41 15 D2
Fairfax Ave
Kingston upon Hull HU5 139 F3
Selby YO8 148 B4
Fairfax Croft YO23 132 B2
Fairfax Dr HU12 72 C8
Fairfax House* YO1 156 C2
Fairfax Rd DN34 152 B3
Fairfax St YO1 156 B1
Fairfield Goole DN14 149 F6
North Cave HU15 53 D2
Rawcliffe DN14 79 B8
Fairfield Ave
Grimsby DN33 113 E8
Kingston upon Hull HU10 138 C1
Fairfield Cl
5 Broughton DN20 97 E3
Nafferton YO25 125 F7
Fairfield Croft 8 DN9 105 E6
Fairfield Ct 4 DN35 103 D1
Fairfield Dr
25 Barton-upon-Humber DN18 84 F8
Messingham DN17 107 D7
Fairfield La LS25 61 A6
Fairfield Rd
Bridlington YO15 122 D1
Grimsby DN33 113 E8
Kingston upon Hull HU5 139 F3
Scunthorpe DN15 150 C8
Fairfield View 5 HU15 68 D5
Fairfields Dr YO30 126 B5
Fairholme La HU7 56 F7
Fairisle Rise 5 DN40 101 C8
Fairlawn HU17 136 C6
Fairmont Cres DN16 151 B6
Fairmont Rd DN32 153 A3
Fairtree Wlk 21 DN8 93 A8
Fairway Waltham DN37 113 E7
York YO30 130 A8
Fairway Ave DN21 117 B2
Fairway Ct DN35 103 E1
Fairway Dr 18 YO26 12 F1
Fairway The
Kingston upon Hull HU10 143 A8
Thorne/Moorends DN8 79 B2
Fairways The
Kingston upon Hull HU8 142 A6
Scunthorpe DN15 150 B6
Falcon Cl 10 YO32 13 F5
Falcon Ct HU4 144 D2
Falconer St 1 YO24 129 F3
Falconers The DN21 108 F2
Falkirk Cl 7 HU7 57 A7
Falkland Rd HU9 147 E8
Falkland St YO1 156 B1
Falkland Way DN18 69 F1
Fallowfield Rd DN33 113 D8
Falmouth St HU5 140 C3
Falsgrave Cres YO30 130 B7
Falsgrave Gr HU4 144 D7
Fannystone Rd DN34 152 B3
Far Bank La DN7 92 C8
Far Comm Rd DN7 93 A4
Far Field Cl 15 DN3 92 A2
Far Field Rd DN3 92 A2
Far Ings La DN18 69 C1
Far Ings Rd DN18 69 D1
Far La YO25 35 A5
Faraday St HU9 141 E2
Fardell Rd DN16 151 D3
Farebrother St DN32 152 E1
Farfield YO26 129 C6
Farfield La YO19 26 E8
Faringdon Rd DN31 153 A6
Farm Cl
6 Edenthorpe DN3 92 A1
Gunness DN15 95 E6
Farm Ct YO43 135 C5
Farm La 2 DN17 106 D8
Farm Way YO8 148 B7
Farmers Way YO23 132 B3
Farmhouse Mews 11 DN36 114 A7
Farmlands Rd 1 YO24 132 D8
Farms La DN14 66 A8
Farmstead Rise YO32 127 D7
Farndale Ave
Kingston upon Hull HU9 141 E1
York YO10 131 D4
Farndale Cl 1 YO32 13 F5
Farndale St YO10 130 D2
Farndale Way 1 DN15 83 A5
Farnella Cl HU3 145 A5
Faroes Cl 1 HU9 142 A3
Farrand Rd HU12 72 C7
Farrar St YO10 130 E3
Farriers Croft 2 YO23 132 B3
Farringdon St 2 HU5 140 E1
Farrishes La DN18 84 A8
Farthing Ave DN15 150 E8
Farthing La YO25 125 C4
Fauconberg Ave 6 DN33 102 E1
Faulding La DN40 86 F2
Faulding Way DN37 102 B4
Faversham Ave HU4 144 B6
Fawcett Cl HU5 140 D1
Fawcett Gdns 9 YO25 124 F4
Fawcett St
27 Gainsborough DN21 117 B1
York YO10 156 C1
Fawkes Dr YO26 129 C4
Fawley Cl HU5 140 E3
Faxfleet La DN14 67 A3
Feasegate YO1 156 B2
Featherbed La YO42 29 C4
Felbridge Cl 1 HU9 142 E2
Feldane HU6 139 E8
Fellbrook Ave YO26 129 B4
Felstead Rd DN34 102 C3
Fen La DN36 114 D1
Fen Wlk DN36 115 C5
Fenby Cl 3 DN37 102 B3
Fenchurch St 1 HU5 140 E1
Fenland Rd 12 DN8 93 B7
Fenton St DN15 151 B7
Fenwick Comm La DN6 77 D2
Fenwick Ct DN36 114 A5
Fenwick La DN6 77 B1
Fenwick Rd DN33 102 D1
Fenwick St YO23 130 C2
Fenwick's La YO10 133 D7
Feoffee La YO42 28 C5
Ferens Art Gall* HU1 155 B2
Ferens Ave HU6 140 B4
Ferens Ct 2 HU9 141 D1
Ferens Gdns HU16 138 F8
Ferensway HU2 155 A3
Ferguson Rd 2 HU17 55 B7
Ferguson Way YO32 127 F1
Fern Cl
Kingston upon Hull HU2 155 A4
York YO32 128 A4
Fern Croft 18 DN9 105 E6
Fern Ct HU13 144 A1
Fern St YO31 156 C4
Fernbank 1 DN9 105 D7
Ferndale Ave HU10 138 D1
Ferndale Dr DN8 79 B1
Ferndale Gr DN14 149 C6
Ferndale Rd YO8 148 C4
Ferndale Terr 11 YO15 122 E2
Ferndown DN37 102 B5
Ferndown Dr DN40 87 C2
Fernhall Cl 11 DN3 92 A2
Fernhill 5 DN37 102 B4
Fernhill Rd HU5 139 D3
Fernland Cl 15 HU15 68 C5

Fernlea Cl YO8 ...148 D4
Fernley Gn Cl 6 WF11 ...61 A2
Fernway YO10 ...131 C3
Ferriby Gr HU6 ...139 F5
Ferriby High Rd HU14 ...69 B5
Ferriby La DN33 ...102 E1
Ferriby Rd
Barton-upon-Humber DN18 ...84 E8
Hessle HU13 ...143 B1
Scunthorpe DN17 ...150 E1
Ferriby Sta HU14 ...69 A4
Ferries St HU9 ...146 D7
Ferry Cl 11 YO8 ...49 F1
Ferry Farm Cl 2 YO19 ...36 D8
Ferry La Airmyn DN14 ...149 A8
Bishopthorpe YO23 ...133 B4
Bubwith YO8 ...50 C5
Goole DN14 ...65 B5
Snaith & Cowick DN14 ...63 C1
Thorganby YO19 ...38 B5
Winteringham DN15 ...68 B1
Woodmansey HU17 ...56 C7
Ferry Rd
Barrow upon Humber DN19 ...70 C1
Fishlake DN8 ...78 F1
Goxhill DN19 ...85 F8
Haxey DN9 ...105 D1
Keadby with Althorpe DN17 ...95 D4
Kilpin DN14 ...65 B5
Kingston upon Hull HU13 ...143 E1
Scunthorpe DN15 ...150 D8
South Cave HU15 ...53 E1
Wawne HU7 ...56 D8
Ferry Rd E DN19 ...85 C8
Ferry Rd W DN15 ...96 A7
Ferryman Pk HU12 ...72 A5
Fetherston Cl 19 YO42 ...29 A3
Fetter La YO1 ...156 B2
Feversham Cres 4 YO31 ...130 C7
Fewson Garth 26 HU12 ...72 D7
Fewster Way YO10 ...156 C1
Fewston Dr 9 YO30 ...126 F1
Field Ave YO8 ...48 B1
Field Cl 10 Laceby DN37 ...101 F1
Snaith DN14 ...78 C8
Field Head
Laceby DN37 ...101 E1
Wilberfoss YO41 ...27 F6
Field La Eastoft DN17 ...81 A4
Gowdall DN14 ...77 F8
Hambleton YO8 ...48 B1
Hensall DN14 ...62 D2
Heslington YO10 ...131 C2
Morton DN21 ...116 F3
Rawcliffe DN14 ...64 A1
Thornton YO42 ...39 A8
Wistow YO8 ...48 C7
Wroot DN9 ...104 D5
Field Lane Sports Ctr YO8 ...48 B1
Field Rd
Bridlington YO16 ...122 C4
Crowle DN17 ...94 D7
Stainforth DN7 ...92 C6
Thorne/Moorends DN8 ...93 A8
West Haddlesey YO8 ...62 A5
Field Side DN8 ...93 A8
Field St HU9 ...146 B7
Field View YO31 ...130 C7
Fieldend La HU12 ...59 B2
Fieldfare YO25 ...125 B5
Fieldfare Dr YO25 ...125 B5
Fieldhouse Rd
7 Humberston DN36 ...103 D1
Humberston DN36 ...114 D8
Fields Cl 2 DN9 ...105 D7
Fields Cl Rd HU12 ...73 E4
Fields Rd DN9 ...105 E2
Fieldside Blyton DN21 ...117 F5
Crowle DN17 ...94 D7
Epworth DN9 ...105 D6
Fieldside Garth HU6 ...56 D5
Fifth Ave
Bridlington YO15 ...123 A4
Fixborough Ind Est. DN15 ...82 A1
Goole DN14 ...149 C5
Scunthorpe DN17 ...150 B2
York YO31 ...130 F4
Fifth Avenue Prim Sch HU6 ...140 A6
Fiftyeights Rd DN10 ...104 B2
Figham Rd HU17 ...137 B3
Figham Springs Way HU17 ...154 B1
Fildes St DN31 ...152 D3
Filey Rd Grimsby DN32 ...153 A1
Hunmanby YO14 ...3 A8
Filey Terr YO30 ...130 C7
Fillingham Cres
Cleethorpes DN35 ...103 C2
Gunness DN15 ...150 B7
Fimber Ave HU16 ...139 A5
Finch Croft 5 HU7 ...141 D7
Finch Pk HU17 ...136 D5
Finchcroft La HU17 ...43 B2
Finchley Cl HU8 ...141 F5
Findlay Cres DN36 ...114 A7
Findon Cl 28 HU7 ...56 F6
Fingall Mews 1 HU5 ...139 D3
Finkle La DN18 ...69 F1
Finkle St
2 Bishop Burton HU17 ...43 A2
Hensall DN14 ...62 D2
Finkle St *continued*
Kingston upon Hull HU16 ...139 A6
Market Weighton YO43 ...135 D4
2 North Cave HU15 ...53 D3
Selby YO8 ...148 C5
Stainforth DN7 ...92 C7
Finningley Garth 14 HU7 ...57 A5
Finnley's La DN14 ...78 C7
Finsbury Ave YO23 ...130 C1
Finsbury Dr 7 DN33 ...102 D1
Finsbury St YO23 ...130 C1
Fir Cl DN16 ...96 D2
Fir Heath Cl 5 YO24 ...129 C1
Fir Tree Cl YO8 ...48 B2
Fir Tree Dr 11 DN6 ...76 E2
Fir Tree La YO8 ...48 B2
Fir Tree Way YO8 ...48 B2
Fir Trees HU10 ...143 D6
Fir Trees The YO8 ...48 B2
Firbank Cl 9 YO32 ...14 A7
Firethorn Cl 3 HU3 ...145 D5
Firsby Cres DN33 ...102 D1
First Ave
Bridlington YO15 ...122 F4
Flixborough DN15 ...82 A1
3 Goole DN14 ...149 C4
Grimsby DN33 ...102 E2
Scunthorpe DN17 ...150 C2
York YO31 ...130 F6
First Comm La YO8 ...48 D4
First La
Kingston upon Hull HU10 ...144 A5
South Cave HU15 ...54 A2
Firth Field Rd DN7 ...92 F4
Firth La DN9 ...104 D5
Firtholme Rd HU12 ...91 A4
Firtree Cl
4 Earswick YO32 ...127 F7
York YO24 ...129 E3
Firtree Dr DN20 ...98 F7
Firwood Whin 5 YO32 ...127 F3
Fish Dock Rd DN31 ...152 F6
Fish La HU15 ...52 D2
Fish St HU1 ...155 B1
Fishemore Ave HU13 ...143 F2
Fisher Cl HU10 ...138 D2
Fisher La YO25 ...22 E5
Fisher Pl DN35 ...153 D3
Fisher Sq HU17 ...154 A2
Fishergate YO10 ...156 C1
Fishergate Prim Sch YO10 ...156 C1
Fisherman's Wharf DN31 ...152 D4
Fishermans Wlk 2 HU3 ...145 C4
Fishlake Nab DN7 ...92 C7
Fishpond Hill YO42 ...29 C4
Fishwick Ave 5 HU13 ...143 E1
Fiskerton Cl 20 DN34 ...102 C2
Fiskerton Way DN31 ...102 C6
Fitling Rd HU11 ...59 B5
Fitties La DN36 ...115 C5
Fitzroy St HU5 ...140 D2
Fitzwilliam Mews 2 DN35 ...103 C1
Flag Wlk 1 HU6 ...140 C8
Flag Yd YO16 ...122 C4
Flamborough Head Nature Reserve* YO15 ...5 D2
Flamborough Rd
Bempton YO15 ...4 E1
Bridlington YO15 ...122 F4
Bridlington YO15 ...123 C8
Flamborough Sch YO15 ...5 A2
Flarepath The DN20 ...99 A8
Flashley Carr La DN6 ...77 F1
Flat La YO42 ...28 D4
Flatgate DN14 ...65 B7
Flavian Gr YO30 ...129 F8
Flaxdale Ct HU5 ...139 E1
Flaxley Ct YO8 ...148 B5
Flaxley Rd YO8 ...148 A7
Flaxman Ave YO10 ...131 A4
Flaxman Croft YO23 ...132 B3
Flaxmill Wlk 2 HU15 ...66 D7
Flaxton Rd
Kingston upon Hull HU5 ...139 D1
Strensall YO32 ...14 B7
Fleet Garth 11 HU12 ...72 D7
Fleet La DN14 ...64 A7
Fleetgate 11 DN18 ...69 E1
Fleets Cl DN7 ...92 C7
Fleetway DN36 ...115 A3
Fleetwood Cl 4 DN33 ...113 E8
Fleming Ave 3 YO31 ...130 E5
Fleming Wlk HU4 ...144 D2
Flemingate HU17 ...154 C2
Flemingdale HU7 ...140 F7
Fletcher Cl
Kingston upon Hull HU13 ...143 E2
6 Scunthorpe DN15 ...96 B7
Fletcher Ct 14 YO32 ...13 E5
Fletcher Gate HU12 ...72 C7
Fletcher Rd DN34 ...102 C4
Fletcher's Croft YO23 ...132 C3
Flinton Gr HU9 ...142 A1
Flinton Rd
Aldbrough HU11 ...58 F8
Humbleton HU11 ...59 A7
Flinton St HU3 ...145 B3
Flixborough Rd DN15 ...82 A4
Floral Hall HU18 ...134 D5
Florence Ave HU13 ...143 F1
Florence Gr YO30 ...126 D2
Florence Nightingale 3 HU5 ...139 F4
Florence St DN32 ...152 E1
Flour Sq DN31 ...152 E5
Fog La YO42 ...38 E4
Folkestone St HU5 ...140 D2
Folks Cl 13 YO32 ...13 F5
Folkton Ave HU16 ...139 A4
Follies The DN15 ...97 E7
Folly La LN7 ...110 C5
Football Gn HU18 ...134 C3
Forber Ave HU9 ...142 C2
Forbes Ave HU6 ...140 C8
Ford La DN20 ...108 F5
Fordlands YO8 ...48 B2
Fordlands Cres YO19 ...133 E5
Fordlands Rd YO19 ...133 E6
Fordon La Willerby YO12 ...1 E7
Wold Newton YO25 ...2 A6
Ford's Ave 9 DN41 ...101 F5
Foredyke Ave HU7 ...141 A4
Foredyke Prim Sch HU9 ...142 A1
Forest Cl 27 YO32 ...13 E5
Forest Dr DN36 ...103 D1
Forest Gr YO31 ...130 F6
Forest La Fulford YO19 ...26 A2
Strensall YO32 ...14 A8
Forest of Galtres Prim Sch YO30 ...12 F5
Forest Way
24 Humberston DN36 ...103 D1
Humberston DN36 ...114 D8
York YO31 ...130 F6
Forester Way HU4 ...144 D3
Foresters Way YO16 ...123 A7
Foresters Wlk YO41 ...15 C1
Forester's Wlk YO24 ...129 B1
Forestgate YO32 ...127 C7
Forge Cl
Huntington YO32 ...128 A2
Melbourne YO42 ...39 B6
South Kelsey LN7 ...110 A1
8 Thorngumbald HU12 ...72 E5
Forge Cres 3 DN39 ...86 A1
Forge La YO19 ...37 A7
Forge Pl HU16 ...138 B7
Forge The YO25 ...124 E3
Forge Way 3 DN36 ...114 A6
Forkedale DN18 ...84 E8
Formby Cl HU6 ...139 E5
Forrester St 21 DN20 ...98 B2
Forrester's Cl 3 DN6 ...76 E2
Forster St 26 DN21 ...117 B1
Forsythia Dr DN33 ...102 E1
Fort Paull Battery* HU12 ...72 B4
Fort Terr 6 YO15 ...122 F2
Forth St YO26 ...129 F6
Fortuna Way 2 DN37 ...102 B4
Fortune Cl HU8 ...141 F4
Forty Acre HU10 ...143 F7
Forty Foot La DN39 ...99 F6
Forty Steps HU10 ...143 F7
Fortyfoot YO16 ...122 F4
Fortyfoot Ct YO16 ...122 E4
Fortyfoot Gr 1 YO16 ...122 F4
Forum Ctr* YO15 ...122 F2
Fosham Rd HU11 ...46 D2
Foss Bank YO31 ...156 C3
Foss Ct YO31 ...127 E1
Foss Field La YO23 ...36 B8
Foss Garth YO41 ...27 F5
Foss Gr HU8 ...142 B6
Foss Islands Rd YO31 ...156 C3
Foss Wlk YO26 ...129 B8
Fossdale Cl HU8 ...141 E6
Fosse Hill Jet Ski Ctr* YO25 ...34 C1
Fossgate YO1 ...156 C2
Fossland View 4 YO32 ...14 A7
Fossway
Stamford Bridge YO41 ...15 D1
York YO31 ...130 D7
Foster Gate YO8 ...148 D4
Foster Rd 9 DN8 ...93 A8
Foster St HU8 ...141 A2
Fostergate YO8 ...48 A8
Foston Gr
Kingston upon Hull HU9 ...142 A1
4 York YO31 ...130 F8
Foston La Beeford YO25 ...22 B1
North Frodingham YO25 ...21 F1
Fotherbie Garth 11 HU12 ...72 C7
Fotherby Rd 4 DN17 ...96 C2
Fotherby St DN31 ...152 E5
Foundry La 5 WF11 ...61 A2
Fountain Cl
Kingston upon Hull HU13 ...143 C3
Kingston upon Hull HU2 ...155 A4
6 Waltham DN37 ...113 D7
Fountain Hill DN10 ...116 B3
Fountain Hill Rd DN10 ...116 B4
Fountain Rd HU2 ...140 E1
Fountain St
16 Caistor LN7 ...111 B4
Kingston upon Hull HU3 ...145 D6
Fountains Ave YO16 ...122 D7
Fountains Way HU15 ...53 D3
Fountayne Rd
13 Hunmanby YO14 ...2 F8
13 Hunmanby YO14 ...2 F8
Fountayne St
Goole DN14 ...149 E5
York YO31 ...130 C7
Four Acre Cl HU10 ...143 C6
Fourth Ave
Bridlington YO15 ...123 A4
Fixborough Ind Est. DN15 ...82 A1
Goole DN14 ...149 C4
Scunthorpe DN17 ...150 C2
York YO31 ...130 E5
Fourways 9 DN36 ...114 D4
Fowler Ct 3 DN15 ...83 A5
Fowler Rd DN16 ...151 C3
Fox Covert
Hibaldstow DN20 ...108 F5
York YO31 ...127 F2
Fox Covert La DN10 ...116 D4
Fox Covert Rd WF8 ...76 C1
Fox Ct DN17 ...94 D8
Fox Garth YO26 ...126 A3
Fox Glade YO41 ...15 C2
Fox Hill (Tumulus)* YO25 ...21 D8
Fox Hill La YO8 ...148 A3
Fox La
Chapel Haddlesey YO8 ...62 C5
Hambleton LS25 ...61 D8
Laxton DN14 ...65 E3
Thorpe Willoughby YO8 ...48 B1
Fox St DN15 ...150 F7
Foxcroft 3 YO32 ...127 C7
Foxdale Ave YO8 ...48 B1
Foxglove Cl 16 HU7 ...56 F5
Foxglove Gdns 5 DN34 ...102 C3
Foxhill DN37 ...102 B4
Foxhill Cl HU9 ...142 E2
Foxhill La YO8 ...148 A3
Foxhill Rd DN8 ...93 B7
Foxhills Comp Sch DN15 ...96 C7
Foxhills Ind Pk DN15 ...96 C8
Foxhills Rd DN15 ...96 C7
Foxholme Rd HU7 ...141 D7
Foxthorn Paddock YO10 ...131 D3
Foxton Cl YO24 ...132 C8
Foxwood La York YO24 ...129 A1
3 York YO24 ...129 C1
York YO24 ...132 C8
Foynes Gn 6 HU8 ...142 C5
Frampton Cl HU7 ...141 B6
Frances Askew Prim Sch HU4 ...144 E4
Frances Ct 8 DN37 ...113 D7
Frances St
Scunthorpe DN15 ...151 A7
York YO10 ...130 D1
Francis Ave 10 HU19 ...75 A6
Francis Ct 7 YO8 ...48 B2
Francis St HU2 ...155 B3
Francis Way 3 HU12 ...74 D1
Frankland Cl DN20 ...98 E3
Frankland Pl DN35 ...153 D3
Franklin Cres DN16 ...151 E2
Franklin Rd DN21 ...107 C4
Franklin Sixth Form Coll DN34 ...152 B1
Franklin St HU9 ...146 C8
Franklin Way DN38 ...99 F5
Fraser St DN32 ...152 F3
Frazer Ct YO30 ...129 E8
Frederic St YO30 ...156 A3
Frederick Gough Comp Sch DN16 ...96 E2
Frederick Holmes Sch HU6 ...140 A5
Frederick St
Cleethorpes DN35 ...153 E2
Goole DN14 ...149 E5
Grimsby DN31 ...152 D4
Frederick Ward Way DN31 ...152 D3
Freehold St HU3 ...145 D7
Freeman Ave 4 HU15 ...68 C5
Freeman Ct DN36 ...114 B5
Freeman St DN32 ...152 F4
Freemans La DN20 ...84 C2
Freeport Wharf DN31 ...152 E4
Freeschool La or Gr DN14 ...52 A2
Freeston St DN35 ...153 B4
Freetown Way HU2 ...155 A3
Freightliner Rd HU3 ...144 F2
Fremantle Ave HU9 ...142 D2
Frensham Cl 9 HU7 ...56 F6
Fresh Fields 16 HU15 ...68 C5
Freshney Bog Nature Reserve* DN34 ...102 B3
Freshney Dr DN31 ...152 C4
Freshney Places Sh Ctr DN31 ...152 D3
Friargate YO1 ...156 B2
Friars Cl YO19 ...26 D7
Friars La HU17 ...154 B2
Friars Mdw YO8 ...148 C8
Friars Rd DN17 ...150 E2
Friar's Wlk YO31 ...130 E8
Friary Ct 5 HU3 ...140 D1
Friendship Ct 2 YO8 ...148 C6
Frith Mews 4 YO8 ...148 C6
Frobisher Ave DN32 ...153 B2
Frodingham Footpath 2 DN15 ...151 B7
Frodingham Inf Sch DN15 ...151 B6
Frodingham La HU12 ...74 D4
Frodingham Rd
Brandesburton YO25 ...34 B4
Scunthorpe DN15 ...151 A8
Frodingham S Rd DN16 ...151 E5
Frodsham St HU9 ...147 B7
Froebel House Sch HU17 ...136 C6
Frome Rd HU8 ...142 C7
Front La HU12 ...59 A3
Front St
Alkborough DN15 ...82 C8
Burton Fleming YO25 ...2 E3
East Stockwith DN21 ...116 E5
Elsham DN20 ...98 F7
Gainsborough DN21 ...117 A2
Grasby DN38 ...110 E7
Langtoft YO25 ...8 C5
Laxton DN14 ...65 E4
Lockington YO25 ...32 B2
Middleton YO25 ...31 C4
Naburn YO19 ...36 D8
Ulceby DN39 ...86 A1
Wold Newton YO25 ...2 A4
York YO24 ...129 C3
Froscoles Cl 6 HU15 ...53 D3
Frusher Ave 7 DN33 ...102 E2
Fryston 11 HU15 ...68 C6
Fryston Comm La LS25 ...61 A8
Fuchsia Croft DN15 ...150 F6
Fuchsia Dr HU4 ...144 B2
Fulbeck Rd DN16 ...151 C2
Fulford Cres
Kingston upon Hull HU10 ...144 A8
3 New Holland DN19 ...70 E2
Fulford Cross YO10 ...130 D1
Fulford Cross Specl Sch YO10 ...130 D1
Fulford Pk YO10 ...133 D7
Fulford Rd YO10 ...133 D8
Fulford Sch YO10 ...133 E7
Fulfordgate YO10 ...133 E7
Fulham La DN14 ...76 E7
Fulham Pk 2 DN33 ...102 D1
Fuller St DN35 ...153 D4
Fulmar Cl HU7 ...141 D8
Fulstow Cty Prim Sch LN11 ...121 E8
Fulstow Gr 22 DN33 ...102 D2
Furlong Rd 23 YO41 ...15 D2
Furness Cl 8 HU7 ...57 A7
Furness Dr YO30 ...126 E1
Furnwood 2 YO32 ...127 D7
Furze Rd HU12 ...60 B2
Fussey Gdns DN20 ...84 C1
Fylingdales Ave
6 York YO30 ...126 E1
York YO30 ...129 E8

G

Gable Pk YO23 ...24 C6
Gables Cl 8 DN14 ...61 D4
Gadwall Cl 2 HU15 ...52 F1
Gain Hills Balk YO16 ...10 D4
Gainas Ave DN21 ...117 B1
Gainford Gr HU9 ...142 E2
Gainford Rd DN8 ...79 B2
Gainford Sq 18 DN8 ...79 B2
Gainsborough La DN20 ...108 F8
Gainsborough Rd
Blyton DN21 ...117 E4
20 Kirton in Lindsey DN21 ...108 B1
Kirton in Lindsey DN21 ...119 A8
Scotter DN21 ...107 B3
Gainsthorpe Rd E DN21 ...108 D4
Gainsthorpe Rd W DN21 ...108 C4
Gale Farm Ct 6 YO24 ...129 C3
Gale La Thorganby YO19 ...37 F4
York YO24 ...129 C2
Gale The YO19 ...36 D4
Galecarr La YO42 ...39 E6
Galegate YO43 ...53 E7
Galfrid Rd HU11 ...142 F7
Galley Ct HU9 ...146 C6
Galligap La YO10 ...131 C4
Gallops The YO24 ...132 B8
Galloway Ct 4 YO25 ...124 F4
Galloway La 3 YO25 ...124 F4
Gallows Bridge Rd HU11 ...59 A7
Gallows Hill* YO25 ...9 A2
Gallows La HU17 ...136 D5
Galmanhoe La YO30 ...156 A3
Galtres Ave YO31 ...131 B7
Galtres Gr YO30 ...129 F7
Galtres Rd YO31 ...131 B7
Galtres Sch YO31 ...131 B5
Ganstead Gr HU9 ...142 A2
Ganstead La HU11 ...142 D6
Ganton Ave HU16 ...139 A5
Ganton Ct 3 HU8 ...142 B5
Ganton Hill YO12 ...1 B7
Ganton Pl YO24 ...132 E7
Ganton Rd YO25 ...1 C4
Ganton Specl Sch HU10 ...144 A7
Ganton Way HU10 ...143 F8
Gap Rd YO14 ...3 D8
Garbett Way 1 YO23 ...133 B3
Garburn Gr 3 YO30 ...126 E1
Garbutt Cl 2 HU12 ...58 D1
Garbutt Gr YO26 ...129 D5
Garbutt Pl 3 DN35 ...103 D2
Garden Dr DN36 ...114 A8
Garden Flats La YO19 ...26 E7

Garden La 11 WF11 61 A3
Garden Pl YO1 156 C2
Garden St 13 Brigg DN20 98 C2
Grimsby DN32 152 D3
York YO31 156 B4
Garden Wlk 12 YO15 122 E2
Gardeners Cl 8 YO23 132 B3
Gardeners Row YO25 7 B3
Gardens The HU3 145 C5
Gardham La YO25 35 A6
Gardham Rd HU17 42 E5
Gare La DN14 66 A6
Garends Rd 4 YO15 5 A2
Garfield Cl HU9 142 D1
Garfield St 22 DN21 117 B1
Garfield Terr YO26 129 F5
Garibaldi St DN32 152 F5
Garland Cl HU9 142 C4
Garland St 2 YO26 129 E4
Garlands The YO30 130 A8
Garman Carr La YO8 48 D6
Garner St DN32 152 E2
Garnet Gr 6 HU3 145 A4
Garnet Terr YO26 129 E5
Garnett St DN35 153 D4
Garrick Cl Brayton YO8 148 B1
Kingston upon Hull HU8 141 F4
15 Pocklington YO42 29 A3
Garrison Rd HU9 155 C1
Garrison St YO15 122 F2
Garrow Hill YO10 130 F2
Garrow Hill Ave YO10 131 A3
Garroway Way YO10 26 A4
Garrowby Hill YO41 16 F3
Garrowby Rd YO42 16 F2
Garrowby St YO41 16 E3
Garrowby View 5 YO41 15 D2
Garth Ave
Kingston upon Hull HU11 58 A3
4 North Duffield YO8 50 A7
Garth Cl 6 YO8 48 D6
Garth Ends Rd HU17 43 A2
Garth Glebe 8 YO8 49 B5
Garth La Goole DN14 65 C4
Grimsby DN31 152 D4
Garth Mill 1 DN14 61 D4
Garth Morrell YO8 148 C2
Garth Rd YO32 127 F4
Garth Terr YO30 130 B7
Garth The HU16 139 A5
Garthends La
3 Hemingbrough YO8 49 F1
Mappleton HU11 47 B5
Garthorpe Rd
Luddington & Haldenby DN17 81 C4
Twin Rivers DN14 81 E7
Garths End 20 Haxby YO32 13 F5
Pocklington YO42 29 A4
Garth's End YO10 133 E8
Garths End La YO42 29 A8
Garthway
13 Holton le Clay DN36 114 A5
4 York YO32 127 D3
Garton Balk YO25 20 D8
Garton Gr
Grimsby DN32 153 A1
3 Kingston upon Hull HU4 144 C7
Garton Hill YO25 19 E7
Garton Rd HU11 47 C1
Garton Sch YO25 20 A6
Garton Slack YO25 19 D6
Gas House La 13 DN14 65 B7
Gashouse La DN9 106 B3
Gate Arts Ctr The* DN14 149 C4
Gate La 11 DN33 102 E1
Gate Way DN31 152 C6
Gateforth New Rd YO8 62 A8
Gatehead La YO42 38 D7
Gatehouse* DN39 86 B5
Gatehouse Rd DN19 85 F7
Gatehowe Rd YO17 17 A7
Gateland Cl YO32 127 C7
Gateland Field La DN14 64 B6
Gatesby Rd DN14 149 C6
Gatewood La DN7 92 E1
Gatherums The DN35 153 E1
Gatwick Garth 15 HU7 57 A5
Gaufer Hill YO43 41 D3
Gautry La DN9 106 B4
Gay Mdws YO32 14 D2
Gayles Mews 3 HU5 139 D3
Gayton Rd DN35 103 D2
Gedney Cl 8 DN37 102 B4
Gee St HU3 145 C5
Geeseness La DN14 78 D2
Geldof Rd YO32 127 F1
Gembling CP Sch YO25 22 A3
Gembling La YO25 22 A4
Gemel Rd HU12 59 C2
Gemsbok Cl 3 HU4 144 D2
General La YO42 38 E6
Geneva Sq DN8 79 C2
Geneva Way HU7 141 B5
George Ave DN17 95 D5
George Butler Cl 16 DN37 101 F1
George Cayley Dr YO30 127 A3
George Ct YO31 156 C3
George Hudson St YO1 156 B2
George Janney Ct DN32 153 A5
George La HU17 55 D8
George Mews 8 LN7 111 B4
George St
2 Barton-upon-Humber DN18 84 F8
Beverley HU17 154 B3
Bridlington YO15 122 C1
Broughton DN20 97 D3
Cleethorpes DN35 153 E1
Gainsborough DN21 117 A1
Great Driffield YO25 124 E4
Grimsby DN31 152 D3
28 Hedon HU12 72 C7
Keadby DN17 95 D5
Kingston upon Hull HU16 139 A7
Kingston upon Hull HU1 155 B2
11 Kirton in Lindsey DN21 108 B1
Pocklington YO42 29 A4
Scunthorpe DN15 151 A8
4 Selby YO8 148 D6
Snaith DN14 63 C1
7 Wistow YO8 48 D6
3 Withernsea HU19 74 F7
York YO1 156 C1
George Terr 1 YO8 49 B4
George Yd HU1 155 C2
Georgian Mews
Bridlington YO15 122 C1
4 Great Driffield YO25 124 F3
Georgian Way YO15 122 C1
Georgina Ct 8 DN18 84 E8
Gerard Ave YO31 131 A5
Germain Rd YO8 148 E4
German Nook La HU17 56 D8
Germany La YO19 133 E6
Gershwin Ave HU4 144 B4
Gertrude St DN32 152 E1
Gervase St DN15 151 A7
Giant Hill* HU11 57 D6
Gibraltar La DN37 101 F1
Gibraltar Way HU7 56 E5
Gibson La HU14 68 E4
Gibson Rd 4 DN7 104 A8
Gibson St YO25 124 E5
Gifford Cl HU7 57 A6
Gilberdyke Prim Sch HU15 66 D8
Gilberdyke Sta HU15 66 D7
Gilbert St YO16 122 D3
Gilbey Rd DN31 152 B5
Gilcross Rd HU12 90 C6
Gildane HU6 139 E8
Giles Ave YO31 131 A5
Giles St DN35 153 E2
Gillamoor Ave YO31 131 B5
Gillamoor Cl 16 HU8 141 E7
Gillann St 15 WF11 61 A2
Gillatts Cl DN20 98 D4
Gillett St HU3 145 B4
Gilliatt St DN15 151 A7
Gilling Mews 4 HU5 139 D3
Gillingwood Rd YO30 126 F3
Gillshill Prim Sch HU8 141 D5
Gillshill Rd HU8 141 D4
Gillus La 5 YO15 4 D3
Gillygate YO31 156 B3
Gillyon Cl 3 HU17 137 B3
Gipsey Cnr YO19 26 E3
Gipsy La
Holton le Moor LN7 110 C1
Owston Ferry DN9 116 F8
Girton Cl 5 DN16 96 D2
Girvan Cl YO24 132 B7
Gisburn Rd HU13 143 F2
Givendale Gr 3 YO10 131 C4
Givendale Hill YO42 29 C6
Givendale La YO42 29 A8
Glade Rd YO19 37 B2
Glade The
Beverley HU17 137 B3
Escrick YO19 37 A6
York YO31 131 B7
Gladstone Dr DN16 151 C5
Gladstone St
Kingston upon Hull HU13 143 E1
Kingston upon Hull HU3 145 C6
York YO31 156 C4
Gladstone Terr 6 YO15 122 F3
Glaisby Ct YO31 131 A6
Glaisdale Cl YO16 122 F7
Glaisdale Gr HU9 146 F8
Glaisdale Rd DN16 151 E1
Glamis Rd HU13 143 F2
Glanford Gr 6 DN19 85 D8
Glanford Rd
22 Brigg DN20 98 C2
Scunthorpe DN17 96 C2
Glanford Way DN15 150 B7
Glanville Ave DN17 150 F4
Glanville Cres DN17 150 F4
Glasgow St HU3 145 A5
Glass House Row HU8 141 A1
Glebe Ave
Full Sutton YO41 16 A2
York YO26 129 D5
Glebe Cl
Burton upon Stather DN15 82 A5
5 Holton le Clay DN36 114 A6
Humberston DN36 114 C8
3 Strensall YO32 14 B7
2 Wawne HU7 56 E7
Glebe Lands The 4 YO43 135 E4
Glebe Rd Brigg DN20 98 C2
Campsall DN6 76 E1
Cleethorpes DN35 153 E2
Grimsby DN33 102 F1
Humberston DN36 114 C8
Kingston upon Hull HU7 141 A4
Scunthorpe DN15 151 B8
Thorne/Moorends DN8 93 B8
Wawne HU7 56 E7
Glebe Way
Barton-upon-Humber DN18 85 A8
26 Haxby YO32 13 E5
Glebelands HU12 59 D2
Glen Almond HU11 142 D6
Glen Ave YO31 130 E5
Glen Cl YO10 133 E6
Glen Cres YO42 39 A7
Glen Hall Rise 11 DN19 85 C8
Glen Rd YO31 130 E5
Glen The
Beverley HU17 137 B2
Kingston upon Hull HU10 138 B1
Glencoe Cl 22 DN7 92 D4
Glencoe St
Kingston upon Hull HU3 144 F6
1 York YO30 130 B7
Glendale Cl HU10 138 C1
Gleneagles 15 DN37 113 D6
Gleneagles Cres 4 DN19 70 E2
Gleneagles Pk HU8 141 F6
Glenfield Ave YO43 135 D4
Glenfield Dr HU10 138 B1
Glenfield Rd DN37 102 B4
Glenholme Ct YO25 32 E7
Glenridding YO24 132 D7
Glenrock Pk HU15 68 B6
Glenwood Cl HU8 141 C3
Glenwood Dr 2 HU4 144 B6
Glimpse The YO16 123 A7
Gloria Way 3 DN37 102 B4
Glossop Rd DN15 150 B6
Gloucester Ave
Grimsby DN34 102 D2
Scunthorpe DN16 151 B3
Gloucester Rd HU10 138 E2
Gloucester St HU4 144 E3
Glover Rd DN17 150 E4
Glovers Ave DN17 95 D4
Goathead La DN14 78 E8
Goathland Cl HU3 145 A6
Goble Cl DN18 85 A8
Godbold Cl HU17 154 C3
Goddard Ave HU5 140 B2
Goddard Cl 9 DN18 84 E8
Godfrey Rd 11 DN8 93 A8
Godman's La HU10 143 B8
Godnow Rd DN17 94 C6
God's Cross* DN9 104 B6
Godwinsway 18 YO41 15 D2
Gold Thread La 5 YO8 48 B8
Goldcrest Cl
1 Kingston upon Hull HU7 141 D8
Scunthorpe DN15 96 B7
Golden Ct 10 HU9 142 A3
Golden Gr HU11 142 D6
Goldgarth DN32 153 A1
Goldings The DN9 105 D2
Golf Links Dr HU15 68 B6
Golf Links Rd HU6 139 E5
Gollands La DN9 105 B2
Goodfell Rd HU17 137 A6
Goodhand Cl DN18 85 A8
Goodhart Rd HU7 141 B8
Goodmanham Rd
Market Weighton YO43 135 D5
Middleton YO25 31 C3
Goodmanham Way 6 HU16 138 E6
Goodramgate YO1 156 B2
Goodrich Cl HU3 140 E1
Goodsyard The YO8 148 D5
Goodwin Par 1 HU3 145 D5
Goodwood DN17 96 B2
Goodwood Gr YO24 129 F1
Goole & District Hospl DN14 149 C6
Goole Coll DN14 149 B4
Goole Gram Sch DN14 149 B5
Goole L Ctr DN14 149 D3
Goole Rd Goole DN14 65 C3
Swinefleet DN14 80 C8
Goole Sta DN14 149 C4
Gooseacre DN17 107 D7
Goosenook La HU17 45 A8
Gordan Pk HU16 139 C6
Gordon Gdns DN33 113 E8
Gordon Rd YO16 122 C4
Gordon St Goole DN14 149 C4
4 Kingston upon Hull HU3 145 B5
York YO10 130 E3
Gore La DN14 77 B5
Goring Pl DN35 153 D3
Gormire Ave 2 YO31 127 E2
Gorse Cl Hatfield DN7 92 C3
Selby YO8 148 C2
Gorse Hill 1 YO19 26 F7
Gorse Paddock YO32 127 F2
Gorsedale HU7 140 E7
Gorton Rd HU10 143 E7
Gorton St DN31 152 F6
Gosport Rd DN34 152 A2
Gossips Wood Rd DN14 79 B8
Gothenburg Way HU7 140 E6
Goths La HU17 154 B4
Gott Cl YO25 124 C2
Gouldesborough Ct 2 HU5 140 C3
Goulton St HU3 145 B3
Gouthwaith Cl YO30 126 F2
Government House Rd YO30 130 A6
Government St 1 DN14 149 D4
Gowdall Broach DN14 77 E8
Gowdall La
Pollington DN14 77 F7
Snaith & Cowick DN14 63 B1
Gowdall Rd DN14 62 E2
Gowdall Way 1 DN14 65 A7
Gower Rd
Kingston upon Hull HU4 144 B3
York YO24 132 E8
Gowthorpe YO8 148 C5
Gowthorpe La DN14 66 E4
Goxhill Airport DN19 86 B8
Goxhill CP Sch DN19 86 A8
Goxhill Gdns 17 DN34 102 C2
Goxhill Rd DN19 85 E8
Goxhill Sta DN19 85 F8
Grafton St
Grimsby DN32 153 A5
Kingston upon Hull HU5 140 C2
Gragdale Cl HU8 141 E7
Graham Ave HU4 144 C2
Graingers Rd HU18 134 D3
Grains Gate LN11 115 E1
Grainsby Ave
Cleethorpes DN35 103 B2
Holton le Clay DN36 114 B5
Grainsby Healing* DN36 113 F3
Grainsby La
Grainsby DN36 113 E1
Tetney DN36 114 D3
Graizelound Fields Rd DN9 105 D1
Grammar Sch La DN20 98 C3
Grammar Sch Rd
Brigg DN20 98 C2
Kingston upon Hull HU5 139 E2
Grammar Sch Rd S 6 DN20 98 C2
Grammar Sch Wlk DN16 96 E2
Grammar Sch Yd HU1 155 B1
Grampian Cl 4 YO32 127 F5
Grampian Way
23 Grimsby DN33 113 E8
Kingston upon Hull HU7 57 A6
Thorne/Moorends DN8 93 A7
Granary Cl DN21 117 A3
Granary Croft 7 DN9 105 D2
Granary Ct YO1 156 B3
Grandale HU7 140 E7
Grange Ave
12 Barton-upon-Humber DN18 84 E8
Hatfield DN7 92 D4
14 Laceby DN37 101 F1
Misterton DN10 116 D5
Grange Cl
2 Buckton/Bempton YO15 4 C3
Full Sutton YO41 16 A2
5 Hatfield DN7 92 D4
Kingston upon Hull HU2 155 B4
Misterton DN10 116 D4
Skelton YO30 126 B5
Grange Cres
Kingston upon Hull HU10 143 E6
Tickton HU17 137 F8
Grange Dr
Kingston upon Hull HU16 139 A7
Misterton DN10 116 D4
Grange Farm La 20 DN36 114 A7
Grange Field DN20 98 D8
Grange Garth YO10 130 D2
Grange Gr 3 DN8 79 B2
Grange Jun & Inf Sch DN34 102 C3
Grange La
Covenham St Bartholomew LN11 121 F6
Molescroft HU17 137 A7
North Kelsey LN7 110 A3
Rufforth YO26 129 A2
Utterby LN11 121 C4
Grange La Football Club HU14 69 B4
Grange La Inf Sch DN16 151 D1
Grange La Jun Sch DN16 151 D1
Grange La N DN16 151 D3
Grange La S DN16 151 D1
Grange Park La HU10 138 B2
Grange Pk
1 Brough HU15 68 C5
Gainsborough DN21 117 A3
2 Kirk Sandall DN3 92 A2
Swanland HU14 69 B6
Grange Rd
3 Bridlington YO16 122 D5
8 Campsall DN6 76 E1
Gainsborough DN21 117 D1
Garthorpe & Fockerby DN14 81 E8
Goole DN14 149 B4
7 Leconfield HU17 43 D6
Grange Rd *continued*
North Frodingham YO25 34 B6
Snaith DN14 78 C8
Thorne/Moorends DN8 79 B2
Thorngumbald HU12 72 F5
Grange St YO10 130 D2
Grange Way HU17 136 E7
Grange Wlk
Grimsby DN34 152 A2
Misterton DN10 116 D5
Granger Ave YO26 129 C4
Grangeside Ave HU6 139 F5
Gransmoor La YO25 22 A5
Gransmoor Rd YO25 22 D5
Grant St
Cleethorpes DN35 153 E3
Grimsby DN31 153 B5
Grantchester Cl HU5 139 C1
Grantham Ave
Grimsby DN33 102 E1
11 Kingston upon Hull HU7 56 F6
Grantham Dr YO26 129 E4
Grantley Gr HU9 142 C2
Grants Ave YO10 133 E8
Granville St
Grimsby DN32 152 F2
1 Kingston upon Hull HU3 145 A6
Granville Terr 4 YO10 130 E3
Grape La YO1 156 B3
Grasby All Saints C of E Prim Sch DN38 110 E8
Grasby Cres DN37 102 B4
Grasby Rd
Great Limber DN37 100 C3
Kingston upon Hull HU8 142 A4
North Kelsey LN7 110 D5
Scunthorpe DN17 150 E1
Grasby Wold La DN38 110 F8
Grasmere Cl
Gainsborough DN21 117 C1
Goole DN14 149 D5
Grasmere Dr YO10 131 B4
Grasmere Gr
11 Humberston DN36 103 C1
5 York YO30 126 F1
Grassam Cl 3 HU12 58 D1
Grassdale Pk 3 HU15 68 B5
Grassholme YO24 132 C7
Grassington Cl 11 HU7 57 A6
Gravel Pit Hill DN20 109 D6
Gravel Pit La DN39 100 A6
Gravel Pit Rd
Barton-upon-Humber DN18 84 D8
Scotter DN21 107 C4
Gravelhill La DN14 76 F7
Gravelholes La DN10 116 C4
Gravelpit La
Kirkburn YO25 19 F1
Sancton YO43 41 E2
Graves La YO42 39 B6
Gray Friars DN37 102 B4
Gray Rd DN17 150 D2
Gray St Goole DN14 149 C5
York YO23 156 A1
Grayburn La HU17 154 A2
Grayingham Rd
19 Kirton in Lindsey DN21 108 B1
Kirton in Lindsey DN21 119 B7
Grayling Cl 15 DN37 102 B4
Grays Croft HU12 59 C2
Grayshon Dr YO26 129 B5
Greame Rd YO16 123 A5
Great Barn St 4 YO16 122 D5
Great Cl YO8 48 B8
Great Coates Prim Sch DN37 102 B5
Great Coates Rd
Grimsby DN37 102 B4
Healing DN41 101 F5
Great Coates Sta DN37 102 B5
Great Field La HU9 147 C8
Great Gutter La HU10 55 C1
Great Gutter La E HU10 138 C2
Great Gutter La W HU10 138 A2
Great Hatfield Rd HU11 46 D4
Great Meadow Rd YO16 122 E5
Great North Way YO26 129 B8
Great Passage St HU1 155 A1
Great Thornton St HU3 145 D6
Great Union St HU9 155 C3
Grebe Rd HU15 52 F1
Greek St HU3 144 F5
Green Acres HU10 143 C6
Green Balk YO42 17 D1
Green Bank DN8 93 D6
Green Cl
Kingston upon Hull HU6 139 F6
York YO30 130 A8
Green Dike YO32 127 C8
Green Dikes La YO25 8 F1
Green Dykes La YO10 130 F3
Green Hill 10 DN35 103 B2
Green Hills YO60 15 B7
Green Island HU9 142 E5
Green La
Appleton Roebuck YO23 36 B6
Barmby on the Marsh DN14 64 A6
Barrow upon Humber DN19 85 D8

Green La *continued*
Barton-upon-Humber DN18 84 F8
Belton DN9 94 D2
Bishopthorpe YO24 133 A6
Brigsley DN37 113 D4
Broughton DN20 97 E3
Buckton/Bempton YO15 4 D3
Cottingwith YO42 38 C5
Fimber YO25 18 F6
Hatfield DN7 92 E1
Heck DN14 77 D8
Kingston upon Hull HU16 138 E6
Kingston upon Hull HU13 144 A1
Kingston upon Hull HU2 155 B4
Langtoft YO25 8 D5
Moor Monkton YO26 24 A8
Nafferton YO25 125 D7
North Duffield YO8 49 F8
North Kelsey LN7 110 A4
Pilham DN21 118 A4
Selby YO8 148 A3
Skidby HU10 138 B4
South Cave HU15 53 D1
Swine HU11 57 E7
Tibthorpe YO25 19 D2
Tickton HU17 137 F8
Weaverthorpe YO25 8 A8
Wetwang YO25 18 D5
Wigginton YO32 13 D5
Wressle DN14 64 D8
York YO30 127 A1
York YO24 129 D2
Green Lane Mid Sch DN8 93 B7
Green Marsh Rd HU12 72 E4
Green Mdws YO31 131 A7
Green Rd
Gringley on the Hill DN10 116 A1
15 Hedon HU12 72 C7
Green Sward YO31 131 A8
Green The
5 Brough HU15 68 D6
20 Dunnington YO19 26 F7
Great Driffield YO25 125 A4
Lund YO25 31 F3
Market Weighton YO43 135 D4
Rawcliffe DN14 64 A1
20 Scotter DN21 107 C3
1 Skelton YO30 126 B5
Sproatley HU11 58 D5
1 Swanland HU14 69 B7
20 Thorne/Moorends DN8 93 A8
Wistow YO8 48 D6
York YO26 129 C3
Green Top Fst Sch DN8 93 A7
Green Way YO32 127 F4
Green Ways 2 YO8 48 D6
Greenacre Cl YO42 29 B3
Greenacre Pk
Gilberdyke HU15 66 D8
Hornsea HU18 134 C1
Greenacres
4 Swanland HU14 69 C7
York YO32 127 F4
Greenacres Cl 3 YO8 48 D1
Greenacres Cres 7 YO8 48 D1
Greenacres Dr 4 YO8 48 D1
Greenacres Gr 3 YO8 48 D1
Greencliffe Dr YO30 130 A6
Greencroft Ct 14 YO19 26 F7
Greencroft La 17 YO19 26 F7
Greenfield Cl 6 DN3 92 A3
Greenfield Dr
6 Brayton YO8 48 D1
Hibaldstow DN20 109 A5
Greenfield Garth HU6 56 D5
Greenfield La YO25 31 C4
Greenfield Pk Dr YO31 131 A7
Greenfield Rd
Bridlington YO16 122 B2
Middleton-on-the-Wolds YO25 31 C4
Greenfields DN14 77 F6
Greenfinch Dr 8 DN35 103 C1
Greengales Ct YO19 38 A8
Greengales La YO19 38 A8
Greengarth DN17 96 C1
Greengate DN9 105 E6
Greengate La Cliffe YO8 49 F6
2 Goxhill DN19 86 A8
South Killingholme DN40 86 E3
Greengate Rd WF8 76 C1
Greenhill 8 DN20 97 D3
Greenhill Rd DN9 105 C2
Greenhoe Rd DN17 96 B2
Greenhow Cl HU8 141 E7
Greenland La DN14 78 F7
Greenlands YO25 124 F5
Greenlands Ave 18 DN36 114 A7
Greenlands La YO8 48 C3
Greenoak La DN14 66 B7
Greens La
Burstwick HU12 73 B8
Burton Pidsea HU12 59 C1
Wawne HU7 56 E7
Green's Rd DN7 92 C3
Greensborough Ave 3 YO26 129 B5
Greenshaw Dr YO32 127 C8
Greenshaw La HU12 74 D1
Greenside
18 Dunnington YO19 26 F7
Greenside *continued*
8 Flamborough YO15 5 A2
Greenside Cl 24 YO19 26 F7
Greenside Wlk 23 YO19 26 F7
Greenstiles La HU14 69 C7
Greenway
8 Barton-upon-Humber DN18 69 F1
10 Waltham DN37 113 E6
Greenway The
2 Haxby YO32 127 C7
Hornsea HU18 134 C2
1 Kingston upon Hull HU4 144 C6
Greenways
Great Driffield YO25 124 F5
2 North Ferriby HU14 69 A5
Greenways Cl YO16 122 F6
Greenways Dr 1 YO8 48 D6
Greenwich Ave HU9 142 C4
Greenwood Ave
Beverley HU17 154 C3
Kingston upon Hull HU6 139 E5
Greenwood Gdns HU17 136 F7
Greenwood Gr YO24 132 C8
Greetham's La DN32 153 B1
Greet's Hill YO17 16 E7
Gregory Cl YO30 126 C5
Grenley St 8 WF11 61 A2
Grenville Bay HU11 142 D6
Grenwich Cl 5 YO30 126 E3
Gresley Ct 3 YO26 129 B4
Gresley Way DN40 87 D2
Greville Rd HU12 72 D7
Grey St
Gainsborough DN21 117 A1
Kingston upon Hull HU2 145 D7
Greyfriars Cres HU17 154 A1
Greyfriars Rd DN20 97 E3
Greygarth Cl 14 HU7 56 F6
Greystoke Rd YO30 126 E1
Greystone Ave HU4 144 E7
Greystone Ct YO32 127 C7
Greystones Rd DN21 117 A2
Griffin Prim Sch HU9 142 C3
Griffin Rd HU9 142 C3
Griffiths Way 18 HU12 73 C4
Grime St DN31 152 E4
Grimsby Coll DN34 152 C1
Grimsby Docks DN32 152 F5
Grimsby L Ctr DN34 152 A4
Grimsby Maternity Hospl DN33 102 E2
Grimsby Rd
Caistor LN7 111 C4
Cleethorpes DN35 153 D4
Fotherby LN11 121 D1
Humberston DN36 103 B1
Laceby DN37 101 F1
Swallow LN7 112 B6
Waltham DN37 113 E7
Grimsby RUFC DN33 102 E1
Grimsby Town Football Club DN35 153 C5
Grimsby Town Sta DN32 152 D3
Grimscott Cl 2 HU7 56 F5
Grimston Rd
12 Hunmanby YO14 3 A8
5 Kingston upon Hull HU10 143 F6
Grimston St HU1 155 B3
Grimthorpe Hill YO42 29 B7
Grimwith Garth YO30 126 F2
Grindale La YO16 122 A7
Grindale Rd
Bempton YO16 4 A3
Grindale YO16 3 F2
Grindell St HU9 146 D8
Gringley Rd
Misterton DN10 116 B4
Walkeringham DN10 116 C2
Grinsdale Rise YO25 125 F7
Grizedale HU7 140 F7
Grosmont Cl HU8 141 E7
Grosvenor Ave DN14 149 A5
Grosvenor Cres 1 DN32 152 D3
Grosvenor Ct DN7 92 D8
Grosvenor Pl HU17 136 D2
Grosvenor Rd
Hornsea HU18 134 D4
York YO30 156 A4
Grosvenor St
Grimsby DN32 152 D2
Kingston upon Hull HU3 145 D8
Grosvenor St N DN15 151 A8
Grosvenor St S DN15 151 A8
Grosvenor Terr YO30 156 A4
Grove Cl HU17 154 B4
Grove Gdns 12 YO26 12 F1
Grove Hill HU13 143 E1
Grove House View HU5 140 D3
Grove La DN37 113 E6
Grove Pk 7 Barlby YO8 49 B5
Beverley HU17 154 A4
Misterton DN10 116 C5
Grove Rd DN7 92 D8
Grove St
Kingston upon Hull HU5 140 D1
Kirton in Lindsey DN21 108 A1
Grove Terr La YO31 156 C4
Grove The
Barrow upon Humber DN19 85 D8
Beckingham DN10 116 D1
Grove The *continued*
Kellington DN14 62 A3
York YO24 132 E6
Grove View YO30 130 A6
Grove Wharf* DN15 95 E7
Grove Wood Rd DN10 116 C5
Grove Wood Terr DN10 116 C5
Grovehill HU17 137 C4
Grovehill Rd HU17 154 C3
Grovenor Ct 11 DN35 103 D1
Groves La YO31 156 C4
Groves The YO25 125 A3
Grundale HU10 143 C6
Grundell's Yd 4 YO16 122 D4
Grundill La
Hatfield HU11 46 A8
Seaton HU11 35 A1
Guardians Rd 2 HU12 74 D1
Guernsey Gr 1 DN40 101 C8
Guest Field HU11 47 B1
Guildford Ave HU8 141 D4
Guildford Cl HU17 136 E1
Guildford St DN32 153 A4
Guildhall Rd HU1 155 B2
Guilicarr La LN7 109 E4
Guisefield Rd 5 DN9 105 D6
Gullane Dr HU6 56 D5
Gunby Pl 9 DN35 103 C2
Gunby Rd Bubwith YO8 50 D5
Scunthorpe DN17 150 E1
Gunbywood Rd YO8 50 D6
Gunness & Burringham C of E Sch DN17 95 E5
Gunness La DN15 95 F8
Gunthorpe Rd DN9 116 F8
Gurnell St DN15 151 A8
Gurnell Street C of E Sch DN15 151 A8
Gurth Ave DN3 92 A1
Gus Walker Dr YO42 29 B4
Guy Garth 3 HU12 72 D7
Gypsey Rd YO16 122 B4

H

Habrough La
Brocklesby DN39 100 C6
Kirmington DN39 100 B6
Habrough Rd
Immingham DN40 87 A1
South Killingholme DN40 86 E2
Habrough Sta DN40 100 E8
Hackforth Wlk HU5 139 D4
Hackness Gr 2 HU5 144 D8
Haddlesey Rd WF11 61 D5
Haddon Rd YO16 122 D7
Haddon St HU3 144 F4
Hadds La DN8 78 F3
Hadds Nook Rd DN8 78 F2
Hadleigh Cl 4 HU3 140 E1
Hadleigh Gn 4 DN17 95 D4
Hadleigh Rd DN40 87 C1
Hadrian Ave YO10 131 B3
Hag La YO42 38 C4
Hagg La Belton DN17 94 E3
Cottingwith YO42 38 E8
Dunnington YO19 26 F6
Hemingbrough YO8 49 F3
Haggs La Fenwick DN6 77 D2
Kingston upon Hull HU10 138 E3
Haig Ave DN16 151 B5
Haig Rd DN8 79 B2
Haig St YO8 148 B6
Haigh La DN14 77 A6
Haigh St DN35 103 D3
Haile Rd DN36 103 D1
Hailgate DN14 65 A7
Hailgate Cl 8 DN14 65 B7
Hainton Ave DN32 152 F2
Haith's La DN36 114 B1
Haldane St DN21 117 A1
Hale Hill La DN7 92 E3
Hales Cl 3 DN16 96 D1
Hales Cres 12 HU12 72 C7
Hales Entry HU9 146 C6
Hales La YO8 63 E5
Haley's Terr YO31 130 D8
Half Acre Wood 1 DN17 95 D4
Halfacres La YO42 40 A6
Halifax App DN20 99 A8
Halifax Ave DN14 149 C6
Halifax Cl 8 YO42 28 F4
Halifax Ct 7 YO30 127 A1
Halifax Way
Elvington Airfield YO41 27 A3
Pocklington Ind Est YO42 28 E3
Halkon Cl DN17 81 D3
Hall Cl 5 Airmyn DN14 64 E4
Cawood YO8 36 D1
Nafferton YO25 125 E7
7 Snaith DN14 78 C8
Hall Ct DN17 81 A3
Hall Farm Cl 4 YO19 48 F8
Hall Gdns DN15 83 B5
Hall La Elsham DN20 98 F7
Stainforth DN7 92 A6
Hall Mdw DN20 84 C2
Hall Park Rd YO14 2 F8
Hall Pk Swanland HU14 69 C6
Wistow YO8 49 A5
York YO10 131 B1
Hall Rd Goole DN14 149 D1
Hornsea HU18 134 D5
Kingston upon Hull HU6 139 E5
Market Weighton YO43 135 D4
Hall Rd *continued*
Sproatley HU11 58 D5
Hall Rise 12 Haxby YO32 13 F5
Messingham DN17 107 D7
Hall Road Prim Sch HU6 139 F4
Hall Spinney The 5 DN14 65 B7
Hall St HU2 145 D7
Hall View DN17 107 D7
Hall Way DN38 99 F5
Hall Wlk 1 Brough HU15 68 D6
Kingston upon Hull HU16 139 B6
Walkington HU17 55 B8
Halladale Cl 1 YO24 132 B7
Hallard Way 7 YO32 14 B7
Hallbrook Ct 4 DN16 96 D1
Hallcroft 1 DN39 86 A1
Hallcroft La YO23 132 A3
Hallcroft Rd 1 DN9 105 D2
Haller St HU9 146 E8
Hallfield Rd YO31 130 E5
Hallgarth DN36 115 B2
Hallgarth Ave DN16 151 B6
Hallgarth Way HU17 154 B2
Hallgate
Kingston upon Hull HU16 139 A6
10 Pocklington YO42 29 A4
Hallgate Cty Jun & Inf Sch HU16 139 B7
Halliwell Cl HU9 147 E8
Halls La 13 Keelby DN41 101 A4
North Kelsey LN7 110 A4
Hall's Rd DN10 116 A2
Hallytreeholme Rd YO25 33 E3
Haltemprice L Ctr HU10 143 E7
Haltemprice St HU3 144 F5
Halton Cl 5 DN21 119 C8
Halton Pl DN35 103 B2
Halton Way DN34 102 D2
Halyard Croft HU1 155 B1
Halycon Ave 1 HU13 143 E2
Hambledon Cl HU7 141 B6
Hambleton Ave YO10 131 C4
Hambleton Terr YO31 130 C7
Hambleton View 10 YO32 13 D5
Hambleton Way YO32 127 F3
Hambling Dr HU17 136 E7
Hamburg Rd HU7 141 A5
Hamden Rd YO42 28 E3
Hamerton Cl 11 YO14 3 A8
Hamerton Rd 10 YO14 3 A8
Hamilton Cl 7 DN34 102 B2
Hamilton Dr
Kingston upon Hull HU8 141 F6
York YO24 129 E2
Hamilton Dr E YO24 129 F2
Hamilton Dr W YO24 129 D2
Hamilton Hill Rd YO25 23 A6
Hamilton Rd
Bridlington YO15 122 D2
Scunthorpe DN17 150 F4
Hamilton St DN32 153 B5
Hamilton Way YO24 129 E2
Hamish Wlk 27 DN40 87 B1
Hamlet The 8 DN14 61 F2
Hamling Way HU4 144 D2
Hamlyn Ave HU4 144 E7
Hamlyn Dr HU4 144 E6
Hammersike Rd YO8 48 A4
Hammersmith Rd 1 HU8 141 F5
Hammerton Cl 3 YO26 129 B3
Hammerton Rd 25 DN17 96 C2
Hammond Rd HU17 154 C4
Hamont Rd DN32 153 B3
Hampden Cres 1 DN7 104 A8
Hampden St YO1 156 B1
Hampshire St HU4 144 E3
Hampstead Ct 6 HU3 140 D1
Hampstead Pk 6 DN33 102 D1
Hampston Cl HU6 140 A7
Hampton Cl 18 DN35 103 C1
Hampton Rd
Hatfield DN7 92 C4
Scunthorpe DN16 151 B4
Hancock La HU15 52 F3
Handel House Sch DN21 117 B1
Handley Cl YO30 127 A2
Hands on History Mus* HU1 155 B2
Hanger La DN14 63 B3
Hankins La YO42 38 D1
Hanley Rd HU5 139 D3
Hanover Ct
Beverley HU17 154 C3
Kingston upon Hull HU1 155 A2
Hanover Sq HU1 155 B2
Hanover St E 5 YO26 129 F5
Hanover St W 7 YO26 129 F5
Hansard Cres
6 Caistor LN7 111 B4
5 Gilberdyke HU15 66 D8
Hansard Dr 6 HU15 66 D8
Hansom Pl YO31 130 C7
Hanson Cl YO43 135 D3
Hanson Way DN32 153 B4
Ha'penny Bridge Way HU9 146 B5
Harborough Cl 20 YO14 2 F8
Harbour Rd YO15 122 F2
Harbour Way HU9 146 C6
Harcourt Cl
Bishopthorpe YO23 133 A4
Wheldrake YO19 37 F7
Harcourt Dr HU9 146 C8
Harcourt St YO31 130 E5
Hardane HU6 139 E8
Harden Cl YO30 126 F2
Hardenshaw La YO8 63 B4
Hardington Cl HU8 142 B7
Hardmoor La YO43 53 C5
Hardrada Way 3 YO41 15 D1
Hardwick St HU5 145 B8
Hardy Rd DN17 150 D2
Hardy St
Kingston upon Hull HU5 140 C3
Selby YO8 148 E4
Hardy's Rd DN35 103 C2
Hardys Rd 4 HU12 72 C7
Hare St DN32 152 F2
Harewood HU17 136 B6
Harewood Ave
Bridlington YO16 122 D6
Kingston upon Hull HU9 142 A3
4 Kirk Sandall DN3 92 A2
Harewood Cl
Rawcliffe YO30 126 D2
5 Wigginton YO32 13 D5
Harewood Gr 17 DN35 103 C1
Hargrave St DN31 152 B5
Hargreave Cl HU17 136 E6
Hargreaves Way DN15 96 D7
Hariff La HU12 73 B4
Harington Ave YO10 130 F4
Harker St 12 WF11 61 A2
Harland La YO25 124 E4
Harland Rd
Bridlington YO16 122 F5
6 Brough HU15 68 C6
Harland Way HU16 138 E8
Harlech Cl 1 HU7 57 A6
Harlech Way DN32 152 F4
Harleigh Ave HU7 141 A5
Harlequin Dr 15 HU7 56 F5
Harleston Cl 5 HU8 142 B5
Harlestone Ct 8 DN34 102 B3
Harley St HU2 155 A4
Harlow Cl
2 Kingston upon Hull HU8 142 C6
1 York YO24 129 F2
Harlow Rd YO24 129 F2
Harlow St DN31 152 B5
Harlthorpe Gn YO8 51 A8
Harneis Cres DN37 101 F1
Harold Ct YO24 129 D3
Harold St
Grimsby DN32 153 A4
Selby YO8 148 F4
Harolds Way 1 YO41 15 D1
Harome Gr HU4 144 C7
Harpenden Cl 12 DN7 92 D3
Harpendon Dr 6 DN7 92 D3
Harper Cl YO42 29 A3
Harper St
8 Great Driffield YO25 124 F4
2 Selby YO8 148 C5
Harpham Gr HU9 142 A1
Harpham La YO25 9 D2
Harpham Rd DN36 115 B2
Harpings Rd HU5 139 F1
Harpswell Hill DN21 119 B1
Harpswell La DN21 118 F1
Harrier Rd 2 DN18 69 F1
Harrington Pl DN16 151 A1
Harrington Rd YO16 122 B2
Harrington St DN35 153 B5
Harris St HU3 144 F5
Harrison Cl
Sproatley HU11 58 D5
Winteringham DN15 83 B8
Harrison St
Grimsby DN31 152 C3
York YO31 130 F6
Harrow Cl 12 DN21 117 C1
Harrow Gdns 12 DN17 96 C2
Harrow Glade 5 YO30 127 A1
Harrow St HU3 145 B4
Harrowdyke 10 DN18 84 E8
Harry Moor La YO8 48 B2
Harrybeck La YO43 53 D4
Harry's Ave HU8 141 B3
Harrys Dream 3 DN20 97 E3
Harsell La HU11 34 F2
Harswell La
Everingham YO43 40 D5
Holme-on-Spalding-Moor YO42 40 C2
Hart Dr 26 YO42 29 A3
Hart Hill Cres YO41 16 A2
Hart La DN15 83 B5
Hart St DN35 153 C4
Hartendale Cl 22 YO15 5 A2
Harthill Ave HU17 43 D6
Harthill Dr HU3 145 C5
Hartland Cl HU7 140 F8
Hartley Bridge HU9 146 C6
Hartley Ct YO15 122 D1
Hartley St HU18 134 D5
Hartoft Rd HU5 139 E2
Hartoft St YO10 130 D2
Harts Cl HU18 134 B4
Hartshead Ave DN15 150 C7
Harvest Ave 19 DN18 84 E8
Harvest Cl 18 DN3 92 A2
Harvest Cres 4 DN37 113 D6

Harvest Rise 1 DN19 85 C8
Harvester Cl DN9 105 F6
Harwood Dr 1 HU4 144 B6
Haslemere Ave YO15 122 E3
Hassacarr La YO19 26 F6
Hastings Ave 1 HU5 140 E2
Hastings Cl 4 YO30 127 A1
Hastings Gr HU4 144 E7
Hatcliffe Cl 20 DN33 102 D2
Hatfield & Dunsville Cty Prim Sch DN7 92 D3
Hatfield & Stainforth Sta DN7 92 C5
Hatfield Cl 3 YO30 126 E3
Hatfield Comp Sch DN7 92 D4
Hatfield Cty Prim Sch DN7 92 D4
Hatfield High Sch DN7 92 D4
Hatfield La
Barnby Dun DN3 92 A4
Edenthorpe DN3 92 A1
Hatfield Pl DN14 149 C1
Hatfield Rd Hatfield DN7 93 A6
Thorne/Moorends DN8 93 A7
Hatfield Water Pk* DN7 92 E5
Hatfield Woodhouse Cty Prim Sch DN7 93 A3
Hathersage Rd HU7 141 C4
Hatkill La YO41 16 B1
Hatters Cl YO23 132 B3
Hatton Gr 32 DN33 102 D2
Haugh La YO8 61 F8
Haughton Rd YO30 130 C7
Hauling La YO23 36 C8
Hauxwell Gr HU8 142 A5
Havelock Cres YO16 122 D3
Havelock Pl YO16 122 D3
Havelock Sch DN32 153 C2
Havelock St
Bridlington YO16 122 D3
Kingston upon Hull HU3 145 A4
Haven Ave
2 Brough HU15 68 B5
Grimsby DN31 152 C4
Haven Basin Rd HU12 72 C6
Haven Cl DN21 117 F5
Haven Garth
1 Brough HU15 68 B5
2 Hedon HU12 72 D7
Haven Gdns DN31 152 A5
Haven Rd
Barton-upon-Humber DN18 69 E1
North Killingholme DN40 87 A6
Patrington HU12 89 C8
Haven Staithes 24 HU12 72 C7
Haven Terr DN31 152 C4
Haven The
Kingston upon Hull HU9 146 B6
2 Walkington HU17 55 D8
Havercroft Rd 15 YO14 3 A8
Haverstoe Pl 7 DN35 103 B2
Hawdon Ave YO8 148 D5
Hawerby Rd DN37 101 F1
Hawke Garth 5 YO14 3 A8
Hawkesbury St HU8 141 E3
Hawkins Gr DN32 153 B2
Hawkins Way 3 DN40 86 E3
Hawkshead Cl 3 YO24 132 B8
Hawling Rd YO43 135 C2
Haworth Cl DN15 150 D8
Haworth St HU6 140 C4
Hawse Rd YO8 63 E8
Hawthorn Ave
2 Brigg DN20 98 C2
Gainsborough DN21 117 B1
1 Immingham DN40 87 D2
Kingston upon Hull HU3 144 F5
Hawthorn Cl
Healing DN41 101 F6
5 Newport HU15 52 F1
Wootton DN39 85 E2
Hawthorn Ct 1 HU3 144 F6
Hawthorn Dr
Wilberfoss YO41 27 E5
Wistow YO8 49 A5
Hawthorn Garth DN14 61 F4
Hawthorn Gate 17 DN18 84 F8
Hawthorn Gr
Gainsborough DN21 117 B1
York YO31 130 E5
Hawthorn Rise 6 DN19 85 C8
Hawthorn Spinney YO32 127 E3
Hawthorn St 1 YO31 130 E5
Hawthorn Terr DN14 149 F5
Hawthorn Terr Cent 2 YO32 127 D3
Hawthorn Terr N YO32 127 D4
Hawthorn Terr S YO32 127 D3
Hawthorn Way 9 HU15 66 D7
Hawthorne Ave
Cleethorpes DN35 153 D4
29 Grimsby DN33 113 E8
Hatfield DN7 92 C2
12 Haxby YO32 13 E5
Kingston upon Hull HU10 138 D1
6 New Waltham DN36 113 F7
Scunthorpe DN17 150 F4
4 Thorne/Moorends DN8 79 A1
Hawthorne Cl 12 DN15 83 A5
Hawthorne Cres DN17 150 F4
Hawthorne Dr YO43 40 A1
Hawthorne Garth HU17 136 F7
Hawthorne Gdns DN19 86 A8
Hawthorne Gr 5 DN8 79 A1
Hawthorne Rd DN8 79 A1
Hawthorne Rise HU13 143 B3
Hawthorns 3 Riccall YO19 48 F8
2 Riccall YO19 48 F8
Hawthorns The 12 HU8 141 E7
Hawton Cl 1 DN21 117 C1
Haxby Moor Rd
Haxby YO32 13 F7
Towthorpe YO32 14 A7
Haxby Rd Clifton YO31 127 D1
New Earswick YO32 127 D6
York YO31 156 B4
Haxby Rd Prim Sch YO31 130 D7
Haxey C of E Prim Sch DN9 105 D3
Haxey Gate Rd DN10 116 C7
Haxey Grange 8 DN9 105 D2
Haxey La DN9 105 D2
Haxey Rd DN10 116 C6
Hayburn Ave HU5 139 F2
Haycroft Ave DN31 152 C3
Haycroft St DN31 152 C3
Haydock Garth 6 HU7 57 A5
Haydon Cl HU10 143 D8
Hayes La DN7 78 D1
Hayfield Cl
Barnby Dun DN3 92 A4
9 Haxey DN9 105 D2
Hayforth Cl YO30 127 A2
Hayling Mere 29 DN35 103 C1
Haymarket Cl HU8 141 F4
Haymer Dr HU12 72 D7
Haynes Cl 2 DN8 93 B7
Haynes Gdns 16 DN8 93 B8
Haynes Gn 9 DN8 93 B8
Haynes Gr 1 DN8 93 B7
Haynes Rd DN8 93 B8
Hays Cl 3 DN36 114 A5
Hayton Cl DN15 83 A5
Hayton Gr HU4 144 D4
Hayton's La DN15 83 D2
Hayward Cl 3 HU17 55 D8
Hazel Ave HU19 75 A5
Hazel Cl
Great Driffield YO25 124 E3
Messingham DN17 107 C7
York YO32 127 D2
Hazel Croft 5 DN40 87 B1
Hazel Garth YO31 131 B7
Hazel Gr Goole DN14 149 D1
2 Kingston upon Hull HU3 145 D5
Hazel Old La DN14 62 C2
Hazel Rd DN7 92 C5
Hazelbarrow Dr HU10 143 F7
Hazelmere Ct YO32 127 E3
Hazelnut Gr YO30 127 B2
Hazelwood Ave YO10 131 D4
Hazing La DN14 77 B6
Headingley Rd 7 DN6 76 E2
Headland Cl 30 YO32 13 E5
Headlands Cl YO16 122 F6
Headlands Dr
Aldbrough HU11 47 C1
Bridlington YO16 122 F6
Kingston upon Hull HU13 143 C2
Headlands Lower Sch YO16 122 E4
Headlands Prim Sch YO32 127 D8
Headlands Rd HU11 47 C1
Headlands Sch YO16 122 F5
Headley Cl 2 YO30 127 B1
Heads La HU13 143 C1
Healey Gr YO31 130 F8
Healey Rd DN16 151 C4
Healing Comp Sch DN41 101 F5
Healing Prim Sch DN41 101 F5
Healing Rd DN41 101 D6
Healing Sta DN41 101 F6
Heapham Rd DN21 117 C1
Heath Cl 2 YO24 129 F2
Heath Croft YO10 133 F7
Heath Moor Dr YO10 133 F8
Heath Ride YO32 14 B8
Heathcote St HU6 140 D4
Heather Bank
13 Stamford Bridge YO41 15 D2
York YO10 131 C4
Heather Cl
7 Kingston upon Hull HU5 139 D1
Selby YO8 148 C3
York YO32 128 A4
Heather Croft 4 YO31 127 E2
Heather Gr DN16 96 E2
Heatherdale Cl 9 DN33 113 E8
Heathfield Cl 8 DN3 92 A3
Heathfield Ct DN34 152 B1
Heathfield Rd 1 YO10 131 A3
Hebden Ave HU8 142 C5
Hebden Rd DN15 150 C8
Hebdon Rise 2 YO26 129 D4
Heber St DN14 149 C2
Hebrides Cl HU9 142 A3
Heck & Pollington Lake DN14 77 E7
Heck La DN14 77 C7
Heckdyke La DN10 116 F7
Hedgerow Cl 4 DN19 85 C8
Hedgerow La 23 DN20 98 C2
Hedley Cl 7 HU15 53 F1
Hedon Museum* HU12 72 C7
Hedon Rd HU9 146 B6
Heigholm La YO25 34 A1
Heigholme La HU17 44 F8
Height Lands La YO23 24 D6
Heimdal Rd DN33 102 E1
Helen Cres 9 DN40 87 B1
Helene Gr DN32 153 B3
Heliport HU15 68 C4
Hellyers Ct HU4 144 D2
Helm Dr HU9 146 C6
Helms Ave 6 HU12 58 C1
Helmsdale YO24 132 C6
Helmsley Gr
16 Haxby YO32 13 D5
Kingston upon Hull HU5 144 C7
Helsinki Rd HU7 140 F5
Helvellyn Cl 10 HU7 57 A6
Hemble Way HU7 56 F5
Hemingbrough CP Sch YO8 49 F1
Hemlock Ave YO31 127 E1
Hemmingway Wlk HU13 143 E3
Hempbridge Cl YO8 148 A5
Hempbridge Rd YO8 148 A5
Hempdyke Rd DN15 150 E8
Hempland Ave YO31 130 F6
Hempland Dr YO31 131 A7
Hempland Inf Sch YO31 131 A6
Hempland Jun Sch YO31 131 B6
Hempland La YO31 131 A7
Hemswell Ave HU9 147 D8
Hemswell Cty Prim Sch DN21 119 D1
Hemswell Dr 6 DN37 102 C4
Hemswell La DN21 119 A1
Henderson Ave DN15 150 F8
Henderson Avenue Prim Sch DN15 150 F8
Henderson Cres DN15 150 F8
Henderson St DN31 153 A6
Henderson Way DN15 83 A5
Hendon Garth YO30 127 A1
Heneage Rd DN32 152 F2
Hengate HU17 154 A3
Henley Ct 6 DN21 117 B1
Henley Dr HU9 141 E1
Henlow Cl 4 DN21 119 C8
Henry Ct 8 DN8 79 B1
Henry St Goole DN14 149 B4
Grimsby DN31 152 C4
Scunthorpe DN15 150 F7
Hensall CP Sch DN14 62 C1
Hensall Sta DN14 62 C1
Henwick Hall La YO8 148 C1
Hepworth's La DN14 63 C2
Herbert St 6 YO10 130 E3
Herberts Way YO31 130 F7
Herdsman Dr YO23 132 C3
Herdsman Rd 3 YO24 132 D8
Herdwick Cl 1 YO30 127 B1
Hereford Ave DN34 152 C1
Hereford Cl 4 HU17 136 E1
Hereford Rd YO42 28 E3
Hereford Sch DN34 152 B1
Hereford St HU4 144 E3
Hereward Pl DN16 151 E3
Herman Wlk YO24 132 C8
Hermes Cl HU9 142 C4
Hermitage Rd YO16 122 C4
Hermitage The 5 DN8 79 B2
Heron Ave YO24 132 C8
Heron Cl Grimsby DN32 103 A2
16 Hedon HU12 72 C7
10 Scunthorpe DN15 96 B7
Heron Holt 1 DN20 97 D4
Heron Rise YO32 127 F5
Heron St HU3 145 B5
Heron Way 6 DN36 114 A6
Herrick Rd DN17 150 D3
Hersey Rd 24 LN7 111 B4
Hertfordshire Cl 2 HU5 139 D1
Hesketh Bank YO10 131 D3
Hesketh Dr DN3 92 A2
Heslerton Ave HU16 139 A4
Heslin Cl 8 YO32 127 C8
Heslington Croft YO10 133 F7
Heslington Ct 2 YO10 131 B1
Heslington La
Heslington YO10 131 A1
York YO10 133 E8
Heslington Prim Sch YO10 131 C1
Heslington Rd YO10 130 E3
Hessay Pl 2 YO26 129 A3
Hessle High Sch HU13 143 C2
Hessle Lower Sch HU13 143 E3
Hessle Mount Sch HU13 143 C3
Hessle Penshurst Prim Sch HU13 143 F3
Hessle Rd HU1 155 A1
Hessle View DN18 84 E8
Hessleskew La YO43 42 A4
Hetherton St YO30 156 A3
Hewde La DN15 83 A8
Hewitt's Ave DN36 114 A8
Hewitt's Cir DN36 103 B1
Hewitts Manor 3 DN35 103 B1
Hewley Ave YO10 131 A4
Heworth YO31 131 A6
Heworth ARLFC YO31 131 A8
Heworth C of E Prim Sch YO31 130 F6
Heworth Gn YO31 156 C4
Heworth Hall Dr YO31 130 F6
Heworth Pl YO31 130 F6
Heworth Rd YO31 130 F6
Hewson Rd DN36 114 D8
Hewson St DN17 107 D7
Hey St DN35 153 F1
Heythrop Rd DN35 103 C2
Hibaldstow Cl 21 DN34 102 C2
Hibaldstow Prim Sch DN20 109 A5
Hickman Cres DN21 117 B2
Hickman Gr DN21 117 E5
Hiderthorpe Cty Jun Sch YO15 122 C1
High Bridge Rd DN8 93 C7
High Brighton St 13 HU19 75 A6
High Burgage
2 Winteringham DN15 68 B1
Winteringham DN15 83 B8
High Catton Rd YO41 27 D8
High Croft 7 YO14 2 F8
High Eggborough La DN14 62 A1
High Farm Ct HU11 142 F7
High Field YO10 131 D4
High Field Rd DN20 98 D3
High Garth DN17 96 C1
High Hazel Rd DN8 79 B2
High La Carnaby YO25 10 C3
Sutton upon Derwent YO41 27 D3
High Levels Bank
Belton DN8 94 A4
Hatfield DN8 93 A6
High Leys Rd DN17 96 C2
High Mdw Gowdall DN14 63 A1
Selby YO8 148 B6
High Mdws HU10 143 C8
High Moor La YO30 12 C8
High Newbiggin St YO31 156 B3
High Oaks YO31 131 B7
High Ousegate YO1 156 B2
High Peter La YO25 20 D7
High Petergate YO1 156 B3
High Rd
Elloughton-cum-Brough HU15 68 D6
North Cave HU15 53 E3
High Ridge Comp Sch DN15 150 E7
High Risby Medieval Village* DN15 83 A1
High Row YO41 16 D4
High Sewerby Rd YO15 123 C7
High Side YO25 34 A8
High St Airmyn DN14 64 E3
Aldbrough HU11 47 C1
Barmby on the Marsh DN14 64 A7
Barrow upon Humber DN19 85 D8
Barton-upon-Humber DN18 69 E1
Beckingham DN10 116 D1
Belton DN9 94 E1
Blyton DN21 117 F5
Boynton YO16 10 D7
Bridlington YO16 122 C4
Broughton DN20 97 D3
Buckton/Bempton YO15 4 C3
Burringham DN17 95 D4
Burton upon Stather DN15 82 B4
Caistor LN7 111 B4
Carlton DN14 63 C2
Cawood YO8 48 B8
Cleethorpes DN35 153 E2
Corringham DN21 118 A1
Cottam YO25 7 E5
4 Crowle DN17 94 D7
Easington HU12 90 F6
East Butterwick DN17 106 D8
East Ferry DN21 106 B2
Eastoft DN17 81 A3
Eastrington DN14 65 F8
Epworth DN9 105 E6
7 Flamborough YO15 5 A2
Flixborough DN15 82 B1
Garthorpe & Fockerby DN17 81 E5
Goole DN14 65 C4
Great Limber DN37 100 D3
Gringley on the Hill DN10 116 A1
Hatfield DN7 92 C2
Haxey DN9 105 D2
Holme-on-Spalding-Moor YO43 40 A1
Humberside Airport DN39 100 A6
Kilham YO25 9 A8
Kingston upon Hull HU1 155 C1
Kirby Grindalythe YO17 6 D8
Kirton in Lindsey DN21 108 B1
Laceby DN37 101 F1
Langtoft YO25 8 C8
High St *continued*
Luddington & Haldenby DN17 81 C4
Market Weighton YO43 135 D4
Messingham DN17 107 D7
Misterton DN10 116 C5
Nafferton YO25 125 F7
Nettleton LN7 111 C2
North Ferriby HU14 69 A5
North Kelsey LN7 110 A4
North Thoresby DN36 114 A1
Norton DN6 76 E2
Owston Ferry DN9 106 B3
Rawcliffe DN14 64 A1
Redbourne DN21 108 F2
Roxby cum Risby DN15 82 E1
Sancton YO43 41 D2
Scotter DN21 107 C3
Scotton DN21 107 C1
Scunthorpe DN15 151 A7
Snaith DN14 63 B1
South Ferriby DN18 84 A7
Swinefleet DN14 65 D1
Ulceby DN39 86 A1
Walkeringham DN10 116 C3
Waltham DN37 113 E6
West/East Butterwick DN17 95 D1
Wharram YO17 6 A6
Winterton DN15 83 A5
Withernwick HU11 46 D3
Wootton DN39 85 E2
Wroot DN9 104 D6
High St E DN15 151 C7
High St W DN21 107 C4
High Stile HU17 45 B8
High Thorpe Cres DN35 103 B2
High Trees Mount HU7 141 E6
Higham Cl HU8 141 E7
Higham Way HU15 68 D5
Highcliff Gdns DN15 150 E7
Highcliffe Ct YO30 130 A6
Highcourt HU6 139 E7
Highcroft HU17 43 A5
Highdales HU10 143 C8
Highfield
Kingston upon Hull HU7 141 D6
Pollington DN14 77 F7
Withernsea HU19 75 A6
Highfield Ave
Great Driffield YO25 124 E6
22 Immingham DN40 87 B1
Scunthorpe DN15 150 E7
Highfield Cl
Barnby Dun DN3 92 A4
Fangfoss YO41 28 C8
Gainsborough DN21 117 C1
Kingston upon Hull HU7 141 D6
5 North Thoresby DN36 114 B1
Wold Newton YO25 2 A4
Highfield Cres
Barlby with Osgodby YO8 49 B5
15 Barton-upon-Humber DN18 84 F8
Kingston upon Hull HU11 142 F7
9 Thorne/Moorends DN8 79 A1
2 Thorne/Moorends DN8 93 A8
2 Westwoodside DN9 105 B2
Highfield Ct YO8 148 B1
Highfield Dr 1 DN21 108 B1
Highfield Gr 4 DN20 98 C3
Highfield La
Fangfoss YO41 16 B1
Womersley DN6 76 D5
Highfield Rd
Beverley HU17 136 F6
North Thoresby DN36 114 B1
Highfield Rise 1 HU12 58 D1
Highfield View 3 YO8 49 B4
Highfield Way HU14 69 A4
Highfields
10 Barrow upon Humber DN19 85 C8
Crowle DN17 94 D8
South Cave HU15 54 A2
Highgate Balne DN14 77 D6
Beverley HU17 154 B2
Cherry Burton HU17 42 E4
Cleethorpes DN35 153 E1
Highgate Cl HU8 142 A5
Highgrove DN17 107 D7
Highgrove Cl 7 YO30 126 E3
Highland Tarn 31 DN40 87 B1
Highlands Ave 5 YO32 14 B7
Highlands Prim Sch HU7 57 A6
Highmoor Cl YO24 132 D8
Highmoor Rd YO24 132 D8
Highthorn Rd YO31 127 E2
Highwood YO25 124 E6
Hilary Gr HU4 144 B2
Hilary Rd 11 DN33 113 E8
Hilbeck Gr YO31 131 B6
Hilbra Ave YO32 127 D6
Hilda St Goole DN14 149 C5
Grimsby DN32 153 A4
6 Selby YO8 148 C5
3 York YO10 130 E3
Hilderthorpe Cty Inf Sch YO15 122 C1
Hilderthorpe Rd YO15 122 D2
Hildyard Cl
19 Hedon HU12 72 D7
1 Kingston upon Hull HU10 143 F6

Hildyard St DN32 ...153 A4
Hiles Ave DN15 ...83 A5
Hill Brow HU10 ...143 B6
Hill Crest YO19 ...14 F1
Hill Crest Gdns YO24 ...129 F1
Hill Field YO8 ...148 B8
Hill Rd DN21 ...118 B1
Hill Rise Brough HU15 ...68 C6
Market Weighton YO43 ...135 E4
Hill Rise Cl YO43 ...135 E4
Hill Rise Dr YO43 ...135 E4
Hill St Bridlington YO16 ...122 D3
Kingston upon Hull HU8 ...141 A2
York YO24 ...129 E3
Hill The DN20 ...98 D8
Hill Top La DN21 ...117 E5
Hill Top Pl DN34 ...102 B2
Hill Top Rd 4 YO8 ...48 D6
Hill View YO31 ...131 C7
Hillam Comm La LS25 ...61 B7
Hillam Hall La 4 LS25 ...61 A7
Hillam Hall View 3 LS25 ...61 A7
Hillam La LS25 ...61 A7
Hillam Rd YO8 ...61 F8
Hillary Garth 9 YO26 ...129 E4
Hillary Rd DN16 ...151 B1
Hillary Way DN37 ...102 C4
Hillcrest Beverley HU17 ...136 C6
8 Monk Fryston LS25 ...61 A8
Hillcrest Ave
Kingston upon Hull HU13 ...143 C2
Poppleton YO26 ...126 A2
Hillcrest Dr
Beverley HU17 ...136 D6
Burton upon Stather DN15 ...82 A4
Hillerby La HU18 ...134 B4
Hillfield Dr HU11 ...45 D2
Hillfoot Dr 22 DN17 ...96 C2
Hillgarth Ct 4 YO41 ...27 B2
Hilliam H Cl 5 LS25 ...61 A7
Hillman Rd HU13 ...143 F3
Hills Dr 6 DN36 ...114 D4
Hillsborough Terr 5 YO30 ...130 C7
Hillside Cl 9 LS25 ...61 A8
Hillside Cres DN38 ...99 B5
Hillside Dr DN18 ...84 E8
Hillside Gdns YO25 ...8 D5
Hillside Rd DN20 ...97 E4
Hillside Way YO17 ...7 B8
Hillsmere Gr 5 DN15 ...83 A5
Hillstead Cl 5 DN36 ...114 D4
Hillsyde Ave DN10 ...116 C5
Hilltop Ave DN15 ...150 E8
Hilston Gr HU9 ...142 B1
Hilton Ave DN15 ...150 B7
Hilton Cl DN9 ...94 E2
Hilton Ct DN35 ...103 D1
Hinch Garth HU12 ...60 B1
Hinderwell St HU5 ...140 C1
Hinkler St DN35 ...153 E1
Hinkley Dr 2 DN40 ...87 B2
Hinsley La DN14 ...63 C2
Hinton Ave 1 YO24 ...132 C8
Hirncroft Cl 10 HU8 ...141 E7
Hirst Courtney & Temple Hirst CP Sch YO8 ...62 E3
Hirst Rd YO8 ...63 A3
Hive La DN14 ...52 B1
Hob Moor Dr YO24 ...129 E2
Hob Moor Inf Sch YO24 ...129 D2
Hob Moor Jun Sch YO24 ...129 E2
Hobart St HU3 ...145 D5
Hobb La 14 DN21 ...107 C3
Hobgate YO24 ...129 D3
Hobman La YO25 ...32 E7
Hobmoor Terr YO24 ...129 F1
Hobson Cl YO23 ...132 B1
Hobson Rd 5 HU15 ...68 C6
Hobson Way DN41 ...101 F8
Hodder Gr HU8 ...142 C6
Hoddesdon Cres 13 DN7 ...92 D3
Hoddy Cows La YO15 ...4 C3
Hodge Ct 3 HU9 ...146 C7
Hodge La WF8 ...76 B3
Hodgson Ave HU17 ...154 B4
Hodgson La Roos HU12 ...60 A1
Upper Poppleton YO26 ...24 F8
Hodgson St HU8 ...155 C3
Hodsow Fields YO42 ...28 E4
Hodsow La YO42 ...28 F3
Hogg La HU10 ...143 B8
Hoggard La DN14 ...81 E8
Hogsea La HU12 ...60 B4
Holbeck Pl 17 DN40 ...87 B1
Holborn St HU8 ...146 B7
Holbrook Cl 2 HU7 ...141 B4
Holburns Croft 3 YO10 ...131 B1
Holcombe Cl HU8 ...142 B7
Holcroft Garth 10 HU12 ...72 D7
Holden Gdns YO8 ...48 D2
Holderness Cres HU17 ...154 B3
Holderness Rd HU9 ...146 C8
Holgate Bridge Gdn 7 YO24 ...130 A3
Holgate Cl 2 HU17 ...137 B3
Holgate Lodge Dr YO26 ...129 E4
Holgate Pl 12 HU14 ...69 B7
Holgate Rd
Scunthorpe DN16 ...151 D4
York YO24 ...156 A1
Holland Ave DN15 ...150 E8
Holland St HU9 ...146 C8
Holles St DN32 ...152 E3
Hollicarrs Cl YO19 ...37 A2
Hollies The
Barlby with Osgodby YO8 ...49 C4
Beverley HU17 ...137 A7
Hornsea HU18 ...134 D2
Kingston upon Hull HU10 ...138 E2
Snaith & Cowick DN14 ...78 C8
Hollin Bridge La DN7 ...93 A3
Hollingsworth Ave 12 DN40 ...87 B1
Hollingsworth Cl 14 DN35 ...103 B1
Hollingsworth La 22 DN9 ...105 E6
Hollis Cres YO32 ...14 B6
Hollowgate Hill DN21 ...119 A3
Hollows The 9 YO16 ...122 C5
Holly Bank Gr 3 YO24 ...129 F2
Holly Bank Rd YO24 ...129 F2
Holly Cl
Acaster Malbis YO23 ...36 C8
Full Sutton YO41 ...16 A2
18 Scunthorpe DN16 ...96 E2
Stallingborough DN41 ...101 D6
Holly Dr HU16 ...138 E5
Holly Gr Selby YO8 ...148 B3
8 Thorpe Willoughby YO8 ...48 B2
Holly Hill HU15 ...68 E6
Holly Rd DN8 ...79 B1
Holly Tree Croft 2 YO19 ...26 F7
Holly Tree Garth YO32 ...14 E3
Holly Tree La
Dunnington YO19 ...26 F7
Haxby YO32 ...127 D8
Hollycroft YO25 ...23 A6
Hollygarth La DN14 ...61 D4
Hollym Rd
Patrington HU19 ...74 F3
Withernsea HU19 ...75 A5
Hollyrood Rd YO30 ...126 E3
Hollytree Ave 2 HU4 ...144 B7
Hollywood YO8 ...148 B7
Holm Garth Dr HU8 ...142 B4
Holm Rd DN9 ...105 B2
Holme Ave DN36 ...114 A7
Holme Church La HU17 ...154 C2
Holme Cl 18 Brigg DN20 ...98 C2
Holme-on-Spalding-Moor YO43 ...40 A1
Paull HU12 ...72 A5
Holme Cres HU16 ...138 E6
Holme Dene DN9 ...105 C2
Holme Dr DN15 ...82 B5
Holme Farm Cl DN37 ...102 B5
Holme Gdns 11 DN7 ...92 C6
Holme Hall Ave DN16 ...96 D2
Holme Hill La YO10 ...26 C4
Holme Ind Est YO43 ...52 C6
Holme La Holme DN16 ...96 E2
Messingham DN17 ...107 D8
Scunthorpe DN16 ...96 D2
Selby YO8 ...148 D6
Holme Rd YO43 ...135 B3
Holme St DN32 ...152 E3
Holme Valley Prim Sch DN16 ...96 E2
Holme Wood Ct 2 DN3 ...92 A1
Holmefield Cl 3 YO8 ...148 A1
Holmefield Ct 2 YO8 ...148 A1
Holmefield La YO10 ...131 A1
Holme-on-Spalding-Moor Prim Sch YO43 ...40 A1
Holmes Dr 2 YO19 ...37 A1
Holmes House* YO8 ...50 B3
Holmes La Bilton HU11 ...58 A4
Roxby cum Risby DN15 ...83 D5
Holmes Pk DN14 ...51 F1
Holmfirth Rd DN15 ...150 C8
Holmpton Gr HU9 ...142 B1
Holmpton Rd
Patrington HU12 ...74 E1
Withernsea HU19 ...75 A5
Holms La YO43 ...53 E7
Holray Pk DN14 ...63 C2
Holroyd Ave YO31 ...131 A5
Holstein Dr 2 DN16 ...96 D1
Holtby Gdns HU18 ...134 C6
Holtby La Holtby YO19 ...14 D1
Stockton-on-the-Forest YO32 ...128 F2
Holtby's Yd YO16 ...122 C4
Holton Ct 8 DN36 ...114 A5
Holton le Clay Jun Sch DN36 ...114 B5
Holton Mount 7 DN36 ...114 A5
Holton Rd
Holton le Moor LN7 ...110 F1
South Kelsey LN7 ...110 D1
Tetney DN36 ...114 C5
Holwell Rd HU7 ...141 A5
Holwick Mews HU5 ...139 D4
Holy Family CP Sch DN7 ...92 D7
Holy Family RC High Sch DN14 ...63 C3
Holy Name RC Prim Sch HU6 ...139 E7
Holy Well* DN15 ...83 C4
Holy Well La LN11 ...121 D4
Holydyke DN18 ...84 E8
Holyoake Rd DN32 ...153 C2
Holyroad Dr DN15 ...96 B7
Holyrood Ave YO15 ...122 F3
Home Beat Dr DN20 ...97 C3
Home Cl HU4 ...144 C5
Home Gn HU16 ...139 A5
Home Paddock 5 DN37 ...113 E6
Home St DN15 ...151 B8
Homefield Ave 8 DN33 ...102 E2
Homefield Cl YO23 ...132 A2
Homestead Cl
Eggborough DN14 ...62 A2
2 York YO32 ...127 F1
Homestead Garth 3 DN7 ...92 D4
Homestead Rd HU12 ...72 F5
Homethorpe HU6 ...140 A8
Honey Pot 5 YO8 ...50 D7
Honeypots La HU12 ...59 A2
Honeysuckle Cl YO8 ...148 C2
Honeysuckle Ct DN35 ...103 C1
Honiton Rd HU7 ...141 A8
Hood Gr DN14 ...149 B6
Hood Rd DN17 ...150 D2
Hood St HU8 ...155 C4
Hook La DN14 ...149 C8
Hook Pasture La DN14 ...149 C1
Hook Rd DN14 ...149 E4
Hooks La Holmpton HU19 ...75 B2
Thorngumbald HU12 ...72 E4
Hoop End DN36 ...114 D4
Hop Hills La DN7 ...92 D5
Hope St
Cleethorpes DN35 ...103 D3
Grimsby DN32 ...152 F4
York YO10 ...156 C1
Hopewell Rd HU9 ...142 C3
Hopfield DN20 ...109 A5
Hopgarth DN9 ...105 D2
Hopgrove La N YO32 ...128 C3
Hopgrove La S YO32 ...128 E3
Hopkins Ave DN17 ...151 A3
Hopkins St HU9 ...142 A3
Hopwood Cl HU3 ...145 D8
Hopwood La HU15 ...52 F1
Horbury Cl DN15 ...150 D8
Hords La YO25 ...21 D4
Horkstow Rd DN18 ...84 A6
Hornbeam Ave DN16 ...151 A1
Hornbeam Dr HU16 ...139 C5
Hornbeam Wlk HU16 ...139 B5
Hornby Gr HU9 ...142 C3
Horner St YO30 ...130 B7
Hornsby Cres DN15 ...96 C7
Hornsea & District War Meml Cottage Hospl HU18 ...134 C5
Hornsea Burton Rd HU18 ...134 D3
Hornsea Leisure Ctr HU18 ...134 D4
Hornsea Mus* HU18 ...134 C4
Hornsea Par 5 HU9 ...146 C8
Hornsea Prim Sch HU18 ...134 C4
Hornsea Rd
Aldbrough HU11 ...47 B2
Atwick HU18 ...134 A8
Hatfield HU11 ...46 D6
Leven HU17 ...45 B8
Seaton HU11 ...35 B1
Skipsea YO25 ...23 B1
Hornsea Sch HU18 ...134 B4
Hornsey Garth 25 YO32 ...13 E5
Hornsey Hill Rd DN21 ...106 D1
Horse Carr La YO25 ...10 B1
Horse Fair Gn 21 DN8 ...93 A8
Horse Mkt 17 LN7 ...111 B4
Horsefair La YO25 ...124 B5
Horsegate Field Rd DN19 ...86 A8
Horseman Ave YO23 ...132 A3
Horseman Cl 2 YO23 ...132 A3
Horseman Dr YO23 ...132 A3
Horseman La YO23 ...132 A3
Horseshoe Cres YO43 ...40 A1
Horseshoe Dr YO15 ...123 C6
Horseshoe The
Great Driffield YO25 ...124 E3
York YO24 ...132 E7
Horsfield Way YO19 ...26 F7
Horsforth Ave YO15 ...122 D1
Horsman Ave YO10 ...156 C1
Horstead Ave DN20 ...98 C3
Hospital Fields Rd YO10 ...130 D1
Hospital Hill 4 YO25 ...10 A2
Hospital La YO8 ...48 B4
Hospitum The* YO30 ...156 A3
Hotham Ave YO26 ...129 B2
Hotham Dr HU5 ...144 B8
Hotham Rd
Hutton Cranswick YO25 ...32 E7
Kingston upon Hull HU5 ...144 A8
North Cave YO43 ...53 D4
Hotham Rd N HU5 ...139 E3
Hotham Rd S HU5 ...144 B8
Hotham Sq HU17 ...137 B4
Hotham St HU9 ...146 D7
Hotspur Rd 1 DN21 ...117 B1
Hotton Cl HU9 ...142 C1
Houghton La YO43 ...41 C1
Houndale La YO25 ...125 E8
Houndsway 6 YO24 ...132 B8
Houps Rd 10 DN8 ...93 B8
Hourne The HU13 ...143 E2
Housemartin Dr 4 HU8 ...141 D8
Houston Dr HU5 ...140 D3
Hove Rd HU5 ...139 D1
Hovedene Dr DN14 ...65 A6
Hovingham Cl 17 HU8 ...141 E7
Howard Dr YO30 ...126 E2
Howard Gr DN32 ...153 B2
Howard Link YO30 ...126 D2
Howard Rd YO32 ...14 B6
Howard St YO10 ...130 D2
Howdale Rd HU8 ...141 E7
Howden Croft Hill HU15 ...68 A8
Howden Cty Jun & Inf Sch DN14 ...65 B7
Howden La YO19 ...133 E1
Howden Rd 4 Barlby YO8 ...49 B4
Eastrington DN14 ...65 F8
Holme-on-Spalding-Moor YO43 ...51 F6
Howden Sec Sch DN14 ...65 B7
Howdens Hill DN15 ...151 A6
Howdenshire Way DN14 ...64 F6
Howe Hill* DN39 ...85 D2
Howe Hill Cl YO26 ...129 E4
Howe Hill Rd YO26 ...129 E4
Howe La Goxhill DN19 ...85 F8
Kirby Underdale YO41 ...17 A5
Nafferton YO25 ...125 F7
Howe St YO24 ...129 D3
Howes La YO25 ...33 E8
Howes Rd 8 YO14 ...3 A8
Howgate La YO43 ...41 A8
Howl Gate YO41 ...27 E8
Howl La YO25 ...32 E8
Howlett Rd 4 DN35 ...103 D2
Howsham Cl HU9 ...142 D5
Howsham La DN38 ...110 C8
Howville Ave DN7 ...92 F3
Howville Rd DN7 ...92 F3
Hoylake Cl HU6 ...139 E5
Hoylake Dr 6 DN40 ...87 C2
Hoylake Rd DN17 ...96 B2
Hubert St
1 Withernsea HU19 ...74 F7
2 York YO23 ...130 B1
Hucknall Garth 16 HU7 ...57 A5
Huddleston Rd DN32 ...153 B3
Hudson Ave DN15 ...96 C7
Hudson Cl YO41 ...15 D2
Hudson Cres 2 YO30 ...130 A7
Hudson Gdns 2 HU5 ...140 D1
Hudson St
Kingston upon Hull HU3 ...145 D8
6 York YO30 ...130 C7
Hudson's La YO25 ...31 B7
Huggate Dikes* YO42 ...17 F2
Huggate Hill YO17 ...17 E7
Huggate La YO25 ...18 B5
Huggin Carr Rd DN7 ...92 F1
Hugh Field La YO8 ...50 A8
Hugh Field N La YO8 ...38 A1
Hugh Hill La DN7 ...92 D6
Hulberry Cl 11 DN41 ...101 A4
Hull & E Riding Hospl HU10 ...143 E5
Hull & East Riding Mus* HU1 ...155 C2
Hull Arena* HU1 ...145 E4
Hull Bridge Rd
Beverley HU17 ...154 B4
Tickton HU17 ...137 C7
Hull City AFC HU4 ...144 E5
Hull Coll HU3 ...144 F7
Hull Coll of F Ed HU6 ...56 C5
Hull Coll Park Street Ctr HU2 ...145 D7
Hull College of F Ed HU1 ...155 C3
Hull Gram Sch HU5 ...140 C3
Hull High Sch for Girls HU10 ...143 C5
Hull Ionians RUFC HU15 ...68 C7
Hull Kingston Rovers RLFC HU9 ...142 C1
Hull Maritime Mus* HU1 ...155 B2
Hull Maternity Hospl HU9 ...147 A8
Hull Nuffield Hospl HU5 ...140 B1
Hull Rd Aldbrough HU11 ...59 B7
Beverley HU17 ...137 B3
Cliffe YO8 ...49 E2
Coniston HU11 ...57 F5
Easington HU12 ...90 E6
Hatfield HU11 ...46 C5
Hemingbrough YO8 ...50 B1
Heslington YO19 ...131 E3
Hornsea HU11 ...46 D8
Hornsea HU18 ...134 B1
Howden DN14 ...65 B7
Keyingham HU12 ...73 C4
Kingston upon Hull HU16 ...139 D5
Kingston upon Hull HU13 ...143 F1
Kingston upon Hull HU10 ...143 F6
Kingston upon Hull HU12 ...147 F6
Preston HU12 ...72 A7
Rimswell HU19 ...74 E6
Woodmansey HU17 ...137 B2
York YO10 ...131 B3
Hull RLFC HU3 ...145 B5
Hull Road Ave 4 DN14 ...65 B7
Hull Royal Infmy HU3 ...145 C6
Hull RUFC HU7 ...140 B8
Hull Sta HU1 ...155 A2
Hull Trinity Ho Sch HU1 ...155 B2
Humber Bank S DN31 ...153 A6
Humber Bridge* HU13 ...69 E3
Humber Bridge Ctry Pk* HU13 ...69 D4
Humber Bridge Rd DN31 ...153 A5
Humber Cres
5 Brough HU15 ...68 C5
Scunthorpe DN17 ...150 F2
Humber Dock St HU1 ...155 B1
Humber Dr 5 YO32 ...14 B6
Humber La
Patrington HU12 ...74 D1
Skeffling HU12 ...90 D5
Welwick HU12 ...90 A7
Humber Pl HU1 ...155 B1
Humber Rd
Barton-upon-Humber DN18 ...69 E1
North Ferriby HU14 ...69 A4
South Killingholme DN40 ...86 F3
Humber Side La
Easington HU12 ...90 F4
Welwick HU12 ...89 F6
Humber Side Rd HU12 ...90 B6
Humber St
Cleethorpes DN35 ...153 F1
Goole DN14 ...149 D1
Grimsby DN31 ...153 A5
Kingston upon Hull HU9 ...155 C1
Market Weighton YO43 ...135 F4
Humber Terr DN31 ...152 C4
Humber View
Barton-upon-Humber DN18 ...84 E8
Kingston upon Hull HU13 ...143 C2
5 Swanland HU14 ...69 B6
Humberdale Cl 4 HU14 ...69 B6
Humberdale Dr HU14 ...69 C5
Humberside Int Airport DN38 ...99 F5
Humberston Ave
13 Humberston DN36 ...114 D8
New Waltham DN36 ...114 B7
Humberston C of E Prim Sch DN36 ...114 D8
Humberston Cloverfields Prim Sch DN36 ...114 C8
Humberston Comp Sch DN36 ...114 C8
Humberston Rd DN36 ...103 B1
Humberstone Rd DN32 ...153 A2
Humberville Rd DN40 ...87 C1
Humbleton Rd
East Garton HU12 ...59 C6
Elstronwick HU12 ...58 E3
Hume Brae DN40 ...87 B1
Hume St DN31 ...152 C3
Hund Oak Dr DN7 ...92 D4
Hungate
13 Barton-upon-Humber DN18 ...69 E1
York YO1 ...156 C2
Hungate Ct
11 Hunmanby YO14 ...2 F8
Market Weighton YO43 ...135 D5
Hungate La YO14 ...2 F8
Hunger Hills Balk YO25 ...10 C4
Hungerhills Dr HU11 ...58 A4
Hunmanby CP Sch YO14 ...2 F8
Hunmanby Rd
Burton Fleming YO25 ...2 E3
Reighton YO14 ...3 C6
Hunmanby Sta YO14 ...3 A7
Hunsley Ave 3 HU5 ...139 B1
Hunsley Cres DN32 ...103 A2
Hunsley Dr DN41 ...101 E6
Hunsley Rd HU17 ...55 A7
Hunt Ct YO31 ...156 C3
Hunt Rd DN16 ...151 C1
Huntcliffe Comp Sch DN21 ...108 C1
Hunter Cl
1 Patrington HU12 ...74 D1
5 Preston HU12 ...58 D1
Hunter Rd HU15 ...68 C6
Hunters Cl
Dunnington YO19 ...26 E7
10 Haxby YO32 ...127 C8
Hunter's Croft DN9 ...105 D3
Hunters Gate DN37 ...102 B5
Hunters Way
Selby YO8 ...148 B4
York YO24 ...132 F7
Hunters Wlk YO8 ...63 D7
Hunters Wood Way 21 YO19 ...26 F7
Huntingdon Cres 5 DN15 ...82 B4
Huntingdon St HU4 ...144 E3
Huntington Prim Sch YO32 ...127 F4
Huntington Rd YO31 ...156 C4
Huntington Sch YO32 ...127 E3
Huntington Sports Club YO32 ...128 A5
Huntley Dr HU5 ...140 A1
Hunts Cl 7 DN20 ...97 E4
Hunts La DN20 ...108 F5
Huntsmans La YO41 ...15 C2
Huntsman's Wlk YO24 ...129 B1
Hurford Pl DN37 ...113 E7
Hurley Cl HU8 ...141 F3

Hurn Cl HU8 141 E6
Hurns La YO30 126 A7
Hurricane Way YO30 126 E3
Hurst La DN17 96 C2
Hurstlea Dr 10 DN36 103 D1
Hurst's Yd YO1 156 C2
Hurton's La LN11 121 F6
Hushells La DN14 78 C2
Hustler Rd YO16 122 F5
Hutch La DN14 66 C3
Hutchinson Rd DN35 153 D3
Hutchinson St 1 YO8 148 B6
Huteson La DN15 82 C8
Hutt St HU3 145 D7
Hutton Balk YO25 32 D8
Hutton Cl
Kingston upon Hull HU5 139 E2
Poppleton YO26 126 A2
Hutton Rd
Grimsby DN31 153 A6
Hutton Cranswick YO25 32 E7
Hutton St YO26 24 A5
Huzzard Cl 5 HU17 55 D8
Hykeham Cl 17 HU7 56 F6
Hymers Ave HU3 145 B7
Hymers Cl 11 YO25 34 B2
Hymers Coll HU3 145 B7
Hyperion St HU9 155 C3
Hyrst Gr YO31 130 E6

I

Icehouse Rd HU3 145 D6
Idas Cl HU9 155 C1
Idle Bank Epworth DN9 94 A2
Haxey DN9 104 F4
Wroot DN9 104 E2
Ikin Way YO32 127 F6
Ilchester Cl HU7 141 B5
Ilford Rd HU5 139 C1
Ilkeston Ave DN14 149 B5
Ilthorpe HU6 140 A8
Ilton Garth YO30 127 A2
Immingham Dock DN40 87 D3
Immingham Medieval Village* DN40 87 B2
Immingham Mus* DN40 87 C1
Immingham Pelham Inf & Nursery Sch DN40 87 C1
Immingham Sch The DN40 87 C1
Immingham Sports Ctr DN40 87 C1
Immingham St Andrews C of E Jun Sch DN40 87 C1
Immingham Swimming Pool DN40 87 C1
Impala Way HU4 144 D2
Imperial Ave DN35 153 C4
Imperial Cl 12 HU9 142 A3
Ing Nook Rd HU15 52 C2
Inghams La 12 DN36 114 D4
Inghams Rd DN36 114 D4
Ingland Ct HU9 142 B1
Ingleborough Ave YO10 131 B4
Ingleby Cl HU8 141 F7
Ingleby Rd DN17 107 D7
Inglefield Cl 7 HU17 55 E8
Inglemire Ave HU6 140 C5
Inglemire La HU6 139 E5
Inglenook Dr 1 DN8 93 B8
Ingleton Ave HU4 144 C6
Ingleton Wlk 3 YO31 131 A5
Inglewood Dr 4 HU4 144 B5
Ingmires 3 HU15 68 D6
Ingram Ave
Kingston upon Hull HU11 142 F6
York YO30 130 C8
Ingram Cres DN7 92 C4
Ingram Gdns DN20 108 E8
Ingram Gr DN7 92 C4
Ingram Pl DN35 103 B2
Ingram Rd DN7 92 C3
Ingrish La YO23 24 C1
Ings Ct DN14 61 F4
Ings Dr YO43 53 F7
Ings La Beal DN14 61 D4
Bishop Wilton YO42 16 D2
Brough HU15 68 C5
Carlton DN14 63 E2
Cawood YO8 48 D8
Cottingwith YO42 38 C5
Dunswell HU6 56 D2
Ellerker HU15 67 F8
Hensall DN14 62 D2
Hibaldstow DN20 109 A5
Immingham DN40 87 D1
Kellington DN14 61 F4
Keyingham HU12 73 C4
Kirk Bramwith DN7 92 C7
Nether Poppleton YO26 126 B1
North Coates DN36 115 A3
North Ferriby HU14 69 A4
Patrington HU12 74 C1
Riccall YO19 48 E8
Riston HU11 45 C2
South Cave HU15 67 E7
Spaldington DN14 51 C4
Thorganby YO19 38 B5
Utterby LN11 121 E4
Ings La *continued*
Walkerith DN21 116 F3
Waltham DN37 113 E6
West Stockwith DN10 116 F6
Wheldrake YO19 38 B7
Whitton DN15 67 E3
Winterton DN15 83 D7
Wistow YO8 49 A6
Ings Prim Sch HU8 141 F4
Ings Rd Cliffe YO8 49 D2
Kingston upon Hull HU7 141 D5
Kirton in Lindsey DN21 107 F1
Molescroft HU17 136 D7
Snaith DN14 63 C1
Thorganby YO19 38 B4
Wilberfoss YO41 27 E6
Ings View YO30 126 D2
Inman Terr YO26 129 D4
Inmans Prim Sch HU12 72 D7
Inmans Rd HU12 72 D7
Innescourt HU6 139 E7
Innsworth Garth 17 HU7 57 A5
Inrea Hill YO42 29 F5
Intake Ave YO30 130 C8
Intake Hill YO43 135 C8
Intake La
Acaster Malbis YO23 36 C7
Beal WF11 61 D5
Dunnington YO19 26 F7
Heck DN14 77 C8
West Haddlesey YO8 61 F6
Intakefield Rd YO8 50 D7
Intakes La YO42 39 A6
Inverewe Way 2 HU16 138 F5
Inverness Rd 24 DN7 92 D4
Invicta Ct YO24 132 B8
Iona Cl
8 Gainsborough DN21 117 C1
Kingston upon Hull HU8 141 E7
Iona Dr DN36 114 D8
Iona Rd YO16 122 F4
Irby Ct 8 DN35 103 B2
Irby Rd DN17 150 E1
Irvine Rd DN16 151 C1
Irwin Ave YO31 130 E6
Isaac Newton Sch HU9 142 D1
Isaac's Hill DN35 153 E2
Isis Ct HU9 146 B5
Island Carr Rd DN20 98 B2
Island Rd DN17 81 E6
Isle Cl DN17 94 D8
Isledane HU6 139 E8
Itlings La HU13 143 F1
Itterby Cres DN35 103 B2
Ivanhoe Rd DN16 151 C5
Iver Cl YO26 129 C5
Iveson Cl 27 HU12 72 C7
Ivy Cl DN7 92 E4
Ivy Farm Ct 6 DN41 101 F5
Ivy La Grainthorpe LN11 115 E1
Hedon HU12 72 C7
Snaith & Cowick DN14 78 D8
Ivy Mdw HU12 59 C2
Ivy Park Rd DN14 149 E6
Ivy Rd DN8 79 A1
Ivybridge Wlk 5 HU9 142 E1

J

Jack Rd YO43 53 C8
Jack Row La DN7 92 B8
Jack Taylor La HU17 137 B4
Jackey La HU11 58 B8
Jacklin La DN17 81 C3
Jacklins App DN16 96 D2
Jackson La YO41 27 E4
Jackson Mews 7 DN40 87 B1
Jackson Rd DN15 150 E7
Jackson St Goole DN14 149 C4
Grimsby DN31 152 C4
Kingston upon Hull HU3 145 D4
York YO31 156 C4
Jackson's Pl DN36 103 B1
Jackson's Wlk YO23 24 D3
Jacksonville DN14 149 C5
Jacobi Cl YO30 130 A7
Jacques' La YO8 49 E4
Jade Gr 1 HU3 145 A4
Jalland St HU8 141 C1
James Backhouse Pl YO24 129 E3
James Cl 1 HU19 75 A6
James Ct 5 DN8 79 B1
James Nicholson Way YO30 127 A2
James Niven Ct 1 HU9 141 D1
James Pl DN39 86 B1
James Reckitt Ave HU8 141 B1
James St 22 Brigg DN20 98 B2
Goole DN14 149 D2
Grimsby DN31 152 C4
Selby YO8 148 C5
York YO10 130 E4
James Way 23 DN40 87 B1
Jameson Rd YO16 122 C4
Jameson St HU1 155 A2
Jamieson Terr YO23 130 B1
Janton Ct DN36 114 A8
Japan Rd DN21 117 A1
Japonica Hill 8 DN40 87 C1
Jaque's Bank DN8 94 A5
Jarratt Hill La HU15 67 C8
Jarratt St HU1 155 B3
Jasmine Cl
10 Snaith DN14 63 C1
Jasmine Cl *continued*
York YO32 127 D2
Jasmine Gr 17 HU7 56 F5
Jasmine Way DN40 87 C1
Jason Cl YO16 122 E6
Jason Garth 1 HU7 57 B5
Jaywick Cl 3 YO32 14 B8
Jedwell Cl YO32 127 D5
Jefferson Cl Goole DN14 65 C4
Molescroft HU17 136 E6
Jefferson Dr HU15 68 C6
Jefferson St DN14 149 C4
Jeffrey La DN9 94 E1
Jendale HU7 140 F8
Jenkinson La YO25 32 D8
Jenner Pl DN35 153 B4
Jennifer Gr 4 YO24 129 F2
Jenning St HU8 155 C4
Jenny Brough La HU13 143 B3
Jenny Cl HU13 143 B3
Jenny La DN14 77 B5
Jenthorpe HU6 140 A8
Jericho La DN40 86 D7
Jervis Rd
Kingston upon Hull HU9 142 D5
York YO24 132 E8
Jesmond Gdns HU9 141 D1
Jesmond Rd HU16 139 C6
Jetcourt HU6 139 E7
Jevans Ct 2 YO25 124 F4
Jewbury YO31 156 C3
Jewison La
Bempton YO16 4 D1
Flamborough Maltings YO15 123 B8
Jill Gr HU13 143 F1
Jipdane HU6 139 F8
Jobsons Cl 11 HU15 53 F1
Joby La HU17 43 A2
Jockey La YO32 127 F2
John Coupland Hospl DN21 117 A2
John Gray Ct HU10 138 D1
John Harrison C of E Prim Sch DN19 85 D8
John Harrison's Cl 1 DN19 85 D8
John Leggott Coll DN17 150 E4
John Newton Way HU7 56 E5
John St
Kingston upon Hull HU2 155 B3
Scunthorpe DN15 151 B7
Selby YO8 148 D6
York YO31 130 E6
Johnny Moor Long La DN14 79 B6
Johnson Cl DN9 94 E2
Johnson St
Cleethorpes DN35 153 B4
Selby YO8 148 B6
Johnson's La DN17 94 C7
Johnston Ct HU17 136 D7
Johnston's Rd DN7 92 E7
Joiners La YO25 19 B6
Jonquil Ave DN16 96 E2
Jorvik Viking Ctr* YO1 156 C2
Joscelyn Ave HU7 141 B5
Joseph Ogle Cl
6 New Waltham DN36 113 F8
3 New Waltham DN36 114 A8
Joseph Rowntree Sch YO32 127 E5
Joseph St DN31 152 C4
Jowland Winn La YO8 63 A4
Jubbergate YO1 156 B2
Jubilee Ave YO16 122 D4
Jubilee Cres 35 DN21 117 B1
Jubilee Gr 8 YO16 122 D5
Jubilee La HU12 59 C2
Jubilee Rd YO8 48 D6
Jubilee Terr YO26 129 F5
Julia Ave YO32 128 B2
Julian Cl HU4 144 A7
Julian St DN32 153 A3
Julian's Bower (Maze)* DN15 82 C8
Julian's Wlk 8 HU10 143 F6
Junction Rd DN7 92 C6
Junella Cl HU3 145 A4
Juniper Cl YO32 127 D3
Juniper Way DN33 102 E1
Justice Hall La 3 DN17 94 D8
Justice La DN14 81 B8
Jute Rd YO26 129 B5
Jutland Ct 13 DN36 114 A8

K

Karen Ave 10 DN41 101 A4
Kathleen Ave
Cleethorpes DN35 153 D4
Scunthorpe DN16 151 B1
Kathleen Gr DN32 153 C3
Kathleen Rd HU8 141 B2
Kathryn Ave YO32 128 A2
Katrine Cl HU7 141 D5
Kay Kendall Ct 16 HU19 75 A6
Kaye Dr YO8 49 B4
Kaymile Cl 15 DN36 114 A7
Kealholme Rd DN17 107 D7
Keats Ave DN17 150 D3
Keats Cl YO30 129 F8
Keb La DN15 83 D2
Keble Cl YO23 133 B3
Keble Dr YO23 133 A2
Keble Gdns YO23 133 B2
Keble Park Cres YO23 133 A2
Keble Pk N YO23 133 A3
Keble Pk S YO23 133 A2
Keddington Rd 18 DN17 96 C2
Kedrum Rd HU9 141 F1
Keel Ct HU17 137 B3
Keel Rd HU6 140 C8
Keelby CP Sch DN41 101 A5
Keelby Rd
Scunthorpe DN17 150 F1
Stallingborough DN41 101 C6
Keeper's Hill YO25 7 A1
Keeper's Way 2 DN9 94 E1
Keepers Way 11 YO19 26 F7
Keirhardie Wlk 4 DN32 152 E3
Keith Ave YO32 128 A4
Keith Cres DN37 101 E1
Keldale 4 YO32 13 F5
Keldgarth YO25 32 F6
Keldgate HU17 154 A2
Keldgate Cl HU17 154 A2
Keldgate Rd
Beverley HU17 136 C2
Cottingham HU16 138 D7
Keldspring La YO42 28 E4
Kelfield Rd 9 YO19 48 F8
Kelgate Cl 11 HU8 141 E7
Kelham Rd DN32 153 D2
Kelk La YO25 22 B6
Kelleythorpe Ind Est YO25 124 B3
Kellington La DN14 61 F2
Kellington Prim Sch DN14 61 F3
Kelsey Ave DN15 150 B7
Kelsey Cl YO43 135 D2
Kelsey Dr 3 HU12 73 C4
Kelsey La DN17 95 D4
Kelsey Rd LN7 110 D1
Kelstern Ct DN34 152 A1
Kelston Dr 2 HU13 144 A3
Kelvin Hall Sch HU5 139 E3
Kelvin St HU9 141 E2
Kemp Rd
Grimsby DN31 153 A7
North Ferriby HU14 69 B6
Kempton Cl 2 YO24 129 D1
Kempton Dr DN7 92 C2
Kempton Rd HU3 144 E6
Kendal Cl 6 YO19 26 F7
Kendal Rd DN40 87 D1
Kendal Way HU4 144 C7
Kendale Rd DN16 151 E4
Kendale View YO25 124 E6
Kendon Gdns DN8 93 B8
Kendrew Cl 3 YO32 127 F3
Kenerdales La YO43 53 E8
Kenford Ct 1 DN36 114 A8
Kenilworth Ave HU5 139 F3
Kenilworth Rd
6 Cleethorpes DN35 103 B2
Scunthorpe DN16 151 C5
Kenlay Cl YO32 127 D4
Kenmar Rd DN37 101 F1
Kenmore Dr HU6 56 D5
Kennedy Cl DN20 98 D2
Kennedy Dr
Goole DN14 149 D5
32 Haxby YO32 13 E5
Kennet Rd HU8 142 C6
Kenneth Ave 5 DN7 92 C6
Kennington Wlk HU16 139 D6
Kenrick Pl 5 YO26 129 B5
Kensal Rise YO10 130 D2
Kensington Ct 1 YO24 132 F8
Kensington Gdns 14 DN14 65 A7
Kensington Pl 3 DN33 113 F8
Kensington Rd
Rawcliffe YO30 126 D2
Scunthorpe DN15 150 B7
Kensington St YO23 130 B1
Kent Cl HU9 146 C7
Kent Dr DN20 109 A5
Kent Rd
Bridlington YO16 122 A2
Goole DN14 149 B4
Kingston upon Hull HU16 139 A5
Selby YO8 148 A6
Kent Sq YO16 122 A2
Kent St Grimsby DN32 152 F5
York YO10 156 C1
Kentmere Cl 2 HU7 57 A7
Kentmere Dr YO30 126 F1
Kents Gdns 14 DN8 79 B2
Kenwardly Rd HU10 143 E8
Kenwood HU19 75 A5
Kenya Dr 3 DN17 96 C1
Keppel Dr YO16 123 A8
Kerdane HU6 139 F8
Kerries Wlk DN17 150 C2
Kerry Dr HU10 143 C6
Kerry Pit Way HU10 143 C6
Kerver La YO19 26 F7
Kesgrave St DN31 153 A5
Kesteven Ct 6 DN40 100 E8
Kesteven Gr 9 DN17 94 D8
Kesteven Way HU7 56 F5
Kestrel Ave HU7 141 D8
Kestrel Dr YO15 123 B7
Kestrel Rd DN17 150 E2
Kestrel Wood Way YO31 127 F2
Keswick Gdns HU6 139 E6
Keswick Way 5 YO32 127 F5
Kettering Rd DN16 151 C6
Kettlebridge La DN40 86 D6
Kettleby La DN20 98 E3
Kettleby View DN20 98 D2
Kettlestring La YO30 127 A3
Kettlethorpe Hill HU15 53 F4
Kettlewell Cl 2 HU7 56 F6
Kettlewell St DN32 152 E1
Ketwell La 10 HU12 72 C7
Ketwell Lane Prim Sch HU12 72 C7
Kew Rd DN35 153 E2
Kexby Ave YO10 130 F3
Kexby Bridge* YO41 27 C6
Kexby House* YO41 27 C6
Kexby Stray YO41 27 A5
Key Way YO19 133 F5
Keyholme La DN36 115 D2
Keyingham Cty Jun Sch HU12 73 D4
Keyingham Inf Sch HU12 73 C3
Keyingham Rd HU12 73 D3
Keyworth Dr 5 LN7 111 B4
Kidd La Brough HU15 68 D6
Melbourne YO42 39 A6
Kiddier Ave 12 DN33 113 D8
Kidhill La HU11 45 B2
Kilburn Ave HU2 155 A4
Kilburn Rd YO10 130 D2
Kildale Cl HU8 141 E6
Kilham La Kilham YO25 9 E5
Thwing YO25 9 B8
Kilham Prim Sch YO25 9 C3
Kilham Rd YO25 8 D5
Kilkoy Dr 4 HU7 56 F6
Killingholme High Lighthouse* DN40 87 B5
Killingholme N Low Lighthouse* DN40 87 C5
Killingholme Prim Sch DN40 86 E3
Killingholme Rd DN40 86 F1
Killingwoldgraves La HU17 43 C2
Kiln La 18 Brigg DN20 98 B2
Patrington HU12 74 D1
Stallingborough DN41 101 D8
Kilnhouse La HU12 60 C2
Kilnsea Gr HU9 141 F2
Kilnwick Ave HU5 139 C2
Kilnwick Garth 2 YO42 29 A3
Kilnwick La YO25 32 B2
Kilnwick Percy Hill YO42 29 D4
Kilnwick Rd YO42 29 B4
Kilpin Broad La DN14 65 E6
Kilton Ct 12 HU8 141 D7
Kilvin Dr HU17 137 A6
Kimberley St HU3 145 C7
Kimberlows Wood Hill 3 YO10 131 C3
Kimmeridge Cl HU7 141 B6
Kinbrace Dr YO24 132 B7
Kinderscout Cl 15 HU7 56 F6
King Charles Cl HU10 143 E7
King Edward Cres 9 DN8 79 B1
King Edward Fst Sch DN8 93 B8
King Edward Rd DN8 93 A8
King Edward St
Belton DN9 94 E2
Grimsby DN31 152 E5
Kingston upon Hull HU1 155 A3
12 Kirton in Lindsey DN21 108 B1
Scunthorpe DN16 151 A5
King Edwards Terr 4 HU15 68 B5
King George Dock HU9 147 C6
King Georges Ct DN7 92 C5
King Rudding Cl 6 YO19 49 A8
King Rudding La YO19 49 B8
King St
1 Barton-upon-Humber DN18 84 F8
Bridlington YO15 122 E2
6 Cawood YO8 48 B8
East Halton DN40 86 D7
Goxhill DN19 86 A8
Great Driffield YO25 124 F4
1 Hornsea HU18 134 C3
19 Keelby DN41 101 A4
Kingston upon Hull HU16 139 B6
Kingston upon Hull HU1 155 B2
Sancton YO43 41 E2
Scunthorpe DN15 151 B8
Thorne/Moorends DN8 93 A8
Winterton DN15 83 A5
17 Withernsea HU19 75 A6
Woodmansey HU17 137 D1
York YO1 156 B2
Kingerby Rd DN17 150 E1
Kingfisher HU7 141 D6
Kingfisher Cl
Kingston upon Hull HU7 141 D8
1 Leven HU17 45 A8
Scunthorpe DN15 96 B7
Kingfisher Rise HU7 141 E6
Kings Acre YO31 131 B6
King's Ave DN20 98 C2
King's Bench St HU3 145 B5
Kings Cl 5 YO8 49 B5
King's Cl 7 DN7 92 D4
Kings Cl 24 YO42 29 A3
Kings Court Rd 4 DN8 79 B1

King's Cross Cl 2 HU3 145 C6
King's Cswy
Reedness DN14 80 E8
Swinefleet DN14 65 D1
Kings Ct DN20 108 F8
Kings Garth YO25 125 F7
Kings Lea YO8 50 A8
Kings Leigh 1 HU3 145 C6
Kings Mdw YO25 124 D4
Kings Mead
Great Driffield YO25 124 D4
Woodmansey HU17 137 D1
Kings Mews DN35 103 E1
Kings Mill Cl YO25 124 D4
Kings Mill Pk YO25 124 D4
King's Mill Rd YO25 124 D3
Kings Mill Sch YO25 124 E4
Kings Moor Rd YO32 14 D2
King's Pl 29 HU12 72 C7
King's Rd
Barnetby le Wold DN38 99 B5
Cleethorpes DN35 103 D2
Kings Rd DN40 87 D1
King's Sq
Beverley HU17 154 B3
York YO1 156 C2
Kingsbury Way 7 HU7 56 F6
Kingsclere YO32 127 F6
Kingscott Cl 10 HU7 56 F5
Kingsdale DN17 96 C1
Kingsgate
Bridlington YO15 122 D1
Carnaby YO15 10 F2
Kingsland Terr 11 YO26 129 F5
Kingsley Ave HU9 141 E2
Kingsley Cl 6 HU15 68 B5
Kingsley Dr HU10 138 D1
Kingsley Gr 4 DN33 102 E2
Kingsport Cl HU3 145 A7
Kingsthorpe YO24 129 D2
Kingston Ave
Grimsby DN34 152 A2
Kingston upon Hull HU13 143 F1
Kingston Cl 8 DN35 103 D1
Kingston General Hospl HU2 140 E1
Kingston Lower Sch HU4 144 C4
Kingston Rd
Bridlington YO15 11 B4
Kingston upon Hull HU10 138 D1
Scunthorpe DN16 151 A3
Kingston Ret Pk HU1 155 A1
Kingston Rise HU10 138 C1
Kingston Sq HU2 155 B3
Kingston St
Goole DN14 149 C2
Kingston upon Hull HU1 155 B1
Kingston upon Hull Swimming Club HU6 140 B7
Kingston Upper Sch HU4 144 C4
Kingston View 27 DN18 84 F8
Kingston Way HU7 140 F5
Kingston Wharf HU1 155 A1
Kingsway 2 Brigg DN20 98 B2
Cleethorpes DN35 103 D3
Goole DN14 149 D4
Kingston upon Hull HU16 139 B5
Scunthorpe DN15 150 C7
14 Stainforth DN7 92 C6
6 Stamford Bridge YO41 15 D2
Kingsway Jun Sch YO30 130 B7
Kingsway N YO30 130 B7
Kingsway Prim Sch DN14 149 E5
Kingsway W YO24 129 D1
Kingswood Gr YO24 129 D3
Kingswood Ret Pk HU7 56 E5
Kingswood Sch HU7 57 A5
Kingtree Ave HU16 139 B6
Kinloch Way
28 Immingham DN40 87 B1
2 Immingham DN40 101 B8
Kinloss Garth 2 HU7 57 B5
Kinloss Prim Sch HU7 57 B5
Kinsbourne Gn 37 DN7 92 D4
Kinthorpe HU6 140 A8
Kipling Ave DN17 150 D3
Kipling Cl YO25 31 C4
Kipling Cotes Medieval Village* YO25 30 D2
Kipling Cotes Race Course* YO25 30 E1
Kipling Wlk 1 HU4 144 D2
Kiplingcotes La YO43 42 A5
Kiplingcotes Nature Reserve* YO43 41 E6
Kiplington Cl HU3 145 A7
Kir Cres YO24 129 C3
Kirby Cl YO43 135 E2
Kirby Dr HU16 139 B6
Kirby La YO25 7 A4
Kirk Balk YO17 16 E8
Kirk Balk La YO60 15 B7
Kirk Cl HU7 141 D6
Kirk Croft HU16 139 A6
Kirk Gate DN37 113 E6
Kirk La Sykehouse DN14 78 B4
Walkington HU17 55 B7
Kirk Rd 2 HU12 58 C1
Kirk Rise HU10 143 C7
Kirk Smeaton C of E Prim Sch WF8 76 B3
Kirk View 1 YO26 129 C3
Kirkby Rd
Scunthorpe DN17 96 C2
Selby YO8 148 B7
Kirkby St HU2 155 B4
Kirkcroft YO32 127 C8
Kirkdale Rd YO10 131 D4
Kirkden Paddocks DN9 94 C2
Kirkfield Rd HU19 75 A6
Kirkgate
Bridlington YO16 122 D4
8 Pocklington YO42 29 A4
Kirkgate Mews YO16 122 D5
Kirkham Ave 1 YO31 130 E8
Kirkham Cl HU13 143 F2
Kirkham Ct DN14 149 E6
Kirkham Dr HU5 140 B2
Kirkham Rd YO16 122 D7
Kirkholme Way HU17 137 B4
Kirkhouse Green Rd DN7 92 A8
Kirkland Cl YO8 148 D4
Kirkland St YO42 29 A4
Kirklands YO32 14 B6
Kirklands La YO41 16 C2
Kirklands Rd HU5 144 E8
Kirkside 2 DN37 113 E6
Kirkstead Cres DN33 102 D2
Kirkstead St HU8 141 A2
Kirkstone Dr YO31 131 A6
Kirkstone Rd HU5 139 D2
Kirkway HU10 143 B7
Kirkwell YO23 133 A4
Kirman Cres 18 DN17 96 C2
Kirmington C of E Prim Sch DN39 100 A6
Kirmington Gdns DN34 152 A2
Kirncroft Cl 16 HU12 73 C4
Kirton in Lindsey Prim Sch DN21 108 B1
Kirton La DN7 92 E6
Kirton Lane Prim Sch DN7 92 D7
Kirton Lindsey Sta DN21 108 B2
Kirton Rd Blyton DN21 117 F6
Holme DN16 97 B2
Kirton in Lindsey DN21 108 A3
Messingham DN17 107 E6
Scawby DN20 108 C8
Scotton DN21 107 D2
Kishorn Ct
30 Immingham DN40 87 B1
1 Immingham DN40 101 B8
Kissing Gate HU12 59 D2
Kitchen Dr YO8 148 D4
Kitchen La HU17 154 A1
Kitchener St Selby YO8 148 B6
York YO31 130 D7
Kitemere Pl 2 YO24 132 B8
Kitty Garth YO19 38 A7
Kitty Hill (Tumulus)* YO41 16 E3
Knapton Ave 7 HU5 139 E3
Knapton Cl 1 YO32 14 B6
Knapton La YO26 129 B4
Knavesmire Cres YO23 130 B1
Knavesmire Prim Sch YO23 130 B1
Knavesmire Rd YO23 130 A1
Knedlington Rd DN14 65 A6
Knight St DN32 153 B2
Knightly Way HU7 56 E5
Knights Cl Belton DN9 94 E2
8 Laceby DN37 101 F1
Knight's Ct 10 DN16 96 D2
Knights Way HU17 154 B3
Knightsbridge 7 DN36 114 A8
Knightsbridge Ct 7 HU3 140 D1
Knightsbridge Rd DN17 107 D7
Knightscourt HU6 139 E7
Knoll St DN35 153 F2
Knoll The YO24 129 B2
Knottingley England Lane Jun & Inf Sch WF11 61 A2
Knottingley High Sch WF11 61 A2
Knottingley Rugby Union Club WF11 61 A3
Knowles Ave HU6 140 C8
Knowsley Ave HU16 139 A7
Kyffin Ave HU9 142 D2
Kyle Cl HU8 142 C6
Kyle Way YO26 129 B8
Kyme St YO1 156 B1

L

Labrador Dr 11 DN20 97 E4
Laburnham Ave 21 DN37 113 D6
Laburnham Cl 22 DN37 113 D6
Laburnum Ave
18 Gainsborough DN21 117 B1
Gunness DN15 95 E6
Hutton Cranswick YO25 32 E7
Kingston upon Hull HU8 141 C2
11 Thorne/Moorends DN8 79 B2
Laburnum Cl
Rufforth YO23 24 C6
7 Snaith DN14 63 C1
3 Thorpe Willoughby YO8 48 B1
Laburnum Ct 4 YO16 123 A6
Laburnum Dr
Beverley HU17 137 A7
Grimsby DN34 102 C4
3 Kingston upon Hull HU4 144 B7
Laburnum Garth 6 YO31 130 F8
Laburnum Gr
Burton upon Stather DN15 82 B5
Crowle DN17 94 D7
Scunthorpe DN16 151 B3
Stillingfleet YO19 36 D4
Laburnum Wlk 17 HU15 66 D8
Laceby Acres Prim Sch DN34 102 B3
Laceby Rd
Grimsby DN34 102 C2
Scunthorpe DN17 150 E1
Lady Frances Cres DN35 153 C1
Lady Hamilton Gdns YO24 129 E2
Lady Rd YO30 130 B7
Ladybower Cl 4 HU7 141 E7
Ladygate HU17 154 A3
Lady's Well* YO43 135 F7
Ladyside Cl 17 HU7 57 A6
Ladysmith Mews 13 YO32 14 A7
Ladysmith Rd
Grimsby DN32 152 F3
Kingston upon Hull HU10 138 E1
Ladywell Gate 3 HU15 68 E6
Laforey Rd DN37 102 C6
Lagoon Dr HU7 141 D8
Lagoon Rd DN17 150 B2
Lairgate HU17 154 A2
Lairs La YO42 30 A5
Lake Dr HU8 141 E3
Lake View HU8 141 E3
Lakeside YO23 36 C7
Lakeside Dr DN17 150 C1
Lakeside Gr
Kingston upon Hull HU4 144 D4
1 Strensall YO32 14 B8
Lakeside Prim Sch YO30 126 F2
Lakeside Ret Pk DN16 151 F1
Laking La YO25 2 A3
Lalrgate Pl 20 DN36 103 C1
Lamb Inn Rd 9 WF11 61 A2
Lamb La Newport HU15 67 B8
Roos HU12 60 A1
Lambert Ave 16 HU15 68 C6
Lambert Cl YO43 135 E3
Lambert Ct YO1 156 B1
Lambert Park Rd 23 HU12 72 C7
Lambert Rd
Bridlington YO16 122 F5
Grimsby DN32 152 E2
Lambert St HU5 140 D2
Lambourn Ct 25 DN35 103 C1
Lambourne Rise 7 DN16 96 D1
Lambton St HU5 140 C3
Lambwath La HU11 46 A3
Lambwath Rd HU8 141 C4
Lambwell Hill HU15 54 E2
Lamel St YO10 131 A3
Lamorna Ave HU8 141 B3
Lamplugh Cres YO23 133 B3
Lamplugh La 7 YO15 122 F4
Lamplugh Rd YO15 122 F4
Lamplugh Sq 6 YO15 122 F4
Lampton Gr DN32 152 D2
Lamwath Prim Sch HU8 141 F5
Lanark St 3 HU5 145 B8
Lancar Cl 18 YO32 13 D5
Lancaster App DN40 86 D4
Lancaster Ave DN31 152 B3
Lancaster Dr
Kingston upon Hull HU8 141 D4
2 Moorland Prison DN7 104 A8
Lancaster Gate DN36 114 A4
Lancaster Rd
Carnaby YO25 10 D2
Gringley on the Hill DN10 116 A1
Pocklington Ind Est YO42 28 E3
Scunthorpe DN16 151 A1
Lancaster Way YO30 127 A1
Lancelot Ct HU9 146 C6
Lancing Way 24 DN33 113 E8
Land Dike LN11 115 A1
Land Ends Rd DN8 78 F1
Land of Green Ginger HU1 155 B2
Landalewood Rd YO30 126 F2
Landau Cl YO30 129 F8
Landeck Ave DN34 152 B2
Landing La
Asselby DN14 64 D6
Barlby with Osgodby YO8 148 F8
Broomfleet HU15 67 A7
Gilberdyke HU15 52 D1
22 Haxby YO32 13 F5
Haxby YO32 127 E7
Hemingbrough YO8 63 F8
Newport HU15 52 E1
Riccall YO19 48 F8
York YO26 129 E6
Landing Rd YO8 62 A7
Landings The 21 YO32 13 F5
Landor Ave DN17 150 D3
Landress La HU17 154 A2
Lane The YO41 15 B2
Laneham St DN15 151 A7
Lanes The 7 DN36 114 D4
Lang Ave YO10 131 A4
Lang Rd
Bishopthorpe YO23 132 F4
York YO32 127 F6
Langdale Ave
Beverley HU17 154 B3
Grimsby DN33 113 D8
Kingston upon Hull HU5 139 E2
York YO31 131 B6
Langdale Cres HU16 139 A5
Langdale Dr 4 HU12 73 C4
Langdale Gr YO8 148 B3
Langdale Rd YO43 135 E4
Langford Wlk 1 HU4 144 B7
Langham Rd
18 Thorngumbald HU12 72 E5
10 Thorngumbald HU12 72 E5
Langholm Cl HU17 136 D5
Langholme Dr YO26 129 C6
Langholme La DN9 116 B8
Langley Ct 1 YO32 127 F6
Langley Dr DN16 96 D1
Langley Garth YO25 124 F4
Langley Pk 25 HU7 56 F5
Langley Pl 5 DN35 103 D2
Langleys Rd 6 DN6 76 E1
Langrick Ave 9 DN14 65 B7
Langrickgate La YO42 38 C5
Langsett Gr YO30 126 F3
Langsett Rd HU7 141 D7
Langthorpe Rd HU11 45 F2
Langtoft CP Sch YO25 8 C5
Langtoft Gr HU6 139 F5
Langton Cl 16 DN33 102 D2
Langton Ct 1 YO32 14 A6
Langton Dr DN33 102 D2
Langton Rd DN36 114 B5
Langtree Cl HU7 140 F8
Langwith Stray YO10 26 C2
Lansdown Link 17 DN35 103 C2
Lansdown Rd
Goole DN14 149 A5
13 Immingham DN40 87 B1
Lansdown Way 7 YO32 13 F5
Lansdowne Ave DN33 102 E2
Lansdowne Cres 9 YO15 122 F3
Lansdowne Rd YO15 122 F2
Lansdowne St HU3 145 C6
Lansdowne Terr 5 YO10 130 E3
Lanshaw Croft YO30 126 F1
Lanyon Cl HU7 141 C7
Laporte Rd DN40 87 E2
Lapwing Cl HU7 141 D8
Larard Ave 2 HU6 140 C8
Larch Cl
2 Immingham DN40 87 D2
Kingston upon Hull HU5 140 D2
Larch Ct 11 DN21 117 C1
Larch Dr HU12 72 E5
Larch Gr Scawby DN20 108 F8
Scunthorpe DN16 151 B3
Larch Rd 6 DN35 103 B1
Larchfield YO31 131 C7
Larchmont Cl 7 HU15 68 C6
Larden Ave 1 DN33 113 E8
Lark Rise 2 DN21 107 B3
Larkfield Cl 1 YO23 132 A3
Larkfield Rd YO8 148 A4
Larkspur Ave DN41 101 F5
Larmour Rd DN37 102 B4
Larne Rd HU9 142 B4
Larsen Rd DN14 149 A3
Lascelles Ave HU19 74 F6
Lashbrook Garth HU4 144 B4
Lastingham 12 HU15 68 C6
Lastingham Cl HU6 139 F6
Laughton Endowed Sch DN21 117 E8
Laughton Rd
Beverley HU17 154 B4
Blyton DN21 117 B4
Laundry La YO25 124 E5
Laura St DN14 149 C5
Laurel Ave DN8 79 B2
Laurel Cl
10 Gainsborough DN21 117 C1
Gateforth YO8 48 B1
3 Grimsby DN33 102 E1
Kingston upon Hull HU4 144 B7
Laurels Cl 1 DN40 100 E8
Laurels The YO42 28 D3
Laurier St DN35 153 D4
Laurold Ave DN7 93 A3
Lauty La HU11 45 C5
Lavender Gr YO26 129 E5
Lavender Wlk
Beverley HU17 154 A1
1 Kingston upon Hull HU4 144 C7
Lavenham Rd DN33 113 D8
Laveracks Ind Est YO41 27 B3
Lawn La DN6 77 E3
Lawns The
Beverley HU17 136 C6
Bridlington YO16 122 E7
Grimsby DN34 152 C2
Kingston upon Hull HU7 141 D6
Kingston upon Hull HU10 143 D7
Lawnsgarth HU16 139 A7
Lawnswood
Kingston upon Hull HU7 141 D5
Lawnswood *continued*
Kingston upon Hull HU13 143 D2
Lawnswood Dr YO30 129 F8
Lawnway YO31 131 A7
Lawrence Ave
Bewholme YO25 34 E3
Kingston upon Hull HU8 141 F3
Lawrence St
Grimsby DN31 152 C4
York YO10 130 E3
Lawson Ave
Grimsby DN31 152 B3
Kingston upon Hull HU16 139 B7
Lawson Cl
Kingston upon Hull HU6 140 B5
1 Walkington HU17 55 B7
Lawson Rd
Bridlington YO16 122 D4
York YO24 132 F7
Lawsons Cl YO14 2 F7
Laxthorpe HU6 140 A8
Laxton Garth HU10 138 B1
Laxton Gr 5 DN16 96 D1
Layerthorpe YO31 156 C3
Lea Cres HU16 139 A5
Lea Croft 2 YO43 135 E4
Lea Field Rd YO25 31 E6
Lea Garth DN17 107 D7
Lea The HU15 54 A2
Lea Way YO32 128 A4
Leaburn Rd DN17 107 D7
Leaconfield Park House* HU17 43 E5
Lead Mill La YO1 156 C1
Leadhills Way 6 HU7 57 B5
Leadley Croft YO23 132 A1
Leads Rd HU7 141 C6
Leake St YO10 130 E3
Lealholm Ct 11 HU8 141 D7
Leame Cl HU3 145 A7
Leamington Cl DN16 151 C5
Leander Rd HU9 142 B3
Leas Cl DN37 113 E7
Leas Jun & Inf Sch The DN37 113 E7
Leas La HU11 34 F1
Lease La DN40 86 D6
Leases The HU17 154 A2
Leatherdog La HU15 52 E1
Leathley Cl 1 HU17 136 E1
Leavens La HU15 52 D2
Leconfield Cl HU9 142 D1
Leconfield Prim Sch HU17 43 D6
Ledbury Dr 10 DN36 114 A8
Ledbury Rd HU5 139 D2
Lee Ave HU19 75 A6
Lee Fair Gdns DN17 96 C1
Lee Smith St HU9 146 E7
Lee St HU8 141 D3
Leeds Rd YO8 148 A4
Leek Hill 9 DN15 83 A5
Leeman Rd YO26 156 A2
Leeming Garth 3 HU7 57 B5
Lees Wlk HU3 145 A7
Leeside YO24 132 E8
Legard Ave DN16 151 B2
Legard Dr HU10 143 F6
Legarde Ave HU4 144 C6
Leggott Way 1 DN41 101 E6
Legion Cl 11 HU15 68 C5
Legsby Ave DN32 152 E2
Legsby Pl DN32 102 F2
Leicester St HU3 145 D8
Leicester Way YO1 156 C1
Leighton Croft 3 YO30 126 F1
Leighton Gr 2 DN33 102 E2
Leisure Pk YO32 128 A2
Leitholm Cl 2 HU7 57 A6
Lelley Rd
Humbleton HU11 58 F5
Preston HU12 58 D2
Lendal YO1 156 B2
Lenham La HU1 155 A2
Leningrad Rd HU7 140 F6
Lennox Cl 2 YO14 3 A8
Leonard Cl HU12 72 A5
Leonard Cres DN15 150 F7
Leonard St
4 Kingston upon Hull HU3 145 D8
Kingston upon Hull HU2 155 A4
Leopold Cl DN16 151 A2
Lerecroft Rd YO24 132 D8
Lesley Ave YO10 133 E8
Lestrange St DN35 153 C3
Levels La DN9 104 A4
Leven C of E Sch HU17 45 A8
Leven Gr HU9 142 A2
Leven Rd
Scunthorpe DN16 151 D2
York YO24 132 D7
Leverstock Gn 36 DN7 92 D4
Levington St DN32 153 A5
Levisham Cl HU6 139 F6
Levisham St YO10 130 D2
Levita Ave HU9 142 C2
Levitt Lanes YO25 31 F2
Lewis Rd DN35 153 D4
Lexington Dr HU4 144 C5
Leyburn Ave
Hornsea HU18 134 C2
Kingston upon Hull HU6 139 E4

Leyden Cl 18 DN40 87 B1
Leyes The YO10 131 C4
Leyfield Cl 1 YO32 14 A7
Leyland Ave 6 DN7 92 E4
Leyland Rd YO31 131 A5
Leys Ct YO16 122 B4
Leys Farm Jun Sch DN17 96 C2
Leys La Darrington WF11 76 A8
Little Smeaton WF8 76 B4
Skipsea YO25 23 A1
Winterton DN15 83 B6
Leys Rd
Bridlington YO16 122 B4
Darrington WF11 76 A7
Leys The HU18 134 B4
Liberty La HU1 155 C2
Lichfield Ave DN17 150 C3
Lichfield Cl
Beverley HU17 136 E1
Kingston upon Hull HU2 155 A4
Lichfield Ct 6 YO23 130 B1
Lichfield Rd
Grimsby DN32 153 B2
40 Hatfield DN7 92 D4
Liddell St HU2 155 A3
Lidgard Rd DN36 103 D1
Lidgett Cl DN20 108 E8
Lidgett Gr YO26 129 B6
Lidgett Grove Sch YO26 129 B6
Lidgett The 7 DN9 105 D6
Lidice Rd DN14 64 E2
Lighthouse Mus The* HU19 74 F6
Lighthouse Rd YO15 5 B2
Lilac Ave
Beverley HU17 136 F7
Kingston upon Hull HU10 138 D1
Kingston upon Hull HU8 141 B2
Scunthorpe DN16 151 C5
York YO10 131 B3
Lilac Cl YO25 124 D3
Lilac Gr YO32 127 D4
Lilacs The 10 YO42 29 A3
Lilbourne Dr YO30 130 A8
Lilling Ave 3 YO31 130 E8
Lily La YO15 5 A2
Lilywood Rd DN20 97 D3
Limber Ct DN34 152 A2
Limber Hill LN8 120 A4
Limber Rd
Humberside Airport DN39 100 A6
Swallow LN7 112 A7
Limber Vale DN34 152 A2
Lime Ave
Kingston upon Hull HU10 138 E1
Scunthorpe DN16 97 A3
York YO31 130 F7
Lime Cl YO25 124 F2
Lime Gr Goxhill DN19 86 A8
Holton le Clay DN36 114 A5
Humberston DN36 114 C7
Scunthorpe DN16 151 B3
Lime St Grimsby DN31 152 C4
Kingston upon Hull HU8 155 C4
Lime Tree 6 HU15 66 D7
Lime Tree Ave
Beverley HU17 137 A6
21 Gainsborough DN21 117 B1
Goole DN14 149 D5
Kingston upon Hull HU8 141 C2
Kingston upon Hull HU13 143 F2
York YO32 127 D3
Lime Tree Gdns DN14 149 D5
Lime Tree Gr
Selby YO8 148 A6
4 Thorne/Moorends DN8 93 A8
Lime Tree La HU11 142 F6
Lime Tree Mews 15 YO19 26 F7
Limedale View 3 DN3 92 A3
Limedane HU6 139 F8
Limegarth 10 YO26 12 F1
Limekiln Hill YO25 7 B3
Limekiln La YO16 123 A5
Limerick Cl HU8 142 B6
Limes The
2 Beckingham DN10 116 D1
3 South Cave HU15 53 F1
3 Stallingborough DN41 101 D6
Stockton-on-the-Forest YO32 14 D2
Limetree Ave
12 Grimsby DN33 102 E2
Kingston upon Hull HU7 141 D6
Limetree Cl 2 YO8 48 B1
Lincoln Castle Way DN19 70 D2
Lincoln Cl 11 DN17 94 D7
Lincoln Cres 2 DN21 119 C8
Lincoln Dr
24 Barton-upon-Humber DN18 84 F8
Caistor LN7 111 B4
Winterton DN15 83 A5
Lincoln Gate DN36 121 A5
Lincoln Gdns DN16 151 A2
Lincoln Gdns Inf Sch DN16 151 B3
Lincoln Gdns Jun Sch DN16 151 A2
Lincoln Gn HU4 144 C7
Lincoln Rd
Cleethorpes DN35 153 C1
Moorland Prison DN7 104 A8
Lincoln St
23 Gainsborough DN21 117 B1
Kingston upon Hull HU2 155 B4
York YO26 129 F5
Lincoln Way
9 Beverley HU17 55 E8
Beverley HU17 154 A1
Lincolnshire Wolds Rly* LN11 121 C7
Lindale 2 YO24 132 C7
Lindale Ave HU18 134 B2
Lindale Gdns DN16 151 C3
Linden Ave HU16 139 C7
Linden Cl 6 Hatfield DN7 92 D4
York YO32 127 F5
Linden Gr 1 YO30 130 A8
Linden Way 9 YO8 48 B2
Lindengate Ave HU7 141 B4
Lindengate Way HU7 141 B5
Lindholme DN21 107 C3
Lindholme Bank Rd DN7 93 B1
Lindisfarne Ave 4 DN36 113 F7
Lindley Rd YO30 126 F1
Lindley St
Scunthorpe DN16 151 A2
York YO24 129 F3
Lindley Wood Gr YO30 126 E3
Lindrick Wlk 8 DN37 113 D6
Lindsey DN36 114 A6
Lindsey Ave YO26 129 D4
Lindsey Ct 21 DN9 105 E6
Lindsey Dr Crowle DN17 94 D8
Healing DN41 102 A5
Holton le Clay DN36 114 A6
Lindsey Lower Sch The DN35 153 D2
Lindsey Pl HU4 144 D6
Lindsey Rd
7 Cleethorpes DN35 103 C2
Cleethorpes DN35 153 F1
Lindsey Rise 30 DN33 113 E8
Lindsey Sch The DN35 103 C2
Lindsey St 2 DN16 151 C6
Lindum Ave 23 DN40 87 B1
Lindum Gr DN17 94 C7
Lindum Rd DN35 103 C2
Lindum St DN15 151 B7
Lindum Wlk LN7 110 A4
Linecroft La DN10 116 E4
Linegate 4 YO43 135 D4
Ling House La DN7 92 A5
Ling La YO41 27 F6
Lingcourt HU6 139 F7
Lingcroft Cl YO8 63 D4
Lingcroft La YO19 133 E3
Lingdale Rd HU9 142 E3
Lings La DN7 92 D3
Lings Rd HU17 42 E3
Lings Windmill* DN7 92 E3
Link Ave YO30 130 C8
Link Rd
Huntington YO31 127 E2
Kingston upon Hull HU16 139 B5
Link The
Copmanthorpe YO23 132 A3
Kingston upon Hull HU4 144 C5
Selby YO8 148 A4
York YO10 133 E8
Linkfield Rd HU5 139 E4
Links Rd DN35 103 D2
Linkway Hatfield DN7 92 F3
Norton DN6 76 E2
Linley Cl HU17 45 A8
Linleyhill Rd HU17 33 C1
Linnaeus St HU3 145 C6
Linnet Cl DN15 96 B7
Linnet Dr HU7 141 D7
Linnet Way YO24 132 C8
Linthorpe Gr HU10 143 E8
Linton Cl HU17 154 A1
Linton Garth HU17 43 A5
Linton on Ouse Cty Prim Sch YO30 12 A7
Linton Rd YO26 126 A1
Linton Rise DN15 82 A4
Linton St 5 YO26 129 E5
Linton Woods YO30 12 A7
Linton Woods La YO30 12 A8
Linwith La DN14 63 C3
Linwood Ave 17 DN33 113 E8
Lisburn Gr DN33 102 E1
Lisle Marsden C of E Prim Sch DN32 102 F2
Lismore Ave HU9 142 A3
Lissett Cl HU17 43 D6
Lissett Gr HU6 140 C7
Lissett La YO25 22 D4
Lister Rd DN15 150 C7
Lister St Grimsby DN31 152 B4
Kingston upon Hull HU1 155 A1
Lister Way YO30 130 A7
Little Ave YO30 130 B8
Little Beck Rd YO16 122 B4
Little Belt The DN21 117 B2
Little Burton 3 YO25 34 B2
Little Clover HU17 136 F6
Little Coates Prim Sch DN31 152 B5
Little Coates Rd DN34 102 C2
Little Comm La DN14 77 C5
Little Dam La HU12 88 B8
Little Garth YO26 126 A2
Little George St HU8 155 C4
Little Grimsby La LN11 121 D1
Little Hallfield Rd YO31 130 E5
Little Heck Comm La DN14 62 D1
Little John St DN34 152 B3
Little La
Broomfleet HU15 67 C6
Ellerton YO42 38 C1
11 Haxby YO32 13 E5
Little Smeaton DN6 76 D4
Mappleton HU11 47 A5
Shipton Thorpe YO43 40 E5
Watton YO25 32 E5
Wrawby DN20 98 D3
Little London La DN14 78 D8
Little Mason St HU2 155 C3
Little Mdws YO32 127 D8
Little Michael St DN34 152 B3
Little Moor La YO8 148 A8
Little Queen St HU1 155 A2
Little Reed St HU2 155 A3
Little Shore HU11 45 E2
Little Stonegate YO1 156 B3
Little Weighton Rd
Skidby HU16 138 A8
Walkington HU17 55 B7
Little Westfield YO25 8 C3
Little Wlk DN21 116 E5
Little Wold La HU15 54 A2
Littlebeck Cl HU3 145 A7
Littlebeck Rd 4 DN36 114 C8
Littlefair Rd HU9 147 A7
Littlefield Cl 5 YO26 12 F1
Littlefield La
Grimsby DN34 152 B2
Marsh Chapel DN36 115 B1
Littleham Cl HU7 141 B8
Littlemoor Cl HU15 53 D3
Littlewood Rd
Rowley HU17 54 D7
11 Thorne/Moorends DN8 93 B8
Littondale HU7 140 F7
Liverpool St HU3 145 A3
Livesey Rd DN36 121 B6
Livingstone Rd HU13 69 F4
Livingstone St YO26 129 F5
Lloyd Cl YO10 131 B1
Lloyds Ave DN17 150 F4
Loatley Gn HU16 139 C5
Lob La YO41 15 D2
Lochrin Pl 2 YO26 129 B4
Lock Cl DN14 77 F6
Lock Hill DN8 93 A8
Lock La
Holme-on-Spalding-Moor YO43 52 B8
Thorne/Moorends DN8 93 A8
Lock Rd DN36 115 A4
Lockey Croft YO32 127 C8
Lockgate Rd DN14 77 C4
Lockham Rd HU12 90 F4
Lockhill DN31 152 E6
Lockington C of E Sch YO25 32 B2
Lockington Rd YO25 31 F3
Lockton Gr 1 HU5 144 D8
Lockwood Bank DN9 105 E6
Lockwood Cl 6 DN8 93 B8
Lockwood Ct DN15 150 E8
Lockwood Dr HU17 136 E7
Lockwood Rd HU17 136 D7
Lockwood St
Great Driffield YO25 124 E3
Kingston upon Hull HU2 155 B4
York YO31 156 C3
Lodge Ave DN18 84 F8
Lodge Cl HU13 143 F1
Lodge Ct 35 DN7 92 D4
Lodge Farm Ct YO42 39 B6
Lodge Gdns 5 DN14 63 C1
Lodge La
Flixborough DN15 82 B2
Gowdall DN14 62 F1
Kirk Bramwith DN7 92 A8
Snaith DN14 78 D8
Lodge Rd DN15 150 C6
Lodge St HU9 141 E2
Lofthouse La YO41 27 D7
Loftsome Way 11 DN14 65 B7
Loftus Gr HU9 142 E3
Logan Cl HU7 141 C7
Loganberry Dr HU4 144 C4
Lombard St
Grimsby DN34 152 A3
Kingston upon Hull HU2 155 A3
Lomond Gr
1 Humberston DN36 114 C8
9 Humberston DN36 114 D8
Lomond Rd HU5 144 E8
Londesborough Ct YO25 124 C4
Londesborough Gr 5 YO8 48 B2
Londesborough Hill YO43 41 A8
Londesborough Rd
Hutton Cranswick YO25 32 E7
Market Weighton YO43 135 D6
Londesborough St
Kingston upon Hull HU3 145 C7
5 Selby YO8 148 C5
London La DN6 77 D1
London St 15 YO42 29 A4
Long Barrow*
Beelsby DN37 112 D4
Thixendale YO17 17 A7
Willerby YO12 1 E7
Long Close La YO10 156 C1
Long Field Dr DN3 92 A1
Long Field Rd DN3 92 A2
Long Furrow YO32 127 C8
Long Hill YO42 29 D1
Long La Atwick YO25 35 D6
Beverley HU17 154 B2
Bridlington YO16 122 C5
Catton YO41 27 D6
Cawood YO8 48 A6
Driffield YO25 124 F7
Eastrington DN14 65 D8
Ellerby HU11 58 B8
Ellerton YO42 38 F1
Foston YO25 22 A3
Goole DN14 149 E7
Great Driffield YO25 124 F6
Heck DN14 77 D8
Heslington YO10 26 C3
Humbleton HU11 58 F5
Kirk Smeaton WF8 76 B1
Market Weighton YO43 41 B2
Nafferton YO25 20 E8
Pollington DN14 78 A7
Skeffling HU12 90 C5
Willoughton DN21 119 B3
Woodmansey HU17 154 B1
Long Mann Hills Rd YO8 148 B4
Long Marston C of E Prim Sch YO26 24 A6
Long Rampart YO42 38 D3
Long Rd DN15 150 E8
Long Ridge Dr YO26 126 A1
Long Ridge La YO26 126 A1
Long St YO25 9 F6
Long Trods 5 YO8 148 C6
Long Wood Rd DN21 117 D1
Longbrough La HU12 59 E4
Longcroft 2 YO32 13 E5
Longcroft Lower Sch HU17 136 B5
Longcroft Pk HU17 136 C5
Longcroft Sch HU17 136 C5
Longdales La HU11 142 F8
Longden St HU3 145 A7
Longfield Rd 4 DN34 102 C2
Longfield Terr YO30 156 A3
Longford Gr HU9 142 E2
Longhill Prim Sch HU8 142 C6
Longhorn Cl 1 DN37 113 C6
Longmans Hill CP Sch YO8 148 C3
Longmans La HU16 139 B6
Longmeadow Rise 7 DN41 101 A4
Longmeadows Dr DN37 101 F1
Longton Rd 13 DN3 92 A3
Longwood Link 8 YO30 126 E3
Longwood Rd YO30 126 F3
Lonsdale Cl DN36 114 D7
Lonsdale St 5 HU3 145 A6
Lopham La DN37 112 F8
Lord Mayor's Wlk YO31 156 B3
Lord Roberts Rd HU17 154 B2
Lord St Grimsby DN31 152 B4
Stainforth DN7 92 C6
Lords La DN19 85 D8
Lords Moor La YO32 14 C7
Lordship La YO8 148 D8
Lorenzo Way HU9 141 F2
Loriners Dr 7 YO23 132 B3
Lorne Cl HU2 155 B4
Lorne St YO23 130 B1
Lorraine Ave 3 YO41 27 B2
Lorraine St HU8 141 A3
Loten Dr HU18 134 D6
Lothian Way HU7 57 A6
Lotting's La YO42 28 C4
Louis Dr HU5 144 B8
Louis St HU3 145 C8
Louth Rd
Fotherby LN11 121 D3
Grimsby DN33 102 E1
5 New Waltham DN36 113 F7
Louville Ave HU19 75 A6
Lovat Cl HU3 145 D5
Love La
Gainsborough DN21 117 B1
Hedon HU12 72 C7
Londesborough YO43 41 A8
York YO24 130 A2
Loveden Ct 7 DN35 103 D2
Lovell Rd 8 DN17 96 C2
Loveridge Ave HU5 140 A2
Lovett St DN35 153 B4
Low Balk Rd HU17 42 F2
Low Burgage DN15 68 B1
Low Catton Rd YO41 27 C8
Low Comm La HU15 68 D4
Low Croft 6 YO32 14 A7
Low Cross St 7 DN17 94 D8
Low Deeps La DN10 104 C1
Low Farm Rd HU11 57 E5
Low Field La
Carnaby YO25 10 C3
Welton HU14 68 E5
Low Fields Dr YO24 129 C3
Low Garth DN17 96 C1
Low Gate DN36 115 C1
Low Gn
Copmanthorpe YO23 132 B2
13 Knottingley WF11 61 A2
Low La
Heslington YO10 131 D1
Kirk Bramwith DN7 92 A6
Low Levels Bank DN8 93 E3
Low Leys Rd DN17 96 C1
Low Mdw YO8 148 C6
Low Mill Cl YO10 131 D3
Low Mill La HU15 53 C2
Low Moor Ave 3 YO10 133 F8
Low Moor La
Askham Richard YO23 24 D3
Hessay YO26 24 C8
Low Ousegate YO1 156 B2
Low Peter La YO25 124 C8
Low Petergate YO1 156 B3
Low Poppleton La YO26 129 B7
Low Rd
Blyborough DN21 119 B6
Gowdall DN14 63 A1
Healing DN41 101 F5
Kellington DN14 61 F4
Kirby Grindalythe YO17 6 F7
Marsh Chapel DN36 115 A1
North Cave HU15 53 E2
Worlaby DN20 98 C8
Low St
Beckingham DN10 116 E1
Carlton DN14 63 C2
Haxey DN9 105 D2
North Ferriby HU14 69 A5
Sancton YO43 41 D2
South Ferriby DN18 84 A7
Winterton DN15 83 A5
Low Well Pk YO19 37 F7
Low Westfield Rd YO23 132 A1
Lowcroft Ave 3 DN9 105 D2
Lowcroft Cl 4 DN9 105 D2
Lowdale Cl HU5 139 E1
Lower Bridge St DN14 149 C3
Lower Burgess St DN31 152 E4
Lower Darnborough St YO23 156 B1
Lower Derwent Valley Nature Reserve* YO42 50 C8
Lower Friargate YO1 156 B2
Lower Kenyon St 6 DN8 93 A8
Lower Priory St YO1 156 A1
Lower Spring St DN31 152 E5
Lowerdale 13 HU15 68 D6
Loweswater Rd 5 YO30 126 E1
Lowfield YO43 40 B1
Lowfield Cl
10 Barnby Dun DN3 92 A3
18 Kirton in Lindsey DN21 108 B1
Lowfield Dr YO32 13 E5
Lowfield La
East Garton HU12 59 C5
Nunburnholme YO42 29 D3
Rufforth YO26 129 A4
Scrayingham YO41 16 A7
Lowfield Rd
Barlby with Osgodby YO8 49 B5
Beverley HU17 137 A7
Hillam LS25 61 C8
Kingston upon Hull HU10 143 E5
Lowfield Sch YO24 129 D3
Lowgate Balne DN14 77 D5
Kingston upon Hull HU1 155 C2
Lowhill DN8 78 F1
Lowick YO24 132 C7
Lowland Cl 3 HU7 141 D8
Lowmoor Rd YO8 49 E6
Lown Hill YO24 129 C2
Lowndes Pk YO25 124 D5
Lowood Dr YO16 122 B4
Lowther Ct YO31 156 C4
Lowther Dr YO8 148 E3
Lowther St
Kingston upon Hull HU3 145 A7
York YO31 156 C4
Lowther Terr YO24 130 A3
Lowthorpe La YO25 125 F7
Loxley Cl YO30 126 F2
Loxley Gn HU4 144 B7
Loyd St HU10 143 F6
Loyds Cl 12 HU15 53 F1
Lucas Ave YO30 130 C8
Lucas Ct DN41 101 F5
Luck La HU12 58 C1
Lucombe Way YO32 127 D4
Ludborough Pk DN36 121 B6
Ludborough Rd DN36 121 B8
Ludborough Way 21 DN35 103 C2
Luddington & Garthorpe Prim Sch DN17 81 C4
Luddington Rd DN17 81 E5
Ludford St DN32 152 E2
Ludgate Cl 4 DN37 113 D6
Ludlow Ave DN34 152 A3
Ludlow Pl DN35 153 E1
Lulworth Ave HU4 144 A3
Lumby Hill LS25 61 A8
Lumby La LS25 61 A8
Lumley Rd YO30 130 B7
Lumsden Cl YO25 124 B2
Lund Ave HU16 138 E6
Lund Cl YO32 127 C8
Lund La Bubwith YO8 50 C4
Cliffe YO8 49 D4

Lund Rd YO25 32 A2
Lunds The HU10 143 C6
Lundy Cl 10 YO30 127 A1
Lundy Ct DN40 101 C8
Luneburg Pl 14 DN15 96 B7
Luneburg Way DN15 96 B7
Lunedale Cl HU8 141 E7
Lunedale Rd DN16 151 D1
Lunn La DN14 61 D3
Lunn's Cres DN18 84 E8
Luton Rd HU5 144 F8
Luttons CP Sch YO17 7 B8
Lycett Rd YO24 132 F6
Lych Gate DN20 97 D3
Lydbrook Rd DN16 151 A5
Lydford Rd DN40 87 C1
Lydham Ct 2 YO24 132 C8
Lydia Ct 6 DN40 87 B1
Lygon St DN16 151 B5
Lymington Garth HU4 144 A3
Lyndale Ave
10 Kirk Sandall DN3 92 A1
York YO10 131 C3
Lynden Way YO24 129 D3
Lyndhurst Ave
17 Grimsby DN33 102 E2
Kingston upon Hull HU16 139 D6
Lyndhurst Cl
Beverley HU17 137 B4
2 Norton DN6 76 F2
Thorne/Moorends DN8 92 F8
Lyndhurst Dr 1 DN6 76 F2
Lyndhurst Rise 3 DN6 76 F2
Lynesykes Rd YO25 21 F5
Lynhams Rd
Bempton YO15 4 E1
Bridlington YO15 123 B8
Lynmouth Cl 9 HU7 57 A5
Lynmouth Dr DN17 150 C4
Lynngarth Ave HU16 139 C6
Lynton Ave
Kingston upon Hull HU4 144 B3
Kingston upon Hull HU5 145 A8
Lynton Cl Brayton YO8 148 B1
Scunthorpe DN15 150 D8
Lynton Gdns YO8 148 B1
Lynton Rise 10 DN35 103 C2
Lynwith Cl DN14 63 C3
Lynwith Ct DN14 63 C3
Lynwith Dr DN14 63 C3
Lynwood Ave
3 Copmanthorpe YO23 132 A3
Kingston upon Hull HU10 143 E6
Lynwood View 4 YO23 132 A3
Lyric Cl 1 HU3 145 C5
Lysaghts Way DN15 82 C1
Lysander Cl YO30 127 A3
Lysander Dr YO43 135 E4
Lyth Cl 5 YO16 123 A7
Lytham Dr
Barnoldby le Beck DN37 113 D6
Kingston upon Hull HU16 139 D6
Lythe Ave HU5 139 E4

M

M62 Trad Est DN14 149 A3
Mablethorpe Rd DN36 115 A3
Macaulay St DN31 152 B4
Macauley Jun & Inf Sch DN31 152 B4
Macdonald Ct 12 YO42 29 A3
Mace View HU17 154 B1
Machray Pl DN35 153 D3
Mackender Ct 3 DN16 151 B2
Mackenzie Pl 24 DN40 87 B1
Maclagan Rd YO23 132 F4
Maclure St DN31 152 F6
Madeley St HU3 145 C4
Madison Gdns 4 HU5 140 A1
Madron Cl HU7 141 B8
Magazine La YO8 49 B3
Magazine Rd YO8 49 B4
Magdalen Cl 3 DN16 96 D2
Magdalen Ct 8 HU12 72 D7
Magdalen Gate HU12 72 D7
Magdalen La HU12 72 D7
Magdalene Rd 8 DN34 102 C3
Magnolia Cl YO25 124 D3
Magnolia Dr DN36 114 A5
Magnolia Gr YO32 127 D2
Magnolia Rise 9 DN40 87 C1
Magnolia Way DN16 151 A3
Magrath Ct 3 DN20 98 C2
Maida Gr YO10 130 D2
Maiden Cl 1 DN40 87 B1
Maiden Ct 3 HU7 57 B5
Maidensgrave Henge* YO25 2 F1
Maidenwell La LN7 110 A4
Maidwell Way 1 DN34 102 B2
Main App Rd DN16 151 C7
Main Ave
Scunthorpe DN17 150 C2
York YO31 130 F5
Main Rd
Ashby cum Fenby DN37 113 D3
Burton Agnes YO25 10 C3
Burton Agnes YO25 22 C6
Burton Pidsea HU12 59 C2
Drax YO8 63 F5
Gilberdyke DN14 66 B7
Holmpton HU19 75 C2
Kilpin DN14 65 D7
Main Rd *continued*
Kingston upon Hull HU11 142 E6
Mappleton HU11 47 A4
Newport HU15 53 A1
Skeffling HU12 90 D6
Thorngumbald HU12 72 F5
Ulrome YO25 22 E6
Utterby LN11 121 C4
Main St
Askham Bryan YO23 24 F3
Asselby DN14 64 D7
Bainton YO25 31 E7
Barmby Moor YO42 28 D3
3 Beal DN14 61 D4
Beeford YO25 22 C1
Beswick YO25 32 C4
Bilbrough YO23 24 C1
Bishopthorpe YO23 133 A4
Bonby DN20 84 C2
Boynton YO16 10 D6
Brandesburton YO25 34 B2
Bridlington YO16 122 A1
Bridlington YO15 123 C6
Broomfleet HU15 67 C6
Brough HU15 68 C6
Bubwith YO8 50 C7
Buckton/Bempton YO15 4 C3
Bugthorpe YO41 16 D4
Burstwick HU12 73 A6
Burton Agnes YO25 10 A1
Cadney DN20 109 D6
Cadney LN7 110 A7
Carnaby YO16 10 E4
Catwick HU17 45 C8
Cherry Burton HU17 43 A5
Cliffe YO8 49 E2
Coniston HU11 57 F6
Copmanthorpe YO23 132 A2
Cottingwith YO42 38 C5
Crowle DN17 94 E6
Dalton Holme HU17 42 E8
Deighton YO19 37 A7
East/West Stockwith DN10 116 F6
Ellerker HU15 68 A8
Ellerton YO42 38 C1
Elvington YO41 27 C2
Escrick YO19 37 B5
Etton HU17 42 F6
Fishlake DN7 92 D8
Foston YO25 22 A4
Fulstow LN11 121 F8
Ganton YO12 1 A8
Garton YO25 19 F6
Goodmanham YO43 41 D6
Gowdall DN14 63 A1
Grasby DN38 110 E7
Harpham YO25 21 F8
Hatfield HU11 46 C5
Hatfield DN7 92 F3
Heck DN14 77 C8
Hemingbrough YO8 49 F1
Hensall DN14 62 D2
Hessay YO26 24 B8
Horkstow DN18 84 A5
Hotham YO43 53 D5
Humberside Airport DN39 100 A6
Hutton Cranswick YO25 32 E7
Keadby with Althorpe DN17 95 D4
Kelfield YO19 36 D1
Kelk YO25 21 F6
Kellington DN14 61 F3
Keyingham HU12 73 C4
Kingston upon Hull HU10 138 C2
Kingston upon Hull HU2 140 F1
Kirk Smeaton WF8 76 B3
Kirkburn YO25 19 F1
Leconfield HU17 43 D6
Long Riston/Arnold HU11 45 C5
Monk Fryston LS25 61 A8
1 Naburn YO19 36 D8
North Duffield YO8 50 A8
North Frodingham YO25 33 F8
Ottringham HU12 73 E3
Patrington HU12 89 C8
Paull HU12 72 A5
Pollington DN14 77 F6
Poppleton YO26 12 F1
Preston HU12 58 C1
Reighton YO14 3 E5
Riccall YO19 49 A8
Roos HU12 60 A1
Scawby DN20 108 E7
Searby cum Owmby DN38 110 D8
Seaton HU11 35 A1
Shipton YO30 12 F5
Sigglesthorne HU11 45 F8
Skerne & Wansford YO25 21 A2
Skidby HU16 138 B8
Skipsea YO25 23 A1
Stamford Bridge YO41 15 D2
Swanland HU14 69 B7
Swine HU11 57 D6
Thornton Curtis DN39 85 E5
Thwing YO25 2 B1
Tibthorpe YO25 19 D2
Tickton HU17 137 E8
Ulrome YO25 22 E5
Watton YO25 32 D5
Wawne HU7 56 F7
Welwick HU12 90 A7
Wheldrake YO19 37 F7
Whitton DN15 67 E3
Main St *continued*
Wilberfoss YO41 27 E5
Withernwick HU11 46 D3
Womersley DN6 76 C6
Worlaby DN20 98 D8
York YO26 129 A5
York YO10 131 B1
York YO10 133 D8
Maine Ave DN15 96 A7
Mains La YO42 39 E3
Maister Rd 12 HU12 73 C4
Majestic Ct 7 HU9 142 A3
Malbys Gr YO23 132 B2
Malcolm Rd DN34 102 C2
Maldon Dr HU9 146 C6
Malet Lambert Sch HU8 141 E4
Malham Ave HU4 144 C6
Malham Gr YO31 131 B5
Malkinson Cl 11 DN15 83 A5
Mallalieu Ct DN15 150 E8
Mallard Ave
Barnby Dun DN3 92 A4
2 Leven HU17 45 A8
Mallard Cl
Beverley HU17 136 F6
2 Healing DN41 101 F5
Ulrome YO25 23 A3
Mallard Dr LN7 111 A4
Mallard Mews DN32 152 E2
Mallard Rd
Kingston upon Hull HU9 142 B4
Scunthorpe DN17 150 E2
Mallard Way 11 YO32 13 F5
Malling Wlk 13 DN16 96 D1
Mallory Cl YO32 127 D4
Mallory Rd DN16 151 D1
Mallyan Cl 15 HU8 141 E7
Malm St HU3 145 B6
Malmesbury Dr DN34 152 C2
Malmo Rd HU7 140 E5
Malpas Cl 8 HU7 56 F5
Malt Kilns The DN14 149 D4
Maltby Ave DN37 102 B2
Maltby La 12 DN18 69 E1
Maltby Rd DN17 150 E1
Malthouse La 5 YO16 122 D5
Malthouse Row DN14 149 C3
Maltings Ct 6 YO8 148 C6
Maltings The
Beverley HU17 154 C3
Nafferton YO25 125 F6
Maltkiln La 4 DN20 98 F7
Maltkiln Rd DN18 69 F1
Malton Ave YO31 130 E6
Malton La YO17 7 A8
Malton Rd
Hunmanby YO14 2 F8
Huntington YO32 128 A1
Molescroft HU17 136 B6
York YO31 130 F7
Malton St HU9 155 C3
Malton Way YO30 129 F8
Malvern Ave
Grimsby DN33 102 D2
York YO26 129 D5
Malvern Cl
Huntington YO32 128 A5
4 Thorne/Moorends DN8 93 A7
Malvern Cres 9 HU5 139 D2
Malvern Rd
Goole DN14 149 D5
Kingston upon Hull HU5 139 D2
Scunthorpe DN17 150 F3
Manby Rd
Immingham DN40 87 B3
Scunthorpe DN17 96 C2
Manchester Rd YO42 28 E3
Manchester St
Cleethorpes DN35 153 D4
Kingston upon Hull HU3 145 A4
Mancklin Ave HU8 141 D5
Mancroft YO32 127 C8
Mandela Link DN31 152 C3
Manderville Cl 18 HU12 72 D7
Manet Rd HU8 141 C1
Manifold Rd DN16 151 E1
Manlake Ave DN15 83 A5
Manley Cl YO32 127 D4
Manley Ct 1 DN9 105 D6
Manley Gdns
Brigg DN20 98 B2
Cleethorpes DN35 103 C2
Manley St DN15 151 B7
Mann La DN9 94 D2
Mannaberg Way DN15 96 D7
Manor Ave DN32 152 D2
Manor Beeches The 3 YO19 26 E7
Manor C of E Sch YO26 129 C7
Manor Cl
Beverley HU17 154 A4
Great Driffield YO25 124 F4
5 Hemingbrough YO8 49 F1
4 Keelby DN41 101 A5
Kirk Smeaton WF8 76 B3
Nafferton YO25 125 F6
6 North Duffield YO8 50 A7
12 Norton DN6 76 E2
Skipsea YO25 23 A2
Sproatley HU11 58 D5
Manor Court Rd 7 DN9 105 E6
Manor Ct 6 Bubwith YO8 50 D7
Kingston upon Hull HU10 69 C8
Stallingborough DN41 101 E7
2 York YO32 127 F6
Manor Dr Beeford YO25 22 C1
Manor Dr *continued*
Bonby DN20 84 C2
Brough HU15 68 C6
Camblesforth YO8 63 C4
4 Dunnington YO19 26 E7
10 Gilberdyke HU15 66 D8
5 North Duffield YO8 50 A7
Scawby DN20 108 E8
Waltham DN37 113 E7
Manor Dr N YO26 129 D4
Manor Dr S YO26 129 D4
Manor Farm Cl
1 Brayton YO8 148 A1
Carlton DN14 63 C2
Copmanthorpe YO23 132 A2
Kellington DN14 61 F3
Messingham DN17 107 D6
Manor Farm Ct YO8 62 C4
Manor Farm La DN14 78 A3
Manor Farm Rd DN17 150 E2
Manor Fields
Kingston upon Hull HU10 69 C8
Market Weighton YO43 135 D4
Manor Garth
Barmby Moor YO42 28 D3
Haxby YO32 127 B8
Kellington DN14 61 F3
Keyingham HU12 73 C4
7 Norton DN6 76 F2
1 Riccall YO19 49 A8
Skidby HU16 55 C4
Manor Gdns
8 Hatfield DN7 92 E4
6 Hunmanby YO14 3 A8
Manor Heath YO23 132 A3
Manor House St HU1 155 A1
Manor La
Barrow upon Humber DN19 85 D8
Goxhill DN19 85 F8
Hollym HU19 75 A4
Rawcliffe YO30 126 D2
Manor Mid Sch DN7 92 E4
Manor Park Cl YO30 126 E2
Manor Park Gr YO30 126 E2
Manor Park Rd YO30 126 E2
Manor Pk
Beverley HU17 154 A4
Preston HU12 58 D1
Seaton HU11 35 A1
Manor Rd Beal DN14 61 C4
Beverley HU17 154 A3
Crowle DN17 94 C7
Goole DN14 149 C1
Hatfield DN7 92 E4
Kingston upon Hull HU5 144 B8
9 North Cave HU15 53 D3
Northorpe DN21 118 D8
Preston HU12 58 C1
Reedness DN14 65 F1
Scunthorpe DN16 96 D2
South Cliffe YO43 53 B7
Swanland HU14 69 B6
Thorngumbald HU12 72 F5
Twin Rivers DN14 81 E7
Manor St
6 Bridlington YO15 122 E2
6 Keelby DN41 101 A5
Kingston upon Hull HU1 155 B2
Manor Way
Kingston upon Hull HU10 143 F6
York YO30 126 E2
Manorfield Ave YO25 124 F5
Manorfield Rd YO25 124 F4
Manorhouse La HU17 55 B8
Mansel St DN32 153 B4
Mansfield Pk HU5 140 B3
Mansfield Rd DN15 150 B6
Mansfield St YO31 156 C3
Mansgate Hill LN7 111 B3
Mansion Court Gdns DN8 93 A8
Manson Cl 13 DN34 102 B2
Manston Garth 4 HU7 57 B5
Manton Ct DN20 108 F6
Manton La DN20 108 E6
Manton Rd DN21 108 A4
Manuel St DN14 149 B4
Manvers St HU5 140 C3
Maple Ave
Bishopthorpe YO23 133 A3
Crowle DN17 94 D7
Flixborough DN15 96 B7
Grimsby DN34 102 C4
Keelby DN41 101 A4
Kingston upon Hull HU10 143 F8
Maple Cl
2 Bridlington YO16 123 A6
Brigg DN20 98 D2
Gainsborough DN21 117 A2
Hambleton YO8 48 B1
12 Keelby DN41 101 A4
5 Kingston upon Hull HU4 144 C7
Messingham DN17 107 D6
Maple Ct YO10 133 E6
Maple Dr
Beverley HU17 136 F6
Goole DN14 149 F5
Maple Gr 12 Brayton YO8 48 D1
8 Healing DN41 101 F5
3 Immingham DN40 87 C2
Kingston upon Hull HU8 141 C2
7 New Waltham DN36 113 F7
York YO10 130 D1
Maple Pk HU12 72 D8
Maple Rd
Bridlington YO16 123 A6
1 Thorne/Moorends DN8 79 B1
Maple St HU5 140 D2
Maple Tree Ave YO8 49 B4
Maple Tree Cl E DN16 151 A5
Maple Tree Cl W DN16 151 A5
Maple Tree Way DN16 151 A5
Maple Wlk 8 YO25 34 B2
Mapleleaf Ct 9 HU16 138 F5
Maplewood Ave HU4 144 B7
Maplewood Paddock 2 YO24 129 C1
Mappleton Gr HU9 142 A2
Mappleton Rd HU11 46 D6
March St
6 Kirton in Lindsey DN21 108 B1
York YO31 156 C4
Marchant Cl HU17 136 D7
Marcus St Goole DN14 149 B4
Grimsby DN34 152 A2
Marfleet Ave HU9 147 B7
Marfleet Cnr DN36 114 B1
Marfleet La HU9 142 B3
Marfleet Prim Sch HU9 147 C8
Margaret Ave DN17 95 D5
Margaret Gr 1 HU13 143 F1
Margaret Pl 18 DN36 114 A7
Margaret St
Grimsby DN32 152 F3
Immingham DN40 101 C8
York YO10 156 C1
Margrave La
Garthorpe & Fockerby DN17 81 E5
Reedness DN14 80 E7
Marian Way DN37 113 C6
Marigold Cl YO8 148 C2
Marigold Wlk 22 DN35 103 C1
Marina Ave 3 DN14 63 B1
Marina View 6 DN8 93 A7
Marine Ave HU14 69 A4
Marine Dr HU18 134 D5
Marine Valley 2 YO15 5 B3
Marine Wharf HU1 155 B1
Mariners Arms Flats DN17 95 D6
Mariners Cl HU9 146 C6
Mariners St 9 DN14 149 C4
Mark Rise DN21 117 F5
Market Ct 5 DN17 94 D7
Market Hall Sh Ctr DN31 152 D3
Market La
12 Barton-upon-Humber DN18 84 F8
6 Brigg DN20 98 B2
Selby YO8 148 C5
Market Pl
11 Barton-upon-Humber DN18 84 F8
Bridlington YO16 122 C5
9 Brigg DN20 98 B2
11 Caistor LN7 111 B4
2 Cawood YO8 48 B8
5 Epworth DN9 105 E6
Great Driffield YO25 124 E4
31 Hedon HU12 72 C7
Hornsea HU18 134 B4
Kingston upon Hull HU1 155 C1
Market Weighton YO43 135 D4
Owston Ferry DN9 106 B2
Patrington HU12 74 D1
Pocklington YO42 29 A3
11 Selby YO8 148 C5
9 Snaith DN14 63 C1
South Cave HU15 54 A2
Market St
Cleethorpes DN35 153 F2
9 Pocklington YO42 29 A4
14 Winterton DN15 83 A5
York YO1 156 B2
Market Weighton Inf Sch YO43 135 D3
Market Weighton Rd
Barlby with Osgodby YO8 49 B6
Holme-on-Spalding-Moor YO43 40 B2
Market Weighton YO43 135 A2
Sancton YO43 41 D3
Market Weighton Sch Adult Ed & Sports Ctr YO43 135 F4
Marketbridge La YO42 39 E7
Markham Cres YO31 156 B4
Markham Mews DN37 113 E6
Markham St YO31 156 B4
Markham Way DN20 98 E4
Markhams Orch DN33 113 E8
Marklew Ave DN34 152 B3
Markman La YO25 125 D5
Marlborough Ave
Goole DN14 149 C5
2 Haxey DN9 105 D2
Hornsea HU18 134 C1
Kingston upon Hull HU13 143 D2
Kingston upon Hull HU5 145 A8
Marlborough Cl YO30 126 D3
Marlborough Dr DN16 151 B4
Marlborough Gr YO10 130 D2
Marlborough Rd 9 DN8 93 B7

Marlborough Terr
8 Bridlington YO15 ...122 F2
Kingston upon Hull HU2 ...155 A3
Marlborough Way
DN35 ...103 C1
Marlow Rd DN21 ...117 C1
Marlowe Rd DN17 ...150 D3
Marlowe St HU8 ...141 C2
Marmaduke St 3 HU3 ...145 C4
Marmiam Dr 2 YO32 ...14 D2
Marmion Dr DN15 ...83 A5
Marmion Rd DN16 ...151 C3
Marne St HU5 ...145 A8
Marquis Ave DN36 ...114 A8
Marr La HU15 ...66 F7
Marris Dr DN15 ...83 B5
Marritt Way 9 HU12 ...73 C4
Marsdale HU7 ...140 F7
Marsden Dr DN15 ...150 D8
Marsden Gr 3 DN8 ...93 A8
Marsden Landing
HU6 ...140 D8
Marsden Rd DN31 ...153 A5
Marsh Dr HU17 ...154 A1
Marsh End
17 Howden DN14 ...65 A7
Knottingley WF11 ...61 A3
Marsh Hill La DN14 ...78 C4
Marsh La Asselby DN14 ...64 D7
Barlow YO8 ...63 B8
Barnetby le Wold DN38 ...99 B4
Barrow upon Humber
DN19 ...70 C2
Barton-upon-Humber
DN18 ...69 F1
2 Beal DN14 ...61 D4
Cawood YO8 ...48 D8
Keyingham HU12 ...73 B3
Knottingley WF11 ...61 A2
Misterton DN10 ...116 D5
New Holland DN19 ...70 E2
Ryehill HU12 ...73 A4
South Killingholme DN40 ...87 B4
Thorne DN8 ...79 A2
Thorngumbald HU12 ...73 A4
West Haddlesey YO8 ...61 F5
Winteringham DN15 ...68 A1
Marsh Lane Gdns DN14 ...61 F4
Marsh Rd Crowle DN17 ...94 B7
Easington HU12 ...90 E5
Keyingham HU12 ...73 A2
Ottringham HU12 ...88 C8
Walkeringham DN10 ...116 E3
Marsh Way DN36 ...115 C5
Marshall Ave
Bridlington YO15 ...122 E2
Grimsby DN34 ...152 B3
Kingston upon Hull
HU10 ...143 E8
Preston HU12 ...72 C8
Marshall Hill YO25 ...19 D2
Marshall St HU5 ...140 C2
Marshchapel Cl 20
DN35 ...103 C2
Marshchapel County Prim
Sch DN36 ...115 B2
Marshfield Ave DN14 ...149 E4
Marshfield Rd
Goole DN14 ...149 E4
Scunthorpe DN16 ...151 C1
Marshland Rd
Thorne DN8 ...79 B2
Thorne/Moorends DN8 ...79 B1
Marshlands Prim Sch
DN14 ...149 D1
Marske Wlk 1 HU5 ...139 E3
Marston Ave YO26 ...129 B3
Marston Cres YO26 ...129 B3
Marston La
Long Marston YO26 ...24 A8
Moor Monkton YO26 ...12 A1
Marten Cl 2 YO30 ...130 A8
Martin Cheeseman Ct 3
YO24 ...132 C8
Martin Cl HU9 ...142 B3
Martin La YO42 ...29 C6
Martin St HU17 ...137 B3
Martin Way
7 New Waltham DN36 ...113 F8
4 New Waltham DN36 ...114 A7
Martin's Cl DN19 ...85 D8
Martins Rd DN39 ...86 B1
Marton Ave YO16 ...122 E5
Marton Ct 6 YO16 ...123 A7
Marton Dr DN7 ...92 D4
Marton Gate YO16 ...123 A7
Marton Gr
8 Grimsby DN33 ...102 D2
Kingston upon Hull HU6 ...139 F5
Marton La YO25 ...9 F6
Marton Rd
Bridlington YO16 ...122 D5
Ellerby HU11 ...46 B1
Marton View YO15 ...123 B8
Martongate Cty Prim Sch
YO16 ...122 F6
Martyn Rd DN32 ...153 D2
Marvel St HU9 ...146 B7
Marvelgarth La HU11 ...35 A2
Mary St DN15 ...151 A7
Mary Sumner Way
DN15 ...150 E8
Marydene Dr HU6 ...140 C5
Marygate YO30 ...156 A3
Marygate La YO30 ...156 A3
Marylebone Wlk 3
DN33 ...102 D1
Mascotte Gdns HU18 ...134 D3
Mask La YO41 ...27 D4
Mason Dr DN17 ...96 C2
Mason St HU2 ...155 B3
Masons Ct 6 DN18 ...84 E8
Maspin Cl 19 HU7 ...56 F5
Maspin Moor Rd LS25 ...61 C7
Massey Cl
8 Epworth DN9 ...105 D6
Kingston upon Hull HU3 ...145 A5
Massey St
Kingston upon Hull HU3 ...145 A4
Selby YO8 ...148 C5
Mast Dr HU9 ...146 C6
Mathews St DN35 ...153 C3
Matlock Dr DN37 ...102 C4
Matson Cl YO16 ...122 C2
Matson Rd YO16 ...122 B1
Matthew Humberstone Sch
DN35 ...103 B2
Mattison Way YO24 ...129 E2
Mattocks La HU12 ...72 D8
Matty La 10 YO43 ...53 F7
Maude Cl 10 HU12 ...73 C4
Maulson Dr HU11 ...58 A3
Maurice Ave HU8 ...141 A2
Mavis Rd DN17 ...150 E2
Mawson Gn La DN14 ...78 C3
Maxwell Ct 9 DN34 ...102 B3
Maxwell Rd YO42 ...29 A4
Maxwell St HU8 ...141 A2
May Gr HU13 ...143 D2
May St
Cleethorpes DN35 ...153 D4
Kingston upon Hull HU5 ...140 D3
May Tree Ave HU8 ...141 C2
Maybury Prim Sch
HU9 ...142 B3
Maybury Rd HU9 ...141 F3
Mayfair Cres 18 DN37 ...113 D6
Mayfair Ct 3 DN35 ...103 D1
Mayfair Dr W DN37 ...102 B4
Mayfield DN14 ...149 E6
Mayfield Ave
2 Gainsborough DN21 ...117 B2
South Killingholme DN40 ...86 F2
Stainforth DN7 ...92 D7
Mayfield Cl DN33 ...113 D8
Mayfield Dr 5 YO8 ...148 A1
Mayfield Gr YO24 ...132 E8
Mayfield Rd
Brayton YO8 ...148 A1
Bridlington YO15 ...122 D1
Mayfield St HU3 ...145 C8
Mayflower Ave 6 DN40 ...87 C1
Mayflower Cl 2 DN40 ...86 E3
Mayland Ave HU5 ...144 A8
Mayland Dr HU16 ...138 E6
Maypole Gdns YO8 ...48 B8
Maypole Gr 3 YO19 ...36 D8
Maypole St DN21 ...119 A2
Maysfield Ct DN20 ...109 A5
Maythorn Rd YO31 ...127 E2
Maythorpe YO23 ...24 C6
Maythorpe Cl HU3 ...145 A7
Mayville Ave HU8 ...141 B3
McGrath Cl 25 YO42 ...29 A3
McShane Ct 11 YO42 ...29 A3
McVeigh Ct 10 DN41 ...101 F5
Mead St HU8 ...141 D5
Mead The 1 DN37 ...101 F1
Mead Wlk HU4 ...144 C6
Meadlands YO31 ...131 B6
Meadley Ct HU17 ...137 C4
Meadow Ave DN39 ...86 A2
Meadow Bank 2 HU17 ...136 F7
Meadow Cl
5 Beeford YO25 ...22 D1
Thorpe Willoughby YO8 ...48 C2
Meadow Court Greyhound
Stadium DN7 ...92 C5
Meadow Croft
Brayton YO8 ...148 A2
10 Kirk Sandall DN3 ...92 A2
Waltham DN37 ...113 D7
Meadow Ct
Grimsby DN37 ...102 C4
Hibaldstow DN20 ...108 F5
3 York YO24 ...132 E8
Meadow Dr
Barton-upon-Humber
DN18 ...84 F8
Grimsby DN33 ...113 D8
Healing DN41 ...102 A5
Market Weighton YO43 ...135 E4
Misterton DN10 ...116 C5
Thorpe Willoughby YO8 ...48 B2
Meadow Field YO43 ...40 A1
Meadow Garth
Kingston upon Hull HU6 ...56 D5
Thorpe Willoughby YO8 ...48 C2
Meadow La
Driffield YO25 ...125 B4
1 Haxby YO32 ...127 D8
9 Newport HU15 ...52 F1
Meadow Pl 5 YO8 ...148 B6
Meadow Rd
Bridlington YO16 ...122 B2
Great Driffield YO25 ...125 A4
Scunthorpe DN17 ...150 C2
Meadow Rise
Barnby Dun DN3 ...92 A3
Blyton DN21 ...117 F6
Meadow The LN7 ...111 B3
Meadow Vale DN20 ...108 F8
Meadow View
Bainton YO25 ...31 E7
Bridlington YO16 ...122 E7
28 Humberston DN35 ...103 C1
Meadow Way
Kingston upon Hull
HU16 ...138 F5
3 Walkington HU17 ...55 C8
York YO32 ...127 F4
York YO31 ...130 F7
Meadow Wlk 6 HU14 ...69 B7
Meadowbank
4 Belton DN9 ...94 E1
Grimsby DN37 ...102 B4
Meadowbank Rd HU3 ...144 E7
Meadowbeck Cl YO10 ...131 B4
Meadowcroft Rd
YO25 ...125 A6
Meadowfield
Barnby Dun DN3 ...92 A3
1 Bubwith YO8 ...50 D7
Meadowfield Cl 6 YO42 ...28 F4
Meadowfield Rd YO15 ...122 D1
Meadowfields Dr
YO31 ...127 D2
Meadows The
Beverley HU17 ...137 B2
4 Buckton/Bempton YO15 ...4 C3
Burringham DN17 ...95 D4
Carlton DN14 ...63 C3
Cherry Burton HU17 ...43 A4
Dunswell HU6 ...56 D5
Great Driffield YO25 ...125 A4
Howden DN14 ...65 A6
Kingston upon Hull HU10 ...69 C8
Kingston upon Hull HU7 ...140 E7
Leven HU17 ...45 A8
Messingham DN17 ...107 D7
7 Monk Fryston LS25 ...61 A8
Riccall YO19 ...48 F8
2 Skelton YO30 ...126 B5
13 South Cave HU15 ...53 F1
5 Westwoodside DN9 ...105 A2
Meadway YO8 ...48 D2
Meadway Dr YO8 ...48 D2
Measham Dr DN7 ...92 D7
Meaux Abbey (Site of)*
HU17 ...44 F2
Meaux La HU17 ...44 F4
Meaux Rd HU7 ...56 F8
Mechanic La 9 HU3 ...145 D5
Medforth Rd YO16 ...122 C4
Medina Ave YO16 ...122 D3
Medina Rd HU8 ...142 C5
Medium Section Rd
DN16 ...97 A4
Medlar Dr 2 HU15 ...68 D5
Medway Pl DN34 ...152 A1
Meggison's Turnpike
YO25 ...32 F7
Meggitt La DN15 ...68 A1
Megson Way HU17 ...55 D8
Melander Cl YO26 ...129 B4
Melander Gdns 5 YO32 ...127 D7
Melbourne Ave
Bridlington YO16 ...122 D3
18 Grimsby DN33 ...102 E2
Melbourne CP Sch
YO42 ...39 A7
Melbourne Pk YO42 ...39 A6
Melbourne Sq HU17 ...43 D6
Melbourne St
4 Kingston upon Hull
HU5 ...140 C3
York YO10 ...130 D2
Melcombe Ave 11 YO32 ...14 A7
Mellwood View DN9 ...106 A3
Melrose Cl 1 YO31 ...131 A5
Melrose Pk HU17 ...154 A2
Melrose Rd 5 DN21 ...117 B1
Melrose St HU3 ...144 F6
Melrosegate YO31 ...130 F5
Melton Ave YO30 ...129 F8
Melton Bottom HU14 ...68 E5
Melton Dr
Bishopthorpe YO23 ...133 A3
York YO30 ...129 F8
Melton Fields HU14 ...68 F5
Melton Gallows DN38 ...99 A5
Melton Old Rd HU14 ...68 E5
Melton Rd
North Ferriby HU14 ...69 A5
Wrawby DN20 ...98 F4
Meltonby Ave HU5 ...139 C2
Meltonby La YO42 ...28 E6
Melville Cl 10 HU12 ...73 C4
Melville St HU1 ...155 A1
Melwood Cl DN9 ...105 F6
Melwood Gr
Kingston upon Hull HU5 ...140 D2
York YO26 ...129 B5
Melwood Hill DN9 ...105 F6
Melwood View DN9 ...105 F6
Memorial Ave 14 HU19 ...75 A6
Menasha Way DN16 ...151 E3
Mendip Ave
Goole DN14 ...149 D5
Grimsby DN33 ...113 E8
Mendip Cl 2 YO32 ...127 F5
Mendip Rd DN17 ...150 D4
Menson Dr DN7 ...92 D4
Mercer Rd 1 DN21 ...117 A1
Merchant Adventurers Hall*
YO1 ...156 C2
Merchant Taylors Hall*
YO31 ...156 C3
Merchant Way YO23 ...132 B3
Merchantgate YO1 ...156 C2
Mere Cres DN16 ...151 D3
Mere La
Dalton Holme HU17 ...42 F8
Edenthorpe DN3 ...92 A1
Winterton DN15 ...83 A7
Mere View Ave HU18 ...134 B2
Mere Way HU14 ...69 B7
Mere Wlk 6 HU18 ...134 C4
Meredith Ave DN17 ...150 C2
Meredyke Rd DN17 ...81 D3
Mereside 9 YO15 ...5 A2
Mereside Terr HU18 ...134 B4
Meridian Point*
DN35 ...103 D2
Merlin Cl HU7 ...141 D7
Merlin Covert 4 YO31 ...127 F3
Merlin Dr DN20 ...99 A8
Merlin Rd DN17 ...150 E2
Merrick St HU9 ...146 B7
Merryman Garth HU12 ...72 C7
Merryweather Ct 14
DN16 ...96 D1
Mersey Prim Sch HU8 ...141 C1
Mersey St HU8 ...141 C1
Merton Gr 5 HU9 ...141 F1
Merton Rd DN16 ...96 D2
Messingham Cty Prim Sch
DN17 ...107 D7
Messingham Cty Sch
DN17 ...107 D7
Messingham La DN20 ...108 C7
Messingham Rd
East Butterwick DN17 ...106 D8
Scotter DN21 ...107 C4
16 Scunthorpe DN17 ...96 C2
Scunthorpe DN16 ...151 A1
Metcalfe La YO19 ...131 C5
Metham La DN14 ...65 F4
Mews The HU3 ...145 C5
Meynell St DN21 ...117 A8
Micklegate 1 Selby YO8 ...148 D5
York YO1 ...156 A2
Micklegate Bar Mus*
YO24 ...156 A1
Micklethwaite Gr 2 DN8 ...79 B2
Micklethwaite Rd 1 DN8 ...79 B2
Mickley Gr HU9 ...142 C2
Middle Banks 24 YO32 ...13 E5
Middle Barn Hill DN20 ...84 D1
Middle Ct DN31 ...152 E4
Middle Dike La HU16 ...139 D7
Middle Garth Dr HU15 ...54 A2
Middle La Amcotts DN17 ...95 E8
Brayton YO8 ...148 C1
14 Knottingley WF11 ...61 A2
Preston HU12 ...58 B1
5 Seaton HU11 ...35 A1
Middle St
Corringham DN21 ...118 B2
Foggathorpe YO42 ...39 A2
Kilham YO25 ...9 B3
Nafferton YO25 ...125 F7
North Kelsey LN7 ...110 A4
Rudston YO25 ...9 F6
Scotton DN21 ...107 C1
Wilberfoss YO41 ...27 F5
Willoughton DN21 ...119 B3
Middle St N YO25 ...124 E4
Middle St S YO25 ...124 F3
Middle Thorpe Rd
DN35 ...103 B2
Middlebrook Gdns
YO8 ...148 A2
Middlebrook La 23 DN8 ...93 A8
Middleburg St HU9 ...146 D8
Middlecroft Dr YO32 ...14 A7
Middlecroft Gr 2 YO32 ...14 B7
Middlefield La WF8 ...76 A2
Middlegate Cl 9 DN19 ...85 C8
Middlegate La
Saxby All Saints DN20 ...84 B4
South Ferriby DN18 ...84 B7
Middleham Ave YO31 ...130 E8
Middleham Cl 3 HU9 ...146 E8
Middlehowe Gn 2 HU17 ...55 B8
Middlehowe Rd HU17 ...55 A8
Middlemarsh Cl 3 HU8 ...141 B4
Middleplatt Rd DN40 ...87 D2
Middlesex Rd HU8 ...141 F5
Middlethorpe Cty Prim Sch
DN35 ...103 B2
Middlethorpe Dr
YO24 ...132 E7
Middlethorpe Gr YO24 ...132 F7
Middleton Cl
Beverley HU17 ...154 C4
Messingham DN17 ...107 D7
Middleton Ct HU5 ...145 B8
Middleton Hall* HU6 ...140 B4
Middleton Rd
Bainton YO25 ...31 D5
Scunthorpe DN16 ...96 D2
York YO24 ...129 C2
Middleton St HU3 ...145 C8
Middleton-on-the-Wolds C
of E Sch YO25 ...31 C4
Middlewood Cl YO23 ...24 C6
Midfield Pl DN36 ...114 D8
Midfield Rd DN36 ...114 D8
Midfield Way 1 DN41 ...101 A4
Midgley Cl
Kingston upon Hull HU3 ...145 C5
21 Stamford Bridge YO41 ...15 D2
Midland Rd DN16 ...151 D5
Midland St HU1 ...155 A2
Midmere Ave HU7 ...141 B7
Midmere Prim Sch
HU7 ...141 C6
Midway Ave
Bridlington YO16 ...122 D2
Poppleton YO26 ...126 A1
Midway Gr HU4 ...144 E4
Milcroft Cres 13 DN7 ...92 D4
Mildred Gr 5 YO24 ...129 F2
Mile End Ave DN7 ...92 D3
Mile End Pk YO42 ...29 A4
Mile The YO42 ...29 A4
Miles La HU17 ...43 C6
Milestone Ave YO23 ...24 C6
Milford Ave YO16 ...122 C5
Milford Cres 5 YO16 ...122 C5
Milford Gr HU9 ...142 E1
Milford Mews 7 YO32 ...127 D7
Milford Way 8 YO32 ...127 D7
Mill Ave DN31 ...152 C4
Mill Balk DN14 ...77 C8
Mill Balk Pl DN14 ...78 B8
Mill Baulk Rd DN10 ...116 C3
Mill Beck La HU16 ...139 B8
Mill Cl Bridlington YO16 ...122 C5
16 Broughton DN20 ...98 B2
Great Driffield YO25 ...124 D4
Marshchapel DN36 ...115 C2
Monk Fryston LS25 ...61 A8
7 Waltham DN37 ...113 E6
Mill Cres 11 DN21 ...107 C3
Mill Croft Scawby DN20 ...108 F8
11 Scunthorpe DN16 ...96 E2
Scunthorpe DN16 ...151 D3
Mill Ct 10 YO16 ...122 C5
Mill Dr HU17 ...45 A8
Mill Falls YO25 ...124 D4
Mill Field Ct 5 DN3 ...92 A3
Mill Field Rd
Chapel Haddlesey YO8 ...62 B5
Fishlake DN7 ...92 C8
Scunthorpe DN16 ...151 E7
Mill Garth
12 Cleethorpes DN35 ...103 B2
14 Hemingbrough YO8 ...49 F1
Mill Gate YO16 ...122 C5
Mill Hill Ellerker HU15 ...68 A8
Escrick YO19 ...37 B5
Mill Hill Cres DN35 ...153 E1
Mill Hill Dr
6 Scunthorpe DN16 ...96 E2
York YO32 ...127 F4
Mill Hill Rd DN7 ...92 E3
Mill House La DN15 ...83 B5
Mill House Way HU11 ...45 D2
Mill La
Acaster Malbis YO23 ...36 C8
Askham Richard YO23 ...24 D2
Barlow YO8 ...63 B7
Barrow upon Humber
DN19 ...85 C8
Beverley HU17 ...154 B4
Bielby YO42 ...39 E6
Bishop Burton HU17 ...43 B2
Brandesburton YO25 ...34 B2
Brayton YO8 ...62 C8
Bridlington YO16 ...122 C5
Brigg DN20 ...98 B1
Brough HU15 ...68 C6
Broughton DN20 ...97 E3
Caistor LN7 ...111 C4
Carlton DN14 ...63 D3
East Halton DN40 ...86 D6
Eastrington DN14 ...52 A1
Elstronwick HU12 ...58 F3
Foston YO25 ...21 F1
Gainsborough DN21 ...117 A2
Gilberdyke HU15 ...52 D1
Gilberdyke DN14 ...66 B7
Goxhill DN19 ...71 A1
Harpham YO25 ...21 E7
Haxby YO32 ...13 D5
Haxey DN9 ...105 B2
Hayton YO42 ...29 D1
2 Hemingbrough YO8 ...49 F1
Hessay YO23 ...24 B7
Holton le Clay DN36 ...114 B4
Hornsea HU18 ...134 B4
Huggate YO42 ...18 B1
Immingham DN40 ...87 A1
14 Keelby DN41 ...101 A4
Kilpin DN14 ...65 D5
Kingston upon Hull
HU16 ...138 E7
Kingston upon Hull
HU10 ...143 C6
Kirton in Lindsey DN21 ...108 C1
Langtoft YO25 ...8 C7
Laxton DN14 ...65 F3
Marshchapel DN36 ...115 C2
Newbald YO43 ...53 E6
Newland YO8 ...64 A3
Newport HU15 ...52 E1
3 North Cave HU15 ...53 D3
North Dalton YO25 ...31 C7
North Kelsey LN7 ...110 A4
Rawcliffe DN14 ...63 F1
1 Riccall YO19 ...37 A1
Rise HU11 ...45 E6
Scawby DN20 ...108 F8
Seaton HU11 ...35 A2
Seaton Ross YO42 ...39 D4
Skipsea YO25 ...23 B2
Sledmere YO25 ...6 F3
Snaith & Cowick DN14 ...78 C8
South Ferriby DN18 ...84 A7
Walkeringham DN10 ...116 C3
Warter YO42 ...30 A4
Watton YO25 ...32 D4
Welwick HU12 ...90 A7
Wilberfoss YO41 ...27 E6

Mill La *continued*
Wrawby DN20 98 E3
York YO31 130 E6
Mill La W HU15 68 B6
Mill Mere Rd DN21 118 A2
Mill Mount YO24 130 A3
Mill Mount Ct YO24 130 A3
Mill Pl DN35 153 F2
Mill Race DN36 114 E4
Mill Rd Aldbrough HU11 47 C2
Burton Constable HU11 58 D7
Burton Fleming YO25 2 D4
Cleethorpes DN35 153 E1
Crowle DN17 94 D8
Hibaldstow DN20 108 E4
Keadby DN17 95 D5
Keyingham HU12 73 C4
Luddington & Haldenby DN17 81 C4
Skidby HU16 138 C7
Sproatley HU11 58 D5
Swanland HU14 69 A6
Mill Rise
Great Driffield YO25 124 D4
Skidby HU16 138 B8
Swanland HU14 69 A6
Mill Side YO25 9 C3
Mill Side Cl 6 YO25 9 C3
Mill St
Great Driffield YO25 124 E4
Hutton Cranswick YO25 32 E8
Kingston upon Hull HU1 155 A2
York YO1 156 C1
Mill View DN37 113 D6
Mill View Rd HU17 137 B3
Mill Wlk HU16 139 C5
Millard Ave DN7 92 D4
Millard Nook 18 DN7 92 D4
Millbank 11 YO16 122 C5
Millbank St DN14 149 F5
Millbeck Bank HU15 67 E8
Millbeck Cl YO43 135 D5
Millbrook Way 23 DN18 84 F8
Millennium Way DN14 149 F5
Miller Ave DN32 153 C2
Miller Cl
Barmby Moor YO42 28 F4
10 Thorne/Moorends DN8 93 B7
Miller La
Thorne/Moorends DN8 93 B7
Yapham YO42 29 A6
Miller Rd DN21 117 D1
Millers Croft 6 YO23 132 B3
Millers Quay 15 DN20 98 B2
Miller's Wlk HU5 139 F2
Millfield Ave
16 Grimsby DN33 102 E2
York YO10 130 F3
Millfield Cl YO41 27 E5
Millfield Dr YO8 63 D4
Millfield Garth YO25 31 C4
Millfield Gdns YO26 126 A2
Millfield La
Nether Poppleton YO26 129 B8
Poppleton YO26 126 A2
York YO10 131 A3
Millfield Rd
4 Bridlington YO16 122 C5
17 Hemingbrough YO8 49 F1
Hemingbrough YO8 63 F8
Thorne/Moorends DN8 93 A8
York YO23 130 B2
Millfield The DN20 109 A6
Millfields
Barton-upon-Humber DN18 84 E8
23 Caistor LN7 111 B4
Millfields Way 7 DN19 85 C8
Millgate YO8 148 C6
Millgates YO26 129 C6
Millhill Rd DN14 149 E5
Millhouse La DN14 149 F5
Millhouse Street Rise 3 DN40 87 B1
Millhouse Woods La HU16 139 B8
Millington Woods Nature Reserve* YO42 29 D8
Millom Way DN32 152 F4
Millport Dr HU4 144 B2
Mills Dr DN7 104 A8
Mills Service Rd DN16 97 A4
Millthorpe Sch YO23 130 B2
Millview Gdns DN20 98 E3
Milne Rd HU9 142 C4
Milner Rd YO16 122 D4
Milner St YO24 129 D3
Milson Cl
4 Barton-upon-Humber DN18 84 E8
Broughton DN20 97 D4
Milson Gr YO10 131 A3
Milson Rd 8 DN41 101 A4
Milton Carr 8 YO30 126 F1
Milton Cl
5 Gainsborough DN21 117 C1
12 Howden DN14 65 A7
Milton Rd
3 Gainsborough DN21 117 C1
Grimsby DN33 102 D2
Scunthorpe DN16 151 B1
Milton St Goole DN14 149 C4
York YO10 130 F3
Minchin Cl 3 YO30 127 B1
Minehead Rd HU7 57 A5
Minerva Terr HU1 155 B1
Minnow Cl 14 DN37 102 B4
Minshull Rd 12 DN35 103 C2
Minster Ave
Beverley HU17 154 B2
York YO31 127 F2
Minster Cl
3 Haxby YO32 127 C8
Kingston upon Hull HU8 141 D5
Minster Ct
Beverley HU17 154 A2
11 Howden DN14 65 A7
Minster Moorgate HU17 154 A2
Minster Moorgate W HU17 154 A2
Minster Rd
Misterton DN10 116 C5
Scunthorpe DN15 150 B6
Minster Sch The
Beverley HU17 136 D3
York YO1 156 B3
Minster The* HU17 154 B2
Minster View YO32 127 C8
Minster Yd YO1 156 B3
Minster Yd N HU17 154 B2
Minster Yd S HU17 154 B2
Mint Wlk HU17 154 B1
Minter Cl 2 YO24 129 B1
Mintfields Rd HU17 154 C3
Minton St HU5 140 D3
Mires La HU15 53 D2
Mires The YO43 53 F7
Mirfield Gr HU9 142 C1
Mirfield Rd
Grimsby DN32 102 F2
Scunthorpe DN15 150 C8
Mirkhill Rd YO8 148 B6
Misson Bank DN9 104 C3
Misterton Prim Sch DN10 116 C4
Mistral Ct YO31 130 E8
Mitcham Rd HU8 142 A5
Mitchell Cl DN7 92 D5
Mitchell La YO41 27 D8
Mitchel's La YO10 133 F8
Miterdale 4 YO24 132 C7
Mitford Cl 3 YO14 2 F8
Mitford Rd 2 YO14 2 F8
Mitten Ave 10 DN14 78 C8
Mizzen Rd HU6 140 B8
Moat Field YO10 131 C4
Moat House Rd DN21 108 A1
Moat La 4 DN40 86 E3
Moat Way YO8 48 D1
Moatside Ct YO31 156 B3
Modder St DN16 151 B2
Moffat Cl HU8 141 C4
Moira Cl DN7 92 D7
Moiser Cl YO32 127 D4
Molescroft Ave 3 HU17 136 D6
Molescroft Cty Prim Sch HU17 136 D6
Molescroft Dr HU17 136 D6
Molescroft Pk 4 HU17 136 D6
Molescroft Rd HU17 136 C6
Molescroft West Cl 2 HU17 136 D6
Mollison Ave DN35 153 F1
Mollison Rd HU4 144 A3
Mond Ave DN14 149 D5
Money Hill (Tumulus)* YO43 42 A8
Monic Ave HU13 143 F2
Monk Ave YO31 130 F7
Monk Bar Ct YO31 156 B3
Monk Bar Mus* YO31 156 C3
Monk Fryston C of E Prim Sch LS25 61 A8
Monk Fryston Prim Sch LS25 61 A8
Monk La YO8 148 C7
Monkbridge Ct YO31 156 C4
Monkgate YO31 156 C3
Monkgate Cloisters YO31 156 C3
Monks Cl DN7 92 D5
Monks Cross Dr YO32 128 A3
Monks Cross Link YO32 128 B4
Monks Rd DN17 150 F2
Monkton 11 HU15 68 D6
Monkton Cl 10 HU16 138 F5
Monkton Rd
5 York YO31 127 F1
York YO31 130 E8
Monmouth St HU4 144 E3
Mons St HU5 145 A8
Monson Rd DN21 118 D8
Montague Rd YO23 133 A3
Montague St
Cleethorpes DN35 153 B5
Goole DN14 149 C4
York YO23 130 C1
Montague Wlk 6 YO26 12 F1
Montcalm Wlk 8 HU16 138 F5
Montgomery Rd DN35 153 D1
Montgomery Sq YO25 124 C2
Montreal Cres 4 HU16 138 F5
Montrose Ave YO31 130 D8
Montrose Ct DN14 149 F5
Montrose Dr DN14 149 F5
Montrose St
Kingston upon Hull HU8 141 B1
Scunthorpe DN16 151 B6
Moody La DN31 152 A7
Mook St YO60 16 B8
Moor Carr La YO8 49 B5
Moor Cl YO19 37 F8
Moor Cottage Rd YO25 34 D5
Moor Dike Rd DN7 104 A8
Moor Edges Rd DN8 93 B8
Moor End YO43 52 B8
Moor Gn HU4 144 B7
Moor Gr YO24 132 E8
Moor La 6 Barlby YO8 49 B5
Bilbrough LS24 24 B1
Bishopthorpe YO23 132 E2
Burton Agnes YO25 10 C2
Caistor LN7 111 A4
Carnaby YO16 10 E4
Cliffe YO8 49 F4
Copmanthorpe YO23 132 A1
Earswick YO32 128 C8
Full Sutton YO41 15 F1
Harpham YO25 22 A8
Hatfield DN8 93 D3
Haxby YO32 13 D7
Humbleton HU11 58 E6
Kelfield YO19 36 E2
Murton YO19 131 F8
Naburn YO19 36 D8
Newton-on-Ouse YO30 12 C7
Rufforth YO23 24 E6
Skelton YO30 126 D6
Strensall YO32 14 B7
Sykehouse DN14 78 A4
Thorne DN8 79 B1
Wroot DN9 104 C6
York YO24 132 C6
Moor Lee La
Eggborough DN14 77 B8
Heck DN14 62 B1
Moor Owners Rd DN8 93 D8
Moor Rd
Bottesford DN17 96 B1
Bridlington YO15 123 D7
Crowle DN17 94 C8
Hunmanby YO14 3 B7
Rawcliffe DN14 79 B7
Sancton YO43 53 C8
Stamford Bridge YO41 15 D2
Thorne DN8 93 C7
Moor Way YO32 128 A4
Moorbeck Cl HU6 139 F4
Moorcroft Rd YO24 132 D7
Moore Ave YO10 131 B4
Moorends Marshland Fst Sch DN8 79 B2
Moorends Rd DN8 79 A4
Moorfield Cty Jun Sch YO16 122 D3
Moorfield Dr YO41 27 E6
Moorfield Rd YO16 122 D3
Moorfield Way YO41 27 E6
Moorfields 3 YO8 48 D6
Moorfields La
Kilpin DN14 65 D3
Reedness DN14 80 F7
Moorfoot Cl 8 HU7 57 A6
Moorgarth Ave
10 York YO24 129 F2
3 York YO24 130 A2
Moorgate YO24 129 D3
Moorhouse Rd 1 HU5 139 B1
Moorings Ct DN14 65 C4
Moorings The DN20 98 A2
Moorland Ave 3 DN10 116 C3
Moorland Cl 4 DN10 116 C3
Moorland Dr 16 DN36 114 A8
Moorland Garth 2 YO32 14 A7
Moorland Rd
Goole DN14 149 D1
York YO10 133 D8
Moorland Way 12 DN9 105 E6
Moorlands Skelton YO32 13 B5
6 Westwoodside DN9 105 A2
Moorlands La YO30 126 C6
Moorlands The HU15 53 E1
Moors La HU15 53 E2
Moors Rd DN15 150 C7
Moortown Rd
Brandesburton YO25 34 B4
Nettleton LN7 111 A3
Moorwell Rd DN17 96 C1
Moot Hill* YO25 124 E5
Mordacks Dr YO16 123 B8
Mordacks Rd YO16 123 A7
Mordaunt Ave DN33 113 D8
More Hall Dr HU7 141 D7
Morecambe Ave DN16 151 A1
Morehall Cl YO30 126 F2
Moreton Bay HU11 142 E5
Morfield Gr 3 DN9 105 D6
Morgan Way DN19 70 D2
Morley Rd DN17 150 F1
Morley St Goole DN14 149 D1
Kingston upon Hull HU8 141 A2
Morley's Yd HU17 154 A3
Morpeth St HU3 145 D7
Morrets La YO8 48 A1
Morrill St HU9 141 D1
Morris Rd HU3 144 E7
Morritt Cl 3 YO31 130 F8
Morrow Ave HU18 134 D5
Mortal Ash Hill DN16 97 C2
Mortimer Dr HU10 143 F6
Mortlake Cl HU8 141 E5
Morton Cl
4 Gainsborough DN21 117 A2
Immingham DN40 87 B2
Morton La
Beverley HU17 154 B3
Hambleton YO8 62 A8
Morton Rd
Gainsborough DN21 117 B2
Grimsby DN34 152 B3
Laughton DN21 117 E8
Morton St HU3 145 C8
Morton Terr DN21 117 B1
Morton Trentside CP Sch DN21 117 A2
Moseley Hill HU11 142 E6
Moss Green La
Brayton YO8 148 A2
Hirst Courtney YO8 62 F3
Moss Haven DN6 77 D1
Moss Rd Grimsby DN32 152 E3
Kirk Bramwith DN7 92 A8
Moss DN6 77 B1
Moss St YO24 156 A1
Mosscroft La DN7 92 E2
Motherwell Cl HU7 141 C4
Moulton Cl 6 DN34 102 B2
Mount Ave
13 Barton-upon-Humber DN18 84 E8
Bridlington YO16 122 E6
Kingston upon Hull HU13 143 D2
Selby YO8 148 B3
Winterton DN15 83 B5
Mount Cres YO16 122 E6
Mount Dr YO16 122 E6
Mount Ephraim 6 YO24 130 A3
Mount Gr YO8 148 B3
Mount Par YO24 130 A3
Mount Pk YO19 49 A8
Mount Pleasant
Aldbrough HU11 47 D2
Harpham YO25 9 D3
9 Holton le Clay DN36 114 A5
1 Hornsea HU18 134 B4
Kingston upon Hull HU8 141 A1
New Holland DN19 70 E2
Waltham DN37 113 D7
Mount Pleasant C of E Jun Sch YO43 135 D3
Mount Pleasant Rd
Goole DN14 149 D5
North Frodingham YO25 34 A7
Thorne DN8 79 A2
Mount Pleasant Windmill* DN21 108 B2
Mount Royale Cl 4 DN39 86 A1
Mount Sch The YO24 130 A3
Mount The
Great Driffield YO25 124 F5
9 Kirk Sandall DN3 92 A1
Selby YO8 148 B3
York YO24 156 A1
Mount Vale YO24 130 A2
Mount Vale Dr YO24 130 A2
Mount Vernon HU11 142 E6
Mount View HU14 69 A5
Mountbatten Cl 7 DN16 96 D2
Mountbatten Prim Sch HU9 142 E3
Mowbray Cl DN9 105 D3
Mowbray Ct 20 DN9 105 E6
Mowbray Dr YO26 129 C4
Mowbray Rd 18 DN8 93 B7
Mowbray St
Epworth DN9 105 E6
3 Gainsborough DN21 117 B1
Mowthorpe Medieval Village* YO17 6 C6
Moy Ct HU6 140 A6
Mucky La HU12 59 C6
Muirfield 16 DN37 113 D6
Muirfield Croft 4 DN40 87 C1
Muirfield Way 6 YO26 129 B5
Mulberry Ave 12 DN8 79 B2
Mulberry Cl
Great Driffield YO25 124 D3
North Thoresby DN36 114 B1
Mulberry Ct YO32 127 F6
Mulberry Dr
10 Crowle DN17 94 D7
7 Haxby YO32 13 E5
Mulberry La HU11 45 E2
Mulcourt HU6 139 F7
Mulgrave St
Kingston upon Hull HU8 155 C4
Scunthorpe DN15 151 A8
Mull Way DN40 101 C8
Mullion Cl HU7 141 C7
Mulwith Cl YO31 131 A6
Mumby Cl 7 DN36 114 B1
Muncastergate YO31 130 E7
Munroe Cl HU8 141 C4
Murham Ave DN14 149 C6
Murray Cl 3 YO42 29 A4
Murray Cres HU16 138 F5
Murray St
Grimsby DN31 152 F6
York YO24 129 F3
Murrayfield Rd HU5 139 F1
Murrough Wilson Pl 3 YO31 130 C7
Murton Garth YO19 131 F6
Murton La YO19 26 D7
Murton Way YO19 131 E5
Museum of Army Transport* HU17 154 C2
Museum St YO1 156 B2
Muston Ave HU16 139 A5
Muston Rd YO14 2 F8
Mutton La DN10 116 C1
Mylor Cl 13 HU7 57 A5
Myrtle Ave
Bishopthorpe YO23 133 B3
Selby YO8 148 B3
Myrtle Rd DN7 92 C4
Myton St HU1 155 A2
Mytongate HU1 155 A1

N

Nab Dr DN14 149 C6
Nab La DN7 92 C8
Naburn La
Deighton YO19 37 A7
Fulford YO19 133 D4
Naburn Pk Mews YO19 36 E8
Nacton St DN31 152 F5
Nafferton Prim Sch YO25 125 E6
Nafferton Sta YO25 125 F6
Nairn Cl YO24 132 C6
Nalton Cl YO23 132 A1
Nalton Ct HU16 139 A5
Nalton St YO8 148 C5
Nan Sampson Bank DN9 104 B4
Nandike Cl 4 HU10 143 F6
Napier Cl HU17 154 A4
Narrow Boats The 14 DN20 98 B2
Narrow La
Cottingwith YO42 38 D7
Eastrington DN14 52 A2
Kilpin DN14 65 D6
Twin Rivers DN14 81 C8
Narvick Rd HU7 140 E5
Naseby Cl 14 DN7 92 D3
Naseby Dr DN31 152 B3
Nashcourt HU6 139 F7
National Ave HU5 144 F8
National Fishing Heritage Ctr* DN31 152 D4
National Rly Mus* YO26 130 A4
Navigation La LN7 111 A4
Navigation Rd YO1 156 C2
Navigation Way HU9 146 C6
Nayfield Cl 7 YO25 124 F4
Naylor's Row 3 HU9 146 B7
Neap House Rd DN15 95 E6
Neasden Cl HU8 141 E5
Neasden Prim Sch HU8 141 E5
Neat Marsh Rd HU12 58 B1
Neatgangs La DN19 71 A3
Neath Rd DN16 151 A5
Neatshead Garth 9 HU7 57 B5
Nelson Ct HU1 155 B1
Nelson Rd HU5 144 B7
Nelson St
Bridlington YO15 122 E2
Gainsborough DN21 117 B1
Grimsby DN32 152 F5
Kingston upon Hull HU1 155 C1
York YO31 156 C4
Nelson Way DN34 102 B3
Nelson's La YO24 129 F1
Nelthorpe Cl 6 DN39 86 A1
Neptune St
Bridlington YO15 122 E1
Cleethorpes DN35 153 E3
Kingston upon Hull HU1 145 D4
Ness La
Garthorpe & Fockerby DN17 81 E6
1 Preston HU12 58 C1
Ness Rd 5 YO8 148 D6
Nessgate YO1 156 B2
Nestor Gr HU9 142 C5
Neswick La YO25 31 F7
Nether Way 20 YO26 12 F1
Nethergate
Nafferton YO25 125 F7
Westwoodside DN9 105 B2
Netherlands Way DN41 87 E1
Netherton Rd HU4 144 B4
Netherwindings 18 YO32 13 F5
Netherwoods 6 YO32 14 B8
Nettleholme 2 DN7 92 D4
Nettleton Garth 3 HU12 73 A6
Nettleton Rd LN7 111 B3
Nettleton Sch LN7 111 A3
Neville Ave HU17 154 C3
Neville Cl
2 Keadby with Althorpe DN17 95 D4
Kingston upon Hull HU3 145 D5
Neville Cres DN15 83 A5
Neville Dr YO23 133 A3
Neville Garth 27 HU12 72 D7
Neville La DN7 92 A8
Neville Pits La DN14 77 B4
Neville Rd DN16 151 C6
Neville St
Cleethorpes DN35 153 D4
York YO31 156 C4
Neville Terr YO31 156 C4
Neville Turner Way 9 DN37 113 D6
Nevinson Gr YO10 133 E8
Nevis Way YO24 132 B7
New Bridge La YO25 125 F5
New Bridge Rd HU9 146 C8
New Burlington Rd YO15 122 D2
New Carr La DN14 52 A3
New Cartergate 5 DN31 152 D3
New Chapel La 6 DN37 101 F1

New Cl 1 DN33 102 E2
New Clee Sta DN31 153 B5
New Cleveland St
HU8 155 C4
New Cut YO25 22 E5
New Delights DN36 114 F3
New Earswick Prim Sch
YO32 127 D4
New Earswick Sports Club
YO32 127 D3
New Fen La YO8 48 F6
New Finkle Ct HU16 139 A6
New Forge Ct 15 YO32 13 F5
New Garden St HU1 155 B3
New George St HU2 155 B3
New Gn 2 DN7 92 C6
New Haven Terr DN31 152 B5
New Holland C of E & Methodist Sch DN19 70 E2
New Holland Rd DN19 85 D8
New Holland Sta DN19 70 E3
New Inn La DN7 92 C7
New La Beal DN14 61 D3
Bishopthorpe YO23 133 A4
Holme-on-Spalding-Moor YO43 52 C4
Humbleton HU11 59 A5
Huntington YO32 128 A1
Laxton DN14 65 E4
Long Marston YO23 24 B3
Newland YO8 64 A3
Rawcliffe DN14 79 A8
Reedness DN14 80 E8
Selby YO8 148 C5
Strensall YO32 14 B8
York YO32 127 F1
York YO24 129 E3
New Laids La HU12 73 B7
New Michael St HU1 155 A1
New Mill Field Rd DN7 92 E3
New Millgate YO8 148 C6
New Park Est DN7 92 D7
New Pasture Cl 6
YO16 122 C5
New Pasture La YO16 122 B5
New Potter Grange Rd
DN14 64 E2
New Rd
Beningbrough YO30 12 C6
Brandesburton YO25 33 E3
Brantingham HU15 68 C8
Burton Pidsea HU12 59 C2
Cleethorpes DN35 153 F2
Etton HU17 43 A6
Foggathorpe YO42 39 A2
Great Driffield YO25 124 F4
Harpham YO25 21 C8
Heck DN14 62 D1
Hedon HU12 72 C7
Hessay YO26 24 C8
Holme-on-Spalding-Moor YO43 40 B1
Hornsea HU18 134 D4
Hunmanby YO14 2 F7
Keyingham HU12 73 D5
Kirby Grindalythe YO17 6 B6
Laceby DN37 113 A8
Long Drax YO8 63 E6
Nafferton YO25 125 D7
Norton DN6 76 F2
Ottringham HU12 73 E3
Reighton YO14 3 E5
Roos HU12 59 F3
Scunthorpe DN17 150 B2
Stapleton WF8 76 B5
Swinefleet DN14 80 C4
Waltham DN37 113 E6
Wheldrake YO19 37 C7
Worlaby DN20 98 D8
New Row DN17 107 D7
New St 17 Brigg DN20 98 C2
Elsham DN20 98 F7
Gainsborough DN21 117 B1
Grimsby DN31 152 E3
Pocklington YO42 29 A3
York YO1 156 B2
New Trent St DN17 94 E6
New Village Rd
Kingston upon Hull HU16 139 C7
Little Weighton HU20 55 A4
New Walkergate
HU17 154 A3
New Waltham Cty Prim Sch
DN36 114 A8
New Wlk
Beverley HU17 136 D5
Great Driffield YO25 124 F4
North Ferriby HU14 69 A4
New Wlk Cl YO25 124 F4
New Wlk Terr YO10 130 D2
Newbald CP Sch YO43 53 F8
Newbald Gr HU6 139 F6
Newbald Rd HU17 136 A2
Newbald Way 1 HU16 138 E6
Newbegin
Beverley HU17 154 A3
Hornsea HU18 134 C4
Newbigg Crowle DN17 94 C8
Westwoodside DN9 105 B2
Newbolt Ave DN17 150 D3
Newbolt Cl LN7 111 A3
Newborn Ave DN15 150 E8
Newborough St YO30 156 A4
Newbridge La YO41 28 A7
Newbridge Rd HU12 73 B6
Newbury Ave
Grimsby DN37 102 C5
York YO24 129 D1
Newbury Gr 2 DN34 102 C2
Newby La DN14 77 F8
Newby Rd DN31 152 C3
Newby Terr YO31 130 C7
Newclose La DN14 149 D6
Newcomen St HU9 141 D1
Newcroft YO8 148 B4
Newdale 3 YO32 13 F5
Newdown Rd DN17 96 B2
Newfield Cl DN3 92 A3
Newfield La
Burstwick HU12 58 F2
South Cave HU15 53 E1
Newfields Ave DN8 79 B1
Newfields Cl DN8 79 B1
Newfields Dr DN8 79 B1
Newgate YO1 156 B2
Newgate Ct YO1 156 B2
Newgate St HU16 139 B6
Newhall Rd 8 DN3 92 A2
Newhay La YO8 49 E1
Newholme Cl HU6 139 F6
Newholme Dr 8 DN8 79 B2
Newington Ave HU4 144 E5
Newington Prim Sch
HU3 145 A4
Newington St HU3 144 F4
Newland Ave
Great Driffield YO25 124 D4
Kingston upon Hull HU5 140 C2
Scunthorpe DN15 150 E6
Newland Ave Sch
HU5 140 C2
Newland Dr DN15 150 D7
Newland Gr 1 HU5 140 C3
Newland Park Ave
HU6 140 B4
Newland Park Cl
YO10 131 A3
Newland Park Dr
YO10 130 F3
Newland Pk HU5 140 A3
Newland Rd DN14 149 C5
Newland Sch for Girls
HU6 140 A4
Newland St Johns C of E Prim Sch HU6 140 D4
Newland View 11 DN9 105 E6
Newland Wlk DN15 150 D7
Newlands 17 DN21 117 C1
Newlands Dr YO26 129 B6
Newlands La Paull HU12 72 D3
Upper Poppleton YO26 24 E8
Newlands Pk 23 DN36 103 D1
Newlands Rd
Bishopthorpe YO23 132 F4
Sunk Island HU12 89 D6
Newlands The HU6 140 C4
Newlyn Cl
Kingston upon Hull HU7 141 C7
4 Kingston upon Hull HU13 144 A2
Newmarket St DN32 152 F4
Newnham Cres 12 DN16 96 D2
Newport Ave YO8 148 B4
Newport Cl 4 HU3 145 D5
Newport Cty Prim Sch
HU15 52 F1
Newport Dr DN15 83 A6
Newport Rd HU15 53 C2
Newport St
Barton-upon-Humber DN18 69 E1
Goole DN14 149 B4
Newsam Cl 4 YO25 22 D1
Newsham Abbey (Site of)* DN39 100 C8
Newsham Dr DN34 152 A3
Newsham Gdns HU19 75 A5
Newsham Hill La YO16 4 C2
Newsham La DN39 100 D8
Newstead Ave DN36 114 B5
Newstead Cres YO16 122 D6
Newstead Rd DN35 103 C2
Newstead St HU5 145 A8
Newthorpe Rd 2 DN6 76 E2
Newton Dr HU17 154 A1
Newton La LN8 120 A5
Newton Marsh La
DN36 114 F6
Newton Pk YO30 12 B7
Newton Rd DN16 151 E2
Newton St 3 HU3 145 B4
Newton Terr YO1 156 B1
Newtondale HU7 140 F7
Newtondale Garth
YO16 122 F7
Newtown Sq HU9 146 E7
Nicholas Ct 7 DN18 84 E8
Nicholas Gdns YO10 130 F3
Nicholas St YO10 130 F3
Nicholson Cl HU17 137 B4
Nicholson La 2 HU11 35 A1
Nicholson Rd
Healing DN41 102 A5
Immingham DN40 86 E4
Nicholson St
Cleethorpes DN35 153 F1
5 Kingston upon Hull HU5 140 E2
Nicholson Way 6 DN9 105 D7
Nicholsons Ct HU16 139 A6
Nicholson's La HU12 74 B3
Nickey Nackey La YO8 48 B8
Nicolgate La 26 DN20 98 C2
Nicolson Dr 16 DN18 84 F8
Nidd Cl YO26 129 B8
Nidd Gr YO24 132 E8
Nidd St DN14 149 D1
Nidderdale HU7 140 F6
Nidderdale Cl 1 YO16 123 A7
Nigel Gr 7 YO24 129 F2
Nightingale Cl
Scunthorpe DN15 96 B7
4 Walkington HU17 55 D8
York YO32 127 E1
Nightingale Dr YO16 122 F5
Nightingale Rd YO16 122 F5
Nine Dikes Rd YO25 9 D8
Ninescores La DN9 104 B4
Ninth Ave
Fixborough Ind Est. DN15 82 A1
York YO31 130 F5
Nith Gr HU8 142 C6
Nithdale Gdns HU5 140 E2
Noah's Wood Submarine Forest* HU19 75 A7
Noddle Hill Way HU7 141 D8
Noel St 2 DN21 117 B1
Nolloth Cres HU17 154 B4
Nooking La DN37 101 D2
Nooking The DN9 105 D3
Nookings Dr DN20 109 A5
Nordale Cl 9 HU8 141 E7
Nordham HU15 53 D3
Norfolk Ave DN15 82 B4
Norfolk Bank La HU15 67 E8
Norfolk La DN35 153 E3
Norfolk St
Beverley HU17 136 D5
Kingston upon Hull HU2 155 A3
York YO23 130 C2
Norland Ave HU4 144 C6
Norlands La YO16 4 A1
Norman Cl
Barton-upon-Humber DN18 84 F8
7 Thorpe Willoughby YO8 48 B1
Norman Cres DN17 150 F4
Norman Dr
3 Hatfield DN7 92 D3
York YO26 129 B6
Norman Rd
Grimsby DN34 152 B3
Hatfield DN7 92 D3
Norman St 5 YO10 131 A3
Normanby Hall* DN15 82 C3
Normanby Hall Ctry Pk* DN15 82 C3
Normanby Rd
Burton upon Stather DN15 82 B4
Nettleton LN7 111 B2
Scunthorpe DN15 151 A8
Normandy Ave HU17 55 E8
Normandy Cl 4 YO8 148 B6
Normandy Rd DN35 153 D1
Normandy Way DN14 149 C3
Normanton Rise HU4 144 C7
Nornabell Dr HU17 136 E7
Nornabell St 1 HU8 146 C8
Norrison Ave HU6 140 C8
Norsefield Ave 1 DN37 113 E7
Norseman Cl 7 YO19 48 F8
Norseway 2 YO41 15 D1
North Axholme Comp Sch
DN17 94 D7
North Back La
2 Bridlington YO16 122 D4
Kilham YO25 9 B3
North Bar Within
HU17 154 A3
North Bar Without
HU17 136 D4
North Bridge St DN32 152 F5
North Burton La YO14 3 B4
North Carr Dales Rd
HU19 74 F4
North Carr La
Saxby All Saints DN20 83 F3
Tickton HU17 44 D3
North Carr Rd
Scotter DN17 106 E5
West Stockwith DN10 116 E5
North Cave C of E Sch
HU15 53 D3
North Cave Rd YO43 53 D4
North Church Side
1 Easington HU12 90 F6
Kingston upon Hull HU1 155 B2
North Cliff Rd DN21 108 C2
North Cliffe Wood Nature Reserve* YO43 53 A7
North Coates Rd
DN36 115 A4
North Comm Rd DN8 78 F2
North Cotes C of E Sch
DN36 115 B3
North Cotes Rd
Hunmanby YO25 2 C5
Wold Newton YO25 1 E5
North Ctry Ct 2 HU9 141 F1
North Cty Prim Sch
DN21 117 A1
North Dr
Kingston upon Hull HU10 143 E6
Swanland HU14 69 B7
North Duffield CP Sch
YO8 50 A8
North Eastern Rd DN8 93 A8
North Elkington La
LN11 121 B1
North End
5 Flamborough YO15 5 A2
Goxhill DN19 86 A8
Seaton Ross YO42 39 D4
South Ferriby DN18 84 A8
North End Cres 13
DN36 114 D4
North End La LN7 110 A2
North End Rd
Halsham HU12 73 F5
Roos HU12 60 A2
1 Tetney DN36 114 D4
North Farm Rd DN17 96 B2
North Ferriby C of E Sch
HU14 69 A5
North Field La
Askham Bryan YO23 24 F3
Upper Poppleton YO26 24 F7
North Frodingham County Prim Sch YO25 33 F8
North Frodingham Rd
YO25 34 B8
North Holme 8 DN36 114 D4
North Ings Rd DN7 92 E5
North Intake La DN9 116 F8
North Kelsey Cty Prim Sch
LN7 110 A4
North Kelsey Rd LN7 110 F4
North La
Huntington YO32 128 D5
Marsh Chapel DN36 115 C2
Sykehouse DN14 78 B4
Wheldrake YO19 37 F7
York YO32 127 F5
York YO24 132 E8
North Leas Ave YO16 122 E7
North Leas Dr YO16 122 E7
North Leys Rd HU19 75 B4
North Lincoln Rd
DN16 151 D6
North Lindsey Coll
DN17 150 E4
North Marine Dr
YO15 123 A4
North Marine Rd 1 YO15 5 B3
North Marsh Rd HU12 91 B3
North Moor 7 YO32 127 F5
North Moor Dr 1 DN10 116 C3
North Moor Gdns
YO32 127 F5
North Moor La
Bottesford DN17 96 B1
Cottingham HU16 139 D8
Messingham DN17 107 B8
North Moor Rd
3 Flamborough YO15 5 B3
Messingham DN17 107 C6
Walkeringham DN10 116 C3
York YO32 127 F5
North Moss La DN41 101 E8
North Ormsby Medieval Village* LN11 121 A3
North Par
Scunthorpe DN16 151 D2
York YO30 156 A3
North Pinfold Way 2
YO16 122 D6
North Pk HU12 58 F2
North Prom
Cleethorpes DN35 153 E3
Withernsea HU19 75 A7
North Quay DN31 153 A7
North Rd Atwick YO25 35 C6
Bewholme YO25 35 A5
Halsham HU12 73 F6
Hatfield HU11 46 C5
Keadby with Althorpe DN17 95 C6
Kingston upon Hull HU4 144 E4
Lund YO25 31 F3
Ulrome YO25 23 A4
Withernsea HU19 74 F7
North Rise 2 HU12 73 A6
North Sea Aquarium* YO15 122 F2
North Sea La DN36 103 D1
North St Aldbrough HU11 47 C1
Barmby on the Marsh DN14 64 A7
Barrow upon Humber DN19 85 D8
Bridlington YO15 122 E2
Caistor LN7 111 B4
Cleethorpes DN35 153 F2
Crowle DN17 94 D8
6 Gainsborough DN21 117 A2
Goole DN14 149 D4
Great Driffield YO25 124 E5
Kingston upon Hull HU10 143 E6
Kingston upon Hull HU2 155 A3
Leven HU17 45 A8
Nafferton YO25 125 E8
Owston Ferry DN9 106 B3
Roxby cum Risby DN15 83 A4
1 Scunthorpe DN15 151 B8
West Butterwick DN17 95 D1
West/East Butterwick DN17 106 D8
York YO1 156 B2
North Thoresby Prim Sch
DN36 114 A1
North Townside Rd
YO25 33 F8
North Turnpike YO25 23 A4
North View HU20 55 B4
North Walls HU1 155 C2
North Warren Rd
DN21 117 A1
North Way DN36 115 B2
Northampton Rd
DN16 151 C5
Northcote Ave YO24 129 E3
Northcroft 5 YO32 13 F5
Northcroft Dr 18 HU8 141 E7
North-Dale Ct 2 DN21 108 B2
Northdale Pk 3 HU14 69 B7
Northern Ave 3 DN20 98 C3
Northferry La DN9 94 C1
Northfield 3 Barlby YO8 49 B5
Rimswell HU19 74 F7
Swanland HU14 69 B7
Northfield Ave
Great Driffield YO25 124 F6
Kingston upon Hull HU13 143 E3
Northfield Cl
Driffield YO25 124 F6
12 Pocklington YO42 28 F4
1 Scunthorpe DN16 151 C2
5 South Cave HU15 53 F1
2 Tetney DN36 114 D4
West Butterwick DN17 95 D1
Womersley DN6 76 C6
Northfield Cotts DN16 96 D1
Northfield Cres YO25 124 E5
Northfield Inf Sch
YO25 124 F6
Northfield La
Amcotts DN17 81 F2
3 Riccall YO19 36 F1
Thornton Curtis DN39 85 D5
Welwick HU12 90 A8
Willoughton DN21 119 A4
Womersley DN6 76 C7
Northfield Rd
Beverley HU17 136 C6
Bubwith YO8 50 E8
Coniston HU11 57 F7
Great Driffield YO25 124 E6
Kingston upon Hull HU3 144 F6
Market Weighton YO43 135 E4
Messingham DN17 107 D8
Pocklington YO42 28 F4
Wetwang YO25 19 A6
Northfield Rise 7 YO42 28 F4
Northfield Sch YO26 129 B5
Northfield Wlk YO25 124 F6
Northfields
Barmby Moor YO42 28 D4
5 Strensall YO32 14 B8
Northgate
Hornsea HU18 134 C5
Hunmanby YO14 2 F8
Kingston upon Hull HU16 139 A7
Kingston upon Hull HU13 143 E2
Thorne/Moorends DN8 79 B2
Walkington HU17 55 B8
Northgate Gr YO43 135 C4
Northgate La YO41 15 A3
Northgate Vale YO43 135 C4
Northlands Ave
1 Earswick YO32 127 F7
2 Winterton DN15 83 A5
Northlands Rd DN15 83 A6
Northlands Rd S DN15 83 A5
Northminster Bsns Pk
YO26 24 F7
Northmoor Rd DN17 80 C1
Northolme DN21 117 B1
Northolme Circ 2
HU13 143 E2
Northolme Cres
Kingston upon Hull HU13 143 E2
Scunthorpe DN15 150 F7
Northolme Dr YO30 126 E1
Northolme Rd HU13 143 E2
Northolt Cl HU8 141 E6
Northorpe Cl HU9 142 C1
Northorpe Rd DN21 107 D1
Northorpe Rise YO16 122 B5
North's La DN37 112 D8
Northside Haxey DN9 105 C2
Laxton DN14 65 F4
Patrington HU12 74 D1
Northside Ct 6 HU12 74 D1
Northside Rd HU19 75 A4
Northstead Cl HU10 138 E1
Northumberland Ave
Hornsea HU18 134 B5
Kingston upon Hull HU2 155 B4
Northumberland Cl
DN34 152 B2
Northway Fulstow LN11 121 E8
Goole DN14 149 B6
Northwood Dr HU13 143 B3
Norton & Kirk Smeat
WF8 76 C3
Norton Comm La DN6 76 F2
Norton Comm Rd DN6 77 A1
Norton Cty Jun & Inf Sch
DN6 76 E2
Norton Gr HU4 144 D4
Norton La LN8 119 F2
Norton Mill La DN6 76 E2
Norton Priory DN6 76 E2
Norton Rd DN16 151 B1
Norton St HU17 154 A2
Norway Dr YO10 133 D8
Norwich Ave 3 DN34 102 D2
Norwich Ct HU17 136 E1

Norwood HU17 ....154 B4
Norwood Ave DN15 ....150 F6
Norwood Cl 3 HU10 ....143 E7
Norwood Dale HU17 ....154 A3
Norwood Far Gr HU17 ..154 B4
Norwood Gr HU17 ....154 B4
Norwood Rd DN7 ....92 C5
Norwood St HU3 ....145 C7
Nostell Rd DN16 ....151 D5
Nostell Way YO16 ....122 D7
Nottingham Rd 6 HU11 ..47 C1
Nova Scotia Way 4 YO19 ....49 A8
Nuffield Cl 6 DN16 ....96 D2
Nun Monkton Prim Sch YO26 ....12 A5
Nunburnholme Ave HU14 ....69 A4
Nunburnholme Hill YO42 ....29 F3
Nunburnholme Pk HU4 ....144 B7
Nunmill St YO23 ....130 C2
Nunnery Hill* YO25 ....21 F6
Nunnery La YO23 ....156 B1
Nunnery Wlk 4 HU15 ....53 F1
Nunnington Cl HU5 ....140 B2
Nuns Rd DN17 ....150 F2
Nunsthorpe Inf Sch DN33 ....102 D2
Nunsthorpe Jun Sch DN33 ....102 D2
Nunthorpe Ave YO23 ..130 B2
Nunthorpe Cl 17 DN7 ....92 D4
Nunthorpe Cres YO23 ....130 B1
Nunthorpe Gr YO23 ....130 B2
Nunthorpe Rd YO23 ....156 A1
Nurseries The HU17 ....136 D7
Nursery Cl
3 Barton-upon-Humber DN18 ....69 F1
Scunthorpe DN17 ....96 C2
Nursery Ct
14 Brough HU15 ....68 C5
Nether Poppleton YO26 ..126 A2
Nursery Dr YO24 ....129 E3
Nursery Gdns
Beverley HU17 ....154 A1
York YO10 ....131 C3
Nursery Gr YO16 ....122 B5
Nursery Rd YO26 ....126 A2
Nursery Wlk HU16 ....139 D6
Nutana Ave HU18 ....134 C7
Nutfields Gr 8 DN7 ....92 C6
Nuttles La HU12 ....58 E2

O

Oak Ave Brough HU15 ....68 C6
Goole DN14 ....149 D1
Grimsby DN32 ....102 F2
Kingston upon Hull HU10 ....138 D1
Scawby DN20 ....108 F8
Withernsea HU19 ....75 A5
Oak Cl Beverley HU17 ....137 A6
Sproatley HU11 ....58 C5
Oak Cres 7 DN8 ....79 A1
Oak Dene DN14 ....149 E6
Oak Dr
Kingston upon Hull HU4 ..144 B7
Newport HU15 ....52 F1
5 Thorpe Willoughby YO8 ..48 B1
Oak Field YO8 ....148 A1
Oak Glade 6 YO31 ....127 F3
Oak Gr
Barrow upon Humber DN19 ....85 C7
9 Hedon HU12 ....72 C7
Oak Hill HU10 ....138 C2
Oak Rd Healing DN41 ....101 F5
Kingston upon Hull HU6 ..140 D5
2 North Duffield YO8 ....50 A7
Scunthorpe DN16 ....151 B3
Thorne/Moorends DN8 ....79 A1
Oak Rise 4 YO26 ....129 C3
Oak Sq 3 HU7 ....56 E7
Oak St 3 YO26 ....129 E5
Oak Tree Ave 14 DN21 ....117 C1
Oak Tree Cl
Beverley HU17 ....136 D6
Strensall YO32 ....14 B7
Oak Tree Ct 7 YO8 ....50 D7
Oak Tree Dr HU17 ....136 D6
Oak Tree Est 10 HU12 ....58 C1
Oak Tree Gr YO32 ....127 D3
Oak Tree La YO32 ....127 C7
Oak Tree Way 10 YO32 ....14 B7
Oak Way DN35 ....103 B1
Oakdale Ave 3 HU10 ....143 E8
Oakdale Cl 6 DN14 ....78 C8
Oakdale Rd YO30 ....126 F2
Oakdene HU16 ....139 B6
Oaken Grove Sch YO32 ....13 F5
Oakfield Cl DN20 ....98 D2
Oakfield Ct 1 HU6 ....139 F4
Oakford Cl DN17 ....150 D4
Oakhill Cres 3 YO32 ....14 A6
Oakington Garth HU7 ..141 C8
Oakland Ave
33 Hatfield DN7 ....92 D4
York YO31 ....131 A7
Oakland Dr YO31 ....131 A7
Oaklands
Camblesforth YO8 ....63 C5
Gilberdyke HU15 ....66 D8
Hornsea HU18 ....134 D2
Oaklands *continued*
Hutton Cranswick YO25 ....32 E6
6 Strensall YO32 ....14 B7
Oaklands Ave 3 DN14 ....65 B7
Oaklands Cres YO8 ....63 C5
Oaklands Dr
Kingston upon Hull HU10 ....138 C1
Kingston upon Hull HU13 ....143 D3
Oaklands Rd DN40 ....87 C2
Oaklands Sch YO24 ....129 C2
Oaklands Small Sch DN14 ....64 E4
Oaklands Sports Ctr YO24 ....129 C2
Oakleigh 9 DN16 ....96 E2
Oakmoor Gr DN8 ....79 B2
Oakmoor Rd DN8 ....79 B2
Oakney Wood Dr YO8 ..148 D1
Oaks La DN10 ....116 C2
Oaktree Dr 4 HU7 ....141 D7
Oakwell Ave YO16 ....123 A6
Oakwell Gr 2 HU8 ....141 B1
Oakwood Cl HU4 ....144 A7
Oakwood Dr DN37 ....102 B3
Oakwood Pk DN14 ....77 F6
Oakwood Rise 1 DN16 ..96 D2
Oatlands Rd YO16 ....123 A6
Oban Ave HU9 ....142 A2
Oban Ct
32 Immingham DN40 ....87 B1
5 Immingham DN40 ....101 B8
Occupation La
North Kelsey LN7 ....110 A4
Swanland HU14 ....69 B8
Ocean Bvd HU9 ....146 B6
Ocean Dr 7 HU15 ....52 F1
Ochrepit Hill YO42 ....17 A2
Octon Rd YO25 ....9 A8
Ogilvy Dr DN17 ....96 C2
Ogle Rd 10 YO15 ....5 B2
Ogleforth YO31 ....156 B3
O'Hanlon Ave DN20 ....98 C2
Old Annandale Rd HU10 ....143 C8
Old Boys Sch La 4 YO8 ..48 B8
Old Bridge Rd HU18 ....134 C2
Old Brumby St DN16 ..151 A4
Old Carpenter's Yd DN7 ....92 B6
Old Chapel La DN37 ....101 F1
Old Clee Jun & Inf Sch DN32 ....153 B2
Old Coppice 14 YO32 ....13 F5
Old Courts Rd 5 DN20 ....98 C2
Old Crosby DN15 ....96 D7
Old Dairy DN19 ....85 D8
Old Dike Lands YO32 ..127 C8
Old Epworth Rd E DN7 ..92 F4
Old Farm Cl HU12 ....73 E3
Old Farm Ct 5 DN37 ....113 D6
Old Farm Way YO8 ....148 B2
Old Field La DN7 ....92 A5
Old Fleet 2 DN37 ....102 B3
Old Fleet Prim Sch HU9 ....142 E2
Old Forge Rd 4 DN10 ....116 C5
Old Forge Way HU11 ....45 D2
Old Green La YO41 ....28 A5
Old Hall La YO41 ....27 C5
Old Haxey Rd DN10 ....116 C6
Old Howe La YO25 ....22 A3
Old Ironside Rd DN16 ..151 D7
Old La Blacktoft DN14 ....66 C4
Hirst Courtney YO8 ....62 F3
Long Marston YO26 ....24 A6
Reedness DN14 ....80 E7
Sigglesthorne HU11 ....45 F8
Old Lea YO43 ....40 B1
Old Leys La DN21 ....119 C3
Old Main Rd
Barnetby Le Beck DN37 ..113 B6
Irby DN37 ....112 D7
Old Manor Dr DN20 ....108 E8
Old Manor Lawns HU17 ....154 B2
Old Market Pl 6 DN31 ..152 D3
Old Mill Cl YO43 ....135 F3
Old Mill La
7 Broughton DN20 ....97 E3
Whitton DN15 ....67 E3
Wrawby DN20 ....98 D4
Old Moor La YO24 ....132 E7
Old Orch YO32 ....127 D8
Old Orch The
Fulford YO10 ....133 E7
Shipton YO30 ....12 F5
Old Plumtree La 2 DN36 ....114 B1
Old Pond Pl 16 HU14 ....69 A4
Old Post Office La
Barnetby le Wold DN38 ....99 B4
5 South Ferriby DN18 ....84 A7
Old Rd Healing DN37 ....102 B5
Holme-on-Spalding-Moor YO43 ....40 B1
Leconfield HU17 ....43 C6
Ottringham HU12 ....73 E3
Old Rectory Gdns DN16 ....151 A1
Old Row The DN15 ....82 A5
Old Sch The
East Garton HU11 ....59 F6
Kirk Bramwith DN7 ....92 A7
Roxby cum Risby DN15 ....82 F4
Old School Dr DN20 ....108 F5
Old School La
Barlby with Osgodby YO8 ..49 B5
North Kelsey LN7 ....110 A4
20 Scunthorpe DN16 ....96 D2
Old School Yd 8 DN21 ..108 B1
Old Showfields 8 DN21 .117 B1
Old Sunderlandwick La YO25 ....20 D1
Old Tatham YO43 ....40 B1
Old Thorne Rd DN7 ....92 E4
Old Trent Rd DN10 ....116 F1
Old Trough La HU15 ....52 C2
Old Vicarage La 5 LS25 ..61 A8
Old Vicarage Pk DN20 ..108 E8
Old Village Rd HU20 ....55 A4
Old Village St DN15 ....95 E6
Old Village The YO32 ....127 F5
Old Warp La DN18 ....84 A7
Old Waste HU17 ....154 A3
Oldbeck Rd HU17 ....137 C4
Oldfield Ave HU6 ....140 C6
Oldfield Cl
Barnby Dun DN3 ....92 A4
Stainforth DN7 ....92 B6
Oldfield Cres DN7 ....92 C6
Oldfield La DN7 ....92 B6
Oldfield Rd 11 DN8 ....93 B7
Oldlane Gate DN14 ....80 D4
Oldstead Ave HU6 ....139 F5
Olinda Rd 2 YO15 ....122 E2
Oliver Ct DN31 ....152 D4
Oliver St DN35 ....153 D4
Oliver's Cl 18 YO14 ....2 F8
Olivers La YO16 ....122 E3
Olivier Ct HU4 ....144 E3
Olympia Cres YO8 ....148 E6
Ombler Cl 11 HU12 ....73 C4
Omega Bvd DN8 ....92 F8
Omega Cl YO16 ....123 A5
Omega Rd YO16 ....122 F5
On Hill HU14 ....69 B6
Ontario Rd DN17 ....96 B2
Onyx Gr 2 HU3 ....145 A4
Oole Rd DN35 ....153 F2
Or The HU9 ....142 B4
Orb La DN15 ....96 D8
Orby Gr 6 DN33 ....102 D2
Orch The Leven HU17 ....45 A7
14 New Waltham DN36 ....114 A7
Orchard Ave 8 DN21 ....107 C3
Orchard Cl
2 Barrow upon Humber DN19 ....85 C7
18 Barton-upon-Humber DN18 ....84 F8
Blyton DN21 ....117 F5
Bridlington YO16 ....122 E7
3 Burringham DN17 ....95 D4
Burton upon Stather DN15 ....82 B5
Great Driffield YO25 ....124 D5
Hatfield DN7 ....92 C3
Kingston upon Hull HU10 ....143 F7
2 Kirton in Lindsey DN21 ..108 B1
Messingham DN17 ....107 D7
6 Monk Fryston LS25 ....61 A8
Morton DN21 ....117 A3
9 Norton DN6 ....76 E2
10 Pocklington YO42 ....28 F4
Roos HU12 ....74 A8
2 Scunthorpe DN16 ....151 B2
Selby YO8 ....148 A4
York YO24 ....129 E1
Orchard Cotts 4 YO19 ....26 F7
Orchard Croft
3 Epworth DN9 ....105 D7
10 Grimsby DN33 ....113 E8
Kingston upon Hull HU16 ....139 B8
Orchard Ct
3 Market Weighton YO43 .135 E4
10 Waltham DN37 ....113 D6
Orchard Dr
Burton upon Stather DN15 ....82 B5
Goole DN14 ....65 C4
Gunness DN15 ....95 E6
Hatfield DN7 ....92 C3
Kingston upon Hull HU13 ....143 E1
Middleton-on-the-Wolds YO25 ....31 C4
1 Winteringham DN15 ....68 B1
Orchard Garth HU17 ....136 D6
Orchard Gdns
4 Pocklington YO42 ....28 F4
York YO31 ....127 E2
Orchard Gr Hatfield DN7 ..92 D5
Misterton DN10 ....116 D4
Orchard La
Great Driffield YO25 ....124 E5
Hutton Cranswick YO25 ....32 E8
Thorne/Moorends DN8 ....79 B2
Orchard Paddock
34 Haxby YO32 ....13 E5
3 Haxby YO32 ....127 D8
Orchard Park Rd HU6 ..139 D8
Orchard Pk YO42 ....39 B6
Orchard Rd
Kingston upon Hull HU4 ..144 B5
Selby YO8 ....148 A4
Skidby HU16 ....138 A8
Upper Poppleton YO26 ....126 A1
Orchard St DN8 ....93 A8
Orchard View 3 YO30 ....126 B5
Orchard Way
1 Gilberdyke HU15 ....66 D7
Orchard Way *continued*
Hensall DN14 ....62 C2
Howden DN14 ....65 A6
9 Pocklington YO42 ....28 F4
Selby YO8 ....148 A4
Skirlaugh HU11 ....45 D2
1 Strensall YO32 ....14 B7
Thorpe Willoughby YO8 ....48 B2
York YO24 ....129 E1
Orchards The YO25 ....32 E8
Orchid Rise DN15 ....150 F6
Ordnance La YO10 ....130 D1
Ore Blending Rd DN16 ..97 A4
Oribi Cl HU4 ....144 C2
Oriel Cl 6 HU17 ....55 D8
Oriel Gr
Kingston upon Hull HU9 ..142 A1
York YO30 ....130 A8
Oriole Rd DN17 ....150 E2
Orion Cl 8 HU3 ....145 B5
Orion Way DN34 ....102 B2
Orkney Cl 7 HU8 ....141 E7
Orkney Pl
11 Immingham DN40 ....87 C1
3 Immingham DN40 ....101 C8
Ormerod Cres 7 HU5 ....139 D2
Ormerod Rd HU5 ....139 D2
Ormonde Ave HU6 ....140 D4
Ormsby Cl 9 DN35 ....103 B2
Ormsby Rd DN17 ....150 E1
Orniscourt HU6 ....139 F7
Orrin Cl YO24 ....132 C7
Orwell St DN31 ....152 F5
Osbaldwick La YO10 ....131 B4
Osbaldwick Link Rd YO19 ....131 D4
Osbaldwick Prim Sch YO10 ....131 C4
Osbaldwick Village YO10 ....131 C4
Osborne Dr DN36 ....114 A5
Osborne Rd DN41 ....101 E8
Osborne St
Cleethorpes DN35 ....153 F2
Grimsby DN31 ....152 D3
Kingston upon Hull HU1 ..155 A2
Osbourne Dr
Keyingham HU12 ....73 D4
4 York YO30 ....126 E3
Oshawa Dell YO42 ....29 A2
Oslear Cres DN35 ....153 E1
Oslo Rd HU7 ....140 F6
Osmington Gdns 10 YO32 .14 A7
Osprey Cl
Kingston upon Hull HU6 ..140 B8
4 York YO24 ....132 B8
Ostler's Cl YO23 ....132 C3
Ostler's La DN18 ....84 A5
Ostman Rd YO26 ....129 C5
Oswald Rd DN15 ....151 A7
Otley Cl HU9 ....142 C2
Ottawa Cl 6 HU16 ....138 F5
Ottawa Rd 6 DN17 ....96 C2
Otterburn St 6 HU3 ....145 A5
Otterwood Bank 6 YO24 ....129 B1
Otterwood La YO24 ....129 B1
Otterwood Paddock YO41 ....15 C2
Ottringham Rd HU12 ....73 D4
Oubrough La HU11 ....57 F8
Oundle Cl 5 DN16 ....96 E2
Our Ladys RC Prim Sch YO24 ....129 E1
Ouse Acres YO26 ....129 D6
Ouse Bank YO8 ....148 E5
Ouse Carr La DN14 ....65 A5
Ouseburn Ave YO26 ....129 C6
Ousecliffe Gdns YO30 ....130 A6
Ousegate YO8 ....148 D5
Out Gates Foston YO25 ....22 B3
Harpham YO25 ....21 E6
Out Holme La DN36 ....114 E3
Out Newton Rd
Holmpton HU19 ....75 C1
Skeffling HU12 ....90 D6
Outer Trinities HU17 ....154 B2
Outgaits Cl 4 YO14 ....2 F8
Outgaits La YO14 ....3 A8
Outgang La YO19 ....131 D6
Outgang The
Brantingham HU15 ....68 B7
South Cliffe YO43 ....53 B6
Outgate DN17 ....94 E6
Outlands Rd HU16 ....139 D5
Outram Cl HU2 ....155 A4
Outstray Rd HU12 ....89 C7
Oval The Brough HU15 ....68 C6
Grimsby DN33 ....102 E1
Hatfield DN7 ....92 C5
Kellingley DN14 ....61 C3
Kingston upon Hull HU8 ..141 C2
Kingston upon Hull HU10 ....143 E8
Pocklington YO42 ....29 A4
23 Scunthorpe DN17 ....96 C2
Overdale Cl YO24 ....132 D8
Overland Rd HU16 ....139 C5
Overstrand Dr HU7 ....141 D6
Overton Ave HU10 ....143 E8
Overton Ct 6 DN18 ....69 F1
Overton Rd YO30 ....12 F3
Ovington Terr YO23 ....130 B2
Owen Ave HU13 ....144 A1
Owlwood Ct 7 YO19 ....26 E7
Owlwood La 6 YO19 ....26 E7
Owmby Hill DN38 ....110 D8
Owmby La LN7 ....110 C5
Owmby Mount
Owmby Rd DN38
Owmby Wold La
Owst Rd HU12 ..
Owsthorpe La DN
Owston Ave 2 YO1
Owston Ferry Rd
Owston Rd
1 Hunmanby YO14 .
West Stockwith DN10
Owthorne Cl YO16 ..
Owthorne Grange HU19 ....
Owthorne Wlk HU19 .
Ox Calder Cl 16 YO19 .
Ox Carr La YO32 ....
Ox Cl YO41 ....
Ox Pasture La DN17 ...
Oxcombe Cl DN37 ....
Oxen La YO8 ....
Oxenhope Rd HU6 ....
Oxford Cl 6 HU17 1
Oxford Rd DN14 1
Oxford St
Bridlington YO16 12
Cleethorpes DN35 15
Grimsby DN32 15
Kingston upon Hull HU2 ..155
Scunthorpe DN16 151
5 York YO24 130
Oxmardyke La HU15 66
Oxmarsh La DN19 ....70 E

P

Packman La HU10 ....143 B8
Paddock Cl YO23 ....132 A2
Paddock Ct
Bridlington YO16 ....122 E7
Great Driffield YO25 ....124 F5
33 Immingham DN40 ....87 B1
Paddock La
Blyton DN21 ....117 F5
West Butterwick DN17 ....95 C1
Paddock La E DN21 ....117 F5
Paddock Rise 8 DN19 ..85 C8
Paddock The
14 Airmyn DN14 ....64 E4
Beverley HU17 ....136 D6
1 Buckton/Bempton YO15 ..4 D3
3 Burton upon Stather DN15 ....82 B4
13 Gilberdyke HU15 ....66 D8
Kingston upon Hull HU16 ....139 C6
Kingston upon Hull HU4 ..144 B5
1 North Ferriby HU14 ....69 A5
8 Selby YO8 ....148 C6
2 Swanland HU14 ....69 C7
Wilberfoss YO41 ....27 E5
York YO26 ....129 C6
Paddock Way YO26 ..129 C6
Paddocks The
Barnoldby le Beck DN37 ..113 B6
Beckingham DN10 ....116 D1
6 Crowle DN17 ....94 D7
Great Driffield YO25 ....124 D3
Hutton Cranswick YO25 ....32 E7
Kingston upon Hull HU10 ....143 B7
Middleton YO25 ....31 C4
Pademoor Terr DN17 ....81 A2
Padstow Cl 7 HU7 ....56 F5
Pagehall Cl DN33 ....102 E1
Paghill Est HU12 ....72 A5
Pagnell Ave YO8 ....148 E4
Paignton Ct DN33 ....113 E7
Painsthorpe La YO41 ....17 B5
Paisley Prim Sch HU3 ..145 A6
Paisley St HU3 ....145 A7
Palace Ave YO15 ....122 E2
Palanza Terr 8 YO15 ....122 E2
Pale La YO8 ....61 F7
Palmcourt HU6 ....139 F7
Palmer Ave HU10 ....143 D8
Palmer Gr YO8 ....148 A3
Palmer La
Barrow upon Humber DN19 ....85 D8
York YO1 ....156 C2
Palmes Cl YO19 ....36 E8
Pam Cl 19 DN40 ....87 C1
Pamela Rd DN40 ....87 C1
Panama Dr HU11 ....45 D2
Panman La YO19 ....26 F8
Paper Mill Rd DN14 ....79 B8
Parade Ct YO31 ....130 F6
Parade The HU5 ....140 D1
Paradise Cotts YO17 ....17 F8
Paradise Pl 10 Brigg DN20 .98 B2
3 Goole DN14 ....149 D4
Paragon Sq HU1 ....155 A2
Paragon St
Kingston upon Hull HU1 ..155 A2
York YO10 ....156 C1
Parish Church Prim Sch The DN21 ....117 B1
Park Ave Barlow YO8 ....63 C7
Barton-upon-Humber DN18 ....84 E8
Beverley HU17 ....154 A4
1 Brandesburton YO25 ....34 B2
Bridlington YO15 ....122 F3
Crowle DN17 ....94 D7

k Ave *continued*
ole DN14 149 B5
eat Driffield YO25 124 E6
imsby DN32 152 D1
ngston upon Hull
U16 139 A7
ingston upon Hull HU5 140 A1
ingston upon Hull
HU13 143 E3
New Earswick YO32 127 D5
Scunthorpe DN17 96 C2
Snaith DN14 78 D8
Withernsea HU19 75 A6
Park Ave W HU5 140 A1
ark Cl 6 Airmyn DN14 64 E4
Great Driffield YO25 124 E5
Immingham DN40 87 C1
Melbourne YO42 39 A7
Skelton YO30 126 B4
Westwoodside DN9 105 A2
Park Cres
11 Thorne/Moorends DN8 93 A7
York YO31 156 C4
Park Dr Campsall DN6 76 E1
Grimsby DN32 152 E1
4 Westwoodside DN9 105 A2
Park Farm Rd DN15 96 C8
Park Gate YO32 14 B8
Park Gdns 5 DN14 78 C8
Park Gr
Kingston upon Hull HU5 140 C1
Selby YO8 148 B3
York YO31 156 C4
Park Grove Sch YO31 156 C4
Park Hill DN21 108 B1
Park La Balne DN14 77 C5
Barlow YO8 63 C7
Bishop Wilton YO42 16 F1
Burn YO8 62 D7
Humberston DN35 103 C1
Kingston upon Hull
HU16 139 A7
Kingston upon Hull HU5 140 D1
Luttons YO17 7 C8
Redbourne DN21 108 F3
Rowley HU17 55 B6
Saxby All Saints DN20 84 A3
Scawby DN20 108 F8
Snaith & Cowick DN14 78 C6
Tickton HU17 44 D2
Westwoodside DN9 105 A2
Wilberfoss YO41 27 E5
Womersley DN6 76 D6
York YO24 129 F3
Park La E HU4 144 C6
Park La W HU4 144 C5
Park Lane Cl
Bishop Wilton YO42 16 F1
Hatfield DN7 92 C2
Park Lane Rd DN7 92 C2
Park Rd Airmyn DN14 64 E4
Barlow YO8 63 C7
Brough HU15 68 E5
Dalton Holme HU17 42 C8
Kingston upon Hull HU3 140 D1
Sproatley HU11 58 C5
Thorne/Moorends DN8 79 B2
Park Rise 17 YO14 2 F8
Park Rose Pottery & L Park*
YO15 10 F3
Park Row
Hornsea HU18 134 D4
Kingston upon Hull HU3 145 D7
Selby YO8 148 D5
Sproatley HU11 58 C5
Park St
Cleethorpes DN35 153 B4
Hotham YO43 53 D5
Kingston upon Hull HU3 145 D6
Messingham DN17 107 D7
Selby YO8 148 D5
Swinefleet DN14 80 D8
Winterton DN15 83 B5
York YO24 156 A1
Park View
Barton-upon-Humber
DN18 84 F8
2 Bridlington YO16 122 F4
Cleethorpes DN35 153 C3
Crowle DN17 94 D6
Kingston upon Hull HU4 144 E4
Messingham DN17 107 D7
10 Thorne/Moorends DN8 93 A7
Park View Cl DN19 85 C7
Park View Terr DN17 106 C8
Park Wlk HU4 144 B5
Parkdale 15 DN18 84 E8
Parker Ave YO26 129 B2
Parker Rd DN36 114 D8
Parker St
8 Cleethorpes DN35 103 C2
Cleethorpes DN35 153 F1
Parker's La DN16 151 C2
Parkfield Ave HU14 69 A4
Parkfield Dr
Bridlington YO16 122 B5
Kingston upon Hull HU3 144 F6
Parkhill Cres DN3 92 A4
Parkhill Rd DN3 92 A4
Parkhill Rise DN15 83 B5
Parkhurst Cl 4 HU8 142 C6
Parkin Ave YO8 148 E4
Parkin Rd DN17 96 C2
Parkinson Ave DN15 151 A7
Parkland Way YO32 127 D8
Parklands Beeford YO25 34 C8
3 West/East Butterwick
DN17 106 D8
Parklands Cres 10 HU14 69 A5
Parklands Dr 9 HU14 69 A5
Parklands The 2 HU15 54 A2
Parks Cl 8 DN39 86 A1
Parks Rd DN7 92 C4
Parkside Cl
Kingston upon Hull
HU16 138 F6
Kingston upon Hull HU5 140 B1
York YO24 129 E3
Parkside Prim Sch
DN14 149 B6
Parkstone Gr 8 DN7 92 D4
Parkstone Prim Sch
HU6 140 D7
Parkstone Rd HU6 140 C7
Parkway The
Kingston upon Hull
HU16 139 A5
Kingston upon Hull
HU10 143 E8
9 Snaith DN14 78 C8
Parkways 12 Hatfield DN7 92 D4
Selby YO8 148 B3
Parkwood Jun & Inf Sch
DN17 150 C4
Parkwood Rise DN3 92 A3
Parliament St
8 Brough HU15 68 D6
Goole DN14 149 C4
Kingston upon Hull HU1 155 B2
York YO1 156 B2
Parris Pl DN35 153 D3
Parsonage Cl YO25 125 E7
Parsons Cl 10 DN14 64 E4
Parson's La DN14 65 A7
Parsons La YO26 12 E1
Parson's Wlk 11 DN14 64 E4
Parthian Rd HU9 142 C3
Partridge Cl
Caistor LN7 111 B4
Scunthorpe DN17 150 E2
Partridge Dr LN7 111 F2
Parva Rd HU18 134 D4
Pashley Rd Thorne DN8 93 B8
20 Thorne/Moorends DN8 93 B7
Pasture Ave
5 Burringham DN17 95 D4
Goole DN14 149 D5
Pasture Cl Kilham YO25 9 B3
2 Leconfield HU17 43 D6
Market Weighton YO43 135 E4
Skelton YO30 126 B5
2 Strensall YO32 14 B6
Wistow YO8 48 D6
Pasture Farm Cl YO10 133 D6
Pasture Hill YO17 16 E8
Pasture La
Amcotts DN17 81 D1
Beverley HU17 136 D4
Ellerton YO42 38 C1
Garthorpe & Fockerby
DN17 81 D6
Heworth YO31 131 B8
Sproatley HU11 58 D6
Pasture Prim Sch
DN14 149 C5
Pasture Rd
Barton-upon-Humber
DN18 69 F1
Goole DN14 149 C4
Hornsea HU18 134 D4
Pasture Rd N DN18 69 F1
Pasture Rd S DN18 69 F1
Pasture Rise YO16 122 B5
Pasture St DN32 152 E3
Pasture Terr HU17 136 D4
Pasture Way YO8 48 D6
Pastures Ct DN17 107 D7
Pastures La HU12 60 B4
Pastures The
Carlton DN14 63 C3
Hutton Cranswick YO25 32 F7
4 York YO24 132 E8
Pately Pl 1 YO26 129 D4
Patrick Pool YO1 156 B2
Patrick St DN32 152 E1
Patricks Cl LN7 110 A4
Patrington C of E Sch
HU12 74 D1
Patrington Garth HU7 141 C8
Patrington Rd
Holmpton HU19 75 C2
Ottringham HU12 73 F3
Patterdale Dr YO30 126 E1
Patterdale Rd HU5 144 E8
Paul Cres 5 DN36 114 C8
Paul La DN15 83 D1
Paull Lands Rd HU12 72 D5
Paull Prim Sch HU12 72 A5
Paull Rd HU12 72 B6
Pavement YO1 156 B2
Paver La YO1 156 C2
Pavilion Cl HU8 141 B2
Pavilion Gdns DN17 150 F6
Paxdale HU7 140 E8
Payton Cl 17 YO42 29 A4
Peace Haven 3 DN37 113 D7
Peace Wlk 6 HU12 58 D1
Peacehaven Cl 2 HU7 141 B7
Peach Tree Ct 5 HU3 145 D5
Peacock St DN17 150 F1
Peaks Ave DN36 114 A8
Peaks La Grimsby DN32 152 F1
New Waltham DN36 114 A8
Peaks Parkway DN32 152 E2
Pear Tree Ave
Long Drax YO8 63 F7
8 Poppleton YO26 12 F1
Pear Tree Cl
Kingston upon Hull HU8 141 D4
11 Waltham DN37 113 D6
York YO32 127 F4
Pear Tree La
Covenham St Bartholomew
LN11 121 E6
Kirk Bramwith DN7 92 A8
Utterby DN36 121 B5
Pearson Ave HU5 140 D1
Pearson Park Prim Sch
HU3 145 D8
Pearson Rd DN35 103 C2
Pearson St HU2 155 A3
Peartree Cl YO1 156 C3
Peartree Pk 19 DN14 65 A7
Pease St HU3 155 A2
Peaseholme HU13 143 C1
Peasholme Gn YO1 156 C2
Peat Carr Bank DN9 104 C3
Peckham Cl HU8 141 E5
Peckitt St YO1 156 B1
Peel Castle Rd 8 DN8 93 B7
Peel Cl YO10 131 A1
Peel Hill Rd 5 DN8 93 B7
Peel Pl HU17 136 D4
Peel St
Kingston upon Hull HU3 145 D8
York YO1 156 C1
Pefham La YO17 17 F4
Pegasus Rd DN20 99 A8
Pelham Ave 8 DN33 102 E1
Pelham Cl
5 Barton-upon-Humber
DN18 84 E8
5 Beverley HU17 55 F8
Pelham Cres 15 DN41 101 A4
Pelham Dr 1 HU9 146 C7
Pelham Pl
9 Grimsby DN33 102 E1
15 Strensall YO32 14 A7
Pelham Rd
Cleethorpes DN35 153 D3
Grimsby DN34 152 C2
1 Holton le Clay DN36 114 A5
Immingham DN40 87 C1
Pelham Sq DN35 153 E3
Pelham View DN20 108 F5
Pelham's Pillar*
DN37 111 C6
Pem La 7 YO42 29 A4
Pemberton Dr 3 DN36 113 F7
Pemberton St 1 HU8 146 B7
Pembroke Ave 13 DN16 96 D2
Pembroke Gr HU9 142 A1
Pembroke Rd DN34 152 A1
Pembroke St YO30 130 B7
Pembroke Terr YO15 122 E1
Pendeen Cl 7 DN21 117 C1
Pendeen Gr HU8 141 B3
Pendle Cl 18 HU7 57 A6
Pendreth Pl DN35 153 D3
Pendrill St HU3 140 E1
Penistone Ct 2 HU9 146 D7
Penley's Gr St YO31 156 C4
Pennine Cl
Immingham DN40 87 B2
York YO32 127 F4
Pennine Rd DN8 93 A7
Pennine Way HU7 57 A6
Pennington St HU8 146 B7
Pennyman Rd HU17 154 C4
Penrose Cl 9 HU7 56 F5
Penshurst Ave HU13 143 F3
Penshurst Rd DN35 103 B2
Pentland Ave DN14 149 D5
Pentland Cl HU8 141 F7
Pentland Dr YO32 127 E3
Penwith Dr HU10 143 F7
Penyghent Ave YO31 131 A5
Peploe Cres 6 DN19 70 E2
Peploe La DN19 70 E2
Peppercorn Cl 6 YO26 129 E4
Peppercorn Wlk
Grimsby DN32 152 E3
11 Holton le Clay DN36 114 A5
Peppercorns The 2
HU15 66 D8
Peppermint Way YO8 148 A5
Peppin La LN11 121 D2
Peppleton Cl HU8 141 C4
Percival St DN15 151 A8
Percy Cl HU17 43 C6
Percy Dr 4 DN14 64 E4
Percy Rd
14 Hunmanby YO14 3 A8
Pocklington YO42 29 A4
Percy St Goole DN14 149 C1
Kingston upon Hull HU2 155 A3
Scunthorpe DN16 151 B6
York YO31 156 B3
Percy's La YO1 156 C2
Peregrine Cl HU4 144 D2
Perivale Cl HU8 142 A5
Perkins Cl DN37 102 C4
Perran Cl HU7 141 B7
Perry St HU3 145 A6
Pershore Ave DN34 102 B2
Perth St HU5 144 F8
Perth Way 3 DN40 101 B8
Petchell Way DN32 152 E4
Peter Hill Dr YO30 130 A8
Peter La YO1 156 B2
Peterborough Rd
DN16 151 B3
Petercroft Cl 5 YO19 26 F7
Petercroft La YO19 26 F7
Peterhouse Rd DN34 152 A1
Petersfield Cl HU7 141 B6
Petersham Cl 1 HU8 142 A5
Petersway YO30 156 A4
Petre Ave YO8 148 E3
Petuaria Cl HU15 68 B6
Pevensey Cl 1 HU7 141 B7
Peveril Ave DN17 150 F4
Pheasant Cl DN17 150 E2
Pheasant Ct 1 LN7 111 B4
Pheasant Dr 5 YO24 132 B8
Phelps Pl DN32 153 C1
Phelps St DN35 153 B5
Philadelphia Terr 2
YO23 130 B2
Philip Ave
Cleethorpes DN35 103 B2
5 Waltham DN37 113 E7
Philip Gr DN35 103 B2
Philips Cres DN15 150 F7
Phillips La 4 DN37 101 F1
Phoenix Cl HU8 141 F4
Phoenix House Sch
DN32 153 B4
Phoenix Parkway DN15 96 B7
Phoenix St Goole DN14 149 D4
Grimsby DN32 152 E3
Phyllis Ave DN34 152 B3
Piccadilly
8 New Waltham DN36 114 A7
York YO1 156 C2
Pick Haven Garth DN14 61 F3
Pickering Ave HU18 134 D2
Pickering Gr 9 DN8 93 A7
Pickering Pk YO25 31 C4
Pickering Rd HU4 144 C3
Pickerings The 17 HU14 69 A4
Picksley Cres DN36 114 A5
Pidgeon Cote La 3
DN19 86 A8
Pier Rd HU19 75 A6
Pier St HU1 155 B1
Piggy La 4 HU19 75 A6
Pighill La HU17 136 D7
Pighill Nook Rd LS25 61 C7
Pike Hills Mount
YO23 132 A3
Pilgrim Ave DN40 87 C1
Pilgrim St YO31 156 B4
Pilgrim's Cl 5 DN40 86 E3
Pilgrims Way DN40 87 B1
Pilham La DN21 117 E4
Pilmar La HU12 60 B1
Pilots Way HU9 155 C1
Pimpernel Way 15 DN16 96 E2
Pinchbeck Ave DN16 151 C6
Pincheon Gn La DN14 78 D4
Pine Cl DN37 102 B5
Pine Ct 8 DN35 103 B1
Pine Hall Rd DN3 92 A3
Pine Mdws HU10 143 B8
Pine Tree Cl YO8 48 B2
Pine Tree La 1 LS25 61 A7
Pine Wlk 4 Brough HU15 68 C6
Healing DN41 102 A5
Pinefield Ave 4 DN3 92 A3
Pinefield Rd DN3 92 A3
Pinelands 4 YO32 127 D7
Pinelands Way YO10 131 C3
Pinetree Ave 5 DN21 107 C3
Pinetree Cl 4 DN20 97 E4
Pinewood Cl 5 YO42 29 A3
Pinewood Cres DN33 102 C2
Pinewood Ct 4 YO42 29 A3
Pinewood Dr YO8 63 D4
Pinewood Gr
2 Kingston upon Hull
HU4 144 C7
6 York YO31 127 E2
Pinewood Hill 4 YO10 131 C3
Pinewood Rd 3 YO42 29 A3
Pinfold 10 Epworth DN9 105 E6
South Cave HU15 53 F1
Pinfold Cl
4 Bridlington YO16 122 D6
5 Riccall YO19 37 A1
Pinfold Ct
3 Bridlington YO16 122 D6
4 Preston HU12 58 C1
4 York YO30 130 A7
Pinfold Gdns
Bridlington YO16 122 D6
14 Holton le Clay DN36 114 B5
Pinfold Gr YO16 122 C6
Pinfold Hill YO8 48 D6
Pinfold La Asselby DN14 64 F6
Bempton YO16 4 B1
Bridlington YO16 122 C7
Burstwick HU12 73 A6
Fishlake DN7 92 D8
10 Grimsby DN33 102 E1
Holton le Clay DN36 114 A5
Kirk Smeaton WF8 76 B3
Moss DN6 77 D1
Norton DN6 76 E2
Pollington DN14 77 F6
Roos HU12 60 A1
Stallingborough DN41 101 D6
25 Thorne/Moorends DN8 93 A8
Pinfold Mdws YO16 122 C6
Pinfold Mews HU17 154 B3
Pinfold St
Bridlington YO16 122 D5
Eastrington DN14 51 F1
Pinfold St *continued*
Howden DN14 65 A6
Pinfold View DN14 77 F6
Pinfold Way S 2 YO16 122 D5
Pingley La DN20 98 C1
Pingley Mdw DN20 98 C1
Pinkney's La YO25 124 D4
Pinney's Ct 7 DN41 101 F5
Piper Rd YO25 32 E8
Piper's La HU11 46 C2
Pippin Ct 11 DN15 96 B7
Pippin Dr 16 DN16 96 D1
Pit La HU12 73 A4
Pitbalk Hill YO43 53 E4
Pitman Ave DN18 84 E8
Pitmoor La 5 DN39 86 A1
Pitsfold Cl 11 HU7 57 A5
Pitt St HU3 144 F7
Plains La DN8 93 F3
Plane St HU3 145 A5
Plantain Cl 14 DN16 96 E2
Plantation Cl HU17 137 B4
Plantation Dr
Barlby with Osgodby YO8 49 B5
1 South Cave HU15 53 F1
Welton HU14 68 F5
York YO26 129 C6
Plantation Gr YO26 129 C6
Plantation Rd 22 DN8 93 A8
Plantation View YO16 123 A8
Plantation Way 23 YO32 13 E5
Plaxton Bridge Rd
HU17 56 C7
Pleasure Island Theme Pk*
DN35 103 E1
Plimsoll Way HU9 146 B6
Plough Garth The DN14 61 F3
Plough Hill 12 LN7 111 B4
Ploughlands 1 YO32 127 C7
Ploughman's Cl YO23 132 C3
Ploughmans' La YO32 127 C7
Plover Dr 9 HU15 68 C6
Plover Sq 2 LN7 111 B4
Plowden Rd HU3 144 F5
Plum Tree Dr DN36 115 C2
Plum Tree Rd HU11 58 D5
Plum Tree Way DN16 151 A5
Plum Tree Wlk HU15 54 A2
Plumer Ave YO31 131 A5
Plumtree Hill Rd DN7 92 C7
Plumtree La 1 DN36 114 B1
Plumtree Rd HU12 72 E4
Plym Gr HU8 142 C6
Plymouth Cl 8 DN15 83 A5
Plymouth Rd DN17 150 D4
Poacher's Croft 3 DN9 94 E1
Pochard Cl 3 HU15 52 F1
Pocklington C of E Infants
Sch YO42 29 A4
Pocklington Ind Est
YO42 28 F3
Pocklington La
Bishop Wilton YO42 16 F2
Huggate YO42 18 A1
Pocklington Sch YO42 28 F3
Pockthorpe La YO25 8 F2
Poffinder Wood Rd
DN7 92 E7
Poles Bank DN9 104 E6
Pollard Cl YO32 127 E3
Pollington Balne C of E Sch
DN14 77 F6
Polton Cl DN7 92 D7
Polton Toft DN7 92 D7
Pomona Way YO25 124 D3
Pond Side DN39 85 E3
Pond St 3 YO8 148 D6
Ponds Way 6 DN18 69 E1
Pontefract Rd DN14 78 A8
Pool Ct 7 DN14 149 C4
Pool Dr DN17 96 C2
Poolbank La HU15 68 E5
Poorhouse La HU9 142 C1
Poplar Cl
Burstwick HU12 73 A6
Kingston upon Hull HU4 144 A5
Skirlaugh HU11 45 E2
Poplar Ct HU7 141 C6
Poplar Dr
Beverley HU17 136 F6
Bridlington YO16 123 A6
Brigg DN20 98 C3
3 Broughton DN20 97 D3
Goole DN14 65 C3
21 Humberston DN36 103 D1
Poplar Gdns Drax YO8 63 F5
Scunthorpe DN16 151 B3
Poplar Gr
Cleethorpes DN35 153 E3
10 Hedon HU12 72 C7
1 Scotter DN21 107 C3
York YO32 127 E3
Poplar La DN21 118 A2
Poplar Rd
Cleethorpes DN35 153 E3
Hatfield DN7 92 C4
Healing DN41 101 F5
Poplar St YO26 129 E5
Poplars The
15 Brandesburton YO25 34 B2
11 Brayton YO8 48 D1
Knottingley WF11 61 A1
5 Leconfield HU17 43 D6
Poplars Way HU17 136 D1
Popple St HU9 146 B6
Poppleton Hall Gdn
YO26 126 A3
Poppleton Rd YO26 129 E4

Poppleton Road Prim Sch YO26 129 E5
Poppleton Sta YO26 24 F8
Popplewell Cl DN9 94 E2
Popplewell Terr 14 DN9 105 E6
Poppy Cl
2 Scunthorpe DN15 96 B7
Selby YO8 148 C2
Porlock Dr HU7 57 A5
Port Ave HU6 140 C8
Portal Rd YO26 129 B6
Porter St
Kingston upon Hull HU3 155 A1
Scunthorpe DN15 151 A8
Portholme Cres 7 YO8 148 C5
Portholme Dr YO8 148 C4
Portholme Rd YO8 148 C5
Portington Rd DN14 51 F1
Portisham Pl 12 YO32 14 A7
Portland Ave DN32 152 E1
Portland Pl
Bridlington YO16 122 C3
Grimsby DN32 102 F2
Kingston upon Hull HU2 155 A3
Portland St
Kingston upon Hull HU2 155 A3
Rawcliffe DN14 79 B8
York YO31 156 B4
Portmadoc Cl 5 HU7 56 F7
Portman Rd DN15 96 C7
Portobello St HU9 141 F3
Post Office La
Ashby cum Fenby DN37 113 D3
Humberside Airport DN39 100 A6
Whitton DN15 67 E3
Post Office Row DN14 64 A1
Post Office St 12 YO15 5 A2
Postern Cl YO23 156 B1
Postern La YO42 38 D6
Posterngate HU1 155 B2
Postill Sq YO16 122 D4
Potterdale Dr HU20 55 A4
Potterill La HU7 141 D6
Potters Dr 4 YO23 132 B3
Potters Way HU18 134 C1
Pottery La YO31 130 E7
Pottinger Gdns LN7 111 A2
Potts La DN17 94 D7
Poultney Garth 4 HU12 72 D7
Powell St YO8 148 B6
Powells Cres DN16 151 B2
Pratt's La HU11 46 D3
Precentor's Ct YO31 156 B3
Prescott Ave 9 HU15 68 C5
Prescott Gr 23 DN7 92 D4
Preston Cty Prim Sch HU12 58 D1
Preston Dr 1 DN20 98 C2
Preston La DN18 84 F8
Preston Rd Hedon HU12 72 C8
Kingston upon Hull HU9 141 F1
Prestwick Ct YO26 129 B5
Pretoria St HU3 144 F5
Pretymen Cres DN36 114 A7
Price's La YO23 156 B1
Prickett Rd YO16 122 C4
Priest Cl YO14 2 F8
Priest La YO19 26 F5
Priestgate
3 Barton-upon-Humber DN18 84 F8
Kingston upon Hull HU7 141 D6
Nafferton YO25 125 F6
Priestgate Cl YO25 125 F6
Primitive Chapel La DN40 86 F2
Primrose Dr 1 HU5 144 C8
Primrose Gr YO8 148 A6
Primrose Hill 9 WF11 61 A3
Primrose Vale 1 WF11 61 A2
Primrose Way
Humberston DN35 103 C1
1 Scunthorpe DN15 96 B7
Prince Albert Gdns DN32 152 E5
Prince Charles Dr 20 DN18 84 F8
Prince Philip Dr 21 DN18 84 F8
Prince St
Bridlington YO15 122 F2
Kingston upon Hull HU1 155 B2
Princes Ave
1 Hedon HU12 72 C7
Kingston upon Hull HU13 143 E1
Kingston upon Hull HU5 145 C8
Prince's Ave HU19 75 A6
Prince's Dock St HU1 155 B2
Princes Gdns HU17 154 A2
Prince's Rd
Cleethorpes DN35 153 E2
Kingston upon Hull HU5 140 C2
Princes St 16 DN20 98 C2
Princess Alexandra Ct 14 DN17 96 C2
Princess Ave DN7 92 C6
Princess Cl YO43 135 D3
Princess Dr 22 DN18 84 F8
Princess Rd
Market Weighton YO43 135 D3
Strensall YO32 14 B7
Princess Royal Hospl The HU8 142 A6
Princess St
4 Bridlington YO15 122 F2
Goole DN14 149 C2
Immingham DN40 87 C1

Princess St *continued*
Kingston upon Hull HU2 155 B3
Princess Terr 5 YO15 122 F2
Princess Way
8 Beverley HU17 55 E8
Woodmansey HU17 136 D1
Printing Office La 6 DN17 94 D8
Priors Cl DN36 114 A7
Prior's Wlk YO26 129 D6
Priory Ave 18 HU14 69 A4
Priory Cell (Rems of)* DN37 113 A2
Priory Cl
Bridlington YO16 122 E5
10 Swanland HU14 69 B7
Wilberfoss YO41 27 F6
Priory Cres
Bridlington YO16 122 E4
Kingston upon Hull HU16 139 B5
Scunthorpe DN17 151 A3
Ulceby DN39 86 A2
Priory Dr HU5 139 D2
Priory Farm Dr 4 HU4 144 D2
Priory Gr HU4 144 D3
Priory La
Barrow upon Humber DN19 85 D8
Scunthorpe DN17 150 E2
1 Snaith DN14 63 C1
Priory Lane Inf Sch DN17 150 F2
Priory Park Cl 3 LS25 61 A8
Priory Park Gr 2 LS25 61 B8
Priory Prim Sch HU5 139 D1
Priory Rd
Beverley HU17 154 C2
Cottingham HU5 139 C3
Grimsby DN37 102 B3
Kingston upon Hull HU16 139 B5
Scunthorpe DN17 151 A2
Priory Rd or H DN6 76 E2
Priory St YO1 156 A1
Priory Way
Kingston upon Hull HU4 144 A1
1 Snaith DN14 63 B1
Priory Wlk YO16 122 D4
Priory Wood Way YO31 127 F2
Proctor's Way DN20 109 A5
Promenade YO15 122 F2
Promenades Sh Ctr The YO15 122 F2
Prospect Cl
Camblesforth YO8 63 D5
Pollington DN14 77 F6
Prospect Pl
Kingston upon Hull HU9 146 B7
Wistow YO8 48 D6
Prospect Rd DN14 79 B8
Prospect St
Bridlington YO15 122 E2
Kingston upon Hull HU2 155 A3
Prospect Terr
Fulford YO10 133 D6
York YO1 156 B1
Prospect Way YO8 148 D4
Providence Cres DN18 84 E8
Providence Pl
10 Bridlington YO15 122 F3
1 Great Driffield YO25 124 F4
Providence Row HU2 155 A4
Prunus Ave HU10 143 F8
Pryme Rd DN16 151 C4
Pryme St
Kingston upon Hull HU10 143 F6
Kingston upon Hull HU2 155 A3
Prystie Pl 1 DN35 103 B1
Puddiners La DN14 80 E7
Pudding Gate 8 HU17 43 A2
Pulcroft Rd HU13 143 D2
Pulham La YO25 19 B5
Pulleyn Cl 3 YO32 14 C8
Pulleyn Dr YO24 129 F1
Pulman St HU3 145 A7
Pump Hill DN20 109 D6
Pump La YO15 4 C3
Purbeck Rd
Grimsby DN33 113 E8
Scunthorpe DN17 150 C5
Purey Cust Nuffield Hospl The YO31 156 B3
Purton Gr HU7 141 A7
Putney Cl HU8 141 E5
Pyewipe Rd DN31 152 C5
Pykestone Cl 15 HU7 57 A6
Pyruss Dr HU4 144 B2
Pytchley Wlk 1 DN35 103 C1

Q

Quadrant The HU6 139 F4
Quaker Gn 1 YO24 132 C7
Quaker La HU17 136 D4
Quaker Rd HU12 59 F4
Quales Mews 2 HU18 134 C4
Quant Mews YO10 131 B3
Quantock Cl
7 Kingston upon Hull HU3 145 D5
Scunthorpe DN17 150 D4
5 Thorne/Moorends DN8 93 A7
Quantock Rd DN33 113 E8
Quarrington Gr 10 HU7 56 F6

Quarry Ave 20 WF11 61 A2
Quarry Rd DN6 76 F2
Quart La
Eastrington DN14 65 F7
Reedness DN14 80 D6
Quay La DN14 80 C7
Quay Rd
Bridlington YO16 122 D3
4 Thorne DN8 78 F1
Quay St HU1 155 B2
Quay The YO8 148 D6
Quayside 1 DN8 78 F1
Quebec Dr HU16 138 E5
Quebec Rd DN17 96 C2
Queen Anne's Rd YO30 156 A3
Queen Dike* YO17 17 B8
Queen Elizabeth Ave 4 DN18 84 A7
Queen Elizabeth High Sch DN21 117 B2
Queen Elizabeth Rd 6 DN36 114 C8
Queen Elizabeth Way 19 DN18 84 F8
Queen Margarets Sch YO19 37 A5
Queen Mary Ave DN35 153 C3
Queen Mary Ave Inf Sch DN35 153 C3
Queen St
Barton-upon-Humber DN18 69 F1
Bridlington YO15 122 E2
14 Brigg DN20 98 C2
13 Epworth DN9 105 E6
Great Driffield YO25 124 F4
Grimsby DN32 152 E3
Kingston upon Hull HU1 155 C1
Kirton in Lindsey DN21 108 B1
Scunthorpe DN16 151 C6
16 Thorne/Moorends DN8 93 A8
15 Winterton DN15 83 A5
Withernsea HU19 75 A6
York YO24 156 A2
Queen St N HU19 74 F7
Queen St S 15 HU19 75 A6
Queen Victoria Sq HU1 155 B2
Queen Victoria St YO23 130 B1
Queen's Alley HU1 155 C1
Queen's Ave 5 DN18 69 F1
Queen's Cl Goole DN14 149 C4
2 Kingston upon Hull HU16 139 B7
Queens Cres DN17 95 D6
Queen's Cres DN7 92 C6
Queen's Ct 17 DN8 93 A8
Queens Dock Ave HU1 155 B2
Queens Dock Mus* HU1 155 B2
Queens Dr DN14 149 D6
Queen's Dr HU16 139 A7
Queen's Gate HU16 139 B7
Queen's Gate St HU3 145 B5
Queens Gdns HU18 134 B3
Queens Par DN35 153 F1
Queen's Rd DN38 99 B4
Queens Rd
Beverley HU17 154 C4
Immingham DN40 87 D1
Kingston upon Hull HU5 140 C2
Queen's Staith Rd YO1 156 B2
Queen's View Cres DN16 151 D3
Queen's Way HU16 139 B7
Queensbury Way 2 HU14 69 B6
Queensfield LN7 110 A1
Queensgate
Beverley HU17 154 A1
Bridlington YO16 122 E4
Queensgate Sq YO16 122 D3
Queensmead
Aldbrough HU11 47 C1
Beverley HU17 55 E8
Lund YO25 31 F2
Queensway
Goole DN14 149 D4
Grimsby DN37 102 C4
Scunthorpe DN16 151 C3
Woodmansey HU17 56 B8
Queensway The HU6 140 B8
Queenswood Gr YO24 129 D2
Queenswood Rd 7 DN16 96 E2
Quillcourt HU6 139 E7
Quilter Ave HU4 144 B5
Quilter Dr HU11 142 F7
Quinton Rd DN32 102 F2
Quorn Mews 26 DN35 103 C2
Quorum The HU4 144 D3

R

Racca Ave 11 WF11 61 A2
Racca Gn WF11 61 A2
Race La Carlton YO8 63 B4
Wootton DN39 85 C3
Racecourse Rd YO23 133 B8
Rachel Cl 3 DN21 117 B2
Radcliffe Rd DN41 101 F5
Radcroft La YO43 53 D5
Raglan St HU5 140 C3

Raich Carter Way HU6 56 D5
Railway Cres 2 HU19 75 A6
Railway Pl DN31 152 F5
Railway St
Barnetby le Wold DN38 99 B4
Beverley HU17 154 B2
Grimsby DN32 152 F4
Hornsea HU18 134 D4
Kingston upon Hull HU1 155 B1
Railway Terr
Grimsby DN32 152 D3
York YO24 130 A4
Raincliffe St 4 YO8 148 C5
Raines Cl 5 HU12 73 A6
Rainham Cl HU8 141 E7
Rainhill Rd 2 HU5 140 A2
Rainsborough Way 3 YO30 130 A8
Rainsburgh La YO25 2 A3
Rainsbutt Rd DN17 94 C8
Rainswood Cl 8 HU7 56 F6
Raithby Ave 3 DN41 101 A4
Raithby Gr 12 DN33 102 D2
Rake Bridge Bank DN7 92 D1
Raker Cl YO19 37 F7
Rakes Rd HU17 42 E2
Raleigh Dr
Kingston upon Hull HU9 146 D6
Sproatley HU11 58 D5
Ralph Butterfield Sch YO32 13 F5
Ram Bvd DN15 96 C8
Ramsay Cl YO31 156 C4
Ramsden Ave DN18 84 E8
Ramsden Cl YO25 124 A1
Ramsden Ct HU17 154 C3
Ramsden Pl 11 HU16 138 F5
Ramsey Ave YO23 133 B3
Ramsey Cl YO16 122 C2
Ramsey Rd YO16 122 B2
Ramsgate Cl HU8 141 E7
Ramskir La DN7 92 C7
Ranby Cres HU18 134 C2
Ranby Dr HU18 134 C2
Ranby Rd DN17 150 E1
Rands Est 7 HU12 58 D1
Randsfield Ave 17 HU15 68 C5
Rangely Cl 9 HU7 57 A6
Rannoch Cl 6 HU7 57 A6
Ransom Ct DN39 100 A6
Ransome Way 14 HU15 68 C6
Ratcliffe Ct YO30 126 C5
Ratcliffe St YO30 130 B7
Rattan Row YO25 8 C6
Ratten Row
4 Bishop Burton HU17 43 A2
12 North Newbald YO43 53 F7
Rauceby Cl 10 HU7 56 F6
Raven Cl DN20 97 D4
Raven Gr YO26 129 C4
Raven St HU9 146 D7
Ravencroft La 1 DN10 116 D1
Ravendale 18 DN18 84 F8
Ravendale Cl 1 DN36 114 B5
Ravendale Rd 10 DN35 103 D2
Ravendale St N DN15 151 B7
Ravendale St S DN15 151 B7
Ravenhill Cl 14 DN35 103 B2
Ravenscar Rd 9 DN37 102 C5
Ravensfleet Rd DN21 116 F6
Ravenspur Rd HU11 58 A4
Ravenspurn YO16 122 B6
Ravenspurn Gr 1 HU9 142 A2
Ravenspurn Rd HU12 89 C8
Ravenspurn St DN31 152 D4
Raventhorpe Medieval Village* DN16 97 B2
Rawcliffe Ave YO30 129 F8
Rawcliffe Cl YO30 126 E2
Rawcliffe Croft YO30 126 D2
Rawcliffe Dr YO30 129 F8
Rawcliffe Gr HU4 144 D5
Rawcliffe in Snaith Prim Sch DN14 64 A2
Rawcliffe Inf Sch YO30 126 E1
Rawcliffe La YO30 126 F1
Rawcliffe Rd DN14 149 A4
Rawcliffe Sta DN14 79 A8
Rawcliffe Way YO30 126 E2
Rawdale Cl HU15 54 A2
Rawdon Ave YO10 130 F4
Rawling Way HU3 145 C5
Rawlinson Ave 22 LN7 111 B4
Ray Dike Cl YO32 127 C7
Raymond Rd DN16 151 C3
Raywell Cl HU10 143 F7
Raywell St HU2 155 A3
Read Cl YO8 63 F5
Read Sch YO8 63 F5
Reading Gate
Reedness DN17 80 C3
Swinefleet DN14 80 D7
Reading Room Yd 4 HU14 69 A4
Real Aeroplane Mus The* YO8 50 D5
Reangamoor La YO42 39 D2
Reaper's Rise 15 DN9 105 E6
Reaper's Way 6 DN9 105 D2
Recreation Rd 2 YO8 148 D6
Recto Ave DN32 152 F1
Rectory Ave 34 DN21 117 B1
Rectory Cl YO25 125 F7
Rectory Gdns
3 Beckingham DN10 116 D1
York YO23 130 B1

Rectory La
Beeford YO25 22 C1
Preston HU12 58 C1
Roos HU12 60 C3
Rectory Rd HU12 74 A8
Rectory St DN9 105 E6
Rectory View YO25 32 C2
Rectory Way YO43 40 B1
Red House La YO43 135 A4
Red House Prep Sch YO26 12 D3
Red La
Market Weighton YO43 135 E5
South Ferriby DN18 83 F7
Red Lion St 2 DN14 149 C4
Red Tower* YO1 130 E4
Redbourn Cl DN16 151 B5
Redbourn E Rd DN16 97 A6
Redbourn Way DN16 151 B6
Redbourne Mere DN21 108 E2
Redbourne Rd
Grimsby DN33 102 D2
Hibaldstow DN20 108 F4
Waddingham DN21 119 F8
Redbourne St
Kingston upon Hull HU3 145 B5
3 Scunthorpe DN16 151 C6
Redcap La YO42 38 C5
Redcar Gr DN32 153 A1
Redcar St HU8 155 C4
Redcliff Dr 19 HU14 69 A4
Redcliff Rd HU13 69 E4
Redcoat W 1 YO24 132 B8
Redcombe La DN20 98 B2
Redeness St YO31 130 E5
Redfern Cl HU3 145 D5
Redgates HU17 55 B7
Redhall Cl 7 DN3 92 A2
Redhill Field La YO23 24 D1
Redhouse La YO8 63 F6
Redland Cres 2 DN8 93 B8
Redland Dr HU10 143 C8
Redman Cl
15 Gainsborough DN21 117 C1
York YO10 133 C8
Redmayne Sq YO32 14 B8
Redmire Cl HU7 57 A6
Redmires Cl YO30 127 A2
Redruth Cl HU7 141 C6
Redthorn Dr YO31 127 F1
Redwing Cl YO25 125 A5
Redwood Cl YO16 122 E6
Redwood Ct DN16 96 E2
Redwood Dr
7 Cleethorpes DN35 103 B1
6 Haxby YO32 13 E5
Redwood Gdns YO25 124 F3
Redwood Way YO16 122 D6
Redwoods The HU10 138 C2
Reed St HU2 155 A3
Reedholme La DN8 78 F4
Reedness Prim Sch DN14 66 A1
Reedsway 12 YO25 34 B2
Reeves The YO24 129 C1
Refinery Rd DN16 151 F6
Reform St HU2 155 B3
Regency Ct 8 DN18 69 E1
Regency Mews 2 YO24 132 F8
Regent Cl
Kingston upon Hull HU10 138 E1
Kingston upon Hull HU3 145 C6
Regent Dr 13 DN17 94 D7
Regent St
Beverley HU17 154 B2
York YO10 130 E3
Regent St Pavement 8 YO42 29 A3
Regent Terr 7 YO15 122 F2
Regents Ct 14 YO26 129 F5
Regina Cres 2 HU5 140 A1
Reginald Gr YO23 130 C1
Reginald Rd DN15 96 C7
Regis Ct HU9 142 B3
Register Sq HU17 154 A2
Reigate Cl HU8 142 A4
Reighton Ave YO30 129 F8
Reighton Dr 10 YO30 126 F1
Reldene Dr HU5 144 B7
Remillo Ave DN32 152 F1
Remington Ave YO25 34 E3
Remple Ave DN7 93 A3
Remple Comm Rd DN7 92 F2
Remple La DN7 93 A3
Rendel St DN31 152 D5
Rensburg St HU9 141 D1
Renshaw Gdns 8 YO26 129 E4
Reporto Ave DN32 152 F1
Repton Dr
Kingston upon Hull HU7 141 D5
21 Scunthorpe DN16 96 D2
Reservoir Rd HU6 140 F3
Responso Ave DN32 152 F1
Reston Ct 8 DN35 103 D2
Reston Gr 25 DN33 102 D2
Retford Gr HU9 142 E1
Retreat Hospl The YO10 130 F2
Revesby Ave
13 Grimsby DN34 102 C2
Scunthorpe DN16 151 A3
Revesby Ct DN16 151 A4
Revigo Ave DN32 152 F1

Revill Cl 17 DN21 107 C3
Reygate Gr YO23 132 B2
Reynolds Cl HU14 68 E5
Reynolds Inf Sch DN35 153 D3
Reynolds Jun Sch DN35 153 D3
Reynolds St DN35 153 D2
Reynoldson St HU5 140 C2
Rhodena Ave YO16 122 D2
Rhodes St HU3 144 F5
Rhyl Cl 4 HU7 56 F7
Rialto Ave DN32 152 F1
Ribble St 4 HU3 145 B4
Ribblesdale 3 HU7 141 A6
Ribblesdale Cl YO16 122 F7
Ribston Cl 9 DN16 96 D1
Ribstone Gr YO31 131 B6
Riby Ct DN36 114 B5
Riby Rd Cabourne LN7 111 D6
Keelby DN41 101 A4
Scunthorpe DN17 150 E1
Stallingborough DN41 101 C4
Swallow LN7 112 A7
Riby Sq DN32 152 F5
Riby St DN31 153 A5
Ribycourt HU6 139 E7
Riccall Cl HU6 140 A6
Riccall CP Sch YO19 36 F1
Riccall La YO19 36 D1
Richard Cooper St DN14 149 E4
Richard St
Grimsby DN31 152 C4
Selby YO8 148 B5
Richardson Cl DN36 114 D8
Richardson St YO23 130 C2
Richdale Ave DN21 108 B1
Richmond Cl YO43 135 F3
Richmond Dr
Goole DN14 149 F5
10 Scunthorpe DN16 96 E2
Richmond Gdns HU17 136 D1
Richmond Rd
Cleethorpes DN35 153 E1
Grimsby DN34 152 A2
Kingston upon Hull HU13 143 E2
Thorne/Moorends DN8 79 B2
Richmond St
Bridlington YO15 122 D1
2 Kingston upon Hull HU5 145 B8
York YO31 130 E5
Richmond Way 2 HU17 55 E8
Richmond Wlk HU17 136 D1
Rickaby Cl YO16 122 D4
Ridding Cres DN14 64 A1
Ridding La DN14 64 A1
Riddings Infants Sch DN17 96 C2
Riddings Jun Sch DN17 96 C2
Ridge View DN20 98 C2
Ridgestone Ave HU11 142 E7
Ridgeway YO26 129 B3
Ridgeway Rd HU5 144 B7
Ridgeway The DN34 102 B2
Ridgewood Ave 8 DN3 92 A1
Ridgewood Dr DN15 82 A4
Riding Fields Sq HU17 154 C3
Ridings The
Beverley HU17 136 C6
Great Driffield YO25 125 A6
Kingston upon Hull HU16 138 E6
Kingston upon Hull HU5 144 A8
15 North Ferriby HU14 69 A4
Ridsdale HU7 140 F7
Rigby Cl HU17 136 D7
Rileston Pl 12 DN16 96 D1
Rillington Ave HU16 139 A5
Rimswell Gr HU9 142 A2
Ring Beck La HU15 68 A8
Ringley Mdws 5 YO15 4 C3
Ringrose St HU3 144 F5
Ringstead Garth 4 HU7 57 A5
Ringstone Rd YO30 126 F3
Ringwood Cl DN16 151 B1
Ripley Cl
Bridlington YO16 122 D5
Kingston upon Hull HU6 140 B7
Ripley Gr 3 YO32 13 E5
Riplingham Rd
Kingston upon Hull HU10 143 A8
Kingston upon Hull HU10 55 C1
Skidby HU10 138 A1
Ripon Ave HU17 136 E1
Ripon Cl DN17 150 C3
Ripon St DN31 152 C3
Ripon Way HU9 146 C8
Risby Garth HU16 55 C4
Risby Gr HU6 139 F5
Risby Hill HU20 55 A4
Risby La HU17 55 B7
Risby Medieval Village* DN15 83 A2
Risby Pl HU17 154 A1
Risby Rd DN15 82 F1
Rise Cl HU11 45 C5
Rise La Catwick HU17 45 D8
Rise HU11 45 D5
Rise Rd HU11 45 F7
Rise The
7 North Ferriby HU14 69 A5
Scunthorpe DN17 96 C2
South Ferriby DN18 84 A8
Risedale 21 LN7 111 B4
Riseway HU11 45 C5
Risewood YO41 15 B2
Rishworth Cl 5 HU7 57 A6
Rishworth Gr YO30 126 F2
Riston C of E Sch HU11 45 C5
Riston Rd HU17 45 C7
Riston St HU3 145 C5
Rivan Ave 5 DN33 113 E8
Rivan Gr 6 DN33 113 E8
Rivelin Cres DN16 151 A4
Rivelin Pl DN16 151 A4
Rivelin Rd DN16 151 A3
Riveling Way YO30 126 F2
River Cl 2 Barlby YO8 49 B5
Goole DN14 149 F5
River Gr HU4 144 E3
River Head YO25 124 F3
River Head Dr 3 YO25 124 F3
River La Fishlake DN7 92 D8
Market Weighton YO43 40 F2
West Haddlesey YO8 62 A5
River Mdw DN20 98 B1
River St 1 Selby YO8 148 D6
York YO23 156 B1
River View 1 Barlby YO8 49 B5
26 Barton-upon-Humber DN18 84 F8
Goole DN14 65 C3
River Wlk DN14 65 C4
Riverdale 4 DN14 61 D4
Riverdale Rd
Kilpin DN14 65 C1
Scunthorpe DN16 151 A3
Riversdale 17 YO32 13 F5
Riversdale Dr DN14 149 F5
Riversdale Rd HU6 140 D6
Riverside
12 Broughton DN20 98 B2
Great Driffield YO25 124 F3
Rawcliffe DN14 64 A2
Scotter DN21 107 C4
Riverside Area Specl Sch DN14 149 E5
Riverside Cl
1 Elvington YO41 27 C2
6 Great Driffield YO25 124 F3
Riverside Cres YO32 127 F6
Riverside Ct
5 Hessle HU13 69 E4
Rawcliffe DN14 64 A2
Riverside Dr DN35 103 D1
Riverside Gdns
2 Elvington YO41 27 C2
2 Poppleton YO26 12 F1
Riverside Mews 5 YO25 124 F3
Riverside Wlk
1 Poppleton YO26 12 F1
5 Strensall YO32 14 A7
Riversvale Dr 21 YO26 12 F1
Riverview Ave HU14 69 A4
Riverview Gdns HU7 140 E7
Riverview Rd HU17 137 C4
Rivesby Ave DN16 151 A3
Riviera Dr YO15 123 B6
Rix Rd HU7 141 A3
Roall La DN14 61 F4
Robert Cl
Immingham DN40 87 B1
3 Withernsea HU19 75 A6
Robert St DN15 151 B7
Robert Wilkinson Prim Sch YO32 14 A7
Robert Wood Ave HU17 154 A2
Roberts St DN32 153 A3
Robin Gr 6 YO24 129 F3
Robin Hood Cres 7 DN3 92 A1
Robin Hood Rd 5 DN3 92 A1
Robinia Dr HU4 144 C2
Robinson Cl DN15 150 E8
Robinson Dr YO24 129 B2
Robinson La DN31 153 A6
Robinson Rd DN40 87 D2
Robinson Row HU1 155 B2
Robinson St E DN32 152 E3
Robinson's Gr DN20 109 A5
Robinson's La DN36 114 B1
Roborough Cl HU7 141 B8
Robson Ave HU6 140 B8
Robson Rd DN35 153 D3
Robson Way
Kingston upon Hull HU7 141 D7
6 Preston HU12 72 C7
Rochdale Rd DN16 151 A1
Rochdale Road Jun Sch DN16 151 A1
Roche Ave YO31 130 E8
Roche Dr DN14 149 E6
Rochester Ave HU4 144 A3
Rochester Cl DN17 150 C3
Rochester Ct 2 DN35 103 D1
Rockford Ave HU8 141 B3
Rockford Gr HU8 141 B3
Rockingham Ave YO31 131 A5
Rockingham Ct 10 DN34 102 B2
Rod Mill Rd DN16 151 E5
Rodney Cl HU2 155 A4
Roe La LS25 61 C7
Rokeby Ave HU4 144 B5
Rokeby Cl
Beverley HU17 154 A4
Kingston upon Hull HU4 144 B5
Rokeby Pk HU4 144 B5
Rokeby Prim Sch HU4 144 B4
Roland Simpson Cl 1 DN14 78 C8
Rolston Ave 3 YO31 127 E2
Rolston Cl HU9 142 C1
Rolston Rd HU18 134 C2
Roman Ave N 17 YO41 15 D2
Roman Ave S YO41 15 D1
Roman Camps* YO30 127 B2
Roman Rigg YO43 53 D8
Romans Cl YO19 48 F8
Romford Gr HU9 142 E1
Romney Gdns 4 HU5 140 E2
Romsey Ct 11 DN34 102 B3
Romyn Cl YO16 122 B2
Ronaldsway Cl 6 HU9 142 A3
Ronson Cl HU9 142 D3
Rookery Ave 10 DN33 102 E2
Rookery Croft 9 DN9 105 E6
Rookery Rd DN41 101 F5
Rookery The DN20 108 F8
Rooklands 2 DN21 107 C3
Rookley Cl 3 HU8 142 C5
Rook's La DN10 116 C5
Roos C of E Sch HU12 60 B1
Roos Cl HU17 136 F7
Rootas La HU17 43 A6
Rope Wlk
Bridlington YO15 122 E2
Thorne/Moorends DN8 93 A8
Roper St HU1 155 A2
Ropers Ct YO23 132 C3
Ropery Cl 3 YO25 9 C3
Ropery La 1 DN18 69 E1
Ropery Rd DN21 117 A2
Ropery St
Grimsby DN32 152 F3
Kingston upon Hull HU3 145 D5
Ropewalk The
9 Caistor LN7 111 B4
York YO31 130 E5
Rosaire Pl DN33 113 E8
Rosalind Ave DN34 152 B3
Rosamond St 7 HU3 145 B4
Rose Gdns 4 DN40 87 C2
Rose La HU17 43 C5
Rose Lea Cl 2 LS25 61 A7
Rose St YO31 130 C7
Rose Tree Gr YO32 127 D4
Rose Wlk DN15 151 C7
Roseacres DN14 65 C4
Roseberry Ave
Bridlington YO15 122 C1
15 Hatfield DN7 92 D4
Roseberry Gr YO30 126 F3
Rosebery St YO26 129 F6
Rosecomb Way 6 YO32 127 D7
Rosecroft Way YO30 129 E8
Rosedale Leven HU17 45 B8
Scunthorpe DN17 96 C1
Waltham DN37 113 D7
Rosedale Ave
Kingston upon Hull HU9 141 E1
York YO26 129 C4
Rosedale Gr HU5 144 D7
Rosedale St YO10 130 D2
Rosemary Ave DN34 102 C3
Rosemary Ct YO1 156 C2
Rosemary Pl YO1 156 C2
Rosemary Way
Beverley HU17 154 C1
Humberston DN36 103 C1
Rosemoor Cl 19 YO14 2 F8
Rosemount Cl 3 HU6 140 B8
Rosemount Dr DN16 151 B2
Rosemount Grange HU13 143 C3
Roseveare Ave DN34 152 A3
Rosewood Cl
3 Bridlington YO16 123 A6
4 Kingston upon Hull HU4 144 B7
Rosewood Way 25 DN16 96 D2
Rosey Row 4 HU9 146 C7
Rosina Gr N DN32 153 B2
Rosina Gr S DN32 153 B2
Roslyn Cres HU12 72 C7
Roslyn Rd HU3 144 E7
Rosmead St HU9 146 D8
Rosper Rd DN40 87 A4
Ross La Bainton YO25 31 D7
Winterton DN15 83 B5
Ross Rd DN31 153 B5
Rossall Cl 4 DN16 96 E2
Rosslyn St 1 YO30 130 A6
Rostun Rd HU12 60 B2
Roth Hill La YO19 37 E3
Rothbury Rd DN17 150 F3
Rothesay Cl 1 HU9 141 E1
Rothwell Ave 19 DN33 102 D2
Rothwell Rd
Cabourne LN7 111 C3
Scunthorpe DN15 150 D8
Rotsea La YO25 33 B7
Rotterdam Rd HU7 141 A5
Rotton Sykes La DN15 67 F2
Rougier St YO1 156 A2
Round Hill Link YO30 126 F2
Roundhay Rd YO15 122 D1
Roundway
Grimsby DN34 152 C1
7 Immingham DN40 87 C1
Roundway The HU4 144 C5
Routh Ave HU17 154 C3
Royal Dr DN40 87 B1
Row La HU12 90 A7
Rowan Ave
Beverley HU17 136 F7
York YO32 127 D4
Rowan Cl
3 Barrow upon Humber DN19 85 C8
Gateforth YO8 48 B1
2 Keelby DN41 101 A4
10 Thorne/Moorends DN8 79 B2
Rowan Cres 2 DN16 96 E2
Rowan Dr
Healing DN41 101 F5
6 Humberston DN36 114 D8
Rowan Garth HU16 55 C4
Rowan Pl YO32 127 D4
Rowan Wlk HU18 134 D2
Rowans The 1 DN9 105 A2
Rowedale Cl 15 YO14 2 F8
Rowland Rd DN16 151 A6
Rowlandhall La DN14 50 E1
Rowlandson St DN31 152 F6
Rowley C of E Sch HU20 55 A4
Rowley Ct 2 YO32 127 F7
Rowley Gr HU6 139 F5
Rowley Rd HU20 54 F3
Rowlston Gr HU9 142 A2
Rowmans The YO30 126 C4
Rowmills Rd DN16 151 C4
Rowntree Ave YO30 130 C8
Rowpit La HU17 45 C8
Rowston Cl 7 DN21 117 B1
Rowston St DN35 103 D3
Rowton Dr HU11 45 D2
Roxburgh St 1 HU5 145 B8
Roxby Cswy DN15 83 C4
Roxby Rd DN15 82 F4
Roxton Ave DN41 101 A5
Roxton Hall Dr 13 HU14 69 A5
Roxton Medieval Village* DN40 101 A7
Royal Chase YO24 132 F8
Royal Cres YO15 122 F2
Royal Ct 23 DN35 103 D1
Royal Dr DN14 79 A8
Royal Dragoon Guard Association Regimental Mus* YO1 156 B2
Royal Garth HU17 154 A1
Royal Hull Hospitals NHS Trust HU3 145 C6
Royal St DN31 152 E6
Royal Wlk HU16 139 D5
Royd's Rd YO8 61 F6
Royston Gr HU8 141 B1
Ruard Rd DN19 86 B8
Ruards La DN19 71 A1
Ruby St 3 YO23 130 B1
Rudcarr La YO19 14 E1
Rudding Dr YO16 122 D7
Ruddings YO19 38 A8
Ruddings Cl 9 YO32 127 C8
Ruddings La YO42 38 E2
Ruddings The YO8 148 A4
Rudgate La DN14 78 E4
Rudham Ave DN32 102 F2
Rudston Beacon* YO25 9 F4
Rudston Gr HU9 142 A1
Rudston Monolith* YO25 9 F6
Rudston Rd YO25 9 F2
Rue De Nozay 2 DN20 97 E4
Ruffhams Cl YO19 37 F8
Rufford Rd 3 DN35 103 C2
Rufforth Dr HU17 43 D5
Rufforth Garth HU7 141 C8
Rufforth Prim Sch YO23 24 C6
Rugby Rd DN16 151 A4
Rugby St 5 HU3 145 B4
Ruislip Cl HU8 142 A5
Runcorn Garth HU4 144 B3
Runner End YO43 40 A1
Runswick Ave YO26 129 B4
Runswick Rd DN32 153 B2
Rupert Rd 9 DN33 102 E2
Rushcarr La DN17 95 C1
Rusholme La YO8 64 A5
Rushtons Way DN20 108 F5
Rushwood Cl 6 YO32 13 F5
Ruskin St HU3 145 B6
Russell Ct 18 DN35 103 D1
Russell Dr 20 HU12 73 C4
Russell Rd DN14 149 B4
Russell St
Kingston upon Hull HU2 155 A3
York YO23 130 B2
Russell Wlk DN17 107 D7
Russet Cl 12 DN15 96 B7
Russet Dr YO31 131 B5
Rustenburg St HU9 141 D1
Rustic La DN21 117 F6
Ruswarp Gr HU6 139 E6
Rutherglen Dr HU9 142 A3
Rutland Cl YO23 132 A3
Rutland Dr 16 DN36 114 A7
Rutland Rd
Goole DN14 149 D6
Kingston upon Hull HU5 144 E8
Scunthorpe DN16 151 D3
Rutland St DN32 153 A4
Ryburn Cl YO30 126 F2
Rydal Ave
11 Grimsby DN33 113 D8
York YO31 131 A6
Rydal Gr HU16 138 E6
Rydale Ct HU5 140 E3
Rydales The HU5 140 E3
Ryde Ave HU5 140 D3
Ryde St HU5 140 D2
Rye Cl YO32 127 C8
Ryecroft 7 YO32 14 A6
Ryecroft Ave
10 Norton DN6 76 E2
York YO24 132 C7
Ryecroft Cl YO31 131 C8
Ryecroft Dr HU19 75 A6
Ryecroft Gdns DN14 62 A2
Ryecroft Rd DN6 76 E1
Ryedale 4 HU15 68 D6
Ryedale Ave DN15 83 A6
Ryedale Way YO8 148 C3
Ryehill Cl YO32 127 D5
Ryehill Gr HU9 141 F2
Ryehill La HU12 73 A4
Ryelands Ave YO16 123 A6
Ryemoor Rd YO32 127 C8
Rylatt Pl YO26 129 B3
Rymer Pl DN35 103 D2
Rysome La HU19 75 C1
Rysome Rd HU12 90 B7

S

Sable Cl HU4 144 C2
Sackville Cl
5 Beverley HU17 55 E8
14 Immingham DN40 87 C1
Sackville Rd 15 DN40 87 C1
Sackville St DN34 152 C3
Sacred Gate HU12 72 D6
Sadberge Ct YO10 131 C3
Saddlers Cl
1 Copmanthorpe YO23 132 B3
Huntington YO32 127 F2
Saddler's Way DN9 105 D3
Saddlers Way YO26 24 A6
Saddleworth Cl 10 HU7 57 A6
Saffron Dr 6 DN14 63 C1
Saffron Garth 15 HU12 74 D1
Saffrondale HU10 143 E7
Sage Cl HU17 154 B1
Sagefield Cl 6 DN33 113 D8
Sailors Wharf HU9 146 C6
Sails Dr YO10 131 B3
Sainsbury Way HU4 144 A1
St Abbs Cl HU9 155 C1
St Aelreds Cl YO31 130 F4
St Aelreds RC Prim Sch YO31 131 B5
St Aidan Cres YO16 122 E4
St Aidan Ct YO16 122 E5
St Aidan Rd YO16 122 E4
St Aiden Cl YO43 135 E3
St Alban Cl YO16 122 E4
St Alban Rd YO16 122 E4
St Albans Ave DN31 152 A4
St Albans Cl
7 Beverley HU17 136 E1
Hibaldstow DN20 108 F5
Scunthorpe DN17 150 C3
St Alban's Cl HU11 46 D3
St Aldan Way HU9 141 F2
St Andrew Pl YO1 156 C2
St Andrew Rd YO16 122 E4
St Andrew St HU17 154 B2
St Andrewgate YO1 156 B2
St Andrews Ave DN17 96 C1
St Andrews C of E Prim Sch HU7 140 E7
St Andrew's Cl
Middleton-on-the-Wolds YO25 31 C4
Paull HU12 72 A5
Redbourne DN21 108 E3
St Andrew's Dr DN15 82 A4
St Andrews Gr 10 DN7 92 D4
St Andrews La 5 DN40 87 B2
St Andrew's Mount HU10 143 C8
St Andrews Prim Sch HU10 143 C7
St Andrews Quay* HU3 145 A2
St Andrew's St DN21 108 A1
St Andrew's Terr 6 DN14 149 C4
St Andrew's Way
2 Barnby Dun DN3 92 A3
Epworth DN9 105 E7
St Andrews Way HU8 141 C3
St Anne's Cl HU17 137 B5
St Anne's Dr HU16 139 D6
St Annes Rd YO15 122 F3
St Anne's Rd 8 DN41 101 A5
St Annes Specl Sch HU15 68 E5
St Anne's Wlk 9 HU15 68 D6
St Ann's Ave DN34 152 B2
St Ann's Ct YO10 130 D2
St Anthony Rd YO16 122 E4
St Anthony's Dr 24 HU12 72 D7
St Anthony's Pk 25 HU12 72 D7
St Aubyn's Pl YO24 130 A2
St Augustine Ave DN32 152 E1
St Augustine Cres DN16 151 B1
St Augustine Dr HU11 45 E2
St Augustine Webster RC Prim Sch DN15 150 D8

St Augustine's Ct 2 HU5 140 D3
St Augustine's Dr YO16 122 E5
St Augustine's Gate 30 HU12 72 C7
St Augustine's Gr YO16 122 E5
St Barbara's Cres 8 DN15 82 B4
St Barnabas Ct
4 Kingston upon Hull HU3 145 C4
13 York YO26 129 F5
St Barnabas Dr HU14 69 C7
St Barnabas Rd DN38 99 B4
St Bartholomew's Cl 17 DN41 101 A4
St Bedes RC Comp Sch DN16 151 B2
St Benedict Rd YO23 156 A1
St Bernadettes RC Sch DN16 151 C2
St Bernard's Cl 9 DN20 97 E4
St Boltophs Cl 4 WF11 61 A2
St Botolph's Rd DN16 151 C3
St Catherines YO30 126 D6
St Catherines Cl YO30 126 C5
St Catherines Cres 8 DN16 96 D2
St Catherines Ct
6 Grimsby DN34 102 C3
Kingston upon Hull HU5 140 E2
St Catherine's Dr DN7 92 C2
St Catherines Dr HU17 43 C6
St Chad DN19 85 D8
St Chad Cres YO16 122 E4
St Chad Gr YO16 122 E4
St Chad Rd YO16 122 E4
St Chad's Rd DN16 151 D3
St Chads Wharf YO23 133 C8
St Charles RC Prim Sch HU2 155 A3
St Christopher Rd YO16 122 E4
St Christopher's Rd DN36 114 C8
St Clares Wlk 11 DN20 98 C2
St Clement's Gr YO23 130 C2
St Columba Rd YO16 122 F5
St Crispins Cl DN40 86 E4
St Cuthbert Rd YO16 122 E4
St David Cl HU17 154 B2
St David La YO15 5 B3
St David's Cl HU16 139 D6
St Davids Cres DN17 96 C2
St David's View 9 DN14 64 E4
St Deny's Cl 1 DN40 86 E3
St Denys' Rd YO1 156 C2
St Edmunds's Ct 4 HU5 139 D2
St Edward's Cl YO24 132 F8
St Edwins Cl 27 DN7 92 D4
St Ellens Ct HU17 154 B2
St Francis Ave DN31 152 A4
St Francis Ct 1 HU5 139 D2
St Francis Gr DN37 101 E1
St Francis Prep Sch YO25 125 E7
St George's Ave
Bridlington YO15 122 E3
Hatfield DN7 92 C3
St Georges Cl 19 DN8 93 B7
St George's Ct DN21 108 F3
St Georges Gn DN14 149 D6
St George's Pl YO24 129 F2
St Georges Prim Sch HU3 145 A6
St Georges RC Prim Sch YO10 130 D2
St George's Rd HU3 145 A5
St Georges Rd 16 DN8 93 B7
St George's Wlk HU9 142 B2
St Giles' Ave DN33 102 E1
St Giles Ct
Kingston upon Hull HU9 142 C1
York YO31 156 B3
St Giles Rd YO30 126 B5
St Giles Way YO23 132 A2
St Giles's Croft HU17 154 A2
St Hedda's Ct 6 HU5 139 D2
St Helena Gdns 3 HU5 140 E2
St Helens Ave 13 DN33 102 E2
St Helen's Ave YO42 29 B4
St Helen's Cl YO42 29 B4
St Helen's Cres DN37 113 D5
St Helen's Dr 10 HU15 68 D6
St Helen's La YO14 3 C6
St Helen's Rd
Brigg DN20 98 C2
Pocklington YO42 29 B4
5 York YO24 132 E8
St Helen's Rise YO19 38 A7
St Helen's Sq
Barmby Moor YO42 28 D4
3 Market Weighton YO43 135 D4
York YO1 156 B2
St Helens Way DN21 119 B2
St Helen's Well* YO43 41 D5
St Helier's Rd DN35 153 E3
St Hilda St
3 Bridlington YO15 122 E2
Kingston upon Hull HU3 140 E1
St Hilda's Ave DN34 152 B2
St Hugh's Ave DN35 153 D2
St Hugh's Cres DN16 151 C4
St Hughs Hospl DN32 102 F2
St Hughs Sch DN16 151 B5
St Hybald's Gr DN20 108 F7
St Ives Cl HU7 141 C7
St Ives Cres DN34 102 C3
St James Ave
Grimsby DN34 152 A2
Hatfield DN7 92 C3
St James C of E Prim Sch HU7 141 C6
St James Cl
9 Crowle DN17 94 D7
Kingston upon Hull HU7 141 D7
York YO30 126 E3
St James' Ct DN34 152 C2
St James Ct
Rawcliffe DN14 64 A1
Scunthorpe DN15 151 A6
St James Mount YO24 130 A2
St James Pl 5 YO24 129 D1
St James' Rd YO15 122 D1
St James Rd
21 Brigg DN20 98 C2
Welton HU14 68 F5
St James Sch DN34 152 C2
St James St HU3 145 D5
St James Terr YO8 148 C5
St James's Rd DN20 108 E8
St Joan's Dr DN20 108 E8
St John Mews YO8 148 B7
St John St
Beverley HU17 154 B2
York YO31 156 B3
St John's Ave YO16 122 C3
St John's Ave W YO16 122 C2
St Johns Cl 1 HU17 55 F8
St John's Cl
Bridlington YO16 122 C2
11 Pocklington YO42 28 F4
St John's Cres YO31 156 C4
St Johns Ct HU6 140 D4
St John's Gdns YO25 124 E3
St John's Gr HU9 141 F1
St John's Pl 2 YO25 124 F3
St John's Rd
Great Driffield YO25 124 E3
8 Humberston DN36 114 C8
Scunthorpe DN16 151 C2
9 Stamford Bridge YO41 15 D2
St Johns Sch HU17 154 C4
St John's St
Bridlington YO16 122 D4
15 Howden DN14 65 A7
St John's Well*
Harpham YO25 21 F8
Scunthorpe DN16 96 D1
St John's Wlk
Bridlington YO16 122 C3
1 Great Driffield YO25 124 F3
Kingston upon Hull HU13 143 F2
St Joseph Dr HU4 144 C5
St Josephs RC Prim Sch
Cleethorpes DN35 103 B2
Goole DN14 149 D5
St Jude Gr YO16 122 D4
St Jude Rd YO16 122 D4
St Jude's Ct 3 HU5 139 D2
St Julian's Wells HU10 143 D7
St Katherine's Rd 2 HU15 53 F1
St Lawrence Ave
Kingston upon Hull HU16 138 F5
Snaith DN14 78 B8
St Lawrence Rd DN7 92 C4
St Lawrence Sq HU11 45 F8
St Lawrences C of E Prim Sch YO10 130 E3
St Lawrence's Pl DN16 151 D3
St Lawrence's Rd DN16 151 D2
St Leonards Ave YO8 49 B4
St Leonard's Ave DN31 152 A4
St Leonard's Cl 2 YO25 22 D1
St Leonard's Pl YO30 156 B3
St Leonard's Rd
Beverley HU17 136 C6
Kingston upon Hull HU5 140 D2
St Luke's Cl DN7 92 C2
St Luke's Cres 12 DN36 114 C8
St Luke's Ct DN32 152 F4
St Luke's Gr YO30 130 B7
St Lukes Sch DN16 151 D3
St Luke's St HU3 155 A2
St Margarets Ave HU16 138 E6
St Margarets Cl
Driffield YO25 124 E3
Kingston upon Hull HU16 138 E6
St Margaret's Cl 9 DN37 101 F1
St Margaret's Cres 4 DN40 100 E8
St Margarets Ct 3 HU8 142 C6
St Margaret's Terr YO1 130 E4
St Margaret's Wlk DN16 151 C1
St Mark St HU8 155 C4
St Mark's Gr YO30 126 E2
St Mark's Rd 13 DN36 114 C8
St Mark's Sq HU3 145 D4
St Martins Ave 2 HU4 144 E6
St Martins C of E Sch DN9 106 A3
St Martin's Cl
Blyton DN21 117 F5
2 Burton Agnes YO25 10 A2
Fangfoss YO41 28 C8
St Martin's Cres
6 Grimsby DN33 102 E2
Scawby DN20 108 E8
St Martin's Ct HU17 154 A2
St Martins Dr YO16 122 C3
St Martin's Dr 1 YO25 10 A2
St Martin's Gr YO16 122 C2
St Martin's La YO1 156 A2
St Martin's Pl 16 DN41 101 A4
St Martins Prep Sch DN32 152 D1
St Martin's Rd
Scawby DN20 108 E8
Thorngumbald HU12 72 E5
St Martins Sch YO41 28 C8
St Mary Queen of Martyrs RC Prim Sch HU7 140 F7
St Mary's YO30 156 A3
St Mary's Ave
1 Barnetby le Wold DN38 99 B4
12 Hemingbrough YO8 49 F1
Kingston upon Hull HU5 139 D4
St Marys C of E Jun & Inf Sch HU17 154 A4
St Marys C of E Prim Sch YO23 24 D3
St Mary's Cl
Beverley HU17 136 D5
Brough HU15 68 C7
St Marys Cl YO42 38 C5
St Mary's Cl
Grimsby DN32 153 C2
15 Haxby YO32 13 E5
7 Thorngumbald HU12 72 E5
St Marys Coll HU6 140 C5
St Mary's Cres YO16 122 D4
St Mary's Ct
9 Scunthorpe DN15 96 B7
York YO24 156 A1
St Mary's Dr
Hatfield DN7 92 C2
Hedon HU12 72 D7
St Mary's Gr YO10 131 C4
St Mary's La 5 DN18 84 F8
St Marys La HU17 154 A3
St Marys RC High Sch DN33 102 D2
St Marys RC Prim Sch
Brigg DN20 98 C3
Grimsby DN32 152 F4
Market Weighton YO43 135 E3
Selby YO8 148 B2
St Marys RC Sch YO15 122 C2
St Mary's Rd DN7 92 C2
St Mary's Terr
Beverley HU17 154 A3
York YO30 156 A3
St Mary's Wlk
Beverley HU17 154 A4
Bridlington YO16 122 D4
St Matthew St HU3 145 B5
St Matthew's Cl 4 YO19 36 D8
St Matthews Ct HU17 154 B2
St Matthew's Ct HU17 154 B2
St Matthew's Rd 11 DN36 114 C8
St Maurice's Rd YO31 156 C3
St Mawes Cres DN34 152 A3
St Michael's Cl
Kingston upon Hull HU8 142 B5
Skidby HU16 138 A8
13 Thorne/Moorends DN8 93 B7
St Michael's Cres DN16 151 C4
St Michael's Ct DN19 86 A8
St Michael's Dr
Hedon HU12 72 D7
Thorne DN8 93 B7
St Michael's Mount
Kingston upon Hull HU6 140 C5
14 Swanland HU14 69 B7
St Michael's Rd DN34 102 B2
St Michael's Wlk 3 YO15 4 D3
St Monicas Cl YO42 39 B6
St Monica's Ct 3 HU5 140 C3
St Nectan Cl 9 HU3 145 A4
St Nicholas Ave HU4 144 C2
St Nicholas C of E Sch DN39 86 A1
St Nicholas Cl
Copmanthorpe YO23 132 A3
8 Newbald YO43 53 F7
St Nicholas Cres YO23 132 A3
St Nicholas Croft YO23 24 E3
St Nicholas Cty Prim Sch HU17 154 C2
St Nicholas Dr
Beverley HU17 154 C2
Grimsby DN37 102 B3
Hornsea HU18 134 C6
St Nicholas Gate HU12 72 D7
St Nicholas Pk 6 HU19 75 A6
St Nicholas Pl 1 YO10 130 F3
St Nicholas Prim Sch HU6 140 C4
St Nicholas Rd
Beverley HU17 154 C2
Copmanthorpe YO23 132 A3
Thorne/Moorends DN8 93 A8
St Nicholas Way 22 YO32 13 E5
St Norberts RC Sch DN17 94 D7
St Olaf's Dr DN32 152 D2
St Olave's Rd YO30 156 A4
St Olave's Sch YO30 156 A3
St Oswald Ct 5 HU5 139 D2
St Oswald Rd YO16 122 E4
St Oswalds C of E Prim Sch YO10 133 E7
St Oswald's Cl YO41 27 F6
St Oswald's Rd YO10 133 D8
St Patrick's Gn 14 HU12 74 D1
St Paul St HU2 155 A4
St Pauls C of E Prim Sch YO24 130 A3
St Pauls Dr HU17 137 E8
St Pauls Mews YO24 130 A3
St Paul's Rd
Gainsborough DN21 117 A2
Scunthorpe DN16 151 B2
St Paul's Sq YO24 130 A3
St Paul's Terr YO24 130 A4
St Pauls Way HU17 137 E8
St Peter St HU9 155 C2
St Peter's Ave
Cleethorpes DN35 153 E2
Kingston upon Hull HU10 143 E6
Scunthorpe DN16 96 D2
St Peters C of E Prim Sch DN35 153 F2
St Peters Cl DN21 116 E5
St Peter's Cl
10 Holton le Clay DN36 114 A5
16 Howden DN14 65 A7
St Peters Cl
Hutton Cranswick YO25 32 E8
Rufforth YO26 129 A5
St Peter's Cres 7 DN36 114 C8
St Peters Gr DN37 101 E1
St Peter's Gr
9 Scotter DN21 107 C3
York YO30 156 A4
St Peter's Rd Drax YO8 63 F5
19 Scotter DN21 107 C3
St Peters Sch YO30 156 A4
St Peter's Sq 14 YO42 29 A4
St Peters View HU11 142 F6
St Peters Wlk HU12 59 D2
St Philip's Gr YO30 130 A8
St Philips Rd HU12 73 C4
St Quintin Field YO25 125 F7
St Quintin Pk 9 YO25 34 B2
St Quintins Cl 6 HU9 146 C8
St Richards RC Prim Sch HU9 142 C1
St Sampsons Sq YO1 156 B2
St Saviourgate YO1 156 C2
St Saviour's Pl YO1 156 C2
St Silas St HU2 155 B4
St Stephen Rd YO16 122 E4
St Stephens Cl YO25 124 E3
St Stephen's Cl HU10 138 C2
St Stephen's Cres 4 HU15 66 D8
St Stephen's Rd YO24 129 C2
St Stephen's Sq YO24 129 C1
St Stephens St HU2 145 D6
St Swithin's Wlk YO26 129 E4
St Thomas Moore Rd HU4 144 A4
St Thomas More RC Prim Sch HU4 144 B4
St Thomas' Pl YO31 156 B4
St Thomas Rd YO16 122 E4
St Thomas' Rd 14 DN36 114 C8
St Thomas's Cl 2 YO10 131 C4
St Thomas's Grange 2 HU5 139 D2
St Vincent's Ave DN15 96 D7
St Vincents Prim Sch HU5 140 D2
St Wilfred Rd YO16 122 E3
St Wilfrids Cl HU12 73 E3
St Wilfrid's Cl 7 YO32 14 B6
St Wilfrid's Cres 9 YO8 48 D1
St Wilfrids RC Prim Sch YO31 156 C3
St Wilfrid's Rd 8 YO32 14 B6
St Williams Coll YO31 156 B3
St Wulstan Cl YO31 130 E7
Saints Cl HU9 141 F2
Salacon Way 1 DN32 153 A5
Salamander Cl DN31 152 B4
Salcey Cl 23 HU7 56 F6
Sales La DN14 78 B3
Salisbury Ave
Beverley HU17 136 E1
Goole DN14 149 E4
Hornsea HU18 134 C2
24 Waltham DN37 113 D6
Salisbury Cl DN17 150 C3
Salisbury Rd YO26 129 F5
Salisbury St
6 Gainsborough DN21 117 B2
Kingston upon Hull HU5 140 B2
Kingston upon Hull HU13 143 D1
Salmon Gr HU6 140 B4
Salmonby Rd
1 Scunthorpe DN17 96 C2
Scunthorpe DN17 150 E1
Salmond Rd 5 YO24 129 B1
Salsbury Ave DN34 152 B2
Salt End La HU12 72 A7
Saltash Rd HU4 144 A2
Saltaugh Rd HU12 88 B8
Saltburn Gr DN32 153 A1
Saltergate Rd DN17
Salters' La LN11
Saltford Ave HU9 1
Saltgrounds Rd HU15
Salthouse La HU1 1
Saltmarsh La HU12
Saltmarshe Sta DN14
Salton Ave 4 HU5 13
Saltshouse Rd HU8 14
Saltwell Pk 29 HU7 5
Salvesen Rd DN35 153
Salvesen Way HU3 145
Samman Cl HU10 143
Samman Rd HU17 154
Samphire Cl DN36 115
Sample Ave HU17 154
Sampson St DN17 81
Samuel Ave DN32 153 B
Sanbeds La DN9 105 B
Sancton Cl HU16 138 E
Sancton Rd YO43 135 E
Sanctuary Way DN37 102 B3
Sand Hutton C of E Prim Sch YO41 15 B5
Sand Hutton Ct YO41 15 B5
Sand La
Barlby with Osgodby YO8 49 B4
Broughton DN20 97 D3
Bubwith YO8 50 D5
Caistor LN7 110 E4
Manton DN21 108 A5
Messingham DN17 107 A7
Newton on Derwent YO41 28 B5
North Cave HU15 53 D2
Sancton YO43 53 D8
South Cliffe YO43 52 E8
Thornton YO42 39 D7
Wistow YO8 48 E6
Wroot DN9 104 C6
Sand Rd DN17 106 B8
Sandacre Ct YO26 129 D5
Sandale Ct HU5 139 E1
Sandbeck La DN21 117 E6
Sandcroft Cl 4 YO24 132 D8
Sandcroft Rd YO24 132 D8
Sanderson Cl YO25 124 D2
Sanderson's Bank DN10 104 C2
Sandfield Cl
Market Weighton YO43 135 B3
Scunthorpe DN17 150 D1
Sandfield Dr 3 HU15 68 C5
Sandford Cl HU7 56 F5
Sandford St DN31 152 B4
Sandgate Rd YO16 123 A6
Sandhall Dr DN14 149 F5
Sandhall Rd DN14 65 C3
Sandhill La Brayton YO8 48 D2
Sutton upon Derwent YO41 27 E2
Sandhill Rd DN14 81 B6
Sandholme 2 YO32 13 F5
Sandholme Cl 1 HU15 66 D8
Sandholme La HU17 44 F8
Sandholme Rd HU15 66 C8
Sandholme Way 4 DN14 65 A7
Sandhouse Cres DN16 151 C5
Sandiacres 5 YO8 48 D1
Sandlemere Cl 3 HU3 145 A5
Sandmartin Ct YO24 132 D8
Sandmoor Cl HU8 142 B6
Sandown Cl YO24 129 E2
Sandpiper Ct HU18 134 D6
Sandpiper Dr HU4 144 B1
Sandpits La HU11 47 C1
Sandringham Cl
6 Bridlington YO16 122 D6
Haxby YO32 127 C7
Kingston upon Hull HU16 139 A7
Sandringham Cres 15 DN17 96 C2
Sandringham Dr DN14 149 B6
Sandringham Rd DN35 103 B2
Sandringham St
2 Kingston upon Hull HU3 145 A6
York YO10 130 D2
Sands Cl Keadby DN17 95 D6
Reighton YO14 3 D7
Sands Ct 3 HU14 69 A4
Sands La Barmston YO25 22 F5
Bridlington YO15 122 F3
Brough HU15 68 C6
Ellerker HU15 67 F6
Holme-on-Spalding-Moor YO43 39 F1
Hornsea HU18 134 D4
Hunmanby YO14 3 A8
Scotter DN21 107 C3
South Ferriby DN18 84 A7
Ulrome YO25 23 B3
Sands Rd Barmston YO15 22 F7
Hunmanby YO14 3 B7
Sands Top YO43 53 E7
Sandsacre Ave YO16 123 A6
Sandsacre Dr 1 YO16 123 A6
Sandsacre Rd YO16 123 A6
Sandsacre Way YO16 122 F6
Sandsfield Ave YO43 40 E6
Sandstock Rd
Pocklington YO42 29 A4
York YO31 131 B7

Sandtoft Rd
Epworth DN9 94 B3
Hatfield DN7 93 A4
Sandtoft Transport Ctr Mus* DN8 94 A3
Sandwalk YO43 135 C3
Sandway Ave 12 YO8 48 B1
Sandway Cl 11 YO8 48 B1
Sandway Dr
Camblesforth YO8 63 D4
1 Thorpe Willoughby YO8 48 B1
Sandwith La YO8 63 B4
Sandy Cl DN36 115 C5
Sandy Gap YO32 127 C7
Sandy La Harpham YO25 9 E2
Harton YO60 15 B8
16 Haxby YO32 13 E5
North Duffield YO8 49 F8
Stockton on the Forest YO32 14 E4
Sandy Point HU9 142 E5
Sandy Rise YO8 148 C3
Sandycroft Cl HU10 139 A1
Sandyland 29 YO32 13 E5
Sandyridge YO26 126 A1
Saner St HU3 145 B6
Saner's Cl HU16 139 B5
Sapperton Cl 16 HU7 56 F6
Sapphire Gr 7 HU3 145 A4
Sarah Rhodes La DN14 65 C3
Sargent Ave YO23 132 F4
Sargon Way DN31 102 C6
Sassaby Cl HU4 144 C3
Saunby Gr DN35 153 E3
Saunders Cres 21 YO42 29 A3
Saunders Croft 4 HU17 55 B8
Saunders La HU17 55 B7
Saunders St DN31 152 C4
Savage Rd YO15 122 D2
Savery St HU9 141 D1
Savile Cl HU17 136 E6
Saville Gr YO30 130 A8
Saville St HU1 155 B2
Savoy Ct 12 DN36 114 A7
Savoy Rd HU8 141 F4
Sawcliffe Medieval Village* DN15 82 F1
Sawley Cl HU18 134 C5
Sawmill Yd 5 YO15 122 E2
Sawston Ave HU5 139 C2
Sawyer's Cres YO23 132 C2
Sawyers Wlk 9 YO19 26 F7
Saxby Gr 17 DN33 102 D2
Saxby Hill DN20 84 B3
Saxby Rd Bonby DN20 84 B2
Kingston upon Hull HU8 142 A5
Scunthorpe DN17 150 E1
Saxcourt HU6 139 E7
Saxford Way 8 YO32 13 D5
Saxon Cl
Barton-upon-Humber DN18 84 F8
Shipton YO30 12 F5
6 Thorpe Willoughby YO8 48 B1
Saxon Cres DN35 153 D2
Saxon Ct Blyton DN21 117 F5
Scunthorpe DN16 96 D2
Saxon Pl YO31 130 E7
Saxon Rd YO41 15 D2
Saxon Rise HU17 136 D7
Saxon Vale YO30 12 F5
Saxon Way
4 Caistor LN7 111 B4
Kingston upon Hull HU13 143 F1
Saxondale HU4 144 B7
Saxonfield LN7 111 A4
Scafell Cl 4 YO30 126 E1
Scaife Garth YO42 28 F3
Scaife Gdns YO31 130 C7
Scaife St YO31 130 C7
Scalby Gr HU5 144 D8
Scalby La HU15 66 D8
Scalby Pl HU18 134 B4
Scale La HU1 155 C2
Scale La Staith HU1 155 C2
Scallow La DN17 107 D6
Scalm La YO8 48 A4
Scampton Cl DN34 152 A1
Scampton Garth HU7 141 C8
Scandinavian Way DN41 87 E1
Scarborough Cres 8 YO16 122 C5
Scarborough Rd
Bempton YO16 4 A1
Blyton DN21 117 E5
7 Bridlington YO16 122 C5
Great Driffield YO25 124 E6
Langtoft YO25 8 C7
Scarborough St HU3 145 A4
Scarborough Terr YO30 156 B4
Scarcroft Hill YO24 130 B2
Scarcroft La YO23 156 A1
Scarcroft Prim Sch YO23 156 A1
Scarcroft Rd YO24 156 A1
Scardale Ct YO8 148 A2
Scargate Cl YO16 123 A7
Scarrington Cres HU4 144 B6
Scarrow Cl HU3 145 A7
Scarsea Way YO15 4 C3
Scartho Jun & Inf Sch DN33 102 E1
Scartho Pk DN33 102 D1
Scartho Rd DN33 102 E2
Scaudercroft 13 YO19 26 F7
Scawby Hall* DN20 108 F8
Scawby Prim Sch DN20 108 E8
Scawby Rd Brigg DN20 98 A1
Broughton DN20 97 E2
13 Grimsby DN33 102 D2
Scunthorpe DN17 150 E1
Scawton Ave 1 YO31 127 E2
Schiphol Way DN38 99 E5
Schofield Ave HU17 154 C3
Schofield Cl 5 DN19 85 C8
Scholefield Ave HU17 56 B8
School Cl Selby YO8 148 B3
18 Stamford Bridge YO41 15 D2
School Dr DN17 107 D7
School Hill YO16 10 E4
School House La 2 DN10 116 C3
School Houses 6 DN20 97 E4
School La Appleby DN15 83 D1
Askham Richard YO23 24 D3
Beswick YO25 32 B4
Beverley HU17 154 B3
Bishopthorpe YO23 133 A4
Bonby DN20 84 C2
Buckton/Bempton YO15 4 C3
Burton Fleming YO25 2 E3
Cabourne LN7 111 D5
Copmanthorpe YO23 132 A2
10 Flamborough YO15 5 A2
Goxhill DN19 86 A8
Grayingham DN21 119 B7
Holmpton HU19 75 D2
Irby DN37 112 D7
15 Keyingham HU12 73 C4
Kingston upon Hull HU10 143 C8
New Holland DN19 70 E2
5 North Ferriby HU14 69 A4
North Kelsey LN7 110 A5
5 Pocklington YO42 29 A4
23 Poppleton YO26 12 F1
Redbourne DN21 108 F2
Rothwell LN7 111 E2
South Ferriby DN18 84 A7
Tetney DN36 114 C3
West/East Butterwick DN17 106 D8
York YO10 131 B1
York YO10 133 E7
School Rd
Hemingbrough YO8 49 F1
7 Preston HU12 58 C1
Scunthorpe DN16 151 B2
South Killingholme DN40 86 E3
Winteringham DN15 68 A1
School St
Kingston upon Hull HU1 155 A2
York YO24 129 D3
School Wlk DN35 153 C1
Schooner Ct HU4 144 B3
Schubert Cl HU9 142 A3
Scorborough La YO25 43 D8
Scoreby La YO41 15 B1
Scotchman La YO60 15 A8
Scotney Cl 5 HU3 140 E1
Scott Ave DN17 150 C2
Scott Cl 7 DN37 102 C4
Scott Gdns 7 HU19 75 A6
Scott Moncrieff Rd YO32 14 B6
Scott Rd YO8 148 C6
Scott St
28 Gainsborough DN21 117 B1
Kingston upon Hull HU2 155 B3
York YO23 130 C2
Scotter Cty Sch DN21 107 C3
Scotter Rd
Laughton DN21 117 F8
Messingham DN17 107 D5
Scotton DN21 107 C2
Scunthorpe DN17 150 C3
Scotter Rd S
Bottesford DN17 96 B1
Scunthorpe DN17 150 C1
Scotterthorpe Rd DN21 107 B4
Scotton Rd DN21 107 C3
Scotts Croft YO43 135 D3
Scotts Garth Cl HU17 137 F8
Scotts Garth Dr HU17 44 C5
Scrap Bay Rd DN16 97 A3
Scrivelsby Ct 9 DN35 103 D2
Scriven Gr 8 YO32 13 F5
Scrope Ave 4 YO31 130 E5
Scrub La DN40 86 E5
Scrubwood La HU17 136 E6
Sculcoates La HU5 140 E2
Scunthorpe General Hospl DN15 150 E6
Scunthorpe Leisure Ctr DN15 151 B7
Scunthorpe Mus & Art Gall* DN15 151 A6
Scunthorpe Sta DN16 151 A6
Scunthorpe United Football Club DN15 150 A6
Sea La DN36 115 B3
Sea Rd
Cleethorpes DN35 153 F2
Holmpton HU19 75 D3
Sea View St DN35 153 F1
Seabrook Dr DN16 96 D1
Seacroft Rd
Cleethorpes DN35 103 D3
Seacroft Rd *continued*
Withernsea HU19 75 A6
Seafield Ave HU9 141 F3
Seafire Cl YO30 127 A3
Seaford Rd DN35 103 D1
Seagate YO15 123 C6
Seagull Cl HU4 144 E2
Seakel La YO23 24 C2
Seamer Gr DN32 153 A1
Sean La DN14 65 F4
Searby Hill DN38 110 D8
Searby Rd DN17 96 C2
Searby Wold La DN38 99 E1
Seaside La HU12 60 C2
Seaside Rd
Aldbrough HU11 47 C2
Easington HU12 91 A5
Holmpton HU19 75 C2
Withernsea HU19 75 A7
Seathorne HU19 74 F7
Seathorne Rd 1 YO16 122 C5
Seaton Cl YO10 131 C4
Seaton Gr
Grimsby DN32 153 A1
Kingston upon Hull HU4 144 E5
Seaton Rd
Bewholme YO25 35 A4
Hornsea HU18 134 A4
Kingston upon Hull HU13 143 F2
Scunthorpe DN17 150 D4
Seavy Carr La HU15 52 F2
Seavy Rd DN14 149 B3
Seawall La DN36 115 C5
Second Ave
Bridlington YO15 123 A4
Fixborough Ind Est. DN15 81 F1
4 Goole DN14 149 C4
Grimsby DN33 102 D2
Scunthorpe DN17 150 C2
York YO31 130 F6
Second Common La YO8 48 C4
Sedbergh Ave HU5 139 D3
Sedbury Cl 5 HU7 56 F6
Sedge Cl 4 DN18 69 F1
Sedgebrook Gr 18 HU7 56 F6
Sedgewood Way 13 DN15 96 B7
Seed Close La 3 DN37 101 F1
Sefton Ave YO31 130 F8
Sefton St 2 HU3 145 B4
Seg La YO8 63 F3
Segmere St DN35 103 D3
Segrave Gr HU5 144 D8
Segrave Wlk 10 YO26 129 E4
Selbourne Rd 5 DN34 102 C2
Selby Abbey YO8 148 D5
Selby Abbey Prim Sch YO8 148 C5
Selby Coll Selby YO8 148 C5
Selby YO8 148 F3
Selby High Sch YO8 148 B4
Selby Rd
Eggborough DN14 61 F1
Fulford YO19 133 E6
Holme-on-Spalding-Moor YO43 39 F1
Howden DN14 65 A7
Riccall YO19 49 A8
Snaith DN14 63 C1
Thorne DN8 92 F8
Wistow YO8 48 D6
Womersley DN14 77 A4
Selby Rly Sports & Social Club YO8 148 D5
Selby St HU3 145 A5
Selby Sta YO8 148 D5
Selby Town Football Club YO8 148 B5
Seldon Rd YO26 129 E5
Selge Way DN33 102 C1
Selkirk St HU5 145 A8
Sellers Dr HU17 43 D6
Selsey Cl 2 HU5 140 D2
Selvage La DN14 78 A6
Selwick Dr YO15 5 D2
Selworthy Cl 3 HU7 57 A5
Selwyn Ave 14 HU14 69 A4
Seraphim App Rd DN16 151 E5
Seraphim Rd DN16 151 F4
Service Rd 1 12 DN37 102 C4
Service Rd 10 3 DN37 102 C5
Service Rd 11 4 DN37 102 C5
Service Rd 12 5 DN37 102 C5
Service Rd 13 6 DN37 102 C5
Service Rd 14 7 DN37 102 C5
Service Rd 15 19 DN37 102 C4
Service Rd 16 18 DN37 102 C4
Service Rd 17 10 DN37 102 C4
Service Rd 18 11 DN37 102 C4
Service Rd 19 13 DN37 102 C4
Service Rd 2 15 DN37 102 C4
Service Rd 20 14 DN37 102 C4
Service Rd 21 13 DN37 102 B4
Service Rd 22 1 DN37 102 C4
Service Rd 23 2 DN37 102 C4
Service Rd 25 5 DN37 102 C4
Service Rd 26 8 DN37 102 C5
Service Rd 3 17 DN37 102 C4
Service Rd 4 3 DN37 102 C4
Service Rd 5 4 DN37 102 C4
Service Rd 6 8 DN37 102 C4
Service Rd 7 9 DN37 102 C4
Service Rd 8 1 DN37 102 C5
Service Rd 9 2 DN37 102 C5
Service Rd No 1 DN32 152 F5
Service Rd No 2 DN32 152 F5
Services Rd DN16 151 E6
Setterwood Garth 2 HU10 143 E8
Setting Cres 8 HU5 139 D2
Setting Rd HU5 139 D2
Seven Corners La HU17 136 D4
Seven Quay Rd DN40 87 D3
Seventh Ave
3 Bridlington YO15 122 F4
York YO31 130 F5
Severn Gn YO26 129 C8
Severn St HU8 141 C1
Severus Ave YO26 129 D4
Severus St YO24 129 D3
Sewer La HU1 155 B1
Sewerby Ave YO16 122 E5
Sewerby Cres YO16 122 D5
Sewerby Ct 6 YO16 122 D5
Sewerby Hall Mus & Art Gall* YO15 123 C7
Sewerby Headlands YO16 122 F5
Sewerby Heads YO16 122 F5
Sewerby Park Cl YO15 123 C7
Sewerby Rd YO16 122 D5
Sewerby Rise YO16 122 E5
Sextant Rd HU6 140 C8
Seymour Gr YO31 130 F6
Seymour Rd 6 HU12 73 C4
Seymour St HU3 144 F5
Shadwell Rise 5 DN18 69 E1
Shady La 3 YO25 10 A2
Shaftesbury Ave
Goole DN14 149 A5
Grimsby DN34 152 B3
Hornsea HU18 134 C5
Kellingley DN14 61 C3
Kingston upon Hull HU8 141 F4
Shaftesbury Mews 1 DN36 114 A7
Shaftesbury Rd YO15 122 C1
Shakespeare Ave
2 Campsall DN6 76 E1
Scunthorpe DN17 150 C2
Shakespeare Cl 6 HU3 145 D8
Shallowdale Gr 1 YO10 131 C3
Shambles YO1 156 B2
Shannon Rd HU8 142 C6
Shardeloes HU9 142 E5
Shardlow Rd HU18 134 C5
Sharp Ave HU12 73 A6
Sharp Hill La YO8 63 F6
Sharp St HU5 140 B2
Sharpe Cl 20 DN18 84 E8
Sharpe Howe* YO11 2 A8
Sharps La HU17 55 B7
Shaw Dr 1 DN33 113 F8
Shaw La DN6 77 D2
Shaw Park Prim Sch HU6 139 F8
Shaw Rd DN10 116 A2
Shaw St HU9 146 B7
Shawfield Cl 7 DN3 92 A3
Shaw's Terr YO24 156 A1
Shears Ct DN37 113 E7
Sheep Cote La DN7 92 D2
Sheep Dip La DN7 92 C4
Sheep Marsh La DN36 115 B3
Sheep Rake La YO25 8 F4
Sheep Trod La HU12 89 F6
Sheepdike La YO25 21 F2
Sheepdyke La
Bonby DN20 84 C2
Hunmanby YO14 3 A8
Sheepfold St DN32 152 E3
Sheepman La YO25 32 F7
Sheeprake La YO15 123 B8
Sheepswarth La HU20 54 F3
Sheepwalk La YO17 7 B7
Sheepwash La DN14 77 A7
Sheffield Park Ave DN15 96 C7
Sheffield St DN15 151 A8
Sheffield St E DN15 151 A8
Sheffield St W DN15 150 F8
Sheldon Cl HU7 141 B8
Sheldrake Way HU17 136 F6
Shelford Ave DN14 65 A7
Shelford St DN15 151 A7
Shelley Ave
Grimsby DN33 102 D2
Kingston upon Hull HU9 142 C2
Shelley Gr YO30 126 F1
Shelroy Cl DN15 96 B7
Shenley Cl 11 DN7 92 D3
Shepherd La HU17 55 F8
Shepherd's Croft DN9 105 D7
Shepherds Lea 6 HU17 55 E8
Shepherdton Mere YO25 9 B1
Sheraton Dr 3 DN36 114 D8
Sherbrooke Ave HU5 139 E4
Sherburn Cres DN15 150 D8
Sherburn Rd YO8 148 A8
Sherburn St
1 Cawood YO8 48 B8
Cleethorpes DN35 153 F1
Kingston upon Hull HU9 146 D8
Sherbuttgate Dr 13 YO42 28 F4
Sherbuttgate Rd 14 YO42 28 F4
Sheriff Highway HU12 72 C6
Sherringham Dr YO24 132 D8
Sherwood Ave HU9 141 E1
Sherwood Cl
13 Norton DN6 76 E1
4 Walkington HU17 55 C8
Sherwood Ct HU9 142 D5
Sherwood Dr HU4 144 A7
Sherwood Gr
Huntington YO32 127 F1
York YO26 129 B6
Sherwood Rd DN34 102 C2
Sherwood Vale DN15 150 D7
Shetland Cl 6 HU7 141 E7
Shetland Way 4 DN40 101 C8
Shields Rd 2 HU12 72 C7
Shildon Gr DN8 79 C2
Shilton Garth Cl 3 YO32 127 F7
Shipcote Rd DN14 149 D1
Shipley Cl HU9 142 C2
Shipman Rd YO43 135 D3
Shipton Cres 6 HU17 43 D6
Shipton La YO43 40 E3
Shipton Low Rd YO30 12 E5
Shipton Rd
Clifton YO30 129 F8
Rawcliffe YO30 126 D2
Scunthorpe DN16 151 C1
York YO30 130 A7
Shipton St 3 YO30 130 B7
Shipton Street Inf Sch YO30 130 B7
Shipyard Rd YO8 148 E5
Shirbutt La YO26 24 C8
Shirley Ave YO26 129 C6
Shirley Cres DN16 151 B4
Shoemaker's La DN21 107 D5
Shopeth Way HU17 56 B8
Shore Rd DN17 81 F5
Shoreditch Cl 2 HU8 141 F5
Short La Bempton YO16 4 C1
12 Bridlington YO16 122 C5
Fotherby LN11 121 C2
Market Weighton YO43 41 B2
West Haddlesey YO8 61 F6
West Halton DN15 82 E8
Short St
Cleethorpes DN35 153 E2
Kingston upon Hull HU1 155 A2
Shortacre La YO42 38 E2
Shorthill Croft HU17 154 A1
Shorwell Cl 2 HU8 142 C5
Shotel Cl YO30 129 F8
Shropshire Cl HU5 139 D1
Shrubberies The YO8 49 E2
Sibelius Rd HU4 144 B4
Sicey La HU6 56 D7
Side La DN33 113 F8
Sidebottom St DN31 152 F6
Siding La YO8 49 B5
Sidings Ct HU15 68 B5
Sidmouth Prim Sch HU5 140 B3
Sidmouth St HU5 140 C3
Sidney Pl DN35 153 B4
Sidney Rd
Grimsby DN34 152 B3
Scunthorpe DN17 150 D2
Sidney St DN35 153 B4
Sidney Way DN35 153 B4
Sidsaph Hill 2 DN10 116 D3
Sigglesthorne C of E Prim Sch HU11 45 F8
Sigglesthorne Rd HU11 46 B6
Signhills Ave 1 DN35 103 D2
Signhills Jun & Inf Sch DN35 103 D2
Sigston Rd
2 Beverley HU17 137 A6
Beverley HU17 154 C4
Silica Cres DN17 150 D1
Silkstone Oval 15 DN8 79 B2
Sills La YO30 12 B6
Silsden Ave 5 HU6 140 C7
Silver Birch Rise 22 DN16 96 D2
Silver St
Barnetby le Wold DN38 99 B4
Barrow upon Humber DN19 85 C7
Holton le Clay DN36 114 A5
Huggate YO42 18 C2
Kingston upon Hull HU1 155 B2
Owston Ferry DN9 106 B2
3 Riccall YO19 49 A8
1 Stainforth DN7 92 C6
24 Thorne/Moorends DN8 93 A8
Whitley DN14 77 A7
Winteringham DN15 68 B1
York YO1 156 B2
Silverdale Ct YO24 132 D7
Silverdale Rd HU6 140 C6
Silvergarth DN32 153 A1
Silversides La DN20 98 A1
Sim Balk La YO24 132 E5
Simon Howe YO12 1 A5
Simons Pl DN35 153 D3
Simpson Ave 6 YO14 2 F8
Simpson Cl DN19 85 D8
Simpson's Yd 3 YO8 148 C6
Sinclair Cres HU8 141 F6
Sinderson Rd 18 DN36 103 D1
Sir Henry Cooper Sch HU6 56 D5
Sir John Nelthorpe Lower Sch DN20 98 C2
Sir John Nelthorpe Sch DN20 98 C2
Sirius Cl 3 HU3 145 B5
Sirocco Ct YO31 130 D8
Siskin Cres DN16 96 D1
Sissons La HU15 53 B1
Sissons Way HU5 140 E3

Sittingbourne Cl HU8 141 E8
Sitwell Gr YO26 129 C5
Sitwell St HU8 155 C4
Siward St YO10 131 A3
Siwards How* YO10 131 B1
Sixhills St DN32 152 F3
Sixth Ave
Bridlington YO15 122 F4
Fixborough Ind Est. DN15 82 A1
Scunthorpe DN17 150 B2
York YO31 130 E5
Skeckling Cl HU12 73 A6
Skeffling Rd HU12 90 B7
Skeldergate YO1 156 B2
Skelton Ave HU5 139 E2
Skelton Broad La DN14 65 C4
Skelton Cres YO43 135 C4
Skelton Ct 3 YO30 130 A6
Skelton Prim Sch YO30 126 C5
Skelton Rd DN17 150 C3
Skern Gr HU9 142 A2
Skerne Rd YO25 124 F2
Skewsby Gr YO31 127 F1
Skidby C of E Prim Sch HU16 138 A7
Skidby Carr La HU6 56 C6
Skidby Gr HU6 139 F5
Skidby Rd HU20 55 A4
Skidby Windmill & Mus of E Riding Rural Life* HU16 138 C7
Skiddaw YO24 132 C7
Skiff La YO43 52 C7
Skiff Lane Ind Est YO43 52 D6
Skilgate Cl 7 HU7 57 A5
Skillings La HU15 68 C5
Skinners La
3 South Ferriby DN18 84 A7
Waltham DN37 113 E6
Skipper La YO25 1 E3
Skippingdale Rd DN15 96 C7
Skipsea Castle* YO25 23 A1
Skipsea CP Sch YO25 23 B1
Skipsea La YO25 23 A3
Skipsea Rd Atwick YO25 35 C7
Beeford YO25 22 D1
Bewholme YO25 35 A5
Skipwith Cl HU6 140 B6
Skipwith Comm Nature Reserve* YO8 49 E8
Skipwith Rd YO19 37 B6
Skirbeck Rd HU8 141 D5
Skirlaugh C of E Sch HU11 45 E2
Skirlaugh Rd
Ellerby HU11 45 F1
Swine HU11 57 E8
Skirlaw Cl 18 DN14 65 A7
Skitter Rd DN40 86 D8
Skylark Dr DN16 96 D1
Slack The DN17 94 D8
Slates The* LN11 121 B4
Slay Pit Cl DN7 92 F4
Slay Pit La DN7 92 F3
Sleaford Ave 3 HU9 142 E2
Sledmere Gr HU4 144 E5
Sledmere Rd YO25 8 B6
Sledmere Sch YO25 7 B3
Sleightholme Cl 21 HU7 56 F6
Sleights Cl HU3 145 A7
Sleights La Acklam YO17 16 E7
Broomfleet HU15 67 B6
Eastrington DN14 51 E3
Slessor Rd YO24 129 B1
Slingsby Cl HU5 139 D2
Slingsby Gr YO24 132 E8
Sloe La HU17 136 D1
Sluice La DN18 83 D8
Sluice Rd DN18 83 F8
Smales' St YO1 156 B1
Small Sch at Winestead Hall HU12 74 C4
Smary La YO19 26 D7
Smeatley's La DN6 76 C4
Smeaton Gr YO26 129 C5
Smeaton Rd YO41 27 D7
Smedley Cl HU17 154 C2
Smith Cl YO10 133 F8
Smith Field 4 DN36 114 B1
Smith St Grimsby DN31 152 F6
Scunthorpe DN15 150 F8
Smithall Rd HU17 136 E7
Smithfield Rd DN16 151 D2
Smithie Cl YO32 127 D5
Smithy La
7 Barnetby le Wold DN38 99 B4
Bigby DN38 99 B2
Smitton St DN31 153 A6
Smook Hills Rd HU19 75 A4
Smythy La YO25 1 D4
Snainton Gr 4 HU5 144 D8
Snaith Prim Sch DN14 78 C8
Snaith Rd
Pollington DN14 77 F7
Rawcliffe DN14 64 A1
Snaith DN14 78 D8
Snaith Sec Sch DN14 78 B8
Snaith Sta DN14 63 C1
Snatchells La DN14 78 C2
Snowdon Cl YO23 24 D3
Snowdon Way HU7 57 A7
Snowdonia Ave DN15 96 B8
Snowhill Cl 4 HU7 57 A6
Snuff Mill La HU16 139 B6
Sober Hill Dr YO43 40 A1
Soft La DN19 86 A6
Solomon Ct DN35 153 D1
Somerby Rd DN17 150 D1
Somerby Wold La DN38 99 C1
Somerden Rd HU9 147 E7
Somersby St DN31 152 D4
Somerscales St HU2 155 A4
Somerset Cl 6 YO30 126 E3
Somerset Dr 6 DN15 82 B4
Somerset Rd YO31 130 D8
Somerset St HU3 145 D5
Somerton Dr DN7 92 F4
Somerton Rd DN40 87 C1
Somervell Rd DN16 151 C1
Sonia Crest DN40 87 B1
Sophia Ave 7 DN33 102 E1
Sorbus Ct 5 HU3 145 D6
Sorbus View 4 HU4 144 C7
Sorrel Cl HU17 136 E1
Sorrel Dr 5 HU5 144 D8
Sorrel Way DN15 96 B7
Sorrell La DN14 78 D1
Soss La DN10 116 D5
Sotheron St DN14 149 D4
Sour La DN8 92 E8
Soutergate 12 DN18 69 F1
South Ave YO25 31 F2
South Axholme Sch DN9 105 D6
South Back La YO16 122 B4
South Bank DN17 95 D6
South Bank Ave YO23 130 B1
South Bridge Rd HU9 155 C1
South Carr Dales Rd HU19 74 F3
South Carr La DN20 109 B4
South Carr Rd DN20 109 A4
South Carrs HU17 45 A8
South Cave Prim Sch HU15 53 F1
South Church Side
2 Easington HU12 90 F6
Kingston upon Hull HU1 155 B2
South Cl 7 YO25 9 C3
South Cliff Rd
4 Bridlington YO15 122 E2
Kirton in Lindsey DN21 108 B1
South Dale LN7 111 B4
South Down Rd 3 YO32 127 F5
South Dr YO25 31 C4
South Duffield Rd YO8 49 C4
South Ella Dr HU10 143 D7
South Ella Way HU10 143 D7
South End
Seaton Ross YO42 39 E3
Thorne/Moorends DN8 93 A7
South End La DN14 77 B4
South End Rd
Ottringham HU12 73 E3
Roos HU12 60 B1
South Ferriby Cty Sch DN18 84 A7
South Field Ct 5 HU16 138 F5
South Furlong Croft 17 DN9 105 E6
South Gate YO25 32 E6
South Glebe YO25 32 B1
South Gr 8 YO25 9 C3
South Holderness Sch HU12 72 D8
South Hunsley Sch HU14 68 E5
South Ings La HU15 53 C2
South Intake La DN9 116 F7
South La
Bishop Wilton YO42 16 F1
Cawood YO8 48 B7
Kingston upon Hull HU13 143 E1
South Leys Comp Sch DN17 96 C2
South Leys Rd HU19 75 A4
South Marine Dr YO15 122 D1
South Marsh Rd DN41 101 F7
South Moor Rd DN10 116 C3
South Newbald Rd YO43 53 F7
South Par
Grimsby DN31 152 D4
Leven HU17 45 A7
8 Selby YO8 148 C5
Thorne DN8 93 A7
York YO24 156 A1
South Par Inf Sch DN31 152 D4
South Par Jun Sch DN31 152 D4
South Park Rd DN17 96 B2
South Parkway 4 DN14 78 C8
South Pk HU12 60 B1
South Prom HU18 134 D4
South Rd
Keadby with Althorpe DN17 95 C6
Thorne/Moorends DN8 79 B2
South Rise HU16 138 B8
South Rise Cres 20 DN17 96 C2
South Ruddings La YO19 37 F7
South Sea Ave 26 YO15 5 A2
South Sea La DN36 114 D7
South Sea Rd YO15 5 A2
South Side Kilham YO25 9 B3
Winteringham DN15 68 A1
South Side La YO25 9 F6
South St
Barmby on the Marsh DN14 64 A7
South St *continued*
Barnetby le Wold DN38 99 B4
Bridlington YO15 122 E1
Burton Fleming YO25 2 E2
8 Gainsborough DN21 117 A2
Goole DN14 149 C2
Keelby DN41 101 A5
Kingston upon Hull HU16 139 A6
Kingston upon Hull HU1 155 A2
Leven HU17 45 A7
Middleton-on-the-Wolds YO25 31 C4
North Kelsey LN7 110 A4
Owston Ferry DN9 106 B2
Roxby cum Risby DN15 82 F3
West Butterwick DN17 106 D8
Winterton DN15 83 A5
South St Mary's Gate 4 DN31 152 D3
South Townside Rd YO25 34 A8
South View
Broughton DN20 97 D4
Healaugh LS24 24 A2
Holton le Clay DN36 114 B5
6 Humberston DN36 103 D1
South View Ave
Brigg DN20 98 C2
Burringham DN17 95 D4
South Wold HU20 55 A4
South Wolds Sch HU17 43 A7
South Wood Dr 12 DN8 93 A7
Southburn Ave HU4 144 E7
Southburn Rd YO25 20 A1
Southcliff Rd HU19 75 A6
Southcliffe Rd 12 DN21 107 C3
Southcoates Ave HU9 141 E2
Southcoates La HU9 146 E8
Southcoates Prim Sch HU9 141 F1
Southcote Cl 4 HU15 54 A2
Southcroft Dr 8 HU8 141 E7
South-Dale Cl 1 DN21 108 B2
Southern Dr HU4 144 C5
Southern Rd DN40 87 C3
Southern Way DN40 87 C3
Southern Wlk DN33 113 E8
Southfield 1 Belton DN9 94 E1
Kingston upon Hull HU13 69 E4
Southfield Cl
Great Driffield YO25 124 F6
Rufforth YO23 24 D6
14 Thorne/Moorends DN8 93 B7
Ulceby DN39 86 B1
Wetwang YO25 19 B5
Southfield Cres 2 YO24 132 E8
Southfield Dr
1 Beverley HU17 137 A6
4 Epworth DN9 105 D6
North Ferriby HU14 69 A4
Southfield La
Barmston YO25 23 A6
Elstronwick HU12 59 C3
Everingham YO42 40 B4
Kellington DN14 61 E2
Roos HU12 60 C1
Seaton Ross YO42 39 D1
Skipsea YO25 23 B2
Willoughton DN21 119 A3
Southfield Pk YO43 135 D3
Southfield Rd
1 Broughton DN20 97 D3
7 Crowle DN17 94 D7
Elstronwick HU12 59 A2
Great Driffield YO25 124 F6
Grimsby DN33 113 E8
15 Holton le Clay DN36 114 A5
Kingston upon Hull HU5 140 A2
North Kelsey LN7 109 E2
Pocklington YO42 28 F4
Scunthorpe DN16 151 C1
Thorne/Moorends DN8 93 B7
Wetwang YO25 19 A5
Winterton DN15 82 F5
Southfield Well Balk YO25 19 B5
Southfields HU15 52 E1
Southfields Rd YO32 14 B7
Southgate
Hornsea HU18 134 C3
Kingston upon Hull HU13 143 E1
Market Weighton YO43 135 E3
Southgate Cl HU10 138 E2
Southgate Gdns 2 HU18 134 C3
Southlands
4 Haxby YO32 13 E5
16 Hemingbrough YO8 49 F1
Southlands Ave 1 DN21 117 A2
Southlands Cl YO19 37 B6
Southlands Dr 3 DN21 117 A2
Southlands Gdns 2 DN21 117 A2
Southlands Rd YO23 130 B2
Southmoor La WF11 61 B1
Southmoor Rd
Crowle DN17 94 C8
Thorganby YO19 37 F5
Southolme Dr 7 YO30 126 F1
Southorpe Cl YO16 122 B5
Southorpe La DN21 118 D7
Southorpe Rd HU11 134 A1
Southside HU12 74 D1
Southside Rd HU12 73 F5
Southwell Ave HU9 147 E8
Southwell Cl HU17 136 E1
Southwold Cres 25 DN33 113 E8
Southwood Ave HU16 138 F6
Southwood Dr HU16 139 A6
Southwood Gdns HU16 138 F5
Southwood Rd
Kingston upon Hull HU16 138 F5
Sutton upon Derwent YO41 38 C8
Soutter Gate HU12 72 C7
Sovereign Cl 14 DN34 102 B2
Sow Hill Rd HU17 154 A3
Sowerby Rd YO26 129 D4
Sowers La DN15 83 A5
Spa Hill DN21 108 B1
Spa Well La DN14 78 C8
Spalding Ave YO30 130 B7
Spalding Rd DN16 151 B4
Spark Mill La HU17 154 C1
Spark St DN34 152 A3
Sparrowcroft La DN14 66 E3
Speculation St YO1 130 E4
Speedwell Cres DN15 96 B7
Speedwell La 1 HU17 55 D8
Speeton Gate YO15 4 B4
Spellowgate YO25 20 C7
Spellowgate Cl YO25 124 D5
Spen La
Holme-on-Spalding-Moor YO43 39 F2
York YO1 156 C3
Spencer Ave DN15 150 F8
Spencer Cl
22 Hedon HU12 72 C7
Kingston upon Hull HU16 138 F6
Spencer St
Beverley HU17 154 A3
Grimsby DN31 153 B5
Kingston upon Hull HU2 155 A3
3 York YO23 156 B1
Spencer Way 1 HU16 139 B7
Spencers Mead YO25 124 E3
Spencers Way YO25 124 E4
Speng La YO26 24 B4
Spenser St DN14 149 C5
Sperrin Cl 2 HU9 142 A3
Spey Bank YO24 132 C6
Spilsby Rd DN17 150 E1
Spindle Cl YO24 132 C8
Spindlewood 1 HU15 68 C7
Spinnaker Cl HU9 146 C6
Spinney Cl 2 DN40 87 C1
Spinney Croft Cl 12 HU14 69 A5
Spinney The
1 Barnby Dun DN3 92 A3
Grimsby DN34 152 C3
Kingston upon Hull HU16 139 A5
6 Newport HU15 52 F1
7 Swanland HU14 69 B7
York YO24 132 F7
Spinney Wlk HU4 144 C6
Spire View 1 HU13 143 E1
Spital Hill DN21 117 B1
Spital Terr DN21 117 B1
Spittlerush La DN6 76 D2
Spout H YO42 28 D3
Spout Hill HU15 68 C8
Spratton Ct 2 DN37 102 B2
Spring Bank
Grimsby DN34 152 A3
Kingston upon Hull HU2 155 A3
4 North Newbald YO43 53 F7
Spring Bank W HU4 144 D7
Spring Cl YO25 124 D5
Spring Cottage Prim Sch HU8 141 F6
Spring Dale Rd YO43 135 E5
Spring Field Cl HU11 45 F8
Spring Gdns HU8 141 D5
Spring Gdns E HU4 144 B6
Spring Gdns S HU4 144 B5
Spring Gdns W HU4 144 B6
Spring Gr HU3 145 A7
Spring La
2 Buckton/Bempton YO15 4 D3
11 Laceby DN37 101 F1
Long Marston YO26 24 A5
York YO10 131 A1
Spring Rd 1 YO43 135 E4
Spring St
Immingham DN40 87 C1
Kingston upon Hull HU2 155 A3
Spring Vale HU9 142 D5
Spring Wlk YO8 148 A1
Springbank DN20 98 C2
Springbank Ave
Dunnington YO19 26 E7
Hornsea HU18 134 B4
Springbok Cl HU4 144 D2
Springburn St HU3 145 A5
Springdale Cl HU10 143 F8
Springdale Way HU17 154 A1
Springfield
Holme-on-Spalding-Moor YO43 40 A1
6 Howden DN14 65 B7
Springfield Ave
Bridlington YO15 122 E2
18 Brough HU15 68 C6
5 Hatfield DN7 92 E4
Springfield Cl
Barlby with Osgodby YO8 49 B5
Heworth YO31 131 C7
2 Scunthorpe DN16 151 C2
Springfield Cres 3 WF8 76 C3
Springfield Dr
9 Barlby YO8 49 B5
Beverley HU17 137 A6
Springfield Gdns YO43 40 A1
Springfield Prim Sch DN33 113 D8
Springfield Rd
25 Brigg DN20 98 C2
Grimsby DN33 113 D8
Kingston upon Hull HU3 144 F6
Pocklington YO42 29 B3
4 Poppleton YO26 12 F1
Springfield Rise DN20 98 D2
Springfield Way
Hook DN14 149 F6
Kingston upon Hull HU10 143 E7
York YO31 131 B7
Springfields 18 WF11 61 A2
Springfields Ave 17 WF11 61 A2
Springhead Ave HU5 144 A7
Springhead Cl 6 DN14 65 A7
Springhead Ct HU10 144 A6
Springhead Gdns HU10 144 A7
Springhead La HU4 144 A7
Springhead Prim Sch HU10 143 F7
Springs Rd DN10 104 C1
Springs Way DN20 98 B2
Springthorpe Rd DN21 118 B1
Springville Ave HU13 143 F2
Springway Cres DN34 152 A3
Springwood YO32 127 D7
Springwood Cres 7 DN33 113 D8
Sproatley Endowed Sch HU11 58 D5
Sproatley Rd HU12 58 D3
Spruce Cl YO32 127 D2
Spruce La DN39 86 A1
Spruce Rd
Kingston upon Hull HU1 155 A1
Leven HU17 45 B8
Spurn Ave 16 DN33 113 E8
Spurn Lightship* YO23 156 B1
Spurn Rd HU12 91 B2
Spurriergate YO1 156 B2
Spyvee St HU8 155 C3
Square The
4 Easington HU12 90 F6
Goxhill DN19 86 A8
Kingston upon Hull HU13 143 E1
Skerne & Wansford YO25 21 C3
Yapham YO42 28 E7
Squire La YO16 122 C4
Stable La
4 Barton-upon-Humber DN18 69 E1
Barton-upon-Humber DN18 69 E1
Stable Rd YO8 63 D7
Stabler Cl 15 YO32 13 D5
Stablers Wlk YO32 127 F7
Staddlethorpe Broad La HU15 66 D7
Stafford St HU2 155 A4
Staindale Cl YO30 126 E2
Staindale Rd DN16 151 E1
Staines Cl HU8 142 A4
Stainforth Mid Sch DN7 92 C6
Stainforth Moor Rd DN7 93 C3
Stainforth Rd DN7 92 A5
Stainton Dr
Grimsby DN33 102 D2
15 Immingham DN40 87 B1
9 Scunthorpe DN17 96 C2
Staithe St 3 YO8 50 D7
Staithes Cl 4 YO26 129 B4
Staithes Rd HU12 72 B8
Stallingborough C of E Prim Sch DN41 101 E6
Stallingborough Rd
Healing DN41 101 E5
Immingham DN40 87 B1
Keelby DN41 101 A5
Stallingborough Sta DN41 101 E6
Stalybridge Ave HU9 142 E1
Stamford Bridge Prim & Inf Sch YO41 15 D2
Stamford Bridge Rd YO19 26 E7
Stamford Bridge W YO41 15 C2
Stamford Gr HU9 142 E1
Stamford St E 10 YO26 129 F5
Stamford St W 8 YO26 129 F5
Stan Valley 2 WF8 76 C3
Stanbury Rd HU6 140 C7
Standage Rd 12 HU12 72 E5
Standidge Dr HU8 142 A5
Standish La 1 DN40 87 B2
Stanfield Rd 2 DN9 105 D6

Stanford Cl DN37 ....101 F1
Stanford Sch DN37 .....101 F1
Stanholme La DN36 ....114 A1
Stanhope Ave HU9 .....141 E2
Stanhope Pl DN35 .....153 C3
Stanhope St DN14 ......149 C4
Stanhurst La DN7 ....93 A5
Staniland Dr YO8 ......148 A5
Staniland Way 1 DN36 .114 D8
Staniwell Rise DN17 .....150 D3
Stanlewells Dr 9 DN20 ....97 D3
Stanley Ave
Haxby YO32 ....127 D7
Hornsea HU18 ....134 C2
Stanley Gdns 15 DN7 .....92 C6
Stanley Rd
Scunthorpe DN15 ....150 C7
16 Stainforth DN7 ....92 C6
Stanley St Goole DN14 ..149 D4
Grimsby DN32 ....153 A4
Kingston upon Hull HU3 ...145 C7
York YO31 ....156 C4
Stannington Dr HU8 ....142 D6
Stansfield Cl HU9 ....142 D1
Stansted St DN31 ......152 B5
Staple Rd DN40 ....86 F3
Stapleford Cl 4 HU9 ...142 E2
Star Carr La DN20 ....98 C4
Star Hill Rd YO25 ....124 F5
Starboard Ave HU6 .....140 C8
Starcarr La YO25 ....34 A1
Starella Gr HU3 ....145 A4
Starham Rd LN7 ....109 C4
Starkbridge La DN14 ....78 A3
Starkey Cres YO31 .....131 A5
Stather Rd
Burton upon Stather DN15 ....82 A5
Flixborough DN15 ....82 A1
Stathers Wlk 3 HU10 ...143 F6
Station App YO15 ......122 E2
Station Ave
Bridlington YO16 ....122 D2
New Waltham DN36 ......114 A7
York YO32 ....127 D3
York YO1 ....156 A2
Station Ct HU18 ....134 D4
Station Dr HU3 ....140 D1
Station Hill YO25 ....19 B6
Station La
Barmby on the Marsh DN14 ....64 B7
Cliffe YO8 ....49 E3
Hedon HU12 ....72 C8
Holme-on-Spalding-Moor YO43 ....39 F1
Searby cum Owmby DN38 ....110 D7
Shipton YO30 ....12 E5
Station Mews HU18 .....134 D4
Station Rd Bainton YO25 ..31 E6
Blyton DN21 ....117 F6
Bridlington YO15 ....122 D2
Brough HU15 ....68 B5
Burringham DN17 ....95 D4
7 Burstwick HU12 ....73 A6
Burton Agnes YO25 ....10 A1
Carlton DN14 ....63 C3
Cleethorpes DN35 ....153 E3
Copmanthorpe YO23 ......132 B2
East Halton DN40 ....86 D7
Eastrington DN14 ....65 F8
Epworth DN9 ....105 D7
Fulstow LN11 ....121 D7
Garthorpe & Fockerby DN17 ....81 E6
Garton YO25 ....20 A5
Gilberdyke HU15 ....66 D8
Grasby DN38 ....110 E6
Grimsby DN37 ....102 B5
Gunness DN15 ....95 E5
Habrough DN40 ....100 E8
Harpham YO25 ....21 E8
Hatfield DN7 ....92 D4
Haxby YO32 ....13 F5
Haxey DN9 ....116 C7
Healing DN41 ....101 F5
Hensall DN14 ....62 C1
Holton le Clay DN36 .....114 A4
Howden DN14 ....65 B8
Hutton Cranswick YO25 .....32 E7
Keadby with Althorpe DN17 ....95 D6
Keyingham HU12 ....73 C4
Killingholme High DN40 .....87 B5
Kingston upon Hull HU16 ....139 C7
Kingston upon Hull HU13 ....143 E1
Kirton in Lindsey DN21 ....108 B2
Lockington YO25 ....32 D1
Ludborough DN36 ....121 B6
Market Weighton YO43 ....135 D4
Middleton YO25 ....31 C5
Middleton-on-the-Wolds YO25 ....31 C4
Misterton DN10 ....116 D5
Nafferton YO25 ....125 F6
New Waltham DN36 ......114 A7
North Cave HU15 ....53 D3
North Ferriby HU14 ....69 A4
North Kelsey LN7 ....110 A4
North Thoresby DN36 .....114 B1
Norton DN6 ....76 F2
Ottringham HU12 ....73 F4
Station Rd *continued*
Owston Ferry DN9 ....106 A2
Patrington HU12 ....74 C2
Pocklington YO42 ....29 A3
24 Poppleton YO26 ....12 F1
Poppleton YO26 ....24 F8
Preston HU12 ....72 C8
Rawcliffe DN14 ....64 A1
Riccall YO19 ....49 A8
Scawby DN20 ....108 F7
Scunthorpe DN15 ....151 B6
Selby YO8 ....148 D5
South Cave HU15 ....54 A2
South Kelsey LN7 ....110 D2
South Killingholme DN40 ...87 A5
Stainforth DN7 ....92 C5
Stallingborough DN41 .....101 D6
Thorngumbald HU12 ....73 A5
Thornton Curtis DN39 ......85 F5
Ulceby DN39 ....86 B1
Walkeringham DN10 ....116 D3
Waltham DN37 ....113 E7
Wharram YO17 ....6 A4
Whitton DN15 ....67 D3
Wistow YO8 ....48 C6
5 Withernsea HU19 ....75 A6
Womersley DN6 ....76 D5
York YO1 ....156 A2
Station Rise YO1 ....156 A2
Station Sq 4 YO32 ....14 B7
Station St DN10 ....116 C5
Station View YO8 ....49 D3
Staveley Rd HU9 ....142 C3
Staves Ct 10 DN36 .....114 D4
Staxton Ct HU9 ....146 D8
Staxton Hill YO12 ....1 C8
Staynor Ave YO8 ....148 E3
Steadings The DN15 .....82 B1
Steele Cl YO43 ....135 D3
Steep Hill HU15 ....54 B2
Steeping Dr 11 DN40 .....87 B1
Steeple Cl 4 YO32 ....13 D5
Steeton Ave 4 HU6 .....140 C7
Stembridge Cl 1 HU9 ...142 E1
Stephen Cl 2 DN39 ....86 A1
Stephen Cres
14 Barton-upon-Humber DN18 ....84 F8
Grimsby DN34 ....102 C2
10 Humberston DN36 .....114 C8
Stephen's Wlk YO8 .....148 B1
Stephenson Cl
Market Weighton YO43 ....135 C3
York YO31 ....127 E1
Stephenson St HU9 .....141 E1
Stephenson Way YO26 ....129 F5
Stephenson's Wlk HU16 ....139 D6
Stephenwath La YO41 ....16 C5
Stepney Ave 18 YO16 ....122 C5
Stepney Gr YO16 ....122 C4
Stepney La HU5 ....140 E1
Sterling Cres DN37 .....113 D6
Sterne Ave
7 Broughton DN20 ....97 D3
York YO31 ....131 A5
Stevenson Pl DN35 .....153 D1
Stevenson's Way 18 DN18 ....84 E8
Stewart Garth HU16 ....138 E6
Stewart La YO19 ....36 C4
Steynburg St HU9 ......141 D1
Stirling Cl 2 DN21 ......117 C1
Stirling Gr YO10 ....133 F8
Stirling Rd
Barmby Moor YO42 ....28 E3
York YO30 ....126 F3
Stirling St
Grimsby DN31 ....153 B5
Kingston upon Hull HU3 ...144 F6
Stirrup Cl YO24 ....132 B8
Stockbridge Ave HU9 ...142 E1
Stockbridge La YO25 ....32 F6
Stockbridge Pk 2 HU15 ...68 C7
Stockbridge Rd HU15 ....68 B7
Stockhill Cl 1 YO19 ....26 E7
Stockholm Cl 1 YO10 ...133 D8
Stockholm Pk 23 HU12 ...72 D7
Stockholm Rd
Kingston upon Hull HU7 ...140 E5
16 Thorngumbald HU12 .....72 E5
Stocking La Hillam LS25 ...61 B7
Knottingley WF11 ....61 B2
Stockleigh Cl HU7 ....140 F8
Stocks Dr DN14 ....79 B8
Stocks Hill Belton DN9 ....94 E1
Huggate YO42 ....18 C1
Stockshill Rd DN16 .....151 C2
Stockton Hall YO32 ......14 D3
Stockton La
Heworth YO32 ....128 D1
York YO31 ....131 A7
Stockton on the Forest Cty Prim Sch YO32 ....14 D3
Stockwell Gr HU9 ......147 E8
Stockwell La 10 YO25 ....34 B2
Stockwell Prim Sch HU9 ....147 E8
Stockwith La YO8 ....63 A4
Stockwith Rd
Haxey DN9 ....105 E1
Owston Ferry DN9 ....116 E8
Walkeringham DN10 ......116 D3
Walkerith DN21 ....116 E4
Stoke St HU2 ....155 A4
Stone Bridge Dr YO41 ...27 F5
Stone Dale YO42 ....17 D3
Stone Hill DN7 ....93 A4
Stone Hill Rd DN7 ....93 A4
Stone La DN17 ....95 D4
Stone Riggs YO32 ....14 D2
Stonebow The YO1 .....156 C2
Stonebridge Ave HU9 ..142 D1
Stonecarr Ct 2 HU7 ......56 F7
Stoneferry Prim Sch HU8 ....141 A3
Stoneferry Rd HU8 .....141 A2
Stonegate
Hunmanby YO14 ....2 F8
Thorne/Moorends DN8 .....93 A8
York YO1 ....156 B2
Stonegate Cl 3 HU7 ....141 D7
Stoneknowle Hill YO43 ...54 A8
Stonelands Ct 2 YO30 ...127 A1
Stonepit Balk YO17 ....6 C5
Stonepit Hill YO17 ....6 C4
Stonepit La YO15 ....4 E3
Stonepit Rd
Ellerker HU15 ....54 A1
Welton HU15 ....68 E6
Stones Mount HU16 ....139 A7
Stonesdale HU7 ....141 A6
Stonethwaite 5 YO24 ...132 C7
Stoney La HU15 ....53 A3
Stoney Way DN36 ....114 D4
Stony La HU15 ....53 A2
Stool Close Rd DN9 ......94 E1
Stoop Cl YO32 ....127 C8
Storkhill Rd HU17 ......154 C4
Storking La YO41 ....27 F6
Stornaway Sq HU8 .....141 F7
Stortford St DN31 ......152 B5
Story St HU1 ....155 A3
Stothards La 1 DN19 ....86 A8
Stottlebink 17 YO15 ....5 A2
Stovin Cres DN15 ....83 A5
Stow Cl 11 DN37 ....102 B4
Stow Ct YO32 ....127 E3
Stow Rd Atwick YO25 ....35 D5
Scunthorpe DN16 ....151 B3
Straight La YO19 ....26 F8
Straits Rd HU11 ....46 D2
Strand Cl HU2 ....155 A4
Strand Inf Sch DN32 ....153 A5
Strand Jun Sch DN32 ...152 F5
Strand St DN32 ....152 F5
Stratford Ave 4 DN33 ...102 D2
Stratford Dr DN16 ......151 C5
Stratford Way YO32 ....127 E3
Strathcona Ave HU5 ....139 E4
Strathearn St 1 HU5 ...140 D3
Strathmore Ave
Burstwick HU12 ....73 A7
Kingston upon Hull HU6 ...140 C6
Stratton Cl HU8 ....142 B7
Stratton Pk 3 HU14 ....69 B6
Strawberry Gdns HU18 ....134 C1
Strawberry Hill 2 DN37 ....113 C6
Strawberry St HU9 ......146 B7
Stray Garth YO31 ......130 F7
Stray Rd
Sunk Island HU12 ....89 B6
York YO31 ....131 B6
Stray The HU15 ....54 A2
Straylands Gr YO31 .....130 F8
Street YO25 ....9 E1
Street La Bubwith YO8 ....50 F5
North Kelsey LN7 ....110 B4
Street Life Mus of Transport* HU1 ....155 C2
Street The YO42 ....28 A2
Strensall Pk YO32 ....14 A5
Strensall Rd
Earswick YO32 ....128 A7
Kingston upon Hull HU5 ...139 C1
York YO32 ....127 F6
Strickland Rd
Eastoft DN17 ....81 A2
18 Hunmanby YO14 ....3 A8
Strickland St HU3 ....145 C4
Strines Gr 9 HU7 ....141 D7
Stripe La YO30 ....126 B5
Stromness Way HU8 .....141 F7
Stroud Cres E HU7 .....141 A7
Stroud Cres W HU7 .....141 A8
Strouther Cl YO42 ....29 A3
Strubby Cl 6 DN35 .....103 D2
Stuart Cl
Bridlington YO15 ....122 C1
Scunthorpe DN17 ....96 C1
4 Strensall YO32 ....14 C8
Stuart Gr
Eggborough DN14 ....62 A2
9 Thorpe Willoughby YO8 ...48 B1
Stuart Rd YO24 ....129 D1
Stuart Wortley St DN31 ....152 F6
Stub Ings La DN40 ....87 D1
Stubbs La
Cridling Stubbs WF11 ......76 A8
Norton DN6 ....76 E2
Stubbs Rd DN6 ....76 D3
Stubden Gr YO30 ....126 F2
Studcross DN9 ....105 D6
Studley Mdws YO16 ....122 D7
Studley St HU8 ....146 B8
Stump Cross* HU17 ....43 C2
Sturdee Gr YO31 ....130 D7
Sturmer Ct 15 DN16 ......96 D1
Sturton Gr 23 DN33 .....102 D2
Sturton La DN20 ....108 E7
Stygate La DN6 ....76 E1
Stylefield Rd 15 YO15 ......5 A2
Styles Croft HU14 ....69 C7
Subway St HU3 ....145 B3
Subway The DN16 ....97 A4
Suddaby Cl HU9 ....141 F2
Suddle Way 4 DN41 .....101 A4
Sudforth La DN14 ....61 C3
Suffolk St HU5 ....140 D3
Suggitt's Ct DN35 ......153 D4
Suggitt's La DN35 ......153 D4
Suggitt's Orch DN35 ....153 D4
Sullivan Rd HU4 ....144 B4
Summer Hill DN21 ......117 C1
Summerdale DN18 ....84 E8
Summerfield Ave 3 DN37 ....113 E7
Summerfield Cl
Great Driffield YO25 ......124 D5
4 Waltham DN37 ....113 E7
Summerfield Rd
Bridlington YO15 ....122 D1
York YO24 ....132 C7
Summergangs Dr 17 HU12 ....72 E5
Summergangs Rd HU8 ....141 C3
Summergroves Way HU4 ....144 B2
Sunbeam Rd HU4 ......144 D5
Sunk Island Rd HU12 ....88 E8
Sunningdale 12 DN37 ...113 D6
Sunningdale Ave 1 DN20 ....98 C3
Sunningdale Cl 1 YO26 .129 B5
Sunningdale Dr 7 DN40 ..87 C2
Sunningdale Rd
Kingston upon Hull HU13 ....143 F2
Kingston upon Hull HU4 ...144 E4
Scunthorpe DN17 ....96 B2
Sunny Bank
Kingston upon Hull HU3 ...145 B7
3 Knottingley WF11 ....61 A2
Sunny Cnr 13 DN33 .....102 E1
Sunny Hill 9 DN21 ......108 B1
Sunnybank 1 DN18 ....84 E8
Sunnydale 3 YO32 ......127 D7
Sunway Gr DN16 ....151 A1
Sunway Infants Sch DN16 ....151 A1
Surbiton Cl HU8 ....141 F5
Surrey Garth HU4 ......144 B4
Surrey Way YO30 ....129 F8
Surtees St
Grimsby DN31 ....152 F6
York YO30 ....130 B7
Sussex Cl
5 Kingston upon Hull HU5 ....139 D1
York YO10 ....131 C2
Sussex Rd YO10 ....131 C2
Sussex St DN35 ....153 B4
Sussex Way 14 YO32 .....14 A7
Susworth Rd DN17 .....106 D4
Sutcliffe Ave 13 DN33 ...102 D2
Sutherland Ave HU6 ....140 B6
Sutherland St YO23 ....130 B1
Sutor Cl YO23 ....132 B3
Sutton Bridge* YO41 ....27 C2
Sutton C of E Sch HU7 ....141 D7
Sutton Cl HU7 ....141 B8
Sutton Ct HU8 ....141 E6
Sutton Gdns HU7 ....141 B7
Sutton Ho Rd HU8 ......141 D5
Sutton La
Barmby Moor YO42 ....28 B3
Byram cum Sutton WF11 ....61 A4
Sutton on Derwent C of E Prim Sch YO41 ....27 C2
Sutton Park Prim Sch HU7 ....140 F7
Sutton Pl DN20 ....108 F7
Sutton Rd Howden DN14 ..65 A6
Kingston upon Hull HU6 ...140 D6
12 Kirk Sandall DN3 ....92 A3
Wawne HU7 ....56 F7
Sutton St DN14 ....149 D4
Sutton Way
Kingston upon Hull HU9 ...142 B2
York YO30 ....130 B8
Swaby Dr DN35 ....103 B2
Swaby's Yd HU17 ....154 A3
Swaddale Ave HU10 ....138 F2
Swainby Cl HU7 ....141 D7
Swale Ave YO24 ....132 E8
Swaledale Ave HU9 ....141 E1
Swaledale Mews YO16 ....122 F6
Swaledale Pl DN16 .....151 D2
Swales Rd DN36 ....114 D8
Swallow Ct 4 DN9 ......105 D7
Swallow Dr 7 DN41 .....101 F5
Swallow Grange 6 HU8 ....141 D7
Swallow La DN39 ....85 E2
Swallowfield Dr HU4 ...144 B2
Swan Cl YO19 ....37 A7
Swan Farm Ct YO19 ......37 A7
Swan Hill* HU11 ....142 F6
Swan Syke Dr 8 DN6 .....76 F2
Swanella Gr HU3 ....145 A4
Swanfield Rd HU9 ......142 C2
Swanland Ave 3 YO15 ...122 F3
Swanland Butts Cl HU10 ....143 C6
Swanland Cl 17 DN8 ......93 B7
Swanland CP Sch HU14 ...69 B6
Swanland Dale HU14 .....69 B8
Swanland Garth 4 HU14 .69 A5
Swanland Hill HU14 .....69 B5
Swanland Rd HU13 .....143 C2
Swanland Way 3 HU16 .138 E6
Swann St
Kingston upon Hull HU2 ...155 C4
York YO23 ....156 A1
Swannacks View DN20 ....108 F7
Sweet Briar Cl 7 DN37 ..113 D7
Sweet Dews Gr HU9 ....146 D8
Sweyne Garth DN14 .....65 D1
Swift Rd DN17 ....150 D2
Swiftsure Cres 10 DN34 .102 B2
Swinburne La DN17 ....150 D3
Swinburne St HU8 ......141 D2
Swinderby Garth 10 HU7 .57 A5
Swinderby Gdns DN34 ..152 A1
Swindon St YO16 ....122 D3
Swine Bank HU5 ....139 B2
Swine La HU11 ....57 E5
Swine Rd HU11 ....45 C1
Swinefleet Prim Sch DN14 ....65 C1
Swinefleet Rd
Goole DN14 ....149 D2
Goole Fields DN14 ....80 C8
Swinegate
Kingston upon Hull HU13 ....143 E1
York YO1 ....156 B2
Swinemoor Cty Inf Sch HU17 ....154 C4
Swinemoor Cty Prim Sch HU17 ....154 C4
Swinemoor La HU17 ....137 B5
Swineridge Hill YO42 .....29 B6
Swineridge La YO42 .....29 C6
Swinescaif Hill Swine HU15 ....54 A3
Swinescaif Rd HU15 .....54 A3
Swinhope Brats* LN8 ...120 B6
Swinster La DN40 ....86 E6
Swinsty Ct YO30 ....126 F1
Switchback LN8 ....120 A1
Swithin Cl HU13 ....144 A2
Sycamore Ave
15 Grimsby DN33 ....102 E2
York YO32 ....127 D4
Sycamore Cl
3 Barnetby le Wold DN38 ...99 B4
2 Broughton DN20 ....97 D3
14 Gilberdyke HU15 ....66 D8
Goole DN14 ....149 E6
1 Haxby YO32 ....127 D7
Kingston upon Hull HU4 ...144 C7
Nafferton YO25 ....125 F7
8 Preston HU12 ....58 C1
Selby YO8 ....148 A4
Skelton YO30 ....126 C5
12 Snaith & Cowick DN14 ...78 C8
Sycamore Cres YO25 ....32 E7
Sycamore Dr
9 Gainsborough DN21 ....117 C1
3 Thorngumbald HU12 .....72 E5
Sycamore Pl YO30 .....156 A3
Sycamore Rd YO8 ....49 B5
Sycamore Terr YO30 ....156 A3
Sycamore View 17 YO26 ...12 F1
Sycamores The HU17 ...137 B3
Sydney Smith Sch HU10 ....144 A5
Sykehouse Rd DN14 .....78 C4
Sykes Balk YO25 ....21 E8
Sykes Cl 6 HU10 ....143 F6
Sykes La Garton YO25 ...124 A5
Goxhill DN19 ....71 A2
Sykes St HU2 ....155 B3
Sylvan Falls YO25 ......124 C4
Sylvan Lea YO25 ....124 C4
Sylvan Mead YO25 .....124 C4
Sylvester St 13 DN21 ...108 B1
Sylvia Cl HU6 ....139 F5
Symmons Cl 4 HU17 ....137 A6
Symons Cl HU2 ....155 A4
Symons Way 18 YO42 ....29 A3

T

Tabard Hamlet 5 DN14 ...61 F2
Tabard Rd 6 DN14 ....61 F2
Tabards The 7 DN14 ......61 F2
Tadcaster Rd YO24 .....132 F8
Tadcaster Rd Dringhouses YO23 ....132 E5
Tadman Cl HU17 ....136 E7
Tadman St HU3 ....145 D4
Talbot Circ DN3 ....92 A4
Talbot Rd DN40 ....87 C1
Talisman Dr 6 DN16 ......96 D1
Tall Trees HU13 ....143 C3
Tallert Way 28 DN33 ....102 C2
Tamar Dr 14 DN36 ....114 A8
Tamar Gr HU8 ....142 C7
Tamarisk Way DN16 .....96 E2
Tamworth Rd 9 YO30 ...127 A1
Tan Dyke Way HU17 ....154 C2
Tanashi Dori DN17 .....150 E5
Tanfield Gr HU9 ....142 C2
Tang Hall La YO31 .....131 A5
Tang Hall Prim Sch YO31 ....130 F5
Tanner Row YO1 ....156 A2
Tanner's Moat YO1 .....156 A2
Tanpit La DN6 ....76 E3
Tansley La HU18 ....134 D1
Tansterne La HU11 ....59 A7

Tarbert Cres 2 YO24 132 B7
Tardrew Cl HU17 136 E6
Target La 16 YO42 29 A4
Tarleton Cl 3 DN3 92 A2
Tarran Ave HU6 140 B8
Tasburgh St DN32 152 F2
Tate Cl YO8 48 D6
Tattersall Dr 1 HU17 137 B3
Tattershall Ave 14 DN34 102 C2
Tattershall Cl HU2 140 E1
Tatton Cl YO30 127 A1
Taunton Rd HU4 144 A3
Taunton Way 19 DN33 113 E8
Tavella Ct 1 DN9 105 B2
Tavistock St HU5 140 C3
Taylor Ave HU9 142 C3
Taylor Cl DN9 94 E2
Taylor St DN35 153 B5
Taylor's Ave DN35 103 C2
Taylors Field YO25 124 E4
Taylor's La HU19 75 C2
Teal Cl 13 Broughton DN20 98 B2
Walkington HU17 55 B7
Teal Dr YO24 132 C8
Teal Pl LN7 111 A4
Teal Rd 1 HU15 52 F1
Tealby Gr 19 DN33 102 D2
Tealby Rd DN17 150 D1
Teale St DN15 151 A8
Team Gate 1 DN37 102 B3
Teanby Dr DN15 83 A5
Tedder Rd YO24 129 B1
Teddington Cl HU8 141 E6
Tedworth Rd HU9 142 C5
Tee La DN15 82 B5
Tees Gr HU8 142 C7
Teesdale Ave HU9 146 E8
Teesdale Mews YO16 122 F7
Telford St HU9 141 E2
Telford Terr 1 YO24 130 B2
Temper Rd DN16 151 F4
Temperance Ave
DN17 107 D7
Temperton's La DN9 106 A2
Templar Cl DN14 61 F1
Templar Ct 17 DN16 96 D2
Templar Way YO8 148 C2
Templar's Bath* DN16 96 D1
Temple Ave YO10 131 B4
Temple Cl Belton DN9 94 E2
Welton HU15 68 E6
Temple Garth YO23 132 C1
Temple La
Aylesby DN37 101 E1
Carnaby YO16 10 E5
Copmanthorpe YO23 132 C1
Temple Manor* YO8 62 D4
Temple Rd YO23 132 F4
Temple St HU5 140 E1
Temple Wlk 2 HU15 68 E6
Templefield Rd DN21 119 A3
Templemead YO31 130 E8
Temsdale 2 HU7 141 A6
Ten Thorn La YO26 129 A4
Tennant St YO8 148 B6
Tennent Rd YO24 129 B2
Tennison Ct HU16 139 A7
Tennyson Ave
Bridlington YO15 122 E3
1 Campsall DN6 76 E1
Kingston upon Hull HU5 140 A1
7 Thorne/Moorends DN8 93 B8
York YO30 130 C7
Tennyson Cl Brigg DN20 98 C1
Caistor LN7 111 A3
Tennyson Rd
Cleethorpes DN35 153 E3
Scunthorpe DN16 151 D3
Tennyson St
33 Gainsborough DN21 117 B1
Goole DN14 149 C5
Grimsby DN31 152 D4
Tensing Rd DN16 151 C1
Tenterden Cl HU7 141 A6
Tern Gr HU8 142 C5
Terrington Pl 4 DN35 103 B2
Terry Ave YO1 156 B1
Terry St
Kingston upon Hull HU3 140 D1
York YO23 130 C1
Teskey King Sch HU6 140 A5
Tetley Rd DN16 151 C3
Tetley View 2 DN17 94 E6
Tetney CP Sch DN36 114 D4
Tetney La DN36 114 B5
Tetney Lock Rd DN36 114 D4
Tetney Rd DN36 114 C8
Tewkesbury Dr DN34 152 C2
Thanet Prim Sch HU9 142 D6
Thanet Rd
Kingston upon Hull HU9 142 D5
York YO24 129 D1
Thatch Cl YO8 148 C4
Thatchers Croft YO23 132 C3
Theaker Ave DN21 117 C1
Thealby La DN15 82 D5
Thearne Cl 7 HU5 140 C3
Thearne La HU17 56 D7
Theodore Rd DN15 150 E8
Theresa Cl 6 YO31 127 F1
Therm Rd HU8 155 C4
Thesiger St DN32 152 F5
Thief La Barlow YO8 148 F1
York YO10 130 F3
Thimblehall La HU15 52 E2
Thinholme La DN9 105 A1
Third Ave
Bridlington YO15 123 A4
Third Ave *continued*
Fixborough Ind Est. DN15 82 A1
Goole DN14 149 C4
Scunthorpe DN17 150 C2
York YO31 130 F5
Third La DN37 113 D3
Thirkleby Cres DN32 103 A2
Thirkleby Way YO10 131 C4
Thirlmere Ave DN33 113 E8
Thirlmere Dr YO31 131 A6
Thirlmere Wlk DN14 149 E6
Thirsk Mews HU5 139 D4
Thirtle Bridge La HU19 74 C8
Thirtleby La HU11 57 F6
Thirty Acre La 13 HU12 72 D7
Thiseldine Cl 6 YO43 53 F7
Thistle Cl YO8 148 C2
Thistleton Gdns 6 HU5 140 E2
Thixendale Rd YO25 18 A7
Thomas Clarkson Way
HU7 140 E8
Thomas Rd
Scunthorpe DN17 150 F4
17 Stainforth DN7 92 C5
Thomas St
Grimsby DN32 152 F3
Kingston upon Hull HU9 146 B7
6 Selby YO8 148 D6
2 York YO10 130 E3
Thomas Sumpter Comp Sch
DN17 150 E3
Thompson Ave HU17 154 C3
Thompson Cl 9 YO8 49 B4
Thompson Dr
10 Hatfield DN7 92 D4
2 Strensall YO32 14 B8
Thompson Nook 14 DN7 92 D4
Thompson Pl 6 YO26 129 E5
Thompson St
Bridlington YO16 122 D3
Scunthorpe DN15 151 B7
Thonock Rd DN21 117 D4
Thorensians Rugby Club
DN8 93 B8
Thoresby Ave YO16 122 D6
Thoresby Cl YO16 122 D6
Thoresby Mews 7
YO16 122 D6
Thoresby Pl 2 DN35 103 C2
Thoresby Prim Sch
HU5 145 B8
Thoresby Rd
Fulstow LN11 121 D8
North Coates DN36 115 A2
Scunthorpe DN17 150 D1
Tetney DN36 114 D3
York YO24 129 B1
Thoresby St HU5 145 B8
Thoresway Gr 9 DN33 102 D2
Thorganby Rd DN35 103 D2
Thorgill Gr HU5 139 E3
Thorn Bank DN9 104 E4
Thorn Barn Cl HU12 72 F5
Thorn La DN19 86 A8
Thorn Leigh 3 HU3 145 C6
Thorn Marsh Rd HU12 72 E2
Thorn Nook YO31 130 F8
Thorn Rd HU12 72 D7
Thornbridge Cl HU9 142 B3
Thornbury Rd DN40 87 C1
Thorncroft 8 YO19 26 F7
Thorndale HU7 140 E8
Thorndale Croft YO25 19 A5
Thorndale La YO25 19 A5
Thornden Bldgs YO8 148 D5
Thorndike Way DN21 117 D1
Thorne & Dikesmarsh
DN8 79 A2
Thorne Gram Sch DN8 93 B8
Thorne North Sta DN8 93 A8
Thorne Rd Hatfield DN7 92 F5
Kirk Sandall DN3 92 A1
3 Stainforth DN7 92 C6
Thorne South Comm Fst Sch
DN8 93 B7
Thorne South Sta DN8 93 B7
Thorne Swimming Baths
DN8 93 B8
Thorne Waste Drain Rd
DN8 79 D1
Thorneycroft Rd 14 HU12 72 E5
Thornfield Ave 5 YO31 130 F8
Thornfield Dr 7 YO31 127 E2
Thorngarth La DN19 85 C8
Thorngumbald Inf Sch
HU12 72 E5
Thorngumbald Jun Sch
HU12 72 F5
Thorngumbald Rd
HU12 72 B4
Thornham Cl HU15 53 F1
Thornham's Way 6
HU15 68 C7
Thornhill Ave HU8 141 C4
Thornhill Cres 19 DN17 96 C2
Thornhill Gdns DN34 152 A3
Thornhills 19 YO32 13 F5
Thornholme Dr 14 DN16 96 D2
Thornleys HU17 43 A4
Thornton 10 HU15 68 C6
Thornton Abbey (Rems of)*
DN39 86 B5
Thornton Abbey Sta
DN39 86 A5
Thornton Ave DN16 151 A3
Thornton Cl HU13 143 D1
Thornton Cres DN35 103 C2
Thornton Ct DN36 114 A8
Thornton Dam La HU15 66 D8
Thornton Gdns 5 DN41 101 A4
Thornton Gr
7 Grimsby DN34 102 C2
3 Preston HU12 58 C1
Thornton Hall* DN39 85 F5
Thornton La YO25 20 A1
Thornton Moor Cl
YO30 126 F2
Thornton Pl DN40 87 B1
Thornton Rd
Barrow upon Humber
DN19 85 D6
Bridlington YO16 122 B2
Goxhill DN19 85 F6
South Kelsey LN7 110 A1
Thornton St DN19 85 C7
Thorntondale Dr YO16 122 F7
Thorntree Cl DN14 149 E6
Thorntree La
Balne DN14 77 C6
Goole DN14 149 E6
Thornwick Ave HU10 143 E8
Thornwick Cl 2 HU3 145 C5
Thornwick Rd YO15 5 B3
Thornwood Covert 1
YO24 129 C1
Thorny La YO42 16 F2
Thorold Pl 11 DN3 92 A3
Thorold St DN31 153 A5
Thorpe YO25 32 B1
Thorpe La YO8 48 B8
Thorpe Leys YO25 32 B2
Thorpe Rd
6 Brough HU15 68 C5
Howden DN14 65 C8
Thorpe Rd Ave 2 DN14 65 B7
Thorpe St
9 Bridlington YO15 122 E2
York YO23 130 B2
Thorpe Willoughby Cty Prim
Sch YO8 48 B1
Thorpehall Rd DN3 92 A2
Thorpepark Prim Sch
HU6 140 A8
Thorpepark Rd HU6 139 F8
Thrislington Sq 19 DN8 79 B2
Throughleys La YO42 39 A5
Thrunscoe Inf Sch & Nursery
DN35 153 F1
Thrunscoe Rd DN35 153 F1
Thrussendale Rd YO17 16 E8
Thurlow Ave
Beverley HU17 136 E6
22 Pocklington YO42 29 A3
Thurlow Garth YO25 125 F7
Thurlstone Cl 13 HU7 56 F6
Thurstan Cl HU17 136 D2
Thurstan Rd HU17 154 A2
Thwaite St HU16 139 C6
Thwing Rd
Burton Fleming YO25 2 E2
Kilham YO25 9 B5
Thyme Way HU17 55 F8
Tibby La YO25 32 C4
Tichbourne Cl 6 HU3 145 C5
Tickton C of E Prim Sch
HU17 137 F8
Tickton Gr HU6 139 F4
Tickton Mdws HU17 137 F8
Tideworth Hague La
DN14 78 C3
Tiger La HU17 154 A3
Tilbury Prim Sch HU4 144 B3
Tilbury Rd HU4 144 B3
Tilia Cl
Kingston upon Hull HU4 144 B2
Scunthorpe DN16 96 E2
Tilmire Cl 2 YO10 133 F8
Tilworth Rd HU8 141 F4
Timberland DN16 96 E2
Timberley Dr 7 DN37 102 B4
Tindale Bank Rd
DN10 116 C7
Tinker La YO23 24 D6
Tinkler's La WF11 61 D6
Tinley Cl HU16 139 B7
Tintagel Way DN36 114 A8
Tippaty La WF11 61 A4
Tippet La HU17 44 F2
Tisbury Rd YO26 129 E4
Tison Garth HU10 143 F6
Tithe Barn Cl 9 HU12 74 D1
Tithe Barn La
8 Patrington HU12 74 D1
13 Thorne/Moorends DN8 93 B8
Tithe Barn Rd 2 WF11 61 A2
Tithe Barn Way DN14 61 F3
Tithe Cl YO24 129 B1
Tithe La YO25 22 E5
Tithe Rd HU12 58 A1
Tiverton Rd HU7 141 A8
Tiverton St DN35 153 C4
Toadham La DN14 77 C5
Toby Ct YO32 14 A7
Todd La DN21 117 F4
Todds Cl HU14 69 C6
Todds Ct DN17 107 D7
Todds La DN15 82 A4
Todd's La HU15 68 A8
Toft Gn YO1 156 A2
Tofts Rd 2 DN18 84 E8
Toll Bar Ave DN36 113 F7
Toll Gavel HU17 154 A3
Tollerton Rd YO30 12 B7
Tollesby La 9 DN7 92 D4
Tomline Rd 2 DN41 101 A5
Tomline St DN31 152 F5
Tomlinson Ave DN15 150 E7
Tonbridge 21 DN33 113 E8
Tonbridge Gr 2 HU9 142 E2
Tongue La HU15 66 E6
Tonnant Way 6 DN34 102 B3
Toogood St HU2 155 B4
Toothill Gdns 2 DN34 102 C3
Toothill Rd 1 DN34 102 C3
Top La
Copmanthorpe YO23 132 B3
Kirk Bramwith DN7 92 A7
Top Rd
South Killingholme DN40 86 E3
Winterton DN15 82 F6
Worlaby DN20 98 D8
Topaz Gr 3 HU3 145 A4
Topcliff Ct YO8 148 B7
Topcliffe Garth HU7 141 C8
Tophill Low Nature Reserve*
YO25 33 D4
Torbay Dr DN33 113 E7
Torchil Cl HU10 143 C6
Toremill Cl YO32 127 D4
Torksey Dr DN33 102 D2
Torksey Pl 28 DN33 102 D2
Torksey St DN21 108 B2
Tornville Cres DN14 79 B8
Torridge Rd HU8 142 C6
Torridon Pl YO24 132 B7
Torrington Rd DN17 150 C4
Torrington St
Grimsby DN32 152 F1
5 Kingston upon Hull
HU5 140 C3
Tostig Ave YO26 129 C5
Tostig Cl 14 YO41 15 D2
Totnes Rd DN33 113 E7
Tottenham Cl 3 HU8 141 F5
Tottering La DN14 51 B5
Tottermire La DN9 105 D7
Towan Cl 11 HU7 56 F5
Tower Hill
Kingston upon Hull
HU13 143 E1
Westwoodside DN9 105 B2
Tower Hill Dr HU13 143 E1
Tower Hill Mews 2
HU13 143 E1
Tower House La HU12 147 F7
Tower Rd
Rimswell HU12 74 C6
Roos HU11 60 A4
Tower St
Flamborough YO15 5 A2
32 Gainsborough DN21 117 B1
Kingston upon Hull HU9 155 C2
York YO1 156 B1
Tower View
Carlton DN14 63 C2
Kingston upon Hull
HU10 143 C5
Town End Ave DN14 63 C3
Town End Gdns 3 YO32 13 D5
Town End La YO42 18 C2
Town End Rd HU12 72 A5
Town Farm Cl YO25 23 A2
Town Hall Sq DN31 152 E3
Town Hall St 1 DN31 152 E3
Town Hill DN20 97 E4
Town Hill Dr DN20 97 E4
Town Rd DN36 114 D4
Town St Hayton YO42 40 C8
Immingham DN40 86 E4
Nunburnholme YO42 29 F3
Shiptonthorpe YO43 40 F6
Townend Cswy DN14 66 D2
Townend La HU15 53 C3
Townend Rd
Ellerton YO42 38 D1
13 Newbald YO43 53 F7
Walkington HU17 55 B8
Townend St YO31 156 B4
Townsend Cl DN36 103 E1
Townshend Dr 1 HU16 138 F5
Townside DN40 86 D6
Townside Cl 1 YO43 53 F7
Townside Rd YO43 53 F7
Towthorpe La YO43 135 B7
Towthorpe Medieval
Village* YO43 135 B8
Towthorpe Moor La
YO32 14 C5
Towthorpe Rd YO32 13 F5
Towton Ave
9 York YO24 129 F2
1 York YO24 130 A2
Toynton Rd 27 DN33 102 D2
Trafalgar Ave 10 DN34 102 B3
Trafalgar Pk DN36 114 A8
Trafalgar St
5 Kingston upon Hull
HU3 145 D7
Kingston upon Hull HU2 155 A4
York YO23 130 B1
Trafford Rd
Kingston upon Hull
HU10 143 E8
4 Norton DN6 76 E2
Trafford St DN15 151 B8
Traffords Way DN20 108 F6
Train Ave HU6 140 C7
Train Gate DN21 108 B1
Tranby Ave
Kingston upon Hull
HU13 143 D2
York YO10 131 D4
Tranby Dr DN32 103 A2
Tranby La Hessle HU10 143 B5
Tranby La *continued*
Swanland HU14 69 B6
Tranby Mdws Pk
HU13 143 C3
Tranby Ride HU10 143 C5
Trandy La DN14 65 D5
Tranmere Cl HU3 145 B5
Tranmere Pk HU18 134 D3
Tranmore La DN14 62 B3
Travis Ave 18 DN8 93 B8
Travis Cl 16 DN8 93 B8
Travis Cty Prim Sch
DN7 92 E4
Travis Gr 17 DN8 93 B8
Travis Rd HU16 138 F5
Travis St YO15 122 E3
Traviss Cl DN16 151 B4
Trawden Cl HU7 56 F6
Tree Cl 9 DN9 105 D6
Treece Gdns 10 DN18 69 F1
Trees The HU6 140 C4
Treeton Rd DN14 65 A6
Tremayne Ave 2 HU15 68 C5
Trenchard Cl 3 DN40 87 D2
Trenchard Rd YO26 129 B6
Trent Ave 4 YO32 127 F6
Trent Pk 6 HU7 56 F6
Trent Rd DN17 95 D6
Trent Side
4 Amcotts DN17 81 F1
Keadby with Althorpe
DN17 95 D6
Trent St DN16 151 B6
Trent View DN17 95 D5
Trent Way YO24 132 D7
Trentham Cl YO16 122 D6
Trentham Dr YO16 122 D6
Trentham Mews 1
YO16 122 D6
Trentholme Dr
Messingham DN17 107 D7
2 York YO24 130 A2
Trenton Ave HU4 144 B6
Trentside
Keadby with Althorpe
DN17 95 D3
Morton DN21 117 A2
Trentvale Prep Sch
DN17 95 D6
Trevor Cl 15 DN37 101 F1
Trevor Gr 8 YO24 129 F2
Trevor St HU2 155 B4
Triangle Dr HU14 69 A4
Triangle The 11 HU14 69 A4
Trinity Ave YO15 122 F3
Trinity Cl
Burstwick HU12 73 A6
Goxhill DN19 86 A8
Leven HU17 45 B8
Trinity Ct 5 DN20 97 D4
Trinity Garth HU16 138 A8
Trinity Gr
Beverley HU17 154 B3
1 Bridlington YO15 122 F3
3 Kingston upon Hull
HU9 141 F1
Kingston upon Hull
HU13 143 E2
Trinity House La HU1 155 B2
Trinity La
Beverley HU17 154 B2
York YO1 156 A2
Trinity Mews 2 YO15 122 F3
Trinity Rd
Bridlington YO15 122 F3
Cleethorpes DN35 153 E1
Hornsea HU18 134 C2
10 Scunthorpe DN16 96 D2
Trinity St
Grimsby DN31 153 A5
Kingston upon Hull HU3 145 C7
Trinity Wlk 2 DN18 69 E1
Trippett St HU2 155 C3
Triton Rd HU9 142 D3
Troon Cl 2 YO26 129 B5
Troon Ct HU8 142 B6
Troon Rd DN7 92 D4
Troutbeck 7 YO24 132 C7
Troutsdale Ave YO30 126 E2
Troutsdale Cl YO16 122 F7
Troutsdale Gr HU9 146 F8
Trumfleet La DN6 77 D1
Trundle Gate YO43 53 F6
Trundle La DN7 92 C8
Trundle St HU1 155 A2
Trundles La 7 WF11 61 A2
Trunkass La DN37 112 D6
Truro Cl HU7 141 C6
Tudor Cl
Bridlington YO15 122 C1
10 Thorpe Willoughby YO8 48 B1
Tudor Ct HU10 138 C1
Tudor Dr HU6 140 B8
Tudor Rd YO24 129 C2
Tudor Way YO32 14 C8
Tudworth Field Rd DN7 93 B5
Tudworth Rd DN7 93 A5
Tuke Ave YO10 131 B4
Tulip Rd DN15 151 C7
Tummel Ct 4 DN40 101 B8
Tune St YO8 49 B4
Tunis St HU5 140 E2
Tunnard St DN32 153 A4
Tunnel Rd DN20 98 D4

Turbary Rd
Epworth DN9 ... 105 B6
Haxey DN9 ... 105 C3
Turf Moor Rd DN7 ... 93 A3
Turkey La YO16 ... 10 E4
Turks Head Gdns 10
HU15 ... 52 F1
Turmar View HU11 ... 58 A4
Turmarr Rd HU12 ... 89 C8
Turmer Ave YO15 ... 122 F3
Turnberry App DN37 ... 113 D6
Turnberry Dr YO26 ... 129 B4
Turnbull Dr 18 YO42 ... 29 A3
Turner Ave HU19 ... 75 A5
Turner Cl YO43 ... 135 D3
Turner Ct HU3 ... 155 A2
Turner Rd HU17 ... 154 B4
Turner St 5 DN21 ... 108 B1
Turner's Croft YO10 ... 131 A1
Turner's La 16 HU14 ... 69 A5
Turners Sq 9 YO8 ... 148 C5
Turnham La YO8 ... 49 C2
Turnhead Cres YO8 ... 49 B5
Turnhead Ct YO8 ... 49 B6
Turnmire Rd 1 YO24 ... 132 E8
Turpin Cl DN21 ... 117 C1
Turpit La HU12 ... 72 A5
Turrets The 15 HU12 ... 72 E5
Turver's La Beal WF11 ... 61 C2
Kellingley WF11 ... 61 C2
Tuxford Gr HU9 ... 142 E2
Tweed Gr HU8 ... 142 B5
Tween Dykes Rd HU7 ... 141 D6
Tweendykes Sch HU7 ... 141 C6
Twickenham Cl 2 HU8 ... 142 A5
Twin Pike Way 14 YO32 ... 13 D5
Two Riggs HU17 ... 43 A4
Twyford Cl 5 HU9 ... 142 E2
Twyning Pl DN35 ... 153 D3
Tydeman Cl 1 DN16 ... 96 D1
Tyler Ave DN34 ... 152 A3
Tyn Garth YO19 ... 36 D8
Tyne St HU3 ... 145 B4
Tynedale 1 HU7 ... 141 A6
Tynedale Ct 1 DN3 ... 92 A2
Tysons Cl 7 DN18 ... 69 F1
Tythe Garth 8 HU15 ... 53 D3

U

Ulceby Rd
Scunthorpe DN17 ... 96 B2
South Killingholme DN39 ... 86 C2
Wootton DN39 ... 85 F3
Ulceby Sta DN39 ... 86 C2
Ullswater YO24 ... 132 D7
Ullswater Cl HU8 ... 141 D4
Ullswater Gr DN14 ... 149 E5
Ulrome Ct 1 HU9 ... 142 B1
Ulster Ave 5 DN33 ... 102 E1
Ulster Rd DN21 ... 117 B1
Ulverston Rd HU4 ... 144 A3
Ulyett La DN17 ... 106 C8
Undercroft 7 YO19 ... 26 F7
Underwit Rd YO8 ... 63 C4
Unicorn Row 10 DN21 ... 108 B1
Union La YO8 ... 148 C4
Union Rd DN8 ... 93 A8
Union St
Great Driffield YO25 ... 124 E4
Kingston upon Hull HU2 ... 155 B3
Pocklington YO42 ... 29 A4
Union Terr YO31 ... 156 B4
Unity Ave HU13 ... 143 F1
Unity Rd DN32 ... 153 C2
University of Hull
Cottingham HU16 ... 138 F8
Kingston upon Hull
HU16 ... 139 C5
Kingston upon Hull HU6 ... 140 B4
University of Humberside
Kingston upon Hull HU6 ... 140 A4
Kingston upon Hull HU6 ... 140 C4
Kingston upon Hull HU1 ... 155 C2
University of Lincolnshire &
Humberside HU1 ... 155 A2
University of York
Heslington YO10 ... 130 F1
York YO10 ... 130 E3
York YO10 ... 131 B2
York YO30 ... 156 A3
University Rd YO10 ... 130 F2
Upavon Garth HU7 ... 141 C7
Upper Burgess St
DN31 ... 152 D4
Upper Hanover St 6
YO26 ... 129 F5
Upper Kenyon St 5 DN8 ... 93 A8
Upper Newborough St 1
YO30 ... 130 C7
Upper Poppleton Jun Sch
YO26 ... 12 F1
Upper Price St YO23 ... 156 A1
Upper St Paul's Terr
YO24 ... 130 A4
Upper Union St HU1 ... 155 A2
Uppercommon La
DN14 ... 61 F3
Uppercroft 4 YO32 ... 127 C8
Upperthorpe Hill DN9 ... 105 A2
Upton St HU8 ... 141 B1
Uredale Pl DN16 ... 151 E1
Usher La YO32 ... 13 F6
Utgard Way 4 DN33 ... 102 D1
Utterby Cty Prim Sch
DN36 ... 121 B5
Utterby Dr DN34 ... 152 C1
Uxbridge Gr HU9 ... 142 E1

V

Valda Vale 32 DN40 ... 87 B1
Vale Cres YO42 ... 16 F2
Vale of Ancholme Sch
DN20 ... 98 B2
Vale The
Beverley HU17 ... 137 B2
Kingston upon Hull
HU10 ... 143 B7
Skelton YO30 ... 126 B5
Valentine Cl
1 Kingston upon Hull
HU4 ... 144 A2
6 Pocklington YO42 ... 29 A3
Valiant Dr HU9 ... 142 D4
Valletta St HU9 ... 147 D7
Valley Dr HU10 ... 143 B7
Valley View YO19 ... 37 F7
Valley View Dr DN16 ... 96 D1
Vanbrugh Dr YO10 ... 131 C3
Vancouver Cres 5 DN17 ... 96 C2
Vane St HU3 ... 145 D7
Vanessa Dr DN21 ... 117 B2
Varah Cl DN18 ... 84 E8
Varlow Rd LN7 ... 111 B4
Varsity Cl 6 DN7 ... 104 A8
Vaughan Ave DN36 ... 103 A2
Vaughan Rd
10 Campsall DN6 ... 76 E1
1 Kingston upon Hull HU13 ... 69 F4
Vavasour Ct YO23 ... 132 B2
Veal St DN31 ... 152 C3
Ventnor St HU5 ... 140 C3
Vere Terr DN31 ... 152 C4
Vermont St HU5 ... 140 D3
Vermuyden Rd DN8 ... 79 C2
Vermuyden Sch DN14 ... 149 B5
Vermuyden Terr
DN14 ... 149 D2
Vernon Cl YO23 ... 133 A3
Vernon Rd
Bridlington YO15 ... 122 F3
York YO30 ... 126 E2
Vernon St HU1 ... 155 B2
Vesper Dr YO24 ... 129 B3
Vesper Wlk YO32 ... 127 F6
Vicar La Beverley HU17 ... 154 A3
Eastrington DN14 ... 51 F1
Hollym HU19 ... 75 A4
Kingston upon Hull HU1 ... 155 B1
Vicarage Ave DN20 ... 98 D3
Vicarage Cl
Beswick YO25 ... 32 D4
2 Bubwith YO8 ... 50 D7
12 Hunmanby YO14 ... 2 F8
Vicarage Cres DN15 ... 82 B5
Vicarage Gdns
2 Brough HU15 ... 68 C6
Scunthorpe DN15 ... 150 F6
Wrawby DN20 ... 98 E4
1 York YO10 ... 131 C4
Vicarage La
Beckingham DN10 ... 116 D1
Bishop Wilton YO42 ... 16 F2
8 Buckton/Bempton YO15 ... 4 D3
Cadney DN20 ... 109 D6
Elsham DN20 ... 98 F7
Grasby DN38 ... 110 E7
Immingham DN40 ... 86 E4
3 Kingston upon Hull
HU13 ... 143 E1
Naburn YO19 ... 36 E8
Redbourne DN21 ... 108 F2
Scawby DN20 ... 108 E8
Skirlaugh HU11 ... 45 D2
Wootton DN39 ... 85 E3
Vicarage Pk DN15 ... 83 D1
Vicarage Rd
Willoughton DN21 ... 119 B4
Wrawby DN20 ... 98 D3
Vicars Cl YO23 ... 132 B2
Vicar's La HU12 ... 91 A6
Vicar's Wlk 1 DN17 ... 94 D7
Viceroy Cl HU2 ... 155 B4
Vickerman's La HU12 ... 59 A3
Victor St Grimsby DN32 ... 153 A4
2 Kingston upon Hull
HU9 ... 146 C8
York YO1 ... 156 B1
Victoria Ave
Hatfield DN7 ... 92 D4
Hornsea HU18 ... 134 D5
Kingston upon Hull
HU10 ... 138 C2
Kingston upon Hull HU5 ... 140 A1
12 Withernsea HU19 ... 75 A6
Victoria Cl
Marshchapel DN36 ... 115 C2
Stainforth DN7 ... 92 C5
Victoria Ct
Burton upon Stather
DN15 ... 82 B5
15 York YO26 ... 129 F5
Victoria Dock Prim Sch
HU9 ... 146 B6
Victoria Dr
3 Barton-upon-Humber
DN18 ... 69 E1
3 Gilberdyke HU15 ... 66 D8
Victoria Farm Cl YO23 ... 24 C6
Victoria Gdns
Hornsea HU18 ... 134 C6
1 Kingston upon Hull
HU5 ... 140 A1
Victoria Pier* HU1 ... 155 C1
Victoria Rd
Barnetby le Wold DN38 ... 99 B4
Beverley HU17 ... 154 A1
Bridlington YO15 ... 122 E3
Great Driffield YO25 ... 124 D5
5 Keelby DN41 ... 101 A5
2 Pocklington YO42 ... 29 A4
Scunthorpe DN16 ... 151 A1
Woodmansey HU17 ... 55 E8
Victoria St Goole DN14 ... 149 D4
Kingston upon Hull
HU13 ... 144 A1
1 York YO23 ... 156 B1
Victoria St N DN31 ... 152 E4
Victoria St S 3 DN31 ... 152 E3
Victoria St W
7 Grimsby DN31 ... 152 D3
2 Grimsby DN31 ... 152 E3
Victoria Way
Grimsby DN31 ... 152 A6
2 York YO32 ... 130 F8
Victoria's Way HU16 ... 139 B6
Victory Way
1 Barton-upon-Humber
DN18 ... 69 F1
9 Grimsby DN37 ... 102 B2
Viking Cl
2 Immingham DN40 ... 87 B1
Kingston upon Hull
HU10 ... 138 C2
20 Stamford Bridge YO41 ... 15 D2
Viking Dr 5 YO19 ... 48 F8
Viking Rd
Bridlington YO16 ... 123 B6
Stamford Bridge YO41 ... 15 D2
York YO26 ... 129 C5
Villa Cl YO8 ... 49 F1
Villa Fields 4 DN14 ... 63 C1
Villa Gr 2 YO31 ... 130 E6
Village Farm Cl 11 HU15 ... 52 F1
Village Farm Ct 7 DN14 ... 61 D4
Village Farm Rd 5 HU12 ... 58 C1
Village Garth 1 YO32 ... 13 E5
Village Rd
Kingston upon Hull HU8 ... 141 C1
Sunk Island HU12 ... 88 E5
Village St YO30 ... 126 E3
Village The Haxby YO32 ... 13 E5
Skelton YO30 ... 126 B5
Stockton on the Forest
YO32 ... 14 D3
Strensall YO32 ... 14 B7
Ville Rd DN16 ... 151 D2
Villiers Ct 7 HU12 ... 72 D7
Vincent Cl 3 HU4 ... 144 A2
Vincent Way YO24 ... 132 C8
Vine Cl HU16 ... 139 A7
Vine St YO23 ... 130 C2
Vinegarth 2 DN9 ... 105 E6
Vinehall Rd DN9 ... 105 C2
Vinery The 13 DN14 ... 65 A7
Vineyards The 3 HU17 ... 45 A8
Violet Cl 10 DN35 ... 103 C1
Viscount Way 12 DN36 ... 114 D8
Vivars Way YO8 ... 148 D5
Vivian Ave DN32 ... 153 B1
Voases Cl HU10 ... 143 E6
Voases La HU10 ... 143 E6
Volage Ct 13 YO42 ... 29 A4
Volta St YO8 ... 148 E4
Vulcan St HU6 ... 140 F4
Vulcan Way DN7 ... 93 A1
Vyner St YO31 ... 130 C7

W

Waby Cl DN37 ... 102 B4
Waddingham Pl
3 Habrough DN40 ... 100 E8
10 New Waltham DN36 ... 114 A7
Waddingham Rd LN7 ... 109 F1
Waddington Ct HU5 ... 140 B3
Waddington Dr 24 DN17 ... 96 C2
Waddington Pl DN34 ... 152 A1
Wade Ave HU18 ... 134 C6
Wade House La YO8 ... 63 F4
Wadebridge Gr 4 HU9 ... 142 E1
Wadham Gr 4 HU9 ... 141 F1
Wadhurst Cl HU7 ... 141 A6
Wadsworth Ave HU6 ... 140 C8
Wadsworth Rd YO25 ... 124 B3
Waggoners Dr 3 YO23 ... 132 B3
Waincroft 8 YO32 ... 14 A6
Wainers Cl 5 YO23 ... 132 B3
Wainfleet Ave HU16 ... 139 A6
Wainfleet Rd 33 DN33 ... 102 D2
Wain's Gr YO24 ... 132 D7
Wain's Rd YO24 ... 132 D8
Waite Cl 17 YO42 ... 29 A3
Waithe La DN37 ... 113 E4
Wake Ave HU16 ... 139 A5
Wakefield Ave
Kingston upon Hull HU9 ... 142 C2
Scotter DN21 ... 107 D4
Wakefield La HU19 ... 75 A2
Wakerley Rd 13 DN21 ... 107 C3
Walcot Rd DN15 ... 82 B8
Walcott St HU3 ... 145 C4
Waldby Garth Rd HU12 ... 73 C4
Waldegrave Ave HU8 ... 142 A4
Walden Stubbs Rd DN6 ... 76 E2
Waldorf Rd DN35 ... 103 C1
Walesby Cl 8 DN33 ... 113 D8
Walesby Rd
2 Scunthorpe DN17 ... 96 C2
Scunthorpe DN17 ... 150 E1
Walgrave St HU5 ... 140 C3
Walk La
Humberston DN36 ... 114 C7
Irby DN37 ... 112 D7
Walker Ave DN33 ... 113 E8
Walker Cl DN15 ... 82 E7
Walker Dr
Winterton DN15 ... 83 A5
York YO24 ... 132 C8
Walker La YO19 ... 37 F7
Walker St HU3 ... 145 C5
Walkergate HU17 ... 154 A3
Walkergate Inf Sch
HU17 ... 154 A3
Walkeringham Cty Prim Sch
DN10 ... 116 C3
Walkeringham Rd
Beckingham DN10 ... 116 D2
Gringley on the Hill
DN10 ... 116 A2
Walkerith Rd 11 DN21 ... 117 A2
Walker's Cl 2 DN38 ... 99 B4
Walkers Ct DN17 ... 107 D7
Walkers Way DN39 ... 86 B2
Walkington Dr YO43 ... 135 C5
Walkington Heads
HU17 ... 54 D8
Walkington La YO30 ... 12 B8
Walkington Prim Sch
HU17 ... 55 C7
Walkington Rd
Beverley HU17 ... 136 C2
Rowley HU20 ... 55 A5
Wall St DN34 ... 152 A3
Waller St
3 Hornsea HU18 ... 134 C3
Kingston upon Hull HU9 ... 146 C8
Walliker St HU3 ... 145 A6
Wallingfen La HU15 ... 53 A1
Walmgate YO1 ... 156 C2
Walmsgate DN33 ... 102 D2
Walmsgate Pl 24 DN33 ... 102 D2
Walmsley Cl 1 YO15 ... 4 C3
Walmsley St HU3 ... 145 D7
Walney Rd YO31 ... 131 A5
Walnut Cl
Kingston upon Hull
HU16 ... 139 D5
York YO10 ... 131 A1
Walnut Cres
9 Cleethorpes DN35 ... 103 B1
11 Snaith & Cowick DN14 ... 78 C8
Walnut Dr DN20 ... 108 F7
Walnut Gr YO25 ... 125 F8
Walnut Rd 1 DN8 ... 79 A1
Walnut Way DN17 ... 107 C7
Walpole St YO31 ... 130 D7
Walsall Garth HU4 ... 144 A4
Walter St 5 HU19 ... 74 F7
Walter's Terr 6 HU5 ... 140 C3
Waltham Grange 24
DN35 ... 103 C2
Waltham La HU17 ... 154 A3
Waltham Rd
Barnoldby le Beck DN37 ... 113 C6
Brigsley DN37 ... 113 D5
Grimsby DN33 ... 113 E8
Waltham St HU1 ... 155 B2
Waltham Toll Bar Sch
DN36 ... 113 F7
Waltham Windmill*
DN37 ... 113 D6
Walton Ct HU17 ... 154 B4
Walton Gr 3 DN33 ... 102 E2
Walton La YO43 ... 53 E6
Walton Pl YO26 ... 129 B3
Walton St HU3 ... 145 A7
Walton Street L Ctr
HU3 ... 145 A6
Walworth Cl HU8 ... 141 E5
Walworth St N 4 YO26 ... 129 F5
Walworth St S 9 YO26 ... 129 F5
Wand La DN14 ... 62 C3
Wandell's View HU15 ... 68 C8
Wandhill 31 YO32 ... 13 E5
Wandle The YO26 ... 129 A2
Wanlass Dr HU16 ... 139 C7
Wansbeck 3 YO24 ... 132 B7
Wansbeck Prim Sch
HU8 ... 142 D7
Wansbeck Rd HU8 ... 142 C7
Wansford Gr HU9 ... 142 A1
Wansford Rd
Driffield YO25 ... 125 B3
Nafferton YO25 ... 125 F5
Ward Ave HU11 ... 142 F7
Ward Ct YO23 ... 156 B1
Ward Lea YO25 ... 125 F7
Ward St DN35 ... 153 C4
Wardall St DN35 ... 153 F1
Wareham Cl HU7 ... 141 B6
Wares Way DN15 ... 150 B7
Warley Ave DN16 ... 151 C4
Warley Dr DN16 ... 151 C4
Warley Rd DN16 ... 151 C3
Warmer La HU12 ... 90 E7
Warn Ave 18 HU12 ... 72 C7
Warneford Rd DN35 ... 153 D4
Warping Way DN15 ... 150 B7
Warren Cl DN21 ... 117 A1
Warren Farm Cotts
YO42 ... 28 C1
Warren Rd DN15 ... 96 D7
Warrendale DN18 ... 84 E8
Warrenne Cl 31 DN7 ... 92 D4
Warrenne Rd DN7 ... 92 D4
Warter C of E Sch
YO42 ... 30 A5
Warter Rd Etton HU17 ... 42 F6
Middleton YO25 ... 31 A4
Warthill C of E Prim Sch
YO19 ... 14 F2
Warton Ave HU17 ... 137 B4
Warwick Ave 5 DN33 ... 102 D2
Warwick Cl DN7 ... 92 F4
Warwick Dr
Barton-upon-Humber
DN18 ... 84 E8
Molescroft HU17 ... 136 E6
Warwick Rd
Cleethorpes DN35 ... 153 D1
Scunthorpe DN16 ... 151 C5
Warwick St
Kingston upon Hull HU9 ... 146 B7
York YO31 ... 130 D7
Warwickshire Cl 6
HU5 ... 139 D1
Wascana Cl HU4 ... 144 B3
Wasdale Ave HU9 ... 142 D4
Wasdale Cl 2 YO30 ... 126 E1
Wasdale Gn 4 HU16 ... 139 B7
Washdyke La
Elsham DN20 ... 98 E6
Immingham DN40 ... 87 B2
Washinghall La DN17 ... 81 A2
Washington St
Great Driffield YO25 ... 124 E4
Kingston upon Hull HU5 ... 140 D3
Wassand Balk HU11 ... 46 A8
Wassand Rd HU11 ... 35 B1
Wassand St HU3 ... 145 C4
Water Bank DN9 ... 104 E5
Water End YO26 ... 129 E5
Water Garth DN14 ... 61 F4
Water Hill La YO8 ... 148 D6
Water La
Bewholme YO25 ... 35 A5
Camblesforth YO8 ... 63 D5
8 Clifton YO30 ... 127 A1
Dunnington YO19 ... 26 F7
Eggborough DN14 ... 62 A2
20 Flamborough YO15 ... 5 A2
Goole DN14 ... 65 C4
Harpham YO25 ... 21 E7
Hemingbrough YO8 ... 49 F1
Kirby Grindalythe YO17 ... 6 B6
Kirby Underdale YO41 ... 17 A5
Kirk Bramwith DN7 ... 92 C7
Kirk Smeaton WF8 ... 76 C3
South Cave HU15 ... 53 F1
West Halton DN15 ... 82 E8
York YO30 ... 130 A7
Water Side DN15 ... 68 A2
Water Way Garth DN14 ... 77 F6
Waterdale HU7 ... 140 E8
Waterdale Pk YO31 ... 127 E1
Waterhouse La HU1 ... 155 A1
Wateringdike La YO43 ... 135 F7
Waterings 19 YO32 ... 13 D5
Waterland Cl 15 HU12 ... 72 D7
Waterloo St HU2 ... 155 A4
Waterlow Dr 7 DN15 ... 83 A5
Waterman Ct 3 YO24 ... 129 B1
Waters Edge DN20 ... 98 B2
Watersedge YO25 ... 124 F3
Waterside Goole DN14 ... 65 C4
3 Thorne DN8 ... 78 F1
Thorne DN8 ... 92 F8
Waterside Dr DN31 ... 152 C4
Waterside Rd
Barton-upon-Humber
DN18 ... 69 E2
Beverley HU17 ... 137 B3
2 Thorne DN8 ... 78 F1
Waterton La DN7 ... 92 D2
Waterways Mus & Adventure
Ctr The* DN14 ... 149 B2
Waterworks La HU11 ... 142 E6
Waterworks St DN40 ... 87 C2
Watford Ave DN34 ... 102 C2
Wath Gr HU8 ... 141 C1
Wath La YO41 ... 27 C8
Watkin St N DN31 ... 152 C5
Watkin St S DN31 ... 152 D5
Watkinson Cl 8 HU12 ... 58 D1
Watson Ave HU9 ... 142 C2
Watson Cl 9 YO14 ... 3 A8
Watson Dr 30 HU12 ... 72 D7
Watson St
Kingston upon Hull HU7 ... 141 D6
York YO24 ... 130 A3
Watson Terr 2 YO24 ... 130 A3
Watsons Ave YO16 ... 122 D5
Watsons Croft DN7 ... 92 D6
Watson's La YO14 ... 3 D6
Watt St HU9 ... 141 E1
Wattlers Cl YO23 ... 132 C3
Watton Abbey* YO25 ... 32 E4
Watton Gr HU6 ... 140 B7
Watton Nature Reserve*
YO25 ... 33 C2
Watts Rd HU17 ... 154 B4
Waudby Cl 2 HU17 ... 55 C8
Wauldby Cl 4 HU10 ... 143 E7
Wauldby View 2 HU14 ... 69 B7
Wavell St YO8 ... 148 A6
Waveney Cl DN15 ... 82 B5
Waveney Gr YO30 ... 130 B8
Waveney Rd HU8 ... 142 B6
Waverley Cl DN14 ... 63 C2
Waverley St
Kingston upon Hull HU1 ... 155 A1

Waverley St *continued*
York YO31 156 C3
Wawne CP Sch HU7 56 E7
Wawne Lodge HU7 56 F6
Wawne Rd HU7 141 C8
Waxholme Rd HU19 74 E8
Wayfbain La 20 HU12 72 C7
Waynefleet Gr 3 YO10 131 A3
Wayside Cl
Holton le Clay DN36 114 A5
15 Scunthorpe DN16 96 D2
Wayside Cres YO16 122 B4
Wayside Dr DN36 114 A8
Wayside Rd YO16 122 B4
Weald Pk HU7 56 F5
Weardale HU7 140 F8
Weatherill St DN14 149 C4
Weaver Gr HU8 142 C7
Weavers Cl YO23 132 B3
Weavers Croft 8 DN9 105 A2
Webb Cl DN18 84 E8
Webster Ave DN15 150 E7
Weddall Cl YO24 129 F1
Weekes Rd 13 DN35 103 C2
Weel Rd HU17 137 D8
Weeland Ct 16 WF11 61 A2
Weeland Rd Beal DN14 61 E3
Hensall DN14 62 E2
Weelsby Ave DN32 152 E1
Weelsby Gr DN32 102 F2
Weelsby Prim Sch
DN32 153 A4
Weelsby Rd DN32 152 E1
Weelsby St DN32 153 A4
Weelsby St S DN32 153 A3
Weelsby View DN36 114 A8
Weelsby Way HU13 143 C2
Weeping Elm Way
DN16 96 E2
Weeton Cl HU11 58 A4
Weeton Dr YO25 19 B5
Weeton North La HU12 90 B8
Weeton Rd HU12 90 C7
Weeton Way 5 HU10 143 E7
Weghill Rd HU12 58 D1
Weighton Ct 9 DN14 65 A7
Weighton Gr HU6 139 F5
Weighton Hill YO43 135 F4
Weir Cl DN9 105 A2
Weir Rd DN9 105 A2
Weir The HU13 143 E1
Welbeck Pl 9 DN34 102 C2
Welbeck Rd DN35 153 C1
Welbeck St HU5 145 B8
Welborn Cl YO10 131 A4
Welbourn Wlk HU4 144 B6
Welburn Ct 8 YO25 22 D1
Welburn Gr HU5 139 E2
Welbury Gr HU9 142 C2
Weldon Rd DN21 119 B1
Welgarth YO25 31 B7
Welham Cl 10 DN14 65 B7
Welholme Ave DN32 152 D1
Welholme Fst Sch
DN32 152 F2
Welholme Mid Sch
DN32 152 F2
Welholme Mus & Gall*
DN32 152 F2
Welholme Rd DN32 152 E2
Well La Beverley HU17 154 B2
Bridlington YO16 122 B4
Kingston upon Hull
HU10 138 E2
Well St
Messingham DN17 107 C7
Tibthorpe YO25 19 D2
Well Vale 3 DN33 113 D8
Welland Ave DN34 102 C2
Welland Dr DN15 82 B5
Welland Rd HU8 142 C7
Welland Rise YO26 129 D5
Wellbeck Cl 19 DN20 98 C2
Wellbeck Rd 8 DN34 102 C2
Wellesley Ave HU6 140 D4
Wellesley Cl YO30 127 A2
Wellgarth DN32 153 B1
Wellington Ave HU18 134 C2
Wellington Cl 5 YO42 28 F4
Wellington La HU3 145 D8
Wellington Rd
Beverley HU17 154 B4
Bridlington YO15 122 E2
Pocklington Ind Est YO42 28 E3
Wellington Row YO1 156 A2
Wellington St
Grimsby DN32 152 F4
Kingston upon Hull HU1 155 B1
York YO10 130 E3
Wellington St W HU1 155 B1
Wellington Way DN20 99 A8
Wellingtonia Dr 5 DN6 76 E1
Wellowgate DN32 152 D3
Wells Cl YO8 148 A5
Wells Cres 3 DN35 103 C1
Wells Gr DN14 149 B6
Wells La DN14 61 E3
Wells Rd DN37 101 D4
Wells St Grimsby DN34 152 B3
Kingston upon Hull HU3 145 A5
Scunthorpe DN15 151 B8
Wellsted St HU3 145 C5
Welshpool Cl 3 HU7 56 F7
Welton Ave
2 Kingston upon Hull
HU16 138 E6
York YO26 129 D5
Welton Cl
17 Barton-upon-Humber
DN18 84 E8
9 Beverley HU17 136 E1
Welton Gr HU6 139 F4
Welton Low Rd HU15 68 C6
Welton Mill* HU15 68 E6
Welton Old Rd HU15 68 E6
Welton Prim Sch HU15 68 D5
Welton Rd HU15 68 C5
Welwick Rd HU12 74 D1
Welwyn Dr YO10 133 E8
Welwyn Park Ave
HU6 140 C7
Welwyn Park Dr HU6 140 D7
Welwyn Park Rd HU6 140 C7
Wembley Park Ave
HU8 141 E5
Wembley Rd DN8 79 B2
Wenchirst La DN14 78 D2
Wendan Rd 7 DN8 93 A7
Wendover Cl
Humberston DN36 114 D8
Messingham DN17 107 D7
Wendover Rd DN17 107 D7
Wendover Rise
6 Cleethorpes DN35 103 C2
Cleethorpes DN35 153 E1
Wendron Cl HU7 141 C6
Wenham Rd YO24 132 C8
Wenlock Dr YO19 37 B6
Wenlock St HU3 145 C7
Wenlock Terr
Kingston upon Hull HU9 141 E1
York YO10 130 D1
Wenning Gr HU8 142 D7
Wensley Ave HU6 139 E4
Wensleydale HU7 140 F8
Wensleydale Cl YO16 122 F6
Wensleydale Dr YO10 131 D4
Wensleydale Rd DN16 151 E2
Wentdale 1 WF8 76 C3
Wentworth Cl
3 Beverley HU17 55 E8
Camblesforth YO8 63 D4
Kellington DN14 62 A2
Kingston upon Hull
HU10 143 F8
Wentworth Cres 1 DN19 70 E2
Wentworth Dr
Goole DN14 149 E5
Messingham DN17 107 D7
Wentworth Gr 5 HU11 47 C1
Wentworth Rd
Bottesford DN17 96 B1
Bridlington YO16 122 C4
Grimsby DN34 152 B3
York YO24 130 B2
Wentworth Way
5 Hunmanby YO14 2 F8
Kingston upon Hull HU9 146 C7
Werneth Rd DN32 152 F4
Wesley Cl
3 Epworth DN9 105 E6
South Cave HU15 54 A2
Winterton DN15 83 A5
Wesley Cres 15 DN35 103 C2
Wesley Ct 7 HU3 145 C5
Wesley Pl YO1 156 C2
Wesley Rd 4 Brigg DN20 98 C2
Scunthorpe DN16 151 E3
Wesley St DN21 108 B1
West Acridge DN18 69 E1
West Ave
Burton Fleming YO25 2 E3
Stainforth DN7 92 C6
West Back Side YO25 10 C4
West Bank
Stainforth DN7 92 B7
York YO24 129 E3
West Butterwick C of E Sch
DN17 106 D8
West Carr La HU7 140 F6
West Cl Fangfoss YO41 28 C8
Nafferton YO25 125 E6
Newport HU15 52 E1
West Coates Rd DN31 152 B6
West Comm Cres
DN17 150 F4
West Comm Gdns
DN17 150 F2
West Comm La DN17 150 F3
West Comm N Rd
DN17 107 A8
West Comm Rd DN17 150 F3
West Crayke YO16 122 F6
West Cross St 16 DN21 108 B1
West Ct 8 Riccall YO19 48 F8
8 Thorne/Moorends DN8 93 A7
West Dale Cres DN21 108 B2
West Dock Ave HU3 145 B4
West Dock St HU3 145 B3
West Dr YO25 125 F6
West Edge Rd WF8 76 A3
West Ella Rd
Kingston upon Hull
HU10 143 A7
Swanland HU14 69 C7
West Ella Way HU10 143 C7
West End Bainton YO25 31 E7
Dalton Holme HU17 42 E8
Garthorpe & Fockerby
DN17 81 E6
Kilham YO25 9 B3
Lund YO25 31 E2
Pollington DN14 77 F6
Rawcliffe DN14 64 A2
Seaton Ross YO42 39 D4
West End *continued*
South Cave HU15 53 F1
Strensall YO32 14 A7
Swanland HU14 69 B6
Ulceby DN39 86 A1
Walkington HU17 55 B7
Winteringham DN15 68 A1
West End Cl
North Duffield YO8 50 A8
9 Strensall YO32 14 B7
West End Farm Cl 6
HU15 53 F1
West End Gdns DN14 77 F6
West End La DN36 115 B1
West End Rd
Epworth DN9 105 C7
2 Habrough DN40 100 E8
5 Habrough DN40 100 E8
Kingston upon Hull
HU16 138 F7
Norton DN6 76 E2
Ulceby DN39 85 F1
West Field La
1 Swanland HU14 69 B6
Upper Poppleton YO26 12 E1
West Garth Kilham YO25 9 B3
Rowley HU20 55 A4
West Gate YO25 124 E5
West Gn
Kingston upon Hull HU10 69 C8
Messingham DN17 107 D7
Pocklington YO42 28 F3
West Gr
Barton-upon-Humber
DN18 69 E1
Kingston upon Hull HU4 144 D4
West Green Dr YO42 29 A3
West Hall Garth 10 HU15 53 F1
West Halton La DN15 82 C8
West Hann La DN19 70 C1
West Haven Way DN40 87 B3
West Hill 1 HU13 69 E4
West Ings Cl 4 WF11 61 A3
West Ings Cres 5 WF11 61 A3
West Ings Ct 1 WF11 61 A3
West Ings La 2 WF11 61 A3
West Ings Mews 6
WF11 61 A3
West Ings Way 3 WF11 61 A3
West La Burn YO8 62 C6
Burton Fleming YO25 2 E3
Keelby DN41 101 A4
Laxton DN14 65 D2
Sykehouse DN14 77 F2
Winterton DN15 83 B5
West Lambwath Rd
HU11 46 D3
West Lea DN33 113 E8
West Leys Pk HU14 69 B6
West Leys Rd HU14 69 B6
West Marsh La
Barrow upon Humber
DN19 70 B1
Goxhill DN19 71 A3
West Mid Mere Rd
DN40 86 D3
West Mill Rise 4 HU17 55 B7
West Moor Rd DN10 116 C3
West Newton Rd HU11 58 D8
West Par HU3 145 C7
West Parklands Dr 8
HU14 69 A5
West Pk YO8 148 A4
West Prom YO25 124 D4
West Rd
Keadby with Althorpe
DN17 95 C6
Sigglesthorne HU11 34 E1
Thorne/Moorends DN8 79 B2
West Road Fst Sch
DN8 79 B2
West St Mary's Gate
DN31 152 D3
West St
Barnetby le Wold DN38 99 B4
Beverley HU17 137 C4
Bridlington YO15 122 E1
Cleethorpes DN35 153 F2
21 Flamborough YO15 5 A2
9 Gainsborough DN21 117 A2
Goole DN14 149 C5
Hibaldstow DN20 108 F5
Kingston upon Hull HU1 155 A2
Leven HU17 44 F8
North Kelsey LN7 110 A4
Roxby cum Risby DN15 82 F3
Scawby DN20 108 E8
Scunthorpe DN15 151 A7
Thorne/Moorends DN8 93 A7
West Butterwick DN17 106 C8
West Halton DN15 82 E7
Winterton DN15 83 A5
West Terr
Beverley HU17 154 C2
19 Brigg DN20 98 B2
West Terrace St 3 DN17 94 D7
West Thorpe YO24 132 D8
West View
Messingham DN17 107 C7
12 North Ferriby HU14 69 A4
Scunthorpe DN17 96 C2
West View Cl 9 DN41 101 A4
West Wood La YO23 24 E4
Westbeck Hill YO42 30 A5
Westbeck La DN21 118 F5
Westborough Way
HU4 144 B6
Westbourne Ave
Bridlington YO16 122 D3
Kingston upon Hull HU5 140 A1
3 Kingston upon Hull
HU13 143 E2
Westbourne Ave W
HU5 140 A1
Westbourne Dr DN17 94 D7
Westbourne Gdns
YO8 148 C4
Westbourne Gr
Goole DN14 149 D6
15 Grimsby DN33 113 E8
Kingston upon Hull
HU13 143 D2
Selby YO8 148 C4
Westbourne Rd
Hornsea HU18 134 D4
Selby YO8 148 C4
Westbourne St 5 HU3 145 A4
Westbrook Cres 3 HU15 66 D7
Westbrook Rd 12 HU15 66 D8
Westbrooke Gr 18 LN7 111 B4
Westburn Ave 2 DN19 70 E2
Westbury Pk 10 DN35 103 D1
Westbury Rd DN35 103 C1
Westcliff Gdns DN17 150 F3
Westcliffe Jun & Inf Sch
DN17 150 D2
Westcliffe Rd 16 DN21 107 C3
Westcott Prim Sch
HU8 141 C3
Westcott St HU8 141 D2
Westcroft 11 YO43 53 F7
Westend Falls YO25 125 E6
Westend La DN14 77 B6
Westenders Way HU1 155 A1
Westerdale 4 HU14 69 B7
Westerdale Cl 8 HU12 73 C4
Westerdale Ct 2 YO30 130 A6
Westerdale Gr HU9 146 E8
Westerdale Rd DN16 151 D1
Western Ave DN20 98 C3
Western Comp Sch
DN34 102 C3
Western Dr 7 DN18 69 E1
Western Gailes Way
HU8 142 B5
Western Gn DN15 68 A1
Western Outway
DN34 102 D2
Western Rd DN14 149 C6
Westfield
Patrington HU12 74 C1
Selby YO8 148 B4
Westfield Ave
Beverley HU17 136 D6
3 Eggborough DN14 61 F2
Goole DN14 149 D5
11 Grimsby DN33 102 E2
Rawcliffe DN14 64 A1
Selby YO8 148 B4
Westfield Cl
Easington HU12 90 F6
2 Eggborough DN14 61 F2
21 Haxby YO32 13 E5
Kingston upon Hull
HU16 138 F6
Nafferton YO25 125 E6
3 Pocklington YO42 28 F4
Westfield Cres YO43 135 C4
Westfield Cty Inf Sch
YO24 129 B2
Westfield Cty Jun Sch
YO26 129 A2
Westfield Dr
Messingham DN17 107 D7
York YO10 133 D8
Westfield Garth
1 Crowle DN17 94 E6
1 Walkington HU17 55 B8
Westfield Gr
4 Eggborough DN14 61 F2
Grimsby DN35 153 D2
12 Haxby YO32 13 D5
Westfield La
East Garton HU12 59 D5
Fishlake DN7 92 B8
Hook DN14 149 D8
Kirk Bramwith DN7 78 B1
Norton WF8 76 C2
Preston HU12 58 B1
Thorganby YO19 38 A5
Westfield Pk HU15 68 C6
Westfield Pl
19 Haxby YO32 13 E5
York YO24 129 A1
Westfield Prim Sch
HU16 138 F6
Westfield Rd
Barton-upon-Humber
DN18 69 C1
Easington HU12 90 F5
1 Eggborough DN14 61 F2
4 Goxhill DN19 86 A8
4 Hatfield DN7 92 E4
20 Haxby YO32 13 E5
Kingston upon Hull
HU16 138 F6
Kingston upon Hull HU4 144 D5
Kirk Bramwith DN7 92 A8
Market Weighton YO43 135 C4
3 North Duffield YO8 50 A7
Pocklington YO42 28 F4
Rawcliffe DN14 64 A1
Scunthorpe DN17 150 B2
Scunthorpe DN16 151 C2
Selby YO8 148 B4
Westfield Rd *continued*
Skidby HU16 138 A5
Waltham DN37 113 D6
Westfield Rise
Beeford YO25 34 B8
Kingston upon Hull
HU13 143 D2
13 Withernsea HU19 75 A6
Westfield Sq DN14 149 D6
Westfield Terr YO43 135 C4
Westfield Villas 3 DN7 92 E4
Westgarth Ave HU6 139 F5
Westgate
Bridlington YO16 122 B4
Grimsby DN31 152 D5
Hornsea HU18 134 B4
Nafferton YO25 125 E6
North Cave HU15 53 D3
North Newbald YO43 53 E7
Patrington HU12 74 D1
Scotton DN21 107 C1
Westgate Manor 4
HU12 74 D1
Westgate Mdws YO25 125 E6
Westgate Rd DN9 94 D2
Westhill Rd DN34 152 A1
Westholme Ave HU18 134 C7
Westholme Cl 10 DN15 82 B4
Westholme Dr YO30 126 E1
Westholme La DN38 99 C5
Westkirke Ave 2 DN33 113 F8
Westland Rd
Kingston upon Hull
HU10 143 B7
3 Westwoodside DN9 105 B2
Westlands Ave
Grimsby DN34 152 C1
Tetney DN36 114 D4
Westlands Cl 13 HU12 72 C7
Westlands Dr HU12 72 C7
Westlands Gr YO31 130 F7
Westlands Mews
YO25 124 D5
Westlands Rd
Hedon HU12 72 C7
Kingston upon Hull HU5 144 B8
Sproatley HU11 58 C5
Westlands Way HU17 45 A8
Westminster Ave HU8 141 E3
Westminster Ct DN14 149 E6
Westminster Dr
Grimsby DN34 152 C2
Hatfield DN7 92 C2
Westminster Rd
2 Broughton DN20 97 D4
York YO30 130 A6
Westmoreland Ave 3
YO15 122 F2
Westmoreland Cl DN9 105 A2
Westmoreland Gr 2
YO15 122 F2
Westmoreland St
1 Kingston upon Hull
HU2 140 F1
Kingston upon Hull HU2 155 B4
Westoby La
Barrow upon Humber
DN19 85 C7
Rowley HU15 54 E3
Weston Gr 3 DN40 87 B2
Westover Dr DN15 82 A4
Westparkside DN14 149 A6
Westpit La YO32 14 A7
Westport Rd 27 DN35 103 C1
Westridge Rd YO15 122 C1
Westrum La DN20 98 C1
Westside Rd DN31 152 C6
Westview Cl YO26 129 B7
Westward Cl DN34 152 C1
Westward Ho DN34 152 B1
Westway Ave HU6 139 F6
Westwick 25 HU12 72 C7
Westwinds Gdns DN15 83 A5
Westwinds Rd 10 DN15 83 A5
Westwold Rd 20 LN7 111 B4
Westwood 4 DN20 97 D4
Westwood Ave HU18 134 B4
Westwood Cl HU7 141 C6
Westwood Dr 3 HU4 144 B6
Westwood Gate HU17 154 A1
Westwood Hospl
HU17 136 D3
Westwood Mews 12
YO19 26 F7
Westwood Rd
Beverley HU17 154 A3
12 Healing DN41 101 F5
Westwood Terr YO23 130 B1
Westwoodside C of E Sch
DN9 105 B2
Wetherby Cl HU6 139 F7
Wetherby Rd YO26 129 B3
Wetwang C of E Sch
YO25 19 B5
Wexford Ave HU9 142 E1
Weyford Rd 9 DN35 103 D1
Weymouth Cl HU7 141 B6
Weymouth Cres DN17 150 C5
Whales La DN14 61 E3
Wharf Rd Crowle DN17 94 D7
Misterton DN10 116 C5
Wharf The DN36 115 A5
Wharfdale Cl DN15 95 E5
Wharfe Dr YO24 132 D8
Wharfedale Ave HU9 141 E1

Wharfedale Dr YO16 ...122 F7
Wharfedale Pl DN16 ...151 D2
Wharncliffe Rd N
DN31 ...153 A7
Wharncliffe St HU5 ...145 A8
Wharnscliffe Dr YO30 ...126 F2
Wharram Field 3 YO25 ...22 D1
Wharram St HU2 ...140 F1
Wharton Ave YO30 ...130 B7
Wharton Rd
Blyton DN21 ...117 D5
8 Stamford Bridge YO41 ...15 D2
Wharton St DN31 ...152 B3
Wheatcroft 6 YO32 ...14 A6
Wheatcroft Ave HU10 ...138 E2
Wheatfield Cl
9 Barnby Dun DN3 ...92 A3
Epworth DN9 ...105 F6
2 Kingston upon Hull
HU4 ...144 D2
Wheatfield Dr 2 DN37 ...113 D6
Wheatfield La YO32 ...127 C8
Wheatland Cl YO42 ...29 B3
Wheatlands Dr HU17 ...136 C6
Wheatlands Gr YO26 ...129 C6
Wheatley Dr
Bridlington YO16 ...123 A6
Haxby YO32 ...127 C8
Wheatley Gdns HU8 ...141 D3
Wheeldale Cl 2 HU7 ...141 D7
Wheeler Prim Sch
HU3 ...144 F5
Wheeler St HU3 ...144 F6
Wheelhouse The 4
YO30 ...126 B5
Wheels La YO8 ...63 F3
Wheelwright Cl
Copmanthorpe YO23 ...132 B2
Sutton upon Derwent
YO41 ...27 C1
Wheldrake C of E Prim Sch
YO19 ...38 A8
Wheldrake Ings Nature
Reserve* YO19 ...38 C7
Wheldrake La
Deighton YO19 ...26 B1
Escrick YO19 ...37 B5
Whenby Gr YO31 ...127 F1
Whernside Ave YO31 ...131 A5
Whernside Cl 12 HU7 ...57 A6
Whimbrel Ave HU18 ...134 C2
Whimbrel Way 12 DN36 ...114 A8
Whin Cl 3 Strensall YO32 ...14 B6
York YO24 ...132 F7
Whin Garth YO24 ...132 F6
Whin La Burstwick HU12 ...73 C7
South Cave HU43 ...54 B6
Whin Moor La HU15 ...68 A7
Whin Rd YO24 ...132 F6
Whincroft Ave DN14 ...149 C6
Whinhill La HU12 ...73 F4
Whinns The HU17 ...154 C1
Whinny Hagg La YO8 ...48 A2
Whinny La YO60 ...15 A7
Whins Gate DN17 ...81 A4
Whins La HU11 ...45 D6
Whip-ma-whop-ma-gate
YO1 ...156 C2
Whisby Ct DN36 ...114 B5
Whiston Way 9 DN18 ...69 F1
Whitby Ave YO31 ...131 A7
Whitby Dr
Grimsby DN32 ...153 A1
York YO31 ...131 A7
Whitby St HU8 ...146 B8
White Cross* HU11 ...45 A6
White Cross Rd YO31 ...130 D7
White Cross Way YO41 ...16 A2
White Gap La HU20 ...54 E5
White Gap Rd HU20 ...54 F4
White Horse Cl 6 YO32 ...127 F5
White Horse La HU12 ...73 E3
White House Cl
10 Hatfield DN7 ...92 D4
Kingston upon Hull
HU10 ...138 C2
Kirk Bramwith DN7 ...92 C7
White House Dale
YO24 ...129 F1
White House Dr YO24 ...129 F1
White House Gdns 4
YO24 ...130 A2
White House Gr 1 YO41 ...27 B2
White House La DN15 ...82 E8
White House Rise
YO24 ...129 F1
White La DN8 ...92 F8
White Ley Rd DN6 ...76 C1
White Lodge YO8 ...148 B4
White Rose Ave 3
YO32 ...127 D3
White Rose Cl YO26 ...126 C1
White Rose Gr 5 YO32 ...127 D3
White Rose Way YO26 ...129 C8
White Sprunt Hill YO17 ...1 A1
White St
Kingston upon Hull HU3 ...144 F5
Selby YO8 ...148 B6
White Wlk HU10 ...143 C6
Whitebeam Cl HU3 ...145 D5
Whitecarr La YO42 ...39 E8
Whitecross Rd HU11 ...45 B6
Whitecross St DN18 ...84 F8
Whitefield Bglws DN14 ...76 F8
Whitefield La DN14 ...61 E1
Whitefields Cl HU17 ...136 E7
Whitefriargate HU1 ...155 B2
Whitegate Hill LN7 ...111 C3
Whitehall Gdns 3 HU5 ...140 A1
Whitehall Rd 5 DN35 ...103 D1
Whitehead Cl HU17 ...154 B2
Whitehope Cl 13 HU7 ...57 A6
Whitehouse Wlk HU6 ...56 D5
Whitelands YO25 ...124 D5
Whitemoor La YO8 ...49 C6
Whiterose Dr YO41 ...15 D2
White's Close La HU12 ...59 A2
White's Rd DN35 ...153 F1
Whitestone Dr YO31 ...127 E2
Whitestone Rd DN17 ...150 C2
Whitethorn Ave 11 HU19 ...75 A6
Whitethorn Cl YO31 ...127 E2
Whitethorn Way HU8 ...141 D4
Whitewell Cl 3 DN21 ...108 B1
Whitfield Rd DN17 ...150 D2
Whitgift Cl 18 DN37 ...101 F1
Whitgift Sch DN37 ...102 B4
Whitley & Eggborough Cty
Prim Sch DN14 ...61 F1
Whitley Bridge Sta
DN14 ...61 F1
Whitley Cl YO30 ...127 A1
Whitley Rd YO41 ...27 A3
Whitley Thorpe La
DN14 ...76 F7
Whitman Rd DN17 ...150 C2
Whitstable Cl 3 HU8 ...141 E7
Whitstone Cl HU7 ...140 F8
Whitton Pl YO10 ...131 C4
Whitton Rd DN15 ...82 C8
Whitworth St HU9 ...141 E2
Whoofer La DN21 ...117 B7
Wickenby Cl 18 DN34 ...102 C2
Wickenby Garth HU7 ...141 C8
Wickham Rd DN31 ...153 A6
Wicklow Ave 22 DN33 ...113 E8
Wickwane Rd HU17 ...137 A6
Wicstun Way YO43 ...135 C3
Wide La YO14 ...3 E5
Widford Gn 7 DN7 ...92 D3
Widop St DN14 ...149 C5
Wigginton Prim Sch
YO32 ...13 D5
Wigginton Rd YO31 ...156 B4
Wigginton Terr YO31 ...130 C8
Wike Gate Cl 7 DN8 ...93 B7
Wike Gate Gr 6 DN8 ...93 B7
Wike Gate Rd DN8 ...93 B8
Wilbar Gr HU5 ...140 B2
Wilberforce Ave YO30 ...130 B7
Wilberforce Coll HU8 ...142 A5
Wilberforce Cres
HU17 ...154 C4
Wilberforce Dr HU1 ...155 C3
Wilberforce House Mus*
HU1 ...155 C2
Wilberforce Monument*
HU1 ...155 C3
Wilberforce St HU3 ...145 D6
Wilberfoss Sch YO41 ...27 E6
Wilbert Gr HU17 ...154 B3
Wilbert La HU17 ...154 B3
Wiles Ct HU17 ...154 C2
Wilfholme Rd YO25 ...32 F3
Wilflete Ct HU9 ...142 B3
Wilfreds Gr 8 YO8 ...49 B4
Wilfreds Rd 5 YO8 ...49 B4
Wilkie Cl DN15 ...150 C7
Wilkinson Ave DN8 ...79 B1
Wilkinson Way 3 YO32 ...14 A7
Willerby Carr Cl 2 HU5 ...139 B1
Willerby Dr 2 DN14 ...65 A7
Willerby Low Rd
HU10 ...138 D3
Willerby Rd HU5 ...144 C8
Willesden Cl 4 HU8 ...141 F5
William Barcroft Jun Sch
DN32 ...153 C3
William Gee High Sch
HU5 ...139 D3
William Jacques Dr
YO8 ...49 E2
William Plows Ave
YO10 ...130 E2
William Rd YO8 ...49 B4
William St
Cleethorpes DN35 ...153 E1
Kingston upon Hull HU1 ...155 A1
Scunthorpe DN16 ...151 B6
Williams Dr DN39 ...86 B1
Williamson St HU9 ...146 C7
Willing Way DN32 ...152 F4
Willingham Garth 4
HU12 ...72 E5
Willingham St DN32 ...152 E2
Willingham Way HU10 ...138 B1
Willis St YO10 ...130 E3
Willitoft Rd YO8 ...50 F6
Willoughby Gr 12 DN34 ...102 C2
Willoughby Rd DN17 ...150 E1
Willoughby Way YO24 ...132 B8
Willoughton CP Sch
DN21 ...119 A4
Willow Ave
2 Misterton DN10 ...116 C5
Thorne/Moorends DN8 ...79 A1
Willow Bank YO32 ...127 E4
Willow Cl
18 Gainsborough DN21 ...117 A2
Laceby DN37 ...101 E1
Pollington DN14 ...78 A6
Snaith DN14 ...78 B8
Willow Cres DN8 ...79 A1
Willow Ct
Hutton Cranswick YO25 ...32 E6
Kexby YO41 ...15 C2
Kingston upon Hull
HU10 ...138 E1
9 Pocklington YO42 ...29 A3
Willow Dr
11 Barton-upon-Humber
DN18 ...69 F1
Bridlington YO16 ...123 A6
Goole DN14 ...65 C3
Kingston upon Hull
HU10 ...143 D8
Messingham DN17 ...107 D7
1 North Duffield YO8 ...50 A7
1 Thorngumbald HU12 ...72 E5
Willow Garth
Eastrington DN14 ...51 F1
Pollington DN14 ...78 A6
Willow Garth La DN6 ...77 A1
Willow Gdns 2 DN19 ...85 D8
Willow Glade YO32 ...127 F3
Willow Gn 7 HU15 ...66 D8
Willow Gr
3 Aldbrough HU11 ...47 C1
Beverley HU17 ...136 D4
Earswick YO32 ...128 A7
Keadby DN17 ...95 D6
Kingston upon Hull HU5 ...140 C2
Pollington DN14 ...78 A6
Scawby DN20 ...108 F8
Scunthorpe DN16 ...151 B3
3 Thorne/Moorends DN8 ...79 B1
York YO31 ...130 F7
Willow La Goxhill DN19 ...86 A8
Pollington DN14 ...78 A6
Woodmansey HU17 ...154 B1
Willow Park Rd YO41 ...27 F5
Willow Rd
Burstwick HU12 ...73 B6
9 Campsall DN6 ...76 E1
10 Knottingley WF11 ...61 A3
6 Thorne/Moorends DN8 ...79 A1
Willow Rise YO8 ...48 B1
Willow Tree Garth 5
HU17 ...136 F7
Willowbridge Rd WF8 ...76 C2
Willowbrook Dr DN20 ...98 D2
Willowdale HU7 ...140 F8
Willowfield HU6 ...140 A6
Willows Ave HU9 ...141 F3
Willows Dr HU18 ...134 C4
Willows Prim Sch
DN37 ...102 C4
Willows The
Kingston upon Hull
HU13 ...143 E4
8 Strensall YO32 ...14 B7
Willy Howe* YO25 ...2 C3
Wilson Cl
Market Weighton YO43 ...135 D3
7 North Ferriby HU14 ...69 A4
Wilson St
Cleethorpes DN35 ...153 D4
Gainsborough DN21 ...117 A1
5 Goole DN14 ...149 C4
Kingston upon Hull
HU10 ...143 E6
4 Kingston upon Hull
HU9 ...146 B7
Wilsthorpe Gr 1 YO10 ...133 F8
Wilstrop Farm Rd
YO23 ...132 A2
Wilton Rd
Hornsea HU18 ...134 D3
Humberston DN36 ...114 B8
Wilton Rise YO24 ...129 F3
Wilton St HU8 ...146 B8
Wiltshire Ave DN15 ...82 B4
Wiltshire Rd HU4 ...144 E2
Wimbledon Cl 4 HU8 ...142 A5
Wimborn Ave DN34 ...152 B2
Wimbourne Cl HU7 ...141 C6
Wimpole Cl 6 YO30 ...127 A1
Winceby Ave DN31 ...152 A4
Winchcombe Ave 3
DN34 ...102 C2
Winchester Ave
5 Beverley HU17 ...136 E1
Grimsby DN33 ...102 D2
Kingston upon Hull HU9 ...142 B4
3 York YO26 ...129 E4
Winchester Cl HU9 ...142 B4
Winchester Dr DN16 ...96 E2
Winchester Gr 1 YO26 ...129 E4
Winchester Rd 20 DN7 ...92 D4
Wincolmlee HU2 ...155 C3
Windermere YO24 ...132 D7
Windermere Ave
DN33 ...113 D8
Windermere Cres
9 Humberston DN36 ...103 C1
10 Kirk Sandall DN3 ...92 A2
Windermere Dr DN14 ...149 E5
Windgate Hill La YO8 ...48 B6
Windham Cres 1 HU7 ...56 F7
Windle Ave HU6 ...140 C7
Windlesham Ave 10
DN33 ...113 D8
Windlestone Sq 11 DN8 ...79 B2
Windmill Gdns YO8 ...148 B7
Windmill Hill YO25 ...124 E5
Windmill La Norton DN6 ...76 D1
York YO10 ...131 B2
Windmill Mdws YO41 ...27 E6
Windmill Rise YO26 ...129 E3
Windmill Way HU13 ...143 F1
Windsor Ave HU10 ...143 E7
Windsor Cl
Beverley HU17 ...137 B5
3 Keelby DN41 ...101 A5
Kingston upon Hull
HU16 ...139 B5
Windsor Cres
Bridlington YO15 ...122 E2
Crowle DN17 ...94 C7
Scunthorpe DN17 ...96 C1
Windsor Ct DN7 ...92 C2
Windsor Dr
Caistor LN7 ...111 B4
Goole DN14 ...149 B5
2 Haxby YO32 ...13 D5
Windsor Garth YO24 ...129 D1
Windsor Gr DN19 ...71 A1
Windsor La DN17 ...94 C7
Windsor Rd
Cleethorpes DN35 ...153 C1
Crowle DN17 ...94 C7
Kingston upon Hull HU5 ...139 F1
Windsor St 1 YO23 ...130 B1
Windsor Way
Barnetby le Wold DN38 ...99 B5
Broughton DN20 ...97 E4
Winestead Gr 3 HU9 ...142 A2
Winestead Ings La
HU12 ...74 A1
Winestead La HU12 ...74 B3
Wingate Rd DN37 ...102 B4
Wingfield Rd HU9 ...142 C2
Wingfield Way HU17 ...55 E8
Winifred Holtby Sch
HU7 ...141 B7
Winn St 1 DN16 ...151 B6
Winscar Croft 8 HU7 ...141 D7
Winscar Gr 9 YO30 ...126 E3
Winsetts Rd HU12 ...90 D5
Winship Cl 4 HU3 ...145 C5
Winslow Dr DN40 ...87 B1
Winslow Gr 15 DN34 ...102 C2
Winston Ave DN34 ...152 B2
Winston Cl HU12 ...73 A7
Winston Dr HU16 ...138 F5
Winston Way DN20 ...98 D2
Winteringham County Prim
Sch DN15 ...68 A1
Winteringham La DN15 ...82 E8
Winteringham Rd DN15 ...83 B6
Winterscale St YO10 ...130 D2
Winterton C of E Inf Sch
DN15 ...83 A5
Winterton Comp Sch
DN15 ...83 A6
Winterton Rd
Roxby cum Risby DN15 ...82 F2
Scunthorpe DN15 ...151 B8
Winteringham DN15 ...83 B8
Winthorpe Rd
Grimsby DN33 ...102 D1
4 Kingston upon Hull
HU13 ...144 A3
Wintringham Rd DN32 ...152 E2
Wintringham Sch
DN32 ...102 F2
Wirral Ave 15 DN34 ...102 C2
Wise Cl HU17 ...136 E7
Wisker La YO32 ...128 C7
Wisteria Dr DN41 ...101 E5
Wisteria Way DN16 ...151 E1
Wistow Gr HU4 ...144 D5
Wistow Parochial C of E Prim
Sch YO8 ...48 D6
Wistow Rd YO8 ...148 A8
Wistowgate YO8 ...48 B8
Witch La YO25 ...3 B2
Witham HU9 ...155 C3
Witham Dr
Burton upon Stather
DN15 ...82 B5
York YO32 ...128 A6
Withern Rd DN33 ...102 D2
Withernsea Cty Jun Sch
HU19 ...74 F7
Withernsea High Sch
HU19 ...74 F7
Withernsea Hospl
HU19 ...75 A6
Withernsea Inf Sch
HU19 ...74 F7
Withernsea Rd
Hollym HU19 ...75 A4
Holmpton HU19 ...75 C3
Rimswell HU19 ...74 D8
Roos HU19 ...60 C1
Withernsea St HU8 ...141 A1
Withernwick La HU11 ...47 A4
Withernwick Prim Sch
HU11 ...46 D3
Withernwick Rd
Aldbrough HU11 ...47 A2
Hatfield HU11 ...46 C5
Witty St HU3 ...145 A3
Wittys Paddock 4 HU11 ...35 A1
Wivell Dr DN41 ...101 A5
Wivern Rd HU9 ...142 D3
Woad La DN37 ...102 C5
Woburn Dr DN14 ...149 E5
Woburn St HU3 ...144 F4
Wold Ave YO43 ...135 E3
Wold Garth YO42 ...29 A3
Wold Hill HU15 ...53 E4
Wold La YO12 ...1 E8
Wold Newton GM Sch
YO25 ...2 A4
Wold Newton Rd YO25 ...2 E3
Wold Prim Sch HU5 ...139 B1
Wold Rd
Barrow upon Humber
DN19 ...85 D7
Kingston upon Hull HU5 ...139 B1
Kirby Grindalythe YO17 ...6 E8
Market Weighton YO43 ...135 F2
Nafferton YO25 ...125 E8
Pocklington YO42 ...29 A4
Walkington HU17 ...54 E7
Worlaby DN20 ...84 E1
Wold Rise YO43 ...41 E2
Wold View Brigg DN20 ...98 C2
Caistor LN7 ...111 B4
Elloughton-cum-Brough
HU15 ...68 C6
Fotherby LN11 ...121 D2
Fridaythorpe YO25 ...18 B5
6 Holton le Clay DN36 ...114 A5
Rothwell LN7 ...111 F2
3 South Cave HU15 ...54 A2
Wold View Rd N YO25 ...124 E3
Wold View Rd S YO25 ...124 E3
Woldcarr Rd HU3 ...144 F6
Woldcroft YO41 ...27 C2
Woldgate
Bridlington YO16 ...122 A3
Carnaby YO16 ...10 E6
Harpham YO25 ...9 D3
5 North Newbald YO43 ...53 F7
Woldgate Sch YO42 ...29 B4
Woldgate View 1 YO42 ...29 A3
Woldholme Ave YO25 ...124 D3
Wolds Cl 12 DN17 ...94 D7
Wolds Gliding Club
YO42 ...28 F3
Wolds The HU16 ...138 E6
Wolfe Ave YO31 ...130 F5
Wolfe Cl 7 HU16 ...138 F5
Wolfreton Dr HU10 ...143 F6
Wolfreton Garth
HU10 ...143 D8
Wolfreton La HU10 ...143 F8
Wolfreton Lower Sch
HU10 ...138 D1
Wolfreton Rd HU10 ...143 F7
Wolfreton Sch HU10 ...138 D1
Wollaston Rd DN35 ...153 E2
Wolsey Ave YO8 ...48 B8
Wolsey Dr
3 Barrow upon Humber
DN19 ...85 C7
Bishopthorpe YO23 ...133 A3
Wolsley St YO10 ...130 E3
Wolviston Ave YO10 ...131 C3
Wombwell Gr 3 HU8 ...141 B1
Womersley C of E Prim Sch
DN6 ...76 C6
Womersley Rd
Grimsby DN31 ...153 A6
Knottingley WF11 ...61 A2
Wood Carr La DN9 ...94 C2
Wood Cl
8 Grimsby DN33 ...113 E8
7 Strensall YO32 ...14 A7
14 Thorpe Willoughby YO8 ...48 B1
Wood Dr 1 HU14 ...69 A4
Wood Gate YO42 ...29 D7
Wood Hill Rd DN21 ...107 A3
Wood Hill Way HU16 ...138 C8
Wood La
Acaster Selby YO23 ...36 B2
Beverley HU17 ...154 A3
Birkin WF11 ...61 D6
Bubwith DN14 ...51 A5
Cottingham HU16 ...139 B4
Fishlake DN7 ...92 D8
13 Thorpe Willoughby YO8 ...48 B1
Wressle DN14 ...51 B2
Wood St Grimsby DN32 ...152 F4
York YO31 ...130 E6
Wood Vale DN16 ...96 E2
Wood View Airmyn DN14 ...64 E3
Messingham DN17 ...107 D8
Swanland HU14 ...69 B7
Wood Way YO32 ...128 A4
Woodale Cl 3 DN15 ...96 B7
Woodall Ct 9 YO8 ...48 D6
Woodapple Ct 2 DN41 ...101 E6
Woodbine Ave DN20 ...98 C2
Woodbine Cl HU2 ...155 A4
Woodclose Rd DN17 ...150 D2
Woodcoates Cl 1 HU17 ...136 F7
Woodcock Cl 9 YO32 ...13 F5
Woodcock Rd 1 YO15 ...5 A2
Woodcock St HU3 ...145 A4
Woodcroft Ave HU6 ...139 F5
Wooden Beck Hill
DN10 ...116 B2
Woodfield Cl 4 DN36 ...114 D8
Woodfield La HU13 ...143 C1
Woodfield Rd
Gainsborough DN21 ...117 C1
Goole DN14 ...149 B6
Woodford L Ctr HU8 ...141 E2
Woodford Pl 1 YO24 ...129 D1
Woodgarr Ave 1 DN17 ...95 D6
Woodgate La HU5 ...144 F8
Woodgate Rd
Kingston upon Hull HU5 ...144 F7
Newbald YO43 ...54 A8
Woodgates Cl 6 HU14 ...69 A5
Woodgates La HU14 ...69 A5
Woodgates Mount 3
HU14 ...69 A5
Woodhall Dr
1 Beverley HU17 ...136 D6
Waltham DN37 ...113 D6

Woodhall La
Hemingbrough YO8 ....50 B3
Womersley DN6 ....76 D6
Woodhall Pk HU17 .....136 D7
Woodhall St HU8 ....141 A2
Woodhall Way HU17 ....154 A4
Woodhill Ave DN21 .....117 C1
Woodhill Cl 2 HU10 ....143 E7
Woodhill Rise HU13 ....143 C2
Woodhouse Gr 4 YO31 .131 A5
Woodhouse Green Rd
DN7 ....92 B8
Woodhouse La
Beeford YO25 ....22 C1
Belton DN9 ....94 E2
Hatfield DN7 ....92 D2
Pocklington YO42 ....29 A5
Riston HU11 ....45 B3
Woodhouse Rd
Scunthorpe DN16 ....151 E4
Thorganby YO19 ....38 A3
Woodhouse St HU9 ....146 D7
Woodings Ct 5 DN14 ....65 A7
Woodland Ave
17 Brough HU15 ....68 C6
14 Gainsborough DN21 ...117 A2
Goole DN14 ....149 C6
Woodland Chase
YO30 ....127 B1
Woodland Dr
Broughton DN20 ....97 D4
1 Elsham DN20 ....98 F7
Kingston upon Hull
HU10 ....143 C6
Woodland End HU4 ....144 C5
Woodland Pl YO32 .....127 E4
Woodland Rise YO25 ...125 A6
Woodland View
5 Barnetby le Wold DN38 ..99 B4
Scunthorpe DN15 ....150 C7
Woodland Way
8 Airmyn DN14 ....64 E4
19 Epworth DN9 ....105 E6
York YO32 ....127 F4
Woodland Wlk 6 DN35 .103 C1
Woodlands
Beverley HU17 ....136 D4
Escrick YO19 ....37 B5
Woodlands Ave
Haxby YO32 ....127 C8
Immingham DN40 ....87 C2
Keelby DN41 ....101 A4
Woodlands Cl
4 Barrow upon Humber
DN19 ....85 C7
Bridlington YO15 ....123 B7
Woodlands Dr HU17 ....136 D4
Woodlands Gr YO31 ....131 A7
Woodlands La
8 Brough HU15 ....68 C6
Hillam LS25 ....61 B7
Woodlands Prim Sch
DN33 ....102 D1
Woodlands Rd HU5 .....144 B7
Woodlands Rise
5 North Ferriby HU14 .....69 A5
Norton DN6 ....76 E1
Woodlands Sports Ctr
DN40 ....87 C2
Woodlands The
Kingston upon Hull
HU16 ....138 F7
Kingston upon Hull HU5 ...140 B2
Preston HU12 ....72 B7
2 Stallingborough DN41 ..101 D6
Woodlands View YO8 ....49 B4
Woodlea Ave YO26 .....129 C4
Woodlea Bank YO26 ....129 D4
Woodlea Cres YO26 ....129 D4
Woodlea Gr YO26 ......129 D5
Woodleigh Cl 2 YO32 ....14 A6
Woodleigh Dr HU7 .....141 C5
Woodmansey C of E Sch
HU17 ....56 C8
Woodmarketgate 26
HU12 ....72 C7
Woodrow Pk DN33 .....102 E1
Wood's La HU1 ....155 A1
Woods La DN40 ....86 F2
Woods Mdw DN20 ......108 F6
Woods Terr 7 DN21 .....117 B2
Woodside
10 Gilberdyke HU15 ....66 D7
Kingston upon Hull
HU13 ....143 D1
Woodside Ave YO31 ....131 A6
Woodside La DN9 ......104 D6
Woodside Rd YO12 ....1 A8
Woodsley Ave
5 Cleethorpes DN35 .....103 C2
Cleethorpes DN35 ....153 E1
Woodstock Cl HU16 ....138 F6
Woodstock Rd DN16 ...151 D4
Woodthorpe Prim Sch
YO24 ....132 C7
Woodville Terr YO8 .....148 E3
Woolam Hill HU12 ....73 A6
Woollin Ave DN17 ......151 A2
Woolnough Ave YO10 ...131 B3
Woolsthorpe Gr 20 HU7 ..56 F6
Woolwich Dr 2 HU4 ....144 B2
Wootton C of E Sch
DN39 ....85 E3
Wootton Rd
Grimsby DN33 ....102 D2
Wootton DN39 ....85 F2
Worcester Ave DN34 ...152 A1
Worcester Cl 11 DN16 ....96 D1
Worcester Dr YO31 .....131 B5
Worcester Rd HU5 .....139 C1
Worcestershire Cl 1
HU5 ....139 D1
Wordsworth Ave 4 DN6 ..76 E1
Wordsworth Cres
YO24 ....132 D7
Wordsworth Rd DN17 ..150 D2
Wordsworth St HU8 ....141 D2
Workington Ave 8 HU4 .144 B6
Worlaby Prim Sch
DN20 ....98 D8
Worlaby Rd 1 DN33 ....113 D8
Worldwide Way
Immingham DN41 ....101 F8
Stallingborough DN41 ......87 F1
Wormley Hill La DN14 ...78 E2
Worral Ct 1 DN3 ....92 A1
Worsborough Cl 10
HU7 ....141 D7
Worsendale Rd YO42 ....16 F2
Worship St HU2 ....155 B3
Worsley Cl
7 Holton le Clay DN36 ...114 A5
Immingham DN40 ....87 D1
Worsley Fst Sch DN34 ..102 C4
Worsley Rd DN40 ....87 C1
Worthing St HU5 ....140 D3
Wortley St DN16 ....151 A6
Wragby Rd DN17 ....150 D1
Wragby St DN32 ....152 F3
Wrangbrook Cl 3 DN14 ..65 A7
Wrangham Dr 1 YO14 .....3 A8
Wrangman Dale Rd
YO43 ....54 A8
Wrawby C E Sch DN20 ...98 E3
Wrawby La HU12 ....58 D2
Wrawby Postmill*
DN20 ....98 E3
Wrawby Rd Brigg DN20 ...98 C2
Scunthorpe DN17 ....150 E1
Wrawby St 7 DN20 ......98 C2
Wray Cl Beverley HU17 ...154 B4
9 Waltham DN37 ....113 D7
Wray St 14 DN21 ....108 B1
Wray's Ave YO31 ....127 E1
Wren Cl 4 Healing DN41 .101 F5
17 Scunthorpe DN16 ......96 D1
Wren Cres DN33 ....102 D1
Wren Hall La YO8 ....63 E6
Wren La 2 YO8 ....148 D5
Wressle Rd DN20 ....97 E4
Wressle Sta YO8 ....50 D2
Wright Cl YO16 ....122 B2
Wright Cres YO16 ......122 B2
Wright St HU2 ....155 A3
Wrights Gdns 1 DN10 ..116 D3
Wrights La WF11 ....76 B8
Wroot Rd DN9 ....104 A2
Wroot Travis Charity Sch
DN9 ....104 D5
Wroots Ave DN14 ......149 D1
Wroxham Ave DN34 ....102 C3
Wrygarth Ave 7 HU15 ....68 C5
Wyatt Ave DN20 ....97 D3
Wybeck Rd DN15 ....96 D7
Wybers Way DN37 ......102 B4
Wybers Wood Jun & Inf Sch
DN37 ....102 B4
Wycliffe Ave YO10 ......131 B3
Wycliffe La YO15 ....122 E2
Wydale Rd YO10 ....131 D4
Wyham Medieval Village*
DN36 ....120 F5
Wyke Coll HU5 ....139 E2
Wyke St HU9 ....146 D7
Wykeham Cl
2 Bridlington YO16 ....122 C5
1 Kingston upon Hull
HU7 ....141 D7
Wykeman Cl YO25 ......124 D3
Wylies Rd HU17 ....154 A3
Wymark View 26 DN33 ..102 C2
Wymersley Rd HU5 .....144 A8
Wynburg St HU9 ....141 D1
Wyndham Cl 4 HU17 ....43 D6
Wyndham Rd 10 DN36 ..114 A7
Wyndham St HU3 ......145 C7
Wynmoor Rd DN17 .....150 F3
Wyntryngham Cl 14
HU12 ....72 D7
Wyredale Rd DN16 .....151 D1
Wysteria Way HU8 .....141 E7
Wytherstone Cl 3 HU7 ...56 F6
Wyton Gr HU9 ....142 A2
Wyton Rd HU12 ....58 B2
Wyvern Cl DN17 ....94 D8

Y

Yapham Rd
Pocklington YO42 ....28 F5
Yapham YO42 ....28 E5
Yarborough Camp*
DN39 ....99 E7
Yarborough Cl 2 DN36 ..114 A5
Yarborough Cres 6
DN20 ....97 D4
Yarborough Dr DN31 ...152 C4
Yarborough Mid Sch
DN34 ....152 A3
Yarborough Prim Sch
DN34 ....102 C4
Yarborough Rd
24 Brigg DN20 ....98 C2
Grimsby DN34 ....152 A3
Keelby DN41 ....101 A5
Yarborough Rd *continued*
Scunthorpe DN16 ....97 A5
Yarburgh Cl 4 DN14 .....63 B1
Yarburgh Gr 2 YO26 ....129 E5
Yarburgh Way YO10 ....131 C3
Yardley Way 3 DN34 ...102 B2
Yarmouth Ave 3 HU4 ...144 A3
Yarra Rd DN35 ....153 F2
Yarrow Rd DN34 ....102 C4
Yatesbury Garth 18 HU7 ..57 A5
Yeadon Garth HU7 .....141 C8
Yearsley Cres YO31 .....130 D7
Yearsley Gr YO31 ......127 E1
Yearsley Grove Jun Sch
YO32 ....127 F1
Yearsley Swimming Baths
YO31 ....130 D8
Yew Tree Cl
Acaster Malbis YO23 ....36 C8
Rufforth YO23 ....24 C6
Selby YO8 ....148 C6
Yew Tree Mews YO19 ...131 C5
Yew Tree Pk DN14 ....77 A7
Yews La DN37 ....101 E1
Yewtree Dr HU4 ....144 B7
Yiewsley Cl HU8 ....141 E6
Yokegate DN14 ....51 E3
Yordas Ct 3 YO16 ......123 A7
York Abbey* YO30 ......156 A3
York Ave DN16 ....96 D2
York Barbican Leisure Ctr
YO10 ....156 C1
York Castle Mus*
YO1 ....156 C1
York City Art Gall*
YO30 ....156 B3
York City Football Club
YO30 ....156 A4
York Cl YO43 ....135 D4
York Coll of F & H Ed
YO24 ....132 E6
York Cricket & RUFC
YO30 ....129 F7
York District Hospl
YO30 ....156 B4
York Dungeon* YO1 ....156 B2
York La Flaxton YO60 ......14 E8
Huggate YO42 ....18 A2
York Minster* YO1 .....156 B3
York Pl DN35 ....103 B2
York Race Course (The
Knavesmire)* YO24 ...130 A1
York Rd Barlby YO8 ....49 B5
Beverley HU17 ....136 D4
Bilbrough YO23 ....24 B2
Bishop Burton HU17 ....42 F3
Bridlington YO15 ....122 F3
Brigg DN20 ....98 C2
Cliffe YO8 ....49 E3
Cottam YO25 ....8 B2
Driffield YO25 ....124 B5
Dunnington YO19 ....26 D6
Fridaythorpe YO25 ....18 B5
Garton YO25 ....19 D8
Great Driffield YO25 ......124 D5
28 Hatfield DN7 ....92 D4
Haxby YO32 ....127 D7
Kilham YO25 ....8 F3
Kingston upon Hull HU6 ...139 F7
1 Kirton in Lindsey DN21 .119 C8
Long Marston YO26 ....24 A6
Market Weighton YO43 ....135 A5
Naburn YO19 ....36 D8
North Duffield YO8 ....50 A8
Riccall YO19 ....37 A1
Shipton Thorpe YO43 ....40 E6
Sledmere YO25 ....7 E1
Stillingfleet YO19 ....36 D4
Strensall YO32 ....14 A6
Sutton-on-the-Forest
YO61 ....13 C8
York YO26 ....129 C3
York Rd Gallows Hill
YO43 ....135 A6
York Rugby League Club
YO32 ....128 A2
York Sixth Form Coll
YO24 ....132 E6
York St
5 Dunnington YO19 ....26 E7
Grimsby DN31 ....152 C4
Kingston upon Hull HU2 ...155 C4
1 Selby YO8 ....148 C5
York Sta YO24 ....156 A2
York Steiner Sch
YO10 ....130 D1
York Terr DN10 ....116 D5
Yorklands YO25 ....124 D5
Yorkshire Air Mus*
YO41 ....26 F3
Yorkshire Cl 3 HU5 .....139 D1
Yorkshire Mus* YO30 ...156 A3
Yorkshire Mus of Farming*
YO19 ....131 F5
Yorkshireside DN17 .....81 A3
Young Pl DN35 ....153 B3
Young St HU19 ....75 A7
Youth Ctr YO25 ....125 A5

Z

Zeigfield Ct 11 HU9 .....142 A3
Zetland St HU3 ....145 A5

Notes

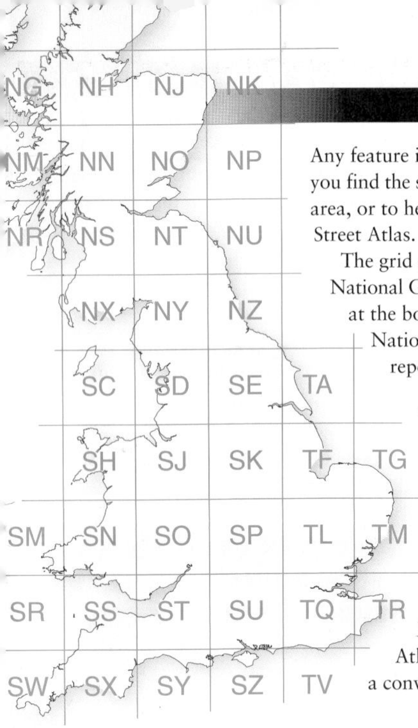

Using the Ordnance Survey National Grid

Any feature in this atlas can be given a unique reference to help you find the same feature on other Ordnance Survey maps of the area, or to help someone else locate you if they do not have a Street Atlas.

The grid squares in this atlas match the Ordnance Survey National Grid and are at 500 metre intervals. The small figures at the bottom and sides of every other grid line are the National Grid kilometre values (**00** to **99** km) and are repeated across the country every 100 km (see left).

To give a unique National Grid reference you need to locate where in the country you are. The country is divided into 100 km squares with each square given a unique two-letter reference. Use the administrative map to determine in which 100 km square a particular page of this atlas falls.

The bold letters and numbers between each grid line (**A** to **F**, **1** to **8**) are for use within a specific Street Atlas only, and when used with the page number, are a convenient way of referencing these grid squares.

Example *The railway bridge over DARLEY GREEN RD in grid square B1*

Step 1: Identify the two-letter reference, in this example the page is in **SP**

Step 2: Identify the 1 km square in which the railway bridge falls. Use the figures in the southwest corner of this square: Eastings **17**, Northings **74**. This gives a unique reference: **SP 17 74**, accurate to 1 km.

Step 3: To give a more precise reference accurate to 100 m you need to estimate how many tenths along and how many tenths up this 1 km square the feature is (to help with this the 1 km square is divided into four 500 m squares). This makes the bridge about **8** tenths along and about **1** tenth up from the southwest corner.

This gives a unique reference: **SP 178 741**, accurate to 100 m.

Eastings (read from left to right along the bottom) come before Northings (read from bottom to top). If you have trouble remembering say to yourself "Along the hall, THEN up the stairs"!

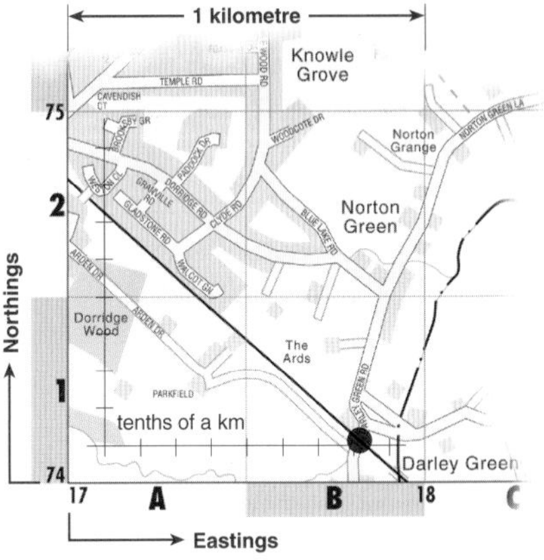

Street Atlases from Philip's

Philip's publish an extensive range of regional and local street atlases which are ideal for motoring, business and leisure use. They are widely used by the emergency services and local authorities throughout Britain.

Key features include:

- **Superb county-wide mapping at an extra-large scale of 3½ inches to 1 mile, or 2½ inches to 1 mile in pocket editio**
- **Complete urban and rural coverage, detailing every name street in town and country**
- **Each atlas available in three handy formats – hardback, spiral, pocket paperback**

'The mapping is very clear... great in scope and value'

★★★★ BEST BUY AUTO EXPRESS

1 Bedfordshire
2 Berkshire
3 Birmingham and West Midlands
4 Bristol and Bath
5 Buckinghamshire
6 Cambridgeshire
7 Cardiff, Swansea and The Valleys
8 Cheshire
9 Derbyshire
10 County Durham and Teesside
11 Edinburgh and Ea Central Scotland
12 North Essex
13 South Essex
14 Glasgow and Wes Central Scotland
15 Gloucestershire
16 North Hampshire
17 South Hampshire
18 Hertfordshire
19 East Kent
20 West Kent
21 Lancashire
22 Leicestershire and Rutland
23 London
24 Greater Mancheste
25 Merseyside
26 Northamptonshire
27 Nottinghamshire
28 Oxfordshire
29 Staffordshire
30 Surrey
31 East Sussex
32 West Sussex
33 Tyne and Wear a Northumberland
34 Warwickshire
35 Wiltshire
36 East Yorkshire and Northern Lincolns
37 North Yorkshire
38 South Yorkshire
39 West Yorkshire

How to order

The Philip's range of street atlases is available from good retailers or directly from the publisher by phoning 01933 443863